The College of Sociology
(1937-39)

Texts by
Georges Bataille, Roger Caillois,
René M. Guastalla, Pierre Klossowski,
Alexandre Kojève, Michel Leiris,
Anatole Lewitzky, Hans Mayer,
Jean Paulhan, Denis de Rougemont,
Jean Wahl, and others

Theory and History of Literature
Edited by Wlad Godzich and Jochen Schulte-Sasse

For other books in the series, see p. 459.

The College of Sociology (1937-39)

Edited by Denis Hollier

Translated by Betsy Wing

Theory and History of Literature, Volume 41

University of Minnesota Press, Minneapolis

The University of Minnesota Press gratefully
acknowledges translation assistance provided for this
book by the French Ministry of Culture.

Published by the University of Minnesota Press
2037 University Avenue Southeast, Minneapolis MN 55414.
Published simultaneously in Canada
by Fitzhenry & Whiteside Limited, Markham.
Printed in the United States of America.

Library of Congress Cataloging-in-Publication Data

Collège de sociologie. English.
  The College of Sociology (1937-39)
  (Theory and history of literature; v. 41)
  Translation of: Le Collège de sociologie.
  Bibliography: p.
  Includes index.
  1. Literature and society—France 2. French
literature—20th century—History and criticism—
Theory, etc. 3. Criticism—France. I. Bataille,
Georges, 1897-1962. II. Hollier, Denis. III. Title.
IV. Series.
PQ142.C5813 1987   840'.9'00912   87-13557
ISBN O-8166-1591-8
ISBN 0-8166-1592-6 (pbk.)

The University of Minnesota
is an equal-opportunity
educator and employer.

Contents

1938-39

APPENDIXES

Foreword: Collage
Denis Hollier

> *The goddess Laverna, who is a head without a body, could not*
> *do better, perhaps, than make advances to "La Jeune*
> *France," which, for some years to come, at least, must*
> *otherwise remain a body without a head.*
> —Edgar Allan Poe, *Fifty Suggestions*

One thinks a lot when afraid. And even more when one is afraid of being afraid. And even more when one is afraid of what one thinks. Afraid to think. Afraid of the thought.

*

Surrealism, which lasted twenty years (1919-39), can be summed up in a single person (André Breton). The College of Sociology (1937-1939) did not last, nor can it be summed up—except as a chorus that is not in unison, the soloists too numerous and their voices too distinct, without unanimity. It had no first person. And, with very few exceptions, it is absent from literature (or sociology) manuals. Black holes elude the surveyor's radar, and the College, too dense for detection, does not show up on maps.

The College falls into a category that could be designated as theory's novelistic side. It happened that one person or another thought, said, or meant this or that. The thoughts themselves are important, disturbing, troubling. But their "aura" comes from the fact that they were thought in this time and this place by this or that person. They happen to have been thought—which is of no help in tracing the transition between system and anecdote. A thought, said Bataille, in *Le Coupable*, is also an event, it belongs to the same world as the one in which trains come into stations. It is just as significant and just as insignificant.

(French-style existentialism came into its own in 1938 with the *Études kierkegaardiennes* in which Jean Wahl developed the negative form of cogito that Kierkegaard called the paradox: Since thinking existence is experience of incompatibility between thought and existence, how is it possible to think or measure the incommensurable? Man is a philosopher more because he exists than because he thinks. Existentialism, philosophy without diplomas, ceased to be a discipline of specialists. It is no longer distinguished from literature. Bataille remembered: "That was what was seductive about this new philosophy right from the first: It was on the same level as life. . . . Wisdom, finally, was no longer a phenomenon of circumstances alien to fear and desire. . . . A man in life's grip was obviously dealing with questions of philosophy as if he were in a stranglehold. In this way philosophy was, in short, reduced to literature.")[1]

*

The trajectory taken by surrealism turned its history into that of a second betrayed revolution. Nadeau could have subtitled his unwittingly Trotskyite account "the surrealist revolution betrayed by its works," or even, "surrealist revolution in the service of cultural reification."[2] By exhibiting and publishing, the movement renounced its revolutionary inspiration. They talked about changing existence but ended up signing paintings, books, and checks like ordinary artists. The end of this history came in February 1938 on the Right Bank: The International Exposition of Surrealism experienced a success free of scandal. At the same time, on the Left Bank, the College of Sociology kindled a brief blaze of inactivity.

But were the concessions made to the artistic institution the real reason for the failure of surrealism? Granted, it never should have gone to work. But this transformation of surrealists into artists is itself only the consequence of a more fundamental betrayal: Their automatic adherence to organizational models borrowed from the political avant-garde (bolshevizing community experience). It is because they began by interiorizing the model of the Leninist groupuscle that when the Stalinism of the end of the thirties made this legacy unbearable, they had no position to fall back on other than the art market.

(Contre-Attaque brought Bataille and Breton together, briefly, in 1936. After it was dissolved, Breton's friends began to turn to "works." Bataille's moved toward the College and its project, bound up with a critique of the monopolization of community by the political. It embodied the necessity for depoliticizing collective experience—that is, it embodied a utopia. This, for those who refused to get down to work, was the only way to avoid the aestheticization of the political that Benjamin had just identified with fascism.)[3]

*

The French in the thirties were ashamed of their system of government: They did not think it was equal to the times. With all the melancholy of parents watching their children leave home, they witnessed the installation of strong governments in Russia, Italy, Germany, and Austria—everywhere except at home.

Times were boiling, but abroad. France had been deserted by current events. The newest thing in politics no longer spoke French. Revolution had stopped being the latest Paris item. Marx made fun of a Germany that made up theories about what other nations did. A century later the situation was reversed: Left behind by current events, shriveled up in its provincialism, gnawed at by decentering, France felt old and thought a great deal about the young Germany. It was severed from revolutions by the theories it made about them (just like in the Kierkegaardian war between the *sum* and the *cogito*). A theory of festival: a bone to chew—for spectators afraid to get cold. The world went into action and France into words. "Paris," said Benjamin, "capital of the last century."

(This was also the period in which Kojève, in his Hegel seminar, dumbfounded these tense years' cream of the intellectual crop by announcing that history was over. Over. A few more wars, some palace rebellions might break out, some sound, even some fury: things no more trivial and no more significant than the arrival of a train at the Gare Saint-Lazare.[4] War had not even broken out yet and history was over!

The thoughts about mimicry that Caillois had been mulling over since 1934 set up a similar schema: Confronted with a threat, certain insects want nothing to do with trouble and they play dead. They regress: back to the inorganic. Death has not yet come but life decides it's all over.)

*

When he examined the answers to his inquiry on directors of conscience, Monnerot discovered (in June 1939) that "not one of those consulted praised, wanted to approve or even excuse parliamentary government."

*

" 'What is the sacred?' Goethe asked. And he answered, 'That which unites souls.' Starting from this definition it may be said that the sacred, as both the aim of this union and the union itself, constitutes the first content of independent architecture. The most familiar example of this is seen in the legend of the Tower of Babel. In the distant valleys of the Euphrates, man erected an enormous architectural work; all of mankind build it in common and this community constituted simultaneously the aim and the content of the work."

In these famous lines from his *Aesthetics*, Hegel assigned to nonutilitarian architecture (the first historical manifestation of artistic activity) a function that is not merely sociological, but also sociogonic. He endowed it with a communifying performative power. In his schema, in fact, the community does not preexist the monument. The monument is what founds, consecrates, and contains the community. Architecture is not society's work, but its setting to work, the resorption of both lack and parergon. There is nothing that requires being exceeded if there is nothing that exceeds. Art, responsible for politics, permits a group to be more than the sum of its parts, to constitute a people, a nation. The sacred is art's fourth dimension.

The College of Sociology went back to Goethe's question. It too wanted to find out what united men and to study the sacred, that is—as Bataille declared in one of his first lectures—human activities "as they create unity." But the College's answer was the opposite of Hegel's: Restoration of the sacred begins by breaking with the world of art. The College is a negative cathedral.

(The Tower of Babel, chosen by Hegel, is a surprising example of sociogonic power: Community could have been the aim of its builders, but, if we stick to the biblical narrative, they did not achieve it. The building was never finished. And concentration of community is not what this biblical episode is traditionally used to demonstrate. Usually it illustrates individualistic dissemination. Cut off from its purpose, the allegorical function of the tower changes categories: It no longer expresses architectural sociogenesis but rather linguistic sociolysis, polyglottic decomposition. The workers would have done better to shut up. Community broke down because of their words. All men had to do was speak in order to stop getting along.)

*

Buenos Aires, May 1941. . .

Roger Caillois had been in Argentina for two years when he published, in Spanish, a small volume not yet available in French, entitled *Sociología de la novela*. The theses he developed there in this indictment of the novel form are not radically new: They link it with a social disconnection (the rise of individualism) and accuse it of undermining the foundations of collective life. Because reading—in contrast to reciting or performing in theater—is a solitary pleasure, when the novel became the dominant literary form, the (domestic) structures of its consumption rubbed off on the contents of the narration. Whereas in its classical forms it remained virginal ("Who would have said, reading these chaste stories, that bodies could embrace?"), ever since the novel became popular, authors have carried on in them more and more as if they were in bedrooms. One lingers over liberties, said Caillois, that people allow themselves only while society is asleep: "Bed is indeed the place where society counts least for man." The conclusions that follow are hardly surprising. "What unites men?" Goethe asked. Caillois answered: not the novel. An irreproachably orthodox Hegelian answer: "Perhaps," he in fact suggested, "one might establish a correlation between the diffusion of novelistic literature and the decadence of monumental architecture." Hugo, in *Notre-Dame de Paris*, proclaimed the end of cathedrals. Caillois's "One will be the death of the other" was gloomier: The novel is an attack on society itself. When the war was over, he would further develop this hypothesis in a work entitled *Babel*.

The crimes of the novel began with modern social vacancy, the draining away of the sacred, the psychasthenia of the collective: Nothing is capable of uniting those who have begun to read novels. Nevertheless, the conclusion contained a surprising prediction, contradicting the account given by these catastrophic motifs. The essay dates from 1941. There was something in the works that, once again, was unifying. There was No Vacancy. It was the hour for joining together, for unanimous resistance, for density, for an activist plenitude: Caillois joined in and linked his personal campaign of resistance against the novel to the resistance to fascism. What divided men? The novel. What was going to unite them? "Once again," announced Caillois, "a period of architecture, of the construction of pyramids and cathedrals, is here." "There is no longer any place for the novel: no emptiness, no interstices, no solitude in which the desire for some other existence could develop." A cathedral is a monument with no bedrooms.

Thirty years later, in 1974, Caillois reprinted this youthful essay in *Approches de l'imaginaire* under the new title of "Puissances du roman" (Powers of the novel), and he had to smile: Allied victory had not had the predicted results. The novel form survived the landing. Mea culpa. Or rather, no, it was really the fault of the College: "I deduced by extrapolation that in the 'full and total' society imagined by the College of Sociology, there would no longer be any place for the novel. I had no inkling that this entirely imagined city was itself no more than a short-lived delusion born of the novel's eternal further enticement." The College: a romantic lie leading one to believe that society could do without the novelistic truth. In any case, it was not through novelistic means that one would escape the novel.

*

Borges's presence in Buenos Aires had nothing to do with the war. But it was during the war, in 1943, that he wrote "The Secret Miracle," fiction set in Prague in March 1939. Six months after the Munich accords, German troops had just entered Czechoslovakia. Jaromir Hladik, the author of *Vindication of Eternity*, was arrested by the Gestapo. He would be shot. The guns of the firing squad were trained on him. Was that the end of the story? A miraculous sophism (Borges went back to this in 1944 in "A New Refutation of Time") permitted Hladik to stop time, to turn its course aside and make a vacuole (a void, a chink), a strange pocket outside time in which, sheltered from the century's brutalities, he would be able to finish his work in progress. Like Caillois's bugs when death threatens.

Sartre's "The Wall" tried to resolve the same dilemma in 1939. But in order to allow Pablo to escape Franco's firing squad, Sartre had recourse to a different narrative strategy.

Borges was not in Paris to hear the Hegelian version of the refutation of time, Kojève's lessons on the end of history. But it would not be surprising if Caillois talked to him about it. On the other hand, we know for sure that Queneau was present, and he too would link the post-Munich anxieties to experiments with time that were oddly similar to Hladik's "refutation": Valentin Brû, the character in *Le Dimanche de la vie*, (The Sunday of Life), was the one who indulged in them. He did the impossible to kill time before the return of Mars.

Do these fictions have some connection with that "blasting out of the homogeneous course of history" evoked by Benjamin in his last text? In order to designate these "Messianic cessations of happening," this "present standing motionless on the threshold of time," he uses the (Kierkegaardian) term "splinters," as well.[5]

(Borges's story, "The Secret Miracle" takes place in March 1939, the same time that, in another temporal series, Anatole Lewitzky read his lectures to the College. In them he demonstrated that shamanism constituted a rebellion of man subjected to the force of time. Four years later, when Borges wrote "The Secret Miracle," Lewitzky was dead. No paradox, no narrative strategy had come to suspend time or to postpone the salvo fired by the Nazi squad.)

*

The College of Sociology rose from the ashes of the Popular Front. Blum had just resigned in June 1937, after one year in power. Six months later, in January 1938, the last Socialists would leave the government. Bad omens and the euphoric discovery of vacations fought each other for a place in the news. The outdoors, camping, and tourism seemed to take over the papers as France treated itself to its first paid vacations. The Universal Exposition opened in May 1937 at the foot of the Eiffel Tower, facing the brand-new Palais de Chaillot. Responsibility for terrorist explosions on the rue Boissière and the rue de Presbourg were claimed by the CSAR (Comité Secret d'Action Révolutionnaire), a secret organization of the extreme right that the press called La Cagoule (the Hood). Céline spewed out his first anti-Semitic pamphlet. There was a lot of talk about the status of refugees, about immigrant workers, about the new family code that was supposed to set the demographic curve straight with its legislation on abortion. In spite of Malraux (despite *L'Espoir* [Man's Hope], despite his flight, his fund-raising trip to Berkeley, despite the film he made in Barcelona), the war in Spain turned into a tragedy for the Republicans. The French gave it some thought: a theory of defeat. Jean-Louis Barrault produced the play *Numance* which Cervantes had been inspired to write by an earlier Spanish resistance that did not turn out any better. The sets were designed by André Masson, the illustrator of *Acéphale*. Giono published his refusal to obey: He would not go to war again. In March 1938—annexation of Austria. In September—Munich. March 1939—Hitler entered Czechoslovakia. Everybody felt the approach of war. But it was vaguely foggy, nobody saw it. As Alain said, they were more and more afraid of being afraid.

Contrary to the announcement of the minister of information, Giraudoux, there was going to be a Trojan War.

*

Leiris worked at the Musée de l'Homme (just opened at the new Palais de Chaillot). Bataille worked at the Bibliothèque Nationale. Caillois, who had just passed the agrégation, taught Latin to pupils of the Lycée de Beauvais north of Paris.

*

The small group of German romantics in Jena who, between 1798 and 1800, put together Schlegels' review, *Athenäeum* is said to have been "the first avant-garde group in history": "There is not the slightest distinction between what our period calls the avant-garde and this inaugural structure surrounding *Athenäeum*."[6]

The first thing romanticism did as the model for avant-garde groups was to make group structure one of the requirements. It placed the avant-garde in the category of plural voice. The group breaks in on the individual. Once community breaks in, voices are divided and speech is pluralized. The group functions as an instance of enunciation that would be the modern equivalent of the (collective) myths of antiquity and the (anonymous) epics of the Middle Ages. Having made a break with any authorial regime, it would allow the resurgence of that anonymous enunciation, belonging to great periods of community, in a contemporary setting. "The art of writing in common," said Novalis, "is a curious symptom that is the presentiment of great progress in literature."

(It is all the more surprising to see a recent work, *Theory of the Avant-Garde*, completely silent about this aspect.[7] Taking the concept of the "work of art" as a starting point, as Bürger does [even if only to denounce its "classic" form] leads one to focus merely on what remains of the failure of these movements. The iconoclastic radicalism of the avant-garde sets salvation through the group [*extra ecclesiam nulla salus*] against salvation through works. It is the radicalism of a revolutionary idleness, the reverse aristocratism of unproductive dandyism. And it is precisely what is implemented by community authority: It requires a number of people to do nothing. How can one, then, blame the avant-garde for having failed "in its attempt to lead art back into social life," when the real content of most of the avant-garde groups was precisely a communal experiment, i.e., an experiment in transforming social life into art?)

*

War and the clergy, in Western tradition, are the ultimate guarantors of a hierarchical segregation of the sexes. "In the great artificial groups like the church and the army," wrote Freud, "there is no room for woman as a sexual object."[8] The social body is engendered by the disjunctive totalitarianism that constitutes the logic of single-party systems: The social phenomenon does not become complete unless it starts by excluding the feminine entities referred to by Lacan as the "not-wholes." There is thus a sphincter politics presiding over the structuring of elites: Men tighten the ranks—no empty spaces, no interstices, no solitude —to expel the gaps, which are feminine. There is nothing accidental about this exclusion: It constitutes the fundamental axiom of a political topography. Woman, in the political vocabulary, will be the name for whatever undoes the whole.

The College had Durkheimian sources and access to collections of data about such rituals of regenerative expulsion. The best example appears in Granet's descriptions of winter in archaic China. Throughout the slack season communication is interrupted, there is no exchange; all contact between things, people and categories is frozen in place. And it is in order to counterbalance the dissemination holding sway in nature—a dissemination in which "philosophers of all ages have recognized a feminine nature (*yin*)"—that the men thus secede. They engage in contests said by Granet initially to have set men against women. The contest ended up being entirely between masculine groups. Women were excluded. Caillois deduced from this that there was a lessening of antagonism between the sexes: Virility hates voids—interstices, solitude—but this was not sexual; it was political. Granet's interpretation was not quite so neutral: He linked the expulsion of women to other prophylactic formulas like the instructionsgiven in *ars erotica* for "combating the harmful influences emanating from woman" (the dissemination, for example, in which philosophers of all ages, etc.).[9]

(Less exotic was the Germanic tradition of Männerbund, which was so important for Dumézil's analyses of the Roman Lupercalians and the commandos of the new order, an order that, as Hans Mayer—who had just barely escaped it— said, was above all a "masculine order."

On several occasions Caillois provided a list of the more or less secret societies that would have composed the College's patrology—monastic and military orders, Templars and Teutonic Knights, Janissaries and Assassins, Jesuits and Freemasons. He even sometimes added the Ku Klux Klan and the Communist Party [*sic*] with which he claimed an affinity.)

*

It was after reading the "Declaration" published by the College at the time of the Munich crisis that Hans Mayer, who was exiled in Paris, came into contact with Bataille.[10]

This declaration, which was well received by the Parisian literary press, condemned "the absence of intense reaction" by the French when confronted by the threat of war. In this absence the College recognized a sign "of man's *devirilization*." The three signatories went on: The cause of such a devirilization, is to be found "in the relaxation of society's current ties, which are practically nonexistent as a result of the development of bourgeois individualism.'' The crimes of democracy therefore are no different from the crimes of the novel. Like the novel, democracy makes men lose their virile unity; democracy, by desocializing, "devirilizes" them ("emasculates" them, Bataille said). It spreads them apart, disseminates them, and dooms them to emptiness, interstices, and solitude.

"What unites men?" asked Goethe. The College replied: They are united by what makes them men because they are not men before they are united. "The creation of a vital bond between men" therefore, is the remedy proposed against the modern detumescence of the social. A man is never alone. To be a man is to be united. Virility is the social bond. Anyone who wanted to escape the spinelessness going around, therefore, had to work at restoring the conditions of a total society. A thick front had to be set up with no gaps or cracks, with nothing missing, nothing different, no solitary dreams, rather a homogeneous and compact body that was completely present and active. A society, said Caillois, must know how to discharge its waste (one might as well say its differences). On the top of the list is emptiness.

Two months earlier, Bataille had made "virility" the leitmotif of his "Sorcerer's Apprentice." Virility, the experience of what he called full existence, was contrasted with the different forms of emptiness. Sacred sociology was to give life "the virile unity of the elements composing it." The one, indivisible substance shrank before the divisions of spread-out substance. And there again, there should be no lack, no splitting apart, no castration, and no dissemination. Virility is the homeophile fulfillment of human wholeness.[11]

*

"Left to itself, the infusorium dies as the result of the imperfect elimination of its products of disassimilation." The hypothesis developed by Freud in this note to *Beyond the Pleasure Principle* is the attribution of responsibility for its death to the organism. Death does not come from the exterior. It is because, on the contrary, there is no longer an exterior that it comes. No exit: The organism dies because there is no out. An organism only dies when it no longer has the energy to maintain the distinction between the internal and the external milieus, between lack and parergon, between what is good for it and what is bad for it. It dies when it no longer has the energy to distinguish itself. It dies, drowned in itself, assimilated by its own wastes, expropriated then and there by its own products of disassimilation. Through wanting to assimilate one's wastes, one vanishes, exhausted, in the lack of distinction between the clean self and its filthy waste.

Caillois borrowed the principal maxim of his politics from this biological model. In "Winter Wind": "A society, like an organism, must be capable of eliminating its wastes." And, in the "Theory of Festival," we find this key theorem to his notion of expenditure: "The very health of the human body requires the regular evacuation of its 'impurities,' urine and excrement, as well as, for the woman, menstrual blood. Social institutions seem not to be exempt from this alternation. They too must be periodically regenerated and purified of the poisonous wastes that represent the harmful part left behind by every act performed for the good of the community.''

*

In *Puissances du roman*, Caillois opposed the bedroom to society: ''Bed is indeed the place where society counts least for man.'' In ''The Sorcerer's Apprentice,'' Bataille seemed to commit himself in the opposite direction: He used the same scale to weigh experiences that took place ''in the sacred place'' and ''in the bedroom.'' The virility he invoked was defined not, as it was for Caillois, by the exclusion of difference and the relationship to the same (homeophilia) but by a certain sort of allopathy in which sexuality acts as the inducer. The ''virile integrity,'' in fact, which this sociology meant to restore as a remedy for modern emptiness, is lost to any man not strong enough to ''respond to the image of a desirable nudity.'' Bataille's reflection here takes on a strange articulation of the sexual and the social, where the sexual would function not as a social experience, properly speaking, but analogically, in compensation—as the center of a utopian projection.

However, although erotic, the set of gestures within ''the lovers' room'' is in tune with Caillois's ''imperialistic attitude'': It is a physical hold and an assertion. Nothing happens here to evoke powerlessness or abandon. On the contrary, what Bataille calls ''an avid and powerful will to be'' is asserted. ''The encounter with a woman,'' he said, ''would be merely a pleasing aesthetic emotion without the will to possess her.'' And for anyone who does not yet have the picture: When life rediscovers ''the virile unity of the elements composing it,'' it asserts itself ''with the simplicity of an ax stroke.''

''The Sorcerer's Apprentice'' appeared in July 1938. Two months later Munich provided the College with the occasion to circulate its declaration. The subject was still revirilization, that is, the *sursocialization* of man. But women can put their clothes back on: The threat of war would do the job as well as they. Virile unity is not the uniting of man and woman. It is man's unity confronted with woman. Virility, like life, is whatever does not let itself be cut apart, whatever resists partition. Etc.

Is all cohesion necessarily damaged by sexual difference? Is the requirement of community conceivable independent from its negative articulation with sexual difference? Is unity an exclusively virile requirement, and does it necessarily imply getting rid of femininity? Does not reinforcing, as Jean-Luc Nancy would have it, the implication of the *Mitsein* in the Heideggerian *Dasein*, come down to confirming and reinforcing the sexualization of Being evoked by Bataille when he makes Being masculine, a *copulus* instead of a *copula*.[12] Democracy devirilizes men when it cuts them off from being together. Can the implication of *Mitsein* in *Dasein* be anything other than the phallicization of *Dasein*? Would being let itself be neutralized?

(In *La Communauté inavouable*, Blanchot evoked various instances of the demand for community: "community of monks, Hassidic community [and the kibbutzim], community of scholars, community with 'community' as a purpose, community of lovers."[13] The list is quite different from the one Caillois read to the College. But is it possible to conceive of a being-together neutral enough to unite in itself both monks and lovers? Is "community" any more than a word used to shelter and keep alive the mythic unity of politics and sex? Why refuse to accept the fusion of finite beings if one is going to sew together things with nothing in common? It is true that with what Blanchot calls "friendship," an androgynous element halfway between the political and the sexual, this joining process had already begun. In this regard, is it not to be feared that a "vague moralism of reconciliation" might divert one from Klossowski's countering quest "for the roots of hatred," especially the reciprocal hatred of the political and the sexual?)[14]

*

Word is out that Lacan had married Bataille's wife. Various people are already busy here and there measuring the theoretical consequences of the anecdotal structures of kinship. A shamelessly restricted theory. The information was plugged into all sorts of other little stories, fascinating minutiae with nothing in common. The deduction market was wide open and bullish. They had nothing to do but ignore that it had nothing to do with anything!

The remarks of a franglophobic gossip: "Around 1935," wrote Étiemble, "in a little group meeting at Jacques Lacan's, it sometimes took all my courage—I, who then was writing *L'Enfant de choeur* (The altar boy)—to resist all the scenes and sets that Bataille came up with."[15]

(The novelistic aspect of the College was not limited to the utopia of the definitive eradication of the novel. It began with what Shoshana Felman has called the "scandal of speaking bodies": It was novelistic first of all in its paradoxes, in its marriage of the divisible and the indivisible. Its impact is to be felt at the hinge that articulates the meeting of the spatial and the nonspatial, the expandable and the inexpansive—the incommensurable. It cannot be reduced to simple gossip. A thought tried to take shape. But each time it did so, each time it took place, and made its time and place known, it merely exposed that which it could not be based on, it demonstrated the nonexistence of its connection with that without which it would not exist.)

*

In 1929, an exchange of insults with Breton provided Bataille (he was already denouncing surrealism for entering the art market) with the occasion to elaborate an initial version of what he sometimes would call heterology, sometimes scatology or even base materialism: a materialism based more on the abject than on the object. Matter there was defined less by its internal properties than by an absolute impropriety, its resistance to any appropriation or assimilation—even intellectual. The residue of discharges, matter is first of all an object of disgust.

(Heterology is not a technique for provoking scandal. Bataille had very little to do with the surrealist provocations, those rituals of cultural aggression that were intended to test the limits of avant-garde tolerance. Heterology is not a product of the aestheticization of the repugnant. Disgust here is not a modality of aesthetic experience but a fundamental existential dimension. Reactions of repulsion do not have to be induced: They are what is given to start with. But rather than discharging them outside (rather than getting rid of them), one should think them. Heterology would be the theory of that which theory expels. In its battle with the angel of repugnance, in the depths of darkness, thought persistently faces the things that repel it. What unites men? The things that repel them. Society stands upon the things it cannot stand.)

*

This heterology had a political dimension. Bataille had never been a communist. But he played what he claimed was a Marxist card against Breton. Work would be to society as sexuality was to the individual—the part that is damned, a center of unbridled energies that are uncontrollable and unassimilable, a locus of expenditures that are inconceivable in terms of a rationalist economy. The proletariat is the abject of private property, family, and State. Speaking of this eruption of the proletariat within and because of capitalism, Marx, in the *Manifesto*, had invoked the sorcerer's apprentice. Its polymorphic, excentric, and excessive violence is fatal for the autocratic forces that unleash it but never will be able to assimilate or reduce it.

Six years later, first at the time of Contre-Attaque and then at the College of Sociology, Bataille developed an entirely different political schema. The European situation, it is true, had changed. The crisis that paralyzed the revolutionary movements from 1930 onward was due to their following outdated models. There was to be no repetition of 1789, 1848 or 1917. "In political thought and analysis," wrote Foucault, "the king's head has still not been cut off."[16] Bataille started with the same acknowledgment in his analysis of the failures of the revolutionary left and the fascist successes: The guillotine is useless when one wants to get rid of a headless power. "Liberal revolutions have been the result of the crisis in autocratic governments. Revolutions of a different sort must necessarily result from the present crisis of democratic governments."[17] The Nazis' taking power constituted the only example of the overturning of a democratic regime. It marked the necessary mutation of revolutionary affects: Antiauthoritarian romanticism had to give way to disciplinary rigor and effectiveness. "It is authority that becomes intolerable in the case of autocracy. In democracy it is the absence of authority."

Which reversed heterologic strategy: Filth changed categories. Originally its abjection, its status as waste, was what valorized the proletariat. Now, when Bataille used the word, it was to insult the ruling class. "Mandatory violence must be opposed *straight out* to this scum, along with the *formation* straight away of fundamental forces of uncompromising authority." Capitalism is filth's power. But that doesn't make it any more attractive: As soon as filth became bourgeois, the former scatophile became a scatophobe. As soon as it changed class, it became the butt of its former lover's insults. Filth can be swept out, was his new opinion. The former apologist of the *informe* now began to denounce the amorphous agitation of the "formless" masses.[18]

(A similar schema was employed by Klossowski in his interpretation of Sade to the College. Aristocratic individualism, of which Sade is a representative, acts like the ferment of decay to undermine monarchic concentration of power. But individuals like Sade remain the nonrecyclable waste of the processes they have initiated. They are incapable of communicating, of making the new society acknowledge their values, even though those values made possible its accession to power. The ideal of a complete man is insignificant in the eyes of the organizers of the new power. Sade, between two deaths, survived the decay of the old regime but was not able to integrate himself with the process of reconstruction taking place.)

*

In December 1937 Bataille wrote a letter to Kojève, who had just delivered a lecture to the College: "The question you ask about me comes down to knowing whether or not I am negligible." Bataille made use of the Kojevian paradox of the end of history to infer a dramatization in which the subject experienced his insignificance, felt himself as negligible. If history is over, "I" has become an unemployed, purposeless negativity, is negligible. No more significant than a train arriving in Gare Saint-Lazare. In order to make a signatory insignificant all that was necessary (in a perverse repetition) was to act as if the Hegelian system had come to an end. It was enough to pretend the system had ended, and the subject—some lucky fall-out from books—would escape the compromise of recognition. In the same letter to Kojève, Bataille evokes the possibility of his own "irrevocable insignificance."

(In these collected texts, at the same time that one reads the traces of some speaking bodies, one should read in the traces themselves their erasure. A trace in the erasure, but also erasure in the trace: a trace glimpsing its own erasure. This collection is not a restoration. There is no prohibition to be lifted, no repression, historic or otherwise, no injustice or neglect to make right. [After it ended those who participated in the College were themselves negligent about it.] One should not take away their aura of insignificance.)

*

Klossowski attested to Benjamin's regular attendance. Hans Mayer did also, recalling their last meeting on the day Caillois gave his lecture on festival.[19] It is undeniable that, for us, Benjamin's frequentation contributes a lot to the aura of the College. But is it because of his presence—or because this presence went unnoticed? Benjamin was there and no one recognized him. When you think that "On Some Motifs in Baudelaire" was to be read at the College, you wonder. And you wonder also knowing it never was.

*

Jean-Luc Nancy is right: What is at stake in such groups is not the fusion of finitudes in an *us*. We have to think of it, rather, as a mechanism of erasure, a machine for desubjectified, impersonal enunciation. Less the production of a collective subject, the integration of various *I*'s into the supplementary self-importance of a *we* than the desubjectification through the multiplication of divided voices, the multiplication of singularities that were not cumulative. The utopia of the group is that of an Arcadia with no "Ego." No first person. Negativity can be unemployed, but that does not keep it from existing. Et in Arcadia nego.

(The literature of the period is strangely obsessed, tempted at the same time that it is terrified by the motif of depersonalization of consciousness. We owe Sartre the most powerful formulation of this dissociation of the "Ego" and the "Cogito." In 1936 this would be the subject of his first philosophical contribution, "Transcendence of the Ego," in which, precisely, he argued against the Husserlian concept of a "transcendental Ego," that consciousness is not pure until it has been purged of "Ego." There is no "transcendental Ego" because the transcendental is not subjective. The transcendental is the healthy version of psychasthenia: a slight depersonalization. As soon as a consciousness [this "absolute existing *by dint of nonexistence"*] says "I," it loses its purity, grows heavy, and sinks into existence. On the contrary, transcendental reduction allows it to regain anonymity, incognito, to get rid of this appendage described by Sartre as "superfluous and harmful."

The privileged position of theater in Sartrian anthropology stems from the actor's being the incarnation of this *épochè*. He is condemned to producing himself as a consciousness without a person: when he uses the first person it is always someone else's. The group is another mechanism by means of which a subjectivity can put itself in parentheses. Those are the terms in which Caillois envisioned it, in his 1939 essay, "Sociology of the Cleric": Community integration engenders an instance of impersonal enunciation. After ordination into the clergy, when an individual speaks it is never in his own name: "His power," says Caillois, "is no longer that of a man, but that of an organism in which his person disappears."[20]

*

While the College was in existence, Blanchot and Bataille did not know each other. (They met at the end of 1940.) Most likely neither of the two had even heard the other's name mentioned when an ex-surrealist now working full-time for the revolution, denounced by turns and in the space of several weeks, the dangers they embodied. Georges Sadoul, the Argus of *Commune*, began with Blanchot, who had written an article in *Combat* (which recently has started ink flowing again).[21] In November 1938, without going to a lot more trouble, he would spare no commonplace to give his readers the worst possible idea of the manifesto published by the College of Sociology in the *Nouvelle Revue française*. He took advantage of the opportunity to throw Bataille's own mud at him.

(Blanchot, in *La Communauté inavouable*: "the same [but no longer the same] . . ." He had said earlier, in speaking of the political development of Friedrich Schlegel, one of the former organizers of the *Athenaeum* and a revolutionary turned reactionary: "Which is the real one? Is the last Schlegel the truth about the first?"[22]

Was it the same Blanchot? But Blanchot himself [if he existed] was he the same? Or his namesake? Which one of the different Blanchots was the one with the other's truth? Is "I" ever any more than its own namesake? "I" is another "I"—in every instance. No one is like himself. The name of an author at the end of a printed text does not count as the name of a subject. "I" has no substantial continuity and each time refers only to the limited occurrence of a singular speech act. Besides, was Blanchot Blanchot before he made Bataille acknowledge him, was he Blanchot before he began to write and no longer to exist? Or might one not [to pick up on Derrida's suggestion apropos Nietzsche] introduce the hypothesis that all of Blanchot's texts would belong to the category "I forgot my signature in some far-right review"? The catalogue of things that are left behind is not confined to umbrellas. How long does it take for a signature, forgotten in some now repudiated spot, to belong to the finder? As for these "I's" that are not identical, would their possible community—an insubstantial, unamalgamated community—be in the category of the unmentionable? In 1965, speaking about Sade and against de Gaulle, Blanchot would say: "Freedom is the freedom to tell all." Did the man who signed these words then remember [and did he include under this definition] the call sent out twenty years earlier in *Combat* against the pollution of "fine French blood," a call attributed to his namesake. Does such unseemly behavior [minor? major?] also stem from the scandal of speaking bodies? Etc.)

(What about this scandal? It does not basically focus on the fact that the same hand could have written this but also that, could have penned such words or signed such sentences. It focuses on a much more primitive scene: Surprise! So he existed too! Literature does not completely prevent existence! Blanchot is not transcendental! He too has—or at least had—a "superfluous, harmful I." [I even saw him once, pale but real, in a committee, in May 1968.]

"Sometimes I think, and sometimes I am," said Valéry. In *La Communauté inavouable*, Blanchot pointed out what was "displeasing" in the chronicle of avant-garde groups: The longing for community was eclipsed by a few dominant personalities who, he said, "existed too much." In his negative sociology the demand for community is that which permits groups to wash away the sin of existing. The more urgent their desire for it, the less its existence. Nonexistence is exigent.)

*

I think I should mention here that I was accused of (or perhaps congratulated for) having "invented" (Florence, January 1985) the College of Sociology.

*

One aspect of the College is that of the unknown masterwork. The masterwork as absence of work. A masterwork of nonrecognition.

*

Mallarmé, in his article on Wagner: "Unless the Fable, free of everything, every known place, time and character, reveals it is derived from the sense latent in everyone's concurrence. . . ." Everyone's concurrence as an opus of operatic idling. The Fable of everyone's concurrence, everyone's concurrence in the Fable. No longer, said Caillois, was there any gap in which the novel could interfere.

*

Blanchot, on the subject of Acéphale: "Those who participated are not sure they ever took part in it." (One would have to be able not to be sure if the College existed).

*

Raymond Aron, in his *Mémoires*, cited two letters by Mauss. After a life spent in the library studying primitive societies, Durkheim's nephew was astonished at the collective ceremonies Across-the-Rhine: "This return to the primitive had not been the object of our reflections," he wrote in 1936. And in 1939: "I think all this is a tragedy for us, too forceful a confirmation of things we had pointed out and the proof that we should have expected this confirmation by evil rather than a confirmation by good.''[23] The criticisms that Monnerot (who was violently anti-Durkheimian) directed at the French school of sociology are focused on precisely this point: The primitive is not so distant from the Sorbonne as the Sorbonne thinks. That was the intuition that gave him the idea of a College of Sociology.

The members of the College, however, started with a schema that was the same as Mauss's: They saw societies evolving further and further away from the sacred. But whereas Mauss was glad, they denounced it as a mutilation. Consequently, sacred sociology did not merely propose to perform an autopsy on the sacred; it also intended to reactivate it. Because a world that was strictly profane lacked the essential.

In his lecture on January 22, 1938, Bataille summed up the two preceding lectures, one by Caillois (on animal societies) and one by Leiris: It can be taken for granted that there exist societies ''where the sacred seems not to intervene,'' some of these are ''presacred,'' like animal societies, others are ''postsacred,'' like the ''societies of advanced civilization in which we live.'' Rarely did Leiris miss an occasion to oppose science and the experience of the sacred. However, that evening he had not spoken as an ethnologist; he had not contrasted the societies his colleagues lived in and those they studied. He spoke not about the absence of the sacred but instead, as his title indicates, about the presence of the sacred in everyday life. Did Bataille consciously reverse Leiris's thesis? It is far more likely that he was unaware of the discrepancy between what his friend said and what he heard. Moreover, one can even imagine that Leiris himself did not see the least discrepancy between what he said and Bataille's summary of it. A problem of the same sort (is the sacred present or absent from modern societies?) would motivate the inquiry about directors of conscience that Monnerot published and commented on in *Volontés* early in 1939.

Is there any sense at all in talking about a profane that would not be opposed to a sacred? Does secularization of a West in the process of steadily becoming profane mark the end of Christianity or the beginning (the return perhaps) of an infinitely more religious era? Does the disaffection of official clergies inaugurate liberal individualism's boasted age of free thought, or does it rather mark the metamorphosis of the traditional directors of conscience into what de Rougemont called directors of unconsciousness?[24] When the profane is no longer distinguished from it, should one conclude the absence of the sacred, or its omnipresence? In the rationalist logic belonging to the profane, opposites exclude each other (the sacred would simply be absent, and the absence of the sacred would be simply profane). But, in fact, by its essential attribute, ambivalence, the sacred escapes that logic: It is thus impossible to distinguish it from its absence. Or its opposite. Enlightenment had to get rid of it. It reemerged in its very heart, a shadow brought by daylight, a sun-scorched scrap. Suddenly light was afraid of its own shadow. Night monsters are less disturbing than noontide demons. And madness is more familiar than lack of reason.

(*Acéphale*, the review founded by Bataille in 1936, opened with a quote from Kierkegaard, dating from the revolutions of 1848: "What looks like politics and imagines itself to be politics, one day will show itself to be a religious movement.")

*

Bataille, who had just written *Le Bleu du ciel*, one of the finest French novels of the century, did not even try to publish it. In 1934, when Caillois broke with surrealism he took the same opportunity to take leave of literature as a whole. His manifesto of breaking away (*Procès intellectuel de l'art* [An intellectual indictment of art]) concluded with this scathing farewell: "This is to say that the crisis of literature is entering the critical stage. And also to hope that this crisis is irreparable."

The rejection of literature is the common denominator of the three texts in "For a College of Sociology." In support of the project, Caillois's "Winter Wind" invoked figures whose works "seem deliberately to situate themselves outside the aesthetic framework." In "The Sorcerer's Apprentice," Bataille denounced artistic activity as a product of the dissociation of the complete man— (*l'homme intégral*): Along with science and politics, it is a result of the division and dissemination of the indivisibly virile. In a letter he had already told Kojève that the man of unemployed, purposeless negativity was unable to find "in the work of art an answer to the question that he himself is." Leiris was not to be outdone. He was then on the verge of publishing *L'Âge d'homme* (Manhood), his first autobiographical performance, which would be defined in the preface as "the negation of a novel." The choice of the autobiographical genre, conceived more on the model of bullfighting than on that of confession, is the Leirisian version of the rejection of fiction: no more games. It is because one is present at "a real act and not a sham" that "The Sacred in Everyday Life" praises sports exhibitions.

The avant-garde dreamed of works that would escape the compromises of cultural recognition. The College thought that in order to escape these compromises they had to renounce works. There was only one insult they could not stand: to be called writers. Naturally it happened. Ever since Rimbaud it was enough for someone to keep quiet for everybody to denounce literature. Anyhow, they never even kept quiet.

*

In the spring of 1937, Caillois spoke before the Convention of Aesthetics and the Science of Art that was held in Paris.[25] But he spoke about something that only negatively concerned the assembly listening: Myth, which is of interest to me, he told his colleagues, does not fall within your province. I am removing it from your sphere. It is of the greatest importance to preclude an aesthetic approach to myth.

In 1938 the essays collected in *Le Mythe et l'homme* would perform different variations on that point of view: Three years after the *Procès intellectuel de l'art* they instruct the jury for another trial, this time a sociological one, of the same suspect. (In *Le Mythe et le livre* [Myth and the book], Guastalla, another speaker at the College, similarly condemned the danger represented to the city by a literature wishing to pass itself off as myth.) Thanks to the appearance of an independent artistic function, the first ferment of dissociation insinuates itself into a social structure, and the novelistic chink is opened where social cohesion inevitably will founder. Myth, which has nothing to do with judgments of taste, has no tolerance for dilettantism, distanciation, anything in the second degree. Its object is not the private aesthetic enjoyment of individuals but their integration within the community: It "involves" the person. Moreover, myth is the very skin of social life and, consequently, is nothing outside its ritual performance. Myth has no other basis than the social body that it unifies and that actualizes it. It has no existence at all outside the collective rites through which it is activated. Lacking any objective material support, nothing remains of a mythology that has become disaffected. It vanishes leaving nothing behind, nothing to preserve in a museum or a library. It lives or dies, but does not survive.

Sartre was entirely right, in speaking about the College, to mention the problems of a secular morality: That which is secular will always suffer for never being truly obligatory. Caillois's major reproach against aestheticization is, in fact, the tolerance and the cultural laxity (detumescence) that go along with it: "a sort of secularization, individualization, and dispersion," a privatization of community. One must escape secular dilettantism through ethics, ethics not of obligation but of constraint: necessity regarded as sacred. This ethics transfers onto myth that which is sublime in moral law.

*

Of all the lectures given at the College, no doubt the one of May 2, 1939, had the greatest impact. That was the session in which Caillois presented his theory of "Festival."

The major portion of the address focused on primitive societies in which the renewal of society was assured by periodic outbursts of orgiastic idleness, which suspended for a time the rule of economics and law: Men were united as soon as they did not work. Caillois contrasted the modern landscape with this schema of expenditure inducing socialization: When our contemporaries stop work it is no longer to join in festivals, it is to go away on vacation. As soon as they are able to escape the rule of necessity they scatter. "The period of turbulence has become one of individualized relaxation."

Once again, then, the complaint was heard in the College that the world no longer had an empty slot for the sacred. What united those men who left on vacation? Virility abhors vacations (in which philosophers of all times have been able to spot a feminine influence) no less than it abhors a vacuum, any emptiness or solitude or other gap through which something novelistic just might insinuate itself. What plenitude could one possibly expect from a society that gave its holidays such a sad name? Vacation—which "(its name alone is indicative) seems to be an empty space"—is, by definition, "incapable of *fulfilling* an individual."

Caillois's final words were solemn: "But we should ask the harsh question. Is a society with no festivals not a society condemned to death? While suffering from the gnawing feeling of suffocation vaguely provoked in everyone by their absence, is not the ephemeral pleasure of vacation one of those false senses of well-being that mask death throes from the dying?" Was society itself not about to be sucked into the implosion of vacations? Before Baudrillard (and parallel to Kojève, who was announcing the end of history) it was the end of the social that Caillois worried about. Societies with vacations are societies without festivals. But what remains social in a society whose festivals have been amputated? The spot for festivals stays empty. Where there were festivals there is a lack—their absence. It is surprising that Caillois forgot to talk about devirilization.

One should ask oneself whether vacations are not society's death sentence, Caillois concluded solemnly. And rapidly. He had to pack his bags. He left on vacation.

But he was not to rush right back from Buenos Aires. Behind the vacations hid a war that the theory of festival had not seen. The sacred was not as far away as he lamented: It is never far from its absence. "Theory of Festival" appeared in December, simultaneously in the *Nouvelle Revue française* and in *L'Homme et le sacré* (Man and the sacred).. The author, no longer in Paris, had been unable to correct his proofs. One can wonder whether he still held to his conclusions. But how could one be sure? The same reasons that would have induced him to revise them also kept him from letting us know.

Only ten years later, Caillois, in Paris again, added an appendix about war to the reedition of *L'Homme et le sacré*. Events, he said, had obliged him to revise the last words of his theory of festival. "What corresponds to festival in modern societies? Initially, I thought of vacations: but it is clear that the nature of vacations and the nature of festivals, far from coinciding, on the contrary are remarkably opposite. It is war that corresponds to festival." One recalls that Bataille, summarizing Leiris's lecture, attributed to him a thesis that was the opposite of the one he had defended. The same thing is happening here. Once again the absence of the sacred is confused with its presence. Revising his conclusions, Caillois corrected an error that he had not committed. He had never suggested that we see vacations as a modern equivalent of primitive festivals; on the contrary, they illustrate the disappearance of festival from the area of the social. Did he also confuse the presence and the absence of the sacred? The first conclusion of the theory of festival made it a theory of defeat. (History is over, Kojève is right. By dint of playing dead, one dies. We have entered *ad eternam* into the slack season of the social, life's Sunday, psychasthenia of vacations, etc.) At the precise moment when Caillois announced that the sacred was on vacation, the context suddenly produced a violent refutation. War broke out—the war that, when it was over, he would try to describe as modern societies having a reunion: festival.

*

Radiguet's novel, *Le Diable au corps* (The devil in the flesh), begins with charming insolence. "Is it my fault if I was twelve a few months before war was declared? Those who already have something against me should imagine what the war was like for so many very young boys: four years of summer vacation." It is the same indecision as that motivating Caillois's textual variations: war or vacation? But here the indecision works in the opposite direction. A first difference concerns the theater in which virility is proved, far less martial for Radiguet (or, at least, his hero) than for Caillois. Pleasure behind the lines did not start with the Summer of 42. But especially, whereas, for Caillois, the vacation was redeemed by the war into which it had been transformed, war dispensed the opposite discovery to Radiguet's adolescent: In the shadow of their great war he had his greatest vacation.

In 1939, in the introduction to *L'Âge d'homme*, Leiris made a discreet allusion to *Le Diable au corps*. The approach of a new war reminded him of the First World War, which he said, he, "like so many other boys of his generation, had gone through seeing scarcely more than a long vacation, as one of them has called it." But if he evokes vacations, it is, like Caillois, with the hope of seeing war put an end to them. In conformity with the post-Munich values of the College, Leiris hoped that this new war would put an end to the vacation started by the first. And would permit him finally to escape the vacant feeling produced by the first. The abhorrence of vacuum is right there. He hoped the war would make him attain the "vital plenitude" of manhood.

Later, in "Les Tablettes sportives" (Sporting notes), he would remember this period. "Despite my fear of it, in 1939 the war seemed to me a sort of escape and salvation on the one hand as the only really important thing that could still happen to me and on the other as dazzling disorientation."[26]

*

A few months after the appearance of *L'Âge d'homme*, Leiris found himself in uniform in southern Algeria. But will be back after the armistice of 1940. Caillois, now a literary Gaullist, would represent free France and the College of Sociology in exile on the banks of the Rio de la Plata. Patrick Waldberg joined the American army. Duthuit went to New York, where he spoke French on the Voice of America. Denis de Rougemont taught in the sociology department at the École Libre des Hautes Études in New York (the francophone university in exile at 66 Fifth Avenue). His course had a strong odor of the College about it: "The rules of the game, or a study of the function of play in arts, societies, and religions."[27] Masson spread the word about Bataille, who apparently came out with a somewhat rapturous description of Paris: "It is smelling more and more like corpse." Wahl, struck from university ranks, imprisoned at la Santé and at Drancy, would also go to the United States. Paulhan, before publishing the clandestine *Les Lettres françaises* and founding the Comité National des Écrivains, was arrested in 1941 and spent a week in solitary confinement. Lewitzky, one of those at the Musée de l'Homme who formed the first group of resistance against the German occupation, would be shot in February 1942. Opinions differ as to the cause of Guastalla's death: According to Paulhan it was suicide, according to Blin he smoked too much—a heart attack.

Berkeley, February 1987

Publications

Since the publication in France of the anthology of the College of Sociology, in 1979, documents and personal memories related to the activities of the group have resurfaced, most of them evoked or provoked by the publication of the volume. This American edition takes some of them into account. The present volume therefore differs, at times significantly, from its French version.

Among the many individuals who contributed in some way to the process of revision and augmentation, I wish to thank particularly Marina Galletti, Jean Jamin, and Renée Morel. The research for its mise-au-point was significantly facilitated by a grant from the University of California at Berkeley.

Asterisked footnotes are those of the individual authors. Numbered notes are the editor's and appear in the Notes section.

The initials *OC* refer to the *Oeuvres complètes* of Georges Bataille, which Gallimard is in the process of publishing. Most of his work (especially that written before the war) is now available in English, some in the volume *Visions of Excess*, edited and translated by Allan Stoekl (Minneapolis: University of Minnesota Press, 1985), some in the special issue of *October* 36 (Spring 1986), edited and translated by Annette Michelson.

NRF refers, of course, to the *Nouvelle Revue française*.

Note on the Foundation
of a College of Sociology

[*This "Note"*[*1] *appeared in July 1937 in issue 3-4 of* Acéphale, *where it was listed in the table of contents as "A Declaration Relating to the Foundation of a College of Sociology." Exactly a year later it would be reprinted, signed by Caillois, in the "Introduction" to the collection entitled "For a College of Sociology" published at the beginning of the* NRF *for July 1938. At that time his text would have an additional final paragraph, but, at the same time, the bunch of signatures would be removed.*[2]

The first issue of Acéphale *had appeared in June 1936, published by the editor G. L. M. (Guy Lévis Mano) who, in October, was going to bring out Bataille's* Sacrifices, *a small volume illustrated by André Masson, as was* Acéphale. *Next to Bataille's name two others were listed as directors of this review: Georges Ambrosino and Pierre Klossowski.*

At the same time (June 1936) the official publishing house of the Communist Party, ÉSI (Éditions sociales internationales), published the review Inquisitions *("Organ of the Group for the Study of Human Phenomenology") directed by Aragon, Caillois, Monnerot, Tzara—though Caillois seems to have been the one most responsible for starting it.*

Jean Wahl compared these two contemporary reviews in a note in the NRF *for August 1936: "Acéphale, Bataille's and Masson's review appeared at the same*

---

[*]This declaration was composed as early as March 1937. The College's activity is to begin in October. To start with, it will consist in theoretical instruction in the form of weekly lectures. For the time being, correspondence should be addressed to G. Bataille, 76 bis, rue de Rennes (6ᵉ).

time as Inquisitions; *Caillois is in search of rigor, Bataille appeals to the heart, to enthusiasm, to ecstasy, to earth and fire, to the guts."*

But Inquisitions *would neither last the summer nor see a second issue. Caillois has recounted, in an interview with Gilles Lapouge, his meeting Bataille around this time at the home of Jacques Lacan, and what ensued: "We saw each other rather frequently afterward and we had the idea, with Michel Leiris, of founding a society for study, which would become the College of Sociology" (La* Quinzaine littéraire, *June 16-30, 1970).*

At the same time as Acéphale, *as if in its shadow, a secret society that was its namesake was the theater of activities still essentially secret today. Bataille was the founder and prime mover. But none of the other directing members of the College would join: Both Caillois and Leiris declined his invitations.*

(Michel Fardoulis-Lagrange's fictional account, G. B. ou un ami présomptueux, *published in 1969, describes* Acéphale, *the secret society. In language whose surrealizing obscurity will disappoint the reader seeking very specific information, he recalls his relations with Bataille during this venture. The volume, published by the Editions "Soleil Noir," is illustrated by Isabelle Waldberg, who, according to the editor, Robert Lebel, would have been "the only woman affiliated with Acéphale." It does seem, however, that Laure, Bataille's friend who died in November 1938, also participated in the group's activities [as the note published by Jérôme Peignot in the volume,* Écrits, fragments, lettres *by* Laure *(Paris, 1978) attests]. Fardoulis-Lagrange would speak once again of the secret society in an interview ["Forgetting: A Divine Art,"* Tel quel, *93 (Autumn 1982)]: "When all is said and done, the existence of a secret society is fruitless, even perhaps to be condemned. Mostly, they are subterfuges for escaping oneself, to privilege some secret shared by a community" [p. 80]. Patrick Waldberg, Georges Ambrosino, and, it seems, Henri Dubief also took part in these discreet fermentations.)*

As for Leiris, his name would never even appear in the table of contents of Acéphale *not even among the initial signers of the "Note" inaugurating the activities of the College. (However, it should be noted that, in 1938, the collection* Acéphale—*whose only publication was this one volume—would publish his* Miroir de la tauromachie, *which was also illustrated with Masson's engravings.) As for Caillois, after the failure of* Inquisitions, *he contributed to* Acéphale. *In the same issue as the "Note," there is a text of his entitled "Dionysiac Virtues" (the issue itself is entitled "Dionysus"). In addition to them, the names of the philosopher Jean Wahl and of the young sociologist Jules Monnerot appear as contributors to the revue.*

"Dionysus" (July 1937) is the final issue of Acéphale. *(Actually, another appears two years later, in June 1939, but in an entirely different form—specifically, it is anonymous. The editor also is changed and the review is located at the "Galeries du livre, 15 rue Gay-Lussac, Paris [5ᵉ]", that is to say, in the very*

bookstore whose back room welcomed the gatherings of the College of Sociology.) Acéphale, *in some way, turned over its territory to the College of Sociology, which would attempt without success to create a publication of its own.]*

1. As soon as particular importance is attributed to the study of social structures, one sees that the few results obtained in this realm by science not only are generally unknown but, moreover, directly contradict current ideas on these subjects. These results appear at first extremely promising and open unexpected viewpoints for the study of human behavior. But they remain timid and incomplete, on the one hand, because science has been too limited to the analysis of so-called primitive societies, while ignoring modern societies; and on the other hand, because the discoveries made have not modified the assumptions and attitudes of research as profoundly as might be expected. It even seems that there are obstacles of a particular nature opposed to the development of an understanding of the vital elements of society: The necessarily contagious and *activist* character of the representations that this work brings to light seems responsible for this.

2. It follows that there is good reason for those who contemplate following investigations as far as possible in this direction, to develop a moral community, different in part from that ordinarily uniting scholars and bound, precisely, to the virulent character of the realm studied and of the laws that little by little are revealed to govern it.

This community, nonetheless, is as free of access as the established scientific community, and anyone can contribute a personal point of view to it, without regard for the particular concern inducing one to get a more precise knowledge of the essential aspects of social existence. No matter what one's origin and goal, this preoccupation alone is considered to be enough to create the necessary ties for common action.

3. The precise object of the contemplated activity can take the name of Sacred Sociology, implying the study of all manifestations of social existence where the active presence of the sacred is clear. It intends to establish in this way the points of coincidence between the fundamental obsessive tendencies of individual psychology and the principal structures that govern social organization and are in command of its revolutions.

GEORGES AMBROSINO, GEORGES BATAILLE, ROGER CAILLOIS, PIERRE KLOSSOWSKI, PIERRE LIBRA, JULES MONNEROT.

For a College of Sociology

[1. The following four texts (by Caillois, Bataille, and Leiris) constituting "For a College of Sociology" were the lead articles in the Nouvelle Revue française *for July 1938. A certain number of special printings were made of these at this time. When they were published the College had already been active for a full year. They roused no great reaction (a brief echo in* Esprit, *a lengthy panning in* Commune): *The crisis in Czechoslovakia was providing other things to get stirred up about.*

It was Jean Paulhan, the managing editor of the NRF, *who invited the College to publish what can be considered as its manifesto there. After this the review would regularly announce the activities of the College (which made establishing a calendar for the year 1938-39 possible). Besides being involved with the* NRF, *to which Caillois and Leiris were regular contributors, Paulhan dealt with the publications* Commerce *and* Mesures. *He had not waited for the College to be founded before publishing its future members ("Lucrèce et Judith" by Leiris in the July 1936 issue; Caillois's "La Mante religieuse," "L'Aridité," and "Ambiguïté du sacré," in April 1937, 1938, and 1939; "L'Obélisque" by Bataille in April 1938 as well as "L'Amitié," which appeared under the pseudonym Dianus in April 1940; finally, in January 1939, Kojève's translation of and commentary on a chapter from Hegel's* Phénoménologie de l'esprit, *"Autonomie et dépendance de la conscience de soi"). Paulhan himself would give a paper at the College at the end of the second year. It would revolve around "sacred language" and be read at the meeting of May 16, 1939 (see Lectures, 1938-1939). By odd coincidence, it is the only meeting that the "Bulletin" of the* NRF *(which very meticulously advertised the activities of the College) would neglect to announce to its readers.*

It is also worth mentioning that shortly after Bataille was supposed to speak on "The structure of Democracies" (December 13, 1938), Paulhan published in the NRF *"La Démocratie fait appel au premier venu" (March 1939). But it is true that this is also the time during which the Third Republic was proceeding to reelect Lebrun to its presidency. Paulhan's use of the concept of "terror" in* Les Fleurs de Tarbes *(subtitled "Terror in Literature," with its revolutionary reference, cannot but evoke certain of the most insistent preoccupations of the College and one of its "commonplaces": the Place de la Concorde. After the war Paulhan would publish in* Les Temps modernes *of March 1946 an essay with a*

7

rather *"collegiate" title: "La Rhétorique était une société secrète."* Moreover, *signing them "Jean Guérin," he stuffed all kinds of bits and pieces into the last pages of his review, particularly between the end of the postwar years (as commentators came to call the period following the Munich agreement) and the declaration of war. These were different sorts of little notes, and under the rubric "Events," three-line bits of news in the style of Fénéon, some of which are reproduced here (see the Appendixes: Events): They give an idea of the period (already so distant) and recall that wonderful anarchy of attention. Also, further on, Paulhan's response to Monnerot's inquiry concerning spiritual directors will be found.*

Of all the members of the College, Caillois seems to have been closest to Paulhan. It was Caillois who served as intermediary between the NRF *and the College in the composition of this manifesto. Later on we will see him questioning Bataille as to how far he had gotten with writing his contribution. He recalls this episode in* Approches de l'imaginaire *(Paris, 1974): "At this juncture, Jean Paulhan invited the group to define its aims in the July 1938 issue of the* Nouvelle Revue française. *For the occasion I composed a sort of statement of purpose approved by Georges Bataille and Michel Leiris. This was included, followed by three texts, one by each of us: 'The Sorcerer's Apprentice' by Georges Bataille, 'The Sacred in Everyday Life' by Michel Leiris, and 'The Winter Wind' by myself."*

2. This statement of purpose, signed with the initials R. C., constitutes the Introduction to "For a College of Sociology." Caillois would republish it in 1974 in the section of his book Approches de l'imaginaire *devoted to the College ("The Paradox of an Active Sociology") where it is titled "A Program for a College of Sociology."*

This Introduction ends with the repetition of the "Note on the Foundation of a College of Sociology," which appeared a year previously, in July 1937, in Acéphale. *In addition, this time there is a final paragraph giving a program of study projected by the College and heralding its conspiratorial repercussions.*

Caillois would repeatedly mention, particularly in the "Préambule pour L'Esprit des sectes," *his reservations about those of the College who, "full of fervor, did not willingly resign themselves to interpretation alone." Behind this plural he doubtless was getting at Bataille. Caillois was, nonetheless, at home with calls to action. We have only to read his Foreword to* Le Mythe et l'homme. *These pages are dated "Paris, June 1937." They are contemporary, therefore, with the conversations preliminary to setting up the College. Caillois states there that from the moment the sociologist gives up his telescope, the investigation of the most virulent social phenomena would turn the academic* caput mortuum *decisively away from a peaceful route and toward an imperative: "Without changing in nature," he writes, the formulations reached by the sociologist "seem no longer to be indicative, but imperative." So it does not seem that Caillois totally escaped contagion from the sociological activism central to the formation of the College.]*

Introduction
Roger Caillois

It seems that present circumstances particularly lend themselves to a *critical work*[1] having as its object the mutual relations of man's *being* and society's *being*: what he expects from it, what it requires of him.

Indeed, these last twenty years have seen as extensive an intellectual *turmoil* as one could imagine. Nothing durable, nothing solid, *no basis*: Everything crumbles already and loses its edges, while time so far has taken only one step. But an extraordinary, almost inconceivable, *fermentation*: yesterday's problems posed again each day with many others that are new, extreme, disconcerting, indefatigably invented by tremendously active minds that are no less tremendously incapable of patience and continuity — in a word, a production that literally floods the market, and is out of proportion to needs and even to the capacity for consumption.[2]

In fact, abundant wealth and many virgin spaces are suddenly open for exploration and sometimes exploitation: the dream, the unconscious, all shapes and forms of the fantastic and the excessive (the one defining the other). A frenzied individualism, turning *scandal* into a value, gave it all a sort of unity of feeling that was almost lyrical. To tell the truth, this was going further than necessary: In any case, it was granting society a great deal to enjoy provoking it so much. There, perhaps, one must see the germ of a contradiction that was bound to grow until it dominated the intellectual life of the period on a certain level: writers awkwardly or arrogantly trying their hand at taking part in political struggles and seeing their intimate preoccupations so out of tune with the demands of their cause that they quickly had to give in or give up.

Neither of these conflicting resolves, research into the richest human phenomena or the urgent appeal from social facts, can be left out without soon being regretted. As for sacrificing one to the other, or hoping that it is possible to pursue both in a parallel direction, experience has endlessly demonstrated how badly these ill-founded solutions let one down. Salvation will have to come from elsewhere.

For half a century now, the human sciences have progressed with such rapidity that we are not yet sufficiently aware of the new possibilities they offer, and are further still from having had the opportunity and audacity to apply them to the many problems posed by the interplay of instincts and "myths" that compose or mobilize them in contemporary society. One particular result of this inadequacy is that an entire side of modern collective life, its most serious aspect, its deep strata, eludes the intellect. And this situation has the effect not only of sending human beings back to the futile capacities of their dreams but also of changing the understanding of social phenomena as a whole and of vitiating at their very basis those maxims of action referred to and guaranteed by that understanding.

This preoccupation with rediscovering the primordial longings and conflicts of the individual condition transposed to the social dimension is at the origin of the College of Sociology. It concludes the text announcing its foundation and defining its program. It is necessary to reproduce this here without further delay.[3]

1. As soon as one attributes a particular importance to the study of social structures, one notices that the few results accepted by science in this realm are not only generally unknown but, moreover, in direct contradiction to current ideas on these subjects. These results, as they are presented, seem extremely promising and open unexpected perspectives for the study of human behavior. But they remain timid and incomplete, on the one hand, because science has been too limited to the analysis of so-called primitive societies, while ignoring modern societies, and on the other hand, because the discoveries made have not modified the assumptions and attitudes of research as profoundly as might be expected. It even seems that there are obstacles of a particular nature opposed to the development of an understanding of the vital elements of society: The necessarily contagious and *activist* character of the representations this work brings to light seems responsible for this.

2. It follows that there is good reason to develop a moral community among those who contemplate pursuing their investigations in this direction as far as possible. This community would be different in part from the one ordinarily uniting scholars and would be bound precisely to the virulent character of the realm studied and of the determinations revealed there bit by bit.

This community, nonetheless, is as accessible as the community of established science, and anyone can contribute a personal point of view to it, regardless of the particular concern bringing him to seek a more precise knowledge of the essential aspects of social existence.[4] No matter what his origin and his goal, this preoccupation alone is considered enough to create the ties necessary for common action.

3. The precise object of this contemplated activity can be called Sacred Sociology, insofar as that implies the study of social existence in every manifestation where there is a clear, active presence of the sacred. The intention is, thus, to establish the points of coincidence between the fundamental obsessive tendencies of individual psychology and the principal structures governing social organization and in command of its revolutions.

There are certain rare, fleeting, and violent moments of his intimate experience on which man places extreme value. From this given the College of Sociology takes its departure, striving to reveal equivalent processes at the very heart of social existence, in the elementary phenomena of attraction and repulsion determining this existence, as in its most marked and meaningful *formations* such as churches, armies, brotherhoods, secret societies. Three principal problems dominate this study: the problems of power, of the sacred, and of myths. Their resolution is not simply a matter of information and exegesis; it is necessary, beyond that, to embrace the person's *total* activity. Of course this necessitates a work undertaken in common, seriously, selflessly, and with critical severity so that not only can the possible results be substantiated, but that this research will command respect from its very outset. However, there is hope of an entirely different order hidden here—one that gives the project all of its meaning: the ambition that the community thus created exceed its initial plan, swing from a will for knowledge to a will for power, become the nucleus of a wider conspiracy—the deliberate calculation that this body find a soul.[5]

The Sorcerer's Apprentice
Georges Bataille

[*Caillois, in the previously mentioned interview with Gilles Lapouge, recalled the times during which the College was fomenting: "Our meetings had begun. The first took place in that dusty cafe at Palais-Royal that the Grand Véfour was then. Specifically, Bataille spoke of the sorcerer's apprentice."*[*1]

This "specifically" refers to Kojève's strong reservations, just recalled by Caillois: In effect, he reproached the conspirators of the College, especially Bataille, for wanting to play at being sorcerer's apprentices. Bataille, as Caillois recalls elsewhere, "little hid his intention of recreating a Sacred, virulent and destructive, that, in its epidemic contagion, would end by reaching and inflaming the one who first planted its seed. During one of our private meetings, he disclosed this to Alexandre Kojevnikov (who later shortened his name to

---

This text does not exactly constitute a sociological study but rather the definition of a point of view that enables us to see the results of sociology as responses to those concerns that are the most virile, and not to a specialized scientific preoccupation. In fact, it is hard for sociology itself to avoid being critical of pure science as a phenomenon of dissociation. If it is the social phenomenon alone that represents the totality of existence, science being no more than a fragmentary activity, the science that contemplates the social phenomenon cannot achieve its objective if, insofar as it achieves it, it becomes the negation of its principles. Sociological science therefore doubtless requires other conditions than those disciplines that are concerned with aspects dissociated from nature. It seems to have developed—particularly in France—to the extent that those who have taken it up have been aware of the coincidence of social and religious phenomena. However, the results of French sociology risk remaining as good as nonexistent, unless the question of totality *is formulated as fully as possible beforehand.*

Kojève). Kojevnikov replied that such a miracleworker, for his part, could no more be carried away by a sacred knowingly activated by himself, than could a conjurer be persuaded of the existence of magic while marveling at his own sleight of hand" (Approches de l'imaginaire, p. 58). *For Kojève, when all was said and done, none of that was magic; nor was there any chance it could be so. You cannot regress from science to magic. Under no circumstances could the* Esquisse d'une théorie générale de la magie *to use here the title of Mauss's and Hubert's famous work, constitute a viaticum for a return trip to wonderland.*

This debate—which revived at the time of the public session on December 4, 1937 (when Kojève spoke; see "Hegelian Concepts") and of which "The Sorcerer's Apprentice" bears many traces—recalls the paradox of the magician that provides the nervure *for* Esquisse d'une théorie des émotions *published by Sartre in 1938. That which was impossible in Kojève's eyes constituted for Sartre the very essence of emotion and magic, the consciousness simultaneously magician and bewitched, "victim of its own trap": All that is required is to believe in it. It was, consequently, a matter of faith, which Sartre would soon call bad faith. But Bataille would call that Luck. We shall come back to this split in terminology.*

Bataille, it seems, had an astonishing ability to get carried away ("getting angry at a chosen moment," reported Caillois). Is that a quick description of a combined practice of magic and the emotions? Be that as it may, the myth of the sorcerer's apprentice represents the contribution to the College of Sociology that is most peculiarly Bataille's: this impatience to make oneself be carried away by the desired storms, and be reaped by tempests sown by the winter wind.]

I. The Absence of Need More Wretched Than the Absence of Satisfaction

A man has a great many needs he must satisfy to avoid distress. But calamity can strike even though he feels no pain. Ill fate can deprive him of the means to provide for his needs; but he is no less stricken when he lacks some such elementary need. The absence of virility most often entails neither suffering nor distress. What is missing for the one who is less a man is not satisfaction; nevertheless, his lack is dreaded as a calamity.

Hence, this is ill of the first order, yet not felt by the one stricken: Only the one who must contemplate the threat of future mutilation sees it as harm.

Consumption, which destroys the lungs without causing suffering, is undoubtedly one of the most pernicious diseases. And the same can be said for everything that causes decomposition without being obtrusive, with no possibility of one's becoming aware of it. Perhaps the worst of all the ills afflicting human beings is the reduction of their existence to the condition of slavish instrument. But no one realizes that it is appalling to become a politician, a writer or a scholar. Hence it is impossible to remedy the inadequacy diminishing anyone who renounces becoming a whole person[2] in order to be no more than one of the functions of human society.

II. The Man Deprived of the Need to Be Man

It would be less harmful if it affected only a certain number of hapless men. The one who takes the fame of his literary works to be the fulfillment of his destiny could be mistaken without human life's being dragged into a universal decline. But nothing exists beyond science, politics, and art—all of which are obliged to exist in isolation, each for itself, like servants of dead masters.

Most activity is slave to the production of useful goods, with no apparent possibility for decisive change, and man is only too inclined to make work's slavery a limit he must no longer overstep. However, the absurdity of such an empty existence also commits the slave to complete his production through a response faithful to what art, politics, or science asks him to be and to believe: There he finds everything in human destiny for which he can be responsible. "Great men" practicing in these realms thus constitute a limit for everyone else. And there is no alarming pain connected with this half-dead state—scarcely the awareness of depression (pleasant if it coexists with the memory of disappointing efforts).

Man is at liberty to love nothing. For the causeless, aimless universe that gave birth to him has not necessarily accorded him an acceptable fate. But the man who is frightened by human destiny, who cannot bear the concatenation of greed, crimes, and miseries, also is unable to be virile. If he turns away from himself, he has no excuse whatever to wear himself out moaning and groaning. Only on the condition that he forget what it really is, can he tolerate the existence that is his lot. Artists, politicians, and scientists are charged with lying to him; those, therefore, who lord over existence are almost always the ones best able to lie to themselves, and consequently the ones who lie best to others. Under these conditions virility declines, as does love for human destiny. We welcome any dodge to keep the heroic and fascinating image of our lot at a distance: Only the useful man can show his unappealing face.

But although this absence of need is the worst thing that can happen, it is felt to be a blessing. Its evil is apparent only when the persistence of "amor fati" makes a man a stranger to this present world.

III. The Man of Science

The "man deprived by fear of the need to be a man" has put his greatest hope in science. He has renounced the *wholeness* that characterized his actions so long as he wanted to live out his destiny. For the scientific act must be autonomous, and the scientist excludes any human interest outside of the desire for knowledge. A man who takes upon himself the burden of science has exchanged his concern for living out human destiny for a concern to discover truth. He moves from the whole to the part, and serving this part requires that the others no longer count. Science is a function that developed only after it took over the position of the destiny that it should *serve*. As long as it was a servant science was powerless.

It is paradoxical that a function could not be carried out except on condition that it present itself as an independent goal.

The body of knowledge that we have at our disposal is due to this sort of fabrication. But while it is true that the human realm is enhanced by it, the existence that benefits[*3] is a crippled one.

IV. The Man of Fiction

The function claimed by art is more equivocal. The writer or artist does not always seem to have agreed to renounce existence, and it is harder to discern their abdication than the scientist's. Art and literature express something that does not seem to run around with its head cut off like erudite laws. The troubling figures they compose, in opposition to a methodically represented reality, do not appear on the scene unless arrayed in shocking seduction. But what do these painted, written ghosts mean, these phantoms created to make the world in which we come alive slightly less unworthy to be haunted by our idle existences? In images of the imagination all is *false*. And false with a falsehood that no longer knows either hesitation or shame. Thus the two essential elements of life find themselves rigorously split. The truth striven for by science is true only if it is devoid of meaning, and nothing has any meaning unless it is fiction.

Those who serve science have excluded human destiny from the realm of truth, and those who serve art have renounced making what an uneasy destiny has compelled them to bring to light into a true world. But for all that, it is not easy to escape the necessity of attaining a real, not fictitious, life. Those who serve art can accept for those whom they create a shadowy and fugitive existence; nonetheless, they themselves are obliged to enter as living beings into the real world of money, fame, and social position. It is impossible, therefore, for them to have a life that is not lame. Often they think they are possessed by what they imagine, but what has no true existence possesses nothing: They are really possessed only by their careers. For the gods, who possess man from the outside, romanticism substitutes the miserable fate of the poet, but it is far from escaping lameness in that manner: It could only make misery into a new sort of career, and it made the falsehoods of those whom it did not kill more annoying.

---

[*]It does not follow that science must be rejected. Its *moral* devastations alone are criticized, but it is not impossible to contravene. As far as sociology is concerned, it is even necessary to contravene in the name of the principle of understanding.

V. Fiction Made to Serve Action

The hypocrisy bound up with the career and, in a more general manner, with the *ego* of the artist or writer, makes it urgent to place fiction in the service of some more solid reality. While it is true that art and literature do not form a world sufficient unto itself, they can be made subject to the real world, contributing to the glory of Church or State or, if this world is divided, contributing to either religious or political action and propaganda. But, in this case, they are no more than the adornment or service of others. If the institutions served were themselves troubled by destiny's conflicting movement, art would be able to serve and express a profound existence. But when it is a question of organizations whose interests are linked with circumstances, with particular communities, art introduces a confusion between profound existence and partisan action that sometimes shocks even the partisans.

Most often, human destiny can be lived only through fiction. Although in fact, the man of fiction suffers for not himself fulfilling the destiny he describes, he suffers because only in his career does he escape fiction. So he attempts to bring the ghosts that haunt him into the real world. But the moment they belong to the world made real through action, the moment the author links them to some particular truth, they lose the privilege they had of completely fulfilling human existence. They are no longer anything more than tedious reflections of a fragmentary world.

VI. The Man of Action

If the truth revealed by science is stripped of human meaning, if only the *fictions* of the mind correspond to the strange human will, these fictions must be *made true* in order for this will to be carried out. He who is possessed by a need to create is only feeling the need to be a man. But he renounces this need if he renounces the creation of anything more than fantasies and lies. He remains virile only in seeking to make reality conform to what he thinks; his every force demands that he subject the abortive world in which he happens to be to dream's caprice.

However, this necessity appears most often only in an obscure form. It seems futile to be content with reflecting reality as science does, and futile to escape it like fiction. Action alone sets out to transform the world, that is to say, to make it like the dream. "Act" resounds in our ear like Jericho's blasting trumpets. No imperative possesses a harsher effectiveness, and the necessity to move to action is immediately and unconditionally imposed on the one who hears it. But he who demands that action realize the will that prompts it quickly meets with strange replies. The neophyte learns that the will whose action is effective is the will that is limited to dismal dreams. He accepts; then gradually he understands that the only thing he has gained from action is the benefit of having acted. He believed he could transform the world according to his dream, and he only transformed his dream in accordance with the most impoverished reality: All he can do is stifle his own will—*in order to be able TO ACT*.

VII. Powerless to Change the World, Action Is Changed by It

The first abnegation action requires of the one who wishes to act is to reduce his dream to the proportions outlined by science. The concern with providing any other field than fiction for human destiny is scorned by political doctrinaires. This concern cannot be dismissed as the practice of extremists who demand that militants put their lives at stake. But man's destiny does not become real simply because he fights. It is also necessary for this destiny to merge with that of the forces within whose ranks he faces death. And the doctrinaires, who dispose of this destiny, reduce it to everyone's equal welfare. The language of action accepts only one formula in conformity with the rational principles that govern science and keep it uninvolved in human life. None of them think that a political act can be personified—defined and represented in the personal form of legendary heroes. For them the only answer to their compulsive avoidance of anything resembling the human face and its expressions of avid desire or joyful defiance in the face of death is the fair division of material and cultural wealth. They are convinced that it is despicable to address the struggling masses as a crowd of heroes already in the throes of death. So they speak in terms of self-interest to those who are, as it were, already streaming with the blood of their own wounds.[4]

Men of action follow or serve *that which exists*. If their action is a revolt, they are still following *that which exists* when they get killed in order to destroy it. They are actually possessed by human destiny when they destroy. And it eludes them as soon as they have no other desire than to organize their faceless world. Scarcely is the destruction complete when, in its aftermath, they find themselves just like everyone else, at the mercy of what they have destroyed, beginning to reconstruct itself. Dreams that science and reason have reduced to empty formulas, those amorphous dreams themselves cease to exist as anything more than dust stirred up in the wake of ACTION. Enslaved themselves, breaking anything that will not bend to a necessity to which they submit before others, men of action blindly abandon themselves to the current that bears them along and gathers speed from their helpless thrashing.

VIII. Dissociated Existence

Broken thus into three parts, existence has ceased to be *existence*: It is only art or science or politics. There where a primitive simplicity had made men rule, there are only scientists, politicians, and artists. Renunciation of existence in exchange for a function is the condition to which each has subscribed. Some scientists have artistic and political concerns; politicians and artists are just as able to look outside their realms. But they are adding up three infirmities and making only an invalid man. Totality of existence has little to do with a collection of abilities and knowledge. It is no more able to be cut into parts than a living body. Life is the virile unity of the elements composing it. It has the simplicity of an ax stroke.

IX. Full Existence and the Image of the Beloved

Simple, intense existence, not yet destroyed by a slavishness to function, is possible only to the extent that it has stopped being subordinate to some particular project such as acting, depicting, or measuring: It is dependent on *the image of destiny*, feeling silently bound up with this seductive and dangerous myth. Human beings are dissociated when they *devote themselves* to a work that is useful but meaningless by itself; only when they are seduced can they find the plenitude of a total existence. Virility is nothing less than the expression of this principle: When a man no longer has the strength to respond to the image of a desirable nudity, he knows he has lost his virile integrity. And in the same way that virility is linked with the attraction of a naked body, a full existence is linked with any image arousing hope and fear. The BELOVED has become the only force in this world in dissolution that has kept the power to bring us back to fervent life. If this world were not endlessly traversed by the convulsive movements of beings in search of each other, if it were not transfigured by the face "whose absence is painful," it would seem to present a mockery to those sprung from it. Human existence would be present as a memory or like a film about "primitive" countries. It is necessary to reject fiction. What there is of tragedy and loss deep within a being, that "blinding miracle," can be encountered now only in bed. It is true that the dust of contentment and irrelevant mundane cares also intrudes in bedrooms; nonetheless, in the almost limitless mental void, locked rooms remain so many islands where the figures of life are recomposed.

X. The Illusory Character of the Beloved

The beloved's image at first appears with a precarious radiance. It enlightens at the same time that it frightens its viewer. He sets it aside and smiles at his childish excitement if what he cares about is his own work. A man who has become "serious" believes it is easy to discover existence somewhere other than in the response that he must make to this appeal. However, even if some other, less plodding, man lets himself be burned by the seduction that frightens him, he must still acknowledge the illusory character of such an image.

For living suffices to contradict the image. Eating, sleeping, speaking empty it of sense. When a man meets a woman and when it becomes obvious to him that here is destiny itself, the things that overcome him then like a silent tragedy are incompatible with this woman's necessary comings and goings. The image in which destiny has come alive for an instant finds itself thus projected in a world that is foreign to everyday fuss and bother. The woman toward whom a man is borne as if toward his human destiny incarnate no longer belongs to the space that money has at its disposal. Her sweetness eludes the real world where she appears while letting herself be no more confined than a dream. Misery would wreak havoc with the mind of anyone who let himself be possessed by the need to make her less. Her reality is as uncertain as a light that flickers but is intensified by the dark.

XI. The True World of Lovers

However, the first doubtful appearance of the two lovers who meet in their night of destiny is not the same as the illusions of theater or books. For theater and literature cannot alone create *a world where beings find each other*. The most heartbreaking visions represented by art have never created more than a transient bond between those touched by them. When they meet each other, those who have been affected must be content with expressing what they have felt in sentences, substituting comparison and analysis for communicable responses. Lovers, on the other hand, communicate, even in the most profound silence when each movement charged with burning passion has the power to bring ecstasy. It would be vain to deny that the hearth thus ignited constitutes a real world—the world in which lovers meet again as they once appeared to each other, having each assumed the stirring countenance of the other's destiny. Thus the tempestuous rhythm of love makes true what was only an illusion on the first day.

The obstacle encountered by activities that are fragmentary and unconscious of others—an action that is ignorant of dreams—is surmounted, therefore, when two people in love join their bodies. Shadowy figures pursued to an embrace are no less marvelous than distant legendary creatures. The sudden vision of a woman seems to belong to the tumultuous world of dreams, but possession plunges the naked dream figure lost in pleasure into the narrowly real world of a bedroom.

The happy act is "dream's sister," on the very bed where the secret of life is revealed to consciousness. And this consciousness is the ecstatic discovery of human destiny, in that protected space where science (as well as art or practical action) has lost its potential to give existence a fragmentary meaning.[*]

---

[*]The description of the "lovers' world in this text, however, has only a *demonstrative* value. This world constitutes one of the rare possibilities in actual life, and its realization presents a character far less distant from the totality of existence than are the worlds of art, politics, or science. It is not, however, the fulfillment of human life. In any case it would be a mistake to consider it as the elementary form of society. The idea that the couple is at the base of the social phenomenon has had to be abandoned for reasons that seem conclusive.

XII. Happenstance

Renouncing the dream, and the man of action's practical intention, are, hence, not the only ways to reach the real world. The lovers' world is no less *true* than the political world. The whole of existence is consumed by it, and politics cannot do this. It is characterized not by traits of the fragmentary, empty world of practical action but by those belonging to *human existence* before it has become reduced to servility: The lovers' world, like life, is built on *a set of accidents that give an avid, powerful will to be the response it desires.*

What determines the choice of the beloved—in such a way that the logically described possibility of another choice fills one with horror—is in fact reducible to *a set of accidents*. Simple coincidences arrange the encounter and compose the feminine figure of destiny that binds a man to it, sometimes until he dies of it. This figure's value depends on demands that have been obsessive for so long, and are so difficult to satisfy, that they color the beloved with this great stroke of luck. The fate of the stakes is decided by the configuration of cards in the game: An unanticipated encounter with a woman has, itself, like an exceptional deal, the power to arrange existence. But the most beautiful hand is meaningless unless the cards fall under conditions that permit one to take possession of the money at stake. The winning figure is only an arbitrary combination; the greed for winning, the winnings themselves, make it real. *Consequences* alone give the nature of truth to a set of accidents that would make no sense unless they were chosen by some human quirk. The encounter with a woman would be merely an aesthetically pleasing emotion without the will to possess her, to make what her appearance seemed to signify come true. But once won, or lost, the fleeting image of destiny ceases to be an aleatory figure in order to become the reality holding fate in check.

An "avid and powerful will to be" is, therefore, the condition of truth, but the *isolated individual* never has the power to create a world (he tries only if he himself is under the influence of forces that make him a *madman*, deranged). The coincidence of wills is no less necessary to the birth of human worlds than the coincidence of face cards in games of chance. Only the lovers' accord, like the agreement of players at a table, creates the living reality, yet undefined, of correspondences. (If that accord is lacking, the inevitable consequence of an early complicity is unhappiness, in which love remains real.) When two or several agree, moreover, it adds to the general belief valuing configurations that already have been described. The meaning of love is established by legends that illustrate the fate of lovers in the minds of everyone.

But this "avid will to be," in keeping precisely with the fact that it is *common*, is by no means similar to the will that deliberates and comes to a decision. It is a will that is like blind dauntlessness in the face of death, and, like one confronting deadly fire, for the most part, it must be left to *chance*. Only the impulse that is *risked* can produce the response required by a secret passion when things that "go together" come up by chance. A great hand has no value unless the cards are shuffled and cut—not previously arranged in a manner that would constitute *cheating*. The player's decision itself must be a *gamble*, made in ignorance of his partners' hands. No more can the secret strength of those who are *loved* and the value of their coming together result from decisions or intentions that are fixed in advance. It is true that even outside the realms of prostitution and marriage the lovers' world is even more given to cheating than gambling is. Rather than any precise line, there are many subtle differences between the artless encounter of persons incapable of ulterior motives and the shameless flirting that relentlessly deceives and maneuvers. But it is only an innocent recklessness that has the power to conquer the miraculous world where lovers come together.[5]

In the fight for life against the teleological tendency, against the ordering of means and ends, luck, chance, divinely, ardently, suddenly makes its appearance and comes away victorious in the same way. Intelligence long ago ceased sensing the universe through reason that reckons. Existence itself recognizes that it is at the disposal of chance when it takes its measure by the starry sky or by death. It recognizes itself in all its own magnificence, created in the image of a universe untouched by the defilement of merit or intention.

XIII. Destiny and Myth

It is impossible, without suffering immediate anguish, to contemplate the crowd that turns away from this "dreadful" rule of chance. This crowd, in fact, requires that a *secure* life depend on nothing other than the right calculation and the right decision. But the life "that measures itself only against death" eludes those who lose their taste for burning, as lovers and gamblers burn, through "the flames of hope and fear." Human destiny requires that it be capricious chance that proposes: That which reason substitutes for luck's luxuriant growth is no longer an adventure to live but rather the empty and correct solution to the difficulties of existence. Actions committed to some rational end are only responses to a necessity to which one slavishly submits. Only actions committed to the pursuit of the seductive images of chance correspond to the need to live by the example of a flame. For it is human to burn, to be consumed to the point of suicide at baccarat. Even if the cards turn up good or bad fortune in a demeaned form, what they represent, winning or losing money, also has the power to signify fate (the queen of spades sometimes signifies death). On the contrary, it is inhuman to abandon existence to a series of useful acts. A portion of human capacities is inevitably devoted to concern for the sufferings from which one must free oneself, such as hunger, cold, social constraints. Life, that which escapes servitude, plays itself, that is to say—puts itself on the luck that turns up.

Life plays itself: Life risks itself: Destiny's plan is realized. What was only a dream figure becomes myth. And *living* myth. Myth, which the dusty remains of intellect know only as *dead* and consider to be a touching error of ignorance, figures fate and becomes *being*. Not the being that rational philosophy misrepresents by giving it the attribute of immutability, but the being that a first name and a patronymic express, and then the double being who loses itself in endless embraces—but also a collective being "who tortures, beheads and makes war." [6]

The man whom art, science, or politics was incapable of satisfying still has *myth* at his disposal. Although love constitutes a world in itself, it leaves its surroundings intact. The experience of love even increases lucidity and suffering: It expands the disquiet and the exhausting sense of emptiness that result from contact with a broken-down society. For one shattered by every trial, only myth reflects the image of a plenitude extending to the community in which men gather. Only myth enters the bodies of those whom it binds together and requires them to have the same expectations. It is the precipitance of every dance; it brings existence "to its boiling point"; it communicates to existence the tragic emotion that makes its sacred innermost recesses accessible. For myth is not merely the divine figure of fate and the world in which this figure moves: It cannot be separated from the community whose creature it is and that ritually takes possession of its authority. It would be fiction if a *people* in festival excitement did not show in their *accord* that it was the vital human reality. [7] Myth is perhaps fable, but this fable is made the opposite of fiction if one looks at the people who dance it, who act it, and whose living *truth* it is. A community that does not succeed in the ritual possession of its myths possesses only a truth that is on the wane: It is living to the extent that its will to be brings all the mythical chances that figure its innermost existence to life. Hence a myth cannot be compared to the scattered fragments of a whole that is broken apart. It is dependent on a *total* existence, and it is the perceptible expression of this.

Myth ritually lived reveals no less than true being: In it life appears no less dreadful, and no less beautiful than the *beloved woman* on the bed where she lies naked. The shadowy light of the sacred place containing the real presence is more oppressive than that of the room enclosing the lovers; what proffers itself for knowledge is equally foreign to laboratory science in the sacred place and in the bedroom. Human existence when it is brought into the sacred place meets with that figure of destiny fixed by the capriciousness of *luck*: The *determinant laws* defined by science are the opposite of this game of fantasy that makes up life. This game draws away from science and coincides with the frenzy that generates figures of art. But whereas art acknowledges the final reality and the superior character of the real world that constrains man, myth enters into human existence like a force demanding that *inferior* reality submit to its rule.

XIV. The Sorcerer's Apprentice

It is true that this return to mankind's old dwelling is perhaps the most anxious moment in a life devoted to the succession of deceptive illusions. Approached by this peculiar process, the old dwelling of myth seems no less deserted than the "picturesque" debris of temples. For the representation of the myth expressing the wholeness of existence is not the result of present-day experience. Only the past, or the civilization of "backward peoples," has made possible the knowledge, though not the possession, of a world that seems henceforth inaccessible. It might be that a whole existence is no longer any more than a simple dream for us, a dream fed by historical descriptions and the secret gleam of our passions. Human beings today could only make themselves masters of a junkheap of existence. This acknowledged truth, however, soon seems to be at the mercy of that lucidity that is governed by the need to live. At the very least a first experience will have to result in failure before the negator acquires the right to the *sleep* guaranteed by his negation.[8] Methodical description of the experiment to be attempted shows, moreover, that all it requires are feasible conditions. The "sorcerer's apprentice," first of all, does not encounter any different demands than those he would have met with following the difficult path of art. Inconsequent figures of fiction exclude a well-defined intention as much as do the barren figures of myth. The requirements of mythological invention are simply more rigorous. They do not, as a rudimentary notion would have it, refer to some obscure faculties of collective invention. But they would refuse any value to figures where the part that is an intentional ordering had not been ruled out with that rigor peculiar to the sense of the *sacred*. From beginning to end, moreover, the "sorcerer's apprentice" must get used to this rigor (supposing that it does not correspond to his own most intimate imperative). Secrecy, in this realm where he ventures, is no less necessary to his strange thought processes than it is to the transports of eroticism (the total world of myth, the world of *being*, is separated from the *disconnected* world by those very limits that separate the *sacred* from the *profane*). "Secret society" is, in fact, the name of the social reality composed of these processes. But this romantic expression must not be understood, as it ordinarily is, in the vulgar sense of "conspiratorial society."[9] For the secret has to do with the constitutive reality of existence that is seductive, not with some act that is contrary to the security of the State. Myth is born in ritual acts concealed from the static vulgarity of a disintegrated society, but the violent dynamic belonging to it has no other object than the return to a lost totality. Even if it is true that the repercussions are critical and transform the face of the world (whereas the action of parties vanishes in the quicksand of contradictory words), its political repercussion can only be the result of existence. That such projects are vague is only the expression of how disconcertingly new is the direction necessary at the paradoxical moment of despair.

The Sacred in Everyday Life
Michel Leiris

[When this text appeared in "For a College of Sociology," it had already been read at the session of January 8, 1938. More information will be found under this same title in the lectures for 1937-38.]

What, for me, is the *sacred*? To be more exact: what does *my* sacred consist of?[1] What objects, places, or occasions awake in me that mixture of fear and attachment, that ambiguous attitude caused by the approach of something simultaneously attractive and dangerous, prestigious and outcast—that combination of respect, desire, and terror that we take as the psychological sign of the sacred?

It is not a question of defining my scale of values—with whatever is of gravest importance to me, most sacred in the ordinary sense of the word, at its summit. Rather, it is a matter of searching through some of the humblest things, taken from everyday life and located outside of what today makes up the officially sacred (religion, fatherland, morals). It is the little things that are required to discover what features would allow me to characterize the nature of what is sacred for me, and help establish exactly the point at which I know I am no longer moving on the level of the ordinary (trivial or serious, pleasant or painful) but rather have entered a radically distinct world, as different from the profane world as fire from water.

It seems obvious that we should first examine everything that fascinated us in childhood and left the memory of that kind of strong emotion. For the material pulled out of the mists of childhood is what, out of all we have available, has some chance of representing the least adulterated.

Thinking back on my childhood, I remember first a few idols, temples and, in a more general way, sacred places. First there were several objects belonging to my father, symbols of his power and authority. His top hat with the flat brim that he hung on the coat rack at night when he came home from the office. His revolver, a Smith and Wesson[2] with its small barrel, dangerous like all firearms and even more attractive for being nickelplated. This instrument he usually kept in a desk drawer or in his bedside table, and it was the attribute *par excellence* of the one who, among other jobs, had the responsibility of defending the home and protecting it from burglars. His money box where he put gold pieces, a sort of miniature safe that was for a long time the exclusive property of the provider, and that, until we each received one like it as a communion present, seemed to my brothers and me the mark of manhood.

Another idol was the salamander stove, "La Radieuse,"[3] adorned with the effigy of a woman resembling a bust of the Republic. A true spirit of the hearth, enthroned in the dining room: inviting with the warmth she gave out and her glowing coals, and formidable, for my brothers and I knew that if we touched her we would burn ourselves. At night when I would wake up with fits of nervous coughing, the spasms symptomatic of "false croup," they would carry me next to her and there, besieged by some supernatural nighttime evil, ravaged by a cough that got into me like a foreign body, I felt myself all at once become someone of importance—like a tragic hero—surrounded as I was by my parents' worry and loving care.

As for places, there was, first of all, the parents' bedroom, which assumed its full meaning only at night when my father and mother were sleeping there—with the door open, so they could look after the children better and where, by the faint glow of the night-light, I could dimly make out the big bed, epitome of the nocturnal world of nightmares that make their way through sleep like dark simulacra of wet dreams.

The other sacred pole of the house—the left-hand pole,[4] tending toward the illicit, in relation to the parental bedroom which was the right-hand pole, the one of established authority, sanctuary of the clock and the grandparents' portraits—was the bathroom. There every night one of my brothers and I would shut ourselves in, out of natural necessity, but also to tell each other animal stories that went on like serials from one day to the next and that we took turns making up. That was the place we felt most like accomplices, fomenting plots and developing a quasi-secret mythology that we picked up again every evening and sometimes copied out in notebooks, the nourishment of the most strictly imaginative part of our life: animals who were soldiers, jockeys, airline or military pilots, launched into contests of war or sports, or detective stories; murky political schemings with attempted coups d'état, murders, kidnappings; drafts of a constitution that was to ensure an ideal government; the poorest of all sentimental affairs that were usually summed up in a happy marriage, followed by bringing a lot of children into the world, but not necessarily foregoing a final episode of widowhood. The invention of instruments of warfare, underground passages, snares, and traps (sometimes even a pit concealed with leaves, its sides provided with very sharp blades and spiked with stakes, to pierce whoever fell in and cut him to bits); many battles, fierce struggles (on battlefields or racecourses); after each battle, detailed statistics with the exact number of prisoners, wounded, and dead for each of the opposing sides, which were, for example, the Cats and the Dogs, the former royalists and the latter republicans. All that we duly recorded in our notebooks, in the form of accounts, pictures, maps, sketches, with tables summarizing it all and with family trees.[5]

Of these long sessions in the bathroom, besides the series of legends we invented and our pantheon of heroes, it was the very secrecy of our meetings that was most clearly marked by the sacred. Granted that the rest of the family knew we were there, but behind the closed door they did not know what we were talking about. There was something more or less forbidden in what we were doing, which, moreover, brought us scoldings when we stayed shut up in there too long. As if in a "men's house" of some island in Oceania—the place where the initiates gather and where from mouth to mouth and from generation to generation, secrets and myths are passed on, we endlessly elaborated our mythology in this room, our clubhouse, and never tired of seeking answers to the various sexual riddles that obsessed us. Seated on the throne like an initiate of higher rank was my brother; I, the youngest, sat on an ordinary chamber pot that served as the neophyte's stool. The flushing mechanism and the hole were, in themselves, mysterious things, and even actually dangerous. (Once, when I ran around the opening pretending to be a circus horse, didn't my foot get stuck in it, and then didn't my parents, called to the rescue, have a terrible time getting it out?) Had we been older and more erudite, we doubtless would not have hesitated to consider these things directly in touch with the gods of the underworld.

Compared to the parlor—an Olympus closed to us on the days visitors were received—the bathroom can be looked on as a cavern, a cave where one comes to be inspired by contacting the deepest, darkest subterranean powers. There, opposite the right-hand sacred of parental majesty, the sinister magic of a left-hand sacred took shape. There it was, also, that we felt the most cut off, the most separate from everyone else, but also the closest to each other, the most shoulder to shoulder, the most in harmony, in this embryonic secret society that we two brothers formed. All in all, for us it was that something eminently sacred that any sort of pact is—like the conspiratorial bond uniting the pupils of the same class against their teachers, a bond so firm and compelling that very few, of all the moral imperatives commanding adult consciences, can be compared to the one with which children forbid themselves to "rat on" each other.

As far as outdoor places are concerned, I remember two that, with time's passage and ideas since formed, seem to have been permeated for me, a religious child in other respects, with a sacred character: the sort of bush-country, *a no-man's-land*[6] that extended between where the fortifications lay and the race-course at Auteuil, and also that racecourse itself.

When our mother or older sister took us for a walk either in the Bois de Boulogne or the public gardens adjoining the Paris greenhouses, it often happened that we would cross this ill-defined space. Contrasted with the bourgeois world of houses, just as the village—for those belonging to so-called savage societies—can be contrasted to the bush,[7] which is the hazy world specific to all the mythical adventures and strange encounters that begin as soon as the duly staked-out world making up the village is left behind, this was a zone where the scarps were really haunting. We were told then, if we happened to stop and play, to beware of strangers (actually, I realize now: satyrs) who might, under false pretenses, try to take us off into the bushes. A place apart, extremely taboo, an area heavily marked by the supernatural and the sacred, so different from the parks, where everything was planned, organized, raked, and where the notices forbidding you to walk on the grass, though signs of taboo, could only endow them with a sacred grown cold.

The other outdoor place that fascinated my brother and me was the racecourse at Auteuil. From a bridle path that skirted it in part, my brother and I could watch the jockeys—in many-colored silks and on bright-coated horses—jump a hedge, then climb a grassy hill behind which they disappeared. We knew that it was there that people (the ones we saw gathered in the stands and whose noise we heard at the finish) made bets and ruined themselves for the sake of those riders in glittering finery; as had my father's former colleague, who, having once been a man with ''horses and carriage,'' had gambled away his entire fortune and now often touched my father for a dollar or so, when he met him at the stock exchange. Of all places the racetrack was most prestigious because of the spectacle that unfolded there, and the considerable sums of money won or lost there; of all places the most immoral, as everything there hangs on good luck or bad, and the place my father, disturbed by the idea that we might become gamblers when we were older, thunderously denounced.[8]

One of our greatest joys was when the starting signal was given near the spot where we stood. The starter, in a redingote, on his horse muscled like a wrestler, a big brute next to the thoroughbreds in the race; the racers dancing in place like roosters, swaying like swans, gathering for the start; then the lineup finished at long last, the pack's sudden gallop and the sound of horseshoes on the ground, whose deepest vibrations we seemed to feel. Though I have never had much taste for sports, from this period I have kept a sense of wonder that makes me look at any sports spectacle as a sort of ritual display. The paraphernalia of the jockeys' tack, the white ropes of boxing rings, and all the preparations: the procession of those entered in the race, the presentation of the contenders, the function of the starter or of the referee; everything one senses of the background, as well, in the way of liniments, massages, dopings, special diets, meticulous regulations. You would say the protagonists act in a separate sphere, both closer to the public and more isolated from it than performers on a stage, for example. For here nothing is false: Whatever might be the importance of the staging, the sports spectacle whose ending is theoretically unforeseeable is a real act and not a sham, in which all events unwind according to what has been determined in advance. Whence, an infinitely greater participation at the same time as a much more intense consciousness of separation since the beings from whom we are here separated are not conventional mannequins—blurry reflections of ourselves, with nothing basically in common with us—but beings like us, at least as solid as ourselves and who might be us.

During this time when we were mad about races, my brother and I often used to imagine that when we were older we would become jockeys—the same way that so many boys from poor neighborhoods can dream of becoming racing cyclists or boxers. Like the maker of a religion, the great revolutionary or conqueror, it would seem that the champion has a destiny, and that the dizzying rise of one so often the product of the most deprived portions of the populace is a sign of unusual luck or magic force—of a mana—that in one leap lets him get to the top and reach a social rank that is, of course, somewhat marginal but out of proportion to anything that common persons have any right to reasonably expect, no matter what their birth. In certain respects, he reminds one of the shaman[9], who, originally, is very often only someone who is deprived, but who takes an astonishing revenge on destiny, as a result of his being absolutely the only one who is hand in glove with the spirits.

Doubtless, my brother and I guessed that vaguely, when we imagined ourselves arrayed in jockey silks as if they were coats of arms or liturgical vestments, that would have distinguished us from others, at the same time that we were joined to them as focal points and as the medium for the collective tumultuous excitement, as the places and receptacles for the convergence of their gazes, which were fixed on our persons like so many pins marking us with prestige. Better than the father's top hat, his small-barreled revolver, and his money box, these thin silk tunics would be the sign of our power, the mana special to people who make every obstacle pass beneath their horse's belly and who, victoriously, are exposed to all the dangers of the fall.

Alongside the objects, places, and spectacles that exerted such a special attraction for us (the attraction for everything that seemed separated from the ordinary world, a brothel for instance—full of nudity and foul, steamy odors—at such a remove from the clothed, fresh-air world of the street, though separated by only a threshold, the concrete form of the taboo condemning the den of iniquity), I discover circumstances, events that were imponderable, so to speak, that gave me a sharp perception of a distinct realm, set aside, with no possible comparison to anything else, and that stood out from the mass of the profane with the same strange, stunning garishness that powdered, shaved bodies have when they irrupt within an inch of the tables, showgirls, at nightclubs where dreary diners sit sweating. I want to speak of certain events of language, of words in themselves rich in repercussions, or words misheard or misread that abruptly trigger a sort of vertigo at the instant in which one perceives that they are not what one had thought before. Such words often acted, in my childhood, as *keys*, either because surprising perspectives were opened through their very resonance or because, discovering one had always mutilated them, suddenly grasping them in their integrity somehow seemed a revelation, like a veil suddenly torn open or some outburst of truth.

Some of these words, or expressions, are bound up in places, circumstances, images whose very nature explains the emotional power with which they were charged. I think of the "Empty Hall,"[10] for example, the name my brothers and I had given a group of rocks forming a sort of natural dolmen, in the vicinity of Nemours, not far from the house where our parents took us several years in a row to spend summer vacation. The "empty hall": It sounds the way our voices sounded beneath the granite vault; it evokes the idea of a giant's deserted home, or a temple whose impressive dimensions were hewn from stone of tremendous age.

A proper name, such as "Rebecca"[11] learned from biblical history, belongs to the strict realm of the sacred, evoking as it does an image that was typically biblical for me: a woman whose face and arms were bronzed, wearing a long tunic, with a full veil on her head, a pitcher on her shoulder and resting her elbow on the well's coping. In this instance, the name itself played in a specific way, making one think, on the one hand, of something sweet and spicy, like raisins or muscat grapes; on the other hand of something hard and unyielding, because of the initial "R" and especially the ". . . cca" that has some of the same effect today in words like "Mecca" or "impeccable."

Finally, another vocable was at one time endowed with the magical merits of a password or abracadabra for me: the exclamation "Baoukta!" invented by my elder brother as a war cry when we played Indians and he was the great, brave, and dreaded chief. What struck me there, as in the name Rebecca, was especially the word's exotic feel, the strangeness it harbored, like a word that might have belonged to the language of Martians or demons, or even had been wrested from a special vocabulary, heavy with hidden meaning, to which only my elder brother, the high priest, held the secret.

Besides these words that—if this can be said—spoke to me by themselves, there were other things in the language that contributed the vague perception of that sort of displacement or gap that still characterizes for me the passage from an ordinary condition to one more privileged, more crystalline, more singular, the shift from a profane to a sacred state. It is, in fact, a matter of very minor discoveries: corrections of what was heard or read that, by bringing two variants of the same word together, with their difference caused a particular distress. One would have said that language was suddenly twisted and that, in the very slight gap separating the two vocables—both of which had become full of strangeness when, now I compared them to each other (as if each of them was only the other one mutilated and contorted)—a breach opened that was able to let through a world of revelations.

I remember one day when, playing with lead soldiers, I dropped one, picked it up and, seeing it wasn't broken, exclaimed: ". . . Reusement!"[12] Upon which, someone who was there—my mother, sister, or older brother—pointed out that you say not "reusement" but "heureusement," which struck me as an astounding discovery. The same way, from the moment when I learned that the name "Moses," Moïse,[13] was not pronounced "Moisse" (as I had always believed when, not knowing how to read very well, I was learning biblical history), these two words took on a resonance that was especially disturbing to me: "Moïse," "Moisse," the very image of his cradle, perhaps because of the word "osier" (wicker) (which the first was similar to) or just because I had already, but without realizing it, heard certain cradles called "moïses." Later, learning the names of the departments, I never read the name "Seine-et-Oise" without emotion because the mistake I had made reading the name in the Bible had attached a certain unusual value in my mind to all words that somewhat resembled "Moïse" or "Moisse."

In a way that was analogous to the way the word ". . . reusement" contrasted with its corrected form "heureusement," in the country where we used to spend vacations with our parents, my brothers and I used to distinguish between the sand pit and the sand quarry, (sablonnière/sablière) two sandy spots that were hardly different from each other except that the second was far larger. Later, we savored a pleasure like the one so-called byzantine discussions can provide, by baptizing two separate types of paper airplanes we used to make, one the *rectilinear* kind, the other the *curvilinear*. In doing this we were acting as ritualists, for whom the sacred resolves itself finally into a subtle system of nuances, minutiae, and details of etiquette.

If I compare these various things—top hat, as sign of the father's authority; small-barreled Smith and Wesson, as sign of his courage and strength; money box, as sign of the wealth I attributed to him as financial support of the house; stove that can burn even though, in principle, it is the protective spirit of the hearth; the parents' bedroom that is the epitome of the night; the bathroom, in whose secrecy we traded mythological accounts and hypotheses on the nature of sexual things; the dangerous area stretching out beyond the fortifications; the race course, where huge sums of money were staked on the luck or skill of important persons, prestigious through their costumes and deeds; the windows opened by certain elements of language, onto a world where one loses one's footing—if I gather all these facts taken from what was my everyday life as a child, I see forming bit by bit an image of what, for me, is the *sacred*.

Something prestigious, like the paternal attributes or the great hall of rocks. Something unusual, like the jockey's ceremonial raiment, or certain words with an exotic resonance. Something dangerous, like the coals glowing red or the bush-country bristling with prowlers. Something ambiguous, like the coughing fits that tear one to pieces but transform one into a tragic hero. Something forbidden, like the parlor where adults perform their rituals. Something secret like the consultations surrounded by bathroom stink. Something breathtaking, like the leap of galloping horses or language's false-bottomed boxes. Something that, all in all, I scarcely conceive of except as marked by the supernatural in one way or another.

If one of the most "sacred" aims that man can set for himself is to acquire as exact and intense an understanding of himself as possible, it seems desirable that each one, scrutinizing his memories with the greatest possible honesty, examine whether he can discover there some sign permitting him to discern the *color* for him of the very notion of sacred.

The Winter Wind
Roger Caillois

["The Winter Wind" first was the subject of a paper given to the Grand Véfour conspirators, who were just about to come to public notice: "I will only say," reports Caillois in a note, "that during a meeting held in a dusty café in the Palais-Royal (the café was the Grand Véfour, half abandoned at that time), I gave a talk that was followed by discussion. The new group was formed at the end of this meeting" (Approches de l'imaginaire, p. 58). Elsewhere: "Our meetings began. The first took place in that dusty café in the Palais-Royal that the Grand Véfour was at that time. Bataille spoke, specifically, about the sorcerer's apprentice. I gave a talk on the winter wind." (interview with Gilles Lapouge).

This talk, whose definitive version, along with that of Bataille's talk, "The Sorcerer's Apprentice" will come to frame Leiris's later contribution in "For a College of Sociology," will be the charter, as it were, for the members of the College, a reference text the equal of the founding "Note," with which it is contemporary. This can be seen, for example, in the way Bataille speaks of it in his July 1939 letter to Caillois (see the Appendixes: Four Letters).

A few remarks about the title. There is the sense that the last lines will develop: glacial rigors and their seasonal delights, which stimulate the deserving. But, along with the furs of the masochistic berserkers (Caillois was more attracted to the chevalier's writings than to those of the marquis), winter was strongly associated with the works of the French sociologists Mauss and Granet. Caillois, their disciple, would frequently refer to them in his lecture entitled "Festival" (May 2, 1939). The seasonal variations whose rhythm in Eskimo societies allowed Mauss to demonstrate that winter was the high point of social

32

life—and even, the high point, the social moment pure and simple, of life. It is the time of group condensation, when exchange, affects, expenditure are intensified. It is the season of fêtes, potlatch, and orgies. But Caillois's ethic brings to mind, especially, Granet's descriptions of the Chinese winter (ushered in and prolonged by the west wind). An Asiatic winter freezing the world's flow with the river's, a season of turning in on oneself, of absolute closure, of withdrawal. Secession is the rule. Its imperative requires an absolute separation of the sexes so that the virile virtues can devote themselves entirely to the task of opposing the dispersive powers that then prey on the world.

*The moral of winter: Nature abhors disorder and society vacancy. Putting it in the plural (*vacance, vacances*), including even paid vacations, is not enough to help it rediscover the secret of inverse entropy.*

N.B.: The cub, the young wolf among Lupercalians, Caillois is the youngest of the College of Sociology. Born in 1913, he was not yet twenty-five when he founded these "Sociology Jugend." An agrégé in grammar, with a diploma in sociology from the École des Hautes Études, he had just finished the École normale. Bataille, born in 1897, though not yet stricken with senatorial seriousness, was in his forties—and Leiris not far behind. These considerations of civil status are important. They pose the problem of the passage to manhood (as Leiris would say).]

Extra ecclesiam nulla salus [1]

Up against a world that is minimally satisfying to them, those who resist it experience their common need for action and suffer in common from the same inability to act. They perceive that they must unite in order to be strong, but fearing that the means is more onerous than the weakness that drags them down, they are afraid that union will make them agree to more sacrifices than those renunciations imposed on them by impotence. Disciples of the great individualists of the last century, they foresee evil in a path where the exigencies of solidarity would soon limit their independence. In a word, they dread that by becoming strong, they would lose their reasons for being so, and at this juncture, they are seized by a sudden malaise. Indeed, the stakes are not trivial.[*2]

I. The Fate of Individualism

The decay of society's morals is a condition under which the

---

[*]These pages, which summarize a talk given in March 1937 to an audience who since, for the most part,[3] have reassembled in the College of Sociology, preserve only its dialectic progression, to the exclusion of any analysis of details or any concrete arguments. Hence their schematic (if not skeletal) aspect. Otherwise, the entire history of the individual's reactions to social life since the nineteenth century would have to be written.

*new ovule or new ovules appear—ovules (individuals) who
contain the germ of new societies and units. The appearance of
individuals is the sign that society has become capable of
reproducing. (Nietzsche,* Volonté de puissance *[Paris, 1935],
vol. 1, p. 361.)[4]*

If one examines the evolution of ideas since the beginning of romanticism, not
only in France but throughout all of Europe, one cannot help but be struck by the
increasing and preponderant influence—truly out of proportion to any other similar phenomenon—of the great individualists whose tradition reaches its culmination with Stirner and its richest expression with Nietzsche. It is remarkable that
works tending in this direction seem deliberately to situate themselves outside
the aesthetic framework, willingly making themselves examples, and with use
assuming the value of watchwords. Although the extreme consequences of the
doctrine have not been generally accepted, less and less have we put up with any
challenge to it as a basic principle. The autonomy of the ethical individual has
become the basis of society. Nonetheless, a crisis of individualism is opening little by little, in which massive and immediately apparent external causes have a
share. The development of sociological work has undermined the postulates fundamental to the structure. More urgently, political and social events themselves
(which scarcely leave one the possibility of living apart, rather, at the very most,
of dying there) have made life in the shadow of ivory towers come gradually to
seem the dullest and dustiest of all lives. These determining factors, which alone
are enough to lead those true to the great individualists to reconsider their attitude, and to give them a taste for an active undertaking that is clearly collective
in character, still do not dispel all their misgivings or prevent their wondering
whether this temptation is leading them to the enhancement of their point of
view, to concession to the tribe, or to capitulation pure and simple.

One cannot hope to resolve this difficulty without examining the reasons that
have led the intellectual to secede from the social group, withdrawing to the
Aventine Hill and there immediately taking an attitude directly hostile to any
constituted society. Now, this abdication is contemporary with an ideology that
bizarrely denies the phenomena of instinctive attraction and cohesion—in which,
later, we shall be looking for the living force of social groupings. All that was
seen in these, of course, was the fact of self-interest and of preoccupations with
distributive justice. These are all considerations with which one's deepest being
feels nothing in common and that, accordingly, turn one away from social existence. To top it all off, they are determining factors clearly absent from a society
that is founded on injustice and privileges, and they immediately make it seem
scandalous and detestable. The conscious individual, consequently, feels only
indifference toward society, when so inclined by a contemplative nature. When
an easily offended nature made the restrictions imposed on the conscious individ-

ual by the group unbearable (restrictions he instantly regarded as nuisances and persecutions), that individual has felt only an open and belligerent hostility. No longer having anything other than defensive reactions toward society, this person naturally reserves sympathy for all those kept on the margin, delinquents, streetwalkers and outlaws, and bit by bit makes a hero of the *intractable convict on whom the prison always shuts*.[*] It is wrong to think of the theme in romantic literature of the prostitute with the heart of gold or the magnanimous thief as characteristics of a mawkish, vulgar sentimentality, when there are few better signs of what is essentially novel about the period. The divorce in values and, by now, almost in morals between the writer and the solid, stable portion of the social body is complete.

However, the individualist, soon carrying this point of view to exaggerated extremes, sets about denouncing as fallacious and tyrannical everything that seems, on any grounds, to be a component of society. Family, State, nation, morality, religion, are denounced to which sometimes are added reason, truth, and science—whether because the bonds they make seem shackles as well, or whether, following the example of the preceding entities, they are to some extent endowed with sacredness. Then a type of methodical iconoclast is born, the desperate person in quest of the profane whom Stirner describes: "Tortured by devouring hunger, crying out in distress, you wander all around the walls enclosing you, in order to find the profane. But to no avail. Soon the Church will cover the whole earth and the *world of the sacred* will be victorious." In these conditions, one single moral action is required: profanation, relentless destruction of the sacred—the only activity capable of giving the anarchist a sense of real freedom.

Actually, that is only an illusion: The sacrilege remains on the level of sarcasm or blasphemy; the acts are so far from coming through with the words' promise that the words seem to be sometimes so abundant and proud just to cover up the absence of action. The greatest individualists have been weak men, minors, misfits, deprived of what roused them to obsession, of all they would have liked to enjoy: Sade imagining his debaucheries within dungeon walls; Nietzsche at Sils-Maria, the solitary, sickly theoretician of violence; Stirner the state employee with an orderly life, extolling crime.

Poetry in the same period was also exalting every form of liberation, but it was a poetry of *refuge* more than anything else, lulling, consoling, bringing oblivion and painting a harsh world with the soothing colors of dream. This dead end could not satisfy forever. Conquest was to be more seductive than *escape*. The problem today is posed in even more urgent terms, but it has become clear that society, by its cohesion, possesses a force that breaks any individual effort

---

[*]Rimbaud [*Une Saison en enfer* ("Mauvais sang"). Caillois had already cited this phrase in "Paris, mythe moderne," *NRF*, May 1937; repeated in *Le Mythe et l'homme* p. 199).]

as if it were glass. Consequently, the moment has come to teach anyone who does not refuse, through self-interest or fear, to know that individuals truly determined to undertake the struggle (on an infinitesimal scale if necessary, but taking an effective course where their endeavor risks becoming epidemic) must confront society on its own territory and attack it with its own arms. That is to say they must constitute themselves in a community and, more than that, cease to regard the values they champion as the prerogative of rebels and insurgents, regarding them, on the contrary, as the principal values of the society they want to see established and as the most social values of all, though perhaps a bit implacable.

This plan supposes a certain education of our sense of rebellion, that would take it from riotousness to a broadly imperialist attitude and would persuade it to subordinate its impulsive, unruly reactions to the necessity for discipline, calculation, and patience. In a word, from being *Satanic* it must become *Luciferian*.[5]

Similarly, it is right for logical individualists to reverse their ideas in regard to power and the sacred in general. On this score, they must almost adopt the exact opposite point of view from Stirner's injunction and concentrate not on profaning but on making sacred. Moreover, it is in doing this that they will most utterly oppose a society that has profaned itself to an extreme degree, with the result that there is nothing upsets it more than the intervention of these values, and nothing that it is less skillful at protecting itself from. And there is something more: The desire to combat society as society governs the constitution of the group. As a structure that is more solid and more condensed,[6] it plans to attack society by trying to establish itself like a cancer at the heart of a more unstable, weaker, though incomparably more voluminous structure. What we see is a process of *sursocialization*[7]. As such the projected community finds that already it is naturally destined to make sacred as much as possible, in order to increase the singularity of its being and the weight of its action to the greatest extent possible.

Individualists now are in a position to mollify their scruples. By undertaking collective action, they would not deny their faith, they would enter into the only path open to them. The moment they decided to escalate from theoretical recrimination to effective struggle, they would only be making the transition from skirmishes to pitched battle. They would foment their holy war. And war, Clausewitz said, is the continuation of politics by other means.

II. The Foundation of Collective Effort

I do not know whether or not I have already said in this work that what has best distinguished men is that those who have accomplished great deeds saw their possibility dawning before others did. (de Retz, Mémoires [Amsterdam, 1717], vol. 4, pp. 177-78) [8]

Just as there exists a primitive, irreducible experience of *self* constituting the basic dynamic of anarchic individualism, the same sort of existential, inalienable basis of collective effort must be brought to light. In no case can the latter take for its affective foundation some given that is entirely retrospective, such as something decisive in a de facto manner—race or language, historical territory or tradition, on which the existence of nations depends and which feeds patriotism.[9] That would be sanctioning the very thing we are conspiring to change, and reinforcing what we hope to see weakened. It is all too clear that a movement originating *within* a society and directed against it cannot be founded on something that marks its limits and reinforces its cohesion by setting it against rivals.

A social nucleus of the kind in question must be based on elements of an entirely different nature. A common will to carry out the same work already implies the elective affinities that alone are able to direct the aggregation of a community, and to constitute the necessary and sufficient reason for it, by providing each one with a double set of complementary experiences of attractions and repulsions toward people. We are dealing with an indisputable fact of everyday life that had already impressed even those who promote individualism: the essential ethical opposition of at least two classes of people, whose reactions are as dissimilar as if they belonged to different animal species, resulting in opposite conceptions of the world and irreconcilable value systems.

Each of us, in relationships with humanity, encounters some who show themselves to be of another moral species, almost of another race. Inevitably, we are led to draw back from them as if they were something strange that was harmful. Their behavior is always the kind we fear, never the kind we hope for, and their vulgarity is worse than anticipated. In contrast, there are others who behave when put to the test just the way we expect, the way it seems we would ourselves in our best moments, and exactly as we hoped they would behave. In that manner, an ideal line of demarcation hardens along which each of us distributes *fellow creatures* and the others. This line is reinforced by the way people behave, which is to say in the world that does not lie, in the world of actions and pressured by realities one would be unwise to evade and that always call one back to order. On this side of the line, the very fact of its presence sets up a community of people who are strongly bound to one another, who spontaneously recognize their kinship and are ready to provide mutual aid without reservation. On the other side, the multitude of wretched people live under their own laws. One has nothing in common with these people, and the feeling of contempt is just and well founded; one instinctively keeps one's distance from them as from things that are unclean. Like a dangerous contagion this multitude spreads its appeal, the latent temptation[10] that the lowest level always exerts on the highest, and which in and of itself is enough to justify for those at the top their pride in being there and their will to stay there.

Those are distinctions not of degree but rather of nature. No one is responsible for the place he occupies in this hierarchy of the qualities of the soul:[11] The weak member is not condemned by judgment but kept apart as a health measure, to protect an integrity. For the same reason that separating intact fruits from diseased ones in a harvest is useful, armed and distant neutrality in respect to unreliable beings is a pure and simple procedure of legitimate defense that is absolutely necessary to avoid contamination. A society, like an organism, must be capable of eliminating its wastes.

Likes and dislikes over which, as we know, one has no control can be thought of as individual, short-lived rudiments of a vital system of this sort that are extremely weak because of their subjective and fragmentary nature. Moreover, it is no coincidence that collective opinion is inclined to represent them as deceptive and, on the pretext of being impartial, recommends ignoring them and not taking them into account when a decision that even remotely concerns society itself, especially the public services, is in question. It seems that society thus senses the need to prevent the formation of any *endogenous* aggregation founded on differential reflexes. It is conscious that a ferment of dissolution for its structure exists there at the same time as living forces beginning to reconstitute themselves and likely to spread from one person to the next—all the more destined to overthrow the social equilibrium for their own benefit because of being disseminated within its very framework. That is why the *socialization* of individual immediate reactions seems, on the contrary, to be the first phase of the development of one social existence at the heart of another. When thoroughly explored and systematized, considered as the expression of a fundamental reality, there is no doubt that they succeed in giving individuals who are most jealous of their independence a group consciousness that is extremely strong, consisting when necessary of a total alienation from themselves.

In fact, when the individualists of the last century imagined a sort of conquest of society (which they never attempted to realize in the least), they always put their hopes on this sort of formation. It cannot be stressed enough how important it was that Balzac and Baudelaire looked with favor on Loyola and the *perinde ac cadaver* of the Society of Jesus, the Old Man of the Mountain and his Hashishins, and proposed them as models. Nor can we emphasize enough the significance that one of them delighted in describing the intrigues of a mysterious association in the midst of contemporary society and the other in imagining the formation of a new aristocracy, based on a mysterious grace that would be neither work nor wealth.[12]

To a great extent these ideas tend to acknowledge that a militant and enclosed association is particularly prepared for battle. It would emulate an active monastic order for the condition of the spirit, paramilitary training for discipline, and, when necessary, the secret society for its methods of existence and action.

These three types of communities are immediately comparable because of the harsh separation that cuts their members off from the rest of society. An analysis would demonstrate that they are less different by their pursuit of their own ends than by conditions that are external to their development. Depending on these conditions they either enjoy the support of the powers that be, are reluctantly tolerated or are reduced to illegality. Affiliation with each type of community is either through initiative or novitiate. Either a complete uniform or an imperceptible sign makes one distinct from others and similar to one another. Their entire ethic is based on this situation; it provides for strict obligations among members and leads them to regard the rest of humanity less as their rightful equals than as the raw material for their ventures.

Thus not only individual attractions and repulsions tend to be sanctioned in the social structure, but soon a distinction of the sort that Nietzsche established between Masters and Slaves tends to be sanctioned as well. Perhaps it is necessary to bring the vocabulary up to date on this point, so that its terms are no longer borrowed from a situation that has disappeared, and which consequently distances the mind from things of the present, and so that, when the result of the doctrine shows slaves to be oppressors and masters miserable, powerless to save themselves from humiliation, these terms no longer seem paradoxical.

It is therefore worthwhile to make this opposition again using a couple of words that are more closely related to contemporary reality, for example "producers" and "consumers".[13] These words simultaneously evoke the economic substratum and translate a vital attitude that, without being completely determined by this substratum, in the simplest cases is often only its direct consequence. One would successfully characterize as consumers those who are turned toward pleasure (*jouissance*); who, unproductive on their own, as parasites of others only assimilate; who, in judging, do not go beyond the principle of what is agreeable. Consumers are incapable of generosity, and all the more so, because the producers' very nature obliges them to make a gift of what they create, which, because the taste for producing is so tenacious that they even scorn leisure and reward, is not for their own use.

Destined to be creators, producers set the standards to which others conform. They instigate the customs that others follow, so that even when stifled and subjugated by the mass of their enemies, producers retain monopoly over risk and initiative. Along with their famous capacity for influence, they maintain an imprescriptible superiority that the consumers themselves, sated and triumphant, are unable to dismiss from their own consciousness, knowing full well that there is no active, effective, fertile principle lying within themselves. Identified with their *self* (whereas the producers are identified with their need to create), consumers are deprived of the sentiment of *sovereign irony at watching themselves live in the tragic moment*. This supreme detachment of strong men that Stirner mentions shows them their worth and assures them of the worthlessness of all those who would be incapable of equal elegance.

III. The Ethic of the Closed Community

*I always thought something could be founded on contempt; now
I know what: morality.* (H. de Montherlant, Service inutile
[Paris, 1935], p. 266) [14]

The nature of masters that allows them so little exchange with others, by the
same token forces them to feel keenly their own interconnection, which they
soon experience as complicity because their least reflex is made out to be a
crime. From the beginning this situation leads to the awareness of a well-defined
ethic, which cannot completely emerge except as the aristocratic structure develops, but which from its starting point allows definition of its principal aspects.

A brief description of this will be necessary here. It is not very hard to consider honesty as the unconditional basis of any ethic. That honesty is an *instinct*
expressing the demand for the unity and totality of a human being, whose every
supplication converges toward a single principle, a single faith, is not for us to
doubt. It is effective proof that this being wants to be pacified, that he tolerates
internal dissensions just as badly as an organism tolerates areas of infection, that
he puts down the riots brewing within and knows how to be wary of desertions
that tempt, debase or disperse him. Honesty is that force that allows each of us
only one face and silences the *raging dogs that tremble within our kings.*[*] But I
recall that a hero is great for having had monsters to do battle with, before being
great for having defeated them.[15] There is nothing to hope for from those who
have nothing to suppress within themselves.

Next come contempt, love of power, and courtesy, virtues that, although not
necessarily cardinal, stem directly from the attitude described and are eminently
characteristic of its originality.

Contempt as a virtue is founded on the experience of the inequality of beings,
which it safeguards, demonstrates and sanctions. Illustrating an actual condition,
it presupposes no pride but would imply that pride should not be frightening. Because individuals are not contemptible through their own fault, they should be no
less despised because it is quite in order to treat them as their nature demands.
Essentially one despises those who do or accept actions that one would be absolutely loath to commit or put up with oneself. It would accomplish nothing to
pretend that there are no delusory aspects, or at least an uncontrollable side to
such a feeling, for there is no one who can affirm that if he were put in the same
circumstances and obliged to act, the conduct he scorns might not be his. Moreover, contempt is creative only if it is exacting. It is nothing if it does not immediately require some severity toward oneself. Once experienced, contempt
must be considered according to the duty it imposes never to deserve it oneself
under the same circumstances, so that each act of contempt appears as a pledge

---

[*] P. Valéry.

of honor and a mortgage against future conduct. But it must also be regarded as giving the right not to treat as equals those whom it separates out—the right not to treat them as adversaries with whom one must respect the rules of war and employ the courtesies required among peers.

As for power, it is important to treat it as a force of nature against which it is senseless to protest, but which one is free to fight and perhaps to master.

Nothing is so futile and pitiful as this hatred of power on principle that saps the best of wills in vain, unequal battles, hardens them in this attitude, and, when all is said and done, makes them deify quirkiness and obstinacy. It is healthy to desire power, whether over souls or bodies, whether prestige or tyranny.[16] Moreover, each one exercises power in a domain that is limited but that he may unexpectedly have the chance to greatly increase. For human relations are such that one often finds power while only coveting freedom, so that domination seems the destiny of the strong, and that even in irons they instinctively look upon it gravely and with respect. Thus they demonstrate that it is love of power that fundamentally distinguishes the conquerors from the slaves.

Precise and meticulous as court etiquette, courtesy, which ritualizes human beings' mutual relationships in their secondary aspects, for that very reason, relieves the mind and increases its ease accordingly. Moreover, it contributes to maintaining a certain internal tension that would be hard to preserve if simple manners were neglected. In a closed type of association, destined to aggravate separations, courtesy is part of the ethic and becomes almost an institution. Codifying the relations of the initiates, its esoteric and conventional character finds itself reinforced because it must serve to differentiate them even further from the uninitiated. The discourteous person, in fact, is not so much one who neglects customs as one who is ignorant of them or pratices those of another group. Therefore, courtesy, a way to recognize each other and to recognize intruders, becomes a practical means of standing aloof. In fact, when one must demonstrate one's hostility or one's contempt for someone, all that is necessary, as we all know, is to affect an extreme courtesy which makes the other as uncomfortable as a reprimand would and immediately excludes any familiarity. In this regard, we should never forget the manner in which certain important individualists, such as Baudelaire, sensed how implacable a weapon perfect correctness concealed, and made dandyism the privileged form of modern heroism.

Such are the principal virtues that an association whose end is itself must first develop. There is nothing in them that individuals cannot accept without mental reservations. On the contrary, they recognize here the extension of certain of his tastes, which they felt but were unable to put their finger on until these tastes were made explicit through possible applications. These tastes made virtues by transposition to a social register are revealed to themselves, and, far from becoming dulled, are given that increased decisiveness and force that define the superiority of lucid consciousness over vague presentiment, groping and confused.

These virtues tend concurrently to sharpen the outlines of the group and to deepen precipitously the moat isolating it within the society of its origin. Those who practice them with this in mind soon find that they form a true *milieu*, a center in the organic sense of the word, an island of heavy density that, as a result, is capable of gathering to it those scattered bodies drifting in a dilute society, and of thus conferring on these active cells a role that is actually positive in place of the unbalanced and sterile agitation they were reveling in before.

This is no longer clement weather. There is a rising wind of subversion in the world now, a cold wind, harsh, arctic, one of those winds that is murderous and so salubrious, one that kills the fragile, the sickly, and the birds, *one that does not let them get through the winter*. And so a silent, slow, irreversible cleansing takes place in nature, like a death tide that rises imperceptibly. Those who are sedentary, in the refuge of their overheated dwellings, exhaust themselves bringing their limbs back to life; the blood congealed in their veins no longer circulates. They nurse their cracked skin and their chilblains—and shiver. They are afraid to venture outdoors, where the hardy nomads, bareheaded, and exulting in their whole bodies, intoxicated with the glacial, tonic violence that beats their stiff and frozen hair against their faces, come to laugh at the wind.

A winter, perhaps a Quaternary—the glaciers' advance—is beginning for this broken-down, halfway collapsing, senile society: a spirit of examination, incredulity that is pitiless and deeply disrespectful, that loves force and judges according to the capacity for resistance—and is cunning enough to swiftly unmask cunning. This climate will be very harsh, this selection will cut very close. Each one will have to prove himself before ears that are deaf to song, but vigilant and practiced, before eyes that are blind to ornament, but piercing. Through eager and skillful hands, through a tact that is extraordinarily well mannered, must pass this sense that is more material, more realistic than others, not fooled by appearances, this sense that perfectly separates the hollow from the full.

Those whose circulation is good will be recognized *in the exceeding cold* by their pink cheeks, their clear skin, their ease, their exhilaration at finally enjoying what they require of life and the great quantity of oxygen their lungs demand. Returned then to their weakness and driven from the scene, the others shrink back, shrivel, and curl up in their holes. The bustlers are paralyzed, the fancy talkers silenced, the comics made invisible. The coast is clear for those who are most able: no obstructions on the roads to impede their progress, none of the countless, melodious warblings to cover up their voices. Let them number and acknowledge each other in this rarefied air; and may winter leave them closely united, shoulder to shoulder, conscious of their strength; then the new spring will be the consecration of their destiny.

Declaration of the College of Sociology on the International Crisis

[The international crisis: It arose in Czechoslovakia and subsided in Munich (Germany). See Jean Guérin's brief news items quoted in the Appendixes: Events.

This "Declaration" appeared simultaneously in the November issues of three reviews: the NRF, Esprit, *and* Volontés *(November 1938). Several of the preceding issues of* Esprit *had already given considerable space to various analyses of the crisis. A large portion of the* NRF, *particularly the whole section "L'Air du mois" (which accepted the College's declaration), is devoted to the Munich accords (Petitjean, Benda, Schlumberger, Arland, Montherlant, de Rougemont, Audiberti, Pourrat, Lecomte)—devoted to denouncing them.*

In the same month's Revue universelle, *Thierry Maulnier spent a whole article on the November* NRF: *"The intellectuals are too late." In reality, only Benda's opinions are in question (the College's text is not mentioned). It was his turn to be worked over by Maulnier, who two weeks before had done the same to J.-R. Bloch, initiating him to his four truths ("Où les responsables accusent").*

The Munich accords were signed during the night of September 29-30. They put an end to a month of war threats skillfully conducted by Hitler, who wanted to annex the Sudetenland (a part of Czechoslovakian territory but with a German population) to the Reich. The democracies gave in, to the great relief of their populations, who spared no applause for the representatives when they returned home.

One could breathe again. The Treaty of Versailles had put an end to the war.

The Munich accords mark "the end of the postwar period," as Robert Aron soon put it in the title of a book inspired by these events.

In Esprit, *the "Declaration of the College of Sociology" was preceded by an editors' note: "The College of Sociology, soon to be discussed with our readers, sends us the following message, which seems to us to throw an accurate light on how the crisis was handled." Three months earlier, in August,* Esprit *had already mentioned in its "Revue des revues" the collection "For a College of Sociology," adding: "We shall return to this." This good intention was signed D. R. (Denis de Rougemont?). But, while the College returned to* Esprit *with this "Declaration," it does not seem that* Esprit *returned to the College.*

In Volontés *as well, the editors had introduced the College's text with a note: "This is not a case of a simple request to be included. We liked the vigor of the text."*

On the subject of Munich, there is a dossier of the crisis that Nizan (winner of the Interallié prize in 1938 for his novel, La Conspiration*) published under the title* Chronique de septembre *(Paris, 1939). On the back cover of this book, published at Gallimard, an advertisement reproduces the table of contents of the issue devoted by the* NRF *to the crisis. The "Declaration" is mentioned there.*

The following December 13, Bataille's lecture on the structure of democracies will be essentially a return to the subject of this September crisis; see Lectures: 1938-39. For a quite different reaction to the crisis from someone who was soon to be involved in the College's activities, see Guastalla's lecture on January 10, 1939.]

The College of Sociology considers the recent international crisis to be an experience of major importance for a number of reasons. It has neither the time nor the means to examine every aspect of the question. Especially, it acknowledges no competence to interpret one way or another the diplomatic evolution that led to keeping the peace, and even more, no ability to determine what part of it was anticipated and what unexpected, what part was agreed to and what inflicted— only, to determine if need be, what part of it was staging and what part sincerity. It knows the simultaneous facility and fragility of such interpretations. Wary of these, it expresses the wish that those whose competence is no greater will follow its example. That is the first point.

The College of Sociology sees its specific role to be the assessment, without indulgence, of the collective psychological reactions aroused by the imminence of war, and that, when the danger was over, fell too quickly into what must rightly be called *restorative* oblivion, or else turned into rosy, almost comforting recollections in a complicitous memory. Those who suffered the most crippling bewilderment end up imagining they acted heroically. The public already gives credence to the legend that it behaved calmly, in a dignified and resolute manner: Did not the Council's president have the cleverness to thank them for it?[1] As it is, we have to say that these are much too pretty names for feelings that only the words "consternation," "resignation," and "fear" had fit until now. The show produced was one of immobilized and silent confusion, a sorry surrender to the event; conscious of its inferiority, it was the unmistakably frightened pose of a people who refuse to accept war as one of the possibilities of its politics when confronted by a nation that grounds its politics in war. That is the second point.

To this moral panic the absurdity of the political positions was added. At the outset the situation was already paradoxical: dictatorships speculating on the peoples' right to self-determination,[2] and democracies putting their chips on the principle of natural frontiers and the vital interests of nations. And afterward these characteristics became more and more extremely pronounced. The son and heir of that Joseph Chamberlain who spoke explicitly of England's universal dominion and who formed its empire[3] could be seen going to beseech Mr. Hitler to consent to any settlement at all, *provided that it be peaceful*.[4] One could read in a communist daily a comparison between the "messenger of peace" and Lord Kitchener, a parallel entirely benefiting the latter. If one had not seen it with one's own eyes, one would have refused to believe that some day the Communists would have to congratulate the man who fought the war in Transvaal for his systematic destruction of the civilian population, for his concentration camps, or for having delivered a great territory to his country (it is true that they did not describe it as "gold and diamond mines for the City bankers"). One should also keep in mind American public opinion, which, from the other side of the ocean, at a safe distance, showed what stupidity, pharisaism and a certain platonic quixotism, which seem more and more characteristic of democracies, are worth.[5] That is the third and last point, before the conclusion.

The College of Sociology is not a political organism. Its members hold whatever opinion they please. It does not think it is obliged to consider the particular interests of France in the venture. Its role is solely to draw the lesson it is bound to draw from the events, and do this while there is still time, that is to say before everyone is completely persuaded that in the heat of the event he effectively demonstrated calm, dignity, and resolve. The College of Sociology regards the general absence of intense reaction in the face of war as a sign of man's *devirilization*. It does not hesitate to see the cause of this in the relaxation of society's current ties, which are practically nonexistent as a result of the development of bourgeois individualism. There is no love lost in its condemnation of the effect: men who are so alone, *so deprived of destiny*, that they find themselves absolutely defenseless when faced with the possibility of death, who, having no profound reasons to fight, find themselves inevitably cowards in the face of battle, no matter what battle—some sort of conscious sheep resigned to the slaughterhouse.

The College of Sociology defined itself essentially as an organism for research and study. It continues to be this. But, on its founding, it reserved for itself the eventual possibility of being, if it could, something else: a center of energy. Yesterday's events suggest, perhaps even demand, that it emphasize this aspect of its self-assigned undertaking. That is why it is taking the initiative of this public declaration. That is why it urges those, for whom the only solution anguish disclosed is the creation of a vital bond between men, to join with it, with no other determining factor than the awareness of the *absolute lie* of current political forms and the necessity for reconstructing on this assumption a collective mode of existence that takes no geographical or social limitation into account and that allows one to behave oneself when death threatens.[6]

BATAILLE, CAILLOIS, LEIRIS
Paris, October 7, 1938

Inquiry: On Spiritual Directors

[His inquiry on spiritual directors, "directeurs de conscience," [1] *was published by Monnerot in issue 14 of* Volontés, *February 1939. This review brought out by Georges Pelorson, will be recalled as one of the publications that issued the statement made by the College after Munich. Queneau was a regular contributor to it (his contributions will be republished in* Le Voyage en Grèce).

Monnerot had been close enough to the College to have figured among those signing the "Note" that announced its founding. He was even close enough to have given it its name (see later in this chapter and the Appendixes: Marginalia). For his beginnings, one can consult the study by Leiris: Contacts de civilisations en Martinique et en Guadeloupe *(Paris, 1955) pp. 107-8, as well as Régis Antoine's* Les Écrivains français des Antilles *(Paris, 1978). Jules Monnerot (Jules-Marcel Monnerot, who began by signing himself Jules-M. or J.-M. Monnerot in order to distinguish himself from his father, also Jules Monnerot, a professor of philosophy and a Communist from Antilles), with several other students transplanted to Paris from Martinique, published in June 1932 the only issue of* Légitime défense. *"It was upon the appearance of a prosurrealist review whose contributors were from Antilles that we came in regular contact with Jules Monnerot,"* André Breton would state twenty years later in the eleventh interview of Entretiens. *Indeed, starting in 1933, Monnerot is seen contributing to the official organ of the surrealist movement, which Breton had put in the service of the revolution. It is there, for the first time, that his signature is side by side that of Caillois, and also that of Georges Sadoul, who was soon to have a fit over the College of Sociology (see Appendixes: Marginalia). Monnerot was next a con-*

tributor to Commune, *the cultural review of the Communist party. A special is-sue of* Commune *appeared on the occasion of the International Congress of Writers for the Defense of Culture held in Paris in June 1935 (among the speak-ers were Gide, Heinrich Mann, Barbusse, Huxley, Babel, Pasternak, Malraux, Benda, and Nizan). The table of contents lists a "Declaration by the Delegation of French Antilleans" signed by Monnerot, who still signs Jules M. Monnerot which begins with this sentence: "As grandsons of black slaves and sometimes of white adventurers as well, whose physical aspect is often a straightforward chal-lenge to the myth of race, we are proud to lend our young voices to the great voices of freedom, of genuine human demands that are expressed in this Con-gress" (Commune, no. 23 [July 1935], p. 1250). The second paragraph of this declaration congratulates Soviet Russia for its political position on "ethnic characteristics" and "national minorities." A year later in June 1936, Mon-nerot along with Caillois (but also Aragon and Tzara) will appear on the board of* Inquisitions, *a short-lived review also published by* the Éditions sociales internationales *and warmly welcomed by the pen of Georges Sadoul in* Com-mune—*anyhow, more warmly welcomed than the College of Sociology would be two years later. By the next year his name begins to appear in tables of contents put together by Bataille: In March 1937, both he and Caillois spoke out during a meeting at the* Palais de la Mutualité *in which Bataille discussed Nietzsche. This was presumably to launch the issue of* Acéphale *on "Nietzsche et les fascistes" that had just appeared. The next number, devoted to "Dionysus," was in press. Monnerot had contributed "Dionysus the Philosopher." The "Note on the Foundation of a College of Sociology" was published in this same issue, and it was the only time that Monnerot actually put his signature to some public expres-sion on the part of the College. Though he was its instigator,* polemos, *conten-tion, soon intervened. The reply the College deigned to give his inquiry (see later in this chapter,* The College of Sociology) *gives some indication of the point to which relations had deteriorated since their baptismal euphoria.*

Monnerot finally recounted this episode himself. His recital of it will be found in one of the appendixes added, in 1979, to the reedition of his Sociologie du communisme *(1963) published by the Éditions Libres-Hallier. Of these few pages of intellectual autobiography, Monnerot's deep opposition to the Durkheimism of the French school of sociology will not be forgotten. It is an op-position whose themes are closely akin to the epistemological transgressions called for by Bataille and Caillois. Nonetheless, this opposition was to pose problems for the College. Its virulence was unacceptable to Leiris (who, more-over, seems not to have put in an appearance in the College until after Monnerot had left it). But Caillois, as well, defined himself as a disciple of Mauss. How-ever much his thought might have been, as Lacan would say, "newly at odds with the sociology in which it was formed," he was far from viewing himself as banished for this from sociology and even less from society. In 1946 Monnerot published* Les Faits sociaux ne sont pas des choses, *whose title* Social Phenomena Are Not Things, *makes no bones about its anti-durkheimian inspiration. The same theoretical inspiration was at the origin of* La Poésie moderne et le sacré *(completed in 1940), a sociology of surrealism considered as a secret society that took its references from Pareto, from the German sociologists, and, among the French, from Georges Sorel and Lévy-Bruhl. At the same time Monnerot reproached French sociology for its claims to objectivism, he criticized it for falling back on secondhand analysis, for limiting itself to perusing and commenting on field studies, and for constituting itself as "a sort of metaethnography": It is frightened at the idea of what might happen to it if it dared study the things that "need urgent understanding" in social life. Since Durkheimian theory had become the official state sociology of the Third Republic, Monnerot soon let himself go in dreams of a College of Sociology that would contrive to reinsert reflection on social phenomena into the private sector.*

Thus it was that "between the two world wars of the twentieth century, some men concerned with this sort of problem—some very young, some less young (it is surprising, moreover, that there were not more of them)—in order to put an urgently needed end to this stagnation, spontaneously were able to contemplate putting sociology into private hands *in our country. At least, that is what I began to think when I read in the review* La Critique sociale *(not when it first appeared but much later), Georges Bataille's text 'La Notion de dépense.' I wanted to know the author. It was easy. Friends we had in common introduced us. And shortly afterward Bataille published in two parts (the last two issues of the review) "La Structure psychologique du fascisme."* [2] *Subsequently, I introduced him to Roger Caillois whom I had met shortly before at André Breton's on the rue Fontaine.*

"Prompted by my keenness for understanding certain dominant phenomena of the first half of the century (communism, fascism), I then conceived of a project for research that as a matter of priority consisted of an approach to the burning questions. *In France the established sociology (in the sense in which the British refer to the established Church) either avoided these subjects or skimmed over them, applying nineteenth-century prejudices that constituted enough of a barrier to counter-indicate any elucidation, what am I saying?—any attempt at elucidation—in this field for those under its jurisdiction. (. . .) It was an area of investigation such as this (though not this alone) that a group that I named to myself 'The College of Sociology', created for this purpose, was to explore. I mentioned this to Bataille and he seemed tempted by it, and also to Caillois, an enthusiastic student of Georges Dumézil whom very few of us were acquainted with at that time. The project I had just formulated thus 'took hold,' but 'out of context.' It rather quickly turned out that our ideas and methods (Bataille's, Caillois's, and mine) for moving to the realization of our concepts were divergent. Often Bataille had more or less created 'groupuscles,' and deserted them*

just as rapidly. All of them were connected to the Trotskyist 'fraction' of the literary set, the dissidents of dissidents. It was characteristic of the period and the milieu, and it seems our friend had the temperament of a heresiarch. Roger Caillois, French-born and a great writer, who already at eighteen had the intellectual authority and grammatical infallibility that we have always since known as his, was waiting for his first—dazzling—book Le Mythe et l'homme *to appear at Gallimard. Both of them envisaged an absolutely immediate public activity made up of lectures and communiqués. I thought it was necessary first, if not to settle on a method, which was far from being done, at least really to get together with each other. I did not expect anything worthwhile to come of improvisation in such matters, and on my insistence we met at Bataille's on the rue de Rennes where I put forward and developed a certain number of propositions on the subject. I remember my reasoning.*

"If, I said, the program of the 'College of Sociology' entails the approach to 'burning questions,' we must expect to be burned ourselves by these inflammable materials.[*] *Describing politics in the making truthfully and relevantly is already intervening: truth's blistering nature . . . Motives hardly matter. I quoted Robert Michels: 'Watch out! It's not a question of treating social phenomena as things.'"*[†]

There is nothing in these remarks that is not in keeping with ideas in the manifestos published by the College between 1937 and 1938. The founding "Note" of June 1937 denounced sociological distancing in the same way; it deplored the discipline's only taking an interest in the remotest societies and protecting itself against any contamination of the "spirit of research" by the possible virulence of what was studied. The signatories there expressed their desire, demanding mobilization of the sociologist as a sorcerer's apprentice who, taking on the "vital elements of society," would have to get involved. The notes added by Bataille to his contribution to "For a College of Sociology" ("The Sorcerer's Apprentice," see notes 1 and 4) are in the same tone: In them the author denounces the "moral devastation" caused by the timid epistemology controlling the practice of official sociology. If the social phenomenon is "the totality of existence," no "specialized activity" would be in a position to give an account of it. Modern history, as Monnerot saw it, can be defined by "the incarnation of Weltanschauungen, *worldviews, in vast groups of men in whose vanguard are activist legions, 'storm troopers'* (Sturmabteilungen): *With the declared project of making its undertaking move imperceptibly from the 'will to knowledge to the will to power' (see the closing remarks of "For a College of Sociology"), it should*

---

[*]A proposition that I was later to be more specific about and develop in *Les Faits sociaux ne sont pas des choses* in the chapter: *Sociologie de la sociologie.*

[†]*Les Partis politiques, essai sur les tendances oligarchiques des démocraties,* Paris, 1914, p.303.

not have been hard for the College to see that as the avant-garde it was acting as the storm troopers of the modern mind.

Since the institution had accepted the program he proposed, where did the quarrel come from? And Monnerot's ensuing departure? Probably friction between personalities played some part. However, Monnerot in the last analysis gives as the reason for the break his colleagues' orientation, which was too literary for him; he had hoped that the venture would get away from any "surrealist overstatement." The same activity could not simultaneously be a matter for sociology and for literature: To pretend that they are concurrent is an insult to "genre distinctions," and, at best, to succeed at this would bring into being something he called a "Sorbonnic Dadaism." "Some time afterward I became aware that the orientation of Bataille, and presumably Caillois, who were contributors to the Nouvelle Revue française, was in the direction of the literary possibilities. Right off I said to Bataille—with a brusqueness and impatience that I have no explanations or excuses for today—that under those conditions I would not take part in the venture. He did nothing to prevent my leaving. I told him it was final, and that's where we left it. Shortly afterward, I had a letter from Roger Caillois containing this sentence: 'If you think we are taking liberties with you, is the real answer abstention? Come and defend your point of view.' But that was what I had already done. So I did not participate at all in the events by means of which the 'College of Sociology' made itself more or less known to the public—before its ultraspeedy and easily predictable dispersal" ("Le Collège de Sociologie ou le problème interrompu," in Sociologie du communisme [Paris, 1979], pp. 541-45).

An undeniable community of interests and concerns, for that matter, would survive this difficult situation—as Monnerot's publications following the war attest. Soon he himself will mention this period of relations with Bataille without alluding to these difficulties at all (see Appendixes: Marginalia). Only he, from among those whose names were associated with the College, would be a member of the first editorial board of Critique, the review founded by Bataille after the Liberation.

1. The text of the inquiry was the lead article in the February 1939 issue of Volontés, occupying the first three pages.

It begins with a question: "Do you think that spiritual direction is an organic function in human communities? Or, on the contrary, that the society in which we live, the community of which we are members, has attained a sort of adulthood that permits it to do without directors?" (Translate, in the terms of Leiris's book published at the same time: Would manhood cause one to renounce confession?) Next an answer is suggested by clarifying the sense of the question: Until the eighteenth century, religion, especially the Catholic religion, held a near monopoly on spiritual direction. What has happened now that rationalism has *considerably weakened it? Has direction simply disappeared, or does it survive in new forms?*

The theme of the second paragraph can be described as the linking of nationalism and universal values. A little history there, as well. But this time it goes back further than the eighteenth century—in fact to the Roman Empire and the Christian religion, which in their time eliminated "tribal religions." These religions in our own time, however, are experiencing a renewed outbreak bearing the colors of "the great postwar national movements (Russian communism, Italian fascism, German nationalsocialism)." In order to "evade, outmatch, and master" this recurrence of what was eliminated—and this is the second question—"we ask if you believe that the irruption into Western history of a new universalism is necessary?"

II. Five months after having published the text of the inquiry, Volontés *published the responses it had received. With a few of Monnerot's comments at the beginning and end, they make up the entire June 1939 issue (no. 18) of the review.*

For an introduction Monnerot clarified certain points of the inquiry that had generated misunderstandings.

1. No, he had not wanted to mix up the respective spheres of the spiritual and the temporal. It is in events themselves that, at every moment, the frontier between them is put in question: "The priesthood's and Empire's quarrel" is one of the forms taken by "the war of souls for the right to investiture, that is to say, for supreme authority."

2. The collapse of religions that followed the advance of enlightenment politicized the sacred, which is now invested in nationalism: "The flag replaces the cross."

3. A final point, about sociological method, recalls once more the "Note on the Foundation of the College" and similar comments by Bataille in "The Sorcerer's Apprentice." Monnerot writes "It is striking that sociologists never write their own sociology. I mean the sociology of the society whose sociologists they are." And he goes on to denounce any venture whose intent would be to infer a moral ethic starting from a science, even if it were from a science of morals.

Then come the replies, divided into three sections by Monnerot. First there were those "answers that meant to help state the issue," by far the most important group. We find there the opinions of Alain, Benda, André Chastel; opinions of a personalist group with Klossowski, Paul-Louis Landsberg, Marcel Moré, and Denis de Rougemont as members; and opinions of Georges Duthuit, Father Fessard, Jean Grenier, René Guastalla, Pierre Libra, Maulnier, Mounier, Paulhan, Georges Pelorson, Gaëtan Picon, Jean Schlumberger, Camille Schuwer, and Jean Wahl. Then there are the "answers offering partial solutions," where we find replies by Paul Guth, Dr. R. Loewenstein, and Armand

Petitjean. The third and last group contains answers from "those who responded to the inquiry without answering the questions": That is where the College of Sociology ends up, in the company of Georges Duhamel, Pierre Mabille, and Ramuz.

III. In the NRF *of July 1939, A. M. Petitjean, himself one of those questioned who replied to the inquiry, commented on the issue of* Volontés *that put together the reactions provoked by Monnerot. First, he saw a sign of the times in the fact that "we feel in much more of a hurry to ask questions than to answer them." He continues: "The answers do not exhaust the questions. Even the questions are barely formulated. Some writers are beginning to be aware that their consciousness lags behind their moral standards. Some intellectuals think the world no longer a beautiful spectacle. And on top of it all, a professor of philosophy, questioned on his raison d'être, humbly concludes his answer: "This is my perception for the moment. It is very vague and I hesitate to send you these useless lines.*

"'Happy New Year, happy new years to men of action.'"

In Les Cahiers du Sud *Jacques Bénet commented on the responses to the inquiry (no. 218, July 1939, p. 629): "Each man on the eve, perhaps, of the fearful adventure, wonders what ideal so many cannons, so many planes, so many future corpses go to defend; each of the animals asks his shepherd where he is being led; each free man demands and requires that everyone sacrifice his life, yet without being able to explain to him why he must die." For that matter, the same J. Bénet had just published an inquiry of his own in* Les Cahiers du Sud *(no. 216, May 1939) that dealt with a related theme: "To oppose the barbarism that is more and more threatening, only a catholicism freed from the impurity and hypocrisy that have nearly changed its spirit and jeopardized its fate seems valid." Gaëtan Picon and André Chastel among others will respond to this inquiry. Pierre Missac, in his reply, mentioned the position of Caillois, in whom, he said, "There is progressively developing a detachment from the object (his ideas on etiquette [see "The Winter Wind"]) and an abandonment to certain tendencies (the underlying causes of his taste for harshness and aridity) that make him receptive to fascism." In the proofs, Missac added a note at the bottom of the page correcting this suspicion: "Since the writing of this reply, Mr. Caillois has declared himself a Communist. I acknowledge that. But that does not basically change my thesis" (P. Missac, "Avec des cartes truquées," Les Cahiers du Sud, no. 216 [May, 1939], p .424).*

Among the replies to Monnerot's inquiry, only those that can be related to the College of Sociology because of their signers or their implications will be found here.]

Pierre Klossowski

QUESTION: Do you think that the society in which we are living, the historical community whose members we are, has reached a sort of adulthood that permits it to do without spiritual directors?[3]

ANSWER: The individual who today enjoys the sweet pleasures of a democratic morality would not want, under any circumstance, to miss an opportunity liable to make him forget its distinctive reality. The fear of finding himself permanently decided on something or committed to something, inspires in him such a phobia for any spiritual authority that the least principle that might establish inner constraints seems to him a psychological agent of some external despotism. Today all individuals are terrified of discovering that they are guilty for the situation in the midst of which they are living. This terror is ambiguous: It is the pure and simple terror of being, all the while desiring to be.

To be guilty or not to be at all, that is the dilemma contemporary man has felt so profoundly that he had to invent psychoanalysis in order to compel himself to lead a guilty existence, all the while giving himself the illusion of having scientifically eliminated guilt. The psychoanalyst will teach him that this feeling is only a dangerous nightmare, only an autosuggestion under whose influence he could not live.

In fact, psychoanalysis is only a secularization of the Christian examination of conscience. But whereas the *spiritual director* establishes a transcendental dependency of the soul in relation to God, psychoanalysts are doing their best to destroy not this dependency, which would be impossible, but the organ that is aware of it, which they call the *superego*.

This *superego* —this is the most usual clinical situation—has prevented the subject's being alive to enjoy the living conditions of his surroundings. In the course of his neurosis the subject has developed an interpretative system that he is no longer able to escape unless one comes to free him from it. But what we are accustomed to call here "neurosis" is really the diversion of fervor from its real goal. In the midst of a basically skeptical world, the subject's fervor, finding no justifying reference, is enclosed in an asocial and incommunicable state. Then, by his very nature incapable of finding a place for the superego in a world of references that he, on the contrary is only seeking to refute, the psychoanalyst dislocates the superego in order to allow the subject to live in a world that has no reference that will justify him.

By establishing the Oedipus complex, orthodox psychoanalysts believe they are able to eradicate original sin which, in their view, constitutes the basic neurosis of our humanity. All life's inhibitions are reduced to this complex. If, indeed, virility is the criterion of psychic health and if the representation of paternal anger has inhibited this virility, the psychoanalyst, on the pretext of destroying paternal censorship within the subject, must take care not to destroy infinitely more: *piety*. Perhaps the objection will be made that the true goal of psychoanalysis is to make the subject become aware of the responsibility that the reality of others imposes on him, particularly in those cases of paranoia that make the subject tend to project onto others what he censors within himself.

Now, if psychoanalysts themselves are explained according to the theory of projection, they in turn could not help seeming to be the *exponents* of the collective paranoia of a given social order. In effect, the community has no other criterion than an instinct for what is injurious to its norm. In relation to that norm, the health of individuals cannot be recognized, insofar as their discriminatory instincts coincide with the community's, except by their faculty of discerning the enemy. Today, while it is true that psychoanalysts fulfill a *social* function, it is only to the extent that they cultivate, on the ruins of guilt, the discriminatory instinct of the individual; and the cure they are able to achieve will only be an adaptation of the subject's soul to the given forms of the collective paranoia.

Far from attesting to its adulthood, the fact that our modern humanity dispenses with spiritual directors and puts itself in the hands of psychoanalysts proves that it dreads being adult; for moral recognition of guilt, or the conscious shouldering of it, has always coincided with complete maturity. But there are situations in which it can seem preferable to humanity to postpone *sine die* the moment at which it will have to pronounce its own sentence. To the same extent that spiritual directors were needed by generations of *mature men* for whom self-accusation, an appeal for pardon and humility, entered into the structure of a virile character, psychoanalysts are needed by a civilization of pubescents, that is, prisoners of a senile adolescence, in which individuals have become incapable of opposing to the multiple solicitations of modern life the resistance that is necessary for a conclusive orientation of character and existence. That is why those who seem to lead the masses are not really in charge but rather are *agents of discharge for guilt*, whether they take on the accomplishment of certain dangerous or criminal acts (agitators, dictators, and in certain cases great criminals), sensationalize reality (journalists, popular writers), or provide the support of a *scientific method* to reduce the feeling of loss (psychoanalysts) or to abolish the apparently economic grounds for social unrest (Marxist sociologists).

Georges Duthuit

A few men, free from any commitment to the institutions and past dogmas responsible in differing degrees for the present bankruptcy, and equally uncommitted to any fraudulent, economico-political ventures of renovation operating on beings who are either fictional or almost completely drained of substance; a handful of adepts, outraged in the same way by morals that are in the process of being compromised, bargained over, evaded, morals that are either eternally or provisionally secure, either material or spiritual, and by "future" systems based on universal, utilitarian degeneration or on the vile mystique of race and State; a relatively small group of seekers ready to carry to its final conclusions their examination of questions of personhood, of the whole person, investigated from its heights to its depths, in its relationship with the social, and ready to model their conduct on these glimpsed conclusions; some patient and resolute individuals with one hope or another but all possessed of the same appetite for privation as for total wealth, cautiously progressing only by a succession of discoveries, dictated by the moment, able, if the case arises, to serve unrestrictedly, secretly if necessary and by guile, the decisions they have taken—no doubt one could find here, in these few, the possibilities for radically influential work. Calculating the immediate results is unimportant.

There have been periods of collective concentration and exhilaration. Spiritual directors then, attempting to tighten their alliance with ties knotted from vile and solemn, impure and sacred, hideous and wonderful things, in order to win over to the common cause wandering instincts and rigorously intractable wills, brought into play every known means of revelation and seduction—poetry, ritual dance, music, architecture, painting, and sculpture. They have left us texts, inspired monuments, even traces of ceremony that can still be recommended. Such vestiges at least will serve to set the destitution or sordid brutality of the parodies of organization and religion, today claiming to settle the destinies of the world, in a glaring light.[4]

René M. Guastalla

I am especially touched that you considered asking me to respond to your inquiry because, on the one hand, I find it more worthwhile, a better way of putting the problems that I think are the essential ones for our time, and, on the other hand, it can only be pleasant to find that one is counted among the young when, as I am, one is a part of the generation that the war took from school and the trenches sent home to battle for our bread; the generation whose tragedy, doubtless, was never to know what youth is and probably to retain an excruciating nostalgia for it always.[5]

Because of this gratitude that I owe you, I am bound to apologize for not answering your entire questionnaire, and being over forty—just barely!—makes it my duty to let reason speak first, telling you why I can answer only a part of your questions.

The more I believe that the problems you formulate are the essential problems, the more I believe that the complexity—though focused—of your questionnaire embraces all of the complexity of reality, at the same time emphasizing the unity that emerges from it, and, for that very reason, the more I feel unable to respond to each point. And if I am to be sincere, I will go so far as to say that it is desirable that each of your correspondents does the same as I. It is only possible to answer everything in the name of an ideology, an idea of the world that is "inspired by passion." And the odds are that the ideologies most of us could claim for our authority are foreign, for two reasons: foreign in fact, colored all Russian red, Italian black, or German brown; foreign in method, as far removed from Claude Bernard as from Descartes.

And this deserves some explanation, I think: Enough attention has not been paid to the fact that, among all living languages, there are only two, English and ours, whose development, from Chaucer to Joyce, from Thuroude to Jules Romains, has continued without those dreadful voids, those renunciations, and those silences that have created blanks and breaks in the seventeenth and eighteenth centuries of Spain, Germany, and Italy and in the Russian steppe that stretches from *byliny* to Pushkin. And that it is precisely present-day France and England that are also the only nations that reject whatever myths are around, resist them, have a guilty conscience in their presence, seems related to this unique continuity in their literary life. The battle in which (I hope soon to prove)[6] the myth and the book have been engaged since the Hellenic fifth century—and on which our civilization, through always precarious and endlessly threatened compromises, has been built, drawing its very energy from this precariousness and these threats—this battle between the book and the myth seems to me to have a sort of confirmation and proof in the symmetry that I was soon to discover between the destiny of English and French literature and the attitude of the two nations confronted with the myths of our times.

Whence the refusal, if we are to think according to the French way of thinking, of a view that is ideological and total. It is up to you to do the algebraic sum of the responses that are given, to isolate the main themes, in your role of simultaneously passionate and impartial witnesses.

The problems you pose are so serious that it seems to me the least you can demand of your correspondents is the modesty of good faith. There should be no question here, where our all is at stake, of elegance or of indulgence. According to the lessons accrued in everyday experience, let everyone, meanly, sordidly, offer what each one of us has learned! That, at least, is what I am going to try to do. It is up to you, either to discard what follows, because you will recognize some futile ghosts in it that are peculiar to the one whom they inhabit, or to take from it, if you think that possible, what seems to you capable of nourishing everyone.

My experience of public life is not profound enough for me to answer, other than very superficially, the first part of your questionnaire.

I shall limit myself to establishing a distinction between what I would like to call *spiritual advisers* and *intellectual advisers*, "directors of conscience" and "directors of reason." The former act in the world of faith, and it would be a possibly very serious abuse of the term if one gave this name to those who, if they are honest, are searching for truths; whereas it only fits those who speak in the name of a Truth that they are certain has been revealed to them by Grace, a Truth that has chosen them and that they have not sought.

It seems to me very revealing of our times that you name the doctor among these spiritual advisers. Confusion between temporal and spiritual healing is the mark of myth, well expressed in the name *medicine man*. Civilization, on the contrary, consists in distinguishing between the two activities.

In the realm of faith, all is given; in the realm of reason, all is painfully sought. And just as the dignity of faith is in submission to what is given, in the same way the dignity of reason is in submitting oneself to a sentence of searching. And presumably it is possible for both dignities to come together in the same person, or in the same society: Nonetheless, they have their own ends and their distinctive laws.

To confuse them can only be disorder, deceiving some and a temptation to deceive for others; bewitchment of the masses, bewitchment of the sorcerer.

It seems to me that the fact, which you mention, that there are zones of silence no longer inhabited by faith must (if we intend to think of the good of all, and at the very least of the good of the majority) oblige us simultaneously to acclaim and preserve the zones in which it is present, and only to speak in the name of reason.

Believers, while going beyond reason, can accept being placed on its terrain. But unbelievers, no matter how they regret a lost faith, no matter what respect they still have (and that is the least of it) for those whom faith inhabits, would not be able to admit or to pretend to admit the laws formulated by faith without a dreadful sacrilege.

Having made this distinction, I think that all those whom you are considering are able to play the role of "intellectual advisers." But they must not—at least, I think—dream of an impossible spiritual power. It will be enough for them to perform their own task well. Actually, from the moment an activity is inscribed as spiritual, one can no longer do it halfway without betrayal. It is better absolutely not to do it at all. But, to compensate, a restricted task that one likes because one has chosen it and in addition performs conscientiously, engages the one accomplishing it and those for whom (no matter how few) it is accomplished, and engages them far beyond what it is worth on its own. On the level of reason it is work that saves, whether an experiment correctly performed, an exact diagnosis, or a minutely studied text. Work that saves, not by the result achieved, but by itself.

I am much more comfortable answering the second part of your inquiry.

To your great credit, you have posed the question very precisely there, better than it is usually done. The following question, to which I shall limit myself, seems especially meaningful: "Do you see in the great postwar national movements (Russian communism, Italian fascism, German national socialism) a return of the tribal religions that were eliminated by the Roman Empire and victorious Christianity, a stunning return to wider territorial zones and more complex social bodies?'' I believe that if the present phenomenon is indeed akin to a return to these tribal religions, there is, however, a rather marked difference between these movements and the myths of the city.

For my part I detest both of these new cults equally. Life in them would be impossible for me for many reasons, but I do not consider myself sufficiently the center of the world to refuse to concede on behalf of others the triumph of one or the other of these myths, if I thought they could make my fellow human beings, or most of them, happy.

This has been necessary to state, since I cannot really give any evidence in what is, perforce, a limited space. And I hope this statement will suffice to prevent accusations of letting my passion speak when I maintain that it seems to me likely that this renaissance of social myths will be of short duration, when measured with the eyes of history.

The tribal religions conquered first by Greek thought and prophetic enthusiasm, and then by Christianity (at the same time heir to them both), will not revive. And for two reasons: First, unlike the natural myths of former times, today's myths are the myths of fiction writers, in that each of them could name its author. We say (and are doubtless wrong) Marxism when speaking of the Russian myth, and Hitlerism (this time rightly) in speaking of the German myth, and if we do not say Mussolinism, it is because Italian fascism has not yet been able to formulate a doctrine. Sometimes it is carried away with Sorel, sometimes with Hitler. Perhaps, because it is harder to make the Italians renounce centuries of individualist civilization. Now, a myth that can name its author is only a fiction like any other, made to measure for the human brain. And it knows that it is this one fact that threatens it: That a person, if isolated, imprisoned, and tortured (Pastor Niemöller), would reject it. Far more, all it takes is another fictionist, more fortunate or more unscrupulous, for a struggle to erupt between the myth and its rival in which both risk perishing. Natural myths, on the contrary, were seen by the citizen who had no desire to encroach on neighboring myths as beyond discussion.

Furthermore, ever since the Hellenic fifth century, white man has become accustomed, bit by bit, to being an individual, to thinking of his own salvation—temporal or spiritual, it hardly matters!—whereas myth has an existence only in the unanimous accord of hardly differentiated beings.

Here Plato's example may be of some use: At the moment in which, beneath the Sophists' blows, myths are dying and the city is dying, Plato, prophet of the *Republic*, with incomparable genius, forges new myths. And he knew what a real myth was himself: Those of his childhood were not so distant. And he knew this so well that, of all those myths forged by people, his are the ones most like natural myths, to the point of remaining spontaneously carved in our memories: the Chargers, the Cave . . . And yet, though privileged in time and in genius, Plato found no way to recreate a cohesion that did not come completely undone again. And he felt his failure himself on the day when, renouncing the enclosed city of the *Republic*, he submitted to the compromises (which were themselves destined for failure) that he attempted in the *Laws*.

Barring total upheaval, the white man is no longer to forget that he ran the formidable risk and sought the perilous honor of being an individual.

Far from believing that we must imitate the fictionists surrounding us, on the pretext that myth should respond to the aspirations of our time, on the contrary, I am confident that myth responds to special circumstances, to accidental misfortunes. We should not be astounded at its blossoming! Saint Mark, recounting Christ's parable, tells us of the seeds that fall on poor and rocky ground: "They sprout quickly, for the dirt is not deep; but when the sun heats, they waste away and, because they have no roots, are quickly dried up." These myths seem to me to be that sort.

The sick man, if he is reasonable, calls on the doctor. If he is in too much of a hurry, or if doctors have disappointed him—through ignorance or nonchalance—he goes to a quack. Spider webs, bat's blood, and magic formulas, if one believes in them, work right away. But medicine, though slower, is right in the end even if it holds no hope for the sick person.

France, though participating in the world's ills, has fortunately been less acutely stricken than the countries who have called on bonesetters. Obviously that is no reason for it to do nothing (as, up until now, it has only too willingly believed). But is it any reason to go looking for a bonesetter?

There is no doubt (Sorel in the wake of many others demonstrated it) that nothing is saved without a myth. Yet, are people so divested of faith that they lack this essential seed? I do not believe so at all. The most "rationalist" among us carry deep within their hearts at least this primordial myth: the belief in tomorrow's dawning, not a metaphorical dawning, but that very one that rises in the sky.

A rational quest can build something on that hope as well. It conflicts so little with the doctor's task that the good doctor relies on it.

Faithfulness to the search, first, and then let each one pursue it in his own direction, with this sole reservation—that everyone promise to submit the search to facts and not to passions.

It is the same moral wish to assure the greatest number that everything will be done so that they keep their right to Hope.

And that is all—in the light of history—that I am able to propose in response to your desire for action.

But do not say that it is not much! It is because its action is determined by basic principles very close to those I have just defined that the group at *La Flèche*[7] has so far accomplished a piece of work that I do not consider useless.

Pierre Libra

A historical community can last a long time, and grow, even if its consciousness is not equal to its action. The history of the Christian West is proof of this. A religion of oriental origin, a Jewish heresy preaching resignation, revelation, and a spirit of equality, did not prevent the development of imperialism, inequality, and science in the West. It is the greatest paradox in history. But after all the West, up until the twentieth century, had no dealings with adversaries as well armed as it; I do not mean armed with courage or natural resources, but with a will to power, and technique. From the day that Islam went to sleep the West grew; later, cannons were persuasive for the colored people. But beginning with the present the Western community needs a consciousness that is equal to its existence.[8]

Western power continued to grow from the sixteenth to the twentieth century; during the same period its consciousness continued to decline. The Roman Catholic Church was able to a great extent to protect the Western character, justifying Inequality (consecration of temporal leaders, and temporal power of spiritual leaders) and Imperialism (under the pretext of a mission), but it was not sufficient justification for science. The scientific spirit was developed in opposition to the Church. What is awful for the West is that this development, at the same time, affected those values of imperialism and hierarchy that the Church enforced. From the sixteenth century until now, each idea that weakens the pontifical authority, Christian revelation, at the same time weakens the temporal values in the Western consciousness that that revelation, by means of that authority, sanctified. Moral values of Christian origin, inimical to Western imperialism, Western inequality, are the beneficiaries of this weakening of religion. Another little paradox. From the eighteenth century onward, prepared for by the Reformation, Western consciousness begins to be more profoundly Christian than in the Middle Ages—preaching kindness and equality seriously; one can begin to detect the Christianizing of the West. (Is the admission, beginning in this period, of the Jewish people, who are the inventors of Christianity and the Russian Slavs, whose spirit is profoundly Christian, into the Western community a coincidence?) Apart from that, nothing changes in actual practice (the Jews and Russians learn imperialism for themselves). In the nineteenth century, Western powers conquer or master most of the world; in the footsteps of this conquest, Western consciousness imposes itself throughout the world. It is actually more Christian than ever then. But it does not matter: The enemies are weaker than ever. Internally, the propaganda of humanitarian ideas serves politicians and financiers, who are in a mutual state of permanent blackmail, as a means of domination. But it does not matter: The technique, colonization, benefits even the peoples. During the youth of our parents, and in this very place, never had the split between consciousness and action been so great. It is the apogee of the Western paradox.

We awoke in 1914. There are a few of us, from the generation born some time around the last world war, who know conclusively that our century is the century in which we must pay for the inconsistency of Western culture since its beginnings, become authentic or disappear. The masses of Europe or elsewhere, profoundly Christianized in their consciousness by the masters of the West just as fast as they were subjected to them, have wanted to pass these years in actual Christianization: the reign of kindness and equality on Earth. That this ideal is profoundly repugnant to the character of the West is something that those who have maintained some definition are in the process of making the masses understand, without hesitating too much over the choice of methods. Beyond the shapeless masses, we realize that there are now nations that are nonoccidental (in origin, at least) whose deepest character remains different from the Western character, but who, educated by the West, are not without their share of imperialism: hence Jews, Russia, Japan. That is the present situation.

In the period of the battle of the Catalannican fields, at the time of the battle of Poitiers, the West was still unformed, as much in spirit as in social organization. Today, for the first time in the course of its actual history, it can be written that the West is in great danger: simultaneously attacked in its imperialism and eroded in its hierarchy. For guidance in action—except in totalitarian countries—it does not have one spiritual supervision. This, as the inquirer remarks, is dispersed; but this dispersal is far from being the worst evil. On the contrary, the evil is in the systematic convergence, under an apparent spiritual anarchy, of almost everyone in business and letters, people of their word (those listed by the inquirer and others) for the furtherance of humanitarian * ideas for the past two centuries, to the detriment once again of Catholicism, even sometimes in the heart of the Catholic Church. On the contrary, the dispersal of consciousness was to the advantage of scientific curiosity (one of the rare Western qualities that still

---

*I will not dwell on this, except for the scientists; for the others one only needs to be familiar with the political and literary history of the last two centuries. For scientists, particularly doctors, I refer to the remarkable book by Dr. Alexis Carrel (*L'Homme, cet inconnu*, 1935, which is among the exceptions proving the rule.[9] I will take the liberty of concluding this remark from his findings: The humanitarianism of scientists and doctors is less striking than that of the ideologues because it is in their professional role and not their thought; the comfort and care they provide without making distinctions about human value favor the weak, even if this consequence is not their intention.

Psychoanalysis deserves special mention. Freud and his disciples, on the basis of just and profound observations, seem to militate in order to *reduce* the importance of *native* differences between individuals, emphasizing education and chance emotional traumas instead. The master and a great number of his followers are Jews. Is that just chance?

apply). It favored also the exemplary quality of certain individuals: Nietzsche, for example, to whom we are indebted for understanding something of what is going on. The evil is in the fact that the celebrated intellectual freedom, of which democratic countries are so proud, through the tyranny of public opinion, at the present boils down to the consent of Western domination and hierarchy to its own ruin.

If that continues, science's turn will not be long in coming—what am I saying? It has come. Here is yet another paradox (we certainly turn up one at every step when we try to explore our present situation in the West). Already, we see that in order to react against what I called the real Christianizing of consciousnesses, Germany and the nations it pulls along behind it are being gradually sucked into a new dogmatism, a caricature of the dogmatism that formerly set scientific curiosity against religion, and that even, wonder of wonders, goes so far as to recall the messianism of the people that Hitler's Germany hates most and claims to despise.* Of course the German nation, by its very existence, is part of the West, but for the moment its consciousness is not. I think we have touched bottom when we see a messianism that seems in imitation of Moses, with its inspired prophet, its sexual taboos, its groups that cannot be assimilated in foreign countries, etc., appearing in one of the great nations of Europe and claiming to be the restorer of Western culture. And where Hitler is not dominant, and minds are obviously very Judaizing, the success of the scientific spirit is no better; indeed, it is rather less of a sure thing, despite the boasts. The open tyranny of Marxist dogma in Westerners of the far left and in Russia (whether it merely goes along with or more firmly fixes some Slavic messianism, it all comes to the same thing for civilization), the underhanded tyranny of an unrealistic humanitarianism in democratic countries, by means of all the liberal processes for discouraging free minds,—particularly in France, through the university,—the tendency is the same. A more and more demanding public opinion wants science to appear to confirm the morality that flatters it. (Hence theories that were born from Western science, whether Masonic, Marxist or racist, now are turning against Western science). Barbarians are everywhere!

Just the same, if we keep to the behavior of the Italian and German leaders, and not their theories, we have to acknowledge that they have begun to expand Europe, and perhaps the whole world by permitting and, you never know, even imposing on the West against its will the consciousness of its own nature and the role it is summoned to play on the Earth by this nature.

What is at the very heart of the national reactions of Italy and Germany is only a taste for strength, and there is nothing more in racism, once unearthed in a pure form than that taste for strength. Racism, relieved of its pedantic justifications, is quite frankly a challenge, a challenge in abusive terms given by some peoples to

---

*Charles Maurras has often returned to this notion, but it is always worth repeating.

other peoples, just like those that Western lords were always permitted, even advised, to hurl at other nobles. Last, thanks to the present-day danger in the West, the military franchise is beginning to revive there, and not just in the behavior of members of a certain caste, but in the relations of nations, of groups tensed with millions of energies! Let's not exaggerate: There is, as we were saying, a pedantic dogmatism in the style of Jews, there is even more not a little unrealistic humanitarianism in the spiritual direction of the totalitarian nations of Europe. There is almost as much talk there as anywhere else about mankind's equality and peace. In spite of everything, ever since the 1914-18 German style of war (the worthless paper, the gas, submarines, etc.), and by way of fascism (remember d'Annunzio's influence especially), Adolf Hitler's racism, which Mussolini takes up, at bottom only masks very real progress. The West is unquestionably indebted to the German and Italian nations for the value newly accorded to the human gesture of defiance, to arrogant defiance, to naked strength. Honor to the brave! Honor to the arrogant! Shame on the talkers, the underhanded nigglers, the cowardly con men! For me this is the noblest Western sense, I would even say the noblest human sense, of what I wish to retain of Hitler's venture.

For it happens that this taste for strength is not just Germanic, it is universally Western, as evidenced by the entire history of the West. . . .

Jean Paulhan (Editor of the *NRF*)

What bothers me somewhat in your inquiry is its timidity. You hesitate (it seems to me) to ask the essential question—to which there would be no other possibility than to answer *yes* or *no*. This is what I mean.[10]

First question: If we continue (you say) without spiritual directors—or are left only to the (mediocre) directives that come to us from newspapers, from science, from editors—isn't catastrophe heading our way?

It's possible. But after all, don't try to frighten me. I am no enemy on principle of catastrophes. Maybe there is something good about them. Maybe they are necessary. If I take a spiritual director, it will be neither out of precaution nor out of prudence. It will be because I have *recognized* that I need one. I mean to say that the human condition is *such* that I am unable to understand, or even approach it except by means of an interposed person.

Is that true? And in the very center of our lives are events taking place such that I am unable to apprehend them directly? That is the whole problem. Don't dodge it.

Second question: Wouldn't it be necessary (you say) to found a new universalism in order to "avoid, surpass, dominate" the tribal religions and their violent returns?

Agreed. I admit it would be indeed necessary. And certainly practical. But in the end would it be *true*? That's the whole question—because if you stick to utility, you will never get anything more than a pale copy of tribal religions.

Is it true? Is there an event, common to us all, that takes place in the very center of our lives, which is such that—and so serious or strange that it must from the moment it is known, or even only sensed, take command over this life and over our reflection? That is still the essential problem.

And don't tell me that I am simply substituting one question for another. No. Rather I am attempting to clarify the *true* meaning of your inquiry—an inquiry I think we are all trying to answer to the best of our ability. It is perhaps not unimportant to specify this meaning. Perhaps, if we don't already sense the solution, we will not even achieve this.

The College of Sociology

The problems your inquiry raises are precisely those that, for the past two years, the College of Sociology has been endeavoring to get to the bottom of and resolve. All its work, its processes, and its gatherings aim precisely toward that end. This conjunction, moreover, is not otherwise astonishing: Your inquirer participated in the discussions from which the College of Sociology arose, his signature is at the end of the declaration announcing its foundation, the association even owes its name to him.[*]

Be that as it may, the College of Sociology would be unable to summarize in a few incomplete and empty lines that which constitutes the essence of its activity. On this occasion it can only recall that it considers its sole task to be *providing* an answer to the questions your inquiry poses and that its ambition is to *be* to the extent that it is able, this answer.

Letter From Pierre Mabille to Monnerot

I have put off writing to you; I had thought I would send you an answer to the inquiry. But in the end I am not going to. It poses questions that are so important that a few hasty, superficial lines are not enough. I would end up making a very long statement, which I have no time for and do not wish to do.

Numerous historical examples would have to account for the opinion given. It would have to go into the secret mechanism of history, that is to say, it would

---

[*]Let us dispel any doubt:

If the College of Sociology has the inquirer to thank for its name, the inquiry, on the contrary, owes no debt to the College.

The relationship of the inquirer with the instigators of the College dates from before its "foundation."

The College, etc., without being puerile, could not claim any monopoly at all, or maintain without bragging that it answers or promises to answer solely by its existence the questions posed here.

These *affectations* are not what the times expect of us. (Inquirer's note.)

have to disclose the existence and functioning of semioccult congregations that possessed or still possess great powers.

In my book *Égrégores* I said, or rather indicated in veiled terms, what I think of these subjects. This work constitutes the best reply I can make to your inquiry, even though it is a bit general. If I did not express myself more clearly or at greater length, it was on purpose. I think this sort of discussion is impossible to institute in public. In order not to pass for a madman, a raving maniac, or some vapid, crazy misinterpreter, in order to be convincing or simply to command attention, it is documentation that is necessary rather than impressions. Consequently, there are some who would be sure to concern themselves with the origin and significance of these documents. They would try to use them for their own benefit or for the group to which they belong.

Having no qualifications they would certainly fail, but they would increase the present chaos to no avail.

Keep in mind that the social and political movements currently proliferating in Europe are all parodies—whether of the past or of the future. Their parodic character is proved by their inability to resolve any problem or bring about complete support; they are not transforming humanity. Nourishing these doomed efforts is not my aim.

Having curbed the first sympathetic impulse, one realizes that your inquiry, to the extent that it doesn't end up as an exchange of banal inanities, would become an extraordinarily dangerous enterprise.

Already, I am not very happy that conversations on these subjects among . . ., . . .,[*] and myself gave birth to this College of Sociology where some professors confuse the Temple with the Circus.

And even then, in the circus, one learns the exercise before performing it, one is not content just to talk about it. The path to initiation is not through scholastic instruction. It is a question not of enriching one's mind but of completing a transmutation in oneself. In transmutation the metal is not painted, it is melted. This great undertaking is open only to true poets.

It would be nice if these intellectual gentlemen would learn someday that thought is not a wreath of artificial roses fashioned from diplomas. What strange workers, these people that serious events always find busy chattering on their perches.

And finally, if you take an interest in the problems whose urgency is emphasized by your inquiry, I advise you to be cautious. Experience has taught that strolling among powder kegs requires certain precautions.

---

[*]Here we omit the names to avoid irrelevant polemics. (Inquirer's note.)

Jean Wahl

What an odd questionnaire . . . How badly the question is put.

I should insist on answering in the first place that the idea of a spiritual adviser implies a religious concept.

But I am stopped by the fact that Marcel Prévost and some woman editor or other in the magazines like *Marie-Claire* are spiritual advisers.

To what extent are a Gide (Gide especially), a Malraux, a Montherlant, for some a Giono, spiritual advisers? Presumably they are much less so than more religious thinkers? Because they address themselves to adults.

There is, to use a word young philosophers are too fond of, a dialectic of spiritual direction:

Worthiest of esteem would be those consciences that did not allow themselves altogether to direct others or to be directed by others. It is among those consciences who want no spiritual direction that it will be most valuable (its value is infinite, when it is impossible).

Let us seek spiritual companions.

There is yet another thing: Spiritual advising is an entirely personal relationship. Hence there is a contradiction between your idea about these journalists that you are talking about, whose papers have a large circulation, and direction of conscience. I do not know what they are directing, but it is not conscience.

But let us put aside this question, which may be only one of terminology.

You ask if "that" can continue without catastrophe. Yes, I would sometimes be inclined to answer; for the catastrophe has taken place.

Once we know this we can hope again.

Moreover, human society has never known a state in which it was happy. It is only a question of degree.

Today what we need to know is whether the collapse of the national-socialist regimes will take place soon enough for the democracies not to have been completely destroyed beforehand.

Next it will be necessary (in all the hypotheses, anyway) that the democracies regain a value, a nobility, raise their family fortune—for their adversity—that they seek an economic doctrine and a political form giving them greater strength to resist.

As far as the economic is concerned, are national socialism and socialism not connected? What with capitalism being sick, socialism being nationalist and nationalism socialist, we should find something else. And, as far as possible, speed right by national socialism . . . Will it be possible?

For the moment, this is what I perceive. It is very vague, and I am very hesitant to be sending you these useless lines.

[There followed three pages of "conclusion." With these Monnerot brought

to a close this issue that Volontés had devoted entirely to publishing the results of the inquiry. After having demanded a "pragmatism" that is not foo far from what Caillois in the same period calls activism ("we have in mind something that is true only if one makes it true, something that demands our strength in order to be"), Monnerot makes things clear—intended perhaps for the ill-intentioned College: "Let's get this straight: There can be no question of ridiculously serving the modern cult of the collective-for-collective's-sake, by setting up in the space of forty-eight hours one 'group,' two manifestos, and four members, and crying, 'Hey! I am founding a religion. I am the pope. Are you with us? Come to think of it, it's a secret society: Look at the prospectus instead.' "

In Inquisitions (which he edited with Monnerot) Caillois entitled the text that was to become the conclusion to Le Mythe et l'homme "Pour une orthodoxie militante." Monnerot, in the same vein, would refuse to mention orthodoxy a propos his "pragmatism": To this end he would create the neologism "orthopraxy." For the epoch is going to go into action. It sets a task that is "intellectual, yes," says Monnerot. "But literally, military also, antipolitical which means political, and religious in the exact sense of the term." The translation of this complex syntagm: It is the task awaiting the French who are "fed up with democracy and contemptuous of fascism."]

Lectures

1937-38

Sacred Sociology and the Relationships between "Society," "Organism," and "Being"
Georges Bataille and Roger Caillois
Saturday, November 20, 1937

[The College of Sociology with this inaugural session moved into the premises where it would meet, twice a month, over the course of two academic years: the back room of the Galeries du Livre, a bookstore (apparently Catholic) located at 15 rue Gay-Lussac.

Both Bataille and Caillois spoke.

First Caillois. But his intervention was not written. No trace of it has been preserved. He himself has forgotten what it was about. Nonetheless, there is a clue in the text of his successor on the "platform," Bataille, whose actual words were, "Caillois having just given a general historical survey of sociologists' thought. . ." But that is all.

With Bataille, the editor's problem is the opposite because there are two manuscripts bearing the title that is on the program for that day. Lacking any certainty, I am publishing first the longer of the two, but with no assurance that it was the only one, or the first one to be read.

This lecture was rather eclectic; echoes of Nietzsche and Durkheim are to be found here, as well as echoes of a certain Belot and of the alternative between a corpuscular and an undulatory discourse that de Broglie's work had recently confronted physicists with, etc. What stands out is the definition of secret societies as elective communities, which for this reason are opposed on the one hand to de facto communities (the fact being geographical or racial) that made up the fascist regimes, but also on the other hand, to what can be called de facto absences of any community, that is to say, democracies.]

I

Caillois's introduction leads me to the development of some general reflections, reflections of a metaphysical order, specifically of an ontological order on the nature of society. Is society a being? Is it an organism? Or is it simply the sum of individuals? In general, questions that are so far from and also external to science proper are not the sort to create an atmosphere favorable to the development of accurate knowledge. Nonetheless, the question of the nature of society is inherent to any social science and particularly to the domain that we have designated by the name of sacred sociology. It would be impossible, therefore, and futile at the same time, to try to evade this question.

Indeed, for us sacred sociology is not just a part of sociology as is, for example, religious sociology, with which it risks confusion. Sacred sociology may be considered the study not only of religious institutions but of the entire communifying movement of society. Hence, it regards power and the army, among other things, as its rightful object, and it contemplates all human activities—sciences, arts, and technology—insofar as they have a communifying value, in the active sense of the word, that is to say, insofar as they are the *creators* of unity.[1] In later discussions I shall return to the precisely specific *sacred* character of everything in human existence that is *communifying*. But, from the outset, I must insist that when sacred sociology is understood in this manner, it supposes that the question of *being* is resolved. More accurately, it is a response to this question. It acknowledges that *in addition* to the individuals who make up society, there exists an overall movement that transforms their nature. It keeps its distance, therefore, from any notion according to which social existence would only add contracts to individuals,[2] that is to say, precisely from the notions on which the whole present-day culture is based. It would even be surprising if it did not contradict the way most of us react mentally (or at least contradict our biases). Having simply acknowledged this, and Caillois having just given a historical survey of sociological thought, I shall attempt to develop a general description so that a consistent representation of society will become possible.

1. Society as different from the sum of the elements that compose it

A human society is in the world as a distinct, but not isolated, existence. It is distinct not only from the rest of things and beings but also from other societies: It is composed of a multitude of elements that are more or less identical to those that compose the neighboring society, but they belong exclusively to it in a sufficiently stable manner. A group of human beings living on an island make up Great Britain. Yet an appreciable number of British subjects are to be found off the island. Vice versa, the island's population includes a certain number of foreigners. Great Britain exists, no less for all that, in an entirely distinct fashion, excluding these foreigners and including, in addition to the islanders, the multitude of Britons scattered throughout the world. Hence, on the one hand, there are Britons and, on the other, there is Great Britain.

If we now consider an atom as present-day ideas represent it, there are on the one hand, electrons and, on the other, the atom formed by the coming together of electrons in a particular movement.[3] A molecule presents the same double aspect: It is both the given number of atoms that compose it (which could exist alone) and the molecule, that is to say, something that greatly differs from atoms that are entirely similar except that they are not combined into a molecular formation. Some molecules are also able to form micelles that are themselves different from the sum of the molecules not yet brought together.

In another direction, crystals form extremely unified wholes within which molecules lose their autonomy. The micelles entering into the composition of colloidal units are situated on the threshold of living matter. This latter presents a double aspect at least as clearly as does inorganic matter. Everyone knows that a cell is different from the juxtaposition of the parts composing it, which are molecules and micelles. And farther up on the scale of beings a multicellular organism cannot be regarded as a simple coexistence of cells. Hence we come back to society, which, combining organisms at the highest level, makes them into something other than their sum.

Even if the facts require some reservations, this enumeration of them encourages one to generalize: The formation of a being composed of simpler beings seems a completely banal process, or even a fundamental process of everything that exists, whether or not it is inert. (For it is understood that the great astral units and the galaxies grouping them do not escape from this modality of beings). Under these circumstances, it ceases to be paradoxical to speak of society as a being. Quite the contrary, the paradox is in the difficulty we often have in becoming aware of the presence of this being. The paradox is in exclaiming ironically "Truth this side of the Pyrenees . . ." and not in recognizing—whether hostile to it or seduced by it—the *existence* of the country and the flag, which effectively limit the mental boundaries of all those constituting it.

2. Atom, molecule, micelle, cell, organism, society

A very general description of the composition of beings is so unfamiliar to our minds that it immediately comes up against the imprecision of vocabulary. The consistency of expression breaks down because society is presumed to be composed not of organisms but of individuals. The notion of individuality can be applied just as well to inert corpuscles as to living beings; it can even be applied to societies. The word "individual" cannot be used, therefore, to designate a degree on the scale of forms. On the other hand, the word "organism" is sometimes applied to the cell. Obviously, it is necessary to overcome such great inaccuracy. Atoms, molecules, micelles and cells are well enough defined, but "organism" must be reserved for groups of cells and in this sense substituted for *individual*. It will still be necessary to distinguish between simple organisms and linear organisms. The name "simple organism" must be reserved for animals with no symmetry, or with axial or radial symmetry, such as sponges, starfish, jellyfish. These animals together form colonies uniting connected elements, and not societies. To the extent that we still take the theory of a colonial origin of organisms into account, we can say that simple organisms, by grouping, form compound organisms. The organisms contemplated by the colonial theory are actually composed of segments that are linearly disposed from head to tail. In some instances, these segments maintain their autonomy. Worms, for example, earthworms, classified by naturalists among the oligochaetes provide the simplest example of this sort of association; higher animals, insects and vertebrates, in their embryonic development, then in their nervous system or in their skeletons, retain something of the segmented character of the worms. Doubtless, science has not settled this point: It is even currently demonstrating a sort of repugnance with respect to the colonial theory. But we still must hold onto the fact that society, which is the most complex structural form in a particular direction of the compound development of beings, is formed only on the basis of linear organisms.

3. The notion of "compound being"

Now, if I want to go back over these reflections I have just made—to get some sort of overall picture of them—I will simply state the sequence: atom, molecule, micelle, cell, simple organism, linear organism, and society. I will add that the atom and molecule are perhaps only the most coherent constructions possible for the mind and that the distinction between simple organisms and linear organisms is much more difficult to make than the others. Subsequently, I will show why these reservations do not seem troublesome to me. All I have to do for the moment is to remark on a new vocabulary inadequacy: I actually have no word to designate in general the elements I have just enumerated. The words "whole," "group," "association," "totality," "body," "structure," are far from making obvious what characteristics distinguish formations such as atom or cell from very different formations that, for their part, are neither easily nor clearly designated: Concretely, I have in mind something like a pile of sand or of rocks, or of a glass of water. I am led, therefore, to propose that we speak of a mass when it is a question of associations that do not modify the parts that form them, and of "compound beings" when it is a question of atoms, cells, or elements of the same order.

I believe it is possible to define these "compound beings" by saying, first, that they present something more than the mass composing them, namely, a specific movement that it is possible to call "communifying movement," at least when it is a question of a linear organism or of a society;[4] and second, that they present a more or less pronounced difference in relation to a mass formed of elements that are similar but not compounded.

4. Society is a compound being

With this ponderous and tedious task of fundamental terminology completed, it is possible to contemplate a first intelligent answer to the question: What is society? It is not a mass. It is not an organism either. Assimilating it to the organism makes no more sense than assimilating it to the molecule (as did Durkheim in some ways). But it is a "compound being."

The rigidity of some is positive: They link their ideas to strict identifications. That of others is negative: They limit themselves to challenging identifications. I want to give an example of such an unnuanced rigidity. It is taken from a recent publication by a French astronomer, Émile Belot, in the international journal *Scientia* (the exact publication date is July 1937).[5] The comparison Belot establishes between living organisms and stars has the merit, besides, of introducing us into a domain that I neglected just now because, in order to simplify, I described only one of the lines of composition of beings. After having attempted to describe the evolution characteristic of the phases of existence of a star, Belot adds that

> the separate study of the origin of the stars and their evolution, of novas and the planetary system, etc., cannot be sufficient for the cosmogonist; he must discover the comparative evolution of such diverse stars and hence arrive at the general laws of biology and biogenetics in all the beings of the Cosmos. We will specify these:
>
> (1) Dualism is at the origin of the stars, at the origin of spiral nebulas, at the origin of the planetary system through the impact of a giant star on a nebula; the dualism at the origin of living beings is called *sexuality*. (2) In the latter, there is *schizogenesis* through cellular division and in the annelids through the division of whole beings. Among cosmic beings, through its condensation a star arrives at a *Barbell* form as H. Poincaré and Jeans have demonstrated, in which case it divides in two like a simple cell. The planetary vortices can leave small planets (Mars, Jupiter, Saturn) in their wake—a phenomenon of *schizogenesis*. The spirals of unstable spiral nebulas divide in fractions whose mass depends on the unit of length of the spiral. (3) In all beings *fertilization* and *birth* are abrupt phenomena (novas for the birth of the planetary rings). (4) In sexuality, before birth there is a *short period of gestation* in comparison with the duration of the perfected being; for planets, a few centuries of nebulous gestation before hundreds of millions of years of life.
> (5) Embryos live temporarily in a milieu that is different from that in

which the perfected beings will live; for planets, the nebular milieu, then the sidereal void. (6) Embryos have temporary forms that are sometimes very different from those of the perfected beings (metamorphoses from larvae, chrysalides, etc.) (vortices, rings for cosmic beings). (7) It is only in the adult state that living beings are able to reproduce. For a star the adult state is reached when, through ellipsoidal condensation, its centrifugal force at the equator is near that which allows its equatorial matter to escape. (8) The Mendelian theory of heredity demonstrates that the species are due to multiple combinations of *dominant characteristics in the two parents.* The varieties of cosmic species are hence sufficient to demonstrate to us that their origin is dualist. (9) Living beings *choose the food* likely to accelerate their evolution through assimilation. Stars passing through a nebula assimilate the dense materials that will increase their density and repulse the materials that are unlikely to accelerate their evolution. The major difference between living beings and cosmic beings is that the former *are born small and grow* whereas the latter *are born gigantic and become small*; this difference is due to gravity, which has only minimal effect on living beings. Hence, *there exists in our universe a unity of genetic plan for all cosmic or living beings.*

Although he is not one of those scientists who stick their necks out only after having very slowly eliminated any chance of error, Émile Belot cannot be classed with the occultists who talked of "geon" and of "living earth." Even if the passage I have just read is a simple digression, Émile Belot is representative of science. Moreover, no reason exists for denying stars the quality of "compound beings," once this quality is recognized in the various formations that human existence encounters on the Earth. It is impossible to deny a minimum of "unity of genetic plan" for all "compound beings." But this minimum can be reduced to the principle that compounding adds and differentiates. It is not necessary to be an astronomer or soothsayer to suppose that it is likely that the development of science will reveal the superficial character of most of the *rigid* comparisons whose disconcerting pronouncement I have just read. The negative responses that are sure to follow will be no less rigid, moreover, than these peremptory assertions; in nature itself, however, everything will remain vague, composite, and rich enough in its potential for different forms to doom human intelligence to endless humiliation.

I have insisted on the vague character of the notion of compound being that I am attempting to introduce. This character is simultaneously vague and, when all is said and done, precise, if we oppose it to the rigidity, which in actual practice is imprecise, of the usual discussions. Actually, I used the word "being" on purpose because it represents the vaguest, most indeterminate idea of all. Émile Belot also uses the word "being." It is true that for my part, I defined exactly what I meant by "compound being," and it seems that that frees me from the excessive vagueness attached to the word "being." I could, therefore, pursue my approach—lingering no longer in the metaphysical bog, where it sometimes seems a serious person should go only for a good laugh. But it happens, on the one hand, that the word "being" suggests the idea of "consciousness" (*conscience*)[6] and, on the other hand, that at least one of those categories listed, the linear organism (if one looks at the whole picture and if one sticks to its most convincing aspect), is characterized by consciousness. This is all that is needed to introduce an ambiguity that, frankly, I must say I have not sought to avoid. On the contrary, it has seemed to me that the extremely vague nature of human knowledge on this point is actually maintained by the expression I am proposing, and I believe that this vague nature must be explicitly maintained. I think that the most educated person is at about the same point in this regard as a peasant. In fact, the way other consciousnesses are known cannot be worked out to any extent at all by science. A horse seems to us endowed with consciousness as does an insect; it is harder to ascribe consciousness to a sponge, but since all degrees from sponge to bee exist . . . we come down to the infusorian, to the cell! There are a certain number of people who can agree to admit that a threshold exists. Consciousness would begin with life, with the cell; it seems rather arbitrary. Why not ascribe a sort of consciousness to corpuscles, to inert matter? Why would the cell become conscious if the particles that compose it are not conscious to any extent? Truthfully, certain of the notions that will follow would encourage more the belief that the birth of consciousness, starting from nothing, at the threshold of life makes no sense at all. Nietzsche bestowed perception and, consequently, knowledge on inorganic matter—even to the point of insisting that only the inert is able to attain the truth; the organic, because it is bound up in complex interests, is doomed to a utilitarian interpretation and to error.[7] I only cite this for the record. It is fair to add that I read these texts by Nietzsche to which I have just alluded with a great deal of interest, seeing that for a long time I have been inclined to view things in the same manner. But even this second fact I cite just for the record. It is not possible to linger on such distant factors, and clearly Nietzsche, in his time, did not linger either.

But this question of the consciousness of beings has two aspects, according to whether we descend the line of the composition of beings or start from ourselves to ascend to the level of society. The second aspect, moreover, is the only important one from the sociological point of view. Here again, in a new form, we come upon the metaphysical question of the nature of society. Specifically, it was the quality of "compound being" that brought up the issue of knowing whether society is a conscious being. Now, the vague and elusive nature that is proper to the very object of the question, consciousness, must in this instance be asserted even more emphatically and seductively than when it concerned the cell or inert matter.[8] The conscious life that we are tends to situate itself as the basis of things, which is not at all absurd, but above all it claims for itself the fundamental unity by means of which, as an irreducible reality, it confronts the rest of the world. Now, it is the fact that consciousness considers itself as indivisible that remains the strongest obstacle to the recognition of a collective consciousness. But that is only a crude belief: Even if it is true that we feel deeply our unity in the face of death, what is obliterated in death is none other than the "communifying movement" that belongs to the parts composing us. Those parts, under the right conditions, would be able to survive us. Are there, between this conscious "communifying movement" that we are and the "communifying movement" of society, differences of nature, or differences of degree? A certain number of processes, which we will come to describe during the sequence of discussions that are planned, seem indeed to demonstrate that there is no clear difference. Between the crowd crying out with a unanimous voice and a state of consciousness that is torn apart, it is difficult to decide where unity is most lacking. And if it is easily recognized that social unity is the more precarious, that a single society can form several crowds at the same moment that are equally unanimous,[9] but that are unaware of each other and then disperse, there is no reason to ignore that there is a particular structure to which institutions, rites, and common representations contribute, which provides the deep supports for collective identity. Above all, there is no reason to forget the composite character of the organisms we are, or the transient nature of personal consciousness. Later, it will even become possible to demonstrate how the phenomena of consciousness in each category of compound beings could be systematically attributed to the interaction of distinct parts. In any case, nothing allows us to content ourselves with the unique importance that the human consciousness of the lone individual assigns to itself. Moreover, I insist on the negative character of these arguments. Basically, I am not concerned with asserting the existence of a collective consciousness; rather, I want to demonstrate that the knowledge of what we call consciousness results only in a very vague notion, which is such that we have no right at all to dispute that society itself has a consciousness. Why not bluntly acknowledge that we are here in the most obscure domain of knowledge?

Moreover, this domain is all the more obscure since it is always difficult when we are in the presence of phenomena of consciousness in the individual sense of the word—always difficult to decide whether they belong exclusively to the person or if they are the expression of society's "communifying movement." For we must not forget that we are no better examples of linear organisms, as a category of compound beings, than are the cells that form us out of the living, autonomous cell. The human being exists only in society and consequently is situated on the scale of beings in the same way as the atom, the molecule, the micelle or the cell that are linked. In the same way that the sheep in a herd driven by a single impulse is a linear organism that is *linked*, that is to say, entering into a compound. Now, from the beginning we have accepted that the elements that thus enter into the formation of compound beings were profoundly changed by this. In human society this change is above all psychic in nature. But I am far from having made a final statement of all the difficulties that the analysis of individual phenomena of consciousness runs into. As human beings we are not solely "linked linear organisms"; by and large we use part of our forces to break, partially or totally, the bonds that unite us with society, with the hope of becoming free individuals. I propose to reserve the name "person" for the compound being that results from this secondary action.[10]

On the other hand, this is an extremely simplified way of representing reality. The tendency to dissociation does not simply oppose individuals to group; it opposes, even within the same whole, several parts that can be composed of the same elements for that matter, but at successive moments of its duration. That it is currently possible for a bishop to be a reserve officer gives some idea of this very complex mode of composition. In the same way, a man in the Middle Ages could belong to his guild, be the king's subject, a bourgeois of his city, and faithful to a Church acknowledged as universal. Secret societies, religious orders, brotherhoods, parties, the army, add to the extreme complexity of the picture that loses even its geographical unity in this way.[11] It is self-evident that these internal formations—very different from the organs of an organism—do not necessarily work toward dissociation; they can just as well be used for preservation or even recomposition. But when tendencies toward dissociation, toward a sort of social interrepulsion,[12] are predominant, these formations are immediately put to use in this direction. (The individual does not attempt to break the social bond and become free on his own; he makes use of internal oppositions. In this case, besides, it is not very important to him that the struggle of a given function does not have as its real object his liberty; he supports this struggle in order to achieve the general weakening—which is, moreover, temporary—of the bond that makes him subordinate). In any case, the general description of the scale of compound beings—along the line from the atom to human community—will hence include a new element. The internal formations that regroup individuals on a new plane are able to take the name "community". However, community will not be able strictly to designate a division subordinate to the primitive formation. In effect, the new communities combine with the old organization—the one stemming only from blood or the soil—and sometimes they will even become more important. Hence, the development of new communities is such that the primary formation itself, when all is said and done, takes on a value equivalent to that of the secondary formations. From then on it can be regarded as one of the communities forming society and take the name of *traditional* community, differing from the new communities, the most important of which are the *elective* communities.[13] These result from a choice on the part of the elements composing them, and they show a characteristic totality—such as religious orders and secret societies.[14]

I have completed here the introduction to a sacred sociology that I wanted to make. I have indicated the major terminological modifications necessary to the development of this realm of knowledge. At the same time, I have sought to demonstrate in what manner the object of this particular investigation is situated within existences as a whole. From the beginning I indicated the direction of this endeavor, by indicating exactly what the sacred was for me, the specific phenomenon of the communifying movement of society. This is what I shall attempt to make intelligible in the course of subsequent discussions.

But before ending today, and while stressing the fact that the endeavor of the College of Sociology must be situated exclusively on the plane of scientific objectivity, I insist on openly acknowledging the personal concern to which this research, whose results I shall reveal, has long been connected. It is not the first time, for that matter, that I will manifest a predilection for what I have just designated as *elective community*.[15] But having taken care to fix the meaning of the terms with rather great precision, I like to make a clear distinction between the principle of *elective community* and the principle of the *traditional* community to which I, in fact, belong but from which I insist on dissociating myself. At the same time I like to contrast it just as clearly with the principles of individualism that result in democratic atomization. This is acknowledged here in order to indicate honestly the preoccupations that perhaps survive in me—even when I am trying to set them aside temporarily—when I am trying to work scientifically. I shall, therefore, content myself with general information, considering that the debate that is opened today must have knowledge, not practice, for its object.

[The second manuscript has been entitled, like the first, "Relationships between 'Society,' 'Organism,' and 'Being.'"][16]

II

We have undertaken to define a realm of knowledge to which we have given the name "sacred sociology," and we propose, starting now, to put forward the few ideas it is possible to elaborate and develop in this realm. These notions are not dependent on some philosophical reflection or other; they do not depend on a given metaphysical doctrine. To a great extent they will be borrowed from works whose authors do not even necessarily have a single opinion on the essential problem of sociology, namely, the nature of society, regarded by some as a being, by others as an organism, and by still others as a simple, more or less contractual, arrangement among autonomous individuals. We are nonetheless bound to pose this metaphysical question about the nature of society from the very outset. It is possible that each one of us will answer it differently without this preventing our coming to an agreement on certain points. But the metaphysical conclusions it is possible to produce for each description will subsist as so many inevitable directions of thought in motion. We have, therefore, an essential interest in giving in advance a description that is sufficiently vital, full of imagery, and, especially, sufficiently critical of those places where our thought processes might end up. Why, for that matter, would one now forget that these places are not merely the ground of an intellectual debate but rather are precisely the theater where political tragedy is playing? According to whether human beings consider the unities they form as piles of dust or grain, as waves made of molecules that are united only by motion, or, on the contrary, consider them as organizations possessing all the rights over the parts that compose them, they arm themselves in one camp or in the opposite one, and the game of death between them begins.

Usually, reflections such as those to follow begin with basic elements borrowed from the history of philosophy. Aristotle took the first step and Comte, as the inventor of the word "sociology" itself, follows him. Espinas, Durkheim, and Tarde represent the recent period. The logical development of ideas in a scholarly form is repeated in a number of works. But elaborated ideas that develop logically from one philosophical task to another are not all that exist: There also is an actual development that belongs more to life than to discursive thought. Now it seems that not many authors have given any appreciable reflection to this actual development. Yet it is easy to characterize these conditions in a few words and to show in this way all of their significant value. Actually, on the whole, when someone thinks about the existence of society, objectively but with a particular concern, whether it is intellectual or practical concern, he tends to consider it as a being. But as soon as he gets away from the serious *concern* with such an object, it is the individual that his thought, explicit or implicit, expressed or not, represents to him as the being. This paradoxical opposition, moreover, is represented particularly clearly by the present state of mind in France: *Faculties*, having *sociology* as their object, represent society alone as real; a few political partisans—of both the right and the left—base their action on a similar representation. But unquestionably there emerges from all of the thought expressed a vague but most dominant belief in the fundamental reality of individual existence.

If one considers social structure as a whole historically, it seems that contemporary societies do not represent the first stage in the formation of human units. A European nation results not from a union of individuals but from a union of provincial groups that formerly displayed a cohesion that was particularly their own and autonomous, as it were.

Hence, contemporary society can be considered to a certain extent as an aggregate of societies that are located at a stage below on the structural scale.[17] These constituent parts, however, cannot be seen as analogous to the cells that compose simple organisms or the atoms that compose molecules because they lose their individuality in the structural composition. The substitution of departments with arbitrary boundaries for provinces of feudal origin demonstrates how precarious the great internal divisions are. In fact, the group that results from the merging of smaller societies must, once the union is achieved, be considered as made up not of regions but of cities and localities of various sizes with a connecting network, namely, the administrative organization and its hierarchy of county towns, which is changeable. Even the capital itself can be moved. Within society, and at a structurally inferior stage, only the city constitutes a well-defined unit.[18]

Moreover, it is necessary to decide exactly what is meant in a rigorous nomenclature by ''city.'' When considering the compositional structure, one must consider any stable built-up area to be a city on condition that it present a minimum of required organization—council, mayor, church, priest. There is no good reason—at least for the contemporary period—to differentiate between rural and urban conglomerations. They both have the same structure. From smallest to largest, they represent formations at the same stage. Only their ramification, subordinating some to others, introduces differences in function, in themselves implying a more or less complete, but always imperfect whole. Even the locality that is the seat of central power remains subordinate to this power that is external to itself and that depends on it not at all. In this sense, an overcrowded locality—the capital or major city of the region—London or New York—can be compared with the smallest village in the same way that the elephant can be compared with the ant. Such compound existences merely have different intensities of movement, depending on the number of elements they unite and on the concentrations of certain functions performed in the largest conglomerations.

A distinction can be made, however, between localities according to their origin. Though this rarely happens, an initial conglomeration can proliferate. In this case the oldest keeps a central importance, and the others are immediately subordinated to it. But in general this is not what happens. A given town simply becomes more important than the neighboring towns, which, only secondly, become subordinate. In both cases the result is the same: The central institutions are, at first, mixed with the local institutions of the privileged town where they are produced.

Hegelian Concepts
Alexandre Kojève

Saturday, December 4, 1937

[The text of this second lecture has not been preserved. Perhaps Kojève never wrote it out, just as he did not always write out his classes at the École des Hautes Études, where he taught in the division of religious sciences as an assistant to Alexandre Koyré. That was why Queneau, who edited his Introduction à la lecture de Hegel *in 1947, would be obliged to establish the text of large sections of the work on the basis of his own notes as an auditor.*

Kojève was born in Moscow in 1902. In Paris from 1928 on, in 1932 he contributed several reading notes to the first issue of the Zeitschrift für Sozialforschung. *In 1935, with Henry Corbin (Heidegger's first French translator), he published (under his Russian name, Kojevnikov) a translation of Henri de Man's book* L'Idée socialiste. *He was a regular contributor to the volumes of* Recherches philosophiques *(which would publish Klossowski, Bataille, Caillois) with numerous reviews (essentially of works on Husserl or Heidegger, but there is a note on Granet's* La Pensée chinoise *in volume 4, p. 446) alongside those by Bachelard, Levinas, Brice Parain, H.-Ch. Puech, Koyré, Leo Strauss, Corbin, Wahl, Raymond Aron, and Jacques-M. Lacan. After the war, he was to become a high official in the French administration: a sensible Hegelian biographical solution. He described himself as a Marxist of the right. He died in the early days of June 1968.*

Kojève's seminars from 1933-39, in which he initiated the future intelligentsia of Paris to The Phenomenology of Mind, *are counted among the legendary events of this era. The list is still incomplete of the great thinkers of the postwar period who found their inspiration there. In his* Mémoires. Cinquante Ans de réflexion politique *[Paris, 1983], pp. 94-100), Raymond Aron recalls this voice: "Kojève first translated several lines of the* Phenomenology, *emphasizing certain words, then he spoke, with no notes, without ever stumbling over a word, in an impeccable French made original and fascinating as well with his Slavic accent. He captivated an audience of superintellectuals who were inclined toward doubt or criticism. Why? Talent, dialectical virtuosity had something to do with it. I do not know if his talent as an orator survives intact in the book recording the final year of his course, but this art, which had nothing to do with eloquence, stemmed from his subject and his person." The book in question, the* Introduction à la lecture de Hegel, *edited by Queneau in 1947, actually spans the entire course, officially devoted to "Hegel's religious philosophy." In* Mesures *in January 1939 Paulhan had published what was to become the volume's opening pages: Kojève's translation of and commentary on chapter 4 of the* Phenomenology *("Autonomie et dépendance de la Conscience de soi: Maîtrise et Servitude"). For reference, it will be recalled that Jean Hyppolite's translation of* La Phénoménologie de l'esprit, *the first complete French translation of Hegel's work, appeared in 1939 also.*

QUENEAU: *"From 1934 to 1939, Bataille would attend Kojève's courses . . ." ("Premières confrontations avec Hegel,"* Critique, *no. 195-96 [August-September 1963], p. 695). In fact, notes taken by Bataille in these courses were found in his papers—a thick enough stack of them that we don't have to take too literally the ironic touch Queneau adds to his portrait of Bataille at the École: ". . . he was not a listener whose attentiveness was exemplary . . . sometimes he even happened to doze off." Be that as it may, it was through Kojève that Bataille came to know Hegel and his Hegel would remain Kojèvian to the end.*

In his interview with Lapouge, Caillois tells of Kojève's relations with the College: "We tried to obtain the assistance of Kojève, who was, as you know, the principal exegete of Hegel in France. Kojève exerted an absolutely extraordinary influence on our generation. I have to say our project did not find favor with him. I remember. It was at Bataille's on the rue de Rennes that we explained our project to Kojève . . . Kojève listened to us, but he dismissed our idea. In his eyes we were putting ourselves in the position of a conjurer who wanted his magic tricks to make him believe in magic. We did, however, keep in close contact with Kojève. He even gave a lecture at the College, on Hegel. This lecture left us all flabbergasted, both because of Kojève's intellectual power and because of his conclusion. You will remember that Hegel speaks of the man on horseback, who marks the closure of History and of philosophy. For Hegel this man was Napoleon. Well! That was the day Kojève informed us that Hegel had seen right but that he was off by a century: The man of the end of history was not Napoleon but Stalin."

Two days after this lecture, Bataille wrote a letter to Kojève in which he talks

about the unemployment to which negativity and its "representatives," the in-
tellectuals, are condemned by this end of history. It takes their bread right off the
table. It is in this letter of December 6 that the concept of "unemployed nega-
tivity" appears for the first time. Bataille would publish part of it ten years later
in one of the appendixes to Le Coupable. *The phrase "unemployed negativity,"*
created by Bataille, can be related to the title Denis de Rougemont gave to one of
his books of the time, Journal d'un intellectuel en chômage *(Journal of an unem-*
ployed intellectual) (reprinted in Journal d'une époque *[1926-1946] [Paris,*
1968]). The unemployment of the negative element for D. de Rougemont stems,
above all, from the fact that history was hard; for Bataille it is from the fact that
it was over.

In his lecture the following January 22 (see Lectures: 1937-38), Bataille
would briefly evoke Kojève's lecture which, he said, "posed, with intentions that
were rather negative I may add, the problem of founding a sociological
science."

Since I have found nothing in the Introduction à la lecture de Hegel *that might*
be related to this specific problem, I will quote two short passages in which the
subjects evoked by Caillois's memories and Bataille's response are treated. In
the first, the man on horseback, the world soul, appears. (I leave it to the reader
to correct it in line with the erratum mentioned by Caillois—instead of "Napo-
leon" read "Stalin.") In the second is the noble romantic soul, the intellectual
who continues to talk revolution when the revolution has become a thing of the
past. These pages are taken from the 1936-37 course on Hegel (Introduction
. . ., pp. 153-54 and pp. 151-52), which focused on the last sections of chapter
6 of La Phénoménologie de l'esprit. *Following this the text of Bataille's letter*
will be found.]

A. From the Christian point of view, Napoleon is the realization of Vanity: He
is, hence, the incarnation of Sin (the Antichrist). He is the first to have dared actually to attribute an absolute (universal) value to human Individuality. For Kant
and Fichte he is *das Böse*: the amoral being par excellence. For the liberal and
tolerant romantic, he is a traitor (he "betrayed" the Revolution). For the "divine" poet, he is only a hypocrite.

For Napoleon, there is only a universally valid morality for *others*; he himself
is "beyond Good and Evil." He is thus, if you like, a "hypocrite." But Kantian
morality does not have the right to make this judgment. Nor does the romantic
Urteil have any more right to accuse Napoleon of egoism and crime; for *every*
Action is egoist and criminal, as long as it does not succeed—and Napoleon succeeded. Moreover, Napoleon's enemies did not *act* against him, did not destroy
him; so their judgment is sheer worthless chatter. They are utter inactivity, that is
to say, a *Sein*, hence a Nothingness: If Germany (hence German philosophy) refuses to "recognize" Napoleon, it will disappear as a *Volk*; the Nations

(*Besonderheit*) who wish to oppose the universal Empire (*Allgemeinheit*) will be annihilated.

But Hegel recognizes Napoleon and reveals him to Germany. He believes he is able to save Germany (through his *Phenomenology*) and preserve it in a sublimated form (*aufgehoben*) in the heart of the Napoleonic Empire.

We have really come down to a duality: Realizer-Revealer, Napoleon-Hegel, Action (universal) and Knowledge (absolute). On the one hand, there is *Bewusstsein* and, on the other, *Selbstbewusstsein*.

Napoleon is turned toward the external World (social and Natural); he comprehends it since he acts successfully. But he does not comprehend himself (he does not know that he *is* God). Hegel is turned toward Napoleon, but Napoleon is a man, he is Man who is "perfect" through his total integration with History; comprehending him is comprehending Man, comprehending oneself. Hence, by comprehending (= justifying) Napoleon, Hegel perfects his *self* consciousness. And thus he becomes a Wise Man, a "perfect" philo-sopher. If Napoleon is God revealed (*der escheinende Gott*), Hegel is the one who reveals him. Absolute Spirit = the plenitude of *Bewusstsein* and *Selbstbewusstsein*, which is to say, the real (natural) World implied by the universal and homogeneous State, realized by Napoleon and revealed by Hegel.

However, Hegel and Napoleon are two different men; hence, *Bewusstsein* and *Selbstbewusstsein* are still separate. But Hegel does not like dualism. Is it a matter of eliminating the final dyad?

That could be accomplished (and more besides!) if Napoleon "recognized" Hegel, as Hegel "recognized" Napoleon. Did Hegel expect (1806) to be summoned by Napoleon to Paris to become the Philosopher (the Wise Man) of the universal and homogeneous State, whose duty it was to explain (justify)—and perhaps direct—Napoleon's Activity?

Always, ever since Plato, the great philosophers have been tempted by this. But the text of the *Phenomenology* relating to it is (willfully?) obscure.

Be that as it may, History has ended.

B. *Die schöne Seele*. The romantic post-revolutionary Man is not yet satisfied: He is not yet *universally* recognized in his "uniqueness" (his genius).

Either: He *imposes* his Convictions; he acts; he ceases being the revolutionary Intellectual; he becomes the Citizen (Napoleon).

Or: He does not want to act, he even has the convictions necessary for not acting. All he needs is to "express himself" and not encroach on the convictions of others. How would he do this? Through Language. In this Society in which the romantic lives, one can, in fact, *say* anything at all; everything is "tolerated" and almost everything is found to be "interesting" (even crime, madness, etc.).

And so this Man believes that he will be able to be "satisfied" by *words*: words, of course, that Society will have *accepted* ("recognized"). In this way, he believes that he *himself* is universally accepted and that he is satisfied with it. Thus he must lead a purely literary existence.

A difference from the Intellectual of the Bestiary (chapter 5, C, a): He is no longer fleeing himself, but on the contrary, describes himself, cheerfully reveals himself to all. He flees the World, not himself—the only *Selbst* that he knows, or that interests him.

It is Man's final flight from the World: refuge in oneself ("the ivory tower").

The height of romantic expression will be the novel's novel, the book's book. (Analogous to the "Phenomenology," which explains how this Phenomenology itself is possible. But the latter has a *real* content: Man as the agent of History).

This Man: First, is a thought that thinks itself (= the pagan, Aristotelian God); already, hence, anthropotheism. But to identify with a pagan divinity is to be easily satisfied (Hegel wants to be Christ).

Second, creates a World from nothing, with the sole aim of making himself be "recognized" (= the Christian God, who creates the World in order to "reveal" himself in it; only the romantic's "World" is just a fiction).

The romantic imagination, creator of "marvelous," "fictional Worlds," reaches its peak with Novalis[1] (as does political action, creator of a real World—with Napoleon). But even Novalis does not take his "divinity" seriously (Napoleon, on the contrary, is to be *der erscheinende Gott* indeed). The Poet is never recognized except by a small number, by a "splinter" (not even a whole Church!) (Napoleon, on the contrary, is vital to all). The Poet who reduces himself to himself in the end exhausts himself, and vanishes utterly in his own nothingness. This is *die absolute Unwahrheit*, the lie pushed to the utmost that obliterates itself. This sublimated, vanishing romantic is the *schöne Seele*: = the unhappy (Christian) Consciousness that has lost its God.

The romantic Poet wanted to be God (and he was right to want it), but he did not know how to go about it: He destroyed himself in madness or suicide. Which is a "beautiful death" but death just the same: total, definitive failure.

[Bataille wrote the following letter to Kojève several days after this lecture was given. Part of it appeared in 1944 in one of the appendixes of Le Coupable. *I have reconstituted the original version (or at least its draft form) from notes in the* Oeuvres complètes *(vol. 5, pp. 369-71).]*

Letter to X, Lecturer on Hegel . . . *

Paris, December 6, 1937

Dear X,

I am writing the following because it seems to me the only way to continue the

---

*This unfinished letter was not recopied, but the draft was sent to the addressee.

conversation we have pursued in several forms. From the outset, I must say that your criticism of me helps me express myself more precisely.

I grant (as a likely supposition) that from now on history is ended (except for the denouement).* However, I picture things differently (I don't attribute much importance to the difference between fascism and communism; on the other hand, it certainly doesn't seem impossible that, in some very distant time, everything will begin again).

If action ("doing") is—as Hegel says—negativity, the question arises as to whether the negativity of one who has "nothing more to do" disappears or remains in a state of "unemployed negativity." Personally, I can only decide in one way, being myself precisely this "unemployed negativity" (I would not be able to define myself more precisely). I don't mind Hegel's having foreseen this possibility; at least he didn't situate it at the conclusion of the processes he described. I imagine that my life—or, better yet, its aborting, the open wound that is my life—constitutes all by itself the refutation of Hegel's closed system.

The question you ask about me comes down to knowing whether I am negligible. I have often asked myself that question; the negative answer haunts me. Furthermore, as the representation I make of myself to myself varies, and as it often happens that I forget, in comparing my life to that of more remarkable men, that mine might be mediocre, I have often said to myself that perhaps there is nothing at the summit of existence except what can be neglected; in effect, no one could "recognize" a height that is as dark as night. A few facts—such as the exceptional difficulty experienced in making myself be "recognized" (on the simple level at which others are "recognized")—have led me to assume the hypothesis of an irrevocable insignificance, seriously though cheerfully.

That doesn't bother me and I see no reason to take any pride in it. But I would be no longer human if I put up with it without a fight (by accepting I would seriously chance becoming not just comically insignificant but bitter and vindictive: then I would have to find my negativity again).

What I am saying about it encourages you to think that all that takes place is just some misfortune, and that's all. Confronted with you, my self-justification is no different from that of a howling animal with its foot in a trap.

Really, the question is no longer one of misfortune, or of life, but only of what becomes of "unemployed negativity," if it is true that it becomes something. I am following it in the forms it engenders, though not in myself right at first but rather in others. Most often, negativity, being impotent, makes itself into a work of art. This metamorphosis, which has real consequences, usually is not a good answer to the situation left by the completion of history (or by the

---

*Wrongly perhaps, wrongly at the very least, as far as the next twenty years were concerned, X imagined the revolutionary solution of communism to be near.

thought of its completion). A work of art answers by evading or, to the extent that it gives a lasting answer, it answers no specific situation. It answers worst of all to the end situation, when evading is no longer possible (when the *moment of truth* arrives). As far as I am concerned, my own negativity gave up on being used only when it no longer had any use; it is the negativity of a man with nothing left to do, and not that of a man who prefers to talk.[2]

But the fact—seemingly incontrovertible—that when negativity turns away from action it expresses itself in a work of art, is no less charged with meaning as far as the possibilities remaining for me are concerned. It is an indication that negativity can be objectified. This fact, moreover, does not just belong to art: religion, better than a tragedy, or than a painting, makes negativity an object of contemplation. But neither in the work of art, nor in the emotional elements of religion, is negativity "recognized as such" at the moment when it enters the workings of existence as a stimulus to major vital reactions. To the contrary, it is introduced in a process of nullification[3] (here the interpretation of facts by a sociologist such as Mauss is extremely important for me). There is, then, a fundamental difference between the objectification of negativity as the past has known it and that which remains possible *at the end*. In effect, the man of "unemployed negativity," not finding in the work of art an answer to the question that he himself is, can only become the man of "recognized negativity." He has recognized that his need to act no longer has any use. But since this need cannot follow art's false leads indefinitely, sooner or later it is recognized for what it is: a negativity empty of content. The temptation to reject this negativity as a sin resurfaces—such a convenient solution that we did not wait for the final crisis to adopt it. But since this solution has already come up, its effectiveness has been previously exhausted. The man of "unemployed negativity" can hardly ever use it any more; to the extent that he is the consequence of what has preceded him, the sentiment of sin no longer has any power for him. He is confronted by his own negativity as if by a wall. No matter how disquieted he is by it, he knows that henceforth nothing can be ruled out since negativity no longer has any prospect.[4]

But the horror he feels looking at negativity within himself is no less likely to end in satisfaction than in the case of a work of art (not to mention religion). For it is precisely in needing to act that he has recognized negativity; and this recognition is bound up with a conception that has it be the condition of all human existence. Far from stopping in this investigation, he finds a total satisfaction in the fact of becoming the man of "recognized negativity." He will no longer rest as he begins the effort to pursue this recognition to its very end. In this way science, to the extent that its object is human negativity—especially the sacred left—becomes the middle term of what is only a process of awareness. Thus it brings into play representations extremely charged with emotive value (such as physical destruction or erotic obscenity, an object of laughter, of physical excitation, of fear and of tears). But at the same time these representations intoxicate him, he strips off the straitjacket that has kept them from contemplation and he sets them objectively within the eruption of time that nothing changes. He understands then that it is his good, not his bad, luck that brought him into a world where there was nothing left to do, and he offers what he has become now, despite himself, to be recognized by others. For he cannot be the man of "recognized negativity" except to the extent that he makes himself be recognized as such. Thus, once again, he discovers something "to do" in a world where, from the point of view of actions, nothing is done any more. And what he has "to do" is to satisfy the portion of existence that is freed from doing: It is all about using free time.

For all that, moreover, he is not up against any less resistance than the men of action who have preceded him. Not that this resistance is able to manifest itself from the outset, but if he does not make a virtue of crime, he generally makes *the* virtue of *the* crime (even if he objectifies crime, making it thus neither more nor less destructive than it was before). It is true that the first phase of resistance must be pure elusion, for no one can know what he is after in confronting others as one who sees in a world of the blind. All around him he encounters people who shy away and who prefer to escape immediately to the side of the blind. And only when a sufficient number achieve this recognition can it become the object of a positive resistance because the blind will be unable to see that something must be expelled until enough of it has been brought into play to make them conscious of its presence.

Moreover, for the man of "recognized negativity," at the moment in which he recognizes negativity in himself, what will then take place does not count (at least regarding the precise form that things are to take). For what is important to him is precisely the fact that he is doomed to conquer or to compel recognition. He knows that his destruction is certain if he does not win in the two possible phases of the struggle. First of all, in the phase of elusive resistance, in his isolation he risks being dedicated to a moral disintegration against which, at the outset, he has no recourse. (He can be one of those for whom losing face in his own eyes does not seem preferable to death). It is only in the second phase that there can be a question of physical destruction, but in both cases, insofar as an individual becomes the man of "recognized negativity," he disappears if the force he brings into play is not greater, first of all, than the force of elusion and, later, than the force of opposition.

I have spoken here of the man of "recognized negativity" as if it were not solely a question of myself. I have to add, in fact, that I do not feel that I am absolutely isolated except insofar as I have become completely aware of what is happening to me. But if I want to complete the story of the owl,[5] I must also say that the man of "unemployed negativity" is already represented by numerous dangers and that the recognition of negativity as a condition of existence has already been carried, in an uncoordinated state, very far. As for what is exclusively mine, I have only described my existence after it has reached a definite stance. When I speak of recognition of the "man of recognized negativity," I speak of the state of my requirements now: Description only comes afterward. It seems to me that until then Minerva can hear the owl.

Only from this precise point does extrapolation take place and it consists of representing everything as a fact, what must follow being produced as the arrival at a position of equilibrium in a well-defined play of forces. Hegel even permitted himself an extrapolation of the same order: moreover, his elusion of a possible later negativity seems to me harder to accept than the description I give of forms of existence that have already been produced—in myself in a very precise manner and independent of a description that frankly came later and in a rather vague way. I add this last thought: In order for phenomenology to have a meaning, Hegel would have to be recognized as its author (which perhaps only genuinely happens with you), and it is obvious that Hegel, as a result of not accepting the role of man of "recognized negativity" to the end, risked nothing: He still belonged, therefore, to a certain extent, to the *Tierreich*.[6]

Animal Societies
Roger Caillois

Saturday, December 18, 1937

["At the close of the discussion that took place following Caillois's lecture on animal societies, I presented a few ideas that I want to return to today." (Bataille's words, January 22, 1938). As with most of what he said, Caillois's text was not preserved—probably was not even written down. On the other hand, Bataille's notes on animal societies have been found among his papers. It is not impossible to think that they formed the framework of his presentation after Caillois had spoken. It is these notes that follow.]

To contemplate animal societies is to contemplate societies as a whole.

1. To situate the social phenomenon within the world as whole.

> Link: star (planet)
> Part of a stellar system
> Molecular mass
> Galaxy

the compositional principle throughout the world.

2. Society as the end of a process on the surface of a cooling star.[1]

> Molecule. micelle. cell. organism.
> Society.
> Line of deterioration.
> Death entering into it more and more.
> Man conscious of death.

Human society surrounding the planet
with a sort of net. a child's string bag
for his ball. planet support.

3. Animal society as a step along this route? Or more as a different *branch*.

Where this branch will fit in.
Difference between colonies and societies.
                    colony = organism

4. The animal colony.

Its characteristics. the material link
for the parts.
The colony is produced by budding.
Rabaud and the absence of interattraction.
The material link proves nothing.
                    sponge

little difference   notion of multiple
between   degrees of
organisms   interattraction
                    sponge
                    colony

Inadequacy of my knowledge of biology.
Regret that there is no biologist here.
Sense of the College. This is equally valid
for the following proposition.

5. Passage from the state of colony-organism to the social state is produced only from a certain metameric form that is seen at the so-called colonial state as in the organic state—only organisms that have become metameric end up as societies.

Insects. birds. mammals.

6. Animal societies form a very limited realm of science and can be defined as groups of metamerized organisms connected by a bond that is not material or, at the very least, not somatic.

Difficulties with this definition.
          meaning of the word "group" (*ensemble*).
Greatly varied solutions.
A personal solution that is not rigid, anticipating differences of degree that go from the vaguest association all the way to one that tends to destroy the autonomy of the parts and to achieve a unity that is in-

divisible: which is only very imperfectly achieved in the most favorable instances.

The degree stems from the extent of the immaterial bond —the grounds for dispute.

>Soul
>Communifying movement
>>Interattraction
>>and interaction?
>>>Division of labor
>>>Morphological
>>>difference.

7. Different theories:

>Impossible rationalism
>Organicism
>Biologism
>That sociology belongs to compound ontology.[2]

8. Rabaud's biologism.

>Interattraction
>Negation of interattraction
>Lone individuals.
>What is interattraction?
>Rabaud's definition p. 101.[3]
>Thigmotropism of the catfish. the
>contagion of motion.
>Relationship between interattraction and
>recognition of the socius.
>
>Notion of contagion: society revolves around
>a group of individuals among whom contagion
>is possible—recognition being
>implicated in this.
>Only explanation: special case of
>compound ontology.
>No necessity. Interrepulsion is
>possible there.
>Lack of stability of society
>thus defined: passage from one to the other.

> There must also be sufficient
> attraction to a common object
> for there to be stability. Nest.

the herd
and the ox.[4]

    9. Secondary importance of interaction.

> This is one result, which Rabaud denies.
> A strange bias that, however, emphasizes certain quick answers.

  10. Psychoanalytic organicism
  11. Difference between animal society and human society.

> Different schools. Durkheim opposed to Rabaud.[5]
> Durkheim not a biologist and related to what I am saying.

  12. Possibility of maintaining identity yet difference in the mode of bonding.

> Development of Durkheim's ideas
> Formation of a nucleus
> Nucleus of repulsion. nucleus of attraction.
> Birth there of power and constraint.

Conclusion: We arrive thus at what is essential, at the very object of the activity pursued here, since this is an express case of sacred sociology. The object of sacred sociology is, in fact, the complex and mobile nucleus formed by sacred things, of the right and of the left. It seems that, on the surface of this planet, when all is said and done, existence revolves around things that are, so to speak, charged with the dread they excite—with a dread that is indistinguishable from the dread of death. It is true that religion very frankly aims to transform unlucky things into lucky and primarily potent things, thereby escaping dread. But knowledge, even later knowledge, discovers the original process again. By establishing the essential nature of the nucleus around which human existence revolves, it clearly reveals human nature, which is, after all, strange and disconcerting for man himself. Very clearly, a major discovery is in question, not merely the discovery by man of what he is—but above all the discovery of the fact that deep within, he is exactly, simultaneously, that which he detests the most and that which makes him burn with desire to the point of reaching an explosive state that is greater than himself.

The Sacred in Everyday Life
Michel Leiris

Saturday, January 8, 1938

[The text read by Leiris at this meeting of the College would be his only important contribution to the institution's activities. It certainly seems that whereas for others the College was the focus of many ambitions and afterthoughts, Leiris never supported the former heart and soul, nor shared in the latter. The first sign was the absence of his signature at the end of the "Note" in Acéphale. *By the time we have reached the correspondence of July 3, 1939 (see the Appendixes: Four Letters), there are no longer just signs: There is overt disagreement. Caillois, moreover, in recollections to which he returns in* Approches de l'imaginaire, *reports that "Michel Leiris participated rather little in the activities of the College." In the eyes of many contemporaries, the consequence of this withdrawal will be to transform the triumvirate into a duumvirate. For Denis de Rougemont or Benda, for example, the College was Bataille's and Caillois's thing. One historian who followed this adventure in vivo would go so far as to speak of the College of Sociology of Georges Bataille, Roger Caillois, and Jean Wahl (Henri Dubief,* Le Déclin de la Troisième République (1929-1938), *vol. 13 of* Nouvelle Histoire de la France contemporaine *[Paris, 1972-76], p. 141).*

"The Sacred in Everyday Life" was published in July 1938 in "For a College of Sociology," six months after the meeting at which Leiris read it. That is where it appears in the present volume. It seems, however, that the text read aloud by the author had been reworked or, at the very least, touched up after the lecture, with publication in mind. In the account of the event given to the next month's NRF *(no. 293, February 1, 1938), Jean Wahl, in fact, mentions several points not found in the text we know. Among others, there is no mention of the "Pari-*

sian peasant," Aragon's beloved brothels, nor any reference to the "spells of Abyssinian sorcerers." (This is, doubtless, the 'medico-magical' rite of the jet du danquârâ that Leiris studied during the Dakar-Djibouti mission's Ethiopian stay, and on which he reported to the Société des Africanistes in February 1935 and published a study in Aethiopica the same year).

At the time of the College's founding, Leiris (except for several small volumes that were surrealist-inspired and of very limited printing) had written only one book, L'Afrique fantôme, which is, moreover, not a literary work in the true sense of the word. It is a personal journal of the Dakar-Djibouti mission that Malraux published in the collection "Les Documents bleus" at Gallimard (Paris, 1934).

The Miroir de la tauromachie would be published by the press G. L. M. (Guy Lévis Mano) at the end of 1938, illustrated by André Masson. The writing of this essay—which must be considered as the first and most important of the manifestos defining a postsurrealist aesthetic—only shortly preceded the beginning of the College's public activities. It is dated October-November 1937, and it was November 20 of the same year that the first lecture took place. (Prior to its publication several pages of the Miroir would appear in the NRF for November 1938, the issue ending with the "Declaration of the College of Sociology on the International Crisis," cosigned by Leiris). The Miroir appeared in the collection "Acéphale" (in the series "L'Érotisme"). It was, however, the sole publication of the collection. (It seems that Tableau de l'amour macabre by the sadologist Maurice Heine was supposed to follow but finally had to be abandoned because of its excessive length). This publication, which Leiris dedicated to the memory of Colette Peignot, the friend of Bataille's who had just died, constitutes Leiris's only (and rather feeble) act of allegiance to the endeavors sponsored by "good old Acephalus"—the Bataillesque equivalent of Jarry's Père Ubu. Although he always refused (as did Caillois) to take part in the activities of Acéphale, the secret society, it turns out that even his signature (unlike Caillois's) does not appear in the contents of the review that was homonymous with it.

As for L'Âge d'homme, the work that in some way would make Leiris's literary existence official, it would not come out until 1939, a year after the "Sacred in Everyday Life" was published in "For a College of Sociology." It should be remembered that, as first published, this autobiographical volume (reviewed by Pierre Leyris in the NRF) is not yet preceded by "De la littérature considérée comme une tauromachie"—to be its preface after the war. And it does not yet open with the dedication to Georges Bataille that is contemporary with this preface. However, although the publication of L'Âge d'homme came after that of the "Sacred," it was written before. The manuscript of the book had been completed in November 1935. Moreover, several extracts had already appeared in reviews: Mesures (1936, no. 3) published the chapter "Lucrèce et Judith," and SUR, the review published by Victoria Ocampo in Buenos Aires, *translated "La Tête d'Holopherne" ("La Cabeza de Holofernes") in its March 1938 issue.*

Leiris continued to remain rather close to surrealism and to Breton despite their hostility to the College. In 1938, the Cahiers G. L. M. *(no. 7), composed by Breton and devoted to the dream, published sixteen of Leiris's dreams. It was also the year in which Breton traveled to Mexico, where, with the painter Diego Rivera, he founded the FIARI (Fédération internationale de l'art révolutionnaire indépendant). The review* Clé, *published after Munich, would be its mouthpiece. Among the reactions to the manifesto published in its first issue is that of Leiris. ("Dear friend, Thank you for your appeal which I read with sympathy. But why Diego Rivera, whose painting [what little I know of it] seems the sort to foster the worst confusion about what we could mean by revolutionary art? Even more, isn't it this very expression "revolutionary art" that is open to all the confusion? Sincerely yours, Michel Leiris.") Leiris is the only member of the College who replied. His letter is introduced in very diplomatically courteous terms: "This is a specious argument that Michel Leiris, to whom we are bound by the many ways that we think in common—despite the confused activity of the 'College of Sociology,' attempts against us.") (It is also in 1939 that Leiris puts together, at the Galerie Simon, in* Glossaire: j'y serre mes gloses, *the "lyric puns" [as he would later call them] that he had published in* La Révolution surréaliste *in 1925 and 1926. This volume would be included in the collection* Mots sans mémoire, *in 1969. But, though a reactivation of the surrealist past, this publication is no less a symptom of the fact that the gestation of* La Règle du jeu *has now begun. The interest in language events to which this testifies, nevertheless, puts it at a great distance from the preoccupations of the College; here it had no other backing than the lapidary linguistics of Paulhan, that "outsider.")*

It is in 1939 that Leiris and Bataille finally will publish, in a noncommercial edition, a first collection of the notes left by Colette Peignot, who died at the end of the preceding year. It would appear under the name of Laure, a pseudonym she had taken for herself. Its title, Le Sacré *is also the title of the article on which Bataille was working while his companion was dying. Several of the notes gathered in Laure's volume can be seen as the more or less direct echo of the 'Sacred in Everyday Life.' One can even find there a page that begins with the question with which Leiris's text concludes: "What color does the very notion of the sacred have for me?" (see the volume edited by Jérôme Peignot:* Laure, Écrits, fragments, lettres *[Paris, 1978], pp. 111 ff.)*

"The Sacred in Everyday Life" *(a title in which one may read a discreet homage to Freud's* Psychopathology of Everyday Life, *on which* La Règle du Jeu *could be said to be modeled) because of its date and its material, constitutes the pivot linking* L'Âge d'homme *to the future* La Règle du Jeu, *without, however, belonging to either one or the other. Leiris, who never reprinted this text (it does not appear in* Brisées), *seems to have felt as uncomfortable with it as he did with participating in the College itself. The only reference that* La Règle du jeu *makes to it is found in "Tambour-trompette," the final chapter of the first volume,* Biffures *(1948). It takes the form of an allusion, as short as possible and hardly explicit, to a text that the author visibly finds it difficult to take into account. In the pages where he retraces the genesis of the autobiographical project that was to occupy more than thirty years, he reviews the various essays that he thinks have a right to be considered as antecedents of* La Règle du jeu. *Then, in parentheses, as if he were mentioning in extremis a text he was going to forget, he slips in an allusion to the "Sacred in Everyday Life": "Without taking into account," he writes, "a few old pages where the description of several of these events took shape." (These are the "language events" footnoted in this volume with the indications of the passages of* La Règle du jeu *in which Leiris picked them up again and developed the description rapidly sketched of them in "The Sacred.")*

But "The Sacred" is also the pivot between Leiris's literary activity and his "second profession," his ethnographic career. Not only the institutional structure where this essay has come to fit (for which it is intended, within which it is read, by which it is published), but also the thematics organizing most of its analyses can be identified as falling within the province of what is understood by secret society. A theory and practice of cryptology jointly develop there. The secret, just as much as the sacred, under the cover of celebrating an idiolect, leaves its scarcely perceptible mark on the surface of everyday life. Under these circumstances, it is not without interest to remember that the study of marginal groups structured by initiation had also become the specialty of Leiris, the ethnographer. Without its being necessary to make more use than is proper of the etymological sense of the word "secretary," it was as such that Leiris was invited by Griaule to join the Dakar-Djibouti mission. At the same time as he found himself entrusted with the office of secretary to the undertaking (L'Afrique fantôme was to come of this), he also was given the specific task of studying "societies of children, senile societies, and religious institutions" (Marcel Griaule, "Mission Dakar-Djibouti. Rapport général," Journal de la Société des Africanistes, *2 [1932], p. 120). It is the same interest that led him to choose the subject of his doctoral thesis :* La Langue secrète des Dogons de Sanga.

Jean Jamin has placed "The Sacred in Everyday Life" in relation to all of Leiris's work: "Quand le sacré devint gauche," L'Ire des vents, *nos. 3-4, (1981), pp. 98-118 .*

After Leiris's lecture, Wahl put together his impressions for the NRF *(February 1938, no. 293, "L'Air du mois") in the following note.]*

At the College of Sociology
Jean Wahl

I am the worst student of the College of Sociology, but a very assiduous one.

Here is this sociology, of which I was never a very devoted follower, taking hold of young minds that are eager for rigorousness, who think they have found in it an answer to questions that they previously thought could be resolved by surrealism, by revolution, and by Freudianism. We must try to understand this phenomenon, which is itself sociological.

Bataille and Caillois, who preside over the destinies of this college, had invited Michel Leiris to speak. It was, I believe, the first meeting in which one had the feeling of some intensity from the beginning to the end of the lecture. From his father's top hat, from the salamander stove that was the spirit of his childhood's winter days, to the cries and spells of Abyssinian sorcerers, by way of those houses that a night walker who was a Paris bourgeois formerly celebrated, he pulled out the disparate forms of the sacred without any sleight of hand. And little by little he defined it as something heterogeneous and ambiguous with which we are in collusion.

At certain moments in earlier meetings—when Caillois brought up secret societies and the solitude of the great beasts, and all that was irrational (the obsessive fear of which drove him toward investigations that were, perhaps, either too rational or not rational enough), or when Bataille spoke of sacrilege—each time one could make out the secret motives leading them in the direction of what they believe is science, the audience already had this sense of some reality. Some among them, however, still had some doubts about the rigor of the positive results. No doubt it will still take a long time for a science of human realities to be constituted, and even for us to have some inkling of the form it might take. But with Leiris, and with Landsberg's observations,[1] for lack of science (is "for lack of" even right?) we are rather continuously in contact with something real.

Attraction and Repulsion I:
Tropisms, Sexuality, Laughter and Tears
Georges Bataille
Saturday, January 22, 1938

[Two meetings will be devoted to the theme "Attraction and repulsion." Bataille speaks at both.

These opposing terms tie in with those French sociology had set up to handle primitive thought. They were frequently used in very different contexts during the thirties. Two examples. Freud has recourse to them to formulate the dualism of instincts (life drive, death drive) in Nouvelles Conférences sur la psychanalyse *(1932): "This opposition is perhaps mixed up in the other one of attraction and repulsion, whose existence in the inorganic world is accepted by physical sciences." And Eddington (to cite a physicist, and a physicist who cites Bataille): "It is almost inadvertently that Einstein added a dispersive force that is repulsive to the attraction of Newton's bodies. This is the force that we call* cosmic repulsion*" (The Expanding Universe, 1933). One could also mention Heidegger's definition of nothingness in* What is Metaphysics? *(1929): "Nothingness attracts nothing to itself; on the contrary, it is essentially* repulsion.*"*

As we have already seen, Bataille's descriptions hesitate between two models for reading social space: the model of nodalization (that is, nodal, centralized attraction) and the model of wavelike contagion. But what is most important is to see the point at which this hesitation is produced: precisely where attraction-repulsion as a pair break down and where repulsion becomes attractive, negativity positive, etc.

Five days before this lecture, Bataille opened a short-lived "Society of Collective Psychology," where he read a text many of whose points are repeated here. For its first year this society had set itself a theme to consider: "Attitudes

When Faced with Death." It was founded by Dr. Allendy, Bataille, Dr. Borel, Leiris, and Dr. Paul Schiff. Among the lectures (were they just planned, or did they take place?) were Leiris on Dogon funeral rites, Lagache on the work of mourning, and Duthuit on the artistic representation of death.]

We were brought together here, first of all, in order to try to define what can be understood by the word "society." I personally have defined society as a "compound being," as a whole presenting something more than the sum of its parts.[1] (Apropos, I think Caillois meant approximately the same thing when he spoke of biologism or of neo-organicism.)[2] Then we examined the question of whether a science of society thus defined was possible and we shall certainly have to return to this fundamental question. But, perhaps, now it will suffice to refer to the Hegelian terms used by Kojève[3] to pose (with rather negative intentions moreover) the problem of the foundations of sociological science. Having debated these general points, we have now arrived at an initial factual description that was focused at first on nonhuman societies not seeming to offer any elements that could be defined as sacred,[4] then on the present social state, directly experienced by us, where sacred elements appear, above all, as survivals.[5]

It has been stated most emphatically that the sociology we intended to expound here was not the generally accepted sociology, nor was it a religious sociology, but rather, very precisely, sacred sociology. Actually, the realm of the sacred goes beyond the realm of religion, but it cannot be identified with the totality, the whole of the social realm. Hence, we have entered the sacred realm that is the object of our specific investigation, first, in attempting to describe animal societies that appear as "presacred," and second, by analyzing, in an existence that has become almost entirely profane, in some ways "postsacred," certain traces and surviving elements of a past in which the sacred could have a constitutive value.

Obviously, it would be absurd if, by expressing myself in this way, I left anyone believing that the sacred does not exist any more, that it is no longer able to exist now except in the form of a survival. But we will have to come back to that question—which, moreover, might very well be our final question. Today I only want to derive some first results, draw some first conclusions from the facts previously described by Caillois and Leiris. Some societies exist where the sacred seems not to intervene—animal societies; some societies exist where the sacred seems, at least initially, in the process of disappearing—societies of advanced civilization in which we live. It is a question of extracting the meaning of these two things together. I assume that by the end of my paper—if I have succeeded in making myself exactly understood, if I have succeeded, I must add, in being sufficiently convincing as to the accuracy of my analysis—it will seem that I have spoken of none other than the essential moving forces of human machinery. At the same time, I hope, it will seem that I have successfully made rather good progress in penetrating this machinery, which is the most complicated, in any case, the most disconcerting, to be found.

At the close of the discussion that took place following Caillois's lecture on animal societies, I presented a few ideas that I want to return to today.[6] They might actually be of fundamental value.

I began with the fact that Rabaud attributes the origin of animal societies *exclusively* to interattraction, that is, to a troposensitivity directing individuals of certain species toward each other.[7] In addition to the numerous difficulties that such a theory raises, I insisted on the point that it could not account for the conglomerations that we find in nature unless these conglomerations were indefinite. If, indefinitely, bees could incorporate one after another, into a swarm, if a stray bee could incorporate indiscriminately into a new swarm, then interattraction could be regarded as a satisfactory explanation. But, in fact, animal societies are individualized, and they usually even display marked interrepulsion when confronted with other societies of the same species. Some other factor is required to explain the phenomena, a factor of individualization.[8] It is not enough that individuals are attracted to each other. It is also necessary that they be conscious of some attraction or other—it might even be quite secondary—to a specific object, to a unique object. This object can be a locality, such as a nest or a hive; it can be an individual, for example, a queen. That is less important; it suffices that it be distinguished by its unique character from a mass that is indefinitely extendable. It is even possible to allow that in a given species stable and limited conglomeration might be produced belatedly without a factor of individualization. The animals, in this case, each time they gather, would go back to the conduct, the social behavior involving the individuality of the formation, whether the conglomeration is the result of chance or of the will of others—especially of the human will. But this social behavior capable of individualizing society presupposes, at the very least, former conditions in which it was necessitated by some factor of individualization, precise conditions without which this behavior would not have been acquired.

I do not imagine this somewhat complex explanation of artificial phenomena such as herds, which are the result of human intervention, introduces any real difficulty.

Following Caillois's paper stating this principle—the necessity of a factor of individualization—I insisted that, in this respect, human societies display an entirely different aspect from that displayed by animal societies. In the latter, the factor of individualization does not appear to be very important: It can be external to the individuals themselves or it can be constituted by one of them. But whether it is a place or a being that is in question, the animals seem only slightly changed by the phenomenon of social formation. Bee or wasp nests can be considered as individual nests that are juxtaposed. Caillois, however, the other day mentioned that there is an exterior cover to the nest, which indisputably introduces a change. The queens' conditions of existence, on the other hand, may have contributed to the pronounced morphological differentiation they display, but even that is not sure, and be that as it may, it seems obvious that interattraction remains the dominant thing. Clearly, it is not just luck that made the theory of interattraction to be born in the mind of a man who has passed his life studying the behavior of insects.[9]

Consideration of human matters leads to a very different view. Contemplating mankind, it is hard to form a precise idea, or even any idea at all, of what the factor of individualization of human societies under the original conditions might have been. Indeed, this factor has been subjected to such a social transformation that nothing still remains of its original nature. It does not seem that the original factor could have been place since the social forms that appear most primitive to us are blood communities, not place-related communities. However, attributing this power to some individual or other, designated by personal strength or by parental situation, would remain at the level of a completely problematic conjecture anyhow. In fact, what constitutes the individual nucleus of every conglomerate of human society is displayed in the most primitive conditions as a reality neither personal nor local—and whose nature has obviously been profoundly changed by social existence. What we are talking about is a set of objects, places, beliefs, persons, and practices that have a sacred character, all of which—objects, places, beliefs, persons, and practices—belong exclusively to one group and not another. But whereas a nonhuman social existence introduced nothing perceptibly exceeding immediate interattraction, this sacred nucleus at the heart of human movements seems to be a formation quite distinct and even disconcerting in its specificity. In fact, this nucleus is external to the individuals, and not only because it is not formed by one or by several persons who are different from the other. In every case, it is much more complex, including more than persons. It is primarily external to the beings who form the group because for them it is the object of a fundamental repulsion. The social nucleus is, in fact, taboo, that is to say, untouchable and unspeakable; from the outset it partakes of the nature of corpses, menstrual blood, or pariahs. Other sorts of filth, in comparison with such a reality, represent only a dissipated force of repulsion: They are not completely untouchable, they are not completely unnameable. Everything leads us to believe that early human beings were brought together by disgust and by common terror, by an insurmountable horror focused precisely on what originally was the central attraction of their union.[10]

The facts one might cite in support of this idea are widely known and extremely numerous, and I do not believe it is necessary for the moment to dwell on them. I would like, in fact, to go on to reflections of a different sort. I do not think that it is possible to move on immediately to a more organized and closely argued description of the central nucleus. Two weeks from now, this description will be the subject of another discussion focusing on social structure.[11] First of all, it seems to me necessary to demonstrate how the existence of such a nucleus divides ordinary human existence from animal existence. I have insisted that immediate interattraction dominates the activity of social animals. It is precisely this interattraction, at least in its simple form, that ceases to play a major role in human groups.

Human interattraction is not immediate, it is *mediated*, in the precise sense of the word; that is, the relations between two men are profoundly changed as a result of their both being situated within the orbit of the central nucleus. The basically terrifying content of the nucleus around which each one's existence is revolving intervenes in their relationship as an inevitable middle term.[12]

I have just expressed myself in a hopelessly abstract manner. I understand that I have just given definitions that are very hard to understand. I only have one way to excuse myself, to justify having recourse to such muddled and apparently unwarranted constructions. I can only try to use this indefensible tool as a key. If a door that had always remained shut opens—no matter how unwieldy the method used—the one who turns the key will appear human again.

Besides, now I am ready to talk about the most familiar things.

There are two existing forms of perceptible human interattraction, first sexual interattraction—which cannot be considered social in the precise sense of the term—then laughter, which, I will now demonstrate, constitutes the specific form of human interattraction. It will be easy for me to show that in human terms these two forms of interattraction exist in an immediate state but that they are not commonly found except in a *mediated* state.

And, in order to make myself understood, I shall start with clear examples of the categories I am contrasting. I shall even choose examples in such a way that they constitute the central theme, the heart of this discussion. I think it will be impossible not to remember what they describe. And retaining them will be enough: Everything I shall add is likely to be linked to these symbols.

A child, who is a few weeks old, responding to an adult's laughter, represents unambiguously the classic example of immediate laughter.[13]

On the other hand, a young girl full of charm and full of humanity who cannot help laughing each time she is told of the death of someone she knows, as I see it, laughs a *mediated* laughter.

I have borrowed this latter case with its obvious point from a psychologist who is an English scholar, well acquainted with this young girl.[14]

I shall only be at a loss to cite a case of immediate sexual excitement: Even the very simple excitement provoked by nudity is as clearly mediated as it is possible to be. I shall have to be content with saying that, taken as a whole, every sexual experience must include some part that is immediate; or, in different terms, it at least supposes very brief states akin to animal activity.

For an example of *mediated* sexual excitement, I shall deliberately choose a case in which the object is the same as that of the young girl's laughter. It concerns a man who could not see a burial without having an erection. But he must have been a respectful son because he suddenly had to flee the scene of his father's funeral.

The difference between the contrasting forms symbolized by these examples provides a clear account of the profound alteration of human life that is due to the action of the social nucleus. Moreover, the analysis I am about to undertake will offer what I believe is a correct answer to the problem of laughter.

I have several reasons for beginning with the analysis of laughter, the most superficial being that we have here one of psychology's most complex and maddening problems. But first of all, I must justify the assertion I just made, according to which laughter would be the "specific form of human interattraction."

Rabaud, seeking to define what is, according to him, the sole factor of social aggregation, expresses it this way:

> The word "attraction," in the biological sense, evokes positive phenomena."[15]

There is a simplifying bias here that is quite in line with the requirements of exact sciences. But it is possible to wonder whether this is a case of a simple phenomenon or of a simplified phenomenon. Actually, Rabaud is leaving out a basic difficulty: The fact that one individual is attracted by another or by others supposes a discernment, a recognition of one's fellow creature, whether or not it is conscious.[16] Of course, Rabaud, to the extent he envisages a stimulant, only envisages very simple elements. Concerning wild bees, *Halictus*, about whose social behavior he had, at length, made outstanding studies, he assumes (without bringing in any basis of proof) an olfactory stimulant. It is unfortunate that some other example of social conduct did not attract him, some example where any assumption simplifying things would be impossible. The catfish forms large groups similar to those many species of fish form. The process of forming this group was analyzed experimentally by Bowen in 1930.[17] A dispersed grouping reforms in half an hour. Cutting the olfactory nerves does not change the conduct of the catfish at all; it still aggregates at the first encounter. On the other hand, fish deprived of their eyes no longer aggregate. And there is a reaction to motion: If an artificial fish is put into the water and if it is made to move like a real fish, the catfish will follow it. It will also follow a fish of another species. But in both these instances, it will quickly notice its mistake and move away: Community of movement is not continued.

Interattraction and aggregation, at least in this case, seem to be linked to recognition. Conversely, the very fact of recognition of fellow creatures, which unquestionably plays a large role not only in human life but also in animal life, doubtless must be linked to processes that are just as simple as those displayed by the catfish. Pierre Janet in a recent article in *Annales médico-psychologiques*[18] demonstrated the absurdity of former conceptions, or perhaps more exactly, former ignorance about the problem. Janet's explanation of the nineteenth-century psychologists' way of seeing is that, according to them, "man knows immediately."

It seems to me possible from here on in to conclude this discussion with facts that touch simultaneously problems of interattraction and of recognition by introducing a precise interpretation: Like organisms, in many instances, may well experience group movements. They are somehow permeable to such movements. What is more, I have thus only stated in other terms the well-known principle of contagion, or if you still want to call it that, fellow feeling, *sympathie* but I believe I have done this with sufficient precision. If one acknowledges permeability in "group movements," in continuous movements, the phenomenon of recognition will appear to be constructed on the basis of the feeling of permeability experienced when confronted with an $\frac{\text{other}}{\text{socius}}$.

Now I will go back to the child's laughter as a basic example of permeability to a common movement. It happens when confronted with adult laughter. It establishes between adult and child a communication that is already so profound that it later will be able to be enriched and amplified by multiplying its possibilities without its intimate nature being changed. Contagious weeping and erotic contagion are the only things that, subsequently, will be able to deepen human communication. Moreover, the laughter two individuals share is already the same as the shared laughter of a roomful of people. No doubt it may seem strange to assert that at that moment we are in the presence of the fundamental phenomenon of interattraction since, both in the roomful of people and in the child's laughter, there is no movement of individuals toward each other and even less any movement of the child toward the adult. Identification of laughter with interattraction, in fact, supposes a somewhat different representation than the one introduced by Rabaud. It would consist not in a movement concentrating individuals who are distant from each other but in the intervention of a new element at the moment in which the individuals come close, something analogous to the production of an electric current uniting, in a more or less stable manner, individuals who came into contact almost by chance. Laughter would be only one of the possible currents since unifying movements, transmissible from one person to another, are able to take different forms as soon as permeability frees a passage.

If we now take into account the order in which different kinds of laughter appear in the very young child, it must be said that the laugh of recognition is not exactly the first that is produced. The laugh of satisfaction that follows taking nourishment or a warm bath, that follows appeasement, comes before the laugh of recognition. Given the explosive character of laughter, a sort of discharge of too much energy, this is not surprising. That is to say, in its raw state, laughter is first the expression of an intense joy and does not represent a simple current of communication that is established between two people or several people laughing together. There is no pure and simple communication; what is communicated has a sense and a color, what is communicated is joy. And this immediate joy will persist through the social alteration of laughter.

We must not, moreover, visualize all this too superficially, imagining, for example, human society linked by laughter and delight. Not only, as we are going to see, is the social delight that reveals itself in laughter something very suspect and even very dreadful, but laughter is only an intermittent phenomenon: It breaks off very often, in fact, in the course of social relations that cannot be exclusively happy. Thus it marks moments of intense communication only within the limits of relations lived between two persons, but—this point must be insisted on—the intensity in this case is one that is devoid of personal significance. To a certain extent, in principle, laughter between two people supposes a state that is open to all comers. This is how, as a whole—but only as a whole, human aggregation is held together by being put in touch with joy—by a contact—whose aggregative value depends on life's being satisfying and exuberant.

If we return now to mediated laughter, the laughter a young girl could not hold back when told someone she knew had died, we are suddenly face to face with a strange mixture of satisfaction and distress. What causes the delight, the exuberance, is precisely what usually causes despondency. It is true that we have here an extreme case, so extreme that communication with other people, introduced by normal laughter, as we have seen, must immediately be cut off. The utmost uneasiness must even result from it, instead of the usual communication. But the ordinary, often repeated, analysis of all the cases of mediated laughter demonstrates that the situation is always approximately the same. It is always a distress; it is always something dispiriting that causes advanced laughter. At least, it is necessary for there to be a great difference in tension between the one who laughs and the object of laughter. The only generally required condition is that the distress be weak enough or distant enough to not inhibit a reaction of joy. Obviously this required condition is not fulfilled in the case of the young girl, and one might say that this is a case of abortive laughter. But it is precisely this excess that makes the example significant: It emphasizes something that usually is barely mentioned. Laughter about falling is already in some manner laughter about death, but since the distress involved is minimal, it does not prevent a communicative laughter. Here it is clear that what is revealing is the anomaly where inhibition is lacking.

Here we have come to the essential point of the problem.

How can it be that distress was turned into joy—something that should have been shattering turned into exuberance—the deepest depression turned into an explosive tension?

It is characteristic of this paradoxical process that it is automatic, unconscious, and expressly produced not in solitude but within ordinary communication. Alone, it is impossible to transform the despondency one feels into a tension; but what the course of individual life is unable to realize, the course of a reaction traversing from one to the other realizes. From the beginning, therefore, the process is of a social nature. Yet, for all that, we do not see the mechanism that is involved. It is obviously not enough to say that we are dealing with a social phenomenon. We also would have to explain how it is possible for social existence to transform depression into tension.

Precisely at this point we must bring into question the existence of a sacred nucleus about which is formed the joyful round of human communication.

I am putting off until the next lecture, as I have already said I would, an extensive and precise description of this nucleus. At that time I shall demonstrate that, its basic content being that which is disgusting and debilitating—as I have already mentioned, menstrual blood, bodily putrefaction—the active function is the transformation of a depressive content into an object of exaltation—in other words the transformation of a left sacred into a right sacred—and to get back to the problem brought up today, the transformation of depression into tension. Now, human nature as a whole, in each group agglomerated around each sacred nucleus, has, to a large extent, by participating in the activity of this nucleus, acquired the faculty of transforming the left into the right, distress into strength. I shall come back to this point—and it is only then, perhaps, that things will clear up a bit—but on the condition at least of referring to something I shall later explain, it has become possible for me to account for what takes place in laughter in common. If in a communicative reaction of exuberance and general joy a third term interferes, one partaking of the nature of death, it is to the extent that the very dark, repulsive nucleus, around which all turbulence revolves, has created the principle of life out of the category death, springing out of falling.

This strange mechanism of mediation, however, is not yet perfectly visible in the example of laughter. The mechanism is less elusive when it is a question of sexual communication, of reciprocal arousal, since these depressive elements can make a more strenuous interference here than in laughter. This is possible, first, because the reaction involved is less easily inhibited, less fragile than joy; second, because the reaction can be specific to one couple and even to a single aroused individual. Consequently, extreme cases can be produced, hence the arousal by a burial that I chose as a symbolic example. In fact, the situation is essentially changed because laughter did not focus attention on its object at all: On the contrary, laughter hid the object from attention and bound the process into an intense and exuberant human communication of joy. When an aroused individual lingers over an object because of his arousal—and even when a connection is made, when arousal results in communication and is bound up in an overall movement—the object does not disappear in the least, nor does its ability to focus extreme attention. So one sees degrees of mediation. Laughter, while unquestionably mediated, retains an aspect of pronounced immediacy in the human relations it controls. Whereas mediation is strenuously maintained, obsessively maintained, often from one end to the other of sexual communication. Between two people whose movements are composed of exuberant life, the theme of reciprocal repulsion focused on sexual parts is present as mediator, as a catalyst increasing the power of communication. Doubtless, the sexual parts are not truly repugnant unless they belong to a person devoid of charm—a fat old woman, for example. But the most desirable woman's organs partake in the unspeakable nature of the organs of the woman who is old and obese. Thus they partake in the nature of the sacred nucleus; which is even less surprising because, as I have mentioned, this nucleus refers to, among other taboo horrors, menstrual blood. Most important here is the fact that a sort of region of silence is introduced between a man and a woman and imposes itself on them in a way that casts a spell on them. In this way their relations are mediated and humanized in the most profound manner, which does not happen between those who laugh.

I cannot continue the development of this today.

I shall put off until the next time speaking of tears whose direct object is what is horrible and unbearable, and I shall just allude, in conclusion, to the profound silence introduced by tears. I would like, thus, to make the nature of the nucleus I have spoken of and the mediation it introduces into existence somewhat palpable. It has seemed to me—and the impression I had then was very strong—that it was as if human relations were empty of meaning if a region of silence did not interfere between them. Immediate, common human relations easily seem unbearable. It seems that it is only to the extent that a silence laden with a certain tragic horror weighs down on life that this life is profoundly human. This is what rarely, but occasionally in the most wonderful way, makes the coming together of two lovers be of human magnitude.[19] But we still have to know the extent to which whatever makes the greatness of the erotic embrace, is not also demanded by social excitement. That is what I shall discuss next time, when I attempt to explain the structure of the sacred center that is necessary to collective human emotion.

Attraction and Repulsion II: Social Structure
Georges Bataille

Saturday, February 5, 1938

[This is the second lecture devoted by Bataille to the way the social mechanism converts initially repulsive impulses into attractive forces. The first two pages had not been found when the second volume of the Oeuvres Complètes *was edited. They appeared for the first time in the French edition of this book; the last page is still missing, however.]*

Two weeks ago I spoke of the profound alterations that take place in the re-lating movements played out between individuals who belong to a limited mass, which is, itself, individualized—specifically in the movements that drive a given society. I represented these alterations as the effect of a central action: as if the nucleus of a structure that is clear-cut and distinct from the individuals adhering to it had the power to really denature the activity that is formed on its periphery. I attempted thus to describe how natural laughter is denatured. Natural laughter would be no more than a very contagious vital exuberance. This simple exuber-ance would be formed with depressing images, with images of failure or death, comparable to just so many emissions from a sort of central nucleus in which so-cial energy would be charged and concentrated. I pointed out, a bit rapidly per-haps, that the same effect made itself felt on sexual attraction, which, like laugh-ter, is formed with images whose most immediate value is repugnant. All these phenomena of denaturation would make up the specificity of human existence within nature, the basic essentials of which would be given, of course, in the de-naturation that is operative in the heart of the central nucleus. I said very little last time about this central nucleus, only that it was complex, simultaneously composed of places, objects, persons, beliefs, and sacred practices, and also that a paradoxical transmutation of depressant into stimulant was to be seen there. I was able to give a spectacle such as ''tragedy'' as a typical example of this trans-mutation.[1] I could have added that the doubling of tragedy by comedy gives an already rather complete picture of the whole that I am trying to describe. Situated within a sort of sacred enclosure is the tragic action that carries the spectators' tension along, if not to the point of tears, at least to a state close to tears. Around this enclosure a clearly profane region is traversed by great waves of laughter, waves that build up and start again around images like those of comedy. This is, doubtless, a very simplified schema, perhaps only a suggestive image or pure al-lusion, but as far as I am concerned it expresses the essential and in a sensible manner, in a manner that can be acutely felt—specifically the fact that union be-tween human beings is not immediate union but is accomplished around a very strange reality, an incomparable and obsessive force; that if human relations stop passing through this middle term, this nucleus of violent silence, they are emp-tied of their human character.

But before pursuing this description, I want to develop some ideas relating to method. How important is this elaboration in relation to the various approaches that are legitimately possible for knowledge? Can it be posited as the develop-ment of a science that is analogous to other sciences—sociology, just as there is biology or astrophysics. It is not just coincidental that I ask this question at this precise moment. It seems to me that the image I have just used introduces an el-ement that could not be encountered either in biology or in physics, an element that I have not hesitated to characterize precisely when I said of this image that what was essential was expressed there in a *sensible* manner. No doubt it is not absolutely certain that there is *nothing* that can be felt that has *ever* intervened in the exact sciences. Some sort of intuitive representation of phenomena accom-panies the positing of laws, but that is only a sort of weak moment for the sci-entist and is somehow external to science, properly speaking, which tends to re-duce sensibility to a minimum. Quite the contrary, I have emphasized, and will continue to do so, that the phenomena I attempt to describe are lived by us. And they are not only lived. A moment ago I used the term ''essential.'' I think, in fact, that they constitute the essential of what is lived by us and, if you like, the heart of existence animating us. And even more: I consider the act of recognizing what this heart of our existence really is to be a decisive act in human develop-ment. In other words, I believe that nothing is more important for us than that we recognize that we are bound and sworn to that which horrifies us most, that which provokes our most intense disgust.

I really think that here I should be obliged to choose: If things are as I have just said, I am obviously distancing myself from what I gladly refer to as science's deep slumber. I understand that I have been instructed to acknowledge this openly. Why should I not admit, in fact, that it is possible that I am creating a phenomenology and not a science of society?[2] Even that might be granting my-self more than others are willing to concede. Would it not, after all, be just a question of something deserving the name of ideology? Would what I am setting forth here be anything more than a combat ideology? That is to say, by defini-tion, a necessary delusion.

I think I have better things to do than to answer the difficulties raised by my initiative by demonstrating that I make use of data of various origins, and that, all in all, it is interesting to be engaged in a broad confrontation. Why not, I might ask, why not join the facts of the sociology that is, or claims to be, scien-tific with the rather purely phenomenological facts of Hegel. It is possible that what I am attempting to do lets itself be reduced to this confrontation. But I have to represent things in a more complicated manner. I believe my attempt has an entirely specific character that I must bring to the surface. I have just said that I think it is a decisive act for us to acknowledge what is really at the heart of our existence. But that is meaningful only if we realize something other than what we expect, and there would be something absurd in claiming to find something profoundly disconcerting merely with a phenomenological method, that is to say, by simply describing apparent lived experience. From these two things, then, this one: Either the detours of objective science will bring external data, foreign to immediate lived experience, or nothing really new will have taken place and my interpretations are unacceptable from the start. In other words, what I am attempting presupposes that revealing the unconscious is possible, and by definition, the unconscious is placed beyond the reach of phenomenological description. It has been impossible to have access to it except through methods that are scientific. These methods are well known: We are talking about sociol-ogy of primitive peoples and about psychoanalysis, disciplines that certainly raise many difficulties in the register of method, but which cannot be reduced to phenomenology.

It is no less true that man's recognition of himself, which I have described as the basic object of my endeavor, cannot occur except on the phenomenological level. That is, there would be no recognition if what is lived were not the last in-stance. This problem has already found a solution precisely within psychoana-lytic experience. We know that it is not enough to *explain* to a neurotic the com-plexes that are controlling his unhealthy behavior, they also must be made *sensible*. Therefore, psychoanalysis alone has already had to solve practically the entire problem I sought to describe—namely, the passage from unconscious to conscious. At this point, moreover, psychoanalysts are reduced to bending the scientific principle in an exceptional manner: Their method is communicated only through *subjective* experience—every psychoanalyst having first to be psy-choanalyzed since objective understandings are clearly insufficient. At this point, there is no justification other than success. It should even follow from this that only those who are psychoanalyzed would be able to recognize the value of psychoanalytic data. But nothing of the sort: Psychoanalysis and the twist it employs have brought into circulation *objective* data that are rather generally and even adequately recognized. That way, at least, the unconscious has been able to become an object of knowledge.

It is obvious that my turn will come to have to prove with success that my endeavor is fully justified. I just wanted to indicate from the outset that given the goal I have set for myself, I am unable to proceed in any other fashion. And it seems to me difficult in any event, after what I have just said, to claim that I will necessarily end up thus with a combat ideology, a necessary delusion. There is no doubt, I admit it to be a very common truth, that it is impossible to create anything other than different accents in all the various forms of man's representation of things. This much being clear, I don't mind admitting that the principles I set forth are a combat ideology as well, that there is no doubt that error plays a not completely avoidable part. I have already had occasion to say that I am not unduly concerned about this—I do mean: unduly. But now I want to insist that, unable to get anywhere except through the detour of cold science—without which the endeavor would no longer be meaningful—I am obliged to accord just about as much weight to my own assertion as to this cold science. It will be said that in these matters, even the coldest science is still off the track; indeed it is, but I claim that it is humanly possible to be content with the authority of a Mauss or of a Freud.[3]

Nonetheless, I must here acknowledge that a Hegelian will have an apparently decisive argument in opposition to all these ideas that I have just elaborated. The *Phenomenology of Mind*, written in 1806, did without Mauss's, as well as Freud's, data. It is no less true that contrary to the principle I just stated—according to which phenomenology could not get at the unconscious—Hegelian method seems to have penetrated deeply at least into our dark regions. Hegel himself attached very great importance to what I describe as the heart of our existence. For him the basis of human specificity is *negativity*, which is to say, destructive action. Hegel indeed recounted how, for several years, he had been terrified by the truth as his mind portrayed it to him, and how he thought he was going mad. This period of extreme anguish comes before the *Phenomenology* but several years after one of his pupils, who had doubtless understood him better than the others, leaving his class with a sense of oppression, wrote that he believed he had heard Death itself speaking from the podium.[4] I must acknowledge in turn that Hegel's penetration allowed him, to a great extent, to go beyond the realm available to common consciousness, but how can one not be struck by a strangely contradictory fact? Namely, Hegel was able to organize, set forth, and publish his doctrine, but it does not seem that (with one exception that I have just quoted) what disturbed him disturbed the others. Even if it was true that for Hegel there was a passage of the unconscious into consciousness, it occurred solely for Hegel. The *Phenomenology* was not recognized itself as recognizing negativity.[5] Hegel, thus, by no means carried out the decisive act that I have called into question. But the critique that can be made of Hegel from the point of view I occupy is not limited to that. Whereas it is true that Hegel turned expressly in the direction in which the essential can be discovered, it does not follow that the immediate method of investigation at hand could have allowed him to give a true and correct description of facts. Only the intervention of objective science as it has been carried out for several decades by sociologists and psychologists has permitted the remarkably precise apprehension and representation of something that, remaining heterogeneous to the conscious mind, could not be apprehended and represented in Hegel's mind except from the outside. Perhaps what Hegel described is actually only the shadow projected through the conscious region of the mind by a reality that, as unconscious, remained unknown, or very dimly known by him. Moreover, the profound difference due to different methods of investigation can be clearly established from the outset. Hegelian phenomenology represents the mind as essentially homogeneous. On this point, recent data on which I rely agree in establishing a formal heterogeneity among different regions of the mind. It seems to me that the marked heterogeneity established between the sacred and the profane by French sociology, or between the unconscious and the conscious by psychoanalysis, is a notion that is entirely foreign to Hegel.

It would make no sense then for us to limit ourselves here to repeating or interpreting the *Phenomenology of Mind* as Kojève does magnificently, moreover, at the Hautes Études. Among the various objects of Hegelian description, negativity remains without a doubt a representation that is simultaneously rich, violent, and charged with great expressive value. But the negativity I will speak about is of another nature. I have represented it at first as projecting its interference into laughter or into sexual activity. Now I shall represent it in its concentrated form. And, doubtless, I shall continue to give the facts I describe an interpretation that is my own personal one in part, but this time I shall stick very close to classic descriptions and interpretations.

If one imagines a very simple human agglomeration, a French village, for example, it is difficult not to be struck by its concentration around the nucleus that the church constitutes. It is possible to have sentiments that are even aggressively anti-Christian; that does not prevent the feeling that the church and the houses surrounding it realize as a whole a vital equilibrium such that radical destruction of the church would be in some ways a mutilation. Generally this sentiment is attributed to the aesthetic value of the religious edifice, but it is obvious to us that churches have not been built with the aim of beautifying landscapes, and it seems possible that the need they fulfilled can be perceived even through aestheticized impressions. The description I shall try to give seems to me, in any case, immediately to have a value that has remained intelligible for everyone. The church constitutes a sacred place in the center of the village, at least in the sense that profane activity stops at its enclosure and cannot penetrate within except through fraud. A certain number of images that are charged with a supernatural meaning give the church interior an expressive value for complex beliefs. A substance that is essentially sacred in the sense that it cannot be touched, and cannot even be seen except under conditions that are rarely met, is preserved in the central portion of the edifice. Moreover, a person who is ritually consecrated is assigned to the church, where every morning he performs a symbolic sacrifice. In addition, in many cases, bodies have been buried under the paving stones, and in all churches a saint's bone has been sealed under the altar during the consecration of the edifice. All the dead bodies from the agglomeration may have been buried within the immediate confines as well. The whole possesses a certain force of repulsion that generally guarantees an interior silence, keeping the noise of life at a distance. At the same time it possesses a force of attraction, being the object of an unquestionable affective concentration that is more or less constant on the part of the inhabitants, a concentration partly independent of sentiments that can be described as specifically Christian.

Furthermore, from the point of view of attraction, within this nucleus there exists a rhythm of activity that is marked by Sunday or yearly feast days. And the activity within honoring these very feast days experiences a moment of increased intensity, a moment of prostrate silence interrupting the sound of the organ and of song. Hence, it is possible to perceive, even in events that are very close to us, a moment of solemn repulsion introduced at the very heart of the spirited attraction that gathers the crowd for a feast day. The gesture required of the faithful at the moment in which the sacrifice is accomplished is one of guilty anguish. The priest's elevation of the sacred object requires heads to be lowered; that is, eyes must be averted and individual existences obliterated, prostrated beneath the weight of a silence charged with anguish.

But the nucleus of human agglomeration is not simply the center of a movement of repulsion and attraction driven by a periodic rhythm. It is even quite worthy of note that it has the power to attract corpses—each time a death interrupts the normal course of common existence. Then it is the locus of a movement that doubtless presents a different aspect than that of feast days but that, however, can be boiled down to the same elements of repulsion and attraction. The crowd of the dead person's kin and acquaintances gathers around the body in the church, but only at a respectful distance since the crowd, despite having been drawn there, does not cease to be subjected to the great force of repulsion belonging to lifeless bodies. This force of repulsion is made especially noticeable— as in the case of the elevation during mass—by the region of oppressed silence that falls around the dead. In any case, it is necessary to insist that the activity of the agglomeration's nucleus during the simultaneously attractive and repulsive presence of a coffin is no less significant than during the periodic feast days.

Baptisms and marriages in Christian ritual, on the contrary, are evidently much less rich in meaning. Only royal coronations, which, it is true, are accomplished only in a single privileged edifice for a given nation, may well provide yet another major element of the description of those sacred nuclei subsisting in present-day society.[6] Performing a coronation at the very center of the movements of repulsion and attraction that drive this society is, in fact, an indication that the power necessarily emanates from such a nucleus, that the energetic charge condensed at the center of social repulsion and attraction is necessary in order to confer on a king the dynamic, simultaneously attractive and dreadful nature that is his attribute.

It is self-evident that Christian theology does not account for these facts in a satisfactory manner. And besides it is not necessary to have gone very far into the science of religions to know that analogous facts independent of Christianity are found everywhere and in every period, as far as investigation has been able to go. Certain elements no doubt may be lacking. The building is absent in a great number of cases. Then the nucleus is mobile and diffuse, and it becomes impossible to speak of anything other than a unity of sacred places, objects, people, beliefs, and practices. That, moreover, is the general definition I introduced at the beginning of this presentation. The nucleus can still be mobile, even if a building is constructed. The diffuse character changes very little in the rhythm of the movement; for it is scarcely important that the concentration takes place successively in different places. It is even possible to point out generally that directed movement is more important than its occasional object, which can change without the nature of the movement changing. All one can add is that there must be a tendency toward concentration, at least at the formation of a principal nucleus.

But if the difference in the degree of concentration of the nucleus is relatively insignificant, that does not hold true for the difference in the richness of forms of activity, and this last difference clearly favors non-Christian rituals. We are even led to think that the facts we have been allowed to know immediately are impoverished, attenuated facts. In itself alone the passage from bloody sacrifice to symbolic sacrifice makes this abundantly clear. I want to refer here to a rather rare personal experience, one permitted to Michel Leiris during his voyage to Africa. I insist on the rarity of such an experience because I do not think that whites often have the same great permeability to the contagion of very strong movements that unites gatherings of blacks. According to Leiris, the essential moment of the sacrifice, the moment of putting to death, is a moment of extraordinary intensity.[7] Undoubtedly, according to what he told me several times, it is of an intensity that cannot be compared with what I was describing when I spoke just now of the silence that accompanies elevation during the mass. I do not believe, however, that he would contest the value of the comparison. Elevation and putting to death seem to be, respectively, the sacrifice's central point and its terrible moment. Nor do I believe that Leiris will contradict me if I present the movement traversing those present both at the black sacrifice and in the white village as a movement that translates the involvement of an intense repulsive force being brought into play.

But at this point in my presentation I am ready to be specific about where these rather complex thought processes are headed. In fact, I have been openly jumping ahead, and unless I am precise about what it consists of, the structure of the exposition I am attempting will become unintelligible.

I have certainly described a unity of morphological and dynamic phenomena in a manner that does not deviate perceptibly from that of a biologist describing the cell and its nucleus. Such a bare description at least could be found in what I have just represented—but on the condition that first it be stripped of a great many considerations that are the expression of lived experiences. Along those lines, I was even led to add Michel Leiris's lived experience to my own. And, for a good reason, I could not do otherwise: Without recourse to a fixed factual experience, it would have been very hard for me not only to express but even to perceive the specific movements of repulsion in the activity of the central nucleus. Doubtless, having discerned the force of active repulsion by experiencing it—at least in memory—it was possible for me to describe its external effects. And these effects are plain enough and significant enough for me to be able to claim to have finally attained biology's objectivity. I have no doubt, however, that I would have perceived nothing if my thought had not, at the beginning, followed a process that is entirely foreign to that of a biologist's thinking, namely, the analysis of lived experience.

So it seems that I had scarcely any grounds for impugning the phenomenological method just now. And, indeed, that would be the case if the lived experiences I speak of—whether Michel Leiris's or mine—could be compared with common experience. But, even though any assertion of this sort may seem disagreeably pretentious, I am obliged to insist to the contrary that the nature of experiences typical of minds profoundly affected by certain objective knowledge is obviously completely altered and obviously foreign to an ordinary mentality. Not only do Leiris and I take for granted the essential premises of psychoanalysis (we have both been psychoanalyzed),[8] but we have been about equally influenced by what French sociology, particularly, has taught us. Under these circumstances our lived experiences may be considered to a certain extent to be fabricated. And it will be easy for me to show that such tampering and fabrication were necessary to become conscious of the essentially repugnant character of sacred things. There is no doubt indeed that there exists an intimate connection between repulsion, disgust, and what psychoanalysis calls repression. And the repression that drives a good many vital elements into the unconscious (still according to the premises of psychoanalysis) is itself an unconscious mechanism. Hence, the action of repulsive forces itself is driven from consciousness each time at least there is production by and of the unconscious: It is, in any case, driven from consciousness each time there is production by and of the sacred.

Movements of repulsion would not have been able to enter the realm of consciousness, therefore, without detours. It is only to the extent that a mind has been led to recognize the fundamental identity between the taboo marking impure things and the purest forms of the sacred that it is able to become conscious of the violent repulsions constituting the specificity of the general movements that create human community. Therefore, I was thinking ahead when I described them as being immediately apparent. My being able to put forward this idea was due to an abnormal conscious perception subsequent to scientific discoveries assimilated throughout the course of a life devoted in part to systematic knowledge.

Now, before moving on to a general interpretation, I am at the point of describing recently discovered facts, to which I alluded when I said that non-Christian religions offered nuclei or, in any case, sacred connections with richer forms of activity than those surviving in our midst. But I am not going to try to repeat in detail the descriptions to be found in a great many easily accessible works. Everything about the institution of the *taboo* is generally rather well known, and I shall just remind you that it consists essentially in the expulsion of certain objects into a region that is impossible to penetrate. These objects have, if you will, the power to send away, or at least keep at a distance, all the individuals who participate in the institution. It is, in essence, not a case of objects consecrated by beliefs or fixed rituals—it is corpses, blood, especially menstrual blood, menstruating women themselves. There is, additionally, the fact that certain persons in particular are taboo for certain others from the limited standpoint of sexual relations, which is what is called the incest taboo. These objects, at any rate, are impure and untouchable, and they are sacred.

But here I come to terms that are much less familiar. In the sacred realm these objects do not occupy just any place: They belong to the left-hand side of this realm that is essentially divided into two parts, the left and the right, or in other words, the impure and the pure, or even unlucky and lucky.[9] On the whole, that which is left entails repulsion and that which is right entails attraction. This does not mean at all, by the way, that the various sacred objects are divisible into left objects and right objects, and, in fact, inside the domain each object has a left side and a right side, with one able to be more important than the other. Also it must be added that the relatively right or left side of a given object is mobile: It varies in the course of ritual practices. Thus it is that widely throughout civilization, a corpse is clearly situated on the left; it is essentially unlucky during the period following death. But once putrefaction is ended, the remains are purified, bleached bones being relatively lucky and pure.[10] Furthermore, the transformation cannot be produced equally in any direction: I have already had occasion to mention that in politics betrayal is always in the direction of the right. That is commonly observed and rarely seems to be contradicted. Now, even if it seems that the connections permitting the association of political left and right with sacred left and right are disputable, it is a fact that sacred objects, in the same way as political figures, are never consistently transmuted except from left to right. The very object of religious practices consists in this essential transmutation, which is openly legible and perceptible in many places in the rich realm of non-Christian religions and still very perceptible in Christianity, where the divine person issues from a tortured body, stamped with vile abuse.

Just now I managed to describe the sacred nucleus of a contemporary agglomeration, a white village, and thanks to some elementary knowledge, I could discern a double movement of attraction and repulsion surrounding this nucleus. Consideration of primitive phenomena, permitting the discernment of the principle of transmutation of the left sacred into the right sacred, allows me to arrive now at a general interpretation of the internal activity of the nucleus. The proposition I posited at the beginning now can be introduced as a correct explanation of these described phenomena as a whole: The central nucleus of an agglomeration is the place where the left sacred is transformed into right sacred, the object of repulsion into object of attraction, and depression into stimulation. From the outset the way the corpse passed through the church was revealing of this process, and on the whole the effects of adhesion and of repulsion maintaining adhesion at a certain distance from the center correspond well to the activity of internal transformation revealed in detail by the rituals studied outside the Christian realm by sociologists.

In order to further penetrate the paradoxical process I wished to present, I now must return to the example of tragedy, attempting that way as well some sort of genetic explanation. A performance of tragedy has the power to draw a crowd around itself, while offering only apparently depressing images of horror, death or mutilation. And, indisputably, it produces a stimulating effect on the spectators—Nietzsche proposed measuring the stimulation on the dynamometer. Initially, the object of tragedy is precisely a crime that consists in the breaking of a taboo—that consists, consequently, in breaking the barrier of repulsion protecting sacred things. It makes sense to acknowledge that such a breach can have a violent dynamic effect.

Let us suppose, following the German theoretician Preuss, that sacred things are essentially discharges emitted by the human body, and in some manner spent forces.[11] Let us further suppose that the barrier of repulsion established by these spent forces establishes a sort of balance by opposing an obstacle to continued expending. This comes down to saying that the integrity of human existence is put at stake each time sacred things are originally produced—I am referring here to the left sacred, of course, the object of an immediate taboo. Obviously, extreme expenditure puts at stake the community's as well as its participants' integrity. The death of an individual can be considered one of the most alarming expenditures for human beings united in a group. The corpse is treated, in fact, as a reality that could threaten to spread. Moreover, as the counterpart of the tendency to limit expending forces, there exists a tendency to expend, even to expend as much force as possible and eventually to the point of complete loss. And it is impossible to imagine an energetic movement within a human group not comprising such a central expenditure of force. Thus the first reaction when confronted with spent things might be to recoil, but there would always be a potential change of heart: The possibility would remain open for the crime that breaks the barrier opposing the expenditure of forces. Crime would thus put into circulation massive quantities of energy in a free state. In regard to this, we must not lose sight of the fact that among so-called backward populations, every death is generally considered the result of a magic crime. And in certain instances, at least in the case of a chief, a death may be followed by immediate pillage and orgy throughout the entire community.

In fact, the central nucleus of primitive agglomerations seems to be no less a place of license than a place of prohibition. The prohibition is obviously the primitive phenomenon that stands there in the way of expending forces, but, if it is at this particular spot that it stands in the way, it is because that is precisely where expenditure can take place. Subsequently, this expenditure lends its energy to the dynamism of the good power, lucky and right, that prohibits crime, that prohibits the very principle of expenditure, that maintains the integrity of the social whole and in the last analysis denies its criminal origin.[12] But this ultimate negation in no way deprives the crime of the energetic value that is necessary to bring the overall social movement and prohibitive power itself into play.

Tragedy, which we have considered secondly, is thus a more significant example and less obscure demonstration of the central movement of society than the Christian Church. Furthermore, it is the counterpart of the Church in the sense that it offers the criminal for the compassionate communion of those present, whereas the Christian ritual no longer has the power to do more than designate the victim.

Before concluding I want to try to summarize my main points, and I will once again lay out a few propositions by way of conclusion. The greatest loss of energy is death, which simultaneously constitutes the ultimate end of possible expenditure and a check on social expenditure as a whole. But without free loss, without expense of energy, no collective existence, or even individual existence is possible. Consequently, as human beings we cannot live without breaking the barriers we must give to our need to expend, barriers that look no less frightening than death. Our entire existence (which comes down to saying all our expenditures) is produced, hence, in a sort of swirling turbulence where death and the most explosive tension of life are simultaneously at play. This stir is essentially what is produced in the center of each individualized whole that it forms. And this stir also continues secondarily in peripheral forms of expenditure when men take roundabout ways to laugh together at [sneaky] representations of death or when, erotically, they are thrown toward each other by images that are like wounds open on life.

I think that now I have made some progress on the route leading to the recognition by human beings of what it is that makes them devoted to the thing that is the object of their most intense horror.

Still, however, at the end of this presentation I must mention a lacuna: I should have expanded further on one of the essential facts I came to discuss, the transformation of the left sacred into the right sacred, but, in fact, the next presentation that I shall have to make, Caillois no longer being able to continue . . .[13]

Power
Roger Caillois
Saturday, February 19, 1938

[This time it is not because he did not write it out, but rather because illness made him interrupt his participation in the activities of the College, that we do not have the text by Caillois that is announced in the program. Bataille spoke in his place. And, as he mentions, to the extent that it was possible, he spoke according to Caillois's instructions.

Many of the points tackled in this lecture are to be found in L'Homme et le sacré, *which Caillois was writing during the period the College was active; it appeared during the summer of 1939. Chapter 3 of this work ("Le Sacré de respect: théorie des interdits") groups the analyses as they relate to the problem of power (see, especially, the sections: "La Genèse du pouvoir," "Le Fait du pouvoir, donnée immédiate," "Caractère sacré du pouvoir"). This chapter is the first panel of a diptych where it contrasts with chapter 4, "Le Sacré de transgression: théorie de la fête," which Caillois will read before the College about a year later, on May 2, 1939.*

In the NRF *of October 1937, Caillois published a note on Léon Blum, who had resigned in June. Blum had published under the title* L'Exercice du pouvoir, *the collection of texts he had written and delivered as president of the Council of the Popular Front. What follows is taken from this note: "I take the liberty of speaking," writes Caillois, "about the conception of power that appears in the writings of Léon Blum; I take the liberty of criticizing it independently from the historical circumstances in which this conception was tested and this power exercised. Power, in effect, whether exercised or submitted to, is a kind of immediate conscious data, toward which a being has an elementary reaction of attrac-*

*tion or repulsion. Furthermore, the analysis of social phenomena demonstrates
that power necessarily belongs to the domain of the sacred. The power of one being over others sets up a relationship among them that cannot be reduced to the
pure forms of contract. It draws its power from the very essence of the social
phenomenon and manifests its imperative aspect with no intermediary or loss of
energy. It also seems as if power were impregnated with the sacred, or were,
rather, its very source, so much so that one hesitates to choose which term defines the other. The world of power is indeed tragedy's world; there it is impossible to go back on any act once it is committed. Saint-Just (who was the first to
assert that one does not rule* innocently, *while making a king's head fall with this
maxim) also made a rare and implacable use of power. After the* Sylla *of
Montesquieu's dialogue, Saint-Just's use of power provided the most brilliant
lesson to be contemplated in these matters. Léon Blum does not have this pontifical conception of power. It is clear that, for Blum, legality is the basis of
power. It is to be feared, rather, that it is power that is the basis of legality. All
power is severe; it is almost destroyed and certainly sapped if it is not abused
whenever deemed necessary. The coercer has a terrible and, in a sense, inexpiable responsibility. But either you take it or you leave it; when coercion must be
exerted, when order must be born, even respect for the law is null and void."*

*Bataille's elaborations will not respect point for point Caillois's view on
power as formulated in this note. Particularly, where Caillois identifies power
with tragedy, Bataille once again distinguishes them from each other. He opposes the power that kills and the power that dies, the lictor's ax that makes unity
rule with a peremptory, cutting gesture and the cross that propagates a tragic
communion of heartrending agony. The military structure of power exports the
works of death, the religious structure takes them on itself in order to expiate the
authority with which it is cloaked. But in this Christian type of religious structure, Bataille reverses the consecrated identifications: Now one must identify no
longer with Christ but with his executioners, not with the king who dies but with
the regicide. It is by means of this displacement that religion becomes tragedy
and piety is converted into shamanistic energy.]*

First I must excuse Caillois. He was to have made the presentation that I shall
make today in his place. His health has made it necessary for him to give up temporarily any activity, at least as far as circumstances permit. Just in the past few
days I have been able to see him and project with him what he would have said
if I had not had to replace him. Frankly, it is difficult for me purely and simply
to replace Caillois and limit myself to saying what would have seemed to him essential. In fact, I am bound to continue the development of what I have already
begun on the subject of power. I am bound to relate the essential facts about
power to the body of principles I have attempted to introduce here. If Caillois
had spoken today, he would have detailed the facts at great length. After his pre-

sentation I would have been led to attempt connecting them to general ideas. Replacing Caillois, I shall limit myself to summarizing what is essential of the facts, and, on the whole, what I shall say will be the commentary on and an attempt at analysis of these facts. And naturally this endeavor will be only a continuation of everything that I have already developed in my two preceding presentations.

Therefore, at the outset, I should recall the essentials of these two presentations. Afterward I shall move on to the facts that have to do with power, and to conclude, I shall attempt a general interpretation.

As I go back to what I have said, I shall not content myself, moreover, with repeating or summarizing it. This time I shall try to give a precise form to the statement of several fundamental propositions, which up until now have not clearly emerged from the description as a whole.

It is possible to consider the conglomeration—town, city, or village—as the fundamental element of human society. We shall soon see that conglomerations are able to join together, forming unities, even unities that are vast. The conglomeration, in any case, is at the root of all empires somewhat as the cell is at the root of every organism—or also as individual persons are at the root of every conglomeration. I chose the example of a French village in order to study the structure of the human conglomeration in its simplest form. But perhaps I did not insist enough on the fact that what was in question was a formation that is not complete, that is not primitive, and moreover is obviously degenerate. The contemporary French village is something whose functioning is clogged, something barely alive, even compared with the French village of a century ago. As it is, however, the traces of a powerful "overall movement" animating the village population are still very easily perceived there. This overall movement is made up of two opposite forces, one centripetal, the other centrifugal. The center is a church forming a stable nucleus with a well-defined sacred character. The opposite forces are, moreover, composed in a very special way. There is an attraction toward a group of ritual objects and acts, but the force of repulsion increases as the force of attraction is active, with the result that individuals who are attracted are held within the power of the sacred center at a respectful distance. The two forces are somehow functions of each other. The overall movement that consecrates the conglomeration's unity, moreover, is not constant. It takes place on regularly repeating dates and also each time some event occurs to modify the established relations among those revolving around the center—birth, marriage, or death.

Last time I insisted on the fundamental character of this movement, and I took advantage of the very simplified character it provides in some examples close at hand in order to base a very general, but still perfunctory reflection on the facts. Today, however, I shall have to insist on the extreme complexity peculiar to the "overall movements" animating human communities. If things are so simple in a village, it is because a village no longer represents a totality. It is not up to the village to take on itself the entirety of human functions. Certain integrations necessary to the affective activity of society are produced only in the capital, which alone realizes the extreme complexity of the movement. All that is necessary, however, is to go back to a relatively recent period, one in which the monuments or ruins are still numerous, to rediscover the memory of this complexity—at least in a number of villages where the church was doubled by a fortified castle. In the Middle Ages, a simple conglomeration could actually possess almost total autonomy, constituting by itself a complete picture of social life.[1] The power was concentrated in the person of the feudal lord, who struck coins, rendered justice, and had an armed force at his disposal.

Taking this new aspect of things into account, I have been led to formulate some general propositions, this time quite precise and more complete.

A conglomeration presents a specific overall movement around a nucleus—mobile or stable, a complex of sacred places, objects, persons, beliefs, and practices. If it possesses autonomy—as in primitive or feudal civilizations—it also presents a movement of concentration of power that is linked with the movement produced around sacred things.

This all must seem very obscure. Initially it was very hard for me to represent convincingly the fundamental and vital animation, which the sacred engenders through shock as it were. And now I am speaking of another kind of animation linked—by what obscure connections?—to the first. This other kind of animation is the concentration of *power*, and as to the nature of this *power* about which essentially I shall be speaking today, I have to first limit myself to getting rid of the current interpretation.

Obviously I am eager to joggle the accepted truth, which has it that if the police lock me up in prison it is because they are stronger than I. It is power that creates the force of the police, not the police who create power.[2] Armed force without power, without the authority that makes use of it, could never have any more meaning or applicability than the force of a volcano. But what then does this power mean—this power that we must admit, no matter how revolutionary and capable of challenge we are, reduces us to trembling before it—because, at a certain point, offending it means death.

A month ago now, in order to make myself understood, I took a roundabout way and sought to make those effects produced in the center of social things perceptible by analyzing the ones produced on the periphery, like the contagious movement of laughter.[3] I am not entirely certain that this method really made me more intelligible up to this point, but I believe in the virtue of persistence, and again today I shall take the same roundabout way I did a month ago.

I assume that a certain number of my present listeners have seen (I think this goes back to 1936) a newsreel showing the unveiling of a monument to the English dead at Vimy.[4] At the proper moment President Lebrun[5] appeared on the screen in his morning coat and rushed headlong onto a platform from which he began to shout stirring words. At that moment most of the audience began to laugh. I myself could hear the unrestrained laughter that had taken hold of me spread throughout the rows of a movie theater. And I have heard that the same thing was repeated elsewhere.

I do not think the fact that dead men were involved could have contributed in anything other than a secondary manner to the excitement thus manifested in roars of laughter. But—precisely—President Lebrun embodies this *power* that I have described as representing, at least if we take into account the passions obscurely urging us on to excess, a threat of death. I know that these obscure passions are normally held in check and even banished from the realm of consciousness. I know that whatever the case, the threat of death represented by power is also banished from the realm of consciousness. However, on the whole, power remains a simultaneously seductive and fearful reality for human beings, and it is always somewhat disappointing for the ordinary mentality if the external aspect of power has nothing seductive or fearful about it. At the very least, such a disappointment is still compensation for another sort of satisfaction that may be regarded as more estimable. But if the external aspect goes as far as the absence of dignity, if it offers no more than the awkward and empty solemnity of someone who has no direct access to greatness—who must seek it out by some artificial means, in the same way as people who do not really have power at their disposal but who are reduced to nervously aping greatness—the futile hoopla making its appearance where motionless majesty is expected no longer provokes just disappointment: It provokes hilarity. Those present—at least before an image projected on a screen emphasizing absurdities and greatly mitigating any feeling of reality—those present no longer communicate in the double movement of attraction and repulsion that keeps a unanimous adherence at a respectful distance; rather they regain their communion by laughing with a single laughter.

As those who have heard my previous presentations can see, I have just repeated the two essential themes I have already developed: the theme of the formation at the center of a human group of a nucleus of attraction and repulsion, and the theme of peripheral laughter stimulated by the continual emissions of a specific energy, of sacred forces, which are made from the central nucleus.

All I shall do today is carry on with these themes, but for the first time I shall be able to attempt a representation of the overall movement.

Having reintroduced the fundamental problem I was eager to pose, I shall now move to laying out the facts, that is to say, specific forms in which *power* appears to us. Starting with these facts, these general forms, I shall latch onto an example that is much more explicit than any other of the formation of *power*, namely, the formation of *power* constructed on the basis of the ignominious crucifixion of Jesus. Then I shall return to the monument to the dead at Vimy in order to complete the cycle. I have already widely used the terms left and right to define a fundamental opposition between the ignoble and the noble, the impure and the pure. This time I shall attempt to describe from beginning to end the dynamic transformation of left into right, then of right into left, moving from the horrible image of a torture victim to the majesty of popes and kings, then from the majesty of sovereigns to the Vichy morning coat[6].

But first of all, what are the common forms in which what we call power appears?

It is possible to say that in the great majority of cases power appears individualized, that is to say, embodied in a single person.[7] The name ''king'' is ordinarily given to this person, and it is possible to maintain this by taking into account the fact that certain differences of name in a given area do not mean much. So the name caesar, kaiser, or czar, after having signified the Romans' phobia for the term *rex*, ended up by simply meaning the great king, or the king of kings—something analogous to the Persian shahanshah. Similar elements, in any case, are found in the sovereigns of every region and every period.

On the whole, the king represents a dynamic concentration of all the impulses socially animating individuals. He is somehow charged with all that is willed—impersonally—within society.[8] Every human community requires that the order of the world, the order of nature, be maintained. Catastrophes must be averted and conditions favorable for the hunt, for breeding stock, for harvests, must be realized. But this requirement is not manifested only as desire, it is also immediately felt as an effective power. And this power to realize the common desire is transferred to the king, who becomes solely responsible. The king, precisely, is the guarantor of the order of things: Hence, if things are disrupted, he must be incriminated.[9]

I shall not detail facts here. The eleven volumes of Frazer's *Golden Bough* were devoted to studying the prerogatives of primitive kings and the taboos imposed on them. It will suffice to recall that Frazer took for his departure practices relating to the priest of Nemi and his ritual slaying.[10] Frazer remarked that the priest originally was royal and that the murder could be linked to his being so. He recognized that kings, in fact, could be put to death by their people and that the royal office often had been less to be envied than to be feared. Because the king is the object of a concentration of collective feelings, he is simultaneously, in fact, the object of precautions that are distrustful and very awkward for him. He is treated like a sacred thing, and sacred things have to be protected from contacts by means of a great many paralyzing prohibitions. And if it so happens that the process ceases to be effective, if it happens that the order of things is disrupted despite royal action, the king can be put to death and sacrificed as a scapegoat,[11] charged with the sins that were in conflict with the normal course of nature. The repulsion that, up until that point, had kept the subjects in a veritable religious terror is abruptly transformed into a murderous repulsion.

The concentration of feelings or reactions of the social body onto one person obviously must result in an ambiguous situation, which is, moreover, analogous to the situation of sacred things in general—objects of attraction and repulsion. Furthermore, it can take other forms than that of the relatively rare killing. To make up for his power, the king can even be stricken with some flaw: He may be impotent, castrated, deformed, or obese. Mythology and ritual bear witness to this tendency. Today I shall merely refer you to the remarkable work on Uranus-Varuna by Dumézil.[12]

In actual fact, the crippled king—or, as they said in the Middle Ages the *roi méhaigné* —is a toned-down version of the king who is put to death. And the toning down is emphasized even more because in the latter case there is no question of real actions or events. The impersonal and unconscious desire of the subjects—the desire for the castration and impotence of the king—seems to have been expressed only in the form of purely symbolic rituals and especially in the form of myths, legends—such as the myth of the castrated Uranus or the legend of the mutilated king, the *roi méhaigné* of the Breton romances.

This "overall social movement" that animates a human community is far from reducing individuals or individual interests. It endlessly traverses the mass that it forms, but each person, to the extent that he is untraversed by great movements external to himself, continues to behave as if alone, attending to his own interests. And, of course, the social structure is the result of social movement, of almost constant social convulsion, but this result is endlessly altered and thwarted by the fact that each individual tries to use it for his own profit. It is self-evident that no one is in a better position in this respect than the king. Or more precisely, nobody is in a better position than the person for whose benefit the social concentration is produced. There are great enough advantages to such a situation that opportunities arise to do away with the possibility of such violent drawbacks as being killed. The paralyzing taboos that could not be broken, could, at least, slowly be neutralized and changed. But the personal interest of the king could not work for the sole benefit of an individual. Any change in the royal situation necessarily was produced for the benefit of the institution itself. And, in fact, royal power as we know it certainly seems to be the result of this modification of the immediate social movement. It supposes in the first place a concentration around a person that is analogous to the concentration produced around sacred places, objects, and actions. Above all, it supposes that the person who had won a power that was originally purely religious or magic had the potential of forming around him a second concentration, that of armed force, which is of another nature and much more stable. Next time I shall speak of the army and its affective structure[13] but for the time being I must limit myself to demonstrating that military relations do not seem to imply the killing of a leader, undoubtedly because the movements of murderous repulsion are normally diverted against the enemy. This merging of military strength with religious strength was necessary to the constitution of the stable and regulating power exercised by the king against society. For military strength alone means nothing: It means nothing insofar as it remains external to the social concentration, external to the "overall movement" animating the society it dominates but to which, at the same time, it belongs. There is no example of a lasting society in which an army and its leader were foreign to the people in the same manner as the occupying forces of another country are in a colony.[14]

Doubtless such military structures could be found at the origin of a royal power. Many institutions representing the composite type I have just described had an origin that was clearly military: the leader of an army becoming king. But it was important that the leader of the army not be content with his immediate and external power. A caesar was doomed to become a god, that is to say, to put himself at the center of an overall movement, of society's religious concentration.

I must now summarize the facts I have just set forth and do so in a formulation amounting to a precise definition of *Power*.

Power in a society would be distinct from the production of a religious force, from a sacred force concentrated in one person. It would also be distinct from the military strength of a leader. *Power* would be the institutional merging of the sacred force and military strength in a single person who makes use of them for his own individual benefit and only in that way for the benefit of the institution.

In other words, *power* is what escapes the tragedy required by the "overall movement" animating human community—but it escapes tragedy specifically by diverting the forces requiring it to its own benefit.[15]

Now when I come back to considering the structure of human groups, no longer taking as my example incomplete elements, such as a village integrated into a modern society, but a human reality in its entirety, I am prepared to say that there is added to the nucleus of repulsion and attraction that composes social animation a formation that derives from it but is external to it. This formation is capable of diverting all energy, all internal dynamism to its benefit, and, outside, it is condemned to indulge in any regulative, administrative, or police function likely to ensure its stability: condemned not to develop, in fact, or even merely exist, unless it exercises a material domination over the whole.

Here I shall make a sort of aside. I think I have been ambiguous: It should be possible to claim that I have just criticized what I call power, but it would not be impossible, however, to assert that I have just spoken in praise of it. Discussions of this sort, furthermore, are in danger of introducing many ambiguities; in fact, it was possible last time to take what I had said as a sort of apology for Christianity. In fact, I represented churches as living realities—functional. As far as possible, I should like to avoid misunderstanding of this sort. I do not believe that last time I made any apology other than an apology for human existence. Now I know of no more radical condemnation of this existence than Christianity.

Besides, the facts that I set forth, the concentration of a village around a sacred place, have nothing to do with Christianity; they are found everywhere and it can even be asserted that there is something about them quite foreign to the Christian spirit. It is fine that this spirit penetrates and profoundly modifies them. They nonetheless constitute the survival, altered as it may be, of paganism's free religious solemnity into our times. I can only add, as far as *power* is concerned, a remark of the same sort: From beginning to end, on the whole, what I have to say can only have the value of an affirmation of existence, and I mean that to be an affirmation of the "overall movement" beyond individual interests animating it. Now the definition I have just given for *power* designates it as a fatal alteration of this movement. Most often there is a struggle between the creative disturbance of sacred forms and the conservative authority of the modification—of the *alienation* that originally constituted power. That does not imply hostility with regard to the powerfulness emanating from interaction of human force but rather a profound aversion toward anything that takes this powerfulness for purposes of conservation.

Having laid out all the facts, I am now prepared, after this brief aside, to try following from beginning to end the formation of a social authority, a *power*, so that it will be easy to grasp the senses in which it is still alive in us.

We know that in Rome, after a long political battle, after internal rifts of long duration, the de facto power fell into the hands of the one general who succeeded in exterminating the others. The triumph of Octavius put an end to partisan struggle in much the same way as did the triumph of Mussolini or of Hitler. Now, in certain respects, partisan struggle represents something equivalent to that "overall movement" that, in my opinion, constitutes social life. Last time we saw that the terms "right" and "left" were found there with meanings similar to those we can give them in speaking of the sacred. I shall have an opportunity to come back to this characteristic of political agitation. It is only of secondary importance that political agitation represents a precarious form of movement and, for all that, almost entirely deceptive. In this case, as in the others, the formation of *power* is always produced to the detriment of the "overall movement" animating the community.[16] Whatever the appearances, from then on Roman society had a reduced existence. The old religious forms were largely exhausted and unable to profit from the need for internal movement, which, under these conditions, created a profound unrest. The movement then reformed itself around the myths of Christianity.

Christianity is a phenomenon whose complexity is perfectly apparent: I shall just recall here the structure of social power to which it has given rise, without imagining that I have exhausted its content in this way. First of all, Christianity put a high value on the paupers, the outcasts, and the unclean. It set up a king in the person of Jesus, but this king associated with the wretched. What is more, Jesus let himself be treated like a criminal and reduced to the condition of a tortured body, thus identifying himself with the left and immediately repulsive form of the sacred. The myth emphasizes the infamous nature of death on the cross by adding that he took on himself the sins of the world, that is to say, the sum of human ignominy. Nonetheless, the torture instrument itself already bore the title *king*, the I.N.R.I., Iesus Nazarenus Rex Iudaeorum. The animation was thus recomposed starting from horror, and as fast as it was composed, it became a creator of force. What was repulsive became the object of an ecstatic seduction and gave rise to the blossoming of a majestic glory. The crucified went to sit at the right hand of his omnipotent Father. Thus he united permanently in his person the pure and fearsome king with the executed king. But he took on himself the very crime of executing the king. And this bizarre mythological figure was associated with a rite of regicide, endlessly repeated by priests who identified themselves with the victim, living themselves as executed kings, taking in turn upon themselves the crime of the whole world. At the same time all limits were pushed back before this continual creation of powerfulness. Christ merged, or more exactly, was now only *one* with a unique, omnipotent, eternal God.

From then on power in the Roman world was divided. On the one hand, the emperor was the expression of military force and continued to form the totality of *power* by relying on the remains of vital movement in the sacred forms of paganism. But a crisis was developing because there was nothing there anymore except an inescapable and dreary de facto power, and the underlying animation of society was turning away from this in order to constitute the purely religious and inoperative power of God.

From that time on the institutional union of sacred force and military strength—those being the terms I have used to define *power*—required an intimate association of the divine person and the imperial person that was possible only after Constantine. And, as always, it implied the *alteration* and *alienation* of the free sacred activity from which it took its force. The wretched, executed king took the robe of the Byzantine emperor: The ignominious victim became a military and hieratic sovereign, and from then on it would have been possible to exclaim as Luther did: "It isn't man but God who hangs, beheads, uses a wheel to break men, slits their throats and makes war."[17] Now God was nothing more than the emperor whose sacred robes he glorified on the church walls, in the same way that the emperor was, for his part, the image of God on earth.

The underlying duality of the specifically Christian sacred power and of *power* was not possible except under conditions utterly different from those of either the Roman or Byzantine Empire. It was possible only in the framework of Western civilization, owing to the profound division of the antagonistic military forces, from the beginning characteristic of those regions of Europe escaping domination by the Roman Empire, which had become the Byzantine Empire. The duality was expressed in the Middle Ages by the terms "spiritual power" and "temporal power," but the vocabulary was utterly deficient and implied already the evolution that had the Roman pontiff be a sovereign among others, strictly analogous to the others. This evolution could have no other result, in fact, than this "institutional union of sacred force and military strength." These are the terms, I repeat, that I have used to define *power* in general. But for all that, one should not underestimate the underlying duality at the basis of the civilization that we are still living. This duality found its expression in the form of an obsessive representation of killing the king. There is no doubt, in fact, that the image of the crucified figure dominates the West right up to our times, and even that it has no possible competition. Certainly it has lost the force of its original meaning, but the duality has continued in other forms. In any case, it is only in the past few years that the crucified figure has been threatened in Germany[18] and in Italy by images of power that exclude any idea of tragedy, any idea of killing the king. Moreover, the Italian fasces as it is seen on every locomotive's belly is in this respect more charged with a precise meaning than is the swastika. The lictor's fasces in Rome was, in fact, the insignia of magistrates to the *imperium* such as consuls and praetors. It represented essentially the military power that belonged to these magistrates and that happened to be regularly linked to the specifically religious power of augury. It must be especially emphasized that the lictor's ax was nothing but the instrument of beheading. Consequently, the instrument for killing subjects is what is conspicuously opposed to the image of the king who is tortured to death.

Now I am able to go back to the overall picture in a rather schematic manner. At the center of human turmoil is the crime that engenders those sacred things that are of the left and untouchable. These impure sacred things themselves give rise to a fearful force that is also sacred, but right and glorious: But this force personified is again subjected to the threat of crime. For the crime's recurrence is necessary to the intense movement producing itself at the center of human groups.[19] It is the crime that essentially constitutes the tragic act, and it is self-evident that some day or other it draws the criminal himself, the violent one, into death. Two opposite answers have been given to the question, so charged with all of human anguish, resulting from this strange situation. Both of these answers are given on the symbolic level, and, at least for the whole it is enough that it be so. Tragedy offers human beings the identification with the criminal who kills the king: Christianity offers identification with the victim, the slain king. The Christian solution up until now has prevailed. But all this movement takes place in a world that thwarts it. Power is constituted above and beyond this turmoil, which it turns to its own profit and, to the extent that the turmoil seems to be no longer useful to it, strives to paralyze it by raising the threat of the executioner's ax against the threat of crime. *Power* is the only force that blindly seeks to eliminate the earth's crime whereas all religious forms are in some way drenched in it.

But as *power* finds its source in bringing sacred things into play, it is weakened as a direct result of its tendency to empty sacred things of their criminal content. It consequently favors the rationalism that kills it and, bit by bit, loses the force to assume the simultaneously religious and military aspect essential to it. Faded and attenuated forms then appear that represent a return to a primitive situation—except for the intensity that has disappeared. The crime, the killing of the king, results in a tragic emission of sacred force. But it is no longer possible in this manner to achieve anything more than equally forceful comic emissions. The sovereign is no longer put to death but rather is disguised as a wretched lord and, moreover, is personally deprived of force. There is no longer the essential fall from living king to dead king; there is only degradation—the emission of energy that can take form only in peripheral laughter where it intervenes like a strange tickling, turning a state of simple, open, and communicative exuberance into an explosive discharge.

This situation in turn, for very general reasons, engenders discontent. The dominant class, as a result of the weakness of power, has lost the capacity to use for its own profit the diversion of the central social forces that permitted the appropriation of wealth. It therefore is smitten with an irresistible nostalgia for that *power* that permits settling the order of things to its own advantage. But, being simultaneously too immediately interested and too cowardly, it is incapable of regenerating this through the criminal creation of sacred forces. It has recourse, therefore, to immediate violence, to the constitution of a new force of a military sort that it links to whatever remains of the sacred forces, particularly the sacred forces that are directly connected with power, such as the fatherland.

Then it creates the situation in which we now find ourselves and that I shall not seek to define in a precise manner until a little later. I must, in fact, stop here today. Moreover, before getting to establish the problems posed for us and their possible solution, I shall have to attempt a detailed analysis of the forms that at the present time, as always, are opposed to any movement, namely, the military forms; then an analysis of the secondary dynamic forms that have always introduced the possibility of reactivating the social tragedy. In this way I shall once again reenter the domain Caillois has reserved for himself, namely the domain of secret societies (or if one wishes, elective communities) that I just referred to in speaking of dynamic forms, and consequently borrowing an expression of Dumézil's that is a strikingly apt description. Caillois, I might add, is to give me beforehand a written paper that I shall read when the time comes, and to which I shall add only a commentary connecting the facts to the body of ideas I am presenting here.

The Structure and Function of the Army
Georges Bataille
Saturday, March 5, 1938

[There is no text among Bataille's manuscripts that bears the title announced by the program of the College for this date. However, there are a number of scattered pages inserted by Bataille in the file labeled "Sociological Studies" that seem to be contemporary with the activities of the College and that analyze the military phenomenon, its position within the social body as a whole, and the inner forces that make it function. Without claiming to have restored the text, I reproduce here only a montage of these pages.

In the preceding lecture ("Power"), Bataille gave a general idea of what he had to say on these questions when he mentioned that "military relations do not seem to imply the killing of a leader, undoubtedly because the movements of murderous repulsion are normally diverted against the enemy."

Bataille's analysis contrasts the army, on the one hand, to the rest of society, to its civilian economy (the opposition army-factory), and, on the other hand, to the religious realm (the opposition war-tragedy). The first point can be related to Mauss's condemnation of totalitarian regimes, the militarization of every area of social space, occupation of the whole by a part, a camp economy imposed on a civilian life. The second point would be set at the junction between Freud's reflections in Chapter 5 of Psychologie collective et analyse du moi *("Deux Foules conventionnelles: l'Église et l'armée") and Dumézil's works in which he demonstrated the double nature of the sovereign function, by turn simultaneously both religious and armed.*

In the background, there is obviously the German army whose history Benoist-Méchin had just related in four astounding volumes. In 1934, Ernst

Jünger's Der Kampf als inneres Erlebnis (Le combat comme expérience intérieure) *(Combat as inner experience) was translated as* La guerre notre mère *(War, our mother).* Caillois extracts long passages from this at the end of his book Bellone ou la pente de la guerre *(Paris, 1963). On the other side of the Rhine would develop (according to the title of one of the fragments reproduced here) a "mystical" conception of the army. It is the idea suggested by Dumézil in a small book published in 1939,* Mythes et dieux des Germains, *later explicitly formulated in his* Horace et les Curiaces *(1942): The military art of northern peoples "has remained on a more archaic, more mystical level."*

(On two occasions, Paulhan was to publish in the NRF *a note on Dumézil's* Mythes et dieux des Germains, *which he signed each time with his pseudonym, Jean Guérin. The first note appeared in the September 1939 issue: "A fascinating and amazingly topical study of the passage of an Indo-European-type sacerdotal society to a magico-military society. Conceived in that manner, mythology revives sociology" [p. 527]. The second, right in the middle of the phony war, in February 1940: "Myth expresses an obsessive fear and makes it possible to single out 'certain psychological constants.' Odin, 'the violently inspired,' is leader of leaders. His chosen ones form 'a sort of magico-military society that is specifically Germanic.' How is Odin to be disarmed? G. D.'s lucid and restrained treatise is fascinating." Drieu la Rochelle also would find in Dumézil's theses a grid through which events of the times fit into the order of things; see "Éternelle Germanie,"* Je suis partout *[January 12, 1940], reprinted in* Chronique politique *[Paris, 1943], p. 213. For his part, rather than reedit* Mythes et dieux, *Dumézil chose to rewrite it; consequently, in 1959 the book would become* Les Dieux des Germains. *This work, revised to the point of being a completely new book, is nonetheless presented in the introduction as the reedition of* Mythes et dieux *1939, which it replaces. That does not prevent Dumézil from disowning his theses of 1939: The date and the haste that were too evident in its publication "are sufficient explanation, I hope, for the unevenness of an exposition outmoded as quickly as it was out of print."*

Forgetting that Munich had already taken place when this small volume appeared, Étiemble mused after the war on what might have happened if reading it had prevented the democratic negotiators from being taken in by Odin/Hitler: "Neither Daladier, nor Léger [the diplomatic name of Saint-John Perse], I suppose, read this book in the plane taking them to Munich. Everything was predicted in it in black and white: Prague, Danzig, the lot" "Einstein, Dumézil," Hygiène des lettres, *vol. 3 (Paris, 1950), p. 243].)*

The year 1938 also saw the publication by de Gaulle of La France et son armée.

The following lines, which are related to the subject of the lecture, are taken from a review by Caillois of Maurice R. Davie's work, La Guerre dans les sociétés primitives *(NRF, August 1936). War "eminently favors the establish-*

ment of autocracy, and, more generally, it multiplies the number of social imperatives and their coercive force (for the sole and exclusively technical reason that discipline constitutes the 'principal force of armies'). It seems under these conditions that society's tendency to increase its density (in the Durkheimian sense of the word) already constitutes a permanent and natural invitation to war, which reinforces the effective unity of the group by opposing it to enemies, and replaces its relaxed peacetime organization with a totalitarian structure. Then, at the same time, one understands that a society in which individualist tendencies can freely develop (a liberal democracy, for example) is less apt to make war and, especially, to set a high value on it *than is a society of the type referred to as 'totalitarian,' whose structure is adapted to war in advance, simultaneously by the framework it uses and by the psychology it provokes: identification with the leader, etc." And the following: "Secret societies have a considerable influence on the decisions concerning war as if the latter were there only in order to aggravate and justify a certain ideal of collective formation that finds in war itself its most intense exaltation . . ."*

All that to be connected with the notes Bataille wrote in 1941 (OC, vol. 5, p. 540): "When I say that I have not liked war, I mean above all that I have never been sensitive to that sort of release, the pursuit of which war constitutes. The exhilaration and bursting pride it offers conquering regiments would have been denied me, even if the occasion presented itself, I think. For me, anything resembling these feelings (or having an affinity with them) is stifled the moment I am called on in person. I have discussed these things in order to understand them from the outside.

"How little I am attracted to war can easily be shown. Contemporary live battle is less arresting for me than the more appalling trench warfare. In war what is arresting for me is a means of agonized contemplation. For me that is still connected to a nostalgia for ecstatic states, yet this nostalgia today seems dubious and lugubrious to me: It never had, I must say, any active value. I never fought in any of the wars in which I might have been involved."]

The aggressive or defensive force of a society takes the name of "army" each time it is clearly distinguished from the whole.[1] There is only one word to designate the armies of populations that are civilized in diverse ways. And yet the military organizations are very different from one another. The place they occupy in the society is variable as well. That is why it is difficult to generalize about them.

This difficulty does not hinder me to the extent that I do not want to discuss any real army. I shall speak of the army as I might speak of "father" or "riot" or any other human reality by describing the necessary connections the name evokes for me. What I shall express will, therefore, be no more than the mystique of the army that is inscribed within me as it is inscribed in the mind of the simplest of persons: a collection of beliefs and reactions that I hold in common with living men like myself. (These beliefs, these reactions, belong also to those who deny them since they deny them for having felt them).

I know that this reality to which I am bound (because the society on which I depend itself depends on the fate of its army) is the portion of the population that trains or is trained to fight.

Men fighting is not enough to make an army: It is necessary, first of all, for the bonds and reactions that are formed in drilling to have profoundly changed their hearts, minds, and bodies.

It seems to me that the difference between soldiers and other men is as striking as the changes seen in chemical reactions. When a body crystallizes, the molecules are newly organized, appearance and properties change. The same thing happens with recruits in the barracks. Doubtless it will be remarked that in the first instance the transformation is natural and in the second, artificial. But the distinction thus made depends entirely on the definition of "artificial." If the transformation of recruits is not natural, it is only to the extent that man is opposed to nature: that which is human is not for all that artificial. The painful transformation of the barracks is, moreover, one of the undertakings of men that least brings to mind a production imitated from nature.

Within society the army thus forms before me a "constituted body," a world closed in on itself, different from the whole, different from other "constituted bodies." It cannot be reduced to its function—which is war. It endlessly sets up powerful bonds among a great many men whose behavior and nature are changed by them. And, in this manner, it changes human nature. Because it does not simply act on those whom it incorporates. It parades itself before others and offers itself for their admiration. It even claims to be the embodiment of their existence and their fate.

Society as a whole unites its members only by bonds that are comparatively loose. It gives them neither a job to fill nor a raison d'être. It abandons them to their own particular destiny, whether it is good or bad. "Constituted bodies" alone offer (or impose) tight bonds: They require that the men forming them join their fate to the fate of the "constituted body"; this destiny becomes the raison d'être for everyone, so much so that each one gets a job and must content himself with fulfilling it honorably in order to achieve it.

If the army were only in the business of attack or defense, in the same way a factory is in the business of producing, I would not insist on what it has engraved on my mind. A factory produces without binding workers to its fate, but the army does not send one to death for a bit of cash. The glory of the military and its code make the soldier be a part that cannot be disconnected: The glory of the army, the reward it most pursues, is everyone's common good, but, in compensation, the code does not permit anyone to escape discipline and danger. Likewise, a factory does not try to pretend it is the utmost goal of existence; the army, on the contrary, making up a sort of intangible bloc unified in its movements, directs a constant challenge toward the rest of the men.

In the midst of other men given over to the pursuit of their private ends, it is the army that has glory, that rises above any specific or general utility. The army is not merely a means as are factories or agriculture; it is glorious, and it teaches to live, suffer, and die in the pursuit of glory. It is sufficient unto itself and only in addition does it serve society. It is generally acknowledged that the army is there for the others and not the others for the army. The truth is that the army has the advantage of doing almost entirely without theory. To the extent that it makes a pretense, it borrows the language of the others and brags about its usefulness. But when it obeys the stark impulses that make it strong, each man would have to consider himself content with contributing humbly to its glory.

The Army as a Totality with Its Own Autonomy

There are armies whose structures are very different from one another; furthermore, the insertion and function of these armies within society vary according to the situation. A feudal army is utterly different from a national army and even more different from a professional army; and finally, an army of revolutionary partisans shows exceptional but temporary characteristics. Nonetheless, one can think of the army in a general manner, in the same way that one can think of a stalk in connection with plants regardless of any specific forms.

The army is that distinct part of society that fights or prepares itself, or trains in advance for fighting.

It is not a simple function, a simple organ of the community; it presents itself equally well as a totality sufficient to itself, a sort of being that is complete in itself, attached to the noncombatant population by connections that are not even intangible. The fact that the army can exist *by* itself, moreover, is of only secondary importance. It is still more remarkable that inside the community whose aggressive or defensive force it is, the army exists *for* itself; it constitutes a whole whose meaning is found in itself.

The army has an aesthetic all its own: It adorns itself with bright uniforms and is led by a band to show off its brilliance and give rhythm to movements like those of a virile and austere ballet corps. Its morality deviates from religious or philosophical morality both because of its superficial casualness and because of its violent physical and formalistic consequences. And although its technical operation makes use of all possible resources, it forms an isolated whole distinguished by hasty performance, tumultuous speed, and, at the same time, peremptory negation of anything that might curb it. The lucidity and speed of decision that it requires and realizes in battle in the end confer on the mentality it represents an intellectual value sufficiently undeniable to have often served as a model for other activities. The army has then the capacity to stir human groups into a movement where all of life and all the aspirations of the individuals composing it are brought into play. Nevertheless, all this diverse wealth of the army is still only the condition for its human autonomy. Totality of existence comes for the army only at the moment in which it links to its destiny the life of each of those whom it unites into a single aggressive body and a single soul. In order to firmly fix a correct and formal realization of this common fervor, the army groups its soldiers around a sacred emblem in the same way that a church clusters the houses that form a village around it. Most often this emblem is an object, colors, or a flag; it can also be a person (such as the noble maiden accompanying the nomads of Arabia into battle on a richly adorned camel). A leader can also have played the part of emblem regardless of his action as one who leads. These emblematic leaders and persons, these ensigns and flags are treated as the analogue of a *soul* by the *body* possessing them: It is better to die than have it taken away by the enemies. And conversely, it is *easy* to die for this conquering soul so eager for conquests.

The Rudimentary Character
of Sacred Elements in the Army

The attraction of armed men around a vital center is similar to the city's attraction to its sacred places (even more than the attraction of the village around its church). It is through this striking adherence of life to what unites it that the army by itself can be considered similar to human communities as a whole and regarded as a whole itself. It is true that an army is usually included within a society and is only the army of that society, but this insertion is always to a certain extent that of "a State within a State." More precisely, the connection of society and its army could be compared to an almost absolutely consistent connection, in which a small strong male would be joined with a large weak female[2]: Male and female each would possess a whole animal life, with the reservation that being habituated to each other takes away their capacity to live alone. However, human reality is not so simple: in one of its most familiar forms it could correspond to the predominance of the female who would *possess* the male and could show his presence at will, by borrowing his external appearance (giving an expression, a face to the society of [   ],[3] in fact, is one of the most consistent functions of the army).

Sacrifice as Expression of the Intimate
Harmony of Death and Life

It is easy to see the intensity of excitement produced at the point at which the mortal game of violent destruction and creation is played out.[4] However, when one casts the light of consciousness on whatever is strangest in human existence, what appears is not some simple fact but a remarkable complexity. The hesitant and uneven gravitation that we see takes place not around a single center but around several, and the nuclei formed in these various centers do not simply coexist; often they are opposed to each other. Between the "men whose death is military" and the "men whose death is religious" or sacrificial, there are doubtless many connections, but what directs them is still divergent and conflicts are still possible. This is so because the military literally buries death in the vainglorious rumble of battles, whereas the priest reels around death in fascination, remaining in tragic turmoil until he has raised from it an image that is bloody but at the same time completely radiant and such that a sacred silence is required in its presence. For the man who fights, meeting death is simply a chance encounter, whereas it is the fate of the sacrificer who must each time divert it onto the victim. The soldier contents himself with saying: "There is death. You are to brave it without giving it a thought. You are to laugh at it." The man of sacrifice gives death a grander fate. For him, "there is death" is not a mere observation that is regrettable or not, for there *must* be death. The victim, human or bovine, *must* die, for existence, *being* tragedy since there is death, is not fulfilled unless the victim is held fascinated by the lot that has fallen to it, captivated by tragedy and the inevitable death to the point of intoxication. In this way the sacrificer alone can really create a *human* being. The soldier cannot do this because sacrifice is necessary for the fascinated victim to hear the only words that make him man: "YOU ARE tragedy."

Consequently, it seems that the military would not go beyond the simple state of a warring animal unless it addressed itself to beings who have already become aware of the tragic nature of their destiny. And it is only in becoming aware of this nature that the soldier's heroic potential is established. It is the sacrificial blaze, not the animality of war, that has made men arise, those paradoxical beings, made greater by the terrors that enthrall them and that they overcome.

Sacrifice Hypocritically Presented in Christianity as the Result of Sin

But sacrifice is still not becoming aware in the fullest sense; in fact, from earliest times, none of those who performed sacrifices was aware of what they were doing in our sense of the word. What was done was consistently experienced and acknowledged as an obscure emotion, but it was impossible to state the raison d'être either of the emotion that was felt or of the actions making its experience possible. And not only was clear understanding of what happened inaccessible, but superficial interpretations or distortions could have free rein. And as the inner truth concealed within sacrifice is agonizingly cruel, the interpretations occurred as evasions. The unyielding harshness that was an attribute of the sacrificer gave him a guilty conscience, and an afflicted conscience results in lying. Thus the Christian priest does not present himself as the real sacrificer, the real priest of his God. The real priests, theologically, are the sins of the world, human crimes, which alone are guilty of the divine killing. The priest's heart, however, joins in every fiber to the sacrifice; and though he himself is only the ascetic prudently avoiding any sin, each morning he does again the work of the sinner; he spills once more the blood of Christ.

The *share*[5] that must be accorded violence and, in another sense, the inadequacy of the limits that can be set for it, never implying any conclusive guarantee, can never contradict certain principles of qualification according to which one category of specific humans and not another must be offered up to the ravages of war. The division of social functions is primitive: Even if, for attack and defense as well, some group or other might do well to arm its surplus women against the men of a neighboring society, it seems that the principle of masculine qualification is universally respected. In developed societies qualification excludes not only the feminine population but certain entire social categories that are not qualified or are differently qualified. Thus slaves, merchants, families, or people dedicated to religion are often kept out of the military profession, whose access is reserved for two specific classes of men: the *nobles*, who make up the brilliant portion of the army, and the mercenaries (the army rabble), who make up its sinister portion. The two classes, moreover, in the form of *participation* constantly exchange their own, proper, qualities. Nobles, the leaders in war, cannot have access to all of the military splendor without participating in the sinister character of the brutes who compose their troops. And conversely, the troops could not develop the full force of their characteristic purulent lewdness without participating in the glory of the decorated men commanding them. As a whole the group, in relation to society as a whole, appears to be something *completely other*, a foreign body. Its function, whose ambiguous aspect corresponds exactly to that of the social structure, is carnage, the tools for which it wears conspicuously but in such a way that the richest garments seem wretched in comparison with this sinister finery. Hence the soldier is to the butcher as a sweet scent is to the stench of genitals; in both cases something brilliant and showy is substituted for something vile, and in both cases the brilliance is derived from the vileness of its opposite.

Brotherhoods, Orders, Secret Societies, Churches
Roger Caillois
Saturday, March 19, 1938

[This lecture, whose subject Bataille says came more or less unexpectedly to him and Caillois, touches the heart of the College of Sociology, the heart of its project, the heart of its dreams, the heart of its very being. Here we discover the secret, passionate core in which these sociologists, who wanted to unmask society and wrest its secret from it, held their communion.

But it is also the lecture in which the distance between the two heads of the College, Bataille and Caillois, is most clearly sensed, even if this distance cannot be directly expressed—partly because of the situation that forced Bataille to perform as a ventriloquist: speaking simultaneously for himself and in place of Caillois.

It is likely that Caillois did not read in the same light as its author the letter (from Mauss to Élie Halévy) that he asked Bataille to quote. Mauss condemns Bolshevism, showing its very project to be fascistic but in words that, for Caillois, make this same Bolshevism fascinating. They transmute a political apparatus charged with representing the interests of the working class into a romantic clandestine organization, the reincarnation of the Society of Jesus, destined by its discipline for a boundless omnipotence. For internationalism, severely condemned by Mauss, becomes one of the major grounds for joining, but it is an internationalism of hierarchs. Hence, for Caillois, the College of Sociology must become a sort of Order of Sociologists (in the sense in which one might speak of the Order of Teutonic Knights), a dense nucleus from which plot and conspiracy (at the same time, in La Conspiration, *Paul Nizan, the Communist novelist, denounces the conspiratorial temptation to which young Communist intellectuals too easily fall prey) are to spread.*

145

Bataille's position is much less political, much more mystical, the product of a shamanism performed for its own sake. For him there is no question of using the secret society as a means to obtain some outside result or other: It has no other end than itself. Its end lies in its very existence. In this sense, on different grounds than Mauss, he is suspicious of and dissociates himself from conspiratorial societies that imply a mastery in which the very essence of the secret is betrayed. For the secret is never a professional secret, which is why, when faced with it, one could never become any more than a sorcerer's apprentice.

There is hence a discrepancy between Bataille and Caillois, for which Caillois offers a way out—dialectically. He argues for an order that he defines as hypertelia. It is above all specific ends, has no use at all, does not let itself be used but holds sway alone. It is the end of ends. When it rules it is not by election, tradition, or revolution; it is by definition. Its rule is not an end external to itself. It is its essence, its essential attribute. So it, in turn, has this "existential" value that Bataille opposes to the projects of conspiracy. Michelet had already pointed out, speaking of the Jesuit order, the tendency every order has to develop what he calls "a fierce religion of itself."]

I already let you know that I would have to present Caillois's excuses today. Because of illness he has had to turn over to me the presentation he expected to make on secret societies. I must say that I regret his absence even more because I am obliged to speak on a subject I know much less well than he. Fortunately, a schematic text he sent me will enable me more or less to answer the main questions posed by the existence of organizations appropriately named brotherhoods, churches, orders, secret societies or so-called elective communities.

However, I am not going to read Caillois's text until later. First, I want to connect the presentation I am going to make now with those that have preceded it. Under the present circumstances especially, I want to insist on pointing out the order that forms a number of ideas that I have sought to introduce. At this moment I must emphatically insist on the opposition I have attempted to point out between a religious world, a world of tragedy and *inner* conflicts on the one hand and, on the other, a military world that is radically hostile to the spirit of tragedy and endlessly turning aggressivity toward the outside—*externalizing* its conflicts. Last time I represented the revolutionary upheavals that have racked Europe for several centuries as a development of religious ferment, that is to say, tragic stirrings. I showed that this development demonstrated the tragic world's capacity for a destruction sparing nothing. And I was able to say that this world had itself worked endlessly for its own annihilation: Before our very eyes, this annihilation resulted in the death of the revolutionary spirit that, today, can no longer exist in a person without making that individual the locus of agonizing contradictions. But above all, I insisted that revolutionary struggles, by annihilating a religious world that had become empty, then by annihilating themselves, have left the field clear for the military. In other words, it is possible to say that the main result of the great European revolutions has been the development of national militarisms. At this very instant, in the face of our impotent remonstrations, the military spirit *alone* dictates the fate of hypnotized human masses, some overwrought, the others appalled.

Last time I limited myself to these pessimistic conclusions, merely mentioning that I would speak two weeks later about the hopes that, considering some factors I introduce, can still be invested in the future of human societies.

I should not have to mention that in no way whatsoever was I thinking about the sort of hope most people still pin on democratic armies. I shall be happy to explain later, if someone thinks it necessary, what I think about this too topical subject. Deep down I think there is something wretched, something obnoxious, about opposing a reality, such as the one threatening human existence today, with discourses alone, assertions of law, a whole blaring discord and the armies belonging to this discourse and this discord. I do not believe it is possible to oppose the rule of arms with anything except some other rule: and, other than the rule of arms, only that of tragedy exists. But it seems to me that today I shall be able to leave no doubt on this point: The spirit of tragedy can truly take possession of human beings; it has the power to constrain them and reduce them to silence; it is tragedy, in fact, that holds real sway. For it is alone in its ability to found an unrestricted empire, whereas arms are unable to exist for long on their own. In other words the armed force can easily become aware that it exists to serve people, but the man who bears tragedy within him is the only one strong enough to convince it of its servile nature: Those who possess only discourse and law are incapable of this.

All in all, there exist three types of men who play or attempt to play a decisive role: The characteristics distinguishing these three types may sometimes come together, but, in general, they make up distinct forces. The first type is the armed lout who violently turns everything that excites him to the *outside*, who never allows for any inner conflict and looks on death as a source of external pleasure: Death, for the armed man, is above all what he is preparing for the enemy.

The second type is the tragic man who thinks throwing everything terrifying back onto others is a joke: The tragic man is essentially the one who becomes aware of human existence. He sees the violent and contradictory forces that stir him; he knows he is prey to human absurdity, prey to the absurdity of nature, but he affirms this reality which has left him no outlet other than crime.

The third type is the man of law and of discourse. From our vantage point today we can take him for the man of comedy. I think it is easy to see that the lout has no difficulty putting the man of discourse in his service but that the man of tragedy cannot be subjugated under any circumstances. The man of tragedy has only to stay alive to make the lout recognize him, as the former is existence itself while the latter is only an available force, only a force in search of an *existence* to serve.

But precisely at this point arises the main question about social life. If the man of tragedy bears within him the reality of inmost human existence lost in the immensity of the universe, it is clear that the community—the only place this existence is realized—will have meaning in human terms only to the extent that it provides a place for tragedy, to the extent that it acknowledges the tragic spirit as its own reality. Now, the domination of the military order, of the armed lout, implies the negation of any inner conflict (and, by the same token, the—rarer—domination of the juridical order rejects tragedy insofar as it is an expression of crime). However, faced with threats appearing on every side, the tragic spirit does not necessarily become aware of the destiny that will impose its rule: Quite the contrary, it is unable to stop itself from the movement of self-destruction that is its peculiar nature. The tragic spirit is freedom, and this freedom that is its life can distract it from worrying about making itself recognized as a human being's inmost reality. Tragedy goes on around us, in fact, only in isolated existences; only individuals today still have in their particular destiny the inexorable integrity of life—its depths, its bursts of light, its silences, and its undeluded heartbreak. These individuals are not necessarily aware that if they stop caring that the real *rule*, the *empire*, they belong to be recognized, this integrity will slip away from them: that their radiance and heartbreak, bit by bit, will become literature, and then made light of as comedy. But even though hardened virility would show them the destiny that—unless they accept an obvious downgrading—they are obliged to answer, they would still find only vast emptiness before them. For just knowing that an individual, being isolated, is impotent does not change the powerless individual into a powerful organization. This is, perhaps, only one more tragic heartbreak, in the existence of the man of tragedy, when he becomes aware of his *rule*, of the power that belongs to him. How, faced with the burdensome realities of the world today—which are daily reduced to a terrifying military reality—is it possible for a man to dream of imposing silence on his surroundings? What difference would its being a tragic silence make, and how could that carry any weight at all? Is it not obvious that it is totally unimportant to the world—as we know it today—if the *existence* he carries within himself falls into mute slavery? Is it not obvious that this world is and is determined to be the world of necessity, unreservedly at the disposal of an economic necessity that is brutally translated into military necessity?

There can be no doubt that for everyone today the horizon seems walled in, and it is self-evident that present-day reality conforms indeed to how it seems to us. But it is possible that this reality is temporary. I see no answer to the anxiety bringing such a bitter taste to our throats. Today's world will be subjected to its fate, and the discourses of war that will accompany the hecatombs, however they are uttered, will only create a desire for deafness, powerful and sick at heart. Before this storm already darkening the sky, there is no longer any protection or any way out. But no matter what squall beats down, existence will survive it; and no matter what the military outcome, existence will be in as much turmoil as ever before over contradictory desires. And even if military domination—I mean by that fascist domination—spreads then beyond its present limits, there would be absolutely no possibility that it could resolve these contradictions. In fact, military domination exists only *against* others. As long as fighting is a possibility, domination is incomplete, whereas if the possibility of fighting disappears the military order immediately loses its raison d'être. This last hypothesis does certainly seem nonsensical, but it is a good demonstration of the conditional and servile nature of the realm that claims to subjugate us. Some day or other such a realm definitely will fall under the rule of others, and will recognize a domination more real than itself. The power of the nationalist stupidity preying on us now is as fragile as it is inordinate, and in fact, there has never been an epoch in which nationalism has gone so far beyond its tolerable limits as it has today. That is, on the one hand, the separation of religious and national life and, on the other, the subjugation of every religious organization to other organizations, followed by their destruction, giving free rein to the unbridled demands of the military order. If there existed a virulent religious organization, new and uncouth from head to toe, one sustained by a spirit incapable of a servile structure, a man might yet learn—and retain—that there is something else to love other than this barely concealed image of financial necessity that one's country is when up in arms. There is something else worth living for, something else worth dying for! And although it is true that such an organization can in no way halt the firestorm we seem already into, its presence in the world could be seen from now on, however, as token of the later victories of MAN over his arms!

I think this was a necessary introduction to the presentation I am about to make on elective communities—using Caillois's papers. In fact, elective communities do not simply represent one form of association studied by sociology; they also represent the means offered to those who have felt the necessity to impose their power on other men; they represent exactly the answer to the main question I just asked: "How, in the face of the realities of the world today, is it possible for the man of tragedy to impose silence on what surrounds him?" My answer is that the man of tragedy belongs to an empire that can be realized by means of the elective community, and, in addition, it is the only possible means of realizing it. I assume that the "elective community" or "secret society" is a form of secondary organization that possesses constant characteristics and to which recourse is always possible when the primary organization of society can no longer satisfy all the desires that arise.

Now I shall move on to Caillois's texts. I shall read each paragraph separately and follow each reading with whatever explanations seem necessary to me.

But, first, in order to make clear precisely what Caillois's text means, I shall read a passage from one of his letters concerning it.[1] Then I shall move on to the notes themselves.

I

"Secret" societies:
Within one group an entirely different sort of grouping develops and asserts itself. It is

    —more restricted
    —more closed: secretive
    —more activist

It can be limited to a specific society or linked with other groupings of the same sort existing in neighboring societies.[2]

> Universal nature not at all necessary but possible.

> The original grouping stemming from blood and soil to which one belongs without decision is of necessity turned in on itself.

> If there is some choice, there may be extension, universality.

> Extension outside.

> Extension inside (slaves in the Dionysiac brotherhoods)

II. Restricted

To society—each individual belongs by right of birth. To a "secret" society or brotherhood, the right of entry must be acquired: It is acquired by succeeding a deceased member, by purchase (often potlatch) or else by murder (one kills a member, which gives one possession of his coat of arms, and as a result makes one inherit the rights attached to it).

> Specific to certain societies
> Orphism
> Freedom of choice, but (iniatic) ordeals.

III. Secretive

A brotherhood is not "secret" in the proper sense of the word: Its gatherings are public and it is known who its members are. But its living force is drawn from an *undisclosable* mysterious element belonging exclusively to it. This element is either knowledge of magic or technical knowledge (the brotherhood develops then in the direction of a guild, e.g., a brotherhood of smiths: The technique is judged dangerous, conferring power and prestige, in this instance, the use and working of *iron*, a metal that is magical and powerful), or the knowledge of particular myths (sometimes connected with the techniques that are the monopoly of the brotherhood).

The brotherhood, hence, is a center of instruction and consequently of prestige

of power

Centering on a *mysterious space* (a clearing in the brush, a place for ceremonies) where initiation ceremonies take place (the newly incorporated member is torn from the family group).

initiation

The brotherhood: irruption of the forces of the tangled realm of underbrush into the organization of the *cleared realm*.

Confusion with conspiratorial societies.[3]

Nietzsche's words: And especially no secret society, the consequences of your thought must be appallingly ruthless.[4]

The connection between Dionysiac brotherhood and the smiths.

Freemasonry.

Add to the techniques and ritual rhythms.

IV. Activist

Brotherhood: a winter organization.

—Importance of seasonal variations in primitive societies.

Society's annual cycle following the vegetation.

A brotherhood is not active except in winter, a trying time, *critical*, sometimes for a very brief period.

Society (administrative) is *encrusted*: The *turbulence* of the brotherhood gives it back its youth and life.

Irruption of bands of maskers (cf. carnival) during a period of *license: jostling* of the *heavy* elements of society (rulers, government, old men, priests) by the light elements (young people, slaves, etc.).

Element of "terrification."[5]

V. Dichotomy

Whence the following sociology (a generalization of Dumézil's studies and interpretations in the Indo-European realm).

Dichotomy within society.[6]

1. A *cohesion*, static, regular, administrative, public, official: *heavy* and *slow*.

2. A *ferment*, dynamic, irregular, secretive, exalted, having as its external characteristics:

—intoxication (bacchants, drinkers, the violent);
—lightness (dancers)————————→vertigo◄
—rapidity (runners or riders)

    —they feed on *living flesh*,
    —drink *strong alcohol*,
    —abduct *women*.

VI

There is a polarity in the sacred that corresponds to this polarity of society.

First, a sacred bound up with social cohesion: guaranteeing rules and taboos, acting as a context, a framework that is an *external support*, a discursive, magico-religious knowledge (formulas and rites). Its priests are forbidden the excesses that are the raison d'être of the others;

Second a *sacred* consisting in the outburst of violations of the rules of life: a sacred that *expends*, that *spends itself* (the orgiastic sacred).

A force *within* man (within the young, unserious, light man) and that *spreads* to the outside: the intensity both of invigoration and pacification

—collective ecstasy
—paroxysmal death

A limitless and individual form: the source of continual innovation and improvisation of the sacred. A direct link with the teeming and mysterious world, and rejection of any other authority (whence the ceremonies *driving off* old men, powerful men).

VII. The Correspondence with Age Classes

(Whence the occasional confusion in manuals and works on brotherhoods between these and age classes, and the reduction of the former to the latter. The connection is striking but that it is the result—or an element—of a more universal opposition that has to do with society's functioning goes unremarked).

VIII. "Youth Society" and "Mature Society" Linked to the Forms of Political Organizations

Compare the connection with Communist and Fascist parties in occupied territory, *encamped with neither artillery nor fleet* but like *secret sects* (Marcel Mauss, letter to Élie Halévy, *Bulletin de la Société Française de philosophie*, October-December 1936, pp. 234-35).[7]

What is essentially new in this depiction of social phenomena is the definition of the secret society as a function, specifically as a function serving to rejuvenate a society grown old. It seems to me that if this is subsequently confirmed, there might be a discovery whose importance could not be exaggerated: a discovery that in comparison to the Icarian conquest of the sky, would be of interest in being of no use to the development of armed forces, quite the contrary. Although this is not particularly important, it just happened during our conversations about how to organize the presentations we have developed here, that the possibility of a theoretical construction granting the "secret society" the value of a rather constant function came simultaneously to Caillois and myself—at least, insofar as it is possible to be exact about the first vague appearance of an idea that, at that point, is still almost insignificant. In any event, this hypothesis came much later than the interest we had long had in the principle of the "secret society." Moreover, the concern with founding an "order" exerting on society some apparently not always definable action haunts many modern minds. Without discussing Balzac and Baudelaire (already referred to by Caillois during a meeting preceding this sequence of lectures last year),[8] and without discussing Nietzsche (about whom I have just had occasion to speak),[9] it seems to me that since the end of the Dada period the project of a secret society charged with providing a sort of active reality to aspirations defined in part under the name of surrealism has always been a preoccupation, at least in the background. But no one thought—Caillois himself did not at first think to represent the organizational mode (glimpsed, moreover, very vaguely) as a transformational mode that would be scarcely less necessary to society than certain functional activities are to the organism. Now we are ready, not exactly to make a definite assertion, but to formulate a clear question. Would not the "secret society" or "elective community" represent in every stage of historical development the means, and the sole means, for societies that have arrived at a real void, a static non-sense, that allows a sort of sloughing off that is explosive?

It stands to reason that it always will be difficult to move on to an actual assertion. In fact, or at least it seems to me, it is obvious that something like this must be what always takes place. But we shall run into a great deal of difficulty if we try to go on and formulate it precisely. And, at the very least, these difficulties themselves can be made specific. Is it not misusing language to speak of a "secret society" the same way one speaks of forms that are relatively well-defined and stable, such as king, noble, sorcerer (all forms more or less encountered from one end of history to the other). Is it permissible to unite under this single phrase the CSAR (Comité Secret d'Action Révolutionnaire), the Carbonari, Hashishins, primitive Christian sects, Orphic, Eleusinian, or Dionysiac brotherhoods, Freemasons, a few others and in addition, African or Polynesian societies?[10] However, it seems to me possible, in the case of secret societies, to proceed to a long and detailed analysis, and it seems that this analysis from the beginning can be connected to a fundamental problem touching on the absence of any stability in such formations. Hence the primitive Christian sect in the long run results in a national Church, for example the Anglican Church. It keeps, however, traces of its original character: In principle, conversion maintains the elective nature of participation, but only in principle since this participation takes place automatically, at least during a long period in Protestant England.

I am led, therefore, to propose a sort of law of secret societies in this form: Within a society the secret societies that develop are evolving themselves and gradually move from being dynamic societies to a structural stage that is stable and stabilizing. As I see it, this is true not just of Christian Churches but of Freemasonries as well. As for constantly maintaining the "secret society" in a dynamic state, that presupposes the absence of any evolution. Dynamism, however, tends to turn up again through monastic orders, and through movements of protest against increasing stability, such as Lutheranism, Puritanism, etc., and better yet, through strange sects like the ones in Russia. On this subject, it must be said that Freemasonry seems to have far fewer revivals of this sort: Martinism might possibly be put in this category, but I have to say, at this point, that I know too little about this question, which is only of secondary interest, to speak at greater length about it. I assume that Freemasonry could be considered generally and irremediably a dead society.

Consideration of Freemasonry introduces, however, a second point of view and a second distinction. One must distinguish not only between old, debased secret societies and young societies. One must also distinguish between those "secret societies" whose function has to do with changing existence generally and those designated by Marcel Mauss as "conspiratorial societies."[11] Conspiratorial societies, moreover, are not specific to an advanced civilization: They are found equally in the backward kingdoms of Black Africa. And often it is difficult to distinguish them from the others, for it is always possible for a purely *existential*[12] "secret society" to conspire. It is even normal for all organizations of this type to intervene in public affairs. Hence it seems to me necessary to reserve the name "conspiratorial society" for those secret societies formed expressly with an action in mind distinct from their own existence: in other words, societies formed to act and not *to exist*. (Those societies that are formed to exist, and which, however, act, must necessarily be considered purely and simply as existential.)

It is obvious that such distinctions risk corresponding to a reality so mobile that categories become meaningless in it. It is not impossible, in fact, for a "conspiratorial society" united for one express purpose to become existential itself. I think, however, we can come to this conclusion: It is possible to imagine the *existential* "secret society" as a genre, as a form constant enough to be defined, and it alone can be the object that Caillois and I are attempting to begin to examine here.

But now it seems necessary to stress what I mean to say when I make use of the perhaps inadequately defined term "existential." Although I have not used it until now, I have nonetheless already had occasion to speak about something it designates. I have spoken of the character of totality distinguishing the army, for example, if one compares it with an industrial or administrative organization. The army possesses all the forms and all the functions that characterize the social body: It is analogous in structure to this social body just as a crab's head is analogous to a man's head (the crab's head, like that of a man, has a mouth, eyes, etc.). But essentially, when I spoke of totality, I was seeking to designate a reality existing for itself, a reality in which the pure and simple pursuit of existence, the pure and simple will to be, is what matters, regardless of any particular goal. Obviously, this existential character belongs, strictly speaking, more to the "secret society" than to the army. And that is precisely what marks its profound originality and its power in the world in which we are living. This world, as I emphasized just now, is held in virtually complete servitude under the thumb of harsh necessity. It has become inconceivable to contemplate doing anything other than the jobs, work, tasks that one *must* fulfill. And this world deems it absurd when human beings claim the essential objective of their gathering together is existence.

Now, the innermost power of the very principle of the "secret society" is precisely that it constitutes the sole radical and working negation, the sole negation that does not simply consist in words, of that principle of necessity in the name of which all contemporary mankind collaborates to waste existence. It is that way, and that way alone, that human aspirations absolutely escape from the real embezzlement and fraud operated by political structures. These structures utilize a natural tendency toward explosion and violence, directing them to achieve any conceivable violent negation of this explosive tendency—proceeding consequently in the same manner as the military organization—founding and expanding the rule of necessity.

For my part, I consider that a decisive step will be taken when people assert that they dismiss prerequisite conditions: that what they intend is to *exist*, without delay or evasion. And I do not believe that such an affirmation can be separated in one sense or another from the will to expend, to burst forth. No bursting forth is possible if one is not determined to *exist*. And any will to exist is vain if it is not this outpouring.

In conclusion, I shall recall what Caillois says about the "secret society": that it is bound up with a sacred that consists in an outburst violating the rules of life, with a sacred that expends, that expends itself. At the same time I remind you that tragedy stems from the Dionysiac brotherhoods and that the world of tragedy is the world of the bacchantes. Further, Caillois says that one of the ends of the "secret society" is collective ecstasy and paroxysmal death. The rule of tragedy cannot be accomplished by a dismal and depressed world. It is evident that power is not to be retained by people who are all talk. Only *existence* in its integrity, implying turbulence, incandescence, and a will for explosion undeterred by the threat of death, can be regarded as the one thing that, itself impossible to subjugate, must necessarily subjugate anything consenting to work for others. When all is said and done, the rule is to belong to those whose life will be so much an outpouring that they will love death. I am not unaware of how offensive this all is. I know that I have strayed from the limits a sociological presentation should set for itself. But I must say, in all honesty, that these limits seem arbitrary to me. The sociological domain is the domain, in fact, the only domain, of life's major decisions. These decisions can be dismissed only by atrophying. It is true that there is another side to this: When investigations and decisions are connected, the former risk being subordinated to the latter. I also think that investigations are at great risk of being subordinated to absence of decision. Their result, in the latter case, has great difficulty in being anything other than a dim reflection of a neutral mind. There is no doubt, however, that certain investigations carried out rather indifferently result in a lively representation of reality. There is an equal chance, slight but real it seems to me, when research coexists with life.

Sacred Sociology of
the Contemporary World
Georges Bataille and Roger Caillois
Saturday, April 2, 1938

[This title and date are announced on the program the College had had printed of its activities. Just as with Bataille's other lectures, the manuscript has, instead of a title, only the date written in his hand (here it heads the only two pages that have been preserved of this lecture).

They begin with a report calling for a first annual assessment of their activities: "We have now come to the end of the cycle of lectures begun last November." From what one can infer from the first lines, it seems, indeed, that this session, at least as far as Bataille's intervention is concerned (but was Caillois now well?), was presented as a summary of the theoretical knowledge acquired during the past year. In order to measure this knowledge against the original ambitions of the College, the summary was accompanied by the rereading of what Bataille calls "the first text that united us." Of course, this text is still to be identified. It can as easily be the "Note" published a year earlier by Acéphale *(see p. 5) (and soon to be resumed, expanded, and completed by Caillois in his introduction to the collection "For a College of Sociology"), as any of the texts read during the preliminary meetings that took place at the Grand Véfour in March 1937 (in particular Caillois's "Winter Wind" and Bataille's "Sorcerer's Apprentice," probably now being written).*

But assessment or no, in one voice or two, and whatever its contents, this lecture was to lose in the following weeks its proclaimed position. It was not to be the last lecture in 1937-38: One certainly, and perhaps two others, followed it in May. Certain is the meeting of May 19, during which Klossowski would read his translation of Kierkegaard's Antigone *and Denis de Rougemont a chapter of his forthcoming* L'Amour et l'Occident. *A possible second: The session of May 19 was, says Klossowski, "devoted to tragedy," and the* NRF *announced in its May bulletin: "At the College of Sociology, Bataille and Caillois will speak on the subject of myth," which would certainly lead one to suppose yet another meeting.]*

We have now come to the end of the cycle of lectures begun last November.

I do not think it is pointless to reread today the first text that united us and that rather clearly shows the goal we set ourselves. I do not think it is pointless because it seems to me that, to a rather great extent, we have carried out the project we formulated.

I remind you that, as we moved toward its realization, we began by referring to the results achieved by contemporary sociology. It was right here that Caillois enumerated the works that have been our points of departure. This enumeration was to result in the publication of a brief bibliography—which we have temporarily had to abandon, especially because of Caillois's illness. Nonetheless, we gathered quite a lot of material, in good enough order that this publication can be envisaged in the near future.[1]

Since the facts we relied on were clear enough, we attempted to define our personal position. Caillois spoke of neo-organicism and biologism. Without accepting too restrictive a definition, it is true, my statements were along the same lines as Caillois's. In any case, we follow Durkheim in agreeing that there is something other than a sum of individual actions in the social phenomenon. Personally, during the numerous presentations I came to be in charge of, I attempted to represent society as a field of forces whose movement, it is true, can be discerned in us, but forces that are, in any case, external to the needs and conscious will of each individual. I insisted on the fact that at each level of beings, from atom to molecule, from polymolecular formation to micellar formation, from cell to organism and to society, the structures composed are different from the sum of their components in being joined by an *overall movement*. It is this overall movement, and it alone, that disappears with our death. If you follow me, there would no longer be any grounds to speak of life as a principle. Nor would there be any grounds for placing a given form of life, as, for example, human life, on the same level as the cellular processes to which it seems possible to reduce it. Existence would change nature each time it passed from one structural level to the structural level above it. This comes down to saying that the molecule composed of atoms is an inconceivable reality for a mind that knew only atoms because the molecule *adds* the molecular *overall movement* to atoms. From one stage to the next, from structure to more complex structure, it is possible to arrive at society and to show that the process of not seeing a social phenomenon external to individuals would be as absurd as not seeing[. . .].[2]

Tragedy
Pierre Klossowski and Denis de Rougemont
Thursday, May 19, 1938

[The program the College had printed up for its first set of lectures stopped on April 2 (and Bataille's contribution on that day repeated that this was a closing session, [see the preceding lecture]. However, its activities resumed again the following month and two sessions were, it seems, held in May. The exact date of the first is not known, but a notice published in the April NRF *informs us that "Bataille and Caillois are to speak on the subject of myth at the College of Sociology." The second took place on May 19 (Thursday, instead of the usual Tuesday). Klossowski, in* Les Nouvelles Lettres, *introducing the translation of Kierkegaard read there by him, gives the details: "The present text was read at the College of Sociology on May 19, 1938, at the session devoted to tragedy, with remarks from Georges Bataille, Jean Wahl, and Denis de Rougemont."*

1. On the subject of the first of these two meetings, the renewed interest in the idea of myth must be mentioned. Anthropology is mixed up with politics, and art with religion. Caillois has just brought out Le Mythe et l'homme, *his first book (published at Gallimard on* March 28, 1938), *and in the last pages of "The Sorcerer's Apprentice" (to appear in July in "For a College of Sociology"), Bataille treats extensively what could be called the politics of the myth that the College hoped to use as its model. In a similar though lesser vein, Guastalla will publish the following year* Le Mythe et le livre *to be read in part at a session of the College. Myth permeates the atmosphere. A lexical study would no doubt be revealing. There are those who reproach modern life for having lost the secret of myth, whereas others, on the contrary, accuse it of rediscovering it. The debate*

159

swings from politics to the study of customs, from Mythe du XXe siècle *by Rosenberg, the Nazi theoretician, to Lévy-Bruhl's* La Mythologie primitive.

A sample follows of the hundreds of examples of this preoccupation with myth of the late thirties to be found in tables of contents.

a. In January 1938, Esprit *publishes a lecture by Landsberg, "Introduction à une critique du mythe," in which the renaissance of myths is denounced as "the absolute end of* Western activism" *(pragmatic values like utility, and life taking away any respect for truth), Georges Sorel is described as the "first sociologist of myth" and "the man of myth," as a "*mythomaniac in Janet's sense.*" There follows a discussion with Jean Lacroix, who especially denounces the modern form of myth that the myth of the science of myth represents. Landsberg goes further: "What I reproach modern myths for is less their being myths than their being fabricated, inauthentic myths, products of a cynically conscious, pragmatic mythologism, making use of an apersonal mechanism of proganda." And: "Myth changes character radically as soon as one knows it is a myth." The structure of this condemnation is like the one (according to Caillois) made by Kojève when he objected to the illusions of Bataille's sorcerer's apprentice: between faith and knowledge,* tertium non datur. *The sorcerer knows too much about it to be taken in his own game, and, whereas it is possible for articles of faith not to become completely disrupted by science, the fact remains that only a perverse blindness can expect that science elaborate objects of faith. But behind this condemnation of modern myths as superficial, it is not hard to hear the nostalgia confident of a time in which they would have been natural.*

Much less pessimistic than Landsberg, Dumézil celebrates with enthusiasm (which is not simply epistemologic) the revival of ancient German myths in the national socialist space over the Rhine. "The 'beautiful legends' of the Germans have been not only repopularized but remythologized," *he writes in* Mythes et dieux des Germains *(Paris [1939], p. 155). "They have become once again myths in the strict sense, because they justify, sustain, and provoke individual and collective behaviors all of which are characteristic of the sacred." But not all of Durkheim's heirs took things as well. In his* Mémoires, *Raymond Aron cites two letters in which Mauss, with rather less optimism than his comparatist student Dumézil, mentions this continuation (or this echo) of certain Durkheimian theories, which have come in contact with the concrete. In November 1936: "This return to the primitive has not been the object of our reflections." In May 1939: the course of events seems to him "too strong a confirmation of things we had shown and the proof that we should have expected them to be verified through evil rather than through good" (50 ans de réflexion politique [1983], p. 71). A good article by Koyré had appeared in 1936 in the* Zeitschrift für Sozialforschung *("La Sociologie française contemporaine"); the author demonstrates there that, politically, totalitarianism is what is behind the Durkheimian school's sociological schemata.*

*We should remember here that the College of Sociology reproached the tra-
ditional study of social phenomena for being "too limited to the analysis of so-
called primitive societies, while ignoring modern societies" (see "For a College
of Sociology"). This is not completely untrue. But a suspicion had already
arisen that there was a certain dangerous primitivism in modernity. The return
of myth was one of the main symptoms of this.*
    b. Volontés, *in February 1939, publishes an article by Queneau, "Le Mythe
et l'imposture." As the title sufficiently indicates, he too lays into the* mytho-
mania *of his contemporaries: "Myth is an imposture when it is constructed,
either by reason, or by antireason. In one instance it can be no more than an al-
legory at best, and at worst a trap. In the other, it can be no more than the inconsistent expression of more than one individual subconscious. The thirst for
myths that currently is found in some, otherwise remarkable, intellects, seems to
me to indicate a* lack, *the sign indeed, of the inadequacy of an antirational position." "They aspire to invent myths—but myths are not invented. Either one
finds them alive, in a community in which one really participates. Or else one
can aspire to a* revelation *to which someone who denies More in order to adore
Less, who jeers at Yes in order to be swallowed up in No, can only remain foreign." That Bataille is the target of these remarks can be inferred by a reference
to the guillotine: "There is no antipathy," says Queneau, "between reason and
that which exceeds it, whereas antireason only cures myopia with enucleation
and headaches with the guillotine." (The article is reprinted in* Le Voyage en
Grèce.*)*
    In an earlier article in Volontés *(June 1938), Queneau specifically congrat-
ulates Étiemble and Yassu Gauclère for the demythification of Rimbaud begun in
their 1936 book. Also in 1938, Étiemble registered as his thesis topic* Le Mythe
de Rimbaud, *which he would defend and publish in two volumes (Genèse du
mythe and Structure du mythe) in 1952. He proposed not only to set out in
search of a mythless Rimbaud but, more ambitiously, to describe in the evolution
of the cult, with Rimbaud as its object, the genesis of a modern myth. "Le Mythe
de Rimbaud" is employed as a title by Étiemble for the first time in an article
contemporary with this project, which was published by the* Revue de littérature
comparée *in January, 1939. To oppose the image of a satanic or luciferian
Rimbaud, Étiemble refers to V. Cerný's thesis on titanism, also presented by
Caillois in the* NRF *in November 1937 (referred to in Lewitzky, "Shamanism,"
note 8). This "Myth of Rimbaud" will become, by means of a* mise en abyme,
merely number 1,218 in the vast compilation constituting the Genèse du mythe,
the first volume of Le Mythe de Rimbaud.*
    Besides this Rimbaud *written in collaboration with Y. Gauclère, Étiemble
published a novel,* L'Enfant de choeur. *Closely connected with the Communists,
he occasionally contributed to* Commune. *His signature appeared in the only issue of* Inquisitions *(he claims paternity of the* s *in the title; see "Deux Masques*

de Roger Caillois,'' in the homage to Caillois in NRF no. 320 [September, 1979]). He published a rather positive review of the issue of Acéphale entitled *"Réparation à Nietzsche"* in the April 1937 NRF.

With a degree in grammar like Caillois, in 1936 Étiemble taught in the lycée at Beauvais with him. But the following year, he is in Chicago, where he will remain for several years. Two years later he writes from there to thank Caillois: *"Your fine* Vent d'hiver *reminds me that I never belonged to the New Church"* (Roger Caillois, Cahiers pour un temps [Centre Georges Pompidou], 1981, p. 207). At the end of his letter Étiemble mentions what he calls *"our investigations of the myth of Rimbaud.''* What part did Caillois play in this project? It is a fact that Étiemble, whose leftist intellectualism had not yet turned into that limited form of antibabelism called franglophobia, did not bring much pataphysical humor into his divestiture of Rimbaldological hagiography. As seriously as an antipope, he intended *"to study everything transforming Rimbaud according to the laws of religious sociology.''* Le Mythe de Rimbaud *is literary history in the service of religious history. Do we have to specify that even if his presence in Paris had led him to mix more closely with the College, Étiemble's Marxisizing Voltaireanism, would have had some difficulty being sympathetic to certain harmonic vibrations heard there. This said, the names he mentions in the introduction to his thesis, Dumézil, Mauss, Caillois, show that he was steeped in the same sort of bibliography. When Étiemble was in Chicago, Paulhan had the* NRF *regularly delivered to him and asked his opinion on the College's events (Jeannine Kohn-Étiemble, 226 lettres inédites de Jean Paulhan [Paris, 1975], p. 165; none of Étiemble's replies are published).*

c. In Europe, in June 1939, Sartre is even more explicit in attacking myth's vogue. Speaking of Denis de Rougement's book L'Amour et l'Occident (which he links to Caillois's work), the writes: "This notion of myth, moreover, is itself a product of the period, and one much in fashion ever since Sorel. Wasn't it Jean-Richard Bloch, not long ago, who called for a myth for the twentieth century? And didn't André Malraux, in fact, discuss myths of love in the preface he wrote for a translation of D. H. Lawrence? This has gone so far that today, I fear, there is a myth of myth, which should, itself, be the object of a sociological study" (reprinted in Situations, vol. 1 [Paris, 1947]).

II. The May 19, 1938, session was devoted to tragedy, a theme already taken up during several of the preceding meetings of the College. There were four speakers: Klossowski, Bataille, Wahl, de Rougemont.

Denis de Rougemont gives his own report of the circumstances of his intervention during the session held by the College that day. He had just launched into writing L'Amour et l'Occident. "From the end of February to the beginning of May, I wrote books I through V. In May, as expected, I gave four lectures in Switzerland, a presentation of book V on Love and War at Bataille and Caillois's College of Sociology, and wrote a long article on nazism based on my Frankfurt *notes: This will be the central text of my* Journal d'Allemagne. *From the end of May to the twentieth of June, in a little château near Brunoy, I completed books VI and VII, the preface, and the final revision of the typed text. The evening of June 21, summer solstice, Day's last triumph over a Night whose rule will slowly spread right into the very heart of the coming summer, they gave* Tristan *at the Opera. I took the last two free seats."*

This note appears in the pages entitled "Vers la guerre" in the volume Journal d'une époque (1926-1946) *where, in 1968, the author gathered his complete (and slightly augmented), less private than personal journals of the past forty years:* Le Paysan du Danube (1926-1929), *the* Journal d'un intellectuel en chômage (1933-1935) *the* Journal d'Allemagne (1935-1936), *and the* Journal des deux mondes (1939-1946). *The last of these was written in his travels between Europe and the two Americas during the war. He was in North America, landing in New York in September 1940, but also in South America where Victoria Ocampo, director of* SUR, *invited him to give a series of lectures in Buenos Aires during September 1941. There he had occasion to meet Caillois, with whom he participated in several roundtable discussions (see* SUR, *no. 84 [September 1941]).*

Born in Switzerland in 1906 and a practicing protestant familiar with German culture, Denis de Rougemont was a frequent presence, from about 1936 on, at the NRF, *where Paulhan entrusted him to put together a memorable "Cahier des révendications." Here the claims and protests of ten or so young discontents from Nizan to Thierry Maulnier, and including representatives from diverse personalist or voluntarist strains, promised democracy a certain number of changes that had nothing in common other than that they called themselves radical. A close acquaintance of Mounier's, de Rougemont would contribute to* Esprit *as well. His* Politique de la personne, *followed by* Penser avec les mains *(1936), made him one of the most visible propagandists for the intellectual's engagement. The period of compulsory leisure, to which his* Journal d'un intellectuel en chômage *(Journal of an unemployed intellectual) owes its title, came to an end when Otto Abetz, the representative of the Nazi party to the Parisian intellectuals, proposed that de Rougemont teach French literature for a year (1935-36) as an assistant at the University of Frankfurt. The* Journal d'Allemagne *would result from this stay. It appeared at Gallimard some two years later (1938) at the moment the Munich crisis flared up. Denis de Rougemont, as mentioned, completed the final version of this work just after having spoken before the College.*

Denis de Rougemont came back with a lesson from this year spent with the Nazis, or put another way, this Erlebnis *of nazism: Democracies must immediately, at any cost, resolve a religious problem (not a social or economic, nor even a political one), which, however, they are not yet even capable of seeing. A page of his* Journal d'Allemagne, *on this point, strongly echoes the dominant preoccupations of the College. It is called "Une Cérémonie sacrée" (A sacred ceremony). German troops have just reoccupied the left bank of the Rhine in the* *final blow remaining to be dealt the Treaty of Versailles and the Locarno accords demilitarizing it. Hitler plans a speech to celebrate such productive aggression and gives it on the Opera square. Denis de Rougemont is in the crowd. Then he has a definitive illumination: He attains the revelation of something he had not understood. "What I am now feeling,"* he notes, *"is what must be called* sacred horror. *I thought I was at a mass meeting, at some political demonstration.* But they are celebrating their religion!*" Easter vacation comes two days later. Denis de Rougemont spends the holiday in Paris where he describes what he has just seen. But it is hard to express these things in French, and he feels a certain difficulty in communicating. He understood something, having lived* (miterlebt) *it on the spot, yet now attempting to describe it to people who were not there, he is accused of propagandizing. However, he defends himself as not in the least a partisan of Hitler. In May 1937, for example, he would review in* Esprit *the last issue of* Acéphale, *which was devoted to repairing Nietzsche. Congratulating Bataille for the undertaking, he suggests that the same might easily be done for Luther ("They also say, no doubt for the rhyme: Luther precursor of Hitler!"). "The age's most potent realities are affective and religious,"* he complains. *"And all I hear is talk of the economy, political technology, and law." Several years later, in his study on "Le Pouvoir charismatique"* (reprinted in* Instincts et société [1964]*), Caillois would quote at length the description of the "sacred ceremony" that the author of the* Journal d'Allemagne *had brought back from his stay in Frankfurt.*

Denis de Rougemont, a Protestant, was well acquainted with Kierkegaard, whom he would even name as his "principal spiritual director" in the reply addressed to Monnerot's inquiry in Volontés *(June 1939). At the same time he defined contemporary leaders as "directors of collective unconsciousness." When he returned for good to France at the end of the university year (June 1936), he could have read, listed among other epigraphs, on the first page of a thin review whose first issue had just appeared, a quote from Kierkegaard corresponding to his own conclusions: "What wore the face of politics and imagined itself to be political, one day will be unmasked as a religious movement." This review was* Acéphale. *The next year Denis de Rougemont would acclaim its issue devoted to the defascisizing of Nietzsche.*

As for L'Amour et l'Occident, *since that is the book (to appear in 1939) connected with the remarks made by de Rougemont at the College on May 19, 1938, it is a history of amorous passion as represented by eight centuries of European literature. The myth of Tristan and Isolde is proposed as the archetype of a necessarily adulterous, fettered, and painful eroticism. In the first pages, the author adopts as his own and develops the opposition of myth and literature to which the period liked to refer. (As Queneau was just seen declaring that myths could not be invented). "Paris, mythe moderne" by Caillois (1937, reprinted in* Le Mythe et l'homme*), opened with the same distinction. There one reads that it can be* *asserted that "it is precisely when myth loses its moral, constraining power that it becomes literature and an object of aesthetic enjoyment." From this hierarchizing opposition there ensues a devaluation of fiction that is very close to the theses that Guastalla developed at the same moment in* Le Mythe et le livre *(see the lecture he delivered at the College on January 10, 1939). Caillois was soon to give this a radical and almost sophistic form in* Puissances du roman *(Marseille, 1942): The College had backed the myth of a society condensed enough to escape the temptation to fictionalize. As for de Rougemont, he brings his own variations to this period motif. The work of art, he proposes in turn, is distinguished from myth, which is anonymous, whereas the work of art is the product of its sole author's individual talent. It must comply with a code of verisimilitude where myth, simultaneously unconscious and compelling, does not have to bother with a rational cover.*

"Love and War," Book V of L'Amour et l'Occident *(the one presented by de Rougemont to the College), sketches a rapid history of the forms taken by war in Europe, from medieval chivalry to total war in modern times. The connecting thread running throughout this outline is given by the following hypothesis: "Any change in military tactics can be considered as relating to a change in conceptions of love, or vice versa." The reader will decide to what extent the analysis set forth in this rather brief chapter corresponds convincingly to the ambitions of such a program. It proceeds from the opposition of two polemical styles, one aiming at conquest, the other at destruction of the enemy. The Middle Ages cultivated a courtly war, simultaneously humane and virile. It obeyed models elaborated by chivalrous restraint and pursued, in the amorous as well as warlike sense of the term, the conquest of its object, its seduction, its capture: It must obtain surrender. War, therefore, according to a quote from Marshal Foch given by the author, "spiritualizes matter" by subjecting it to the orders of an aesthetic whose cardinal values are elegance and economy: Moderate in victory, it knows how to be sparing. In contrast to this medieval war, de Rougemont proposes a picture of modern war in which mechanical and unmanning violence is seen to be given free rein, unleashing passions and instincts, pursuing—in a narcissistic blindness leading straight to catastrophe—the annihilation of its object. The tournament could be considered as the apogee, the climax of heterosexual drives sublimated in war. The mechanization of the modern army, on the other hand, as pictured by the author, would have the effect at best of plunging the soldiers into a "generalized impotence," and at worst of leading them "to chronic onanism and homosexuality."*

In the Journal d'Allemagne, *a brief dialogue preceded the description of the "sacred ceremony" that Hitler's visit to Frankfurt allowed him to attend. There de Rougemont confesses he does not believe in the collective soul. "And you, do you believe in the collective soul? Is it not a grandiloquent phrase for denoting the absence of a personal soul in individuals swept up in the mechanical move-*

ments of a crowd?'' Total war which, according to L'Amour et l'Occident, *would be characteristic of modern aggressive logic, thus corresponds to a society intending to appropriate for itself the affectivity of its members. Any movement of passion, transferred from the private to the public, ordered out of the context of an individual life that must be abandoned to ennui, finds itself consequently channeled and gathered entirely into the collective: Collective stirrings demand individual asthenia in return.*

So it was to tragedy that this session of May 19, 1938, was devoted. Bataille spoke as well. His remarks have not been preserved, but it is probable that on this occasion he returned to comments on this subject developed in earlier discussions, especially on February 5 and 19, as well as on March 15. These comments would have been partially in agreement with de Rougemont's view of things (all things otherwise being equal and ignoring the fact that the latter viewed religion much more positively than Bataille—de Rougemont's religion having nothing anti-Christian or atheological about it). Bataille contrasted military death and religious, sacrificial death: War seeks the death of another who is considered the enemy, whereas the condition for effective sacrifice is the identification of the one making the sacrifice and his victim. This is the reason that only sacrifice has a tragic dimension. In the ''Chronique nietzschéenne'' in Acéphale *(July 1937, see* OC, *vol. 1, p. 482), Bataille had already opposed to the fascist world, which he defined as that of ''military repression,'' the experience of an authentically Nietzschean community that would, he said, have for its object ''existence itself,* EXISTENCE, WHICH IS TO SAY TRAGEDY.'' *Speaking of Cervantes's play,* Numance, *with its particularly tragic resonance with the Spanish civil war, which was the reason Jean-Louis Barrault had just produced it (André Masson painted the scenery), the same article a few pages later returned to the opposition of the army and tragedy. Whereas the (''caesarian'') military community is rallied around a leader, it is tragedy that unites the ''*HEADLESS'' *community. It is in this period that Bataille speaks (in ''L'Obélisque'') of ''the tragic times of Greece'' and that he writes ''La Mère-tragédie.'' One final note: ''La Menace de guerre,'' which appeared in June 1939 in the last issue of* Acéphale, *once again formulates the hypothesis of a society (or rather a church) that would place ''Tragedy'' above all. This issue of* Acéphale, *composed entirely by Bataille, was not signed, as if anonymity would give it the dimension of a mythic utterance.*

No clue has been found that would permit us to reconstitute the remarks of Jean Wahl during this session. We will recall simply that he had just defined himself three months earlier as a ''very assiduous'' student of the College (see Leiris, ''The Sacred in Everyday Life''). D. de Rougemont's presence at the forum, but especially the nature of Klossowski's remarks, may have encouraged him to speak of Kierkegaard: It is in 1938, in fact, that his memorable Études kierkegaardiennes *appeared. It is also in 1938 that his collection of poems,* Connaître sans connaître, *was published by G. L. M., the editor of* Acéphale *as well as of Leiris's* Miroir de la tauromachie.

Consequently, of the four interventions for which this session of the College provided a theater, only one, Klossowski's, has been preserved in writing. This is the first time that he takes the podium to speak.

What we have here is the translation of Kierkegaard's Antigone *(an extract from* L'Alternative*), which was published, with the translator's commentary, simultaneously in the review and in offprints by* Les Nouvelles Lettres *in August 1938 (the review's second issue). The first issue of this publication, directed by Jean Le Louët, had come out in June 1938. Its table of contents lists a text by Maritain, poems by Wahl, and the note on Chamfort (see Klossowski, "The Marquis de Sade and the Revolution," note 1). Maritain and Wahl will reappear. The names Landsberg and Picon also will turn up again. The review would come to an end as 1939 swept on.*

In Acéphale, *a little before, Klossowski had already published a note on Kierkegaard which he was to repeat in the first edition of* Sade, mon prochain, *but would remove from later editions.*

Preceding the translation of Antigone *was the following translator's note: "The French text is based on the German translation (by Christophe Schrempf and Wolfgang Pfleiderer [Jena: Eugen Diederichs, 1911]), taking into account the Danish. I wish to express here my gratitude to M. Frithiof Brandt, professor of Philosophy at the University of Copenhagen; Ulf Jespersen and Friedrich Brahe, who were kind enough to check the French and German texts against the Danish. The present text was read at the College of Sociology, May 19, 1938, at the session devoted to tragedy, with interventions by Georges Bataille, Jean Wahl, and Denis de Rougemont."]*

Kierkegaard's *Antigone*

Possibly someone could say to me: Tragedy still is tragedy. I would not have much of an objection since any historical development is realized only within its own idea; if this person truly claims to make a statement, not just following the repeated expression "tragedy" with ellipses, an empty parenthesis, then this person's meaning will be that what is contained in the idea of tragedy, rather than destroying the idea, has only expanded and enriched it. Doubtless no attentive observer will miss that there is an essential difference between modern tragedy and ancient tragedy, this certainty being something that theater audiences and readers of drama believe they long since acquired as the dividend for today's aesthetic exploitation. Yet if someone else wanted to assert an absolute difference and (first surreptitiously, though finally with violence, perhaps) separate ancient and modern tragedy, what would be the point? He would only saw off the branch he is sitting on and prove that what he wanted to separate is interdependent and united.

Opposed to any such unilateral attempt at separating ancient tragedy from modern tragedy, there is also the fact that aestheticians still refer to what Aristotle said about tragedy, considering that his definitions and his requirements have exhausted the idea. And are we not all gripped by a certain bitterness to think that no matter how the world has changed, just as it is still human nature to shed tears, representation of the tragic has stayed essentially unchanged? This may seem reassuring to someone who wants absolutely no separation, absolutely no break, but this does not make the difficulty I wanted to point out exist in the world any less; indeed rather more, it appears in an even more formidable form. Anyone with any knowledge of modern aesthetics, who will have seen how rigorously Aristotle's directives are abided by today, will grant that it is not simply out of respect or habit that Aristotelian aesthetic is what is referred to. But, as soon as one examines these directives in detail, the difficulty becomes obvious. Aristotelian definitions are so general, in fact, that one can simultaneously agree and disagree with Aristotle. Not to jump ahead in the exposition that is to follow, I shall be content with a few brief and identical reflections on comedy. If an old aesthetician were to say that comedy presupposes characters and situation, there is no doubt that one could constantly refer to this definition; but as soon as one has seen how many different ways a person can be made to laugh, it appears that the rule of characters and situation is remarkably supple. Those who have made their own or others' laughter the object of their observations, those who then discover less what was fortuitous than what was common, those who notice then the psychological interest of how different the things exciting laughter are at each stage of life, can easily persuade themselves that the immutable rule for how comedy must provoke laughter is extremely variable in relation to the different representations of absurdity produced throughout the mind's development. Must not this difference even be large enough for the physiological expression of absurdity to be transformed—for laughter to become tears? The same is true for tragedy.

The task proposed by this brief study is absolutely not to establish the relationship between ancient tragedy and modern tragedy; rather it seeks to demonstrate the manner in which ancient tragedy essentially lets itself be absorbed by modern tragedy so that true tragedy is expressed there. And the study will limit itself to this. I shall think of this restriction less as one imposed by our times because the contemporary world is evolving far more in the direction of comedy than in the direction of tragedy. Individual doubt undermines all our existence and isolation continually gets the upper hand. Our social aspirations are an unequivocal sign of this; insofar as they are working against isolated aspiration they are themselves an expression of isolated aspiration. For isolation is produced anywhere that one is emphasized as a number; where an individual is emphasized as a single one, anyone sees the isolation; but there is precisely the same isolation when a hundred individuals insist on being noticed solely as a hundred, which is what those favoring association neither can nor would want to see. If only the crowd is counted, then it hardly matters what number is obtained: Whether it is one, or a thousand, or fifteen hundred million who people the earth, it is one and the same. As a result, the spirit of association is as revolutionary in principle as the spirit the association fights. To prove his magnificence David had his peoples counted; nowadays peoples count themselves to prove their importance relative to a superior power. In other respects, associations show signs of being arbitrary: Frequently they are formed with some chance aim or other that the association naturally still determines forever. Countless today, associations prove that the ties of the epoch are coming undone, and they contribute themselves to rapidly untying them. These infusoria inside the organism of the State are evidence of its complete decomposition. When did hetaerae begin to be common in Greece? Was it not during the period that the State was in danger of collapse? And does not our epoch bear a striking resemblance to the one Aristophanes depicted, doubtless making it no more ridiculous than it really was? From the political point of view have not the ties that invisibly united the organs of the States been broken? And in religion, has not the power upholding the invisible been weakened and destroyed? Do not statesmen and priests have in common with ancient oracles that they cannot look at themselves without laughing? Yet our period is distinguished from this period of Hellenic history by a specific trait: It is more self-important, more profoundly desperate. Thus our epoch has enough trouble accepting life to know that something like responsibility exists and this is rather important. But although everyone wants to rule no one wants to be responsible. In recent memory a French statesman, when again offered a ministerial post, would not accept it unless the secretary of state would be responsible. The king is not responsible, but the minister is. The minister in turn refuses responsibility: He is willing to be minister but not responsible. Let responsibility fall on the secretary of state. In this roundabout way only night watchmen and policemen end up bearing responsibility. Wouldn't this story of responsibility, stood on its head, be a subject worthy of Aristophanes? Governments fear nothing worse than responsibility. Why? Because they fear the party of the opposition, which by similar hierarchic means passes responsibility back down from rank to rank. That being the case we are presented with the following spectacle: The two powers face each other but are unable to come to blows because each is concealed from the other, being only a cypher of itself, which is certainly not unfunny. There is plenty of evidence throughout history to demonstrate that the knot binding the State together has come undone; the resulting isolation is comic by its very nature, particularly comic in that subjectivity wants only to assert itself as a pure and simple form. An isolated personality wishing to assert his accidental nature against the necessity of evolution will be comic. Moreover, the most heartfelt comedy one can imagine would consist in a chance individual's conceiving the universal idea of saving the world. This is why the appearance of Christ is in one sense the most profound tragedy (in another sense it is infinitely more) because Christ appeared in the fullness of time and—something that must be particularly remembered for what is to follow—bore the sins of the world.

Aristotle held up two elements as being at the origin of action in tragedy: διά-νοια καί ηθος but at the same time he remarks that the τέλος is the most important and that the action of individuals is not meant to represent the characters but rather that the characters are there for the action. This, as we shall easily see, is where modern tragedy moves away from ancient. It is characteristic of the latter that action does not simply proceed from the characters (it is not subjectively reflexive enough for that), although it contains relatively more suffering. Also, did ancient tragedy not develop dialogue to an unsurpassable degree of reflection, so much so and so well that everything would be resolved there? In ancient tragedy monologue and chorus respond to moments when the dialogue is discreet. The chorus approaches sometimes the substantiality of the epic, sometimes the soaring of lyricism. Both conditions express an excess that is not successfully reduced to individuality; the monologue is more of a lyrical concentration and is charged with that excess that cannot be reduced to action or to situation. Action itself in ancient tragedy consists of an epic moment, and it is event as much as action. The reason for this lies naturally in the fact that the ancient world did not reflect subjectivity in itself. Doubtless, individuals move with a certain freedom, but they remain within substantial determining categories such as the State, the family, and fate. These substantial categories constitute what is pregnant with destiny in ancient tragedy; they make ancient tragedy what it is. That is why the hero's fall is not simply the consequence of his actions; it is at the same time something he suffers. In modern tragedy, on the whole, the hero's fall is not suffering but action. This is why modern tragedy is essentially based on situation and character. The tragic hero is then reflected subjectively in himself, and this reflection not only reflects him in his immediate relationship to the State, the clan, and fate, but often even in his relationship to his past. What interests us here is the completely determined moment in which his life becomes his action. In fact, that is exactly how the situations and roles of tragedy became exhausted: The process is resolved; there is no leftover immediacy. The result is that modern tragedy has neither epic foreground nor epic background. The hero lives and dies by his own actions.

The things I have just explained rather clearly though briefly here will serve to establish a difference between ancient and modern tragedy, which seems to me extremely important: I mean the different sorts of tragic guilt. Aristotle, as we know, requires the hero to have αμαρτία. But like action, guilt, in Greek tragedy, is an intermediary between acting and suffering, and that is what comprises the tragic clash. On the other hand, the more subjectivity is reflexive, and the more one sees the individual abandoned to himself in a completely Pelagian fashion, the more guilt acquires an ethical character. Greek tragedy is situated between these two extremes. If the individual has no guilt, he presents no tragic interest because the tragic clash lacks tension; on the other hand, he is no more interesting to us in a tragic sense if he is absolutely guilty. Consequently, it is when contemporary tragedy tends to turn everything pregnant with fate into individuality and subjectivity that it doubtless has misunderstood the essence of tragedy. From this point on we are told nothing of the hero's past life. He is purely and simply charged with the burden of his entire life as his own action; he is made responsible for everything, and aesthetic guilt is thereby changed into ethical guilt. The tragic hero then becomes evil, and evil becomes the very object of tragedy; however, evil offers no aesthetic interest; sin is not an aesthetic element. This misunderstanding no doubt proceeds from the fact that our period leans so heavily toward comedy. Comedy resides in isolation; when one tries to introduce tragedy into isolation, one obtains evil for the sake of evil and not at all guilt, which is specifically tragic in its equivocal innocence. Examples are easily to be found in modern literature. Thus it is that Grabbe's play, *Faust und Don Juan*, inspired in many ways, is based on the principle of evil. I shall be wary of taking all my arguments from a single work, however, and shall refer to the universal consciousness of our times. Suppose an author blamed his hero's fall on the action of destructive impressions from an unhappy youth; this is something the spirit of our time would judge inadmissible, no matter how remarkable the poetic representation might be. It does not want to know any such nurse's tales because it applies another criterion, because it makes the individual purely and simply responsible for the course of his life. But this makes the individual not tragic at all but evil in his fall. Just as if the whole human race were nothing but a world of gods to which I too undeniably have the honor of belonging. Alas, the force we display, the courage with which we attempt to shape our own destiny, indeed our own selves, is only illusion: Thus tragedy is lost and despair replaces it. It is the very nature of tragedy to produce both bitterness and healing, which is by no means a contemptible result. But when one attempts to find oneself as unnaturally as does our epoch, one becomes lost and comic. No matter how odd a person may be, are we not all children of God, children of our times, our people, our families, our friends, and is that not precisely where our particular truth lies? If, relative as each of us is in every respect, we wish to be the absolute, we make ourselves absurd. In many languages there are words that, because they are frequently used for a specific case, end up becoming independent as adverbs in this particular case. Such a word, in the eyes of a specialist, has suffered irreparable damage: If then the same word had pretensions to being declined with five cases like a substantive, that would not fail to be laughable. And the individual is just as laughable when, pulled from the maternal breast of his times with immense difficulty, he claims to be something absolute in spite of his infinite relativity. Tragedy comprises an infinite gentleness, whose relation to human life is, from an aesthetic point of view, on the order of grace and divine mercy, but, softer, more feminine, than the latter, tragic gentleness consoles the one who is suffering with a deeply maternal love. Ethics, on the other hand, is harsh and severe. When a criminal defends himself before a court by arguing that his mother had a tendency to steal, especially during pregnancy, the court will require an examination of his mental condition, at the same time that it informs the thief that he, rather than his mother, is being dealt with here. Now, to the extent that this is a case of crime, there could be no question of the sinner's taking refuge in the temple of aesthetics. Yet aesthetics will offer him a mode of expression able to attenuate his suffering. The sinner himself, of course, ought not to have recourse to this sort of release, nor seek this sort of attenuation: His path leads not to aesthetics but to the religious realm. What is aesthetic is behind him, and it would only add to his sins to content himself with aesthetics. What is religious is the expression of paternal love, it attenuates the ethical for the sinner by the same continuity that gives tragedy its gentleness. Aesthetics, however, has a soothing effect before the sin's contradiction is produced, whereas the religious does so only after this contradiction has been lived in all its terror. At the very moment the sinner risks succumbing to the weight of universal sin, which he took upon himself with the feeling that the guiltier he was the more he could hope for deliverance, at the instant of most intense horror, the comforting idea dawns on him that this too was the condition of universal sin manifesting itself through him. Now this consolation is a religious consolation; anyone believing he could attain it by some other means, for example, by taking refuge in aesthetics, will never find it. In a certain sense the epoch's need to make the individual responsible for everything that happens to him corresponds to a correct sense of reality. But our epoch is not profound or intense enough in doing this; whence its compromises. It is sure enough of itself to be able to scorn the tears of tragedy, sure enough of itself to be able to do without mercy. And yet what would human life be at all, what would the human race be, if deprived of tears and of grace! The only ways out are bitterness or else the deep concern and intense joy of religion. This happy people! Is it not melancholy and bitterness, running through all it has left us of its art, its poetry and its joys, that gives us the most intense emotions?

Up to now I have reduced the difference between ancient and modern tragedy to the differences tragic guilt presents. Now, this is the crucial point to bring out all the specific differences. In fact, if the hero's guilt is unequivocal, the monologue disappears and so does fate; thought becomes transparent in dialogue, action in situation. The different sort of guilt is reflected in the condition of the soul that tragedy provokes. Aristotle requires tragedy to simultaneously arouse fear and pity in the spectator. Hegel in his *Aesthetics* returns to this observation in order to use each of these two points as a basis for a twofold factor that, nonetheless, does not exhaust the problem at all. In Aristotle's distinction between fear and pity, one could relate fear to the impressions accompanying the details of the episode, and pity to the final impression of the whole. It is the latter that I would like to emphasize because this overall impression corresponds to tragic guilt and obeys the same dialectic. Hegel's observation about this is that there are two sorts of pity: ordinary compassion, addressed to the finite aspects of suffering, and true tragic compassion. This is correct, but not particularly important for me, because I consider that the general emotion is a misunderstanding that can occur as easily with ancient tragedy as with modern tragedy. However, what Hegel adds regarding true tragic pity is very powerful and true: *True pity or compassion, by contrast, is the act of sympathizing with the moral justification of the one who suffers* (Hegel, *Aesthetics*, vol. 3). Now, whereas Hegel considers pity more generally, drawing attention to the different forms it can take in the individual, I shall attempt to show the different forms of compassion corresponding to the different forms of tragic guilt. (To characterize them I shall take apart the roots of the word [*compatir*], separating *com* from *pâtir* and replacing the *com* only when I see in the spectator's state of mind differences that are not subjectively accidental, but different reflections corresponding to the different sorts of tragic guilt.) In ancient tragedy suffering is more profound, grief less; in modern tragedy it is suffering that is less and grief that is greater. Now suffering always contains something more substantial than grief.[*1] Grief is based on constant reflection on the fact of suffering, a reflection that is absolutely foreign to suffering. It is extremely interesting psychologically to watch a child when he sees someone older suffer. The child is not sufficiently reflective to feel grief and yet his suffering is incredibly intense. He is not reflective enough to be able to conceive of guilt or sin: He would be incapable of any such ideas at the sight of someone older who suffers; though the motive of the suffering remains hidden for him, an obscure premonition of this motive, nonetheless, is mixed in with his suffering. The suffering of the Greeks is of this order but in a more perfectly harmonious form, and that is why it is so sweet and so deep. If, on the other hand, someone older, an adult, sees someone younger, a child, suffering, the adult's grief is greater and his suffering less. Thus, grief has a direct relationship, and suffering an indirect relationship, to guilt. In ancient tragedy suffering is more profound. That is, it is more profound in the state of consciousness corresponding to it for, of course, there is nothing arbitrarily subjective there. But each is part of the other: Anyone who wishes to understand profound suffering in Greek

---

*Kierkegaard's words were *Smerte* (*douleur*) and *Sorg* (*peine, chagrin*). I have preferred to translate the second term by *souffrance* rather than by *peine*, *souffrance* implying *endurance of pain* imposed on the subject by the force of external things, and in this sense, contrasted with *douleur*, suffering the subject imposes on himself through his own reflection. [This translator's note by Klossowski will explain my choice of the words "suffering" and "grief" rather than the usual English rendering of Kierkegaard's *Smerte* and *Sorg* as "sorrow" and "pain."—Trans.]

tragedy has to penetrate Hellenic consciousness. Current admiration for Greek theater is too often nothing but pure verbiage. For one thing is certain: Our epoch feels not the least affinity with the suffering that is peculiar to the Greek mind. *It is a terrible thing to fall into the hands of the living God**. This, in short, is the content of Greek tragedy.[2] This is why there is hideous suffering in it but less grief than in modern tragedy. For in the latter, the hero is completely conscious as he suffers his guilt, whereas the Greek hero's guilt remains equivocal. As was the case with tragic guilt, the question arises here of identifying true aesthetic suffering and true aesthetic grief. The bitterest grief is obviously remorse, but remorse has an ethical, not an aesthetic, reality. It is the bitterest grief because guilt has become entirely transparent for it, absolutely obvious, and that is why it cannot be aesthetically interesting. The brilliant light surrounding remorse obscures it on an aesthetic level: It refuses to be seen by anyone, least of all a spectator, and aspires to some entirely different translation. Without a doubt, modern comedy has brought remorse to the stage, but that only proves the poet's misunderstanding; for the psychological interest solicited by the representation of remorse is not of an aesthetic order. Similar blunders arise from the general confusion of ideas afflicting our epoch; things are sought where they should not be sought, and, what is worse, they are found where they absolutely should not be found: edifying impressions in the theater, aesthetic sensations in the church. We ask novelists to convert us, religious writers to bring us pleasure, philosophers to preach, priests to teach. Remorse, I say, is not an *aesthetic* grief, but nevertheless our epoch always is reduced to remorse when it wants to achieve the greatest tragic result. The same is true for the tragic guilt corresponding to this remorse. Our epoch has lost all substantial determining factors: It no longer conceives of the particular individual in the organic whole of family, State, human race, but abandons him entirely to himself; and the individual thus becomes his own creator, his guilt becomes his sin, his grief his remorse. From this moment tragedy is abolished and drama, strictly representing the hero as prey to his suffering, has lost all tragic interest, because the power that sends these sufferings has been disempowered. The spectator calls out to the hero: Help yourself and heaven will help you! In other words, the spectator has become incapable of compassion, whereas compassion from an objective and a subjective point of view is the specific expression of tragedy.†

To make things clearer, before pursuing the development of my thoughts, I

---

*Hebrews 10:31.

†The choice of verses from Paul to define Greek tragedy as well as the reflections on substantial determining factors are entirely characteristic of the ambiguous spiritual state of Kierkegaard, who is willing to express himself here only in the guise of Victor Érémita. When Kierkegaard comes out from behind his pseudonym, he will have invested every substantial determining factor with the consciousness of sin: Self then *is born* in *knowing* its potential eternity as guilt before God.

shall be more specific about truly aesthetic suffering. Suffering and grief each move in opposite directions, so that it is possible for me to state that the more complete innocence is, the deeper suffering is. Doubtless it is important not to force conclusions from this idea, or we risk doing away with what is tragic. In fact, tragedy requires a moment of guilt that, however, has no subjective reflection; this is why suffering is so profound in Greek tragedy. If you want to take this as far as possible, I will say that it passes from aesthetics into another realm; the unity of absolute innocence and absolute guilt depends on its being determined no longer aesthetically but metaphysically. This is the reason we are always afraid to call Christ's life a tragedy; we feel it would be improper to use aesthetic factors of judgment here. The real motive for this is doubtless more profound: All the factors of aesthetic judgment are neutralized in this phenomenon. Aesthetics has the relative as its object. Tragic action is simultaneously suffering, tragic suffering is simultaneously action, but what is aesthetic lies in relativity. The identity between absolute action and absolute suffering surpasses the possibilities of aesthetics and falls into the metaphysical realm. This identity is in the life of Christ. His suffering is absolute because it is absolutely his act; his action is absolutely his suffering because it is absolute obedience. Consequently, tragedy requires a moment of guilt, but this guilt is not subjectively reflected and that is what makes this suffering so profound. Tragic guilt is much more than subjective guilt, it is hereditary guilt; but both hereditary guilt and hereditary sin are substantial determining factors, and it is this substantial nature that deepens the suffering. Sophocles' trilogy, *Oedipus Rex, Oedipus at Colonus,* and *Antigone,* admired through the ages, revolves in essence around this authentically tragic interest. Now, hereditary guilt has a central contradiction: It is simultaneously guilt and nonguilt. The guilty individual becomes guilty through piety, but this guilt acquired through piety has nonetheless every possible aesthetic amphibole. At this point one might be tempted to say that the Jewish people have produced the most profound tragic elements. Is it not said of Jehovah that he is a jealous God who visits the sins of the fathers on the children even unto the third or fourth generation? And reading the terrifying curses of the Old Testament, would one not easily find tragic material? Yet Judaism is much too ethically advanced and Jehovah's curses, terrible as they may be, are nonetheless legitimate punishments. The same was not true in Greece: Not only did the wrath of the Gods have no ethical character, but it was *aesthetically* ambiguous.

In Greek tragedy, for example, in *Philoctetes* which is in the strict sense a tragedy of suffering, we find a transition from suffering to grief. Here, however, objectivity still predominates to a great extent. The Greek hero still appears to be resting in his fate; this fate is unchangeable, and consequently, there is no more to be said about it. That is why his grief remains suffering. His grief makes its first appearance with this first doubt: Did such a thing *have* to happen to me, to *me?* Might it not have been different? Doubtless, Philoctetes presents us with a reflection that carries this contradiction that is brilliantly depicted and so true in human terms—the innermost contradiction of his grief—very far. But Philoctetes' reflection remains integrated with the objectivity that is the basis of everything. It does not go any deeper into itself, and when Philoctetes complains that no one knows his grief, this complaint is essentially Greek. It is extraordinarily true, but at the same time it reveals how far this grief is from a reflective grief that always desires to remain alone with itself and that seeks some new grief in its solitude.

True tragic suffering requires an element of guilt, true tragic grief an element of innocence; true tragic suffering requires a certain transparency, true tragic grief requires a certain opacity. I think this is the best way for me to express the dialectic of grief and suffering, the things separating and connecting them; I think I have rendered the dialectic inherent in tragic guilt the same way.

Since it is not in the spirit of our association to present complete works or more extensive and definitive reflections; since we are not inclined to construct a Tower of Babel that the living God, in the name of his justice, can destroy at any moment; since we are conscious that this confusion is produced itself without ceremony, and that we recognize that what is peculiar to all true human aspiration is that it is fragmentary (which is what specifically distinguishes it from the constancy of nature); that, in other respects, the richness of an individuality consists in its aptitude for a productivity that is fertile in a fragmentary way; that in laboriously perfecting its ideas, this individuality no more spoils its own pleasure in producing than the pleasure others take in receptivity, but rather lets the ideas spring up in sparks that are fleeting, a form containing infinitely more for both creator and re-creator than any detailed elaboration, for the creator because it is the expression of the idea, for the re-creator because it encourages his own production; since that, as I have said, is not in the spirit of our association and since this periodic sentence that I am reading to you could easily be considered detrimental to the interjectory style, where the idea surfaces without, however, emerging—the style in use in our community; I call your attention to the fact that my way of proceeding could not be seen as unorthodox, the connection unifying this periodic sentence being so loose that the contradictions it contains aspire unmanageably enough to an aphoristic independence so that consequently my style has only sought to make itself appear to be—something it is not—revolutionary.

Since our association aims at rejuvenation and rebirth in each of our meetings, to this end it requires that the sense of its action be manifested by symbols that are always new. Let us then define today our leanings as the attempt of fragmentary aspirations in the art of composing posthumous works. A fully developed work does not permit us any relationship with the personality that produced it; on the other hand, posthumous writings, because of their abrupt, desultory character, awake in us the need to collaborate with the poet's personality. Posthumous works are ruins, and ruins present a residence that is obviously appropriate for those who are dead to the world. We, who are also dead to the world, must practice the art of giving a posthumous character to what we are creating; art that consists in imitating a slovenly style, a carefree accidental style moving in anacoluthons; art that consists in obtaining a pleasure that will never be *present* but will always contain an element of the past; a pleasure that, consequently, will not enter consciousness except as something past, as the term "posthumous" suggests. In a certain sense, everything a poet has produced is posthumous; but no one would think to call a work that is brought to perfection posthumous, even if it had not been published during the author's lifetime. Now, according to our ideas, is that not what is remarkable about all typically human production—that it is posthumous because it has not been granted to human beings to live like the gods in a contemplation outside of time. So I shall call what is produced within our circle "posthumous," artificially posthumous; I shall call the quality of genius by which we recognize the highest rank "posthumous indolence"; and *vis inertiae*, the natural law we venerate. Having said this, I think I have met the expectations of our sacred habits and customs.

And now, my dear Συμπαρανεκρώμενοι, come close, circle around me as I send my tragic heroine all over the world, giving this daughter of suffering grief for her dowry. She is my work, and yet her contour is so imprecise, her features so nebulous, that each of you will be able to fall in love with her and love her in your own way. She is a creature of my mind, her thoughts are mine. And yet, during a night of lovemaking, while I rested beside her, did she not confide her most secret thoughts to me, breathing them under my embrace, her whole soul ready to be transformed that very instant and disappear from sight, so that it was only in the condition in which she left me that I felt her reality; whereas, on the contrary, born of my condition then, she should have grown and increased in a more and more substantial reality? I am the one to inspire her words, and yet did I not take advantage of her trust? Is she not standing behind me? Does she not look at me reproachfully? Yet what happens is the opposite: It is, in fact, in her mystery that she becomes clear. She is my possession, she is legally mine and yet sometimes I feel the need to go back to her, despite the fact that she is before me and exists only to the extent that I produce her before you. Antigone is her name, a name that I shall keep, like the body of ancient tragedy, even though everything in it appears in a contemporary light. I have good reasons for deliberately choosing a feminine figure, especially because the feminine figure most clearly displays this difference I want to demonstrate. As a woman, my Antigone has enough substantiality, and as a human being, who belongs to a reflective world, enough reflection to experience suffering and grief. In order for suffering to come alive in her, tragic guilt must waver between guilt and innocence, and the consciousness of guilt must constantly be mediated by some substantial determining factor. But for tragic guilt to take on this character of uncertainty, there must be no infinitely manifested reflection. This, in fact, would risk reflecting its subject somewhere outside of guilt because, in its infinite subjectivity, it would not let the element of hereditary guilt that determines suffering survive. Now, since the awakening of reflection could not be prevented, this reflection, once awakened, will reflect its subject not outside of suffering but within it, and will at every instant transform suffering into grief.

The race of Labdacus is exposed to the wrath of the gods. Oedipus has killed the Sphinx and liberated Thebes; Oedipus has killed his father and married his mother, and Antigone is the fruit of this union. These are the contents of the Greek tragedy. This then is where I permit myself a slight divergence: I let everything stay the same and yet I change everything. Oedipus has killed the Sphinx and liberated Thebes, everybody knows that part; and at the present, venerated and admired, he is living happily married to Jocasta. As for the horror hidden beneath this tranquillity, no one is aware of it, except just one person: Antigone. How could she have learned it? That is unimportant from the point of view of tragedy. Once, earlier, before reaching maturity, her heart was warned by dark signs of some terrible secret until finally the stunning certainty drove her to profound anxiety. And I consider this deep anxiety one of the elements defining modern tragedy. In fact, anxiety is reflection and in that way is essentially different from suffering. Anxiety is the organ through which the subject appropriates and assimilates suffering for himself. Anxiety is the energy of the movement with which suffering enters the heart. This movement is not swift, though, like an arrow's; it is successive: It is not completed all at once but is constantly stopping. Just as erotic passion attracts its object by lustful looks, deep anxiety focuses on suffering in order to attract it. As a faithful and persevering love wraps the beloved object in its web, so does anxiety relentlessly attend to suffering. But anxiety simultaneously loves and fears its object, and consequently, it is even more tenacious than love. Anxiety acts in two ways. It lurks around its object, touches it all over and finds suffering that way, or else, at some particular moment, it creates suffering as an object for itself; but it does this in such a way that even this moment is instantly reduced to a successive movement.

Understood in this manner, deep anxiety is one factor authentically determining the tragic and the old saying *quem deus vult perdere, primum dementat* is here only too true. Anxiety is also a determining attribute of reflection: We feel deep anxiety when *faced with something*, hence, we separate anxiety from its object and we add this object to ourselves in anxiety. Moreover, anxiety implies a reflection of time; I cannot be made anxious by something present, but only by something past or future. The thing that is present is the only thing able to immediately determine the individual; the past or future can do so only by reflection. Hellenic suffering, however, like all of Hellenic existence, is completely and entirely present; this is why suffering in it is profound, grief less so. Anxiety is thus an essential element of tragedy.[*] Hamlet is tragic because he apprehends his mother's crime. Robert le Diable wonders how he happens to commit so much evil. Högni, the Troll's son, sees his reflection in the water and wonders why he deserves such a face.

And so the difference between the ancient and the modern becomes readily apparent. In Sophocles' tragedy Antigone is not haunted in the least by her father's wretched fate. Like an opaque and impenetrable suffering, this fate hangs over their heads; the whole family feels its weight. Antigone's life is as carefree as any other young Greek girl's, and the chorus, as if it disregarded this unfortunate birthright of the family, pities her because she must die so young without having tasted the greatest delight of life. It would be a mistake to take this as thoughtlessness, and it would be absolutely wrong to draw the conclusion that the individual is here isolated in his egoism, with no concern for his relation to his race. What must be remembered here is that, for the Greek, the conditions of existence are granted once and for all, just like the sky beneath which he dwells. Dark and cloudy this sky may be, but it is immutable. It sets the fundamental key for the soul, on a note of suffering and not of grief. For Antigone the tragic guilt is concentrated in one specific act: She buried her brother despite the king's forbidding it. If, then, this is considered as an isolated event, as a conflict between a deeply pious, sororal love and the human, arbitrary nature of the royal interdiction, Antigone is no longer a Greek tragedy but a tragic theme that is absolutely modern. Tragic interest, in the Greek and Sophoclean sense, lies in the fact that the brother's unfortunate death and the sister's situation reflect the sad fate of Oedipus: His tragic destiny has ramifications for each of the family's progeny.

This totality is what makes the spectator's suffering so profound. It is not an isolated individual who perishes but a little universe in its entirety. Suffering as a natural force is turned loose; from this moment it is borne along by the weight of its own consequences, and in Antigone's sad fate is echoed her father's fate, manifested as potentialized suffering. When, despite the king's command, Antigone decides to bury her brother, what we see is less a free initiative than necessity heavy with fate visiting the fathers' crime upon their children. There is, without a doubt, enough freedom in her action for us to like Antigone's sororal piety; but in each new blow that will strike not only Oedipus but his whole race, we hear a rhymelike repetition of the necessity of *fatum*.

The Sophoclean Antigone has a carefree existence; had she not collided with the king's will she might even have led a happy life. In contrast, our Antigone is done with life. I would go so far as to say that I have not given her a weak constitution: It is said that the right word at the right moment is like a golden apple under a silver skin. So I put the fruit of suffering inside a skin of grief. Her

---

[*]That is, modern tragedy.

dowry is no ephemeral glory, it is nothing that moths and rust can eat away; it is an eternal treasure that runs no risk of being stolen by thieves; she herself keeps it under close surveillance. Her life does not turn out like that of the Greek Antigone; its movement is completely interior, inside her very self, the setting is spiritual. I do not know, my friends, whether I have succeeded in interesting you in this young girl. A little *captatio* might not be completely superfluous. You see, she too does not belong to the world in which she exists; her life properly speaking, no matter how healthy and wholesome, takes place in secret. She too, though she lingers among the living, in a certain sense is absent from this world. Her days flow by in silence, and not a single moan is heard by the world; it is in the depths of her soul that she moans. There is no need to remind you that she is not at all a weak and sickly woman but one who is proud and forceful. The human being whose heart hides a secret, is, as it were, ennobled by it, and no doubt is as ennobling as a secret. Life takes on a meaning that, however, it has only for this person who is thus freed from any superficial attention to the outside world: This self-sufficient being rests serenely in his secret, which is nevertheless the most wretched of secrets. This is our Antigone. She is proud of her secret, proud of having been chosen by remarkable means to save the glory and honor of her race; and when the grateful people acclaim Oedipus, she feels her own significance. The secret goes deeper in her soul, so deep that no longer would a living person be able to reach it. Then she feels the weight of everything put into her hands, and that is what gives her the stature of a tragic character. For she must be interesting to us as an isolated character. More than a simple young girl, nonetheless she is still a young girl; she is betrothed, yet completely virginal and pure. As a fiancée, woman has achieved her specific purpose, and that is why a woman generally can only be interesting to the extent that she is given some specific relationship to this purpose. We have analogies for this. It can be said of a woman that she is betrothed to God; she puts her confidence in what is contained in her faith and in her spirit. I might, perhaps, say of our Antigone that she is betrothed in a finer sense of the word. And she is even more: She is mother, she is, from a purely æsthetic point of view, *virgo mater*; she carries her secret beneath her heart and no one suspects.

She is completely engrossed in silence; her secret forces her back again and again into her deepest self, and that is what gives her bearing an element of the supernatural. She is proud, she is jealously possessive with her suffering, for her suffering is her love. And yet this suffering is not a dead, motionless possession: It never stops moving, it gives birth to grief, it is delivered in grief. When a young girl decides to sacrifice her life to an idea, when she takes her place in existence wearing a crown of sacrifice on her brow, she is like a fiancée; in fact, the great idea that excites her transforms her, and the sacrificial crown becomes the crown of betrothal. She knows no man, yet she is betrothed; she does not even know the idea that excites her—that would not be feminine—yet she is betrothed.

Our Antigone is, thus, betrothed to suffering. She sanctifies her life and consecrates it to suffering for her father's fate, for her own fate. Misfortune like her
father's clamors for suffering, yet no one can suffer for this misfortune because
no one knows anything about it. And just as Sophocles' Antigone cannot bear
that her brother's remains not be given the last tribute, it would be unbearable for
our Antigone to have what causes her anguish remain ignored and unmourned.
And she is quite ready to give thanks to the gods because, at least, it weighs
heavily on her. Antigone, thus, is great in her grief. Here again I can point out a
difference between the ancient and the modern. Philoctetes laments the fact that
no one knows how much he suffers; that is specifically Greek and answers to a
deep human need: The others must learn what he has to bear. That is a need unknown to reflective grief. Antigone is incapable of wanting anyone to know she
suffers; on the other hand she thinks it justified that her father's crimes be known
by someone who suffers because of knowing them: Aesthetic justice requires that
punishment intervene where a crime has occurred. In Greek tragedy Antigone's
suffering bursts forth only at the moment in which she learns that she is going to
be buried alive:

> O unfortunate that I am!
> Rejected by the living
> I shall importune the dead.

Our Antigone, on the other hand, could say as much for her entire existence.
The difference is obvious. For the Greek Antigone there is a factual truth in these
words that attenuate suffering. If our Antigone spoke the same words, they
would have to be understood in a figurative sense, and it is precisely the fact that
she can only say it in a figurative sense that forms her particular grief. The
Greeks do not express themselves indirectly because the reflection necessary to
such expression is not part of their existence. Consequently, when Philoctetes
bemoans the fact of living alone and abandoned on a desert isle, he is expressing
an external truth. When our Antigone, in her solitude, experiences her grief, she
is alone only in a figurative sense and that is what makes her grief real.

As far as tragic guilt is concerned, on the one hand, it lies in the fact that she
buries her brother despite being forbidden to do so and, on the other hand, in her
fate's relation to the grievous destiny of her father, which we know by the two
previous tragedies. Let us now go back to the peculiar dialectic that relates the
guilt of a race to the individual. It resides in the fact of heredity. In general, dialectic is seen as relatively abstract, as a logical movement; life teaches us, however, that there are numerous dialectics and that almost every passion has its own
specific dialectic. The dialectic placing the guilt of race or family in relation to
the isolated subject, so that the latter not only suffers the consequences of guilt
(that is a purely natural and insurmountable result) but also shares the guilt itself
and participates in it, is a dialectic that has become foreign and without obliga-

tion for us. Consequently, to resurrect ancient tragedy would be impossible unless each individual were born again, not merely spiritually, but socially, from the maternal bosom of the family and the race. The dialectic placing the individual in relation to the family and the race is not a subjective dialectic for precisely the latter only suppresses the relation, removing the individual from the group; the dialectic establishing the bond is, on the contrary, completely objective, it is essentially piety. This is something the individual can sustain without being harmed by it. These days we customarily rate as a natural condition whatever we do not want to accept as a spiritual condition. We do not want to be isolated, however, to be so much opposed to nature that we do not acknowledge the family as a whole where one member cannot suffer without all the others suffering with him. Why does nearly everyone fear that some member of the family might cover him with shame, unless it is because he feels he would have to suffer for it himself. Now, like it or not, the individual *has* to agree to this suffering. But because we are taking the individual, not the familial, point of view, this constraint only emphasizes the suffering. We sense that man cannot make himself the absolute master of natural conditions, yet we still hope he will succeed as far as possible. On the other hand, if the individual recognizes his natural determination as an element of his essential truth, this natural relation is transmuted into a spiritual condition. The individual then feels himself guilty along with the family; he participates in the familial guilt. That is a result that is inconceivable for many, and consequently, they are unable to conceive of what it is that constitutes tragedy. Either the individual is isolated, that is to say, absolutely the creator of his own fate, in which case tragedy disappears and is replaced by evil (the fact that a blinded individual gets lost inside himself is not tragic either, because he does it deliberately); or else isolated individuals are only pure modifications of the eternal substance of being-there; and that is not tragedy either.

Now, if the ancient is absorbed by the modern, the conditions for the manifestation of tragic guilt also change. The Greek Antigone participates in the father's guilt with all her filial piety, and so does the modern Antigone. But for Sophocles' Antigone the father's guilt and suffering are an external fact, an unsurmountable fact that does not affect her suffering (*quod non volvit in pectore*), and, insofar as subjected to the natural consequences of things, she does suffer from the father's guilt, she still is concerned only with an objective reality. This is not the case with our Antigone. I am assuming that Oedipus is dead. During his lifetime she knew his secret without ever being brave enough to confide in her father. Upon the death of Oedipus, the sole possibility for freeing herself from his secret disappears. From then on to confide in a living person would be to cover the memory of her father in shame, and thus his life takes on a sacred meaning because every day, at every moment, she is paying her last respects. Besides, there is something she has been unable to determine: Did her father himself know? There again we find a modern element. This uncertainty makes her suffering anxious, gives her grief an ambiguous nature. She loves her father with all her heart, and this love, emerging from her self, places her inside the father's guilt. Moreover, she feels herself a stranger among human beings; the more she loves the father, the more she experiences his guilt, and it is only beside him that she can find peace. Companions in guilt, together they bear the suffering. But as long as her father lived she could not confide her suffering in him. Would she not have risked plunging him into an abyss of grief like her own? Yet, if he was unaware of it, his guilt would be less as a result. Note the extent to which everything is relative here. If Antigone did not know precisely how the events were linked, she would lose her importance; she then would have to struggle only with an apprehension which would not be tragic enough to interest us. But she knows everything, and the sort of uncertainty that this knowledge conceals serves only to keep her suffering alive and continually transform it into grief. Moreover, she exists in a constant state of tension with those around her. Oedipus continues to exist in his people's memory as a worthy, honored, and happy king. Antigone herself admires her father as much as she loves him. She participates in every demonstration of joy and praise devoted to him; in all the kingdom there is no other young woman so full of enthusiasm for her father. Her thoughts constantly turn to him, and the entire country sees her as the model of an affectionate daughter; and yet, for her this enthusiasm is the only way to give vent to her grief. Her father does occupy her thoughts constantly, but in what way? That is her grievous secret. She dare not abandon herself to grief and melancholy: She is too aware of all the things depending on her; she is afraid that the sight of her suffering would give away her secret. And this is yet another reason why her suffering must forever turn into grief.

When she is developed in this manner, Antigone certainly merits our interest, and I do not have to reproach myself for fickleness or for having a fatherly lover's soft spot if I dare think that she could no doubt make an attempt at the tragic genre and take part in a tragedy. But for the moment she is only an epic character, and what is tragic about her is interesting only in epic terms.

Imagining a plot in which she might appear is certainly not too difficult: We only have to stick with the motives provided by the Greek tragedy. For example, she might have an older sister who is married, or the mother might still be alive; either of these would remain secondary characters. It is clear that our tragedy like that of Sophocles, contains some epic element; and even though it is unnecessary to emphasize this element, soliloquy, sustained by situation, will play an important part. For everything in the tragedy must be concentrated on the main concern filling Antigone's life; and then the question arises: How will these basic ideas produce dramatic interest?

Our heroine, as she appears in the preceding, is about to skip rapidly over one stage in her life: She wants to open up into a life that is entirely spiritual, which nature opposes. A woman who is endowed with such depth of soul must necessarily love with extraordinary passion. That is where dramatic interest is introduced, and where the tragic clash is produced. Antigone is in love, and sad to say, she is mortally in love. Perhaps we had better qualify our use of the notion of tragic clash. The stronger and deeper the affinity between the conflicting forces, the greater the collision; the more similar the forces, the greater this clash. My Antigone, hence, is in love and the man she loves suspects as much. Because she is unusual she has an unusual dowry: her grief. Without this dowry she would be incapable of belonging to a man; that would seem risky to her. She would be incapable of hiding it from him because the eyes of a lover see too well; she would be incapable of hiding it from him because that would be breaking the rules of her love. But to belong to him with this dowry? If only she could confide her secret in a living person, would this living person be her beloved? Antigone is strong enough to bear her grief alone. The question is not to know whether she must communicate it for her own sake, to ease her heart. If she does it she does it for love of her beloved, and even then she does not cease to suffer. Her existence is too deeply rooted in her secret. But is she able to take responsibility for this with respect to the dead? Therein lies the question. From this point of view the clash is one of feelings. Her life, which up to this point has passed tranquilly and in silence, now becomes troubled and impassioned. Naturally the disturbance is completely interior; her response takes on more and more pathos. She is struggling with herself; she wanted to sacrifice her life to her secret, and now she is enjoined to sacrifice her love. She wins, that is to say, her secret wins, whereas she succumbs. And then the other clash is produced: In order for the tragic clash to be truly profound, the forces that collide must be identical. In the preceding clash, that was not the case; we saw there her love for the father opposed to love for herself. The question is whether the sacrifice of her self-love will be too much for her. The other colliding force is her loving affinity with the beloved. He knows he is loved, so he is daring in his courtship. Her reserve doubtless appears strange to him: He suspects there are rather special problems, which he, nonetheless, hopes to surmount. What is important to him is to convince her that he loves her more than anything in the world, that he could not live if he had to renounce her love. The obstacle only adds to his passion, which becomes so fantastic that it ends up seeming unreal. Each pledge he makes increases Antigone's grief, each of his sighs sinks the arrow of suffering deeper into her heart. He recoils before no method of conquering her. Like everyone else, he knows how deeply she loves her father. He meets her at the tomb of Oedipus, where she had sought refuge. There she wants to abandon herself to the remembrance of her father, in a nostalgia that is doubtless mixed with grief because she does not know how to invoke him, because she does not know if he was aware of his guilt. And so it is there that the beloved surprises her. He beseeches her, for the sake of the love with which she embraces her father's shade. He feels that in this way too he is having an extraordinary effect on her. He exploits this, putting his hopes completely in this method, not in the least suspecting that he is working—against himself.

From this point on what is important is to decide how, in order to conclude, her secret will be stolen from her. It would be vain to have her fall into passing madness, letting her betray herself in that condition. Moreover, the colliding forces are so completely paralyzed that action becomes impossible for the tragic individual. Antigone's grief has been emphasized by her love, by her suffering in sympathy with the beloved. She will find peace only in death: Her life is so totally devoted to suffering that she wants to set a limit to the misfortune that, pregnant with fate, would be reproduced in the next generation. She wants to contain this misfortune. It is only at the instant of death that she is able to admit the fervor of her love, that she is able to belong to the one to whom, in that same instant, she no longer belongs.

When Epaminondas was wounded at the battle of Mantiniea, he left the arrow in his wound until he had learned that the battle was won because he knew that he would die as soon as he pulled it out. In the same way our Antigone bears her secret within her heart, and life plunges the secret like an arrow, deeper and deeper, without depriving her of life; as long as the arrow remains in her heart she can live; as soon as she removes it she dies. The beloved must struggle to draw her secret out of her, and when he is triumphant he kills her. Yet, who is it that has killed her? The living or the dead? The dead in a certain sense. To the extent that it is the memory of her father that kills her, the prediction made to Hercules, when he was told that he would be slain not by the living but by the dead, can apply equally to Antigone. In another sense it is the living: His unfortunate love makes it possible for the memory to kill her.

1938-39

The Structure of Democracies
Georges Bataille
Tuesday, December 13, 1938

*[The program for this second year has been reconstructed following the an-
nouncements that Jean Guérin so hospitably included in the NRF. We see that it
is rather late, at the threshold of winter, when the College recommences its activities. Ever since the beginning of the summer and the Czechoslovakian crisis,
current events had left very little space or time for thoughts. Munich took place
in September. October and November are full of accusatory sound and fury unleashed by these agreements. Reading the report of this meeting made by
Bertrand d'Astorg, we see that the current context was also the subject of this
lecture, a lecture that was consequently more politically engaged than any in the
preceding year had been. We have reason to assume that the great majority of
listeners could call to mind the "Declaration on the International Crisis" signed
by the College, which the NRF and two other reviews had published the month
before.*

*Should we say what happened to these people? On November 7, 1938, Laure
died. Bataille and Leiris are soon to publish two short volumes of her notes,* Le
Sacré *in 1939,* Histoire d'une petite fille *in 1943. In volume 5 of Bataille's*
Oeuvres Complètes, *in connection with* Le Coupable *(pp. 505ff.) there are some
posthumous pages, written a year later (during the phony war), that recount her
dying—the final moments of which Leiris also described in* Fourbis. *Bataille, in
the house he shared with Laure, was engaged in writing the article entitled "The
Sacred" (commissioned by Duthuit for the issue of* Cahiers d'art *that he was in
charge of) when death arrived to cut off communication with his companion.*

Later, in an autobiographical note, in the third person, he confides: "A death tore him apart in 1938."

No text by Bataille has been found with democracy as its subject. But a letter addressed by him to Paulhan on January 6, several weeks after the lecture, informs us that he was busy writing a book about this (even giving the impression that it was nearly completed) and that its central aim was to relate the "carnival spirit" to the "blind beliefs of the democratic world." In his article, d'Astorg makes no allusion at all to the first point. So it is possible that Bataille made the connection that he mentions in the letter to Paulhan, between carnival and democracy, only when he began to develop his initial theses with a book in mind. A "Commémoration de Mardi Gras" by Bataille, moreover, would be announced by the NRF *for the meeting on Tuesday, February 21.*

Given the preoccupations of the College, there is nothing surprising about the subject. The carnival theme is central to Frazer's works (and a number of Dumézil's) from which the College derived a great deal of its information. As for the winter and end-of-winter festivals described by Mauss and Granet, they too, in their own way, are a sort of "Mardi Gras." Carnival can be seen as the one sacred display that has survived in contemporary life, one of the rare moments in which social life escapes the prosaic and ordinary and opens up to metamorphosis. It is also the time of masks.

It is possible that "The Mask," published at the end of the second volume of the Oeuvres complètes, *is related to what Bataille discussed in one of these two lectures. "The mask," he writes, "is chaos become flesh." "Norms and rules, laws of social existence or of nature bring neither god nor mask into subjection. Violence, animality, and antisocial behavior in these* sacred *figures are as important as the goodness or the intellectual nature of a God who stands behind morality and reason." "A mask suffices to cast* Homo sapiens *back into a world he knows nothing about because it is like the timing of weather with its violent, unpredictable changes. This time brings the everlasting old man into the endlessly recurring chaos of its night. He is incarnated in man the lover, young and* masked. *Torrential existence sends* Homo sapiens *back to the platitude of scholarly treatises:* Homo tragicus *rages alone to the sound of the annihilation and mortal destruction of a* history *about which nothing is known because all that is knowable of it is a past buried forever, forever vain."*

While there is nothing unexpected about Bataille's interest in the carnival (even in its contemporary guise as Mardi Gras), the connection that he establishes between carnival and democracy might seem to be more surprising. But Caillois had already advanced the idea of the popular and antiaristocratic nature of the Dionysiac feasts in ancient Greece ("Les Vertus dionysiaques," Acéphale, *July 1937). He will make this carnival version of democracy echo again in his "Théorie de la fête," in which he connects the excesses of Saturnalia with sacrilegious transgressions set off by the death of the king (see*

"Festival," May 2, 1939). We may perhaps have to look for the slogan for the democracy proposed by Bataille in some pages, contemporary with this lecture, in which he describes the Mexican carnival. It would then boil down to the imperative: "Don't die like Louis XIV. DIE LIKE A DOG" ("Calaveras," OC, vol. 2, p. 408).

The lecture discussing power that Bataille delivered in Caillois's place, the preceding February 19, identified plurality—and hence the conflict—of the parties (that is to say, democracy) with the "overall movement that in my opinion constitutes social life." And although this "political agitation" seems precarious to him and "for all that, almost completely deceptive," this identification made him condemn fascism for its "repression" of this agitation. Even earlier, Bataille, in "Propositions sur le fascisme" (Acéphale, January 1937), had denounced the unitarian repression of this overall movement. He specified, however, that "protest against unitarianism does not necessarily occur in a democratic sense" (OC, vol. 1, p. 468). He writes: "The only lively and powerful society, the only free society is the bi- or polycephalic *society"—a phrase in which Denis de Rougemont can see the embryo of a federalist pluralism.*

The use of a mask is an initial version of two-headedness. Through this, the blind beliefs of the democratic world (not to be confused with the utilitarian rationalism of the bourgeoisie!) and its antimonarchical Dionysianism are linked in part to the world of the carnival.

In his report, d'Astorg mentions that it was difficult in the discussion to identify the position of the various participants. How was one to distinguish the "perfidious antidemocrats" from the defenders of an "ideal democracy"? Or those who condemned in Munich the perfect example of democratic rule from those who condemned the Munich accords, on the contrary, for the betrayal of democratic requirements? In any case, it is likely that this hesitation did not apply to Benda, who made himself heard that evening (although in 1935 he happened to publish in the NRF *a particularly chivalrous review of Drieu's* Socialisme fasciste*). And, in Benda's view, it would certainly seem also that it did not apply to the organizers of the meeting: When he alluded to this debate in* La Grande Épreuve des démocraties *(New York, 1942), he did not hesitate to characterize unabashedly the members of the College as "Pedants, hostile to democracy moreover" (see the Appendixes: "Marginalia").*

Another member of the audience would point out that the Nazi state "claims that it is conceived by the people in a different way than is ours." This paradox did not strain the dialectic resources of the time. It is not impossible, moreover, to suggest whose voice this was. When war was declared in September 1939, Paulhan would, in fact, publish in his NRF *a "Retour sur 1914." He recalls there that "Hitler is the elected president of a democracy" and that, what is more, "he has been elected on the platform he now is applying" (Paulhan, Oeuvres, vol. 5, p. 283). In March 1939 (Bataille's lecture on democracy was given in December and Paulhan himself would address the College in May), he would publish, also in the* NRF, *"La Démocratie fait appel au premier venu," (Democracy calls on everyone). It is the eulogy, parodoxical as expected, of a democracy invented, he says, "against sociologists, against realistic politicians, and even against unanimism." Defending it, thus, is first of all protecting it against "any aristocracy of knowledge, of the mind, of eloquence." From this follows the condemnation of the present regime, officially a democracy but in fact an aristocracy: "With us it all takes place between princes" ("princes of the mind" he means, obviously). But who is this "everyone," this "first comer," this "no matter who," this "man of the streets" that he opposes to them. What should he be called? how "designated"? The article ends with: "One would do" (Oeuvres, vol. 5, p. 281). This plain unitarianism would be quelled in monarchism in a letter to Drieu: "The only healthy idea of democracy," Paulhan writes to his successor at the* NRF, *"namely, that one must trust anyone, leads straight to the king who, precisely, is this anyone, chosen not for his visionary characteristics, but simply for the accident of his birth." In a note he adds: "Moreover, that is what makes me an anglophile" (quoted by D. Desanti,* Drieu la Rochelle ou le séducteur mystifié *[Paris, 1978], p. 371). This little account reports that Paulhan, in June 1936, was elected municipal councillor in Châtenay-Malabry (the commune of the southern suburb where he was living), on the ballot with the Popular Front—but with no party affiliation mentioned, which did not prevent his having a reputation as a Maurrassian and even, it is said, a correspondence with Maurras.*

In a letter to Étiemble that is also dated March 1939, Paulhan backs up his political views with a quote from one of his favorite authors, Chesterton: "Hereditary despotism," Chesterton wrote, "is in essence democratic. Though it does not proclaim that all men are able to govern, it proclaims the next most democratic thing, which is that anyone at all, no matter who, *is able to govern" (J. Kohn-Étiemble,* 226 lettres inédites de Jean Paulhan *[Paris, 1975], p. 183). At that time Étiemble is in America. He brings back from a trip to Mexico some invigorating paragraphs stimulated by climbing the pyramid of Tehotihuacan. Paulhan (who would publish them in the* NRF) *begins his letter by connecting his own political fantasies to his correspondent's Mexican reveries. "All my political preferences would go to an absolute monarch chosen on January first by lottery and to be executed December 31. If this solution is ever allowed (actually it simply revives certain customs of the Roman soldiers during* Saturnalia), *we should remember—and why not realize—your ideas about the utility of stepped pyramids." It is more than likely that this mention of Saturnalia refers to the lecture (lectures, if he gave several) that Bataille delivered on the relations between democracy and carnival. We know that Bataille himself, without ever having been to Mexico, did not fail to meditate on the sacrificial use of the Aztec pyramids. In his lecture on power, he cited Frazer's interpretation, where the priest of Nemi, Dianus, was seen as a royal figure. This character was to become essential to his own mythology. He would embody a figure of ephemeral, mortal sovereignty, similar to the one jokingly mentioned by Paulhan in this letter.*

Caillois too would defend the argument according to which fascism would be a scarcely divergent extension of democratic principles. He formulates this in "La Hiérarchie des êtres," published in April 1939, in a special issue of Les Volontaires *entitled "Le Fascisme contre l'esprit." Unlike Paulhan, he does not bring up the power of words and princes of the mind. He starts with the egalitarianism that he sees at the basis of the two political regimes. From this point of view fascism can be considered "as a pathological variety, a sort of perversion of democracy." Caillois contrasts with both regimes another whose fundamental principle would be inequality and which would develop in a hierarchical order: "It is precisely this principle of equal rights, common to all as democracy would have it, restricted as fascism demands, which irrevocably throws out the idea of* order *or of elective community." Readers of this article will probably be astonished to see that when Caillois speaks of order and of elective community, he is thinking of communism, a communism that he advises, however, not to delay in ending a marriage of convenience with democracy where it is foolishly wasting the youth of its brilliant powers.*

Having said this, Caillois was not always opposed to the restricted equality by which he characterized fascism. This defines, for example, the internal relations of the aristocracy of knowledge and mind that he would propose from Buenos Aires in 1940 as an alternative to democracy and fascism. In contrast to Paulhan's position, Caillois's politics set great store by princes of the mind. And, as he makes clear in his "Sociologie du clerc," he sees (contrary to Benda) in the clerisy an eminently political institution. "Generally it is important, it seems to me, to lean in the direction of an organization that gives power in every instance to intellectual competence and moral qualification, that does not easily accept that these must bow to a majority opinion and even less that they rely on the quasi-unanimity of an intoxicated or terrorized mass. May I be permitted the momentary dream of a utopia? I would want each leader solely responsible to his peers who are gathered in a college, he would take his place in their midst only as the first among equals." "Défense de la République," Circonstancielles (1940-1945) *(Paris, 1946).*

The report that follows, which we give in place of Bataille's lecture, was published by Bertrand d'Astorg in issue 5 of Les Nouvelles Lettres *(the same review had published, in August 1938, Klossowski's translation of Kierkegaard's* Antigone, *read and discussed by him before the College in May).]*

At the College of Sociology
Bertrand d'Astorg

Tuesday, December 13, at the College of Sociology, Georges Bataille presented a paper on the September crisis and the structure of democracies. Within this structure, the lecturer distinguished between the "sacred" realm (whose discussion is forbidden), constituted in his view by the integrity of national territory, and the "realm of discussion" in which equivalence and potential exchange are at play—in short, what we might be tempted to call the realm of bargaining. The arguments put forth by the partisans of resistance—the fate of democracies, respect for one's word, and Germany's access to a hegemonic position in Europe—applied to the latter. On the other hand, in the eyes of democrats, the founding principle that governs this "realm of discussion" is specifically: "The principle of discussion is indisputable." And Germany, by playing on grounds divergent from this principle, won the match. It brought the democracies face to face with a sequence of accomplished facts (in relation to which they were, a priori, defenseless) and emphasized that no territorial claims had been drawn up against France (thus situating France outside its sacred domain). Analyzing the atmosphere of passivity in which events developed, emphasizing particularly the ignominy of the radio programs, whose consequence was to be the voice proclaiming either war or peace, Bataille pessimistically pronounced a mortal crisis in which democracies would possibly perish. The ensuing discussion unexpectedly confirmed the crisis of the democracies, or, worse, the spiritual crisis of the democrats. Benda expressed his judgment that it was very unfortunate that the "sacred" had been reduced to territorial integrity, a secondary concern in his view, it seems. He would see the "sacred" lying more in the principle of discussion itself, in which human freedom, magically steered by reason, is expressed.[1] In the final analysis, Benda acknowledged, an act of faith in reason itself was necessary. It remains to be seen whether freedom of expression exhausts the essence of freedom. I, who am neither scholar nor journalist, do not believe it does. The other remarks managed to demonstrate, if this was necessary, the verbalism on which the principles of our democracies are founded. The strange thing was that one could not tell whether the speakers were perfidious antidemocrats or if they were defending a personal conception of an ideal democracy. Parliamentarianism, plebeianism, the right of nations, the bourgeoisie as the "class that is all talk," all these words banged around together sounding shrill and cracked, and new heights of confusion were attained when a spectator innocently asked if, indeed, Hitler had based his demands on one of the great principles and recalled that the Nazi state claims to be democratically conceived along popular lines that are different from ours.[2] But Bataille, whose pessimism must be approaching despair, and who seemed at first to agree with Benda's final recourse to reason, then said something that suddenly sounded both profound and right. The sociologist gave way to the lyric, a human sound arose. There are moments, said the speaker (and I am attempting to remember the substance of his thought on this serious matter), in which man, even when he no longer knows if there are essential values involved in the struggle, must accept being on intimate terms with suffering and death, without wishing to know in advance what reality will spring from it. For Benda, who has discovered no absolute other than reason, democracy's guide, such an attitude must seem an abdication. For us, it is an expansion. Man, finally relieved of the contradictions of a hesitant and usually poorly informed reason, finds himself one and whole within the absolute of his Truth, because on the level of heroism it can only be God's Truth. At this point, his sacrifice serves his country and, on top of it all, the interest of democracies if the democrats guarantee an internal adaptation of institutions that would also be centered on human beings' royal freedom. Democracy, by thus having recourse to the individual (and not to the citizen who is argumentative and a slave to a particular argument), can save itself. What seems particularly grave to me is that the September crisis marked the harmonious blossoming of democracy, as we know it today. If the people, in a terrifying spinelessness, on two successive days accepted first war then peace, if they first went to the frontiers and then cheered Daladier, *it is because not only territorial integrity but war itself is part of the sacred realm. It is simply the form taken by this integrity.* Through a vague notion of the mandate granted by the vote, the French people are so convinced that they are merged with the State and the State with the government, that they are ready as a result to accept any decision at all: war today, peace tomorrow, and, within the same legislature one government by the Popular Front and one by the National Union. This is the real human abdication, this obliteration of the person who expects a solution from someone other than himself. In reality, I am persuaded that, in Germany and Italy, the war provoked resistances that we would have been incapable of. It is significant on the other hand that the men who adopted a straightforward attitude of refusal in September were precisely the ones not contaminated by democratic beliefs: whether they were nationalist partisans represented by the Nietzschean Thierry Maulnier,[3] or revolutionaries (like Giono) who broke spiritually and physically with the civilization of the democratic federation. War would be excluded from the sacred domain if a League of Nations, a super-State, assumed the responsibility for it in the name of an international morality. But at the same time, this League of Nations would take on the responsibility for the defense of territorial integrity (see article 10 of the pact). Would democracy, emptied thus of its blood, of the "sacred" defined by Bataille, collapse? I think not, as long as it is specifically left to people to find within themselves an absolute that is neither political nor social, but personal, indivisible, for whose sake they are free and heroic. A country unable to rouse a hero to defend it, or better yet to cultivate it, is dead. But any system breaking the human will to heroism is criminal.

Letter from Georges Bataille to Jean Paulhan

January 6, 1939

Dear friend,

I am sending you an outline of the work I mentioned. Really a very abbreviated outline: The final paragraph actually corresponds to something developed alone in as much length as what precedes it, but, when expressed in a few sentences, what I want to say about the relation between the ''carnival spirit'' and democracies seems rather wild. What I want to do is come up with a small and very readable book, addressing anyone at all (and distinctly easier to follow than the lecture you heard). The outline would therefore give a false idea of what the manuscript will be if I stated, without explanation, that the beliefs of the democratic world can only develop the basic elements of the carnival (while nascent democracy began with police prohibition of this same carnival, in France from 1790 to 1798).

I am going to take two weeks of vacation to write this book, so it will certainly be finished by February 1.

I counted on coming to see you yesterday but was unable to.

Will it be soon enough if I bring you the declaration of the College of Sociology next Thursday? In any case, I shall have it on Tuesday evening at Gay-Lussac, if you are coming to hear Guastalla. Would you rather I sent it to you?

Sincerely,
Georges Bataille

Bataille's Notes

Morphology

Primacy of morphology supposes organic characteristics.
Simple position of questions.

1. Principle of composition

All beings are created from simpler elements that are distinct from each other.

Difference between interattraction and attraction by an individual:

Headless structure exists: cell.

Headed structure: plain in the bilaterally symmetrical animals.

Reservation about the head.
Passage from organism to society.

2. Distinction between federations equipped with heads and headless federations.

The tribe.
Principle of individuation.
Character of the American federation.

3. General value of the principle of individuation.

Society needs to be individuated.
Heterogeneous character of the individual.
Normal character of the monarchical structure in society.
Two aspects: decay of secondary cities; fragility of democracy.

4. Phenomena observed in individuation:

General links between a being and death

$$\text{Archaic} \begin{cases} \text{Execution of kings} \\ \\ \text{Sovereignty and castration} \end{cases}$$

Lasting nature in several forms:

Principle of division of society.
Polemic and aggressivity.
Birth of communities is a phenomenon of society's division.

Complexity resulting from the phenomenon of division:
heads, different levels, the same individual's belonging to several heads.

An aim just possibly desirable.

Complexity of strong structures.
This situation is the furthest from ours. Seen thus, there are two general possibilities.
reconstitution of a central and general structure;
reconstitution of elementary structures.

Morphology introduces continuum into the hiatus.

Taking into account to the greatest extent possible for me.

However, a point of view exists where the contents must be considered as simple availability—limitless. At a certain moment, the will to be, obviously, must not separate from being's complicity with death, that is to say, with nonbeing.

The Birth of Literature
René M. Guastalla

Tuesday, January 10,1939

[The Hellenist René M. Guastalla, an Italian by origin and a contributor to the Revue des études grecques, *was best known for his pedagogical publications, as the author of textbooks (*Les Textes grecs, La Vie antique*), and editor of selected passages (*Herodotus's Egypt *in 1939). The* Survey of French Literature, *published with Peter Sammartino (Longmans, Green, 1937), describes him as "Agrégé des Lettres, Professeur de Première Supérieure au Lycée Lakanal (Seine)." He left Marseille for the Paris region in 1935.*

His name appeared in 1939 in the table of contents of Mesures, *Paulhan's review, where he and Georges Blin signed a translation of selections from Philo's* Treatise on Divine Monarchy.

But Georges Blin, who knew him well (as Guastalla's pupil at the Lycée Saint-Charles in Marseille then as a student in Paris when Guastalla had an appointment at Sceaux and wrote to him in Paris), has trouble remembering any connection between Guastalla and the activities of the College. "If he was tangential to the College of Sociology, it was doubtless through Jules Monnerot and those of the editors at (Bergery's) La Flèche *who were not moving toward the right in 1937. I myself had lunch at Guastalla's with Émile Bergery and Montherlant around this time. . . . And I also attended sessions at the College of Sociology (I still have a colorful memory of a discussion about Death that was rowdy to say the least).[1] But I approached it from another angle (thanks to Caillois, who was then a student of Mauss and Jean Bayet), drawn there by the rue d'Ulm, but even before by the* Cahiers du Sud, *from my years in Marseilles. I think Guastalla died in Lyon of a heart attack brought on by tobacco (he even smoked in class) together with despair caused by economic circumstances as well as anti-Semitism.''*

Guastalla was a Jew. We learn in a roundabout way, through a letter from Paulhan to Caillois (see p. 378) that, at the end of 1941, rumor in Paris had it that his death was a suicide.

Guastalla was, in fact, one of the regular columnists for La Flèche, a weekly published by Bergery's Front Commun. On March 17, 1937, a pencil portrait of him appeared in the section "People to know," on the page with all the news pertaining to members of the Front. Other contributors to La Flèche, like Denis de Rougemont, would also intersect with activities of the College. Georges Blin's surprise seems no less justified when we recall the Front's resolute pacifism at the time. Bergery, a radical deputy who was the energy behind the party's left wing, had founded the "Front Commun contre le fascisme" (Common Front against Fascism) in 1933, just after Hitler's coming to power. But the course of events that, following the uprisings in February 1934, would end with the formation and then the victory of the Popular Front, was to relegate this earlier organization to an increasingly marginal position. Then when the experiment of the Popular Front came to an end the Common Front's line was extremely indecisive. The watchword for frontism was to protect oneself against foreign interference and to use effective facts to fight against the powers of money. The signatures to be found in La Flèche are extremely diverse, among them Robert Aron, Marcel Déat, Félicien Challaye, Georges Duveau, Daniel-Rops, Claude Mauriac, Emmanuel Berl, Henri Guillemin, François Perroux, and even André Gide. It accommodated heterogeneous anxieties and discontent; its main theme was the bad mood of those intellectuals of good will whose only real point in common was their opposition to war. Bergery (who, in 1940, was to be a leading figure in the collaborationist left) is the only deputy who voted against war on September 2, 1939.

La Flèche attacks in every way possible the bellicose bragging unleashed by the Munich crisis. Anti-Semitism (of which there is more and more in La Flèche) is not the only explanation for the insults that Galtier-Boissière addresses to Benda in the October 28, 1938, issue, in which he calls him an "irresponsible sadist destined to the whorehouse." "As for his young disciples," he adds, "they argue about war in the abstract." The members of the College could be said to be in this category, with their "Declaration on the International Crisis." Several weeks later, Robert Aron, who, with Bergery wrote the lead articles of the paper, published La Fin de l'après-guerre. In each issue of La Flèche a promotional campaign pushed the book: "1918-1938: l'après guerre. 1938-39 . . . : PEACE?" Guastalla himself would review Aron's work in his column on December 30.

It was the following month that Guastalla would give his lecture at the College, in which, it is true, the Hellenist speaks more loudly than the ideologist.

But this presentation implies no criticism whatsoever of the positions adopted during the events surrounding Munich. On May 26, 1939, for example (in an article on Guéhenno's Journal d'une révolution [1937-1938]*), he will return to the September crisis, recalling Hitler's speech which he listened to in the offices of* La Flèche, *with his comrades from the Front "at the height of the battle that we were fighting here for peace, and that we do not regret." A month later, on June 23, reviewing an anti-Munich book by Father Fessard, he expressed the same sentiments: "Obviously, we do not deny anything about our attitude at that time."*

The dominant theme in Guastalla's articles, however, is less pacifism than the refusal to fall into what Caillois called the "inclination toward war." The battle for peace was precisely in opposition to peacefully deserting in favor of war. Thus, on December 18, 1937, he reproaches the author of Les Hommes de bonne volonté *for his description of the approach of the First World War, in the fourteenth volume of his saga. "Jules Romains probably would not have relived so intensely this abandonment of all of Europe to evil inevitabilities, if he had written his book before 1936-1937." A year later (December 2, 1938), concerning a biography of Jaurès he wrote: "Right up to the bullet that killed him, Jaurès refused to believe in the inevitability of war, thus dictating our duty for us." Another note (March 24, 1939) about* La Fin et les moyens *by Huxley, whose brand of "non-resistant Buddhism is, perhaps, as we have frequently said in this journal, the supreme temptation of someone who reflects on the destiny of men and of the world, but it is also the temptation that a people must reject if it does not want to turn the victory over to evil forces."*

(It should also be recalled that on May 26, 1939, La Flèche *would publish Pierre Prévost's article on "The College of Sociology" [see Appendixes: Marginalia]. This is all the more remarkable because the paper did not usually remark on the activities of the intellectual avant-garde. Also, it should be mentioned that on June 16, 1939, Guastalla, with the unanimous agreement of those connected with the College would greet Dumézil's* Mythes et dieux des Germains *with the highest praise: "The author is a religious historian, and, indeed, he is describing the ancient Germanic peoples from before Charlemagne, before Christianity. But I dare say there is no book on contemporary Germany with a better analysis, none advances us further than this one.")*

*Guastalla's final contribution (*La Flèche *ceased to appear after war was declared), in July 1939, concerns a work devoted to Greece (*Harmonies de la Grèce, *by Jean-G. Tricot). A similar Greece is celebrated by Guastalla in* Le Mythe et le livre. Essai sur l'origine de la littérature, *whose publication date at Gallimard was January 28, 1940.*

*In a work that appeared two years earlier and was similarly entitled (*Le Mythe et l'homme*), Caillois had written: "It is precisely when myth loses its moral, constraining force that it becomes an object of aesthetic pleasure." Guastalla develops the same sort of opposition, except that he sets in contrast to* *ancient myths that are collective and anonymous, modern Europe's "literary myths," which, rather than being the work of any community are produced by an individual whose name, moreover, they often bear (Marxism, Hitlerism, etc.). But for Caillois as for Guastalla, literature is the object of a political condemnation: It arises in Greece out of the "divorce between the citizen and the city": "The Eastern scriptures are not literature; Rome received a tradition that was already literary from Greece; therefore, it is in Greece that literature was born." At the beginning of Greek literary history tragedy is still thoroughly mythical. Guastalla compares it to a "totemic feast" and the masked actor to an "Indian sorcerer or a Siberian medicine man." But at the other end of this history, literature rules supreme: "Substituted for the tradition of the city maintained by social cohesion is a tradition of culture maintained by literature." "The individual has become the center of the poem, and already the form of lyricism has begun to lead toward Horace. But also, the lyre is silenced. Paper that is written upon—and Callimachus is a librarian—here replaces the human voice."*

The work, as we shall see, is written in a style in which the reference to Greece is expressed in a rather good-natured manner, with an archaistic regionalism whose Dionysian aspects smell more of garlic than of fire. (Or, as he says in his review of Tricot, it has "the healthy smell of the stadium and coastal pines.") More Giono than Nietzsche. He describes a tragedy that is much more humanistic—much less tragic—than Caillois's or Bataille's version.

Groethuysen would publish a review of Le Mythe et le livre *in the May 1940 NRF. The following is an extract: "The novel, therefore, would be the 'countermyth,' and the novelist would usurp the functions of the city. While the 'natural myth is the most important thing in the city,' the novelist's fragile myth leans in the direction of dissociation." "Guastalla's essay is a valuable document for the crisis of liberal times. The concept of literature that Guastalla's critique presupposes is essentially 'liberal'; it is based on an availability of myths that does not involve deciding between these myths. But does not modern man, at the same time, seek the unique myth that would deprive him of his freedom? Does he not wish to leave literature in order to find the myth that would impose itself on everyone and unite him with his fellows? How can the two be reconciled? Guastalla's lucid and passionate critique, in any case, allows us better to see the problem."*

Queneau, as well, prepared a note about Guastalla's book, which he read when he was drafted, in March 1940: "Read the Guastalla. Memories: the college of sociology," he wrote in his Journal. *The note was supposed to appear in* Volontés, *but the war interrupted the publication of Pelorson's review. Queneau finally published it in 1973, at the end of his book,* Le Voyage en Grèce. *His remarks support Groethuysen's; like him he wonders about the validity of the concept of 'natural myth,' and concludes on the same note of inquiring approval.*

There are also some remarks of interest in the context of the College of Sociology: "If literature is discredited because it is more recent than myth, how much more discredited then must be Western science, which only dates from the sixteenth century, and historical science and sociology, a spring chicken barely fifty years old." "It must be understood that I see no objection to a reintegration of all of literature—but then all of science as well!—in poetry!"

One of the chapters of Le Mythe et le livre *bears the title announced for this lecture: "The Birth of Literature." That is what I am publishing here. But it could have been the subtitle of practically the entire work. Perhaps, like Queneau, we can consider many of his statements to be "commonplaces, ever since Nietzsche"—but that is no reason for them not to have been delivered before the College of Sociology.*

Guastalla's reply to Monnerot's inquiry on spiritual directors appears earlier in this volume.]

For the convenience of language up to this point we set man in opposition to the city. But it is entirely apparent that the latter does not exist without those who constitute it. And the opposition has no value except in the sense in which man, in the epoch of the city, feels himself a member of the social body as much as and more than he feels himself owner of the land, his tools, and even his very body. But, from this moment on, he is not always inside the city, nor even in those more restricted cities represented by tribe, deme, or family. Because of the formation of the Greek people, he has connections with other cities, and in his own city, connections with noncitizens.

It is self-evident then, that, for some persons, when conditions are favorable and force of circumstances loosens the social bond, this loosening may be felt not as troubling but rather as a liberation.

And it might have happened, even in the great Eastern theo-monarchies, that this sentiment made itself felt somewhere or other; in fact, one sees something like it in the speeches of Job's friends. But it is scarcely more than a sentiment.

On the contrary, the vitality of Greece was such, and the Hellene's desire to live, as well as his adaptive capacity, were such that here and here alone this sentiment became conscious thought, and militant thought. Perhaps, there have been people elsewhere who felt themselves to be individuals, but here there were people who willed themselves to be so.

Having once made this distinction—which is essential—the question, it seems, must be thought like this: Once, as far back in the past as we can go, there was a long period in which the most important thing for a person was to belong to a group, a period in which one did not leave one's social group—by marriage, slavery, or death—except to enter (or be thought of as entering) into another social group; this state of affairs was everywhere, except in Greece, stronger than the circumstances that arose to dissolve or distort one social group or another.

In contrast, there is a world, the one in which we live, where—no matter what the "romancers" of myth do—the individual exists, and where at the same time that he is bound to a group, the group does not preexist him, where it is the will (ideally and wholly free) that he has to belong to this group or rather to be a member of it that makes the group itself. At the moment of this writing one of the Nazi leaders makes the statement: "Anyone not a partisan of Adolf Hitler is not German." This demonstrates the impossibility, in the world of the individual, for the "romancers," even those making myth of people and blood, not to take individual membership into account! And only goes to show that today, despite ups and downs and the way things may seem for the moment, we inhabit the world of the individual!

We have seen how this world, whose particular expression—we must not forget—is literature is completely formed in the Hellenistic era, and in the classic era is not yet born.

But what do we mean when we say that it is not yet born in the fifth century, for example? Only this: It does not exist in the clear consciousness of most people, the great majority of them, and writers and orators speaking in the name of this majority are not yet conscious of its birth.

It remains to be seen whether there are the first perceptible symptoms of it. They are perceptible to us, without a doubt, because we know what all this will come to; but, and this is what is important, they are more and more clearly felt by those experiencing these symptoms, felt by the city as well, which rejects them because it does not want to die of them.

Pericles was the choragus of Sophocles and Anaxagoras's friend, as well as the uncle of Alcibiades. This is a conjunction to give us pause. The poet best representing the average sentiments of the city, the one most tenderly acknowledging the city, is side by side here with the exile from Ionia whom Athens, in its turn, will reject. Face to face with both of them is the adolescent who, in the next generation, will be an object of love and terror for Athens, the prince of youth whom both Sophists and Socrates will argue over, this Alcibiades, more of an orator than Lysias, more Spartan than Sparta. Alcibiades, the Asian satrap, who already contains within himself all the contradictions of the new human being.

We have marked out the limits between the two worlds and given notice that between these limits there is no linear frontier but rather a wide zone. We have reached the heart of this zone.

Anaxagoras, Alcibiades—both adventurers, the second already authentically an individual, but suffering because he is and causing the city and Greece to suffer; for the hour has not yet come in which the individual is to discover his law. Still caught in the city's frame of reference that he no longer lives, but rather lives on—like mistletoe on an apple tree—his adventure is what he will seek to carry out, through his action as citizen, instead of rendering tumult and energy harmless by putting them into writing.

And that was what Socrates meant when he counseled him to concern himself not with the city but with his soul.

But Anaxagoras, too, is an adventurer (his adventure is completely intellectual, granted) because he is no longer inside the city and he is conscious of this: Ionian, and Ionian in exile.

We must, in fact, remember the difference we noticed from the beginning between colonial Greece and Greece proper. Both are the offspring of intermixing peoples; both contain the same ferment of individualism, but the climate is different. Citizens who scatter can take with them a torch lit at the hearth of the city, yet they take neither the temples of the gods nor the tombs of the dead.

Where they go, clashes and assimilation with the natives await them; in any event, not the noblest but the strongest kills the enemy and saves his brothers, the handsomest—or most beautiful—marries Medea—or is ravished by Paris.

Little by little, however, the city becomes organized on the model of what took place in the motherland. But with less assurance of its legitimacy, and it is not just chance that the first written laws were colonial. Commerce launched these people onto *the salty expanse* (αλς), which becomes a *passage* (πόντος); one goes here, another there. And both when he faces the sea and when he faces transferable wealth, man is alone: Ulysses is the Ionian hero, no son of a goddess like Achilles, but son of his works and the waves.

And this fringe of cities feels the menace of empires—first Lydia, then Persia. For each of them, the true city, at least in thought, is this ''wooden city'' that Athens failed to build once and for all on the eve of Salamis; but Athens wanted to build the whole thing with men, women, children, ashes of the dead, and statues of the gods. Occasionally the Ionian attempts this adventure, and Marseilles in this manner is Phocaea's daughter. But most frequently, the Ionian ''wooden city'' carries only one man who, to save his life is going to try somewhere else. And saving his life is not simply saving his skin; for the best of them it is also saving himself from the reasons for existence.

Standing alone before the vast sea, image of the vast world, the Ionian no longer is able to be satisfied with collective thought, the explanations provided by the city. In the elements, or in the depths of his solitude, he must seek the reason for everything. At each moment he must reconstruct a collapsing universe unless he is to collapse with it.

Πάντα ῥέει (*Everything falls apart*)[2] and Πάντων μέτρον ἄνθρωπος (*Man is the measure of all things*) are Ionian sayings. And the other great language spoken by the world of the individual, the language that federates (whereas literature isolates)—the language of mathematics, is born there among these same men.

But number, at its birth, assumes that because it explains the relations between things, it can put life in order—the world's life, society's life, each of our lives—according to its own laws. There is a confused sense because the same term λόγος is both *computation* and *reason*. And Pythagoras fails in his dream of making number the god of the new city, of using it like a sword to arm the wise men whom he wanted to crown kings.

Πάντα ῥέει: the seething, contradictory confusion of Ionia, whence, entrusted to these fragile materials—a wooden vessel, papyrus, man's word—forces will set out that will give birth after two centuries of labor to the world in which we live ourselves—for how long?

How right the city was to recognize there its old enemy ὕβρις, immoderation, and to see in Anaxagoras, the modest scholar, its most formidable adversary, the incarnation of the refusal to think in common. Athens had not yet lived through the experience when already it knew that Anaxagoras, existing for a few or, if he had to, himself alone, not seeking to break up the city where he found refuge, still, without wishing to do so laid the ground for men like Alcibiades and Critias. Just as it also knew that Pericles, by demanding the rights of a citizen for the son he had with Aspasia, displayed ὕβρις. Anaxagoras, Aspasia, she from Miletus, he from Clazomenae, both Ionian.

Ionian philosophy is an individual work that created individuals. And history is just as much an individual work.

How could it be surprising that its father was Herodotus, citizen of Halicarnassus, a traveler in Egypt and Asia, a metic in Athens, the citizen of Thourii, a Panhellenic colony, citizen of the world?

He too has no desire to break the ancient, unwritten law of the city. On the contrary, like the Antigone of his friend Sophocles, he calls upon it, endlessly and expressly consults it: Never has anyone spoken so much about ὕβρις and νέμεσις, gods and εὐνομίη. Yet, in spite of himself, Herodotus is another who breaks up the cohesiveness of the city just because he cuts time up (even if badly) and because he founds history, which is to say the individual's grasp of the city and judgment of it. He knows that impartiality is the law of history, and he founds impartiality at the same time as history. But a citizen is unable to be impartial.

It is true that all that is the barest of seeds in him. But it is there. And there is no doubt that the seed took a long time to bear fruit. The same Thucydides who claimed to be an individual and scorned the poetic naïveté of Herodotus would not have been who he was without the example of his predecessor. And in some respects the Athenian, moreover, as we have seen, is inside the city more than the Ionian. That these two judgments can seem contradictory merely proves that these are not simple matters.

It is by taking a course that was invisible to the men who opened the paths, taking a course that, even for us, is still hard to perceive, that we emerge into this new world. And the paths have often been traced however one could, without wanting to and because one could not do otherwise, because life depended on the way out that one would find and because each one had to free oneself from the brambles and brush and find the clearing.

But the ones who will follow these paths, though isolated and inimical to the majority, by following the paths will widen them and they will soon become more numerous. At first in spite of themselves and then consciously, of their own free will, in order to escape these paths, they will trace the perpendicular trails connecting them.

Because there are a few who are aware of this new life where everything depends on them alone, they will make use of this power for action. Most of them will be within the city, still thinking according to citizen categories; but this power cannot act inside the city without acting against it in the long run.

A few, outside the city, and among these the best, seek beyond the city of human beings for the city of God; others are resolutely opposed to any city.

We are back again with Alcibiades and Socrates: "If you had to limit yourself to ruling over Athens, to ruling over Greece, that would not be enough for you, you have to rule over the world." Gorgias is right: "Πάντων μέτρον ἄνθρωπος ("Man is the measure of all things").

But here we are, in the presence also of Socrates and the disciples of Gorgias. Polos and Callicles are each an intellectual Alcibiades. And no doubt the city is wrong, Aristophanes who is the first to speak on its behalf, is wrong to confuse Socrates with the Sophists against whom this philosopher struggled. But he is right—and so is the city—to recognize them as members of the same family.

Socrates never physically left the soil of his fatherland, except to follow the fatherland in the army, a hoplite among hoplites; Socrates dies because he refuses to leave Athens. But even in the army (between two battles) he pursues an investigation of his own, meditating for a whole day and night outside camp. Yet although he obeys the laws that punish him, he is even more obedient to the demon who speaks within and—whether he likes it or not—to the law that results only from his reason; and although he dies because he does not leave Athens, it is in order to rebel against the city. Plato will leave it.

Socrates resembles his enemies, the Sophists, and really is one of them in this way. They come from no city because in every city they find what they want, money and praise. He is from no city because he finds what he values, truth and justice, only in the world of eternal forms. And for us that creates an infinite moral difference between them. For the city, and practically speaking, it makes none. All it can see is that the army of Sophists grows daily, it knows this army is its enemy, and from the very fact that Socrates separates himself from the main body of the troops, it thinks, and in a certain sense correctly, that he commands the army and it is upon him that the city turns its aggression.

And the city is right, knowing it will be the first to die at the hands of the Sophists.

There is no doubt that circumstances count for a lot, particularly the exchanges that, by creating a transferable wealth, separate individuals from the collectivity. But here, as elsewhere, moral forces that are dependent on material circumstances are also causes. One abets the other, as the slope does the avalanche, and it is all connected.

A clear awareness that one's own powers were in conflict with those of the city increases this conflict through the realization. And it is this awareness that was the work of the Sophists.

A few were won over at first, then, because ideas—especially those that go along with the sense of things—are understood even by those who have never heard them discussed, this awareness became the condition for life of a number of people, until finally it became the commonweal—or woe—for all.

Of course, the political struggle between aristocrats and democrats dates in Greece from well before the age of the Sophists. But we must not be taken in by these words. The question is not of the form of the city but of its contents. Outside the γένη, the *families*, whose federation created the tribe and the city, initially there are no citizens; outside the civic cult, hence outside the fatherland, there is only a crowd who are inferior or rather nonexistent in the eyes of the *gennetes*, the well born, the good and fair.

To want to maintain this state of affairs is to be an aristocrat. But to be a democrat is not to want to break it up; it is to want to participate in it, to be inside the closed system. One cannot enter the ancient tribes, so new ones will be made, which, like the others, will be the daughters of a founding hero. In the city thus rebuilt and entered, an agreement will be reached to exclude those who are not from it. Political parties are legacies of the family.

With the Sophists all this changes. It is no longer a matter of being from a party almost in the same way one is from a deme or a tribe; it is a matter of using the party—any one, it does not matter, all equally scorned—for one's own glory, fortune, or venture. Plato saw clearly that the end of the Sophist was to produce a tyrant. And in fact, Peisistrates is the picture of Alcibiades. But only the picture, because the earlier tyrant, busy as he was with his own fortune, simultaneously fox and lion, is not yet conscious of his individuality, whereas his emulator is intoxicated with individuality; because the former acts to satisfy the appetites of the crowd with his own appetites, whereas the new tyrant acts for the satisfaction of acting, of being the conqueror on the Agora like his horses are at Olympia; because the former is an elemental power, the power of his hunger, his thirst, and his genitals, whereas the latter is an aesthete whose only joy is in despising power at the moment that he lusts after it.

Alcibiades differs from the tyrant of earlier days as anxiety differs from stability, that is to say, as the individual differs from things because he judges and measures them.

And that is precisely how Alcibiades, the disciple of Socrates, is truly the new man, the one whom the Sophists wish to see rule, just as the *condottieri* are the sons of the Renaissance and mark the break with Christianity.

But Christianity was a city of the spirit and—in this sense—a Platonic city; the ancient city was a religion of the social body in which the soul was only the sum of citizens' breath. When Christianity was attacked, it could only be from outside because the spirit does not yield completely. But to attack the city was to wreck it thoroughly because its only being was in its very body.

And that was what the Sophists did.

They first taught everyone's mind to play for the pleasure of playing. And the name of Sophism has remained for certain of those games in which the mind tests its power, sees how far it can go, like a pianist with scales and arpeggios: an excellent training for the domination of the multitude, but equally excellent for forming professional writers. Writing is also capturing intellects, making them agree with strange connections: a sort of lie that can be sublime but is nonetheless a sort of lie. And even more so with respect to the city.

Now it is above all important to be right, that is, to play the game better than the adversary—and in every reader there is an adversary.

The sense of rivalry is one of the strengths of the Greek soul. The ἀγών is simultaneously *competition* and *combat*. There have long been physical games where the city is twice rewarded because its warriors—and in Sparta, strong brood mares—are forged there, and because as Pindar demonstrates, it is less each victor who is triumphant than his city through him. Now, for these games that were entirely civic, the Sophists substitute a new game. The gymnasium, where the bodies of citizens exercised as a group—deme by deme, tribe by tribe—becomes the place where intellectual games are played, and in these games each one plays alone.

At the beginning of the *Works*, old Hesiod contrasted two rivalries, the rivalry of doing better, which is good, and that of envying the one who does better than oneself, which is bad. But one can also say that the Good Rivalry is one of εὐνομίη and hence of the city, the Bad Rivalry is one of ὕβρις and of the individual.

With the Sophists, ὕβρις is what is cultivated, and that is how the word changes its meaning. Thus, when the Renaissance taught men that each one is alone in life and that what is essential to each one is his glory, the word "glory" itself, reserved up until then for the city of God (which is the Christian's true city), will end up designating what is most personal in each soul, and it is in this sense that Corneille's heroines will speak of their glory. In an analogous fashion the word that best translates the idea of ὕβρις (*immodération, démesure*) is a pre-Renaissance word become obsolete in modern times.

But the new games of the palestra, games that even the sickly can play, are not the most important thing about the art for the Sophists. This individual who has been taught to measure his strength must be armed for a life in which he will be able to give full measure, with the only goal his own satisfaction. And as long as sophistics remain the privilege of a few, this can only mean dominating the city.

That the Peloponnesian War was instrumental is proven by a famous page from Thucydides, where he analyzes with clinical precision the part played by the war in this breakdown.

But, if we examine it more closely, we will see that this social malady is translated above all as a malady of language, in the historian's diagnosis: Abstract words change meaning according to the appetites of those who utter them. That is the Sophists' lesson and their role.

And perhaps it is what is most grave. Think about it. These abstract words have been, up to now, immobile with the rigidity of gods; they even are gods since they live like the Olympians within (and of) the collective soul. They are immobile in the sense that even where they do change and either take on a new force or else die, it is because the entire people has changed—just as Apollo, the swan-god, became the god with the swan and the mare-goddess Demeter became the goddess with the horses—these abstract words now change at the whim of whoever pronounces them. It is no longer conceivable that Διχή is a goddess when she has been dragged, and will be dragged again, in bloody mud. Old Hesiod easily imagined that there was a time when Διχή lived among men and that it was mens' iniquity that made her leave the earth; but he had her living at the banquet of the gods.

Where then, for the pupils of the Sophists, are both Διχή and the gods now? It all holds together; from the moment that they learn how to make weak language strong and strong weak—by the will of an individual—they can certainly learn that there are other gods than the gods of the city, or even that there are no gods at all. And Hugo, medieval Hugo, eulogist of the city of God, knows very well that

The word is the Word and the Word is God.

By dint of treating venerable words as merchandise, words into which the ancestors had put heart and soul, one can easily treat venerable Hermes and the Venerable Goddesses as objects of ridicule. One morning, when Athens wakes up, she will see the mutilated herms; she will learn that the mysteries of the two Eleusinian goddesses have been parodied.

It might seem astonishing that these jokes played by ill-bred urchins could take on such importance in the eyes of the city, so that nothing else counted—not even war; so that it preferred to lose everything rather than not take revenge. This is because the city understood that everything was at stake in this declaration of a war more serious than the one it waged in Sicily.

And the other side understood too. How fascinating it would be to know the state of mind of those who mutilated the herms! No doubt, this sacrilege was a πίστις, a *token* the conspirators gave each other. But how did they feel when they accomplished such a fearful act? Andocides' defense is not very enlightening, perhaps out of caution, but also because it all must have seemed extremely unclear even for the participants. Because within every one of them two worlds were in conflict, the old world, in which they were sons of the city, nursed on its beliefs, and the new one, the world where they were the disciples of the Sophists, and each one believed only in himself.

What better act to resolve such a debate. By the very fact of declaring war on the city in this way, the conspirators make war on the part of their heart still bound to citizen traditions. By destroying that part of themselves they will become individuals. It is the price for everything.

One must still believe in the gods to turn a sacrilegious hand upon them; otherwise it is only a chunk of carved marble. One must think that there is a connection between the acts at Eleusis and the fate of harvests, the fate of one's soul in the beyond, in order to take pleasure in parodying these acts. To wish to place oneself above common law, one must still somehow believe in this law.

There must be a bond stronger than their necessarily divergent wills among these individuals who unite for action, a bond that federates these autonomies just freshly born into autonomous existence, intoxicated with this birth, and also extremely proud of being the first born to this existence. Then they remember the rituals forming the cities, making the collective existence; they remember all the better for not having been free of them for long. And the better to show that it is in opposition to the city that this union of wills, autonomous by their own doing, is formed, they reverse the city's rituals, they replace them with counterrituals. The herms of the city! The goddesses of the fields! Individual bonds with individual by "desecrating" all aspects of the civic world. The Sophists did their work well.

Here the paths hesitate at a crossroads, but the Sophists have guessed which way men will choose and a great poet turns up to hesitate at the paths, to point out to the people the road that he himself will not take: Euripides.

He is of the past in that he is the song expressing a collective will and of the future in the sense that this will is unclear for those who have it, and will not be clear for their sons except insofar as Euripides will express it. Not to have his laurels until after the tomb, he is truly a posthumous poet.

Now we are able to answer the question we were asking earlier: "*How could his tragedies,*" we asked, "*which serve Aristotle as the norms of tragedy, the prototype for an eternal classicism, how could their newness have seemed so different from what the audience expected?*" And, after having said that this was the central question for this whole project, we added that in order to answer it was necessary "*to define the state of mind of the two publics, the one rejecting Euripides and the one sanctioning him.*"

We see now that the public that sanctioned Euripides is the public that—directly or indirectly—came out of the school of the Sophists. Euripides' true audience is made up of *hermokopids*, the mutilators of the herms, and Alcibiades. Or rather Alcibiades is the Euripides of action, just as Euripides is the Alcibiades of dream. Sophists both.

Accepting the material and framework of tragedy as tradition transmitted it to him, both as the material of his thought and as its framework, even going back to the most ancient models (closer to Aeschylus than to Sophocles in this), he finishes tragedy—and in both senses of the word. By this I mean pushing all factors to the utmost extreme, requiring from each of them—chorus, characters, action, symbol—everything possible and beyond possibility, he provides the finished model of tragedy and, at the same time, breaks the molds he has used.

The chorus remains sometimes, and traditionally, for him the bearer of thought held in common, but in this case the poet is so disdainful of formulating this kind of thought that the moral of a play can perfectly easily be transposed onto another. But, even in the event that the chorus is opposed to the characters, it is as the city now is opposed to the individual. We feel that, far from being able to convict the hero of immoderation, it is drawn to him.

More often, Euripides speaks in place of the chorus and even more frequently, the song of the chorus is no more than the basso continuo above which rises—in a play of virtuosity and the protests of a human being—the actor's monody. These are the songs (their lyrical design still perceptible under the metric scheme, frantic trills that Aristophanes will make fun of), these are the cries and sobs that Euripides treats most tenderly.

For the chorus—any old noisy fuss, the φλτοτότοθρατ of comic parody, created out of pompous words and thoughts worn out with too much use, an empty dummy where the blood no longer circulates. But for the actor—insofar as he is man and expert, all the miracles of rhythm and song; insofar as he is character, all the subtlety of a thought that is the author's own.

And Euripides cares so much about this thought, which is contrasted not only to common thought but also to the basic idea of the play and its central myth, that the principal characters are charged with expressing it, judging men and gods solely according to the laws of Euripidean reason. The poet will even go to the extent of creating characters useless to the action properly speaking, who are charged with formulating this thought or with giving others occasion to formulate it.

What is more, who better can be opposed to the common rules than woman, for whom and by whom they were not created? All the feminine rebellions against the law of the city are his preferred subject; naked woman, wearing the sole truth of her sex, this is Euripides' favorite character.

Sophocles' Antigone rebels against Creon's law, Aeschylus' Electra against the law of Aegisthus. But, vestals of the cult of the dead, they do this to obey the order of the underground gods. When, in the first version of the drama, the one the audience could not stand and whose general outline Seneca's tragedy preserves, Phaedra throws herself into the arms of Hippolyte, she is only obeying the will of her flesh. And perhaps Euripides detests his heroines at the very instant he transposes into the ardor of their bodies the ardor of his mind. But this hatred is still fraternal because an individual is recognizing what is individual and indomitable in the being he paints. Sometimes this is expressed in reasoning that the feminine character (if Euripides kept to the truth of the passion) would be unable either to have or to formulate. It is the poet who follows the line of reasoning, the poet who unmasks to speak and show his face.

At this point (moreover not just with feminine characters) the action stops. Besides, what does Euripides care for action! Not that he is not entirely capable of constructing coherent action, as we see in the two *Iphigenias*; but usually one can feel his indifference to it.

Sometimes he makes his tragedy be a series of *tableaux vivants*, in which the unity is obtained only by a great elemental emotion, as in *The Trojan Women*; sometimes, as in *Hecuba*, he juxtaposes two actions that have nothing in common but the raw grief of a character. But those are occasional means. What is especially important is his haste to get going at the beginning, his haste to quit at any moment and especially at the end.

Hence these prologues where everything is said. They make it clear that the action, even in instances where Euripides has changed the legend and could well be proud of some stroke of genius, counts for nothing in the drama. We understand that all interest must be in the poet, his manner of playing with the traditional themes, the elegance of his verse, the subtlety of psychological analysis, the thought and word play bearing his mark and typical only of him.

Hence, during the course of the action, these unexpected pauses where everything hangs on the poet's fantasies, the Sophist's theories, the acrobatics of the composer and versifier. Hence finally, these denouements where a god who has become a machine for concluding the action intervenes. And this action, once it has been turned this way and that, every aspect examined to the writer's satisfaction, sufficiently commented upon by the subtlety of the moralist (which never was any more than a pretext for all these individual games) when it is reduced only to its own substance as action, interests no one, neither the author nor, it appears, the characters. Then it is only something to get rid of, any way at all.

The god can come spout a monologue, who will listen? The actors think of their voices and of the beaten egg yolks awaiting them in the wings, the audience thinks of anchovies and a glass of water. Euripides—of his next tragedy.

He has great hopes that this next tragedy, better than the one concluded, will allow him to express himself, and this time completely, a hope disappointed with each attempt, desperately reiterated with each attempt, and always the substratum hidden under the various symbols.

For Aeschylus, conflict symbolized the founding of the cities, and confronting the chorus of the Eumenides, appeased at the end of the trilogy, is another chorus summing up the whole city, happy to have received and to keep in trust its founding justice. For Sophocles, the conflict is indeed between the souls of men, but they are opposed in order for ὕβρις to give in before εὐνομία, the individual before the higher law of which he is the bearer. Conflict, thus, is the symbol of the city's existence. For Euripides, the only conflict is between the poet and himself.

Euripides, the first real writer of literature, all ready to be read. Judged by people who could not read.

And this is what explains both the setbacks during his lifetime and his posthumous successes. While he was living he could not be enjoyed, this reader, this loner, except by the tiny handful of the readers alone by themselves in the city: Socrates and his enemy-friends, the Sophists. The city where thought is not distinct from common action renounced itself the five times it gave him laurels. And the last time Euripides was dead: presaging all the laurels that awaited him beyond the tomb, on his head or on Racine's; at the boundary between two ages, his body completely in one, his mind completely in the other. Yes, the first real writer of literature.

Neither soldier nor orator nor a good father nor a good husband, out of place everywhere except in the think tank where Aristophanes puts him, away from the crowd of mankind, there where the whole thing is played out between his paper and himself. Even more an individual than Socrates or the Sophists because he has no need of disciples. What would he pass on to them, in fact? Neither recipes for triumph like the Sophists, because he does not know how to triumph, nor truths like Socrates, because he was never able to find his truth in himself.

One man all alone, needing to express what he carries in the darkness of his heart. Confronting all mankind with it, he waits for mankind to do something good of its own with the message he is passing on. This defines Euripides. And also, already, this is the definition of a writer, confronting the world, outside the world.

Times changed. The boundaries are marked. With Euripides literature was born.

Hitler and the Teutonic Order
Georges Bataille

Tuesday, January 24, 1939

[Nothing has been found in Bataille's manuscripts that can be connected to this lecture announced in the NRF. *Therefore I shall limit myself to developing a few of the likely implications of this subject.*

First, concerning the concept of "order." This is the perfect Varunian concept, one that is decisive for the College, around which it defines itself. Order is not merely an occurrence, but simultaneously a value to be imposed on reality and the instrument with which to impose it. At the same time, it is an imperative idea and an imperialist organization. "L'Ordre et l'empire" is the title of one of the texts Caillois collected in Le Mythe et l'homme. *Order and empire do, in fact, go hand in hand. Moreover, a good many of these avant-garde groups end up together on this theme (see specifically "L'Ordre nouveau"): opposing a defensive idea of order that must be maintained in relation to and against everything, with a dynamic idea of an order that would attract and integrate everything including disorder. Order would no longer be conservative but creative; it would be less the keeper of the past than the conqueror of the future.*

It is self-evident, on the other hand, that religious connotations of the word (ordination) are no discouragement to its use by the College. Bataille had published as a student at the École des Chartes the medieval poem L'Ordre de chevalerie, *etc.*

In the "Préambule pour L'Esprit des sectes,*" Caillois, before going on to mention the College of Sociology, enumerates several contemporary literary works in which nostalgia for an "order" was expressed. There was* Recherche d'une Église *by Jules Romains, one of whose characters is haunted by the mem-*

ory of those "monastic and military orders, the Temple and the Teutonic knights, the Janissaries and Assassins, finally the Jesuits and the Freemasons." Then there was a text by Montherlant, "Les Chevaleries," published in the January 1941 NRF *(it is the first text in* Le Solstice de juin*), where it is stated that "knighthood was also a college" (the phrase spoken at the dubbing ceremony is quoted: "Te in nostro collegio accipio"). Along with these recollections Montherlant recalls a sort of order he had founded with a few college friends at the end of the other war and that he had baptized, baldly, "The Order." Finally, just before the College of Sociology would appear, Caillois quotes* La Gerbe des forces (Nouvelle Allemagne) *by Alphonse de Châteaubriant (published June 15, 1937): "It is time to read again* La Gerbe des Forces *by Alphonse de Chateaubriant. It has been said how much invaluable sympathy for the New Germany there is within the ranks of the French army. It is apparent that the writer, intentionally encouraged to visit the Third Reich, was seduced above all by a certain attempt, then actively pursued, to recreate the ancient orders of chivalry. In fact, in a few forsaken fortresses in the heart of the Black Forest and in the Baltics, there is an endeavor to prepare an elite of young, implacable, and pure leaders for the supreme role of dictators first of the nation then of the world destined for conquest by this nation. Nothing came, it seems, of this attempt. No doubt the party had already chosen its candidates for this task. But the endeavor had fired more than one imagination.*

It was particularly true among those of us who had founded the College of Sociology" (Instincts et société *[Paris, 1964], p. 65, and* Approches de l'imaginaire, *p. 92).*

The chapter of Châteaubriant's book describing these institutions ("Les Ordensburgs") begins with these lines: "This great work of human creation has as its crowning achievement an institution that would not be disavowed by the spirit of the masters of the Teutonic order, an institution that brings this initial institution to impressive perfection, and that can be called: 'The School for Führers'" (p. 273). The initial organization mentioned here was the subject of the preceding chapter: Führerisme *or* Führerprinzip, *which was what enabled national socialism to triumph in Germany and would enable it to triumph everywhere else in the realm of international bolshevism.*

I quote here several passages of the book in order to set the tone. First a meditation before the imposing mass of these castles where the race is improving itself: "Here I slough off my weary Frenchman's skin, wearied with vapid repetitions of a dead thought, and from the depths of my eyes I look at this warriors' abbey that is destined to form the leaders for an Imperial government. By 'look at' I don't mean striving to register the mouse grey color of the walls, nor the clean, sharp edges of their unyielding silhouette on the pallid air. I mean rather, seeing in this conception, this creation, something of 'a great people' about this fortress; something of the immense solitude meant for Templars; something of the school for 'invincible heroes,' as we see it in the romances of chivalry. It is seeing the spiritual aspect of this architecture, the thought that is like the cement in its construction, which is the equal of that controlling the Egyptian pyramids' astonishing convergent edges" (p. 278). And further on: "It seems that some powerful link, yet undestroyed, still indestructible, connects these crenelated and fortified burgs from the age when this ancient Teutonic order existed, with these solid Ordensburgs anchored to the earth as they must be to serve as platforms beneath the feet of those strong men whom the world, as much as Germany, needs today" (p. 286).

In this book where all the eyes prove to be blue once the thick smoke of romantic pipes clears off, Hitler can be seen holding an invisible hand out to "the one called God" while with the other (were we supposed to imagine he had lost one?) he grips tightly the roots of the race. There is also a denunciation of the pact of the Palais-Bourbon with the "Moscow Mephistopheles." We are present at strange confessions like that of the twice-converted German: "I no longer believed in God and it is Hitler who made me believe in him again." "There is no explanation . . . don't ask for explanation" ends innumerable hushed raptures on a note of mystery. The sheaf of powers metamorphoses to become the "fasces of prayers" that becomes firmly entrenched where the race must step: It is not enough to be many; homogeneity is required. For "if the group is not pure, if the individuals are dissimilar because of the character of their spirit, of their innermost interest, or the form of their belief, each man will become individual and the great power of prayer will be lost." Hitlerian racism therefore is thrusting "its organic roots into the productive water of the deep Christian lake." That is why it alone is able to confront not marxism but a "society constructed as if from the outside, on an interpretation of marxism by minds of Israelite, Chinese, Lettic, and Tartar origin." Precisely the same minds against which, in their day, the Teutonic knights fought.

This sentimental and confused rhetoric, this racism of a regionalist aristocrat who was panicked by what he calls "depersonalization," should not pertain too much to Bataille. He had already written in Acéphale*: "The scene of the provisions made in Hitler's Germany for a liberated, anti-Christian enthusiasm, attempting to seem Nietzschean, has come to a shameful conclusion," in* Acéphale. *Châteaubriant's book must have confirmed this judgment. As for the orders, Bataille took off from them to dream about elective communities, but Châteaubriant described them as the last chance at salvation for traditional communities.]*

The Marquis de Sade and the Revolution
Pierre Klossowski
Tuesday, February 7, 1939

[The year 1939 was the occasion for festivities for the Third Republic. It was the 150th anniversary of the Revolution (1939 = 1789 + 150). Klossowski's way of marking the College's participation in these remembrances was to deliver this lecture, in which he makes Sade one of the fathers of the Revolution. His example would be followed because the NRF *several months later was to announce that on April 9, at 2:30 P.M., cité Dupetit-Thouars, Maurice Heine would give a lecture on the Marquis de Sade and the Revolution.*

I am publishing Klossowski's lecture in the form it was given as the first essay in a collection of essays, Sade, mon prochain, *published in 1947.*

In 1939, Klossowski had not yet published a book, except for translations like those in Otto Flacke's work Le Marquis de Sade *(Paris, 1933) and in Max Scheler's book* Le Sens de la souffrance, *followed by two other essays (Paris, 1936). He also worked, with Pierre-Jean Jouve, on the translation of Hölderlin's* Poèmes de la folie, *with a preface by Groethuysen (Paris, 1929), and he signed, with Pierre Leyris, one of the very first French translations of Kafka, the "Verdict," published in* Bifur *in April 1930. But, above all, he is the author of studies on Sade's work ("Le Mal et la négation d'autrui dans la philosophie de D. A. F. de Sade,"* Recherches philosophiques, *4 [1934-35]; "Éléments d'une étude psychanalytique sur le marquis de Sade,"* Revue française de psychanalyse, *no. 6 [1933]; and "Temps et agressivité. Contribution à l'étude du temps subjectif,"* Recherches philosophiques, *5 [1935-36]), which would also be reprinted, with some revision, in* Sade, mon prochain. *His name had been associated with "Contre-Attaque," and it was still connected to*

Acéphale, *which he, Bataille, and Ambrosino directed. He was one of the sign-*
ers of the "Note" published there by the founders of the College. A Catholic,
with ties to the group at Esprit, *Klossowski would also publish in Mounier's re-*
view (see his response to Monnerot's inquiry on spiritual directors).

It was Klossowski who signed the translation of Walter Benjamin's essay,
"L'Oeuvre d'art à l'époque de sa reproduction mécanisée," published in the
Zeitschrift für Sozialforschung, *5 (1936) edited by Horkheimer and Adorno and*
published in Paris by the Éditions Alcan. (He also translated several pages taken
from Benjamin's study on Goethe's novel, Elective Affinities, *"L'Angoisse*
mythique chez Goethe." These were published in the special number of Les
Cahiers du Sud *[May-June 1937] on German romanticism, the issue in which*
Caillois published his condemnation of Novalis, "L'Alternative.")

Klossowski's recollections of Benjamin's passing into the orbit of the College
are in the Marginalia of the present volume, under the heading "Entre Marx et
Fourier." The following lines are from another recollection of the same event,
extracted from "Lettre sur W. B.," Mercure de France *(July 1952). "I met*
him," says Klossowski, "at the time when I was participating in the Breton-
Bataille agglutinations [= "Contre-Attaque"], shortly before 'acephalizing'
with the latter. Benjamin followed all these goings-on with as much consterna-
tion as curiosity. Although Bataille and I were at variance with him then on ev-
ery position, we listened to him with fascination."

A second edition of Sade, mon prochain *in 1967 was thoroughly revised. In*
the first place, the essay entitled "Le Corps du néant," recalling the ambitions
pursued by Bataille during the period of the College, disappeared. On the other
hand, another essay made its appearance: "Le Philosophe scélérat," which
took the present lecture's place as the first essay. As for this lecture, notes will
demonstrate the differences here and there.

I shall just suggest here that the evolution of Klossowski's point of view be-
tween the two editions of his book, is, in the end, somehow involved with what
was going on in Benjamin's text on "mechanical reproduction" of the work of
art he had translated. Shortly after the second edition of Sade, mon prochain, *he*
published a study on Sade and Fourier stating that during "Sade's period, still
one of manufacture . . . the suggestion and the living object of emotion are
merged"—whereas mechanical reproduction was soon to lead to the standard-
ization of voluptuous emotion through industrial exploitation.

As for the Fourierist model of the phalanstery, the College of Sociology, be-
cause of its ambitions, was a product not of this, but rather of the Sadian secret
society par excellence, the "Society of the Friends of Crime"—the crime com-
mitted in common, said by Freud to be what society is based upon.

In the chapter on Sade in La Littérature et le mal, *Bataille would comment on*
Klossowski's studies. In particular, the paragraph entitled "Sade's Thought"

resumes the thesis Klossowski had developed in his lecture at the College (see OC, vol. 9, p. 247).]

I

Revolution, it seems, could only erupt thanks to a wide-ranging combination of contradictory demands: If the psychic forces that were face to face had identified each other at the beginning, their unanimous mobilization would never have occurred. It is owing to a sort of confusion of two different categories of claims that the subversive atmosphere could succesfully build up. In fact, there are two groups in competition: On the one hand there is the amorphous mass of average human beings who require a social regime in which the idea of *the natural man* can be tested—the natural man here being only the idealization of the ordinary man. On the other hand there is a category of individuals who, belonging to the ruling classes and at a higher level of existence, have been able to develop, thanks to the very iniquity of this level of existence, a supreme degree of lucidity. These men, whether upper-middle-class bourgeois or enlightened aristocrats, dreamy or systematic, libertine in thought or practice, have been able to objectify the contents of their guilty conscience: They know what is morally risky about their existence just as they know intimately the problematic structure they have developed. Now, whereas some want to be restored during the social upheaval and to find there a solution for themselves (that is true of Chamfort),[1] others dream above all of making their own problematic structure be accepted as a universal necessity and expect for the Revolution to bring about a complete recasting of the structure of mankind; that, at least, is the case with Sade, who is haunted by the image of the complete man, whose sensibility is polymorphous.[2]

During the Revolution there is a period of collective incubation during which the first transgressions engaged in by the masses give the impression that the population has become susceptible to all sorts of adventures. The effect of this period of psychic regression, which is entirely temporary, is to plunge libertine minds into a sort of euphoria: The most daring elaborations of individual thought have some chance of being translated into experience. Each of these minds, because of the level of decomposition it has attained individually, has ripened something that now seems possible to sow on fertile ground. They are incapable of realizing that, on the contrary, they are the already rotten fruit that is, as it were, coming loose from the social tree. They are going to fall because they are an end, not a beginning, the end of a long evolution. They forget that the earth only takes the seed in, that is to say, whatever portion of their example constitutes a universal lesson for posterity. Their dream of giving birth to a humanity identical to themselves contradicts the very basis of their maturity or their lucidity, and it is only by passing through crises like those they have experienced that other individuals who are also refuse in the collective process are able to meet them at the same level of lucidity and establish then a real filiation.[3]

As soon as the mass's violent and unpredictable decisions intervene, and the principles of the new factions take shape and become laws, while the moral and religious authorities of the old hierarchy are emptied of their content, the problematic men find they suddenly feel strange and disoriented, because they were intimately linked with the sacred values that they shouted down, because their libertinism was meaningful only at the level of existence they occupied in the fallen society. Now that the throne has collapsed, the king has been slapped in his beheaded face, the church pillaged, and sacrilege has become an everyday affair[4] performed en masse, these immoralists appear rather bizarre. They appear as what they really were: symptoms of disintegration who have managed paradoxically to survive disintegration and who are unable to become integrated into the process of recomposition that the sovereign people's principles, the essence of the general will, etc., are accomplishing in consciousnesses. It would suffice that these men go before the people and raise the innate necessity for sacrilege, massacre, and rape to the status of a system—and then, in that very instant, the masses would begin to commit every crime, and would turn on the philosophers and tear them to shreds with no less satisfaction.[5]

It seems at first glance that there is an insoluble problem: The privileged man who has reached the highest stage of consciousness thanks to social upheaval is absolutely incapable of benefiting the social forces with his own lucidity. In other words, this man is incapable of making the individuals from this mass that is amorphous yet rich in possibilities identical with himself for an instant. The morally advanced position that he occupies seems occupied to the detriment of the revolutionary mass. Now, from the point of view of its preservation, the mass is right, for whenever the human mind's expression becomes piercing like Sade's, it risks precipitating the end of all human fate. But the mass is wrong because it is only made up of individuals. The individual intrinsically represents the race, and there is no clear reason why the race should escape the risks an individual's success would entail for it.

The more successful an individual, the more he concentrates the diffuse energies of his epoch, and the more dangerous he is for that epoch; but the more he concentrates within himself these diffuse energies in order to bring them heavily to bear on his own destiny, the more he liberates the epoch. Sade took the virtual criminality of his contemporaries for his personal destiny. He wanted to pay all alone, in proportion to the collective guilt his conscience had invested.

Saint-Just and Bonaparte, on the contrary, knew how to discharge on their fellow human beings everything the epoch had built up in themselves. From the masses' point of view they were perfectly sound men, and these men knew that the masses recognize this resolution to sacrifice them as the best index of a man's health. Sade, still from the masses' point of view, is obviously an unhealthy man: Far from finding some moral satisfaction in the revolutionary fury, he came close to experiencing the legalized carnage of the Terror as a caricature of his system. During his imprisonment at Picpus under Robespierre, he described his stay there in these terms: "Paradise on earth; beautiful house, superb garden, exclusive society, wonderful women, when suddenly the execution grounds were placed absolutely under our windows and the cemetery for those guillotined put in the very middle of our garden. We did away with eighteen hundred of these in five days, a third of them from our own unfortunate house" (29 brumaire, year III).

And later: "What with all of this I am not doing very well, my detention by the state with the guillotine right before my eyes did me a hundred times more harm than all imaginable Bastilles could ever have done." (2 pluviôse, year III). Whence also his need to constantly raise the stakes in his writing; it is not simply because he finally had the right to say all, it is also in some ways in order to have a clear conscience for having delivered a refutation of the truths proclaimed by the Revolution that he then provides the most virulent version of his *Justine*. It was necessary somewhere to strip bare the secret impulse of the revolutionary mass. And this was not done in its political demonstrations since even when they beat to death, drowned, hanged, pillaged, burned, and raped, it was never other than in the name of the sovereign people.

Sade's perseverance in studying only the perverse forms of human nature throughout his life should prove that there is only one thing important to him: the necessity to have all the evil he is capable of dispensing returned to man. The republican state claims to exist for the public good, but although it is obvious that it cannot make good prevail, no one suspects that it fosters the germs of evil deep within. Under the pretext of preventing these germs of evil from hatching, the new social regime claims to be victorious over evil, which is precisely what constitutes a constant threat—the evil that can break out at any moment yet never does break out. This chance of there being evil that never erupts yet any moment can erupt is Sade's constant anxiety. This evil must, therefore, erupt once and for all; the bad seed has to flourish so the mind can tear it out and consume it. In a word, evil must be made to prevail once and for all in the world so that it will destroy itself and so Sade's mind can find peace. But this peace is inconceivable; it is impossible to dream of it for even an instant since every instant is filled with the threat of evil, while Liberty refuses to recognize that it exists only through evil and claims to live for good.

Sade must necessarily feel that the Jacobin Revolution is a hateful rival distorting his ideas and compromising his venture. Whereas Sade would like to institute the reign of the complete man, the Revolution wants to make the natural man live. The Revolution, on behalf of this natural man, takes on all the forces that basically belong to the complete man and that should contribute to his full bloom. There is no worse enemy for the complete man than God. By killing the king, who is God's temporal representative, one must have killed God in people's consciousness at the same time, and this immeasurable murder can have only one immeasurable consequence: the advent of the complete man. Hence the complete man bears the stamp of the crime, the most fearsome crime of all: regicide. *"Here an extraordinary reflection appears,"* he writes, *"But since, despite its effrontery, it is true, I shall recount it. A nation that begins to govern itself as a republic will maintain itself only with virtues because one must always begin with the least to arrive at the most*; but a nation that is already old and corrupt and that, courageously, shakes off the yoke of its monarchical government to adopt a republican one, will maintain itself only through many crimes because it is already involved in crime, and if it wanted to move from crime to virtue, that is to say, from a violent state to a milder one, it would fall into an inertia soon resulting in its certain downfall."[6]

For Sade, revolution occurring in the *old and corrupt nation* would in no way provide a chance for regeneration; there is absolutely no question of inaugurating the happy age of a natural innocence regained once the nation is purged of its aristocratic class. The reign of freedom, for Sade, must and will in fact be neither more nor less than monarchical corruption brought to culmination. *"A nation that is already old and corrupt,"* meaning one that has attained a certain degree of criminality, *"courageously shakes off the monarchical yoke"*; in other words, this degree of criminality to which its ancient masters brought it will provide the tempo for perpetrating regicide in order to adopt a republican government— meaning a social state given access to a heightened criminality by perpetrating regicide. The revolutionary community, therefore, will be profoundly, secretly, but closely, bound up with the moral disintegration of monarchical society since it is thanks to this disintegration that its members have acquired the strength and energy necessary for bloody decisions. And what does corruption mean here if not the degree of advanced de-Christianization of the society that was contemporary with Sade, the practice of the arbitrary being even more unstoppable because its basis lay, if not in atheism, at least in the deepest skepticism?

As soon as this moral skepticism, this atheism (whether instigated or one of conviction), spreads into the monarchical society, it results in disintegration so that the feudal relations between lord and servant consecrated by the theocratic hierarchy are virtually broken off already. The ancient relationship of master and slave is reestablished in actual fact.

II. The Breakdown of Theocratic Feudalism and the Birth of Aristocratic Individualism

In the period between ancient conditions of slavery and the Revolution, theocratic hierarchy was established in the West—the Church's attempt to group the social forces confronting it into an order able to ensure moral significance to each category of individuals.[7] Theocratic hierarchy is supposed to put an end to the ancient law of the jungle. Human beings created in God's image cannot exploit human beings; every person is the servant of God. Inscribed on the pediment of theocratic hierarchy is the proverb: Fear of the Lord is the Beginning of Wisdom. The king, appointed by God, is his temporal servant; the lord, appointed by the king, is servant to the king; and every man who acknowledges that he is servant to his lord is the servant of God. The hierarchy assigns the lord military, judicial, and social functions entrusted to him by the king. For him these are obligations toward the king and toward the people, but exercise of these functions assures him the right to gratitude and fealty from his vassal and servant. The servant, for his part, having put himself under the protection of his lord, to whom he renders homage and fealty, performs an act of faith in his God and his king. Hence, at the last level of the hierarchy, he fulfills his individual significance because he is participating in an edifice whose keystone is God. Now, as the king concentrates power more and more, while the lord abandons his functions one by one, the latter not only frees himself in relation to his obligations toward the king, but he still claims to maintain the rights and privileges ensuing from these. Then the lord only needs to develop an existence for its own sake, making his privileges something he enjoys without accountability to God or anyone else, least of all to his servant—the lord only needs to put God's existence in doubt for the whole structure to totter. The fact of serving at the bottom of the social ladder loses all meaning in the eyes of the servant. And finally, when the lord seems to want to maintain the structure of theocratic hierarchy for the sole purpose of guaranteeing an unwarranted existence, an existence that is the very negation of this hierarchy, an existence that consists in demonstrating that the fear of the Lord is the beginning of madness, then the law of the jungle comes back in full force. The conditions of the ancient relationship strong to weak, master to slave are reestablished.

And the great, libertine lord, especially, on the eve of the Revolution, is no more than a master who knows he is the rightful possessor of power, but who knows also that he can lose it any minute and that he is already virtually a slave. Because he no longer has undisputed authority in his own eyes (whereas he has kept his instincts for it) and there is nothing sacred about his will any more, he adopts the language of the masses. He calls himself a ''roué,'' he looks for arguments in the philosophers, he reads Hobbes, d'Holbach, and La Mettrie, as a man who, no longer believing in divine right, seeks to legitimate his privileged position by rational sophisms accessible to everyone. In this condition, if the great libertine lord is not resolutely atheist, he conceives his own existence as a provocation for the benefit of God and simultaneously for the benefit of the people. If, however, he is resolutely atheist, while doing what he pleases with his servant's life, making him a slave and the object of his pleasures, he lets the people know that he has killed God in his consciousness and that his prerogatives were only the exercise of crime with impunity. The man at the bottom of the hierarchy whose closeness to God was in the act of serving and who has fallen into slavery, now that God is dead at the top of the hierarchy, remains a servant with no lord to the extent that God lives in his conscience. He does not become a slave effectively, except in that, experiencing the death of God in his own consciousness, he continues to be subject to the one who is in fact, the master. And he will only become truly a master insofar as, going along with the murder of God perpetrated at the top of the hierarchy, he wants to annihilate the master and become master himself.

The servant who has become a slave, either through atheism or through his master's sacrilegious existence, in fact rebels. He accepts therefore the death of God, but when it is time to put his master on trial, in the name of what is he to do this, if not in the name of the prerogative of crime? He has no other choice than to become his master's accomplice immediately in the revolt against God and, in turn, take on the crime himself. The only possible outcome of the trial is that the slaves assume the masters' prerogatives, beginning with killing the masters. This, it certainly seems, is the vicious circle[8] of the insidious thesis claiming that a *nation that has shaken off its monarchical yoke can maintain itself only through crimes because it is already involved in crime.* This is the vicious circle to which Sade would confine the Revolution.

The Republic, in short, can never begin. The Revolution is not truly the Revolution except to the extent that it is the Monarchy in permanent insurrection. A sacred value cannot be trampled on unless one has one's feet on it. The theocratic principle is not in question, quite the opposite: It determines Sade's terminology, otherwise what is the meaning of the word crime?

III. Regicide as the Enactment of the Execution of God

The nation's execution of the king is, therefore, only the most extreme phase of the process whose first phase is the execution of God by the revolt of the great libertine lord. The execution of the king thus becomes the enactment of the execution of God. When, after having sentenced the king, whose person remains inviolable until the suspension of monarchy, the members of the Convention are called upon to declare themselves for or against condemning him to death, the argument to rally most of the votes in favor of capital punishment will not and cannot be more than a compromise between the judicial and the political points of view. There are only a few isolated individuals who, taking up the challenge flung at monarchist Europe, will dare to say like Danton: "We do not want to condemn the king, we want to kill him." Even Saint-Just, who was above all preoccupied with inculcating in the nation a strong sense of its rights, asserts that it is less a question of sentencing the king than of fighting him as an enemy because it is impossible to reign innocently.[9] But it is to be Robespierre who, conscious of the necessity for creating a new idea of public law, will decisively state the dilemma: "There are no legal proceedings to institute here. Louis is not a defendant. You are not judges. You are only and can only be men of the State, representatives of the nation. It is not that you must pass sentence for or against a man, but rather that you must take steps for the public safety, and bring to bear an act of national salvation. [. . .] In effect, if Louis can still be the object of legal proceedings, Louis can be absolved; he can be innocent. What am I saying? He is presumed to be innocent until sentenced, but if Louis is absolved, if Louis can be presumed innocent, what happens to the revolution? If Louis is innocent, all the defenders of freedom become libelous; all the rebels were friends of truth and defenders of oppressed innocence.''[10] And Robespierre concludes: ''Louis must die so the country can live.'' By selling his people to foreign despots, the king annulled the social pact that bound the nation; from then on, a state of war existed between the people and the tyrant who must be destroyed as an enemy is destroyed. This is the Revolution's point of view: it will allow the cementing of a republican order. Now those are ideas that are not without effect in Sade's thought. At the moment the blade severs the head of Louis XVI, Sade does not see citizen Capet, nor even a dying traitor; Sade, like Joseph de Maistre and all the Ultramontanists, sees the representative of God dying. It is the blood of the temporal representative of God and, in a deeper sense, the blood of God that falls on the heads of the insurgent people. The counterrevolutionary, Catholic philosophers like Joseph de Maistre, Bonald, Maine de Biran speak of the execution of Louis XVI as a redemptive martyrdom;[11] for them Louis expiates the sins of the nation. *For Sade, the execution of the king plunges the nation into what is inexpiable:* regicides, hence parricides. And it is doubtless because he saw a coercive force in it that Sade wished to substitute for the fraternity of natural man this solidarity with the parricide as the appropriate bond for a community that could not be fraternal because it was Cainite.

IV. From the Godless Society
to the Society without Executioner

The Revolution wanted to institute the fraternity and equality of the mother-fatherland's children. And what a bizarre term: *mère patrie* mother-fatherland.[12] It supposes a hermaphrodite divinity whose equivocal nature seems to translate the complexity of the execution of the king. This term is a product of the ambivalence of the revolutionary act, ambivalence that the members of the Convention are obviously incapable of realizing but that they account for by substituting the mother country for the sacred authority of the father, that is to say, the king. But the rebellious slaves who, by their rebellion against their masters, have made themselves accomplices in their masters' revolt against God, in order to become masters in their turn, could they simply just claim to found a community of innocents? To become innocent they would have to expiate the inexpiable execution of the king. There is no choice but to push the consummation of evil as far as it will go. Robespierre says in his discourse on the trial of the king: ''When a nation has been forced to have recourse to the right of insurrection, it returns to the state of nature with respect to the tyrant. How would it be possible for him to invoke the social pact? He has nullified it. The nation can still preserve it if it decides that it is relevant to relations among citizens; but the effect of tyranny and insurrection is to completely break off relations to the tyrant. It sets them up in a reciprocal warring state. Courts and judicial procedures are for the members of a city.''[13]

Now this is precisely where the crucial point appears, the divergence between Sade and the Revolution, between Sade and terrorism, between Sade and Robespierre. Can the social pact, once the tyrant is annihilated, exist unilaterally for the citizens among themselves? Can courts and judicial procedures live on for the members of the city? How can that be? replies Sade. You have rebelled against iniquity; for you the iniquity consisted in being excluded from its practice. By revolting against iniquity you have only responded with iniquity because you have killed your masters as your masters have killed God in their consciousness. Justice for you, unless you are to return to servitude, your justice (and you have given bloody proof of it) can consist only in the common practice of individual iniquity. How can you appeal, if not to God at least to an identical order that would assure you of tranquil enjoyment of the benefits of insurrection? From now on anything you undertake will bear the mark of murder.

That is what Sade did his utmost to demonstrate in his opuscule *Français, encore un effort si vous voulez être républicains* (Frenchmen, one more try if you want to be Republicans), which is not so much his work as that of Dolmancé, one of the characters in his *Philosophie dans le Boudoir*, where this opuscule appears. Nevertheless, since we have good reason to believe that it was in his fictions that he expressed the heart of his thought, insofar as it had a heart, we must perhaps attach more importance to this strange document than to the numerous professions of republican public spirit with which he honored the revolutionary authorities during his nine years of freedom.

This one declamatory title: *Français, encore un effort . . .* seems very suspicious and lets us glimpse the author's real intentions well enough. The work is composed of two chapters, the first devoted to *religion* the second to *morals*. In the first, where he attempts to demonstrate that *theism is not at all suitable to a republican government*, Sade, to undermine the basis of theocratic society, employs positive rational arguments. The question is put in the following terms: Christianity must be rejected because its social consequences are immoral; only atheism is able to ensure an ethical basis for national education: ''Replace the deific foolishness with which you tire the young organs of your children with excellent social principles; instead of learning futile prayers . . . let them be taught their duties to society; teach them to cherish the virtues you scarcely spoke of before and that, without your religious fables, are sufficient for their individual happiness; make them feel that this happiness consists in making others as fortunate as we wish to be ourselves. If you establish these truths on Christian chimera as you were formerly insane enough to do, your students will no sooner recognize the futility of the basis than they will demolish the edifice, and they will become wicked just because they believe it was the religion they have overturned that forbade them to be so. By making them feel, on the contrary, the necessity for virtue, solely because their own happiness depends on it, they will be decent people out of egotism, and this law that governs all men will be the most reliable one of all.''

Those are positive, materialist principles that, at first glance, seem irrefutable on the rational level and suitable for providing the basis of a new society. These principles can give rise to so-called bold innovations such as the abolition of the family, the authorization of free love—that is to say women being communal for men and men communal for women—finally and above all the nationalization of children, who will know no other father than the State. All these problems are posed by Sade (one can sense certain of Fourier's phalansterian ideas anticipated here, the project of *harmonist society* based on the *free play of passions*),[14] and this is how he solves them. In the second chapter, which is devoted to morals, he immediately backs the *"Republicans"* up against a wall: "Think Citizens, by according freedom of conscience and freedom of the press, *freedom of action* also must pretty well be accorded, and with the exception of whatever directly shakes the basis of government, who knows how few crimes you would have to punish, because in reality there are very few criminal acts in a society based on liberty and equality.'' Does individual happiness really consist in making others as fortunate as we wish to be ourselves, as the moral atheist claims? "It is not a matter of loving one's fellow man as one loves oneself,'' the second chapter immediately replies, drawing the first conclusions of an atheist morality; ''that is against the laws of nature whose instrument must be the sole director of our laws.'' Institute the community of women for men and the community of men for women, but let it be in order to fill the public palaces of national prostitution. Community children? Of course, to make them more accessible for sodomy. Suppression of the family? Certainly, but let one exception prove the rule: incest. Community wealth? By theft, ''because the vow to respect property is not binding on the person who has nothing: punish the man who is negligent enough to let himself be robbed, not the one who robs and who has only followed the foremost and most sacred impulse of nature, that of preserving his own existence no matter what, or to whom the cost.'' But if calumny, theft, rape, incest, adultery and sodomy must experience no penalty in a republican government, the crime this government is least prepared to deal with harshly is murder: "It is proven that the practice of some virtues is impossible for certain men, just as there are some remedies that cannot be suitable for some temperaments. So what would the height of injustice be for you if your law punishes someone incapable of complying with the law? From these first principles, we realize, ensues the necessity to create laws that are mild and above all to wipe out permanently the atrocity of the death penalty, because the law, cold in itself, is incapable of being accessible to the passions that can justify in man the cruel act of murder. The feelings that can make a man pardon this act come from nature; and the law, which is, on the contrary, always opposed to nature and gets nothing from it, cannot be authorized to permit itself the same motives and cannot possibly have the same rights.''

A government born of the murder of God, surviving only through murder, is a government that has lost in advance the right of inflicting capital punishment, and consequently is incapable of declaring any penalty against any other crime: ''A republican government that is surrounded by despots can preserve itself only by means of war and there is nothing less moral than war.'' In politics, is murder a crime? Let us dare admit, on the contrary, that it is unfortunately only one of the greatest resources of politics. Is it not by dint of murders that France is free today? ''Which of the human sciences has more need of maintaining itself by the murder that is only a way of cheating, whose only aim is increasing one nation at the expense of another? . . . This is an odd blindness in man, who publicly teaches the art of killing, who rewards the one who does it best, and who punishes the one who, for a private cause, has rid himself of his enemy!'' . . . 'I grant you mercy,' said Louis XV to Charolais, who had just killed a man for his amusement. 'But I grant it also to the one who will kill you.' Every basis of the law against murderers is found in this sublime word.'' Here we see that Sade is capable of remembering in an extremely opportune moment the principles of existence of the old monarchy, whose immorality the Republic, in short, would have to sanction: ''I ask how one can manage to prove that in a State that is immoral through its obligations, it is essential for the individuals to be moral? I will tell you something else: It is good for them not to be . . . Insurrection is not at all a moral state; nevertheless it must be the permanent state of a republic; it would, therefore, be as absurd as it would be dangerous to require those who must maintain the machine's perpetual upheaval to be moral beings themselves; because a man's moral state is a state of tranquillity and peace; his immoral state a perpetual motion that moves him closer to the necessary insurrection in which the Republican must always keep his government.''

At the beginning of his opuscule, Sade asserts that children will be inculcated with excellent social principles thanks to atheism. Then, one by one, he draws these conclusions: The results will be to precipitate society into a state of perpetual motion, into a state of permanent immorality, that is to say, inevitably to its own destruction.

V

All in all, the vision of society in a permanent state of immorality is presented as a *utopia of evil*; this paradoxical utopia corresponds to the potential state of our modern society. Whereas a utopian awareness of human possibilities elaborates a future vision of potential progress, the Sadian awareness elaborates the future vision of potential regression; looking ahead in this manner is all the more incredible because the *method is placed in the service of regression*. Now, unlike utopias of good whose shortcoming is their disregarding of bad realities, the utopia of evil consists in systematically disregarding not the possibilities of good but one important factor, namely, boredom. Although it most frequently produces evil, boredom increases again once the evil is committed, in the same way that disgust follows a crime, when it was committed just for the sake of committing a crime. Sade retains only the bad realities by suppressing their temporal character: The result in effect is that every moment of social existence is filled solely with evil that destroys one moment with another. Born of Sade's boredom and disgust, the utopia of society in a state of permanent criminality, if taken literally and if the ideologues of evil took it into their heads to put it into practice, would inevitably sink into disgust and boredom. There can be no other remedy for disgust and boredom than an increasing buildup of new crimes ad infinitum.[15]

VI

The conjecture is that underlying the Revolution, there was a sort of moral conspiracy whose aim would have been to compel a humanity that was at loose ends, having lost its sense of social necessity, to become aware of its guilt. And this conspiracy was well served by two methods: an exoteric method practiced by Joseph de Maistre in his sociology of original sin and an infinitely complex, esoteric method that *consists in disguising itself as atheism in order to combat atheism, in speaking the language of moral skepticism in order to combat moral skepticism, with the sole aim of giving back to reason everything this method can, in order to show its worthlessness.*

Sade's pamphlet does not fail to be puzzling; and we are tempted to wonder if Sade did not wish to discredit in his own way the immortal principles of 1789, if this fallen great man did not embrace the philosophy of the "shining lights" solely in order to reveal its dark foundations.

And here we return to the questions with which we began. We can either take Sade at his word, as one of the most advanced *epiphenomena*, the most revealing of a far-reaching process of social decomposition and recomposition. He would then turn out to be an abscess on the sick body, who would believe he could speak in the name of this body. His political nihilism would be only the ostensibly unhealthy episode of the collective process; his apology for *pure crime*, his invitation to persevere in crime, only the attempt to pervert the political instinct, that is to say, the collectivity's instinct for preservation. For the people turn themselves over to the extermination of those opposed to them with a profound satisfaction; the collectivity senses always whatever, for good or bad reasons, is harmful to it, which is why it is able to mingle cruelty and justice with the steadiest of hands, without feeling the least remorse, rites it is likely to invent at the foot of the scaffold releasing it from the pure cruelty whose face and effects it knows how to travesty.

Or else we could stop at certain passages of his pamphlet where we are warned: "Let no one accuse me of being a dangerous innovator. Let no one say there is some danger in dulling, as these writings perhaps do, remorse in the criminal's soul, that the worst thing is in augmenting by my gentle words the penchant certain criminals have for crime. I formally testify here that I have none of these perverse views. I am making known ideas that, ever since manhood, made themselves known to me, whose flow for so many centuries the vile despotism of tyrants has opposed. Too bad for those whom these great ideas would corrupt; too bad for those who can only grasp the evil in philosophic opinions, who are likely to be corrupted by everything. Who knows if they might not be corrupted by reading Seneca and Charron? Those are not the ones to whom I speak; I ADDRESS ONLY PEOPLE WHO ARE CAPABLE OF UNDERSTANDING ME, AND THESE PEOPLE WILL READ ME WITHOUT DANGER."

This is consciousness dawning at its highest level, the very level that allows the whole process of decomposition and recomposition to be embraced. Moreover, while recognizing Sade's nature as a release, we must attribute to him the *function of exposing dark forces that are camouflaged as social values* by the collectivity's defense mechanisms; camouflaged in this manner, these dark forces have an empty space where they can lead their infernal circular dance. Sade is not afraid of mixing with these forces, but he only enters the dance to rip off the masks put on them by the Revolution in order to make them acceptable and to allow the "enfants de la patrie" their innocent practice.

[A note from 1967 (see note 15)]:

This passage, as well as section VI , shows the tendentious deviation of the author's reasoning, during the period that he wrote this study. The "utopia of Evil" disregards not "boredom" but the *functional* that is, the utilitarian aspect, which the institutions of a particular social milieu attribute to the exercise of impulsive forces. If there is a utopia of "Evil" here, it is that Sade, making use of institutional language itself, projects the ideal of a human grouping that, in order to declare itself in "permanent revolt" based on its members' "state of perpetual motion," would be aware of basing itself on none other than the exercise of impulses freed from any ideological justification. This would immediately change the behavior of individuals as well as the nature of their actions. That is what Sade's utopic aim consisted in; for although disgust and boredom follow "crime committed just for the sake of committing a crime," it can happen only in the existing institutional world that the idea of such a crime comes to be born, followed by such a boredom, meaning a drop in intensity. So strong is the functional tendency of institutionally structured impulses that the individual never succeeds, except rarely, at keeping himself on the level of an impulsive intensity, as soon as this intensity ceases to correspond, as a *means*, to an institutionally assigned *end* —that is, in a general manner, to the preservation of institutions, to a transcendent significance, for the Good of all. The real problem would be rather to know what, in a state of "permanent revolt," would come to restructure the impulsive forces, and what would be the actions in which these forces would acknowledge themselves as having no other end than themselves.

The Sociology of the Executioner
Roger Caillois

Tuesday, February 21, 1939

[The NRF *announced a "Commemoration of Mardi Gras" by Bataille for February 21, 1939. There is nothing surprising about the subject, given the preoccupations of the College; moreover, Caillois will mention it, at least in passing, in his lecture entitled "Festival."*

Caillois, on the other hand, said that he had spoken at the College on the sociology of the executioner. In the interview with Lapouge: "I myself gave talks on animal societies, spiritual power, the sociology of the executioner." In Approches de l'imaginaire*: "Every two weeks talks were given in the back room of a bookstore on rue Gay-Lussac. A varied audience squeezed in and participated actively in the discussions. It was there that I developed some hypotheses in particular about festival and the executioner, examples of what we were calling 'sacred sociology.'"*

We can go on to imagine that this sociology of the executioner was what was discussed instead of the announced lecture on the festivals of Mardi Gras, or even perhaps, simply following this lecture. In fact, several of the points made directly echo those discussed by Klossowski on the subject of Sade in the preceding lecture, specifically, the question of regicide. This reflection on the executioner, moreover, is inscribed in the most immediate current events. Deibler, the head executioner, had just died, and his death was all the more important because it left the office vacant just at the moment that the trial of Weidman began. Everyone knew that this trial would end in a death sentence at the very least, and not just because he was a German.

"The Sociology of the Executioner" appeared first in translation in SUR, *Victoria Ocampo's review in Buenos Aires, in May 1939; later, it appeared in*

French in La Communion des forts *(Mexico City, 1943; Marseilles, 1944). This collection of "sociological studies," as its subtitle says, is divided into two parts. The first brings together the "Sociologie du bourreau" (The sociology of the executioner), "Vertiges," and "Secrets trésors," (all three of which will be republished in* Instincts et société). *The second, entitled "Dures vertus," consists of three chapters: "La Sévérité," "L'Aridité," and "Sociologie du clerc." "L'Aridité," which had previously appeared in* Mesures *had been rather severely criticized by W. Benjamin in* Zeitschrift für Sozialforschung. *Of these three texts, only the "Sociologie du clerc" would be published again—in the section of* Approches de l'imaginaire *devoted to the College. There it rubs shoulders with the preface of* La Communion des forts, *now referred to as the preface to a provisional book, and in the table of contents as the preface to a dismembered book. Perhaps those are the texts that Bataille described in his lecture the following July 4 as the kind of thing that "suspended the agreement" in force between Caillois and himself.*

Étiemble was to mention La Communion des forts *in* L'Arche *in 1944: "That this myth of the executioner," he wrote, "was still in full force on the eve of June 1940, and in a republic that sees itself invoking the one that decapitated Louis XVI, is certainly proof that 'social material,' as Caillois calls it, the material upon which every statesman must work, is almost entirely turned over to the dark powers secreted by religions—powers 'at play on account of and on behalf of war,' powers that enthrall us with their 'vertiginous' maelstrom. It is because of the existence of such powers, against which just writing* The Golden Bough *is not enough, that government by an aristocracy is the sole guarantee of wisdom and lucidity." Étiemble concluded this note: "Some day I shall propose a 'legal status for the aristocracy within a socialist republic,' thus offering him [= Caillois] the chance to set the record straight."]*

The Death of the Executioner

February 2, 1939: Anatole Deibler is dead at the age of seventy-six.

Reading the newspaper articles devoted to the death of Anatole Deibler, the Republic's "high executioner," one would say that society discovered the existence of its executioner only through his death. In any case, it is rare that a natural death arouses so much commentary on the life of an obscure individual who did his best to be forgotten by others and whom others, for their part, apparently wished to forget. This man made the heads of four hundred fellow men fall and each time curiosity was directed toward the one executed, never toward the executioner. There was more than a conspiracy of silence where he was. It was as if a mysterious and all-powerful taboo forbade mentioning an accursed person, as if a secret and effective obstacle prevented even the thought of doing so.

He died: His death was announced on the front page of the daily papers with enormous headlines. Neither lyricism nor photographs were spared. Is it that nothing is happening in the world, so we pay attention to a minor news item? Yet Europe's destiny is at stake and, perhaps, is being decided. Unimportant. Long articles recount the dead man's career and that of his predecessors. His position in the State is defined. His professional qualities are commented on, his method, his "touch." Nothing is left unknown about his private life, his character, his habits. It seems there is no detail unworthy of the reader's interest. The excessive publicity given to an accident that one might normally announce in a modest, brief paragraph is surprising. To impute this excess to the public's unhealthy curiosity that demands its daily ration from journalists would be a rather simplistic solution. This solution, in any case, should not spare us from contemplating the *unhealthy* nature of this curiosity, pondering its cause, its function, its end, or determining what disordered instincts it would satisfy. But in this particular case, there is more one can do: The information published about the dead executioner is not, in fact, ordinary. A great deal of it does more credit to the journalists' imagination than to the reliability of their reports.[1] This fact seems all the more remarkable because the different articles, despite the manifest contradictions they present when compared, all paint a similar image of the executioner. This image, depending on the author, is composed of elements that, although divergent, in their mutual organization always end up shaping a face with the same expression. It is as if their imaginations had felt the urgent promptings of the same design, fascination with the same figure, and had set themselves to reproducing this with more or less arbitrary strokes and makeshift devices. It is a question of reconstructing this ideal model that was so persuasive. We can be certain beforehand that this task will not be uninteresting because a strange difficulty is immediately encountered: The authors of the articles agree less about the facts than about legend's halo. Their stories cancel each other out when there is a question of the observable, material, historical incident constituted by the death of an old man, at dawn in a subway station. On the contrary, they corroborate each other in everything that is subjective and uncontrollable and that has been added to the pure event. One does not, in general, expect to find the real diffuse and fragile and the imaginary clear and strong.

It should not be too surprising that the versions of the incident are not in agreement. It would be ridiculous to demand more of journalists than they can provide. They have neither the time nor the means to work as historians. But it is still surprising that, as if through the workings of some preestablished harmony, they come to such agreement on everything else. Possibly they drew on the same source,* but, besides the fact that the reports are far from all referring to the same

---

*Probably in Deibler's memoirs, published in *Paris-Soir*. These memoirs, moreover, start out being stylized already because they were written by a journalist who rented a room in the executioner's home, in order to collect his confidences for the journal.

details, this explanation in no way accounts for the impressive sameness of the tendentious commentaries accompanying these reports.

In the first place, one remarks on the systematic care with which the executioner's character seems contrasted to his function. Because his function causes fear, the man is asserted to be timid and shy. His villa is compared with a blockhouse on the Maginot line because it is so well equipped with safety devices. It is recounted that, refusing to get into an automobile from the Justice Department, sent in an emergency to pick him up at home, he called a taxi and told the minister's messengers, "Excuse me, I never trust strangers" (*Le Figaro*).*
He has a harsh and solemn job, but the executioner is said to be casual and likable. Every morning he walks his little dog, in the afternoon he goes to the racetrack, and when his stomach permits he has his aperitif brought to his house from the nearby cafe; he likes to play cards, especially manille (*Excelsior*), he is described as having a small private income (*Le Figaro*), as being an old-age pensioner (*Paris-Soir*); he has "property" (*L'Intransigeant*). His life is that of a punctual civil servant, of a good "family man" (*Paris-Soir*, title). In his quarter he is called "the bourgeois from Point-du-Jour" (*Paris-Soir*, subtitle), without malice it seems, because the journalist mentioning this detail seems unaware of the expression's sinister double meaning (the executioner does his work at dawn, or *point du jour*). His is the most implacable of professions: He is claimed to be soft-hearted, always ready to be useful to his fellow man and to help the poor (*Le Figaro*). The improvements he brought to the guillotine are explained by his humanitarian disposition (*Le Figaro*, *L'Intransigeant*, etc.). His face is said to wear a sweet, melancholy expression. His profession is lugubrious, brutal, bloody: He is shown as exclusively devoted to refined, delicate tasks (*Le Figaro*). A lover and creator of beauty, he cultivates rare roses with jealous attention, he creates and fires "artistic" pottery (*Excelsior*). Privately he suffers far more agony than he publicly inflicts: A pharmacist's error caused the death of his son at age five. His daughter, who grew old without finding a husband, leads "a persecuted existence." All this is more than enough to fill the days of this tortured executioner's family life with gloom.

This relentless pursuit of contrast leads sometimes to the most capricious connections: A commentator wonders if this man who is devoted to macabre affairs did not choose to live in the rue Claude-Terrasse because it bears the name of a cheerful musician (*La Liberté*). In general, the doubly funereal theme of the executioner's death is a chance to provoke laughter by apt jokes or by recalling witticisms about the individual's profession. For example, they say that the executioner's profession has no "dead season" (*L'Ordre*). Among the funny anecdotes, one, particularly lavish and ridiculous, gives the tone of this attempt at freedom from anxiety, this recourse to sacrilege that laughter constantly repre-

---

*There is no doubt that this is a fabrication: One does not have "emergency" beheadings.

sents on such occasions. Sanson, the executioner who served Louis XV, had such a delicate touch that he was said to work without the sentenced man's feeling a thing. When he executed Lally-Tollendal, the victim asked impatiently, "Well! What are you waiting for?" And what Sanson replied, funny because of the horror itself and because it was addressed to a corpse: "But, Monseigneur, it's done. Look for yourself" (*Le Figaro*). Deibler, however, is represented as a character who is completely indifferent, if not hostile, to stories about executioners and executions. He returned a collection of works of this sort to an Englishman who had given them to him as a present, saying disdainfully, somewhat gravely: "Whenever it concerns the exercise of his functions, the executioner must not know how to read" (*Le Figaro*).

Conversely, in contrast to these anecdotes, a tendency to force the sinister, inexpiable character of the public executioner can be observed. Scarcely has his existence been described as peaceful when it is painted as appalling. Thus he becomes what the headline of an article calls "the executioner with a double life" (*Paris-Soir*). Since childhood he has lived apart from his fellow man. At school, his father's profession, which we are assured he knows nothing about, condemns him to isolation. His comrades persecute him, insult him and exclude him from their games (*Paris-Soir, Ce Soir*). Finally they reveal the "curse" hanging over him. It is a terrible shock to him. Then, taking pride in his ignominy, he plays at guillotining his companions and goes out of his way to terrorize them (*Paris-Soir*).[*] Later, looking for work, he is turned down as soon as they hear his name, "branded with a bloody mark" (*Paris-Soir*). At night he is awakened by his father's raving: "Blood!" (*Le Progrès de Lyon*). His father, in fact, soon resigns. During the executions he felt covered with blood although he stayed as immaculate as the magistrates standing beside him (*L'Intransigeant*). No one was willing to give his daughter to be married to the executioner's son. He asked for the hand of the daughter of the carpenter, Heurteloup, who manufactured scaffolds for the whole world—the only man who made his living, like the executioner though indirectly, from capital punishment. He was rejected: The artisan did not want his daughter to be married to a man who cut off heads (*Ce Soir, L'Intransigeant*, etc.). This is where it becomes romantic, which is to say that, naturally, the executioner is transformed into a romantic hero. Despairing of love, Deibler consented to be his father's successor (*Ce Soir*). The first Sanson also, so they say, decided to enter the career that was to bring fame to his descendants because of an unhappy love (*Le Figaro*). In this way we can see how this story is a form of folklore.

A dramatic tableau is painted of the morning when the young man accepted his destiny. The day of the execution at which he would serve as his father's aide for the first time, his father went to wake him at dawn, saying, "Get up, it's

---

[*] I do not have to emphasize the gratuitousness of all these details.

time.'' We are made to remark that the ''future executioner is wrested from sleep just like a man sentenced to death'' (*Paris-Soir*).

On the other hand, the journalists take pleasure in giving the executioner's death a supernatural setting. Coincidences are perceived that are attributed not to chance but to some dark necessity. They insist that the man who caused sudden death died suddenly. They emphasize that he lost his life at the very moment he was leaving to kill. They remark that he was on his way to an execution that was to take place in Rennes, his birthplace. Providence, they say, is incapable of having an executioner die a banal death (*L'Époque*). This is, perhaps, the most ordinary theme of the daily papers: The death of the public executioner must be the homogeneous and satisfying conclusion to something that has been required, something presented as entirely subjected to fate.

Reality, we must admit, has no reason to be jealous of the myth. The character, in fact, seems unique in the State. Strictly speaking he is not a civil servant but a simple employee who is paid by the Justice Department from a special fund in its budget. It seems they want us to think that the State knows nothing about him. In any case, on one important point he is outside the law: He is left out of the draft registration. The sons of executioners are exempt from military service by tacit agreement. To avoid his fate the deceased executioner spontaneously, without being called up, presented himself at the recruiting office, appearing out of the blue ''before the stunned officers.'' They had to enlist him, lacking legal texts with which to challenge him (*L'Intransigeant*). Better yet: The office of executioner is virtually hereditary. When the fate that hangs heavy over their lives is to be emphasized, executioners are shown to be sons, grandsons, and great-grandsons of executioners (*Le Figaro*). The hereditary character of the job, despite being scandalous in a democracy, rouses no comment. Rather it is brought out in titles composed in large print: ''The last in a dynasty'' (*Ce Soir*), ''a line of executioners,'' ''a family of executioners'' (*Paris-Soir*), ''a tragic lineage.'' Certain papers go so far as to think it *natural* that succession follow a collateral line and that Deibler's office would automatically be transmitted to his nephew, since there was no heir in a direct line (*L'Humanité*, *L'Action française*, *L'Ère nouvelle*). Without emphasizing its exceptional nature, there is talk of the prerogative (typical of sovereign power) that would allow the executioner to designate his successor. It is simply mentioned that the deceased used this prerogative in July 1932, in favor of his sister's son, but no one bothered to explain how, under these conditions, someone else might apply for the post of executioner.

Finally, the ''secular'' tradition is mentioned according to which, after the executioner's death, the sentence of the first man condemned to climb the scaffold is commuted (*L'Humanité*, *Le Petit Parisien*, *Paris-Soir*). This all happens as if the executioner's life redeemed the criminal's. On some level this right to pardon, intervening at the death of an executioner as it does at the birth of an heir to the throne, puts the executioner in the same category as the one holding supreme power.

In fact, this is his sociological reality. It explains his particular privileges and his paradoxical position in relation to the law. On the other hand, it justifies the supernatural atmosphere with which people like to surround him and the ambiguous character they attribute to his existence. He presses the murder button "in the name of the people of France" (*L'Intransigeant*). He alone has the authority to do so. He is called "Monsieur de Paris." This title of nobility, whose solemnity is remarked (*La Liberté*), seems to impress the journalists enough that sometimes they are tempted to explain it. Their explanations naturally originate in crude rationalism, and in a naive preoccupation with the ephemeral, which usually inspire the first attempts at simplifying a myth. They speak here, without dwelling on it, of the man who in the provinces was called "le monsieur de Paris" (*Excelsior*). The suggestion is obvious. There the author is not short on details, gravely asserting that when he stayed in hotels, the executioner advised the personnel not to reveal his identity. Consequently, their reply to the curious who asked his name was: "That is 'le monsieur de Paris' (the gentleman from Paris), (*Le Jour*). Obviously, such a solution is impossible because use of the definite article presupposes that the person mentioned is already known. Moreover, this hypothesis does not explain how the expression was retained or how it spread, and above all how it could have been completely transformed by the loss of its article. Anybody, without its being necessary to stress this, can feel how completely different "le monsieur de Paris" (the gentleman from Paris) is from "Monsieur de Paris" (His Grace of Paris). In reality, we are talking about an official title, parallel to those of provincial executioners, Monsieur de Bretagne, Monsieur d'Alger, etc., where Monsieur has the sense of *Monseigneur*, and which corresponds exactly to the formal title formally customary for high dignitaries in the Church, particularly bishops. Thus Bossuet was commonly called "Monsieur de Meaux," Fénelon "Monsieur de Cambrai," Talleyrand "Monsieur d'Autun." The attempt at exegesis is interesting only in its absurdity. It betrays a mind that is too rationalist faced with facts whose nature eludes it.

Nonetheless, the resemblance between executioner and head of State, and their antithetical situation resulting from institutions, is manifested even in their clothing. The redingote, in fact, is considered a real uniform and almost a ceremonial costume belonging less to the man than to the function, and it is passed on along with the function. In one of the tales of Deibler's life, meant to symbolize his final resignation to his fate, he is reported to have returned home one day with the aide's black redingote (*Ce Soir*). This, combined with a top hat, in which he is claimed to have had a "gentleman's refinement" (*L'Ordre*), transformed the appearance of the executioner into a sort of sinister double of the head of State, who traditionally dressed in the same manner. Similarly, under the monarchy, the executioner's appearance was that of a great lord: He was obliged to "curl and powder his hair, to wear braided trim, white stockings, and black shoes." Moreover, we know that in certain German states, the executioner acquired the titles and privileges of nobility when he had cut off a certain number of heads. What is even more bizarre, in Württemburg he could have himself called "Doctor." In France, he enjoyed special rights: He received a pig's head from the Abbey of Saint-Germain when he conducted an execution on its territory, and on Saint-Vincent's Day he walked at the head of the abbey's procession. In Paris the municipality gave him five lengths of cloth for his clothing. He collected a tax on the merchandise displayed at Les Halles. He went in person to demand the payment. Especially, he was acknowledged to have the right of "havage," which consisted in taking as much as one hand could hold of every grain on sale in the market. Finally, a strange custom, more typically an obligation than a privilege, substituting for the king in very specific circumstances: He had to invite all the knights of Saint Louis who had fallen into destitution to dine at his table. It is said that Sanson proudly used a magnificent set of silverware when he did so.

Executioner and Sovereign

The secret affinity between the State's most honored individual and the one most discredited is revealed even in imagination, where both are treated in the same manner. We have seen how insistently the guillotine's blood and horror are compared with the *tranquil* existence and *peaceful* nature of the executioner. Systematically, on every occasion, whether a coronation or a sovereign's visit, the people like to contrast the royal splendor, the pomp and luxury surrounding the monarchs, with the simplicity and modesty of their tastes, "their bourgeois habits." In both instances, the individual is placed in a setting either dreadful or seductive, but at the same time an effort is made to set him in contradiction to this atmosphere, in order to reduce him to the scale of an average man. One might say the average man feels doubly frightened seeing exceptional beings simultaneously very close and very far from him. He tends to identify with them and to draw back from them at the same time, in one movement of avidity and repulsion. We have already acknowledged the psychological constellation defining man's attitude when confronted with the sacred. It is described by Saint Augustine who confesses how he burns with ardor when he thinks of his resemblance to the divine, and shudders in horror when he recalls how different he remains from it.[*] Both the sovereign and the public executioner are close to the homogeneous mass of their fellow citizens and at the same time violently separated from this mass. The ambiguity each of them displays is apparent between them as well; one unites in his person every honor and every form of respect, the other

---

[*]*Confessions* vol. 11, 9, #1.

every form of disgust and scorn. In minds, as in the structure of the State, they occupy situations that correspond and are felt to do so: Each is unique in his place, and they evoke each other precisely because of their antagonism.[*2]

Hence, sovereign and executioner, one in brilliance and splendor and the other in darkness and shame, fulfill cardinal and symmetrical functions. One commands the army from which the other is excluded. They are equally untouchable, but one would soil the former by touching or even looking at him, whereas one would be soiled by contact with the latter. Consequently, in primitive societies they are subjected to numerous interdictions separating them from common existence.[†] Within recent history the executioner was forbidden to enter a public place. It is hard to marry the king, but it is no less difficult for the executioner to get married. One does not form a union with just anyone, and no one wants to unite with the other. Each is isolated by birth, one in grandeur, the other in ignominy. But, representing the two poles of society, they are mutually attractive and tend to be united above the profane world. Without its being necessary to study here the figure of the executioner in mythology and folklore, nonetheless, we must insist on the frequent tales where love joins the queen with the executioner (or his son) and the executioner with the daughter of the king. This is, specifically, the theme of a legend from around Vienna, from which Karl Zuckmeyer derived his famous play, *Der Schelm von Bergen*.

In other stories, the queen dances during a masked ball with a handsome gentleman who wears a red mask on his face; she falls madly in love with him and he is none other than the executioner. In a third type of tale, the executioner's son makes the conquest of a princess because he is the only one who can break the spell that keeps her in a magic melancholy, deprives her of sleep, or prevents her waking up.[**3] Just as the king sometimes takes on priestly functions, and in any event finds himself classed along with the priest and God, sometimes it happens that the executioner appears as a sacrosanct character who represents society in different religious acts. For example, to him is entrusted the consecration of the

---

[*]It is tempting to interpret in this way certain aberrant details in the articles devoted to Deibler's death. It may be reckless, but the absence of any other explanation is an excuse for proposing this one. The executioner is said to have consoled himself for his unfortunate attachment to the daughter of the carpenter Heurteloup by dedicating himself to the "little queen" (*L'Intransigeant*), an expression that, it seems, designates bicycle races. One can wonder whether the resurrection of this bizarre metaphor was not provoked by the more or less conscious sentiment of the homologous situation of the head of State and the executioner in any society. One journalist asks who is the civil servant, the only one of his kind, whose name contains the letters: L, E, B, R, XX, and R. He claims that the man in the street will reply "Lebrun" and not "Deibler." We should certainly not ask such jokes to provide any more than the little they are able to, but the latter is proof, at least, that the Republic's highest magistrate and its executioner tend to form a couple in the mind.

[†]For the king this is a well-known fact; for the executioner, see, for example, Frazer, *Tabou et les périls de l'âme* (French trans., 1927), pp. 150-51.

[**]This information was communicated to me by Hans Mayer, to whom I am extremely grateful.

first fruits of the harvest.[*4] However, generally he belongs to the irregular, sinister, malevolent side of the supernatural world. He is a sort of sorcerer, a reverse-priest. He can take communion, but he must receive the host from gloved hands, which is forbidden to all the other faithful. When parents are opposed to the marriage of two young people, or when the Church for some reason is not willing to bless their union, the couple seeks out the executioner, who marries them by joining their hands, not on the Bible, but on a sword. What is more, dressed in red, the executioner is more or less likened to the Devil. His weapon carries all the contagion of the sacred: Anyone brushing against it is destined for it, and sooner or later the ax will have him. In a tale by Clément Brentano, a young girl inadvertently puts her head on the executioner's ax. That's it. Despite every endeavor she is destined for the scaffold, and in fact, she has her head cut off by the same blade that she carelessly touched.

There are meteorological phenomena attributed to the executioner, as to some supernatural character. In Saint-Malo, when it snows they say the executioner "is plucking his geese." In order to chase away the fog there is a spell threatening that the executioner will come "with his bitch and his hound" to break its neck. He plays the role of a legendary being whose passage has made a mark on nature and the countryside. In the Norman farmlands there is a stream called "the stream of dirty hands." Once the water was pure. But ever since the executioner washed his bloody hands there, after decapitating someone from the region, the water has remained dirty. By virtue of the law attributing a healing power to everything that causes horror, a spring in Saint-Cyr-en-Talmondois named "Spring of the Red Arm," (because tradition has it that an executioner drowned there) has the reputation of being endowed with curative powers. The women who heal warts and all sorts of other excrescences go there to say their incantations as if "the executioner who makes heads roll had passed on to the water as well the power of making anything that sticks out fall off."[†]

Broadly speaking the executioner is regarded as a sorcerer. He is, in fact, in a good position to have an abundant supply of the numerous ingredients extracted from his victims' corpses that magic fancies for its potions. Hanged-man's fat, which cures rheumatism, is bought from him, as well as human skull scrapings used against epilepsy. Above all, he trades in mandrake root, which grows at the foot of the gallows and procures women, wealth, and power for its possessor. For a long time he has had the right to dispose of the victims' spoils, always superstitiously regarded as talismans. The people of Paris argued greedily over the possessions of the Marquise de Brinvilliers. Here, once again, the link between sovereign power and the dark, powerful forces haunting crime and the executioner can be noted. In the palace of the emperor of Monomatapa, a once pow-

---

[*]Frazer, *Le Bouc Émissaire* (The Scapegoat) (French trans., Paris, 1925), pp. 158, 407n., 440.
[†]P. Sébillot, *Le Folk-lore de France* (Paris, 1906), vol. 1, pp. 86, 119; vol. 2, pp. 282, 374.

erful southeastern African state, there was a room where criminals' bodies were cremated. Their ashes were used to make an elixir kept exclusively for the potentate.

It is useless to conjecture, as sometimes happens, on what tricks were used that could possibly explain these beliefs. We can assume that executioners used subterfuge in certain executions, making an opening in the hanged man's windpipe underneath the rope and omitting the kick to his cervical vertebrae that was meant to finish him off.[*] Not only should there be some reservations about the possibility of such maneuvers, but we must refuse to see anything in them that might have ascribed to the executioner the ability to raise the dead. Whenever such fraud was attempted it was discovered, and this could not have served to attribute to the executioner a power that, moreover, seems never to have been witnessed. The medical knowledge conceded to him, on the contrary, clearly derives from the very nature of his office, the ease with which he is able to obtain substances necessary for the composition of various ointments, and the sort of life he is obliged to live. In the nineteenth century the executioner still set bones and provided the medical doctor with some unfair competition. The one from Nîmes was famous. An Englishman, suffering from a stiff neck that resisted treatment, and abandoned by the professors at the Faculté de Montpellier whom he had crossed the Channel to consult, ended up entrusting himself to the executioner's care. The executioner cured him by simulating his hanging. The anecdote speaks for itself. Just as the young people who have *despaired* of receiving the *legitimate* blessing of the Church authorities go to be married by the one who is accursed, so patients who *despair* of *official* knowledge knock on his door to be cured. Thus the executioner is seen to be in constant conflict with and substituted for organisms that society acknowledges, respects, and upholds. These organisms, in exchange, project on society the veneration and prestige whose object they are. Those who lose faith in these all-powerful institutions, who no longer expect the realization of their hopes, turn toward their sinister, abhorred counterpart who is not incorporated *as a body*, like Justice, Church, or Science, and who lives apart, *on the margin*, whom one flees and persecutes simultaneously, whom one fears and illtreats. When God does not answer, one calls the Devil; when the doctor is powerless, the healer; when the banks refuse, the usurer. The executioner touches both worlds. His mandate is from the law, but he is the last of its servants, the one nearest the dark, peripheral regions where the very ones he is fighting stir and hide. He seems to emerge from a terrible, disordered zone into the light of order and legality. One might say the clothing he uses to officiate is a disguise. The Middle Ages did not allow him to live inside the cities. His house was built in the outlying quarters, the favorite place for criminals and prostitutes. For a long time, if a man's profession as ex-

---

[*]Charles Durand, in an unpublished article quoted in the article "Bourreau" in the *Grand Larousse*.

ecutioner was concealed when a building was rented, it was acknowledged as cause for nullification of the contract. Even today at Place Saint-Jacques the passerby observes with surprise some wretched tumbledown houses dwarfed by high commercial buildings: That is where formerly the executioner and his aides lived and where the scaffolds used to be stored. Whether through chance or bias no one yet has bought them to tear down and build something in their place. In Spain the executioner's house was painted red. He himself had to wear a cassock of white cloth bordered in scarlet and cover his head with a wide-brimmed hat, because he had to call attention to his lair and his person for the loathing of his fellowmen.

Everything connects the executioner to the unassimilated part of the social body. Most often he is a pardoned criminal, sometimes he is the *last* person to take up habitation in the city; in Swabia, the *last* elected alderman; in Franconia, the *last* man married. Fulfilling the function of executioner consequently becomes a sort of entrance fee, a token of aggregation to the community. It is an office entrusted to a person who finds himself in a *marginal period* until some newcomer takes his place as *last comer* and definitively unites him with the other members of the group. Even the executioner's income seems doomed to be too shameful to mention. He rents shops on the Place de la Grève. He owns or is entrusted with administering houses of prostitution. Under the ancien régime he collected a tax on the streetwalkers. Cast out by society, he shares the fate of everything it condemns and keeps at a distance. He is appointed by a letter from the Grand Chancellery, signed by the king himself, but the document is thrown to him under the table, where he has to crawl to pick it up. Above all he is the man who agrees to kill others in the name of the law. Only the head of State has the right of life and death over the citizens of a nation, and only the executioner enforces it. He leaves the sovereign the prestigious part and takes charge of the part that is infamous. The blood staining his hands does not sully the court that pronounced sentence: The executioner takes on himself all the horror of the execution. As a result he is classed with the criminals whom he sacrifices. Those who are protected by the terrifying examples of which he is author keep their distance from him, regard him as a monster, scorn and fear him inasmuch as they dread those from whom they have asked him to deliver them permanently. This has reached such a point that his death seems to ransom the life of a guilty person. He is annexed by the world of perdition on whose frontier he has been placed as a vigilant and implacable sentinel rejected by the very ones who owe their sense of security to him. Joseph de Maistre, at the end of the impressive portrait he painted of the executioner, the terror he inspires, his isolation among his fellowmen, points out precisely that this living depth of abjection is simultaneously the condition and support of all grandeur, all power, and all subordination. "It is both the horror and the bond of human society," he concludes.[5] One could not find a better phrase to show the extent to which the executioner constitutes the counterpart, both support and antithesis of this same society's *horror* and *bond*, of the sovereign whose majestic face presupposes the reverse side of infamy assumed by his terrible opposite.

Under these conditions one can understand that the beheading of the king would fill the people with astonishment and fear, and would seem to be the culmination of revolutions. This act joins the two poles of society, so one is sacrificed by the other, to assure something like a momentary victory of the forces of disorder and change over those of order and stability. Moreover, this triumph lasts only for the moment in which the ax falls, for the deed is less sacrifice than sacrilege. It makes an attempt on majesty, but only to establish another. From the sovereign's blood is born the divinity of the nation. When the executioner shows the monarch's head to the crowd, he attests the perpetration of a crime, but at the same time, he communicates to those present the holy power of the beheaded king, by baptizing them with royal blood.

However paralyzing such an act may be, we must not expect that in later history it ever took on such a precise meaning. Societies in which periodic execution of the king forms a regular part of the workings of institutions, entering into their normal functioning as a rite of renewal or expiation, have been left behind. Such customs are not related to the execution of the sovereign as it is produced during a crisis of rule or dynasty. Its nature, then, is that of an episode with strictly political import, even if it arouses in some people, as is natural, *individual* reactions that are clearly religious. Be that as it may, we can rest assured that *in the popular consciousness*, the beheading of the king unerringly appears as the acme of the revolution. It provides the multitude with the bloody and solemn spectacle of the transmission of power. The imposing ceremony sanctifies the people in whose name, and for whose benefit, it is realized.

Very significant in this respect is the attitude of the French Revolution toward the executioner. We have evidence of numerous events clearly meant to integrate him into the noble, just, and respectable sphere of high society. On December 23, 1789, Father Maury still contested the executioner's rights as an active citizen. The Convention would do more than merely accord these rights. There is no token of honor that is not lavished on him. Leguinio, an assigned representative, publicly embraced the executioner of Rochefort, whom he had invited to dinner and seated facing him at table. One general had the guillotine engraved on his seal. A Conventional decree gave the public executioners the rank of officer in the armies of the Republic. At official festivities executioners were asked to open the ball. The National Assembly reinforced the interdiction against calling them by the libelous name *bourreaux*. The new title they should be given is debated. "Avenger of the People" was proposed. During the debate Mathon de la Varenne praised them: He was indignant that punishment of the guilty should be "degrading for those inflicting the punishment." In his opinion, the ignominy should at least be divided among all those who collaborate in the workings of justice, from the president of the court down to the last clerk.

Corresponding to this promotion of the executioner is the deposition of the king. One is made to enter the law at the same moment the other is made to leave it. The statement delivered by Saint-Just on November 12, 1792, produced such a sensation in public opinion that historians quite willingly regard this as the act deciding the condemnation of Louis XVI. The speech is entirely devoted to justifying the exclusion of the monarch from the protection of the laws. The orator's cold and implacable logic demonstrates that there is no middle course: Louis must "rule or die." He is not a citizen, cannot vote, or bear arms. The laws of the city never concern him. In a monarchy he is above them; in a republic he is outside the society simply for having been king. "One does not rule innocently."* We have seen how the executioner was outside laws in the same way: He too was unable to bear arms and they wanted to take away his right to vote, as if one could not be an executioner innocently. The situation is reversed. The community, this time, drives the king from its bosom and transforms the executioner into an honored representative of popular sovereignty. Saint-Just does not hide the fact that the king's death is to be the very foundation of the Republic and is to constitute for it "a bond of public spirit and unity."[6]

If the decapitation of Louis XVI is thus presented as token and symbol of the new regime's advent, if his deposition appears so precisely symmetrical to the executioner's rise, it is understandable that the execution of January 21, 1793, should occupy, in the course of the Revolution, a position approaching a sort of zenith.[7] It truly represents the highest point of a curve and provides the most condensed and complete illustration of the whole crisis, the most vivid summation of it for memory.

On the contrary, the execution of Marie-Antoinette was by no means an affair of State. It did not revive the majesty of a king in the majesty of a people. The "Widow Capet" appeared before the revolutionary Court, not before the Convention, that is, before judges and not before the representatives of the nation. They went after her private life. It is as much the woman in her as the queen that is condemned. They went out of their way to disgrace her. The crowd insulted her while the cart carried her to the scaffold. A paper recording the execution mentioned that the wretched woman had to "swallow death for a long time."

There is no doubt that this time a certain sadism played a role in the applause of those present watching the queen delivered to the executioner. The scene is like a counterpart of the stories where the queen falls in love with the executioner. Love and death bring the representatives of the two poles of society together in a strange way. The kiss of the queen and the accursed man seemed a redemption of the world of darkness by the world of light. The falling of the

---

*Saint-Just, *Oeuvres complètes* (Paris, 1908), vol. 1, pp. 364-72.

royal head, the ignominious execution of the queen, manifested the victory of the powers of damnation. In general, it aroused more horror and reprobation than the death of the king, it provoked a greater shudder, it aroused more violent reactions. The encounter of the queen and executioner on history's gallows or in masked balls, by transporting the significance into the realm of passion, conferred the most accessible and most directly moving form of meaning onto moments where the opposite forces of society confront each other, intersect, and, like stars, come into conjunction only to immediately separate and return to occupy their position at a respectful distance from each other.

Thus the executioner and the sovereign make a couple. In concert they assure the cohesiveness of society. The one who bears the scepter and crown draws to his person all the honors due to the highest power; the other bears the weight of sins necessarily entailed by the exercise of authority, no matter how just and moderate it may be. The horror he inspires is the counterpart of the splendor surrounding the monarch, whose right of reprieve presupposes conversely the murderous deed of the executioner. The lives of men are in their hands. It is not surprising, therefore, that both are the objects of feelings of horror or veneration, whose sacred nature is clearly acknowledged. One protects everything we respect, everything constituting the values and institutions upon which the whole society rests. The other seems contaminated by the pollution of those whom society has turned over to him; he makes his money from prostitutes and passes for a sorcerer. He is rejected into the darkness outside, into the sinister, teeming, unassimilable world hunted down by the justice whose agent he nonetheless is. So we must not blame the press too much for having devoted so many articles to the death of Anatole Deibler. It has allowed us to see the extent to which the executioner continues to be a legendary character and keeps the important, bygone traits of his former visage within imaginations. It demonstrates that there is no society so totally won over by the powers of abstraction that myth and the realities giving birth to it lose all authority and power within it.

Shamanism
Anatole Lewitzky
Tuesday, March 7, and Tuesday, March 21, 1939

[The text of this lecture was published by Caillois in Diogène, *no. 17 (January 1957) with the title "Mythes et rites du chamanisme." The same review (no. 20, October 1957) provided the following biographical note on the author: "Anatole LEWITZKY: born at Bogorodskoi, near Moscow, in 1901; refugee in Switzerland then Paris; higher education at the Sorbonne, with a diploma from the Institut d'Ethnologie; student of Marcel Mauss at the École pratique des Hautes Études, in the political science division; at the same time that he pursued his education, A. L. worked as an accountant, then a chauffeur, then in a warehouse, etc.; in 1933 he joined the Musée de l'Homme; in 1937 he took charge of the museum's department of Oceania; in 1939 he was charged with creating a department of comparative technology at the museum; he received a grant from the CNRS in 1938; French delegate to the International Congress of Anthropological and Ethnological Sciences in Copenhagen, 1938; shot as a Resistance worker in 1942."*

Two details in this note must be corrected. It should read "religious science" rather than "political science." Moreover, in 1933 the Musée de l'Homme did not exist. It was still only the Ethnographic Museum of the Trocadéro, directed by Paul Rivet. It is Rivet who, between 1935 and 1937, aided by Georges-Henri Rivière, was to reorganize it in order to create the present Musée de l'Homme in the brand-new Palais de Chaillot that had just been constructed on the Place du Trocadéro. Lewitzky took an active part in setting it up again. The inauguration took place in June 1938 (the 27th, to be exact). Leiris, who was also one of the family, briefly notes this occasion in the NRF *of August 1938: "From Ethno-graphic Museum to Museum of Man."*

Under the direction of Mauss and René Grousset, Lewitzky prepared a thesis on Siberian shamanism. Then war broke out. As soon as he was demobilized, in August 1940, Lewitzky returned to Paris and with Boris Vildé and Yvonne Odon set up the resistance network at the Musée de l'Homme, the first to appear in oc-cupied France. On February 11, 1941, the SS surrounded the Palais de Chail-lot. The Musée de l'Homme was searched, and Lewitzky was arrested and taken to Fresnes. The network, whose other members were subsequently arrested, was to be put on trial January 6 of the following year. The trial lasted six weeks and ended in ten death sentences. The women were pardoned. Vildé, Lewitzky, and the five other members of the Resistance were shot by the Germans on February 23, 1942, on Mont-Valérien. (Paulhan, who was involved as the publisher, gave his version of the events in "Une Semaine au secret" (A week in solitary) in Écrivains en prison *[Paris, 1945; reissued in 1956 in volume 1 of his* Oeuvres*]; see also his interviews with R. Mallet,* Les Incertitudes du langage *[Paris, 1970], p. 148. Aragon, in* Le Crime contre l'esprit *[Paris, 1944], devoted sev-eral pages to this affair of the Musée de l'Homme, and there is an entire work devoted to it by Martin Blumenson,* The Vildé Affair: Beginnings of the French Resistance *[Boston, 1977].)*

Leiris published in Nuits sans nuit *two nightmares directly connected to the execution of this colleague in ethnology who chose the Resistance and for whom no secret, miraculous intervention provided time to finish his thesis on the sha-mans—those titans outraged by the order of the world and the omnipotence of the gods. The first of these dreams is dated the night of May 19-20, 1942. In the sec-ond, dated "a week later," the sentenced man's silhouette is fleetingly recalled. It is just at the moment that he went to the place where he was to be executed. "Topped with a soft hat, his face with its slightly mongoloid cheekbones and eyes seemed extremely pale (but really no paler than usual)."*

Because of his familiarity with Russian, his mother tongue, Lewitzky special-ized in the study of Siberian civilizations. From 1932 to 1937 Mauss gave a course on northeastern Asian cosmology at the Hautes Études. In his teaching résumé he twice mentions Lewitzky's contribution to his work: in 1934-35, "Mr. Lewitzky gave three excellent lectures on Buryat and Yakut shamanism, making use of all the Russian documents and particularly treating the beautiful hunting costumes he was able to study at the Trocadéro"; in 1936-37, "Mr. Lewitzky has continued his work on the Goldes with an excellent study of Golde shaman-ism and the mythology of shamanism" (M. Mauss, Oeuvres, *ed. Karady [Paris, 1969], vol. 2, pp. 186-87). Lewitzky also participated in the volume of the* Encyclopédie française *devoted to "The Human Race" (vol. 7, 1936), directed by Rivet (in the index, we can pick out the names Leiris, Métraux, Soustelle, Halbwachs . . .). He also took part in the* Histoire générale des religions *(to which Leiris also contributed) published at Quillet by M. Gorce and R. Mortier. It is from this publication that I have taken the bibliographical references mentioned in the notes to this lecture. The notes he took in preparation for his thesis have been collected by Eveline Lot-Falck, who used them in* Les Rites de chasse chez les peuples sibériens, *published in 1953 in the collection "L'Espèce humaine" that Leiris was in charge of at that time at Gallimard. We know that Bataille made use of this work, which appeared at the moment he was writing his* Lascaux. *Numerous analogies between the valley of the Vézère and that of the Amur would arise from his reading, even to the extent of this surprising landscape description of the "desolate, somewhat Siberian aspect of the Causses."*

The question of shamanism was central to the intellectual preoccupations of the College. Bataille proclaimed himself a "sorcerer's apprentice." And Caillois, in the notice at the beginning of Le Mythe et l'homme, *contrasted "as the representatives of two fundamental attitudes of the mind,* shamanism, *displaying the power of the individual who struggles against the natural order of reality, and* manism, *showing the pursuit through self-abandon of an identification of self and nonself, consciousness and the external world." Both poetry and mysticism are the concerns of* manism *whereas the magician's knowledge and aggressivity are associated with* shamanism. *Caillois would mention shamanism again in a note in the* NRF *devoted to Lévy-Bruhl (no. 299, August 1938, p. 323), referring then to Lewitzky's work: "Lévy-Bruhl's pages on the shaman's function in a leaderless society are, he says, extremely important. Moreover, it is a fundamental question and much to be regretted that its primary literature, almost exclusively in Russian, is so inaccessible. But the few who have been privileged to hear A. Lewitzky's discussions know, as I do, how extraordinarily significant the problem is. We would have liked Mr. Lévy-Bruhl to have done more than mention it in passing."*

I shall end this introduction by quoting the passage of Caillois's interview with Gilles Lapouge (La Quinzaine littéraire, June 16-30, 1970) in which the College's reactions to Lewitzky's double session are mentioned: "Lewitzky gave two lectures on shamanism. The question enthralled me [Caillois is speaking] because in my schema (Mauss's schema), there was a complete antinomy between magic and religion. I was feeling very Luciferian at that time, I regarded Lucifer as the rebel who was effective. Shamanism, consequently, was important to me as the synthesis between religious powers and the realm of infernal affairs. Bataille, for his part, was in approximately the same frame of mind. But the difference was that Bataille wanted really to become a shaman."]

What is shamanism? What is the social nature of this institution that sometimes seems so obviously situated on the margin of society that one is almost tempted to describe it as antisocial? There is no dearth of definitions, of course, but regarding religion there are no definitions that hold; the limits of its phenomena are too vague, the nuances too subtle. The shaman's social position is so variable that it seems scarcely possible to envisage the juridical, as it were, as-pect of the question. On the other hand, in mythology and ritual we find numer-ous elements that indicate the position held by the shaman in collective represen-tations, especially through the general representations of divinities. In seeking to establish the shaman's position in relation to the divinities, as it comes to light in mythology, we arrive at information on his social nature, that is to say, on the way society conceives of the shaman.

What seems unquestionable is that the term ''shamanism'' corresponds to a reality.[1] In fact, among Turko-Mongolians, Finno-Ugrics, Asian Tunguso-Manchurians and Palearctics, as well as among the Tibetans and the North American Indians, we encounter magico-religious practices that show numerous common characteristics. Note the presence of the *drum,* [2] widespread from the Lapps to the Eskimo of Greenland, ecstatic *dances*, the clearly pathological na-ture of the shaman's personality, and finally the idea of a profoundly intimate contact with the representatives of the spirit world, the notion of levitation and, more generally, of penetration into other worlds.

But (accompanying these common characteristics), what a variety of specific forms, and of elements that are superimposed or substituted! Shamanism can scarcely be studied independently of the historical and archaeological study of central and northern Asia; strictly ethnographical methods are not sufficient. We are concerned with populations belonging to several linguistic families, living over a vast terrain, populations who, in the course of their history, were shaken up by innumerable migrations, who founded empires or were incorporated into them. Finally came Buddhism, Islam, and Christianity. At the present time there is great confusion, and yet it does not seem that the ancient beliefs are com-pletely destroyed.

What is a shaman? From whom did he get his power? What is his role?

One becomes a shaman only if one has certain psychic and nervous disposi-tions, which are interpreted as a vocation or even a direct call from the spirits. These dispositions sometimes appear in infancy, or in adults following a shock to the nervous equilibrium by some sickness or accident. Whereas it is a general rule that every magician is suffering a nervous disorder to some extent, shaman-ism is characterized by rites whose very performance requires a morbid nervous organization. Without exception all authors testify to these facts. Radlov ob-serves that, among Altaic Tartars, beginning shamans are subject to attacks of epilepsy and hysteria or display other symptoms of nervous disorders.[3] Hangalov points out that the future Buryat shamans have a quite specific neuropsychic con-stitution, clearly different from that of a normal man.[4] He cites also the case of three famous shamans from the district of Balagansk who, stricken with violent dementia, had to be put to death. Bogoras asserts that for the future shaman the idea of his vocation reaches such intensity that he contracts nervous diseases ex-actly during the period of *revelation*.[5]

A shaman is chosen by the spirits.[6] These spirits come to find him, offer him their friendship, their support, indeed their services. To become a shaman one must have a strong soul. Being noticed by the spirits is proof of exceptional power. One only needs to make the acquaintance of several myths pertaining to shamanism to understand that the shaman is always seen as a being capable of emulating the spirits and, moreover, one who possesses all their specific qualities. The shaman in mythology is more than an intermediary between men and spirits, he is a spirit himself—he has his independence and his own power. Far from being their servant, he makes numerous secondary spirits, over whom he holds authority, serve him. To illustrate this aspect of shamanism, here are a few myths that are quite suggestive:

Yakuts—myth of the first shaman

"His name was An-Argyl-Oyum.

"He was powerful and accomplished great miracles: He raised the dead, restored sight to the blind. The rumor of such miracles went as far as Ai-Toyen (God). He sent to ask the shaman in what god's name he worked these miracles and if he believed in him? An-Argyl-Oyum (the grave, important shaman) answered three times that he did not believe in god and that he accomplished the miracles by his own power and his own strength.

"Ai-Toyen, in a fury, commanded that the shaman be burned.

"But, because Oyum's body was made out of reptiles, a frog was able to escape the flame and went to live in a very high mountain.

"The descendants of this frog are the powerful demons that to the present day still provide the shamans of the Yakuts."

The First Buryat Shaman
(version reported by Chachkov) [7]

"The most famous of all the shamans, Hara-Gyrgen, had unlimited strength; raising the dead, enriching the poor—everything was within his power. This omnipotence worried the god (the most popular of the gods of heaven: Esege-Malan) who feared that the shaman might rebel against him one day. So he decided to test him. He took away the soul from a wealthy young girl. This caused her to fall gravely ill and her father invited the shaman (to cure her). The shaman concentrated all his forces, sat on his drum and flew into the heavens and all over them, as well as into all the spaces of the underground world, in search of the lost soul.

"Suddenly he saw it on the god's table, shut up in a bottle that the god was plugging with his finger. The wily shaman then turned himself into a yellow spider and stung the god hard on his cheek. The god let go of the bottle and put his hand on his cheek. The shaman took advantage of this to steal the soul shut up in the bottle and return it to the dying young girl. But the god did not forgive him for his insolence and took steps to limit his power.''

The second version is more complete.

''The first Buryat shaman was Boholi-Hara; he had a supernatural strength. Boholi-Hara possessed a book of writings that he got from Esege-Malan-Tengeri. At this time there was a very wealthy man living on the earth who had no children at all. He addressed the shaman Boholi-Hara, asking him to help him in his difficulty, by intervening with the god so he would give him a son. So Boholi-Hara went into the rich man's house and began to shamanize, but he did not address the gods or genies with the request that they grant this man with no descendants a son. He himself made a son for him, setting about it in the following manner: He made the bones of stone, the flesh of clay, the blood of river water. He still had to give him a soul, but Boholi-Hara was not at all at a loss: He gathered seventy different flowers and made the boy's soul out of them. At the end of a short time a son was born to the childless moneybags and he grew to be three years old.

''One day the sky (Esege-Mamo) ordered three winged couriers to inspect the earth. The three winged couriers flew all over the earth and found everything in order, except that a childless moneybags had an exceptionally beautiful boy born to him and no one knew who had created him; the winged couriers went back to Esege-Malan and gave him an account of this. So Esege-Malan learned that the boy had been created without their intervention by the shaman Boholi-Hara, who had no right to create men independently of the gods, for only gods could create men; that is why Esege-Malan sent the three winged couriers back, charging them with bringing the boy's soul to him.''

Just as in the previous version, the god shut the soul up in a bottle and the shaman managed to get it out. The text again:

''Boholi-Hara came back down to earth and made the boy's soul reenter his body; then he exclaimed: 'There exists no other man in the world who is capable, as I am, of creating a man and taking his soul back from Esege-Malan.' Hearing that, Esege-Malan was stricken with rage and ordered the shaman to appear before him. The shaman went up into the sky to the home of Esege-Malan who took his shamanist book, tore it up and threw it away. Then he said to Boholi-Hara: 'How do you dare, you, a secular man, to create a man without the gods, who alone are qualified to do it? How dare you cause me pain and take back the soul of someone who is sick?' Finally he cut the shaman's drum in two, which diminished his power.

''At this moment the sky's nine sons came into Esege-Malan's home and said to him: 'We need him, because every day we shoot nine arrows onto the earth and he returns them to us in the sky.' Esege-Malan sentenced the shaman Boholi-Hara to sit astride a black stone until either the stone or he wore out. If Boholi-

Hara wore out before the stone then he would no longer exist and shamans would be powerless. If, however, Boholi-Hara did not wear out, but the stone did, then he would reappear on earth once more in possession of the same power." The myth ends with a theme that is of considerable importance. The shaman, it is said, withstood the test thanks to the support given him by a god, who is one of the guardian gods of the forge. "Boholi-Hara put on iron boots that wouldn't wear out, which had been given him by the god of the sky Zan-Sagan, and that is why, now, Boholi-Hara sits astride the stone and the stone is wearing away, is already halfway gone."

This is a rather impressive myth. Nonetheless, I would hesitate to offer it as a definition of shamanism. The titanic element seems exaggerated in it, in fact, especially when it is compared to mythical tales of other shamanist peoples of Asia.[8] Buryat mythology is highly developed. The notion of god encountered there is not common to the shamanistic world. It seems to have been developed by numerous successive generations of shamans, organized into a veritable clergy. It is already a mythology that is based on a systematized cosmogony.

But there are two things in this myth I would like to pause over: the return of the arrows to heaven and the assistance of the god of the forge. The sky's nine sons every day shoot nine arrows onto the earth and it is the shaman who returns them. In almost every part of Asia there is a widespread rite that consists in shooting arrows into the heavens, on certain specific occasions. What is an arrow if not a vehicle, or more generally speaking, a means of communicating with distant realms? Among the Buryats a man who is killed by lightning is given the status of a shaman; he is buried according to the funeral rites customary for the burial of a shaman: The officiants take nine arrows, and along the route, they shoot one into the sky; they are returning to the sky—they say—the arrow that killed the man. On the way back from the burial they shoot the eight others, destined, no doubt, for eight other gods of the sky. Thus, relations between the sky and the earth are regularly assured, there is a continual exchange of some sort, a kind of reciprocity.[9]

These relations are thought indispensable by the gods themselves, so much so that they intervene in favor of the shaman in disgrace. This notion of indispensable relations between the different worlds, so characteristic of shamanistic mythologies in general, retains all its force in Buryat rites and beliefs. In order to assume the fundamental function of his profession, the shaman has to undergo an apprenticeship in the celestial realms.

A particularly interesting piece of information is reported by Sternberg. "A Buryat shaman," he said, "generally has for his ancestor some great shaman, who has become a spirit, who chooses the most capable of his descendants. He takes their souls to heaven in order to teach them the shamanistic art and familiarize them with the vast heavenly empire, accustoming them to its rules. When they go to heaven, the souls of young shamans stop at the home of the god of the middle world; Tehasar Mankal, the yellow goat, god of the dance, fertility, and wealth, who lives with the nine daughters of Solboni, god of dawn . . . . There the young shaman's soul spends its time in amorous play with the divine daughters, etc.''[10] Let us ignore for the moment this question of the shaman's intimacy with spirits of the opposite sex. What must be especially noted here is that the true initiation takes place in heaven. It could not be expressed more clearly than in this rite.

The ceremony is presided over by an old shaman, assisted by nine young people; ritually these are the shaman-father and his nine sons, the latter symbolizing the sky's nine sons. Nine receptacles, nine wooden bowls, nine stones are prepared; in the village burial grove a certain number of birches and one pine are taken down. The largest birch, pulled up by the roots, is permanently planted in a corner of the future shaman's dwelling, with its top, stuck through the hole over the hearth, rising above the roof. This birch symbolizes the door god, who gives the shaman access to heaven and the different gods. Before the postulant's dwelling a fixed number of birches are planted in the ground: first one, then nine main ones, then three groups of three that are chosen from dry trees, then finally nine more that were to serve for tying up sacrificial rams, etc. A whole system of red and blue cords binds the great birch inside with the birches outside. These cords symbolize the path—literally *the bridge* [11] the shaman must cross to reach the gods. Once everything is in place, the shamans gather in the novice's dwelling and begin to shamanize, that is, to sing and dance, and invoking particularly the first ninety shaman-men and the first ninety shaman-women. At the proper moment they form a procession that makes its way toward the sacrificial animals, who are immolated after a rather complex purification ritual. It is then that the initiate approaches the first of the nine birches, climbs to the top and invokes first the master of the shamans, then his deceased shaman-relatives. He climbs down head first. Then, making nine spirals around each of the eight other trees he climbs them one after the other, and at the top invokes the corresponding spirits. The nine birches that the initiate climbs allow him, of course, to reach the nine heavens. Thus, by direct contact with the nine tengheri,[12] he will have the necessary powers for performing the function conferred upon him. As for the birch planted permanently inside his dwelling, it allows him to reach his patron or, in general, the realms inhabited by spirits at any moment.

In his life, the shaman then seems a person who is obedient to the gods, and the ritual represents him as getting his powers from the gods of heaven. In what is the official, as it were, mythology shamanism is represented as an institution created by the nine gods of heaven who favor humans, with the aim of helping men. In Yakut shamanism, which though rather highly organized, conserves better a number of archaic elements, we find this fine oath pronounced during initiation: ''I promise to be the protector of the wretched, father of the poor, mother of the orphans.'' Initiation, which is shorter than among the Buryats, consists of this: The future shaman, dressed in ritual costume, sticks and drum in hand, is led by his initiator onto a mountain or into the distant countryside. Nine young virgin girls are placed at his right and nine young boys at his left. The old shaman stands behind and pronounces the words of the oath that the initiate repeats. He too engages himself to consecrate his life to the genie who has chosen him, and to obey this genie's orders. It is then that the master reveals to the initiate the place this spirit stays, and the spirit thus becomes the tutelary genie of the new shaman; the master also teaches him the procedures to use to control this guardian genie. In reality, the shaman possesses several tutelary genies, just as every man possesses several souls that are distinguished by specific characters. However, he has one that could be considered the principal one: *ijä-kyl*, the animal-mother, a true personal totem, upon whom his life and death depend. The shaman sees it only three times during his life. The animal-mother dies before the shaman does, but he cannot survive it for long. This totem resides always in the same place; it is eminently vulnerable because fright is enough to kill it. Alongside this totem, the Yakut shaman possesses another principal tutelary genie; this one is active. The shaman's power particularly depends on this genie. These genies are called *shamans* and constitute the counterparts in the beyond of shamans living on the earth. Their battles have a direct repercussion on the fate of earthly shamans.

It is doubtful, however, that one can consider dualism a characteristic of shamanist mythologies. We find in them elements that tend to prove that this is a recent distinction. In fact, the idea of a primitive lack of differentiation is encountered even in the Yakuts. For example, here is the myth of the initiation that takes place in heaven. In the Yakut pantheon there is an important divinity whose name literally translated means *the insatiable glutton-sun*; this divinity is one of the sons of the great god of heaven. The principal attribute of this god is a huge iron stick. During initiation the head of the shaman-initiate, detached from his body, is stuck on the end of this stick in such a way that the whole world can be shown to the head. During this time the initiate's body is cut into pieces and these pieces are thrown below to the secondary spirits; when these have eaten the flesh of the initiate they become his natural servants as a result.

This representation of the shaman's servant-genies is even more apparent in Tungus shamanism, which is certainly much more archaic than that of the peoples who are, strictly speaking, Turko-Mongols.

For most of the Tungus people the initiation ceremony is completely lacking. The man who feels disposed to become a shaman has no need of investiture. His dignity is conferred on him by the spirits. Initiation is the exclusive business of the spirits. It is up to them to judge whether the aspirant is sufficiently prepared for the exercise of his ministry. To be acknowledged, a Tungus shaman must simply show his ability. What is remarkable is that the ritual of initiation is lacking even among those Tungus peoples who possess a hierarchy of shamanic ranks, as do certain of them from the Amurian region. Among the Goldes, the future shaman himself chooses the moment of his consecration, obeying—he believes—his genie's will. When he decides he is sufficiently prepared, he invites all his nearby relatives, as well as his neighbors. Behind his dwelling, beneath a large tree, he plants nine little sketchily carved stakes, which depict the clan's friendly divinities. In the evening, after sunset, he begins to sing in honor of his tutelary genie. Then, leaving the house, he dances his way toward the prepared place and performs nine chants, alternated with dances. When this long show is over he takes the sacrificial animal presented to him—a young pig, a rooster, or a wild duck—bleeds it, sprinkles the idols with blood, and drinks some himself. Next he dismembers the animal, cuts its head off, and removes the liver, the heart, and lungs, which are reserved for the genies. Everyone returns to the house, the new shaman goes in dancing, seats himself on the boards, and begins to sing the story relating his conversion. The ceremony ends with a feast.

This ceremony is sufficient for one to be recognized as a shaman of the first rank, whose principal function is to combat evil spirits, particularly those of illness. The second and third rank give the right to preside over funerals, to take the soul of the dead person, and to lead it into the beyond. The shaman confers these ranks on himself also. Upon the invitation of a spirit, he manufactures the clothing and ritual attributes that correspond. Then, accompanied by two or three assistants, he makes ceremonial visits to the villages inhabited by members of his clan. During these visits, he does not reveal the aim of his trip. When he has reached the limit of his clan's territory, he puts on the distinguishing signs of his new dignity and returns, announcing his inspiration to everyone and inviting his relatives to the great sacrifice of consecration. On the eve of the ceremony, after sunset, nine people perform a dance, in which the whole gathering soon participates. The dancers wear bells around their waists and play drums. The dance goes on until the arrival of the shaman himself. He begins by telling in song his story, his struggles, his hesitations; he invokes his guardian spirits, begins suddenly to speak in their name, and dances. This session is divided into nine stages. When the ninth chant is over, the most senior member of the assemblage pours a glass of eau-de-vie and, kneeling, presents it to the shaman, with these words: "Be our shaman, help us." The next day the sacrifice takes place. As soon as it is morning the shaman begins to stir, he implores his genies not to abandon him and never to refuse him their help, then finally to accept the sacrifice. When all the preparations are finished, the shaman, followed by all the guests, goes to the place designated for the ceremony. Before the figurines, nine pigs are lined up with their hooves tied. At a sign from the shaman, his assistants leap on the animals, bleed them, and collect the blood in wooden bowls, which they present to their master. Afflicted by the most intense excitation, shouting, and shaking, he drinks the blood greedily. Abruptly he goes into a trance, shouts out hysterically, leaps and dances, violently shaking all the bells and pendants on his ritual costume. It can happen that nervous tension reaches such a level of intensity in the ecstatic shaman that he collapses in a faint.

While the shaman rests, the meat of the animals that is meant for the subsequent meal is cooked. The feast usually goes on late into the night. The shaman, after having drunk the first glass of eau-de-vie, does not drink any more and eats only with great moderation. Etiquette demands that he himself serve his guests, and he will soon be the only one in their midst to have his wits about him.

The genie who chose the shaman will serve him throughout his ministry as his agent, performing on his behalf in the invisible worlds. The Tungus from the Amur region call this genie *ajami*: the friend. He is the spiritual support that the shaman can count on under any circumstance, whose faithfulness is not based on self-interest, who supports him through pure affection, indeed through love. Moreover, it is primarily through the intermediary of this genie that the Tungus shaman recruits his other invisible assistants. He has several categories of them generally, of varying strength. There are some he uses as fighters in his mythical battles against his enemies from the other world; others as scouts or intelligence agents; still others as simple couriers or porters. It is not only through the power of attraction of his strong personality that the shaman retains them all. Some he gets through prayers and persuasion; certain less important ones merely find it advantageous to be regularly fed the blood and intestines of sacrificed animals. Whereas the smallest genies are often recruited by force, among the Tungus of Transbaikalia, Shirokogorov points out that the shaman is surrounded by a large group of supporting genies of every sort, and that it is his business to prevent their being harmful.[13] The death of such a shaman provokes dreadful calamities, freeing these genies to descend on people and torture them, causing epidemics and, most particularly, nervous diseases.

The idea of a great god, or great gods, scarcely exists outside the limits of the Turko-Mongolian world, the same is true for the sky's predominance. Even the Yakuts, though their shamans are initiated in heaven, have personal totems whose importance cannot be underestimated. Totems live in some barren spot, under a rock for instance, but never in heaven. And Yakut shamanism acknowledges—like Tungus shamanism—any number of zoomorphic genies, or at least ones whose origin is zoomorphic, whose function is often to help the shaman transport himself into other worlds in general, not just into a celestial world. Besides heaven there is a lower, underground world, but there are also the invisible spaces of the world inhabited by human beings. This is important because a great many of the zoomorphic elements in mythology imply the existence of invisible regions on earth. It is generally conceded that totemism perhaps never even existed in Northern Asia. The problem is too complex to debate here. However one fact seems certain, which is that most of the peoples concerning us today, the Buryats, Yakuts, Altaic Turks, Samoyeds, Ostyaks, and others, from very ancient times conceive of their relations with the animal world in a very suggestive way. The animals are represented as organized in clans, each species forming a particular clan governed by a ruler. This ruler dwells in some invisible place that is out of reach of ordinary mortals. The animal clans have duties vis-à-vis people, just as human clans also have duties regarding animals. An animal must be killed in a certain manner, otherwise the ruler of his clan will not release any more game or will somehow seek vengeance from men. Animal clans are considered on an equal footing with human clans, and are envisaged as their allies, with all the consequences this position implies. Thus, according to myth, certain animal species provide the male for the human clan. Revenge can come just as well from either side. The Chukchee, hence, avoid killing a wolf because they are convinced that the other wolves would come and take vengeance. The Orotches are afraid to kill a squirrel. The Tungus from Yenisei never kill mosquitoes.

When, however, a bear kills a man, for example, The Orotches immediately organize a battue, catch a bear, kill it, eat its heart, throw its meat away, but keep the skin with the head which will serve as the dead man's shroud. Among the Voguls, in a similar case, the dead man's closest kinsman is required to avenge him by killing a bear. The Goldes behave in the same fashion regarding the tiger; they kill it and bury it, making this little speech: "Now we are even, you have killed one of ours, we have killed one of yours. And now let us live in peace. Don't come and bother us any more. Otherwise we are going to kill you."

This somehow social conception of a universe is very clearly apparent among most of the more or less archaic peoples of the area with which we are concerned. It is very likely that the widespread custom in almost the entire center and north of Asia, of having tame animals is connected to these ancient representations. These mythical conceptions of the animal kingdom have given birth to a multitude of spirits of absolutely similar origin. According to Zelenin, these spirits seem to have kept their clannish character over a very long period of time and sometimes even attest to being members of the maternal clan. This fact is reported particularly by such authoritative scholars as Castren[14] and Radlov[15]. Be that as it may, the cult of these spirits seems in every case to be founded on the contractual principle. Here are some examples. Among the Altaic Turks, the genie is dealt with for not having fulfilled his obligations, for example, when a sick person whose guardian he was dies. His effigy is carried into the forest, it is hung from a branch and given a triple offering of eau-de-vie; they beseech it not to get angry and then, paying their respects to it, they go away. In particularly serious cases, the genie can be judged and sentenced. His effigy is beaten and trampled on, then burned to the abuse of those present.

Krasheninnikov describes a scene of the burning of fifty-five Kamchadal fetishes.[16] The Voguls, before they go hunting, come to an agreement with their genies about sharing the spoils, adding: "But if we are unsuccessful, you get nothing." They also occasionally replace certain fetishes with others. At the beginning of the eighteenth century, the Ostyaks, when unsuccessful at fishing, reproach the father of fish, insult him, overturn his effigy, drag it in the mud, trample on it, spit on it, and generally subject it to insulting treatment as long as the fishing does not improve.

The Samoyeds were in the habit of giving their divinities a good thrashing. When they made new fetishes they first subjected them to a test, for example, putting them next to a trap and adopting them only if this succeeded. The Tungus, during the hunt, threw the figurine of the genie of huntsmen into the air, and when it fell face down, which predicted failure, they beat it.

We have just seen that even rather important divinities, such as the Ostyaks' father of fish, did not escape ill treatment. Only perhaps the representations of the head animals of the most powerful species, considered as the rulers of nature, who organized life and dispensed wealth, were treated with more respect.

But what does shamanism have to do with all that? It seems that men dealt directly with their divinities, and what divinities! We are far indeed from the gods in heaven of the Buryat pantheon. We also know that certain religious ceremonies of the clans were accomplished by the collective gathering, presided over by the senior member, assisted by old men. The shaman took no part except as a simple member of the clan, unless his age gave him right to the principal place.

Shamanism, therefore, seems to come after all these zoomorphic pantheons. It adopted them, it helped itself particularly to the anarchic spirits, and tamed them. The shaman did not become the priest of the society, in the full sense of the word, except among some of the Turko-Mongolian peoples. But society accepted him and adapted itself to his presence. Shamanism must have made its appearance at the same time as the invention of metallurgy.

Among the Buryats, the sentenced shaman is aided by the god of the forge, and he puts on iron boots. Among the Yakuts, it is on an iron rod that the god sticks the head of the shaman initiate. And this is what we are told by a Yakut informant: "The smith and the shaman come out of the same nest. . . . they are on the same level. . . . Smiths too are able to cure, give advice, foretell the future. . . . The smith's function is hereditary, and it is in the ninth generation that smiths acquire the exceptional magic skills that, in particular, allow them to forge the iron attributes of the shaman's costume. In general, spirits are afraid of the clanking of iron and the sound of the bellows." Moreover, every shaman's costume is covered with all sorts of iron pendants.

The Altaic Turks have a very similar way of conceiving of things. For them, the shaman has to deal with the god Erlik. According to the myths, this god inhabits a tent of iron, or what is doubtless the same thing, a cave dug in the depths of a mountain that is entirely of iron. The shaman who makes his way there sings: "Bravely let us cross the sky that strikes the iron forest."

This interdependence of the shaman with the smith, or with iron in general, is attested to in almost every part of northern Asia. Among the eastern Tungus the smiths were shamans.

And finally, there is a bird whose importance in this part of Asia, and all the way to China, should not be underrated, the owl or eagle owl. It is the smith's bird and also the shaman's. It symbolizes underground fire. It hunts devils and devours them. That is why owl skins are often hung above cradles or in door frames. The bird has considerable power, consequently the shaman is often adorned with owl feathers.

A shaman seems, therefore, to be a magician above all, but a magician filling a function sanctioned by the community, that is, a sort of priest as well. When he fights the divinities, it is to defend humans.

He is, however, not the only one with this attitude toward divinities. The collectivity itself, when it is necessary, braves the invisible powers, rebels against their intervention. All in all, between the shaman's attitude and that of someone profane, there is only a difference of degree and not one of nature.

The Rituals of Political Associations in Germany of the Romantic Period

Hans Mayer

Tuesday, April 18, 1939

[Hans Mayer was born in Cologne in 1907. In 1931 he defended a thesis Die Krise der deutschen Staatslehre *(The crisis of the German theory of the State). In 1933, the SS searched his house forcing him to go underground, then into exile; from 1933 to 1939, he alternated between France and Switzerland. From 1936 on he contributed to Horkheimer's* Zeitschrift für Socialforschung, *where he regularly published reviews of works of political philosophy.*

What follows is taken from a letter that he wrote to me: "In fact, I did speak on the subject to the College of Sociology in 1939. It was about some work done in connection with my Büchner und seine Zeit, *which would appear only after the war (1946). The discussion took place, as was the custom, with Bataille presiding. It served as introduction to some very interesting debates.*

"What bothers me most about this memory is your date of April 18. I am sure I remember that my lecture was expressly planned as the last meeting before summer vacation. It was even the reason, if I am not mistaken, that it was necessary to put off until the following autumn a lecture that Walter Benjamin was to have given—and which, naturally, was never to take place. That is why the memory of this evening for me is connected to the first days of summer, but, certainly, that could be just confusion.

"There would be much to tell about the way I came into contact with the College. I wrote Bataille during this period, and that is how we met the first time, before working together. During the year 1938-39, I saw Bataille very frequently. We met regularly twice a month."

Since the publication of Le Collège de Sociologie *in French, Hans Mayer has published his autobiography,* Ein Deutscher auf Widerruf. Errinerungen *(Frankfurt*

262

am Main, 1982). The chapter "Paris am Vorabend" (Paris, on the eve) evokes the end of the thirties. There are portraits of Raymond Aron and Paul-Louis Landsberg. It ends with memories relating to the College. "Caillois was a brilliant conversationalist. Bataille sometimes brought to mind those great actors who, by daylight, have an inexpressive face but in the evening, on stage, are capable of embodying anything at all, even what is most totally unexpected, becoming younger or aging as they please. I was paying court to Caillois, but it is clear that during this period Bataille was paying court to me" (p. 239). A little later, apropos Bataille: "At the time I did not realize who this man was I saw so frequently. He maintained a sort of incognito. He just wanted to meet me" (p. 240). He concludes, "Georges Bataille was much more 'German' than I had ever been or could ever become" (p. 243).

The impression that emerges from these memories is that in the last analysis it was luck that was responsible for his embarking on the adventure of the College, an adventure that, forty-five years later, he is nonetheless far from regretting. But it took forty-five years for him to remember it. Of all the many pages Hans Mayer published on French literature, all mention authors whose humanism is more official, and none to my knowledge even mentions this episode in the life of an exiled intellectual.

Benjamin's lecture, which Hans Mayer remembers as being postponed so that he could give his, was to sketch out a sociology of fashion that would be inspired by Baudelaire's texts on Paris. Doubtless, then, we can have some idea of what it would have contained by reading the essay that appeared in the Zeitschrift *of 1939: "On Some Themes in Baudelaire." Benjamin committed suicide, as we know, at the Spanish border, in September 1940.*

We have seen that Caillois, in his lecture on the executioner, thanked Hans Mayer for acquainting him with the German tales pertaining to this subject.

A short book by Hans Mayer has been translated into French: Sur Richard Wagner *(Paris, 1972).]*

The existence and structure of the Third Reich pose numerous problems. Far more numerous than the ways French sociologists and politicians have of analyzing and assessing these numerous facts. With rare exceptions they come down to two. Apparently the traits that are specific to Nazi Germany have to fall under one of two interpretations that, thrown into the bargain, are absolutely irreconcilable with each other.

The first is the more widespread: We might be tempted to name it for Rabbi Ben Akliba, who is supposed to have said that there is nothing new under the sun. Confident of this point of view, aided by some vague historical analogies, this first sort of observer always comes back to the theory of the "Eternal German": an aggressor and spoilsport by heredity, by tradition, by definition. The Reich of William II, President Ebert's Republic, and Marshal Hindenburg's, the Third Reich—everything inspires in them an eternal *ceterum censeo.*

It is not a matter of criticizing here the political consequences of this attitude: It is only the historical and sociological conception it reveals that is called into question. It is ahistorical and almost anti-historical par excellence because according to this conception the German people constitute a sort of heavy substance forever endowed with characteristic attributes and giving the impression of an immovable block of "residues" (to use Vilfredo Pareto's term),[1] which is incapable of being changed or modified by historical events. This methodological error, like any self-respecting error, goes far beyond the borders of any one political party or another. If, in Léon Daudet's contribution to Goethe's centenary, it is expressed in this meaningful title "Goethe à n'en plus finir" (Endless Goethe)[2] it is also what authorizes this sentence from a scholar who is not always particularly straight: "I maintain that, by its morality, the German collectivity is one of the plagues of the world and if all I had to do was push a button to exterminate the whole thing, I would do it immediately."[3] This is the story of the Chinese mandarin slightly warmed over and it is rather entertaining to note that the author of this phrase, a die-hard antimetaphysician here finds himself lined up with an apocalyptic preacher like M. Fr. W. Foerster, who claims (in his book *L'Europe et la question allemande*) that "from Fichte to Hitler is but one step." That, it seems to us, is the disastrous consequence of a mentality that knows nothing of history, which inspired Paul Valéry to challenge historical knowledge[4] and made it necessary for Raymond Aron, going to great lengths to revive it, to note that "the philosophy of history in France is a literary genre so disparaged that no one dares admit to its practice."[5]

The second way of thinking about, or rather misjudging German affairs, is less fraught with consequences, but just as debatable as to its scientific value. It could be defined as an unconscious historicism. Historicism, as we know and as the studies by Dilthey, Troeltsch, and Meinecke have demonstrated, is characterized by the concern for recognizing the event's novel and unique character, different from all previous history. In analysis of the historical event, it would seek to eliminate anything typical or indicative that could be found there, every trace of what Aron (to refer to him once again) calls a "fragmentary consistency." When applied to the birth and structure of the Third Reich, this method comes to the conclusion that only the concrete circumstances in postwar Germany—economic data, the six million unemployed, social change, strategic and tactical errors of the republican parties, can explain the victory of national socialism; that no fact before 1918, let's say, could be taken into consideration when analyzing the birth of the Third Reich. This attitude, carried to extremes, would see Hitler's advent as simply the result of a cabal of the presidential palace against the late General Schleicher, an explanation dear to footnote lovers, perhaps, but completely erroneous. Because, while this sheds light on everything, it does not explain a major point: the tremendous success of Hitler's slogans with the masses, especially the middle strata. Poverty and unemployment explain the

general movement, but not the concrete movement, nor the success of the slogans of total nationalism in its Nazi version.

This raises the problem of political myths: It is a matter of making compre-
hensible the deep-seated reasons for the strong influence of certain slogans and
symbols on the German masses. National socialism has created, invented, nothing in the way of symbols, but it has known how to use what already existed. It
could signal certain half-conscious, almost-erased residues, to raise them, bring
them back to life, and expand them. But these residues, we must emphasize from
the start, are in no way eternal: They are made up of resentments, emotions,
memories that German history, especially the history of the unification of Germany in the last century, produced and put together. All the symbols, all the
forms of association, almost all the concepts of the Nazi movement and the Third
Reich predate the postwar epoch, but most of them do not predate the first awakening of national sentiment in Germany: that is, the second half of the eighteenth
century.

That is the first thesis. Here is a second: It can be seen that, generally, among
the concepts and myths that have made Hitler's fortune, those that were strictly
Nordic or Germanic, neopagan that is, have only played an extremely secondary
role,[6] and always played it to the detriment of truly effective concepts, those connected to a purely German history, to the idea of the Reich and memories of medieval Germany. Moreover, all the history of the Third Reich is there to prove it:
The discrepancy between the sectarianism of certain neopagan clans, for example, the disciples of Madame Ludendorff or of Professor Hauer[7] more than tim-
idly supported by Alfred Rosenberg, and the visionary power of the imperial
myth becomes daily more important. An exact description of the first appearance
of these myths in the history of German nationalism, therefore, cannot help but
be to the point. Against the theoreticians of the Eternal German, it supports the
historically dated and analyzable (indeed changeable) character of this mentality.
And against simplistic historicism, it defends the necessity of descending to the
"Mothers," as Goethe said: to the deepest levels of collective consciousness.

The French translation of Ernst von Salomon's Les Réprouvés[8] created rather
a stir in France, with perhaps even more success than in Germany where a real
inflation of everything connected to the history of irregular troops, to the life and
customs of postwar nationalist associations was produced. There were autobiographical accounts like those of the famous Captain Röhm,[9] falsely romantic
novels, intentionally bestial like Bronnen's book with its subject drawn from the
guerrilla warfare of irregulars against the Polish in Upper Silesia.[10] In the opposite camp there were indictments like those by Dr. Gumbel and the German
League for the Rights of Man against political assassins and assassinations.[11]
From all of that, despite the different points of view, a disturbing atmosphere
emerged, the simultaneously troubling and troubled presence of numerous

groups, sects, "orders" of total nationalism, the image of a sort of life completely out of harmony with the prewar bourgeois existence and with the Western, democratic, and liberal ideal of the republicans of Weimar.

Within these circles the storm troops were formed, the real assault troops of national socialism, and we risk misinterpreting both the evolution of the Nazi movement and the mentality, for example, of the "Black Corps," the organ of the SS and of Himmler, if we do not connect them to the whole evolution of militant nationalism from the years following the war. This point must be insisted upon: Hitler, you might say, invented nothing in the realm of symbols, signs, rituals, and slogans. Everything we now consider as the specific essence and particular mentality of nazism, national socialism shared with numerous groups. But, out of the common patrimony, Hitler was able to make a reality; what had been pure sectarian ideology and conspiracy, he made into a tactic, a successful politics, for the failure of his putsch of November 9, 1923 (another enterprise that is completely classic in the genre of the irregulars) revealed to him the flaws and limits of the putschist conception of closed circles. Nonetheless, the essential features of this sectarian and conspiratorial nationalism are "conserved" (in Hegel's double sense)[12] in the Nazi movement. Almost all the leaders of the Third Reich, especially heads of the party and the paramilitary organizations, passed through the irregulars. The "old soldiers" of the party, the majority of the deputies of the so-called Reichstag, represent the pure formulation of this type. The corps themselves, all these Vikings, Werewolves, O. C. Orgeschs, Oberlands, are dissolved; their cadres have been incorporated into Hitler's party, but they have saved most of their beliefs, myths, rituals, and symbols. The Vehmgericht was an institution dear to almost all the irregular troops and nationalist orders, both a secret court for traitors and an authority that judged and condemned "in contumaciam" the enemies of the movement. In the National Socialist party the Vehmgericht took the form of the famous USCHLA, a committee of inquiry and arbitration that ruled in camera on all the high-ranking civil servants of the party. Its head, not by chance, is a former leader of the irregulars, a reputed executioner, the famous Major Buch—the same who had Röhm and company shot on June 30, 1934. The idea of a great German Reich, and especially the Third Reich, is not Hitler's invention either. It was formulated after the war in a book that is, moreover, rather remarkable, by Moeller van den Bruck and that is called, precisely, *The Third Reich*.[13] The book is antiliberal, antidemocratic, and also antibourgeois, written by a total nationalist, not at all racist for all that although scarcely philosemitic, and, between 1921 and 1923 (i.e., during the period that was decisive in the formation of German nationalism and national socialism), it was something of a bible for the national youth.

It was also Moeller who, well before Rosenberg and *Mein Kampf*, conceived the basic principles of a *foreign policy* for German nationalism. Here is what he said in 1922 in a pamphlet entitled *Socialism and Foreign Policy*. "The Germans have no home. They are spread all over the world; destiny requires that they serve the earth. But they need something to be able to get started and a land to which they can return. They have to have their land. . . . The only thing that is important to us is an orientation toward the East; those still talking about an orientation toward the West today have understood nothing about the Great War.''[14] A nationalist thinker, not a Nazi (it is important to repeat), instead rather hostile to the Führer, Moeller had the ear of the nationalist youth. To these words of his, then, let us add a few sentences from his book *The Third Reich* that form, as it were, its conclusion: "German nationalism fights for the final Reich. The Reich is always promised. It is never realized. It is the perfect realized only in the imperfect. This is the German people's special message, one contested by all other peoples. Now, there is only one Reich, as there is only one Church. What commonly assumes the name 'Empire' is merely a State. But there is only one Reich.'' Obviously, *Mein Kampf*'s well-known program repeats less emphatically and more cynically the same conception. At every moment it is imperative that German nationalism be seen as a whole. When, in December 1923, Moeller was able to write to another young German nationalist, Heinrich von Gleichen, that the idea of the Third Reich expresses a political conception whose aim is "the advent of a German era, an era in which the German people will finally accomplish its mission on earth,'' he was formulating the program held in common by all the postwar German nationalists.

Hermann Rauschning, in his recent book *The Revolution of Nihilism*,[15] forcefully emphasizes the *nihilist character* of all the policies of the Third Reich: the absence of a real program, real myths, integral values. It reveals the art for art's sake of dynamism, a dynamism "in itself," moving in a vacuum, with neither its aim nor its necessity understood. This is not false, but it is not the whole truth. There are nihilists who use certain slogans without believing in them; on the other hand, there are those who are sincerely and eagerly affected by the enchantment of magic formulas. Although Hitler may despise the people, the nation, the Reich, although he may see only his own glory, there are still all those who follow and believe. Pareto has brilliantly explained that it is necessary to distinguish between a nonbelieving nihilist elite, wearing an intellectual facade, and those led by it, for whom it creates myths that are like Épinal images.

According to Pareto, history, of course, is *the cemetery of aristocracy.*[16] But it is also, in a much realer, more down-to-earth sense, *the cemetery of the masses who let themselves be captivated by the charms of the elite.* This teaching, applied to the problem of German nationalism, requires a dual perspective: one seeing the nihilism of those who exploit myths together with the sordid materialism this represents, and one that observes the actual life of the myths, their genesis, how they function, how they fade.

The second task is the only important one here. It is clear that the few concrete cases that have been touched upon, that of the Vehmgericht or that of the Reich, are only given as examples. There are many other concepts, above all that of the Führer, also the concept of national socialism. This is far less true of racist theory because we should repeat that living national socialism, in order to inspire the youth, depends far less on the racism of a Rosenberg, the crudeness of a Streicher, than on the memories, the golden legends of a great German past and the eschatological prophecies of a glorious future for a globalized Germanity. But that is precisely where, in analyzing these problems that are central to contemporary German nationalism, the strands connecting the present to the past become visible so it is possible to *detect* the birth of myths, and consequently the reasons for their effectiveness.

Postwar nationalism, with its myths, its forms of association and recruitment, was not born on virgin soil, which seems to prove that French theoreticians of the Eternal German are right. Nonetheless, even if it is not this nationalism's first incarnation, there is a great gulf between it and *pre*war nationalism. The difference is visible in every area: the social milieu, organizational form, and the final goal, ideas, and images. The German nationalism of William II's Reich had represented an essentially *bourgeois* current. The organizations took the form of bourgeois societies, clubs, bourgeois parties with president, treasurer, newsletter, governmental representatives. Typical associations would be the naval society (Flottenverein) that disseminated Tirpitz's programs for naval construction; the colonial society, center of activity for rich export merchants, shipping companies, an imperialist and conformist petit-bourgeois swollen with national pride; finally the Pangermanic League of the Adviser Class, an association of expansionists and imperialists who were well-to-do, right-thinking, fierce opponents of social reforms and determined partisans of a strict class hierarchy. They had no agenda other than one of annexation and expansion in the style of the Adviser Class's famous *Kaiserbuch* (If I Were Emperor); no myth or symbol other than adoration of William II, his eloquence and his uniforms (the classic description of this mentality is found in the novel *Der Untertan* by Heinrich Mann); no personal obligations for the organization members; complete absence of any quasi-military discipline, or any profound, urgent, and exclusive contact between members. Everything reflected the bourgeois intellect at the epoch of imperialist expansion.

German nationalism of the *postwar* period is the absolute negation of this. Its leaders were not formed among the bourgeois of *Bildung und Besitz*, the possessors of erudition and material wealth, but rather were in opposition to them. General von Schleicher, in December 1932, was able to speak of "anticapitalist nostalgia," which according to him sustained the immense majority of the German people. Well, it definitely animated the top leaders of those who returned from the war, whom Remarque described in his books *Après* and *Trois Camarades*:[17] those returning ghosts described by the poet Kästner as having "been too poorly nourished in body and spirit because we wanted to create too quickly, with their aid, a Universal History.'' They found themselves face to face with war and postwar profiteers; facing the collapse of all values, a society transformed from top to bottom. Whence come their disillusionment, their antibourgeois nostalgia, and what they soon call their "socialism," which the Nazi party's agenda, written by Feder, translated as "antimammonism," to which are added anti-Semitism and antiliberalism. Their ideal is activism, whether in its pure form as dynamism, art for art's sake, a voluptuous pleasure in destruction, or in the form of an antireasoning, irrational, mythic nationalism inspired by images of the battle for the Reich, the final Reich.

This form of association is flagrantly opposed to what was true in the past of bourgeois parties, even those on the "right": the name "party" is dropped in order to adopt that of "front," order, group, "movement." (Even the Nazi party itself likes to be called a "movement"; Munich now is called "Capital of the Movement.") Discipline is military; strict obedience is expected; the individual is uprooted from bourgeois civil life; undefeated, he is linked to others who are undefeated. Woman is excluded, even despised, the symbol of life that is down to earth; the bonds are those of masculine order, of "Männerbund" according to Blüher's terminology.[18] This order excludes every social and economic hierarchy, acknowledging only military hierarchy. "To be German is to be poor," one of the disciples of this movement said in conversation. Every tie with prewar bourgeois nationalism is broken, renounced: Going back more than a century, the cohesive nationalism of those returning from the war united with the early associations shaped by the idea of nationality in Germany at the beginning of the nineteenth century. This is where the past can help us to understand the present and, perhaps, the future.

To pin down where it began we must trace very rapidly the general evolution of national sentiment in Germany from its awakening until the formation of the Reich in 1871. Now, to avoid misunderstanding, we must rigorously distinguish between two sociological ideas. German sociology deserves credit for bringing them to the fore. Knowledge of them is more necessary than ever. It is a matter of the distinction between two concepts, both of which concern the problem of the nation and nationality. The German terms speak in one instance of *Kulturnation* and in the other of *Staatsnation*. *Kulturnation* designates the situation of a community whose members are linked to each other by the same language, the same historical traditions, and identical life-styles. The National Socialists prefer to speak of *Volkstum*, but the term *Kulturnation* is much more precise, thanks to its opposite, *Staatsnation*. The national community designated as *Kulturnation* (or, to use the French term, *nationalité*) completely ignores the question of whether the legal status of the members of this nationality is the same everywhere, whether they live inside the same state or are spread out among the territories of several supranational states. *Kulturnation* designates, therefore, a sort of civilization and not a political state. On the other hand, the *Staatsnation* applies only to the national State, to those of the same language forming a national State among themselves. (It is interesting to see that French language and custom have difficulty bowing to this distinction. France, the oldest national State of Europe, has difficulty conceiving of a *nationalité*, meaning a national civilization that has no national home. Whence the dual sense of the word *nationalité* in French, meaning *Kulturnation*, national civilization, on the one hand, and on the other, civil state, citizenship; thus accepting national civilization as existing only within a well-established national State).

Now, the history of Germany since the second half of the eighteenth century has had only one goal: to transform the German *Kulturnation*, all those whose language, origin, and civilization are German, into one *Staatsnation*, that is, a single and "great" national State. The German problem will never be understood until this fact is grasped: that the German *Kulturnation* has existed far longer than the German national State. The existence of the Germanic Holy Roman Empire does not negate this thesis, for, even disregarding the legal nature of this empire, of this "monstre sui generis" as Pufendorf said in the seventeenth century, one thing is sure: This empire was not a national State in the modern sense. The national idea developed in opposition to absolutism; its conception at origin was democratic and liberal, which it ceased to be. Therefore, there are several reasons not to speak of "national sentiment" in Germany before, let's say, 1740, before Frederick II and Maria Theresa came to the throne. The war between these two sovereigns must have contributed to a new consciousness among the different German branches. In its first phase the national movement scarcely left the apolitical, extrapolitical setting of a battle for the language and civilization of the Germans. It was a battle for the rights of Germanic culture against the hegemony of French civilization—almost the only culture accepted by the princely circles and courts of eighteenth-century Germany, ever since the Peace of Westphalia. Let us not forget that the formation of the German *Kulturnation* necessarily had to be created in opposition to French civilization, against Boileau and Voltaire. Similarly, the formation of the national State's *Staatsnation* will take place in war: first against Napoleon, later against the Second Empire. The same is true for the great dates of cultural awakening: the appearance of an authentic German poet, Klopstock; the elaboration of a German aesthetics and dramatic art by Lessing; the creation of a national theater and later a national opera; the growing awareness of the Germans' past, their national character and their art, thanks to Herder and the young Goethe; all this evolution is marked by some kind of successive, irresistible liberation from French hegemony. Already the initial movements of a wider political awareness were appearing: the inglorious defeat of the Prince of Soubise at Rosbach was celebrated throughout Germany, regardless of the frontiers of states—large or small, as a national victory. Frederick of Prussia became a national hero, at the precise moment that, by strange coincidence, he became the favorite of French opinion in revolt against the government of Louis XV. The great moment of transition, however, which characterized the passage from a struggle for civilization to struggle for the national German State, a unified Germany, must be fixed in 1807 following the battle of Jena and the Treaty of Tilsit. The French Revolution having been transformed from a movement for the liberation of nations into a force of conquest and domination, German nationalism found itself, right away, in its first political appearance, marked by a strong tinge of patriotic resentment, that is, anti-French sentiment. In effect, its first task was war against French domination, and the avatars of European history wanted this to be a mark never entirely erased. Therefore it is not surprising that the great tradition of nationalist associations, after 1918, was never completely diverted from its origins. But this must be demonstrated in more detail.

The first association whose traces can be followed is the "League of Virtue" (Tugendbund), which, starting in 1807 with an imprecise form and an agenda whose details were poorly defined, brought together the principal architects of a Prussian redress, such as Stein, Scharnhorst, Gneisenau, Boyen, and their friends. The association's form was rather the result of a mutual new awareness and of personal friendships. Its agenda consisted of the military, social, and moral reorganization of a vanquished Prussia, and discussion of the best ways to realize this goal. The League was almost exclusively composed of middle-aged men. Since there was no organization, properly speaking, principles of organization were lacking. Above all, there was no question of any secret and illegal activity: Everything took place in confabs and conversations between friends all inspired by the same ideal.

The famous irregulars of Major von Schill already demonstrate more cohesiveness and integration. We are dealing with a veritable military organization here, composed of officers and soldiers of the Prussian army, either from the army Napoleon took on or from the older cadres of the period before 1806. The openly declared goal is an uprising by Germany against foreign countries, the form of organization is that of a military detachment whose central rule is the soldier's discipline. And there, in the ranks of soldiers, whose hearts beat in unison for the same goal, is prepared a miniature version of the modern form of a truly national and popular army—the creation of the French Revolution, the ideal of a Scharnhorst. Schill's uprising fails. The major is killed in the streets of Stralsund, his principal lieutenants are shot by a firing squad in Wesel.

Other sorts of associations are in the works. An extremely odd group, though it never left the stage of gestation, met in Berlin around 1812. It was formed from among the youth who had fervently followed the lessons of Fichte, the philosopher: the famous *Speeches to the German Nation*. Thirteen of those who heard Fichte, young officers, teachers, students discovering their emotional agreement, decided to move from contemplation to realization. They formed a "German association" that is sometimes also called the "German Order"

(*Deutsche Orden*), taking its inspiration, no doubt, from the Teutonic tradition and the idea of a masculine order with a national tendency. The ideal, of course, is still national redress and German unity. A rather odd, even bizarre man, the Kriegsrat Gruner, made contact with the association, which was a secret one this time. Gruner was chief of the Prussian police from 1810 until the summer of 1812, but he was playing a double game: A devoted civil servant of the king of Prussia, Napoleon's ally, at the same time he favored the youth's anti-French and nationalist activity. It has been impossible to establish whether Gruner, in these maneuvers, was guided by ambition or by a national ideal. Karl Immermann, a great German writer and Heine's friend, made no bones abut using this episode in the great portrait he created of contemporary Germany in his novel *Die Epigonen*. There we find Gruner, side by side with August Schlegel and many other contemporaries of romantic Germany; but this bizarre character has become a sort of evil demon who tempts the pure, innocent youth the better to ruin it. Be that as it may, it is indeed Gruner, who on June 28, 1812, suggested to the German Order that it come out in the open and provide itself with bylaws. So the police officer's game was discovered, and he himself arrested; the history of the Order came to an end there. But the idea of this formation was not lost. The German Order, stillborn, led its members straight in the direction of the future secret societies. These formed in the orbit of an Arndt and of the irregulars of 1813, especially the troops of Major von Lützow and his band of "blacks": famous cavalrymen in black tunics, wearing a black cap with the death's head, the model for the Nazi SS.

The name of Ernst Moritz Arndt has been mentioned. In fact, no one else, perhaps, contributed more to the practical and political formation of German nationalism. That Fichte was an infinitely profounder and more far-reaching thinker there is no doubt, but Arndt, all the while deeply imbued with the humanism from the Age of the Enlightenment, hence far from Teutonic fools like Father Jahn, was an inspired organizer. From his writings emerged the principal forms of political associations before and after 1814. It is Arndt who is the spiritual father of the idea of the German *Volkstum* that today is so much to the point, and it is in his patriotic and Francophobe pamphlets that nascent nationalism could find specific directions for its formation. It is interesting to note that Arndt's activity continued after the defeat of Napoleon, thus preparing the next stage of the young German nationalism: no longer war against the foreign invader, but against the restored reigning order in Germany, against Metternich and what was called "his system." The point of departure can be found in a pamphlet published by Arndt in April 1814 with the title *One More Word about the French and Us*, in which he sets forth the measures that in his opinion are the only ones able to ensure the fruits of victory and the realization of the German national State. First among these was an institution, to which, moreover, Arndt devoted another of his writings, *Project for a German Association*. In fact, in both cases it is a question of a sort of patriotic society that was supposed to have ramifications throughout all of Germany, whose goal would be to revive the national spirit—to prevent any obstacle to the rights of the German people. During 1814, a good number of these "German associations" were founded. In 1815 they provided themselves with bylaws that they owed to a Hessian lawyer, Carl Hoffmann, a colonel in the Landsturm. The following is the main text that merits our attention because it creates a bridge between the era of the beginnings of German nationalism and contemporary ideas. Article 1: "Those not German (*teutsch*) by birth cannot be members." Article 2: "Only those confessing the Christian religion are accepted. Those who are decent, sober, honest, devout, and hard-working people are welcome." Article 3: "No one is admitted who freely and willingly served under a foreign country, who is inspired by French principles, or who has acted in conformity with these." Article 19 declares that the society is public, that it disapproves of everything secret, signs, rituals, etc. Its name alone indicates its goal. The following paragraph recalls that the society is "popular" (*völkisch*) in nature, which means that it endeavors "to spread Germanic traditions and virtue and to exterminate foreign vice." Article 24 gives the reasons that can make one unworthy of membership. They constitute a curious mixture of general morality and patriotism. For example, one is unworthy if condemned by common law or if one has rebelled against legal authority; also excluded are cowards, atheists, debauchers, misers, anyone having affection for the language, traditions, and customs of the country's eternal enemies: for France and the French language. The bourgeois character of this movement is revealed as clearly here as its xenophobic patriotism. Each of the association's meetings was opened and closed by a prayer whose text is also known. It invoked the Almighty who "saved our Germany from the spiritual yoke of foreign tyrants"; it prayed for God to "preserve us always from foreign constraint, to inspire and maintain in us sentiments that are truly German and every sort of German virtue." It ended with a prayer for peace.

These groups spread rapidly in the west and southwest of the country during the summer of 1815. Gruner, released in the meantime, slipped in to exploit the movement; but the reactionaries had begun their counterattack: Metternich and the restored princes wanted to hear nothing of liberty or Germanic unity. A series of pamphlets denounced the patriotic movement as revolutionary. Several branches of the association were forbidden; others were dissolved by the members. In October 1815, a general Congress of the German associations was held in Frankfurt that dissolved the society by its own free will. The nationalist movement, if it was to continue, saw itself obliged to become illegal, to change its method, to gather—instead of level-headed, loyalist bourgeois—adolescents who were conspiratorial and fervent. The history of this conspiracy is entirely characteristic. That is where, for the first time, the methods of the patriotic sects of postwar Germany are encountered in all their specificity: from direct and terrorist action to morals.

Throughout this whole period, dating approximately from 1815 to 1819, the main organization was the Burschenschaft. This was a patriotic association of students that was to replace the former student societies of a local or regional cast, with the openly avowed aim of making universities and the setting of a university existence a rallying place for German unification. All the branches of the Burschenshaften, the ones at Jena, the one at Heidelberg, Giessen, and Halle, reserved a major portion of their programs for the question of German unity: Moeller van den Bruck's slogan, Only One Reich, which is, as we know the slogan of present-day Germany, is already found in student speeches and manifestos of this period. The ideal of the one and only great Reich was accompanied by that of a single national Church that would unite Catholics, Protestants and Lutherans under the sign of a single Germanic faith. It should be remarked that this problem of the unification of the different confessions and beliefs in Germany was widely debated in the Germany of romanticism. At a certain moment it seemed that the boundaries between Catholics and Protestants would disappear; the anti-Catholic Catholicism of the Hardenberg-Novalis reformation provides a rather curious idea of this. It is also known that Hegel was working on this question in the months preceding his death. Therefore, it is obvious that the present-day struggle of national socialism against the universalism of the Roman Church and the Protestant ministers has its basis far less, as some believe, in the ideas of neopaganism than in the old desire of German nationalists to link the political unification of the Reich to an analogous ecclesiastical unification. This idea made its first and resounding appearance during the period that concerns us.

The Burschenschaft (or rather the Burschenschaften, because every university soon had its own branch) itself directly descends from the projects of Arndt and the "German associations." Created in 1814, in Halle, under the name "Teutonia," with the slogan Honor, Liberty, Country, it spread very rapidly during the year 1815. The dissolution of the "German associations" gave free rein to this new type of patriotic organization that, this time, took the form of a party of the youth. This changing of generations was translated into changes of tone and method. Whereas the adult organization had been legal, loyal, even bourgeois, the Burschenschaft of this period very soon betrayed its penchant for the secret act, mystical ecstasy, and military discipline. Two waves of ideas met there: a revolutionary democratism that clearly clashed with the monarchical loyalism of the preceding association, and the young, virulent, very aggressive, profoundly anti-French, resolutely Christian in the sense already mentioned (hence anti-Semitic), nationalism. Many factors came together to explain this tendency: horror of the French Revolution, which dreamt up the emancipation of Jews and the ecstatic Christianity of the romantic era; the role of certain Jewish financiers, above all the Rothschilds, in the system of the Holy Alliance and

Metternich's regime; finally, the clearly marked reserve of the German Jews during the wars of liberation in which those who owed Napoleon their liberty and equality did not want to enlist in the armies of his adversaries, preferring payment of an indemnity to active participation in the combat. In any event, the spirit of the Burschenschaften could not have been more nonconformist. Consequently, a split quickly developed between the youth and their elders. The year 1818 saw a discussion of principle taking place at Jena between the mouthpiece for the elders' nationalism, Professor Fries, and the youth's Führer, Karl Follen. Fries did his best to warn the cadets against anything that was a secret order or society; at the most he would allow a "republikanische Religionsverbindung" stripped of any illegal characteristics. But Follen, who preached Revolution and Republic, carried the day. In fact, it is Karl Follen and none other who is the Führer of young German nationalism, and the one is worthy of the other.

A man of remarkable eloquence, extensive culture, stunning beauty, a born conspirator, unscrupulously mixing the cause and his own glory, Follen literally played the role of a prophet among apostles. He saw himself as Jesus Christ and his disciples as apostles. The song of his organization proclaimed: "Thou shalt become a Christ." Here everything was a symbol of death and voluptuous pleasure in death, in the double sense of sacrifice and murder. The historian Treitschke, who detested Follen and saw in him only the "gravedigger" of the Burschenschaft, has passed on to us one of the hymns of this period, which was called "New Year's Song for Free Christians, to Be Sung Marching." It reads: "Brandish knives of liberty! Hurrah! Plunge your dagger in his throat! The victim is already adorned in purple and beribboned, he wears the crown, the altar of vengeance awaits him!"

There is no doubt that we are here in the presence of a true "masculine order," a Männerbund, and that there is a sort of eroticism that binds these rebellious adolescents. There are different levels of membership. The half-hearted are accepted in a simple ceremony, in a secret and nocturnal session, after taking an oath of fidelity and absolute silence. Then there is the little group, the "Unbedingten," rebels whom Follen had gathered around himself, numbering six or seven, including among others, his brother August Follen and the young Karl Ludwig Sand, future assassin of Kotzebue.

It has been much debated whether the rebels really professed the principle: The end justifies the means. The fact remains that Article 2 of their agenda announced: "They will tremble before our daggers!" The image of the young Schiller comes to mind—the manifesto "In tyrannos" that *The Brigands* was. Nietzsche, who did not particularly like Schiller, did not hesitate to reproach him for this; in short, he was all the more justified because the dagger used by the murderer of Kotzebue, the instrument of execution, bore the inscription "In tyrannos." The same state of mind reappeared a century later in the assassins of Erzberger, Rathenau, and many others: This mixture of cynicism and spiritual dedication, of lansquenet and masculine order, the same absence of clear and distinct ideas as well, all are to be found already among the ranks of Follen's apostles. The sacred character of the group is obvious. The same Sand who was to pay with his head and whose blood, spilled by the executioner, was to dampen the handkerchiefs of the faithful, of whom a professor of theology would say that he was the model of the good German—this same Sand had the following conception of the meaning of common action: "The main idea of our festival (this was the famous Wartburg Festival in October 1817, a meeting of the students and gymnasts who were pupils of Father Jahn, a national and antireactionary demonstration followed by an auto-da-fé of proscribed books such as the Napoleonic Code, philosemitic, and liberal writings) is that we have all become priests through baptism and we are all free and equal." One notices the strange mixture of rational and irrational, liberal and antiliberal concepts. Next the hereditary enemies of the German *Volkstum* are denounced. There are three: Romans, monks, and militarism! Only two of these adversaries have survived in our time: Romans, which means the spirit of Roman law vigorously opposed by the jurists of the Third Reich, and the Catholic Church.

Because of the subject's extreme complexity and range we can only touch lightly upon it, just to reveal the survival and continuity of the ideas born at that decisive moment of Germany's national awakening. The problem of the Vehmgericht alone merits a separate study: the romantic epoch had a very peculiar idea of the German's secret courts. The birth of German ethnology and archaeology, the exploration of German medieval history, literature, and customs stirred up many dreams. The combination of hatred of Roman law with an Épinal-like, simplistic image of independent peasants and tenant farmers, and with vague, seductive memories of the Teutonic Order and other masculine orders, resulted in a real obsession with an avenging Vehme. Reconciliation between the spirit of Follen's disciplines and this Vehmgericht was easily accomplished. Suffice it to mention two literary works of this epoch: the scene of the secret court in Kleist's *Das Käthchen von Heilbronn*, and the episode of the peasant court in which justice is dispensed by night with a sword claimed to be Charlemagne's, an episode recounted by Immermann in *Die Epigonen.*

The Teutomania of the gymnasts of Jahn, the picturesque costume that they themselves referred to as "old German," disdaining detachable collars, as well as vests and haircuts, is too well known and, moreover, not rich enough in secret, sacred forms to be discussed in detail. This mixture of Gallophobia, bellicosity, and sniveling loyalism is pretty ridiculous in its exaggerations. We should just mention Article 7 of the gymnasts' rules, which gave them the task of informing on, making it their duty to denounce to their leaders, anyone who, either in writing or speaking, declared himself against Jahn, his ideas, or physical culture in general.

There is still one thing to be said about the end of this first movement of German nationalism. The murder of Kotzebue on March 23, 1819, and another attempted assassination with its intended victim a high-ranking civil servant from Nassau, obliged the German governments to put down this terrorist movement. The federal decrees of September 20, 1819, put an end to the stirrings among high school and university students. People soon began to be resigned. Follen had to go into exile. His breath no longer fanned the flames—which quickly went out. The "Davidsbündler," once exams were over, became philistines. Confronted with magistrates, more than one of them declared his regret for having neglected his "honorable" studies. Follen himself, though desperate, did not lay down his arms. We still have him to thank for a final act that has moments of coming within a hairbreadth of farce, but the events are absolutely authentic. A young teacher, von Sperwitz, went to Switzerland in the spring of 1821. At Chur he met Follen and some of his disciples. Follen persuaded him to return to Germany to secretly organize a "Jünglingsbund," a league of young people who would continue the work of the Burschenschaft, but this time under the orders of a parallel organization of adults, a Männerbund, only one of whose members would be known to the youth, all the others being protected by absolute secrecy. Sperwitz accepted, took an oath, and adopted the program that Follen wrote out in nine articles. These provided for the revolutionary action, the details of the organization of the Männer- And Jünglingsbund, the swearing of an oath and in article 9, the threat of death for the traitor. Back in Germany, Sperwitz gathered all the nonconformist forces from among the national youth; the Youth League came into being and even grew; almost all the universities organized sections. Article 9 became concrete: A lottery was to designate the one who would execute the traitor. Yet what worried the youth was the complete absence of any direct or indirect activity of the league of their elders. It was all very well that it had to be absolutely secret, but some little sign from time to time would be nice. Considering this worry, an illegal congress of the youths decided in the spring of 1822 to send a secret messenger, a certain Wesselhoeft, from one end of Germany to the other, so he could inquire about the situation of the Männerbund. In October he was able to report that there was no trace of any league. The only choice was to conclude "that this league is a ludicrous enterprise dreamed up in Switzerland by some émigrés who would like to reestablish their footing in Germany." And, without the league of the elders, the order of the youth lost its meaning. Consequently, they proceeded solemnly to the dissolution of an organization that had never been able to forget its origins, meaning its emergence fully armed from the mind of Karl Follen. The latter, greatly disappointed, went to Paris in May 1824, where Victor Cousin took him in. Then he emigrated to the United States. Ten years later this caricature was caricatured by Immermann in *Die Epigonen*.

Here the history of the beginnings of a cohesive nationalism in Germany ends. The struggle for unification of what Metternich called a "geographic," rather than a political, nation continued. The stages it passed through in 1848-49, 1864,

1866, 1870-71, to mention only a few, are well known. Still, the entire subsequent history of the nineteenth century did not reproduce anything analogous to the forms, rites, and concepts of the movement we have just discussed. Resistance, in a new stage, the immediate consequence of the revolutions of 1830, appeared in a very different form. It was like the similar movements of European liberalism everywhere. At the festival of Hambach on May 27, 1832 (usually contrasted, rightly or wrongly, to the ceremonies at Wartburg), everything was like the atmosphere of the banquets prior to February 1848. The same students (or their younger siblings) who, on the evening of Wartburg, had cried out their anathema against the Jews, in Hambach acclaimed the exiled Jew, Ludwig Börne. Aggressive nationalism had evolved in the direction of the glorification of a League of Nations. Once again the distinguished man—the lawyer, the academic, the bourgeois was making the decisions. His method was that of the traditional political liberal: the court and the free press, not direct action, not the dagger, not the ecstasy of those who swore by death and who swore to die.

This liberal, national bourgeois spirit, this national liberalism that is open to every shade, color, and tendency, from imperialism to pacifism, is indeed what characterizes the politics of the bourgeoisie of the Second Reich, the one that collapsed on November 9, 1918. It was then that this bizarre spectacle began again, this new proof of the law of the conservation of energy, this return of rites, methods, concepts that we had thought permanently outdated. Prepared already before the war, revived by the disgust felt by the youth in the prewar years over the waste of a bourgeois life, over William II's shining helmet and the fake Renaissance style, consecrated in the *Jugendbewegung* and by the death of those who wanted to go to war carrying *Faust* and *Zarathustra* in their packs, the spirit of 1819 once again begin to spread: the spirit of rebels, myth, and direct action. But history does not stop. What was progressive does not remain so eternally, and the Germany of 1933 is a far cry from the Germanic Confederation that came out of the Congress of Vienna.

Festival
Roger Caillois

Tuesday, May 2, 1939

[This lecture is the counterpart of the one Bataille, following Caillois's notes in the latter's absence, delivered on the subject of power on February 19, 1938. Both of these correspond, in fact, to the two central chapters of L'Homme et le sacré *(HS): the lecture on power to Chapter 3 ("Le Sacré de respect: théorie des interdits,") and the lecture on festival to Chapter 4 ("Le Sacré de transgression: théorie de la fête").*

The lecture took place May 2. It is likely that it consisted in the more or less cursory reading of Chapter 4, in press at that time. L'Homme et le sacré *was to appear shortly, the third volume of the collection "Mythes et religions" directed by P.-L. Couchaud at the publishing house E. Leroux; the first title in the series was* Mythes et dieux des Germains *by Dumézil. There is no publication date, but the foreword, dated March 31, 1939, is followed by a PS dated June 1939: Caillois, "prevented from correcting the proofs of this little book by a trip to South America," is grateful to Georges Dumézil for having taken on this thankless task.*

Chapter 4 of L'Homme et le sacré *would appear again, separately, in the December 1939-January 1940* NRF *under the title "Théorie de la fête."*

In 1950, L'Homme et le sacré *was reissued by Gallimard with the addition of several appendixes. Bataille wrote his article "La Guerre et la philosophie du sacré" (*Critique, *February 1951) about this edition, one of whose appendixes was concerned with war.*

I am publishing here the text of the chapter as it appears in the 1939 edition (HS, 1939). Because its end is significantly different both from the NRF *version and from the version of 1950 (HS 1950), I am giving the successive texts of these final lines. Their pessimism changes key depending on whether they came before or after the break occasioned by the war. Before the war, Caillois was disgusted to see the modern world sinking into vacation, languishing in a slow, stagnating dance—never again to be shaken up by festival. After the war, he saw it on the contrary (and after the fact) doomed . . . to war. "Everything that does not consume itself rots." Those are practically the last words in* L'Homme et le sacré. *They could not find a better application than Caillois's conclusion, which from one edition to the next swings between "fascination with fire and the loathing of rot." In any case, unlike the experience some students had of the previous war, for this Luciferian who, certainly, was the very devil intellectually much more than physically, this war was only a particularly long vacation.*

At the end of July, Sartre announced the latest gossip to Simone de Beauvoir: "Let me tell you, but I'm afraid you won't think this is funny enough, the beautiful Vittoria Ocampo has carried off Roger Caillois. Off they go—to Argentina." In the weeks following this lecture, Caillois indeed left for Argentina where Le Mythe et l'homme *had just been translated (by Ricardo Baeza, Buenos Aires; published by SUR Editions on July 10, 1939). But he did count on returning, as Bataille expected him to do. Yet the* Revue de l'histoire des religions *would announce in its September-December 1939 issue, in the program of courses at the Hautes Études: "Comparative Mythology: Director of Studies, G. Dumézil, in the army. R. Caillois, upon his return from assignment, will give a series of lessons entitled* Le Vocabulaire religieux des Romains." *He was not to return until after the war. These five years in South America certainly warranted Caillois's going back over the last words of his "theory of the festival": It was not a vacation, it was war.*

This lecture, it seems, was one of the "perfect moments," or at the very least an intense moment, in the history of the College. Through the intermediary of the published text, bit by bit, it became emblematic of the preoccupations that inspired it. Neither Sartre nor Simone de Beauvoir attended the sessions on the rue Gay-Lussac. However, the ex-dutiful daughter, toward the end of La Force de l'âge *tells about the fêtes—what Leiris called "fiestas"—apparently worthy of Caillois's descriptions, that were organized, during the enthusiasm of the Liberation, around the alumni of the College (if Leiris and Bataille can still be described this way) and the new boys of existentialism. For his part, Caillois was still in Buenos Aires. But, carried away by the general jubilation, Simone de Beauvoir brought him in, at the bottom of a page in a footnote: "Caillois, in* Le Mythe de la fête *and Georges Bataille, in* La Part du diable *have analyzed these phenomena far more exhaustively." What she wrote was, in fact, bibliographically rather dubious because it is not the "mythe de la fête," but either* Le Mythe et l'homme *or "Théorie de la fête" (moreover, the latter is not in the former) that Caillois wrote. As for* La Part du diable, *Denis de Rougemont wrote it, which is one thing (among others) that distinguishes it from* La Part maudite.

In La Littérature et le mal *Bataille would return once again to the "theory of transgression" developed by Caillois in "this important masterpiece,"* L'Homme et le sacré. *And he expressly refers to chapter 4, "Théorie de la fête" (*OC, *vol. 9, p. 314 and note 3; see also* OC, *vol. 8, p. 250).]*

In contrast with life that is regular, busy with everyday work, peaceful, caught inside a system of prohibitions, taken up by precautions, where the maxim *quieta non movere* keeps order in the world, is the ferment of the festival.* If only its external aspects are considered, festival presents identical characteristics no matter what the level of civilization. It implies a noisy and excited throng of people. These huge gatherings are eminently favorable to the birth and contagion of an intense excitement spent in cries and gestures, inciting an unchecked abandonment to the most reckless impulses. Even today, when anemic festivals stand out so little from the colorless background constituted by the monotony of present-day life, where they seem dispersed, scattered, nearly lost in this monotony, we can still distinguish in them a few pitiful vestiges of the collective eruption that characterized the ancient feasts. In fact, the disguises and few bits of boldness still permitted at Carnival, the drinking and street dances on July 14, even the carousing at the end of the Nuremberg Congress in national-socialist Germany, are evidence of the same social necessity and its continuation. There is no festival, even one that is by definition sad, that does not consist of at least the beginnings of excess and revelry: We have only to recall rural burial feasts. The festival of yesteryear or of today is always defined by dancing, singing, excitement, excessive eating and drinking. It is necessary to go all out, to the point of exhaustion, to the point of sickness. That is the very law of the festival.

I. Festival, Resorting to the Sacred

In the so-called primitive civilizations, the contrast is more marked. The festival lasts several weeks, several months, interrupted by four-to five-day periods of rest. Often several years are required to get together the quantity of food and wealth that will be not only ostentatiously consumed or spent but also destroyed and wasted pure and simple, because waste and destruction, as forms of excess, are rightfully part of the festival's essence.

---

* It is pointless to emphasize that this theory of the festival is far from exhausting its different aspects. Particularly, it needs to be connected to a theory of sacrifice. The latter, in fact, seems a sort of privileged contents of the festival. It has come to be something like the internal movement that sums it up or gives it its meaning. They appear together in the same relationship as soul and body. Unable to insist on this intimate connection (I had to choose), I have done my best to emphasize the *sacrificial atmosphere* that belongs to the festival, in the hope that the reader could thus appreciate that the dialectic of the festival duplicates and reproduces that of the sacrifice.

The festival is apt to end frenetically in an orgy, a nocturnal debauch of sound and movement, transformed into rhythm and dance by the crudest instruments beating in time. According to an observer, the swarming mass of humanity undulates and beats the ground, pivots and jerks around a central pole. The excitement is expressed in any sort of display that will increase it. It is augmented and intensified by anything that will express it: the haunting beat of spears against shields, guttural, heavily accented chants, the jerking and promiscuity of dance. Violence erupts spontaneously. Fighting breaks out from time to time: The combatants are separated and strong arms lift them into the air where they are swung rhythmically until they are quieted. This never interrupts the dancing circle. By the same token, people suddenly leave the dance by twos and go off into the nearby woods, where they couple, then return to their places in the whirl that goes on till morning.

One can understand how festival, representing such a paroxysm of life and contrasting so violently with the petty concerns of daily existence, seems to the individual like another world, where he feels himself sustained and transformed by powers that are beyond him. His day-to-day activity, gathering, hunting, fishing or raising animals, only occupies his time and sees to his immediate needs. He applies his attention, his patience and his skill to it, but on a deeper level, he lives on the memory of one festival and in expectation of another because the festival for him, for his memory and his desire, represents the time of intense emotions and the metamorphosis of his being.

Advent of the Sacred

Durkheim has the honor of having recognized the important illustration afforded by the contrast between festivals and working days, of the distinction between the sacred and the profane. In effect, they oppose intermittent explosion to dull continuity, frenzied elation to daily repetition of the same material preoccupations, the powerful inspiration of common ferment to the tranquil labors in which each one makes himself busy alone, society's concentration to its dispersion, the fever of climactic moments to the quiet toil of the dull parts of his existence.[1] Moreover, the religious ceremonies that occasion them are deeply disruptive for the souls of the faithful. If festival is the time of joy, it is also the time of anguish. Fasting and silence are enforced before the final release. Habitual prohibitions are enforced and new restrictions are imposed. Excesses and extremes of every sort, ritual solemnity, and the prerequisite harshness of restrictions combine also to make the atmosphere of the festival into a special world.

In reality, the festival is often regarded as the actual reign of the sacred. A feast day, an ordinary Sunday, first of all is a time that is consecrated to the divine, a time when work is forbidden, when one must rest, rejoice, and praise God. In societies where the festivals are not spread throughout all of workaday

existence, but grouped in a real *festival season*, one can see even better the extent
to which this season really constitutes the period in which the sacred is supreme.
Mauss's study of Eskimo societies furnishes the best examples of violent contrast
between these two sorts of life, which can always be perceived among peoples
condemned by climate or economic organization to prolonged inactivity for part
of the year. In winter, Eskimo society closes in: Everything takes place or is
done in common, whereas during the summer each family, isolated in its tent in
a huge desertlike expanse, is alone to find the essentials, with nothing intervening to reduce the role of individual initiative. Contrasted with life in the summer,
one almost entirely secular, winter seems a time of "continuous religious exaltation," like a long festival.[2] Among the American Indians of the north, social
morphology is no less seasonably variable. There too, summer's dispersion is
succeeded by winter's concentration. The clans disappear and give way to religious brotherhoods that then perform the great ritual dances and organize the
tribal ceremonies. It is the epoch of the transmission of myths and rites, when
spirits appear to novices and initiate them. The Kwakiutl themselves describe it:
"In summer the sacred is beneath and the secular on top; in winter, the sacred is
on top, the profane beneath."[3] It could not be put more clearly.

In ordinary life, the sacred, as we have seen, is almost exclusively manifested
by prohibitions. It is defined as "reserved," as "separate"; it is set outside common usage, protected by prohibitions destined to prevent any attempts against
the order of the world, any risk of unsettling it or introducing troublesome ferment. It appears hence to be essentially *negative*. That, in fact, is one of the basic
characteristics most often recognized in ritual taboo. And the sacred period of social life is precisely one in which the rules are suspended and license is approved,
as it were. One can no doubt deny that the excesses of the festival have a precise
ritual sense, considering them simply as mere *discharges of energy*. "One is so
far outside the ordinary conditions of existence," writes Durkheim, "and one is
so conscious of this that one feels almost a need to place oneself above and beyond ordinary morality."[4] Certainly, the unruly excitement and exuberance of
the festival correspond to a sort of drive to detumescence. Confucius already
made note of this when, in justification of Chinese peasant feasts, he said that
one must not "always keep the bow drawn without ever releasing it, nor always
released without ever drawing it."[5] The excesses of collective rapture surely do
fulfill this function *also*. Their coming is a sudden explosion after a long, strict
containment. But that is only one of their aspects, more certainly their physiological mechanism than their raison d'être. And this characteristic is far from exhausting the nature of these excesses. The natives, in fact, see them as the condition for their festivals' effective magic. They are the early evidence of the
ritual's success, and consequently, they promise indirectly that the women will
be fertile, harvests rich, warriors brave, game plentiful, and fish abundant.

Excess, Remedy to Attrition

Excess, consequently, is not just a constant accompaniment to the festival. It is not a simple epiphenomenon of the excitement growing out of the festival. It is necessary to the success of the ceremonies celebrated and participates in their holy powers, contributing as they do to revitalizing nature or society. This, in fact, would seem to be the aim of festivals. Time is wearing and exhausting. It is what makes one grow old, what leads the way to death, what wears one down. (In fact, the root of the Greek and Iranian words designating time carries this meaning). Each year vegetation is renewed, and social life, like nature, begins another cycle. Everything that exists must be rejuvenated. The creation of the world must begin anew. This world acts like a *cosmos* ruled by a universal order, and it functions according to a regular rhythm. Rules and moderation sustain it. Its law is that everything has *its own* place and everything happens in *its own* time. This explains why the only manifestations of the sacred are interdictions, taboos, *protections* against anything that could threaten cosmic regularity or else they are expiations, *redress* for anything that might have disturbed it. There is a tendency toward immobility because any change, any innovation endangers the stability of the universe; the desire is to stop its evolution and destroy any chance of its death. But the seeds of its annihilation reside in its own functioning, which accumulates waste and entails the wearing down of its mechanism. There is nothing that seems not to be subjected to this law that is defined and confirmed by all of experience. The very health of a human body requires the regular evacuation of its "impurities," urine and excrement, as well as, for the woman, menstrual blood. Yet, in the end age weakens and paralyzes the body. In the same way, nature yearly passes through a cycle of growth and decline. Social institutions seem not to be exempt from this alternation. They too must be periodically regenerated and purified of the poisonous wastes that represent the harmful part left behind by every act performed for the good of the community, and this involves some pollution of the one who assumes responsibility for this regeneration.

Hence, the gods of the Vedic pantheon seek a creature onto whom they can transfer the impurity they contract by sprinkling blood during a sacrifice. This sort of purging generally takes place in the form of an expulsion or execution, either of a scapegoat who is charged with all the sins committed in that manner, or of some personification of the old year that is to be replaced. Evil, weakness and wear, all ideas that are more or less interchangeable, must be driven out. In Tonkin, rites are celebrated with the express aim of eliminating the impure residue of each event, especially acts of authority. They seek to neutralize the irritation and malevolence of the spirits of people condemned by the government to death for treason, rebellion, or conspiracy. In China, the sweepings, that is, the daily wastes of domestic existence, are piled up by the door of the house and carefully disposed of during the festivals of yearly renewal because they contain, as does everything unclean, an active principle that can bring prosperity if used properly.

The elimination of the slag that every organism accumulates in its functioning, the annual liquidation of sins, the expulsion of the old year are not enough. They serve only to bury a crumbling and encrusted past *that has had its day* and that must give way to a virgin world whose advent the festival is destined to hasten.

Prohibitions have proven powerless to maintain the integrity of nature and society; so there is all the more reason that these prohibitions cannot make nature and society as young as they used to be. Nothing in rules makes them capable of reviving this integrity. It is necessary to invoke the creative powers of the gods and go back to the beginning of the world, turning to the forces that then transformed *chaos* into *cosmos*.

Primordial Chaos

The festival presents itself, in fact, as an actualization of the early stages of the universe, the *Urzeit*, the original, eminently creative era that saw everything, every creature, every institution become fixed in its traditional and definitive form. This epoch is none other than the one in which lived and moved the divine ancestors, whose story is told in *myths*. What is more, for the Tsimshians of North America, myths are distinguished from other legendary tales precisely because they are situated in this time gone by, when the world had not yet assumed its present appearance. Lévy-Bruhl has done an outstanding study of the characteristics of this mythical Great Age in Australian and Papuan cultures.[6] Each tribe has a special term to designate it. For the Aruntas it is *altjira*; for the Aluridas, *dzugur*; for the Karadjeri, *bugari*; for the people of northwestern Australia, *ungud*, etc. These words often simultaneously designate dream, and at the same time, in general, anything that seems unusual or magic. They all are used to define a time when "the exceptional was the rule." The expressions used by observers all tend to bring out this aspect of the primordial age. For Dr. Fortune, this mythical time is the time when "creatures came into existence and natural history began." It is simultaneously set at the *beginning* and *outside* of evolution. Thus Elkin remarks that it is no less the present or the future than the past; "It is a state as well as a period," is his revealing comment.[7] Basically, the mythical time is the origin of the other and continually emerges in it, producing everything disconcerting or inexplicable that arises there. The supernatural is constantly to be found lurking behind what one can perceive, and it tends to manifest itself through this medium. The primordial age is described with remarkable unanimity in the most diverse regions. It is the place of all metamorphoses, of all miracles. Nothing was yet stabilized, no rules had been pronounced, no forms yet fixed. Things that have become impossible since then, at that time, were possible. Objects moved of their own accord, canoes flew on the breezes, men turned into animals, and vice versa. Instead of growing old and dying they shed their skins. The whole universe was plastic, fluid, and inexhaustible. Crops grew spontaneously and flesh grew back on animals as soon as it was cut off.

Creation of the Cosmos

Finally, the ancestors imposed upon the world an appearance that has not changed and laws that have been in force ever since that time. They created human beings, by bringing them out of earth or by transforming already existing creatures of a half-animal nature. At the same time they created or formed the different animal and vegetable species. In making each individual they changed all his descendants yet to come so they would resemble him, without their having to intervene again. They also fixed the sea, dry land, islands, and mountains in their places. They separated the tribes and instituted for each one its civilization, its ceremonies and ceremonial details, its rituals, its customs, and its laws. But because they contained each thing and each creature within given limits, limits that would from then on be *natural*, they deprived them of the magic powers that permitted them to realize instantly their desires and, without experiencing any obstacles, to become whatever they wanted to be on the spot. Order cannot, in fact, adapt to the simultaneous existence of all possibilities or the absence of all rules. The world then experienced insurmountable limitations that confined each species inside its proper being and prevented its getting out. Everything was immobilized and what was prohibited was established so that the new organization and law would not be disturbed. Last, death was introduced into the world, through the disobedience of the first man, or more often of the first woman, by the error of some divine messenger, through the stupidity of the blundering ancestor, The Bungler, who very commonly clumsily does his best to imitate the deeds of the Creator and whose idiotic stubbornness brings about results that are both comic and catastrophic. In any event, with death, like the worm in the apple, *cosmos* has emerged from *chaos*. The era of disorder is over, natural history begins, the rule of normal causality is instituted. Unbounded creative activity is succeeded by the vigilance required to keep the created universe in good order.

Chaos and Golden Age

We realize that mythical times seem cloaked in a basic ambiguity. It is presented, in fact, in antithetical aspects: Chaos and Golden Age. The absence of barriers is as seductive as the lack of order and stability is repulsive. Man looks with nostalgia toward a world where he had only to reach out his hand to gather delicious fruits that were always ripe, where crops obligingly gathered themselves without work, without sowing or harvesting, a world where harsh labor was unknown, where desires were realized as soon as they were conceived without being mutilated, reduced, or annihilated by some material obstacle or social prohibition. The Golden Age, the childhood of the world like the childhood of man, corresponds to this conception of an earthly paradise where everything is provided at first. When this paradise is left behind, it is by the sweat of his brow that man must earn his bread. It is the reign of Saturn or Kronos, where there is no war, no commerce, no slavery or private property. But this world of light, calm delight, an easy and happy existence is, at the same time, a world of darkness and horror. Saturn's time is one of human sacrifices, and Kronos devoured his children. The spontaneous fertility of the soil itself is not without its underside. The first age is presented also as the era of exuberant and wild creations, of monstrous and excessive childbirths. Sometimes the two antagonistic depictions are inextricably merged, sometimes an intellectual effort at coherence separates them, and mythology can be seen to distinguish between and contrast the two, making Chaos and Golden Age successive. They appear as the two faces of a single imaginary reality, the reality of a world without rules from which the regulated world where human beings now live was to come. The world without rules is opposed to the regulated world just as the world of *myth* is opposed to the world of *history*, beginning when the former ends; just as the world of dream, as it is apt to be called, is opposed to the waking world; just as the time of leisure, abundance, and prodigality is opposed to the time of *work*, *lack*, and *thrift*. At the same time, more or less obscurely, this first age represents childhood. To establish this there is no need to invoke that heartfelt regret, that penchant of memory leading the adult to extreme embellishment of the memory of his early years, which suddenly seem to him to have been given over to games, and exempt from care, and which, against all evidence, he regards as the time of eternal celebration in a Garden of Eden. There is no doubt, however, that the two conceptions of the infancy of the world and of the *vert paradis des amours enfantines*, the green and cheeky paradise of children's love affairs, have rubbed off on each other.

Moreover, it is a fact that before the initiation ceremonies introducing him into a social framework, the young person's activity is not subjected to the prohibitions limiting that of an adult; similarly, before marriage, adolescent sexuality is generally as free as can be imagined. It seems that at that time, the individual is not yet included in the order of the world, and consequently does not risk bringing it harm by transgressing laws that do not concern him. He exists, so to speak, on the margins of the regulated universe just as he exists on the edge of organized society. He only half belongs to the cosmos; he has not yet broken every tie with the mythical universe, the beyond, from which the ancestors drew his soul in order to put it in the womb of a woman, his mother, where they make it be born again.

The infancy of the world, in contrast to order and to "natural history," represents a time of universal confusion that cannot be imagined without some anxiety. Among the Eskimo, the contradictory aspects of the primordial era seem intimately entwined. It possesses the characteristics of undifferentiated chaos: All was darkness, there was no light on earth. Neither continents nor seas could be seen. People and animals did not differ from each other. They spoke the same language, lived in similar houses, and hunted in the same way.[8] Nevertheless, in the description of this epoch traits can be recognized that are usually used to depict the Golden Age: Talismans had considerable power then, and one could turn into an animal, a plant, or a pebble. The caribou's flesh grew back on its skeleton after it had been eaten. Snow shovels moved from one place to another by themselves, without one's bothering to carry them.[9] This last possibility shows already, in a meaningful way, a mixture of regret and fear; it illustrates the desire for a world in which everything is accomplished effortlessly, and makes one dread that the shovels might come alive again and suddenly escape from their owners. Consequently, they can never be left unattended in the snow.

II. Recreation of the World

The earliest age—a nightmare for the same reasons that it is simultaneously a paradise—seems indeed to be the *period* and *state* of creative energy from which emerged the present world, which is subject to the vicissitudes of wear and tear and threatened by death. Consequently, it is by being born again, steeping itself again in that ever present eternity as if in an ever flowing fountain of youth, that the world has a chance of being rejuvenated, rediscovering the plenitude of life and strength that will allow it to brave a new cycle of time. That is the function fulfilled by the festival. It has already been defined as an actualization of the time of creation. To repeat Dumézil's apt phrase, it constitutes an *access to the Great Time*,[10] the moment in which men leave evolution to enter the reservoir of ever new and omnipotent forces represented by the primordial age. It takes place in temples, in churches, in holy places that represent in the same way *access to the Great Space*, the one in which divine ancestors evolved, whose sites and sacred rocks are the visible landmarks still associated with the Creators' authoritative gestures. When there is a critical phase of the seasonal rhythm, a ceremony is performed; when nature seems to renew itself, when a change takes place that is visible to all eyes: at the beginning or end of winter in arctic or temperate climates, at the beginning or end of the rainy season in the tropics. With an intense emotion that comes from simultaneous anxiety and hope, a pilgrimage is made to the places formerly frequented by mythical ancestors. The Australian piously retraces their itinerary, stops wherever they stopped and carefully repeats their actions. Elkin has forcefully emphasized this vital religious bond that exists between the native and his country and goes beyond any mere geography. The land seems to him the route that leads to the invisible world, and puts him in contact with "the powers dispensing life and benefiting man and nature."[11] If he must leave the land of his birth or if it is completely disrupted by colonization, he believes he is doomed to death and feels himself withering away because he is no longer able to regain contact with the sources that periodically give life to his being.

Incarnation of the Ancestor-Creators

Festival is thus celebrated in a mythical space-time, and it takes on the function of regenerating the real world. To that end the moment of vegetation's renewal and, if necessary, of the totem animal's reappearing in abundance is likely to be chosen. Everyone goes to the place where the mythical ancestor created the living type from which the group descends. The ancestor's ceremony of creation has been inherited by this group and it alone is able to carry this through to a successful conclusion. Actors mime the deeds and gestures of the hero. They wear masks that identify them with this half-man, half-animal ancestor. Often these props have shutters that, at a given moment, suddenly reveal a second face and thus permit the wearer to reproduce the instantaneous transformations that took place in the earliest times. What is important, in fact, is to make the beings of the period of creation be present and active; they alone have the magical power to confer the desirable effectiveness on the ritual. What is more, no clear distinction is made between "the mythical basis and the present ceremony." Among the Yuma of Colorado, as Daryll Forde has stated categorically, his informants never stopped confusing the ritual they habitually celebrated and the act by means of which the ancestors originally instituted it.

Several different procedures are employed concurrently to revive the fertile times of the dazzling ancestors. Sometimes the telling of myths is enough. These myths, by definition, are secret and powerful narratives that recount the creation of a species or the founding of an institution. They act like magic words. Just repeating them is enough to cause the repetition of the act they are commemorating. Another way of conjuring up the mythical period consists in retracing the rock paintings that represent their ancestors in remote underground passages.[12] By reviving their colors and periodically retouching them (they must not be completely redone at any one time or the continuity would be broken), the beings they represent are called back to life, they are *actualized*; so they will ensure the return of the rainy season, the multiplication of edible plants and animals, the burgeoning of spirit-children who make women pregnant and guarantee the tribe's prosperity.

Often a truly dramatic representation is resorted to. In Australia the Warramunga imitate the life of each clan's mythical ancestor, for example, for the Black Serpent people, the life of their hero, Thalawalla, from the time he emerges from the ground to the time he goes back into it. The actors' skin is covered with down that flies off when they move. Thus they represent the dispersal of the life seeds escaping from the ancestor's body. By doing this they ensure the multiplication of Black Serpents. Men then are revived in turn; they are regenerated and confirmed in their intimate essence by consuming the sacred animal.[13] We have seen that to do this, when it is a question of *respecting* the order of the world and not of *renewing* it, is sacrilegious and forbidden. But now the members of the clan are identified with the beings of the mythical epoch who know no prohibitions and who instituted these prohibitions in the form they will once again take. During the preceding period, the officiants have sanctified themselves through rigorous fasting and observation of many prohibitions that have made them progressively pass from the profane world into the domain of the sacred. They have become the ancestors: The masks and ornaments they wear are signs of their metamorphosis. Then they are able to kill and eat the animal, to gather and eat the plant of which they mystically partake. They realize, thus, their communion with the principle from which they draw their life and force. With it they absorb a new influx of energy. And then they leave it for the other clans. From this moment on they are not to eat freely of this species that they have resurrected and deconsecrated by being the first to make use of this sacred nourishment, identical with themselves, which they periodically need to taste in an act of life-giving cannibalism and fortifying theophagy. Feast and festival are ended, and *order* is established once again.

Fertility and Initiation Rites

These ceremonies of fertility are not the only ones. There are others whose goal is to bring young people into the society of men and assimilate them to the collectivity. These are rites of initiation. They seem to be exactly comparable to the preceding ones and are, like them, based on the representation of myths relating to the origins of things and institutions. They are absolutely parallel. Fertility ceremonies ensure the rebirth of nature, initiation ceremonies the rebirth of society. Whether they coincide or are celebrated separately, they both consist in making the mythical past be real and present in order to bring forth a rejuvenated world. In the *majo* cult of New Guinea, novices who enter the sacred place act as if they were newborn.[14] They pretend to know nothing, and act as if they did not know how to use utensils and as if they were seeing for the first time the food they are given to eat. Then, for their instruction, actors who embody the divine ancestors present each thing to them, *in the order* in which the myths recount the ancestors' intervention to create these things. It would be impossible to point out any better the extent to which the ceremony signifies the return to primordial chaos and the establishment in detail of cosmic law. Order's coming into being does not take place all of a sudden; it is carried out in an *orderly* fashion.

According to Wirz, the *majo* ceremonies are identical, whether it is a case of fertility or of initiation. They differ only in their goals. In fact, society always goes hand in hand with nature. The novice is like the seed buried in the ground, and like soil that has not yet been worked. In the beginning the ancestors transformed the monstrous creatures of the Great Time into men, whom they completed by giving them sexual organs, their sources of life and fertility. Initiation, in the same way, makes neophytes into real men. Circumcision *completes* their penes. The whole ceremony confers upon them various virile powers, particularly bravery, invincibility, and moreover the right and power to procreate. It brings the new generation of men to maturity, just as the rites performed for the reproduction of the totemic species assure the growth of the new crop or new animal generation.

What is more, in mythical times the two sorts of ceremony (initiation and fertility) were simply one. Strehlow is explicit about this in Australia,[15] where, moreover, the rituals of these ceremonies are most clearly distinct from each other. The ancestors take their novices all over the Great Space, teaching at the same time as they *perform* the rites by means of which they created beings or fixed them in a stable morphology. They initiate these novices, hence, not through a "blank," ineffectual ceremony, but through the first, effective unfurling, the brand new gift of their act of creation.

Suspension of Marked Time

In any event, it is important first to actualize the primordial age: *the festival is Chaos rediscovered and shaped anew.* In China the wineskin that represents chaos is considered to be transformed when it has been pierced seven times by lightning. Similarly, human beings have seven facial openings, and a well-born individual has seven in the heart. A stupid person "without openings," with neither face nor eyes, personifies this wineskin-chaos. At the end of a feast the lightning pierces it seven times. Granet emphasizes that this is not to kill it but to make it be reborn to a higher existence, to *mold* it. The arrows drawn against the wineskin seem linked (in the ritual) to a winter festival, *the drinking bout of the long night*, that takes place during the last twelve days of the year and during which every excess, each more extreme than the last, is committed.[16] This is a widespread custom; the festival brings back the time of creative license, the time preceding and engendering order, form and *prohibition* (the three ideas are linked and *together* are the opposite of the idea of chaos). This period has its place ready-made in the calendar, for example, when months are counted by moons and the year by the earth's turning around the sun, during the twelve days that remain in limbo at the end of the solar cycle and make it possible to reconcile the two ways of measuring time. These intercalary days belong to no month and to no year. They are outside time as it is marked off, and at they same time they seem wholly designated for the periodic regenerative return of the Great Time.[17]

These extra days are the equivalent of the entire year, its "replica," as the Rig-Veda calls the sacred days of midwinter in ancient India. Each of these days corresponds to each of the months, and what takes place during the former prefigures what is to happen in the latter; moreover, their names are the same and follow each other in the same order. If the counting is done in two and a half year cycles, as in the de Coligny Celtic calendar, the intercalary period is made up of thirty days that reproduce the twelve-month sequence repeated two and a half times.[18]

The Presence of Ghosts

This time, no matter how long it lasts, witnesses the merging of this world and the beyond; the ancestors or the gods, incarnated by masked dancers, come to mingle with men, and they violently interrupt the course of natural history. They are present in the Australian totemic festivals, in the New Caledonian *pilou* and the Papuan and North American initiation ceremonies. By the same token, the dead leave their abodes and invade the world of the living. For, during this suspension of universal order constituted by the changing of the year, all barriers are down and nothing keeps the dead from visiting their descendants. In Siam, a diabolical character opens the doors to the abyss and the dead return to spend three days in the sun. A temporary king rules the land with all the prerogatives of a true sovereign, while the people devote themselves to games of chance (a classic activity of risk and squandering, the direct opposite of slow and sure accumulation of wealth through work). Among the Eskimo, during winter festivals, spirits are reincarnated in members of the camp, thus confirming the solidarity and continuity of generations in the group. Afterward they are solemnly dismissed so that normal conditions of existence can resume their course. When the festival season is broken up and festivals are spread throughout the entire year, a period in which the dead are free to mingle in the society of the living is always evident. Then, at the end of the time allotted them for their annual invasion, they are sent back to their realm by an explicit exorcism. In Rome, on certain dates, the rock that closes the *mundus* is raised. This hole in the Palatine is held to be the entrance to the infernal world, a shrunken version of this world itself and, symmetrically, as its name indicates, the exact counterpart also of the living world. It is simultaneously the epitome of the Great Space in the presence of the area that is profane, and the orifice permitting their communication. When the rock is raised the spirits are free to wander in the city, as they do on three days in May. At the end of this time each head of a family chases them from his house by spitting beans, which ransoms him and his family from their incursion until the next year.

The return of the dead is still often linked to a time change. Throughout Europe it is mainly during Saint Sylvester's night, that is to say, during the last night of the year, that ghosts, specters, and phantoms are free to hold sway among the living.

III. The Function of Debauchery

This interlude of universal confusion constituted by the festival seems thus to be the time during which the order of the world is suspended. This is why excesses are permitted then. It is important to act against the rules. Everything must be done backward. In the mythical era the course of time was reversed: One was born old and died a child. Two reasons converge here to make debauchery and indiscretion commendable in these circumstances. To be more certain of regaining the conditions of existence in the mythical past, a great effort was made to do the opposite of what one usually did. On the other hand, all exuberance displays additional energy that can only bring abundance and prosperity to the awaited spring. Both of these reasons lead to the violation of prohibitions and to immoderation, to profiting from the suspension of order so as to do the direct opposite of rules of prohibition and, with no restraint, abuse the rules of permission. Consequently, every prescription protecting a good natural and social organization is systematically violated. These transgressions, however, do not cease to be sacrilegious. They attack rules that yesterday seemed, and tomorrow will become, the holiest and most inviolate. They are really the greatest form of sacrilege.

Generally speaking, every circumstance in which society's and the world's existence seem to falter and require renewal through an influx of youthful and excessive energy is *assimilated* to the moving moment in which time changes. Under these conditions, it is not surprising that liberties that are similar or identical to the ones practiced on the intercalary days are resorted to in order to compensate for some plague. One Australian tribe is reported to do this during epidemics, and another during displays of *aurora australis*, which the natives regard as a celestial fire threatening to consume them. The elders order the exchange of wives at such times.

When one observes the actions of the Fijians, there can be no doubt that the natives feel they are restoring the universe that has been attacked in its very being. When there is a poor harvest and they fear a shortage of food, they perform a ceremony they call "creation of the earth." The earth has just shown that it is exhausted, and it must be rejuvenated, brought back to life, while warding off the ruin that lies in wait for the world and men.

Social Sacrileges at the Death of a King

When the life of society and of nature is epitomized in the sacred person of a king, it is the hour of his death that determines the critical moment and releases the ritual license.[19] This license then assumes characteristics corresponding exactly to the catastrophe that has occurred. The sacrilege is of a social nature. It is perpetrated at the expense of majesty, hierarchy, and power. There is no case in which it can be asserted that the unleashing of long-repressed passions is making the most of an inevitable weakness of government or temporary absence of authority. Not the least resistance is opposed to this popular frenzy: It is considered as necessary as obedience to the deceased monarch. In the Hawaiian Islands, when the crowd learns of the king's death, they commit every act that in ordinary times would be considered criminal. They burn, pillage, and kill, and the women are required to prostitute themselves publicly. Bosman reports that in Guinea, as soon as the people learn of the king's death, "each one tries to outrob his neighbor" and these thefts continue until a successor is proclaimed.

In the Fiji Islands the facts are even clearer: The chief's death is the signal for pillage. The tribes that are his subjects invade the capital and commit every sort of violent robbery and depredation. To avoid this, it is often decided to keep the king's death a secret, and when the tribes come to ask if the king is dead (in the hope of devastating and sacking) they are told that his body has already decomposed.[20] Then they leave—disappointed, but docile, because they came too late. This example shows clearly that the time for license is exactly that of the *decomposition* of the king's body, that is, the acute period of infection and defilement that death represents, the time in which it is utterly, obviously virulent, highly active and contagious. By demonstrating its vitality, society must protect itself from this danger, which comes to an end only with the complete elimination of the parts of the royal body that can rot, when nothing is left of the remains but a hard, sound, incorruptible skeleton. The dangerous phase is then judged to be over and things can resume their usual course. A new reign begins after the time of uncertainty and confusion during which the flesh of the Guardian was melting away.

The king, in fact, is essentially a *Guardian*, whose role consists in maintaining order, moderation, and rules. These are all principles that wear out, age, and die with him, and at the same time as his physical integrity decreases, their strength and *efficacious power*, are lost. Consequently, his death opens a kind of interregnum of a reverse *efficacious power*, that is, the principle of disorder and excess that generates the ferment from which a new, revived order will be born.

Dietary and Sexual Sacrilege

In a totemic society, sexual and dietary sacrilege, similarly, aim at guaranteeing food and fertility for the group during a *new* time period. License is tied to the ceremony newly reviving the sacred animal or to the one integrating young people into the adult society. In fact, these rites open a new vital cycle and consequently play exactly the same role as the time change in more differentiated civilizations. They constitute a return to chaos, a phase in which the existence of the universe and of legality is suddenly put in question. The prohibitions normally ensuring that institutions function correctly and that the world runs smoothly, separating what is allowed from what is forbidden, are violated. The group kills and eats the species they revere, and, in a parallel with the great dietary crime, they commit the great sexual crime: the law of exogamy is broken. Under cover of darkness and dancing, in defiance of kinship ties, the men have sexual relations with the wives of the complementary clan who, because they came originally from the same clan, are taboo for these men. Among the Warramunga, when the Uluuru phratry celebrates their initiation ceremony, they take their women in the evening to the men of the Kingilli phratry (who, we recall, made all the preparations for the festival). The Kingilli then have sexual relations with these women, who, nonetheless are members of their phratry.[21] Ordinarily, these incestuous unions rouse a shiver of terror and loathing, and the guilty ones are dealt the harshest punishments. During the festival these unions are both permitted and obligatory.

It must be emphasized that these sacrilegious acts are held to be as ritual and holy as the very prohibitions they violate. Like these prohibitions they fall within the province of the *sacred*. Leenhardt reports that during the great New Caledonian festival, the *pilou*, a masked character appears who breaks all the rules by doing their opposite.[22] He does everything the others are forbidden to do. As the incarnation of the ancestor with whom his mask identifies him, he mimes and repeats the actions of his mythical patron who "pursues pregnant women and overturns emotional and social notions."

Myth and Incest

Once again it is a matter of adopting the behavior that conforms with the legendary example set by the divine ancestors—who practiced incest.[23]

In most instances, the original couple were brother and sister. This is true for numerous Oceanic, African, and American tribes. In Egypt, Nut, the sky goddess, came every night to couple with her brother Keb, the earth god. In Greece, Kronos and Rhea also are brother and sister, and if Deucalion and Pyrrha, who repopulate the world after a flood, are not, they are at least the sort of cousins kept apart by the law of exogamy. Even better, incest is characteristic of chaos: One implies the other. Chaos is the time of mythical incest, and incest as we have seen, is commonly considered to unleash cosmic catastrophes. Among the African Ashanti, if someone who has sexual relations with a forbidden woman, thus compromising the universal order, has not been punished as he should, hunters are no longer able to kill anything in the forests, crops do not grow, women no longer give birth and the clans become mixed and cease to exist. The observer makes the clear conclusion: "Everything in the world is only Chaos then." Among the Eskimo, the dissolute sexuality is a distinct manifestation of a return to the mythical period. Orgies take place during the festival of extinguishing the lights celebrated at the winter solstice. All the lamps in the camp are simultaneously extinguished and then relighted. The time change is made visible; it is localized and illustrated. During the darkness that symbolizes chaos, the couples have sexual relations under the deep bench lining the walls of the winter house. An exchange of all the wives is initiated.[24] Sometimes the principle determining these temporary unions is understood. In Alaska and at Cumberland Sound, a masked actor, personifying the goddess Sedna, matches the men and women according to their names, that is, as the ancestors for whom they are named were matched.[25] Thus the disappearance of the ordinary rules that regulate sexual behavior is no less than a temporary *surfacing* of the long ago time of creation.

The myths of incest are myths of creation. In general, they explain the origin of the human race. The power of a union that is both forbidden and characteristic of the Great Time is added to the normal fertility of sexual union. Erotic practices are especially important to the Kiwai and Marind-Anim of Papua: They only reproduce the ones that the ancestors used to create the useful plants. In the festival, as Lévy-Bruhl remarks, debauchery takes effect through sympathetic magic as well as through participation in the creative power of the beings of ancient times.[26]

The Value of Sexual License

The sexual act already inherently possesses a fecundating power. It is *hot* as the Thonga say; that is, it deploys an energy that is capable of increasing all the forces seen in nature. The orgy of virility occasioned by the festival helps it perform its function simply by encouraging and reviving cosmic forces. But this result could also come from any other excess, any other debauchery. There is clearly not one of these without its role in the festival.

Just as order, which preserves but wears out, is founded on moderation and distinction, disorder, which regenerates, entails excess and confusion. In China, a continuous barrier of prohibitions separates the sexes in all the events of public or private life. Man and woman work separately at distinct occupations. What is more, nothing belonging to one is to come in contact with anything connected with the other. But for the festival, for sacrifices, for ritual labor, for melting metals, for any form of creation, the joint action of man and woman is required. "Collaboration of the sexes," writes Granet, "was all the more efficacious because it was sacrilegious normally and saved for sacred moments."[27] Thus, the winter festivals end in an orgy in which men and women fight and tear off each other's clothes. This was, doubtless, less to be bare than to put on the clothes they had won. In fact, the exchange of clothing, as symbol of reverse values, seems to be the mark of a state of chaos. It took place during the Babylonian

Sacaea, and during the orgiastic festival of Purim among the Jews, in direct violation of the law of Moses. No doubt these rites must be connected with the double disguise of Hercules and Omphale.[28] In any case, in Greece the Argive festival when boys and girls exchange clothes, is significantly named *hubristika*. And *hubris* represents an attack on the cosmic and social order, undue excess. Texts describe it as characteristic of the Centaurs, mythological monsters who are half-man half-animal, who carry off women and eat raw flesh. Centaurs, Dumézil has remarked, are incarnated by members of the confraternity at initiations and by masked figures who make an abrupt appearance at the year change and who, following the example of their legendary counterparts, typically violate every prohibition.[29]

Fertile Excesses

Fertility is born of excess. To the sexual orgy the festival adds the monstrous ingestion of food and drink. "Primitive" festivals, prepared well in advance, display to a high degree this characteristic, still strikingly persistent in more sophisticated civilizations. At the Athenian Anthesteria each one was given a goatskin of wine, and a contest began whose victor was the first to empty his bottle.[30] During Purim, the Talmud indicates one should drink until it is impossible to distinguish between the two cries specific to the festival: "Cursed be Haman" and "Blessed be Mordecai."[31] In China, if the texts are to be believed, food was accumulated "in piles heaped higher than a hill"; ponds were dug and filled with wine where boats could have spun around just as a chariot race could have been held on the pile of food.

Everyone was required to stuff himself as full as possible, filling himself like a distended wineskin. This exaggeration of the traditional descriptions demonstrates another aspect of ritual excesses: the barrage of chatter and boasting that accompanies the waste of these piles of wealth that are *sacrificed*. The role of bragging duels in the feasts and drinking bouts of the Germans, Celts and many other peoples is well known. The prosperity of the next harvests must be forced by lavishly spending the food stores and by going the deed still one better with words. There are open-ended, ruinous competitions for whoever forfeits the most, in a sort of wager with fate to force it to return what it has received with hundredfold interest. Everyone expected to obtain, according to Granet's commentary on the Chinese practices, "better remuneration, a higher return from his future work."[32] The Eskimo make the same calculation. The exchanges and distribution of presents that accompany the festivals of Sedna or the sending back of spirits into the beyond, possess a mystical efficacity. They make the hunt fruitful. "Without generosity there is no luck," Mauss emphasizes,[33] basing this on observation that makes it specific that "the exchange of gifts has the effect of producing the abundance of wealth." The exchange still currently in practice in

Europe, and precisely on the occasion of the *New Year*, seems a weak vestige of a dense circulation of all the treasures that once was destined to invigorate cosmic existence and to test the cohesion of social existence. *Economy, accumulation*, and *moderation* define the rhythm of profane life; *prodigality* and *excess* define that of the festival, the periodic and exhilarating interlude of sacred life that cuts in and restores youth and health.

By the same token, the steady routine of work allowing provisions to be amassed is contrasted to the frenetic turmoil of the banquet where they are devoured. In fact, the festival is made up not simply of *debauches of consumption* involving the mouth or sex, but also *debauches of expression* involving words or deeds. Shouts, mockery, insults, the give-and-take of crude jokes (obscene or sacrilegious) between the public and a procession passing through it (like on the second day of the Anthesteria, at the Lenaean celebrations, at the Great Mysteries, at carnival and at the medieval festival of Fools), jeering assaults between the group of women and the group of men (like at the sanctuary of Demeter Mysia near Pellana of Achaea) constitute the most important verbal excesses. Movement, erotic and violent gestures, and pretend or real fighting are not left out. Baubo's obscene contortions, by making Demeter laugh, wake nature from her lethargy and make her fertile again. One dances until exhaustion and spins until dizzy. Violence is quickly resorted to: In the Warramunga's fire ceremony twelve participants grab flaming torches. One of them charges his counterparts, using his firebrand as a weapon, and soon there is a general melee where crackling torches strike heads and shower the combatants' bodies with burning sparks.[34]

Parody of Power and Sanctity

Forbidden and excessive acts do not seem sufficient to mark the difference between the time of release and the time of order.[35] There are additional *upside-down acts*. Every effort is made to behave in a manner that is exactly the opposite of normal behavior. The inversion of all relationships seems clear proof of a return of chaos, of an epoch of fluidity and confusion. Festivals in which one is committed to reviving the infancy of the world, the Greek Kronia or Roman Saturnalia (whose names are significant), involve the reversal of social order. Slaves eat at the masters' table, order them around and mock them, while the masters serve the slaves, obey them and put up with affronts and reprimands. In each house a miniature State is established: The high functions, the roles of priests and consuls, are given to the slaves who then exercise an ephemeral parody of power. In Babylon also rank was reversed during the festival of Sacaea: In each family a slave dressed as king was head of the household for a limited time. An analogous phenomenon took place on the level of the State. In Rome a monarch was elected who gave his subjects for the day ridiculous orders, such as to go around the house carrying on one's shoulders a woman playing the flute. Certain facts lead one to think that the false king in ancient times met with a tragic fate: He was permitted every debauchery and every excess, but he was put to death on the altar of the god-king Saturn, whom he had personified for thirty days. With the king of chaos dead everything returned to order, and the legitimate government was once again in charge of an organized universe, the cosmos. In Rhodes, at the end of the Kronia, a prisoner was made drunk and then sacrificed. At the Babylonian Sacaea a slave who, throughout the festival had filled the role of king of the city, using the king's concubines and giving orders in his place, providing the people with an example of orgy and lust, was hung or crucified. There is no doubt that these false kings, who were fated to die after having shown, during the annual *retirement* of legitimate power, that they are excessive, extreme, and dissolute tyrants, should be compared with Nahusha (similarly excessive, extreme, and dissolute) who rules over the heavens and earth during the *retirement* of Indra "to the other side of the ninety-nine rivers" after the murder of Vrita. They can be compared as well to Mithothyn, the usurping magician who rules the universe during Odin's *retirement*, when Odin goes into exile to be purified of the defilement contracted on account of his wife Freyja. That is to say, we can compare them more generally with the temporary sovereigns who, particularly in Indo-European myths, take the place of the real ruler of the gods when he must go do penance for the sins that the very exercise of authority has placed upon him.

Everything induces one to see the modern carnival as a sort of dying echo of ancient festivals like the Saturnalia. In fact, a cardboard figure representing a huge, comical, colorful king is shot, burned or drowned at carnival, following a period of jubilation. The rite no longer has any religious value, but the reason for this seems clear: The moment the human victim is replaced by an effigy, the ritual tends to lose its value for expiation or fertility, the double character by means of which it liquidates past defilement and creates a new world. It then takes on the nature of a parody; already this aspect is visible in the Roman festival, and it plays the major role in the medieval festival of the Fools or Innocents.

There is a period of rejoicing for the minor clergy, beginning around Christmas time. A pope, a bishop, or an abbot is elected who is to occupy the throne in travesty until the evening of Epiphany. These priests *wear feminine clothing*, chant obscene or grotesque refrains to the tunes of liturgical chants, transform the altar into a tavern table where they carouse, burning pieces of old shoes in the censer and, in a word, indulging in every imaginable *impropriety*. Finally, with great pomp, a donkey wearing a rich chasuble is led into the church, and the service is held in his honor. Beneath these sacrilegious and absurd parodies, the ancient preoccupation with annually overturning the order of things can be easily recognized. It is perhaps even more visible in the exchange of roles between nuns and pupils in the great convent of the Congregation of Notre-Dame, in

Paris, on the Holy Innocents' Day. The pupils dressed in the nuns' habits and taught classes while their teachers took their places on the benches and pretended to listen. The same festival at the Franciscan monastery in Antibes involved a *reversal* of functions between priests and laymen. The clergy replaced the lay brothers in the kitchen and the garden, while the latter said mass. They dressed for the occasion in ragged vestments turned *inside out*, and they read the holy books while holding them *upside down*.

Regulation and Infraction

No doubt these later manifestations should not be seen as much more than the automatic application to a new setting of a sort of mechanism of reversal, inherited from times when there was an intensely felt necessity to do everything backward or to excess at the moment of the year change. It seems that only the principle of the ritual has been retained, along with the notion of a temporary substitution of the power of comedy for legitimate power. Festival, as we have recognized, represents something far more complex as a whole. It involves the dismissal of time that is used up, the past year, and at the same time it involves disposing of wastes produced by the functioning of any economy, eliminating the defilement connected with the exercise of any power.

Furthermore, there is a return to the creative chaos, to the *rudis indigestaque moles*, from which the organized universe was born and will again be born. It begins a period of license during which the legitimate authorities have retreated. In Tonkin, the Great Seal of Justice was enclosed during this time inside a casket, *face down, to mark that law slept*. Courts are closed and of all crimes only murder is taken into account. Moreover, sentencing those who surrendered as guilty of murder was put off until the return of the rule of law. Meanwhile, power was entrusted to a monarch charged with violating every prohibition and abandoning himself to every excess. He personified the mythical sovereign of the Golden Age-Chaos. General debauchery rejuvenates the world, encourages the life-giving forces of nature that are threatened with death. When later it is time to reestablish order, to fashion the new universe, the temporary king is dethroned, expelled, sacrificed. This, perhaps, makes it easier to identify him with the envoy of ancient times in his incarnation as a scapegoat who was hunted down or put to death. The dead who have returned are sent back again. Gods and ancestors leave the world of men. The dancers who stood for them bury their masks and erase their paint. Barriers once again are erected between men and women, and sexual and dietary prohibitions are again in effect.

Once the restoration is complete, the forces of excess required for rejuvenation must give way to the spirit of moderation and docility, to this fear that is the beginning of wisdom, to everything that preserves and maintains. Frenzy is succeeded by work, excess by respect. The *sacred as regulation*, that of prohibitions, organizes the creation won by the *sacred as infraction*, and makes it last. One governs the normal course of social life, the other rules over its paroxysm.

Expenditure and Paroxysm

In its most complete form, in fact, the festival must be defined as the *paroxysm* of society, which it simultaneously purifies and renews. It is its culmination not simply from a religious point of view but also from an economic point of view. It is the moment of circulation of wealth, the occasion for the most important markets, and the prestigious distribution of accumulated treasure. It seems to be the *total* phenomenon, manifesting the glory of the collectivity and tempering its very being. The group then rejoices in the births that have occurred, which are proof of its prosperity and guarantee its future. It takes to its bosom the new members through an initiation that is to be the basis for their strength. It bids its dead farewell and solemnly swears its loyalty to them. This is the occasion, in hierarchical societies, for different social classes to fraternize. At the same time, in clan societies, it is the occasion for the complementary and antagonistic groups to mix together, attesting to their solidarity and making the mystical principles they incarnate (ordinarily scrupulously separated) collaborate in the work of creation.

One of the Kanaka explains: "Our festivals mark the movement of the awl that is used to bind together the bundles of thatch on a roof, to make there be a single roof, a single speech." Leenhardt does not hesitate to comment on this statement: "The summit of Kanaka society, consequently, is not the head of a hierarchy, a chief, it is the *pilou* itself. It is the moment of communion of the allied clans, who all together, in the fervor of speaking and dancing, exalt the gods, the totems, the invisible beings who are the source of life, the basis of power, and the prerequisite for society."[36] In fact, when these ruinous and exhausting festivals come to an end, through the influence of colonization, society has lost its bonds and comes apart.[37]

Festivals everywhere appear, no matter how differently they are pictured and whether altogether in one season or spread out during the course of the year, to fulfill a similar function. They constitute a break in the obligation to work, a deliverance from the limitations and constraints of the human condition: It is the moment in which myth and dream are lived. One exists in a time and in a condition in which one's only obligation is to use things up and spend oneself. Motives of acquisition are no longer acceptable; one must waste, and everyone outdoes the other in squandering his gold, his provisions, his sexual or muscular energy. But it seems that societies, in the course of their evolution, tend to lose their differentiation, moving in the direction of uniformity, leveling, and relaxation of tensions. As it becomes more pronounced the complexity of the social organism is less tolerant of the interruption of the ordinary course of life. Everything has to go on today just like it did yesterday, and tomorrow just like today.[38] Consequently, the period of relaxation has become individualized. The opposition between vacation and working days seems really to have taken over from the old alternation between feasting and work, ecstasy and self-control, that annually revived order out of chaos, wealth from prodigality, and stability from frenzy.[39]

[NRF *January 1940:*]

A general ferment is no longer possible. The period of turbulence has become individualized. *Vacation* is the successor of the festival. Of course, this is still a time of expenditure and free activity when regular work is interrupted, but it is a phase of *relaxation* and not of *paroxysm*. The values are completely reversed because in one instance each one goes off on his own, and in the other everyone comes together in the same place. Vacation (its name alone is indicative) seems to be an empty space, at least a slowing down of social activity. At the same time vacation is incapable of *overjoying* an individual. It has been deprived of any positive character. The happiness it brings is primarily a result of a distraction and distancing from worries. Going on vacation, first of all, is escaping from one's cares, enjoying a "well-earned" rest. Rather than communication with the group in its moment of exuberance and jubilation, it is further isolation. Consequently vacation, unlike festival, constitutes not the flood stage of collective existence, but rather its low-water mark.[40] From this point of view vacations are characteristic of an extremely dissipated society in which no mediation remains between the passions of an individual and the State apparatus. In this case, it can be a grave and even alarming sign that a society should prove incapable of reviving some festival that expresses, illustrates, and restores it. Doubtless, there can be no question of bringing back the old alternation between feasting and labor, ecstasy and self-control that annually revived order out of chaos, wealth from prodigality, and stability from frenzy. But we should ask the harsh question. Is a society with no festivals not a society condemned to death? While suffering from the gnawing feeling of suffocation vaguely provoked in everyone by their absence, is not the ephemeral pleasure of vacation one of those false senses of well-being that mask death throes from the dying?

[L'Homme et le sacré *(1950):*]

So one must ask what brew of the same magnitude frees the individual's instincts, repressed by the requirements of organized existence, and at the same time results in a sufficiently wide-ranging, collective ferment. And it seems that from the time strongly established States appeared (and more and more clearly as their structure asserts itself), the old alternation between feast and labor, ecstasy and self-control that periodically revived order out of chaos, wealth from prodigality, stability from frenzy has been replaced by an alternation of a completely different order, and yet the only thing offering the modern world a nature and intensity that are comparable. This is the alternation between peace and war, prosperity and destruction of the results of prosperity, stable tranquillity, and compulsory violence.

Sacred Language
Jean Paulhan
Tuesday, May 16, 1939

[The lecture delivered by Paulhan at the College of Sociology has finally been found by Jacqueline F. Paulhan, who published it in 1982 in the second of the Cahiers Jean Paulhan *entitled* Jean Paulhan et Madagascar (1908-1910). *The title, "Sacred Language," fits the contents better than the one announced on the printed program for this third trimester.*

Paulhan, born in 1884, was distinctly older than the members of the College. Caillois was born in 1913, just as Paulhan published his first book, Les Hain-Tenys, *brought back from his three-year stay in Madagascar (and from which, as we shall see, much of the material at issue in his lecture to the College is borrowed). When Paulhan published* Le Guerrier appliqué *(in 1917), Bataille was experiencing a religious crisis that was not atheological in the least, during which he wrote "Notre-Dame de Rheims" which he soon was in such a hurry to forget.*

Paulhan's name appeared in the index of presurrealist, postwar reviews such as Nord-Sud *and* Littérature. *In 1920, Jacques Rivière brought him into the* Nouvelle Revue française *as secretary. When Rivière died in 1925, Paulhan became director of the review. From this position, he is said to have carefully doled out, for more than fifteen years, the occult power of what Monnerot, perhaps, would have called a literary spiritual director. An enigmatic authority (which he found the proverb possessed) was, in fact, commonly attributed to him. This rising star among éminences grises fit right in with secret societies and their imperceptible but totalitarian hold. Paulhan, who gave no evidence of disdaining occult action or clandestinity, liked to publish in his own journal under*

304

*a pseudonym (we have already met Jean Guérin). But fame like this spreads: Raymond Aron had revealed a sort of Père Joseph of the Fourth Republic in the person of Kojève; Paulhan's reputation, too, is bound up with an omnipotence that refuses to make an appearance. One may think his work has suffered for it. Yet it is clear that this secret omnipotence is something not completely foreign to the work. Before the foundation of the College, Paulhan had published Caillois and Leiris in the reviews with which he was connected (*Mesures, *the* NRF*). After it was founded, of all the reviews of the period, the* NRF *would be the one most open to the activities of the College, which never managed to establish its own journal.*

There are gestures that "are not accomplished without some negligence." These words, last, or nearly last, in Fleurs de Tarbes, *could summarize Paulhan's method. It resembles something like an exercise of negligence: attentive, conscientious, meditated absentmindedness. Answers to the darkest questions are within reach. Just don't think about them.*

The proverb tellers evoked by Paulhan in his lecture seem to him to make up a secret society, but one that is very unusual because its "passwords are banalities," as he says. As in the democracy he referred to two months earlier (see "The Structure of Democracies"), the best position to be in is that of first comer, just anybody. Proverbs are somehow commonplaces. The secret society of the commonplace is only opened overtly, with a skeleton key. Thirty years later, in a chapter of Le Clair et l'obscur, *Paulhan would return to this. "Everything takes place as if the men were forming a secret society. . . . And doubly secret," he continues, "if the word forming the members into a group is still obscure for the most assiduous of them. A given man can belong without even knowing it." This half-Kafkaesque, half-Borgesian apologue recalls the metamorphoses that conclude "Sacred Language": when the profane ceases to be marked off from its opposite, the sacred, and when one passes imperceptibly from what is sacred in everyday life to the everyday life as sacred.*

By 1939 Paulhan had spent twenty-five years intermittently reflecting on the semantics of proverbs. He had several times intended to write a university thesis on the subject. The lecture he delivered before the College does not, however, strictly speaking, present any conclusion. It rather describes, as in the earlier texts, the failure to reach any conclusion, and draws the consequences from the inevitability of such a failure. It is presented, in fact, as an epistemological autobiography that would remind one of the Discours de la méthode *if it were not so resolutely balked by a theoretical irresolution. Paulhan, to begin, retraces his progress (rather slow) in Malagasy—and (still slower) in proverbs. And how, without knowing how, he ended up finding himself in the (to him uncomfortable) position of a sorcerer's apprentice, using proverbs quite brilliantly, whereas he had not advanced so much as one iota in analyzing how they function. Kojève countered Bataille and his friends by saying that a magician cannot believe in magic. Paulhan is just as much in the position of Monsieur de Hautemare, the object of Stendhal's irony in* Lamiel, *because he "had helped fabricate a miracle in which* he himself was the first to believe." *And now, to his secret humiliation, he found himself an active member of the proverb tellers' secret society without the least notion what it was, in whatever he had said, that opened the doors for him.*

For Paulhan did not so much want to use proverbs as to capture in the flesh the workings of this language within language. But words, precisely, never let themselves be captured in the flesh. It disturbs them to be watched. The same is true for the sacred, according to Bataille, and that is the reason, according to "The Sorcerer's Apprentice," that sacred sociology can "avoid with difficulty criticizing pure science." By the same token, Paulhan, in 1938 (though he had not waited for this date to admit being a tempted spectator), noted, "There are some spectacles that cannot bear a spectator; these are words" (Oeuvres, vol. 2, p. 191). And, that same year, in "La Demoiselle aux miroirs": "Man does not grasp his mind intact *any more than he sees his neck directly." This early scene of Paulhanian linguistics thus foreshadows what Blanchot, a little later, would call the gaze of Orpheus: It sets as its object what disappears from its sight, slips away at its approach—its own blind spot, what is out of range. Obviously, this inspiring difficulty is not limited to language. Responding to Monnerot's inquiry about spriritual directors (the answer appeared in June 1939), he personalizes the area of his investigation: "Are there some sorts of events that take place in the center of our lives that I can never observe directly?" Marcel Duchamp imagined a faucet that would stop running as soon as one stopped hearing it. Paulhan's fantasies go in the opposite direction. In one of his stories, there is a machine that stops as soon as one looks at it head on. The secret is easy as pie: Just don't think about it.]*

Botzarro, as everyone knows, was silent for twenty years, at the end of which time his language took on such a power that from then on one word of his was enough to put out a fire, and ten words to make a cedar grow.[1]

I never knew him. But for four years I lived in a country[2] where each man, with little effort, could believe he was Botzarro. I am going to detail for you my experience with proverbs, thirty years ago in Madagascar—an experience whose meaning I scarcely understood before today.

The Proverb as Separate

Before I applied myself to understanding proverbial language, I had a rather intense experience of its existence because of the trouble and even, if I may say so, the harm it caused me.[3]

I learned Malagasy by using it, living among the Malagasy people. It was after a year's practice, when I was beginning to speak rather fluently, that I had the sense that there was a profound, perhaps insurmountable difference between my language and that of the Malagasy. This happened when I noticed that at certain passes in the conversation, they had a second language available to them, one that was more solemn and tacitly agreed to be completely effective. Deprived as I was of this language, my words seemed to me without dignity or weight.

I applied myself to the recognition of this language. It was rather easy. It contained archaic words; it was obscure; the phrases were more rapidly pronounced, in one breath as if they were a single word. Sometimes it had rhyme and rhythm. But above all, it was spoken with equally peculiar gravity and detachment. Rabe stood up each time he said a proverb. Ralay leaned forward and spread his arms. Rasoa took on an expression that was both tense and dispossessed.

I saw nothing, therefore, not already known by those who have studied proverbs. When Léon Bloy writes "Who has not remarked the solemn wisdom, the *morituri sumus* of these good souls when they speak sentences bequeathed them by the centuries,"[4] he clearly registers simultaneously the solemn nature of these proverbial phrases and also the dispossession distinguishing them from any other phrase.

Effectiveness of the Proverb

Of course, the difference would have been unimportant if it had no effect. But I also observed, and this was what troubled me, that proverbs were particularly suited to convincing and persuading. The Malagasy do not say "Tell a proverb," but "Stop the discussion, break it, cut through with a proverb." Not that the one in a dispute who had just said a proverb would automatically win, but at least, in order for the dispute to continue, it would be necessary to reply with another proverb—or better still, with two or three proverbs, as if the conversation, once it had reached this superior plane could not demean itself subsequently.

Here again, I saw nothing that has not always been known. There is a sixteenth-century collection of proverbs called: *Ways to Win any Dispute*, and another, *Good Answers to Anything*. From Solon to the Druids, from Pythagoras to Franklin, effectiveness is the characteristic least often denied proverbs. And everyone knows that their other name, "adages," expresses precisely this efficacity: *ad agendum* for acting.

Ambiguity of the Proverb

You can guess what there is left to say: sometimes proverbs fail. And then they are as helpless, as silly, and as ineffectual as they had just been powerful.

You could guess it, but I have to admit it took me a rather long time to realize it. First it was because the moment they sensed failure, the Malagasy whom I listened to were extraordinarily skillful in masking the proverbial quality of their phrase and completing the proverb with a flippancy equal to its original seriousness of tone. Also, no doubt it was because I was resigned in advance to attribute all blunders to myself and scarcely imagined that the Malagasy could be as helpless in respect to their own language as I was. But I had to face facts. Not only did it happen that a proverb would fail, but this failure even invited jokes. People said, "Naturally, with your proverbs. . ." or "When he comes up with a proverb he thinks he's said it all."

Exactly like a French bourgeois would say, "Don't bother us with your ready-made phrases." Or even—I cite Bloy—"The man who makes no use of his faculty of thought is limited in his language to a small number of proverbs."[5] In addition, this ambiguity of proverbs had a social aspect that was the same elsewhere, in Madagascar, as in Europe: Peasants generally respected proverbs more than town dwellers, and old people more than young.

The proverb as Sacred

Proverbs are apt to be called *time-honored expressions*. In short, sacred expressions. They offer the essential characteristics of this sacredness; within the overall language they are *separate*, *effective*, and *ambiguous*. Last, they offer some undefinable aspect that is mysterious and secret, that is not without magic. Plutarch compares them to the Eleusinian mysteries, which conceal a sublime philosophy beneath a vulgarized form. Erasmus compares them to Alcibiades' Sileni whose ugly exterior hides a divine soul. Ecclesiastes has already told us that the Wise Man is the one who has been able to penetrate the secret of the proverbs. Finally it seems that proverb tellers, always and everywhere, have formed something like a secret society.[6]

This, at least, is a rather peculiar secret society: It does not hide, it operates publicly, and its passwords—unlike other magic words—are banalities. Nonetheless, it remains secret, and everything takes place as if an undefinable difficulty, providing sufficient defense against indiscretion, would protect the proverbs.

But I see no reason for this difficulty to detain us. On the contrary: All the conditions that would allow us to carry on seem to come together here. Because, unlike other magic words, the proverb offers, along with its mystery, an apparent meaning. It is like other phrases, other ordinary phrases—but it is also distinct from them. Daily one sees ordinary phrases become proverbial. And consequently it seems that, in order to pry out the secret of the proverb and its sacred character, it would suffice to establish the conditions and the details of this change.

Which is what I am going to try to do. First though, I simply want to lay out three points of method, that will keep us from wandering blindly.

Three Points of Method

The first point is self-evident. We are attempting to explain the positive nature of the proverb. *To explain* an event is, by definition, to reduce it to one or more elements that are already clear and defined. It is to reduce the unknown to the known, which clarifies it. Just like the physicist who discovers that a lithium atom is made up of a nucleus and two layers of electrons. Or the detective who discovers that the murderer lived in the forest and went around with Chinese people.

The second point is no less evident. If I ask myself what, in the case of language, are the known elements that are as clear as the existence of Chinese people or the definition of an atomic nucleus, I find two. In the common consciousness a sharp distinction is made between them. On the one hand, there is the sign and on the other the thing it signifies: the word and the idea that goes with it. Therefore, chances are that the proverb's particular characteristic, the sacred, can be reduced to a specific combination of words and ideas.

The final point is the most delicate. The danger in every observation of language is that it will have the same effect on this language as would some form of awkwardness—and there are few subjects where the observer *disturbs* the object of his study to such an extent. Consequently, it is only upon reflection that the distinction between the word and the idea itself becomes barely perceptible. The speaker, the talker cares little about it. In order to draw his attention, for example, to the *words* he uses, his tongue must slip, or he must lack some word, or else he must find himself suddenly inspired with a scientific concern—like ours. But we shall take care not to push this so far that it prevents our restoring the naturalness, the facility, and the lack of this distinction that are part of everyday language.

I. About One Experience with the Proverb and Its Ensuing Failure

Preparations for the experience. I have said that for me, it was as if there were within the Malagasy language a second language—to all appearances rather close to an argot or a technical language—but whose specific characteristic was that tacit convention seemed to attribute to it a complete effectiveness. Consequently, I had the feeling that authority, whose absence I felt rather painfully in my own language, was of an external and material nature, and that, if I did not possess this it was through simple ignorance. In short, it seemed to me to stem from words—and I have no doubt that the idea we share of "the power of words" played a part in strengthening this feeling of mine. Quite simply, I never inquired—as one ordinarily does—whether this power was inherently laudable or dangerous. I just had to try to get it for myself. I had to learn the words. So that was what I immediately began to do.

I'm afraid that, in all of this, I seem somewhat more naive than normal. But I had set myself the task of learning Malagasy by using it, and only by using it. I really don't know, even today, what was the point of the prejudice keeping me from grammars and dictionaries at that time. It's not very important. Even if absurd, I owed this absurdity some curious experiences from which I am still getting something.

The first success. So I applied myself to remembering the proverbs that I heard said and those that were entrusted to me. I didn't run into as many difficulties as one might fear. I had learned the Malagasy language up to this point by phrases rather than by words. And I kept on. Moreover, these new phrases were particularly easy to memorize. Their *import*, no doubt, seemed simple to me—but their apparent meaning (the meaning they would have had if they were not proverbs) was wonderfully diverse, lively, and cutting: sometimes on the order of a fable, sometimes an anecdote. It was as easy as could be for me to remember the anecdote in proverbs like

> Cicada's voice covers the fields
> Cicada's body is held in a hand

or

> Meadowlark's egg by the side of the road
> I'm not guilty; the meadowlark is.

I didn't have to worry about forgetting later this apparent detail. The proverb was, of course, for me just a single word. But it was at least a word whose etymology could be perceived and was striking. It is possible that French proverbs such as

> L'occasion n'a qu'un cheveu
> À bon chat, bon rat
> [Opportunity has only one hair
> The right rat for the right cat]

have a real meaning that is different from their apparent meaning—in which the hair or the cat is no less absent than *salt* is absent from *salary* and *ligate* or *ligature* from *religion*. But that is unimportant if the hair and the cat work to keep them there.

And I found a second advantage in this.

The sequel to the success. Proverbs go in families. The same surprises, the same sequences are repeated in them. These phrases, according to the group, offered the same internal order, the same composition. Each proverb seemed to me like a mold or a stencil suitable for forming, by means of a few substitutions, a hundred different proverbs. And I passed easily from

> If the teeth are broken, too bad for the head

to

> If the hair is gray, too bad for the head.
> If the eye is put out, too bad for the head.
> If the mouth is thick, too bad for the head.

So the proverb

> The egg is advising the hen

(whose subtler meaning recalls the French proverb "He wants to teach his mother how to make babies") led me naturally to other proverbs, such as,

> A gunshot against thunder: A little boy shooting a man
> A visit to the grave: The visitor does the host's job
> Like the louse: What one has on one's head is what bites

and all the other proverbs evoking an upside-down world. I worried little about this upside-down world. It was invaluable to me, at least, to evoke it long enough to remember the phrase. Sometimes other proverbs would have rhythm or rhyme, like verses. In short, everything about them seemed likely to favor my project.

The difficulties did not come until somewhat later.

A first failure. This was when I found myself with some two or three hundred proverbs in my head and at a loss how to use them.

At first, rather naively, I had imagined that how to use proverbs would come with the rest—which was what happened with common phrases—and that I only had to remember them to immediately profit from their power. The opposite happened, and my awkwardness at dissociating myself from the proverb I had just pronounced further emphasized my failure. I said that proverbs, including those of the Malagasy, remained ambiguous, totally prepared to fail, but also prepared to triumph. My own proverbs were not at all ambiguous but misfired regularly.

I saw the reason rather quickly. A Swiss philologist, Charles Bally, wrote an extremely fine treatise on the dangers of etymology.[7] He demonstrated that children and foreigners would make fewer mistakes about the meaning of words in a language if professors were not in the habit of calling their attention to etymologies—true or false, but usually so far removed from the present sense of the word that all they are good for, at best, is muddling the meaning.

And I had to admit that, in the same way, the apparent sense of the proverbs—and this visible etymology—while it was a strong aid in remembering them, subsequently served only to deceive me about their meaning and their use. Here are three examples.

A. Rabenahy, the *fokonolona*—that is, the communal counselor—mentioned to me some gossip going around about his administration, and he added, "How am I supposed to answer? *A dead ox doesn't chase away flies.*" And I said: "But you're still a live ox." Then one of our friends reproached me, saying, "How can you call Rabenahy an ox?" I would have happily replied that Rabenahy called himself an ox first, if I had not had plenty of occasion to observe that proverbs are almost never taken as metaphors, which it seemed to me they were.

B. Rabenahy, in my presence, said to his son Ralay, "Just the same, you have to make up your mind to marry." Ralay replied, "Well, in that event one might say: *'Who hastens to marriage, runs toward divorce.'*"

I did not notice that this was a proverb, and I said something like: "It is not because one marries young that one gets divorced fast." And it would be exaggerating to say that they didn't listen to me. They didn't even *hear* me. Rabenahy answered with another proverb. I would have a thousand other occasions to remark that the proverb is only an entity that cannot be broken down, and where the sense connections remain invisible.

C. Rabenahy suggested we walk to the market. Ralay answered, *"Respect can be sold. If you walk, they will make fun of you."* I remarked that I did not care much about being respected. And immediately I became aware that I was speaking in a void and for myself alone. But Rabenahy replied, *"Cicada's voice covers the fields. Cicada's body is held in a hand.* You are not wealthy. So don't try to impress everybody." No one paid any more attention to my objection than if it had been made in an unfamiliar language. Picture a hundred similar disappointments. You see there that the proverb differs from its apparent sense to the point of being unrecognizable through metaphor or through an abstract connection or even through the simple words it seems to offer us.

Sequels to the failure. You can see where these failures imperceptibly were leading me. Since language alone remained powerless to assure my effectiveness, this influence must consequently come from something other than words: from thoughts and things. If proverbial language was not a secret language, it remained nonetheless a secret knowledge and each proverb constituted one of its laws. From that point on I proposed to apply myself solely to the study of these laws themselves. A number of different reflections helped to decide me on this method.

One was simply good sense. No matter how different the Malagasy were from us, I did not push the taste for exoticism to the point of wanting them to be extraordinary at all costs. And it is more *natural* for a man to obey a faith and a thought than a mere word.

The other was directly suggested by the Malagasy themselves, precisely because of the visible embarrassment they experienced each time I asked them to explain a proverb to me. Sometimes they would just repeat the proverb to me, as if it were self-evident. Sometimes they set it in an imaginary discussion that it was to resolve, and their explanations had an awkwardness that was symmetrical with mine, as if the proverb had been a simple, irreducible fact to the point of not being open at all to explanation.

Finally, I thought I saw clearly the source of the illusion that, at the beginning, had me believing in the effectiveness of a word. And, in fact, as long as I refused to fathom its meaning, adhere to it, or side with it—simply being sensitive to its external characteristics, its solemnity, its archaism, its rhythm—the proverb for me was only a word. I only had to avoid seeing it any longer reflected through my awkwardness.

II. A Second Experience and a New Failure

In which I begin by succeeding. I launched fervently on this new experience. I have implied that everything Malagasy filled me with a rather thoughtless enthusiasm. I was, I think, like most voyagers who tend to think of themselves as rather divided and inconsistent, but who recognize in primitive peoples the unity and fervor of a cohesive existence. In short, I was ready to admire in the Malagasy customs or aims that would have been completely disagreeable to me in Europe. I did not dislike searching in the proverbs for a profound philosophy, something like key events, whose occurrences (at which we were present) would only be appearances. I looked for this philosophy, and of course I found it. It is the sort of philosophy one always finds when one looks for it.

The feeling that the Malagasy themselves were very concerned with seeking it out with me was also helpful. I currently had an explanation for their proverbial disputes. It was not a question of using, or abusing, the somehow mechanical effect of a proverb, but—to stick more closely to the truth—establishing whether the event that divided them stemmed from this or that law (exactly like two physicists, investigating the cause of a given phenomenon, can hesitate between electricity and heat).

Rabenahy said to his son Ralay, "This time, I think you are going to stop gambling. You have lost fifty francs with your evening."

"So now I have to gamble to get them back."

"Remember the proverb: *What one hopes for never comes, what one holds onto is lost.*"

"Yes, but with a bit of patience the moment comes when it is the *birth of a calf in the autumn: joy and wealth at the same time.*"

The Malagasy are a clever, subtle people, and extremely polite. It did not displease me to imagine them completely taken up in a subtle play of explanations and origins.

In which I find some troubling things. I am afraid that, in the descriptions I am attempting, I am excessively systematic. Of course, during the entire period I mention, I was pursuing progress in the Malagasy language. It is likely that I was continuing also to learn proverbs by heart and to slip them haphazardly into my conversation. But still my attention was turned elsewhere.

I have kept the evidence of this. I had taken it into my head, for example, to outline a classification of the proverbs according to the philosophy or metaphysics—realism, idealism, dialectical—that they seemed to me to spring from and express in their fashion. I was rather successful.

In other respects, I tried to share my own liking for the Malagasy with my friends. In my letters I wrote them proverbs that had seemed to me particularly apt or revealing. I drew up lists of them. I went so far as to read collections of Malagasy proverbs that I had ended up getting—not like I would have read a dictionary, but rather like a sequence of fables or little plays each one of which contained its entire meaning:

> *The little girl who watches games: You see her when she goes away;*
> or *You wait for the spiteful gossip to leave before sweeping the*
> *house.*

One can imagine a thousand short novels about these, and I liked doing so.

In the end, I had a misgiving: It was that, without really admitting it, I was making a choice among the proverbs that were given to me. It was particularly the paradoxical or malicious proverbs that I was remembering. But other proverbs obviously seemed useless for me. I ignored them. All I had to do was find thirty proverbs out of a hundred that were able to intrigue and instruct me, in order to assume that those were the *real* proverbs. And in the long run my procedure seemed to me a bit tendentious.

I met up with something more seriously troubling.

A second failure. I said my progress in Malagasy was advancing during this period. I learned endless new words, and I even occasionally noticed that (without giving it much thought) I had just used a proverb. Each day, as I added new touches to the subtle, rational Malagasy soul that I imagined, a few new proverbs also found their place in my language. In the end I was struck by this fact: They were not the *same* proverbs appearing here and there. As if my thought and my language had been active on two different planes, I had made lists of clever or odd proverbs and yet later I was ill at ease saying them. On the contrary, the most obvious proverbs, the ones apparently most devoid of interest, were the ones I used most readily. Like:

> A piece of stone is stone.
> When tears fall it means the heart is large.
> The one who likes lawsuits bankrupts himself.

I met with other obstacles.

I said that the appearance of a proverb in a discussion somehow lifted this discussion to a higher level, from which it, subsequently, could not lower itself, in the sense that one had to concede or, if one stuck to a position, respond with another proverb. I had noticed also rather quickly, however, that the more proverbs contained in a reply the more weight and dignity it had. Answering with two proverbs to an argument that offered only one, with three to two, four to three, was definitely putting reason on one's side. This use of proverbs is codified in the *hain-teny*.[8] But the simplest conversation already showed it. To Ralay's proverb "birth of a calf in the autumn" that I mentioned earlier, Rabenahy responded with two proverbs:

> Don't wait for misfortune to stop your gambling. Don't do *like the blindman: When he has already been hit he ducks the stone.* Don't do *like the mouse: After it is hit it dodges.*

Thus he was assured of having an advantage.

So I found I was imperceptibly brought back to seeing a purely material, mechanical, and quantitative action in the effect of proverbs.

Some other aspects of the failure. It seems that correct reasoning does not gain anything by being repeated two or three times—certainly not by ten or fifteen repetitions as would happen in some disputes. If, however, three won over two and eight over seven, I had to admit that it was the phrase itself, free of thought, that played its role here and exercised its effect. And evidence of this purely linguistic effect began to come at me from all sides the more I buried myself in a purely intellectual consideration of the proverb. A thousand signs informed me that it was not the idea but the phrase that carried weight. First I was bound to notice, along these lines, an extravagant proliferation surrounding every proverb. It seemed any phrase, even absurd or meaningless ones, had the right to influence as soon as it modeled itself on the proverb's rhythm and composition. For example, from

> Soul of a slave: ravage

came, haphazardly,

> Soul of a child: think of nothing

> Soul of Iketaka: be coy
> Soul of Ikoto: destroy

and thousands of other proverbs, rhyming by chance. I was furious to see that they were all accorded the same authority.

I was no less scandalized to see that, conversely, the proverb that had seemed to me most subtle or apt lost all value and—very nearly—all meaning as soon as I omitted some not particularly meaningful particle or conjunction in telling it; or even when I would happen to change the word order. For instance,

> Laugh at a drumless dancer

was a proverb and was effective. But if, for example, you said, ''That's something to laugh at: He dances without a drum'' or even, ''It is absurd to dance with no drum,'' the proverb didn't work, and the phrase fell flat.

The natural conclusion was that I had to go back to considering the whole proverb as a single word whose meaning was relatively unimportant and that owed its import only to some strictly material quality it had.

A disappointment's paradox. I saw myself, consequently, thrown back on the first opinion I had formed of proverbial effect—and, moreover, too certain that this opinion, in turn, threw me back rather quickly on the opinion I was abandoning. That, indeed, is what happened. I was yet to find myself hesitating several times between one or the other explanation, between a secret language and a secret knowledge, without either one convincing me for long. But the the surest effect each explanation had on me was to throw me back on the opposite opinion. So I was endlessly tossed from word to idea, idea to word, finally losing not just any explanation but even any precise idea of *proverbial effect.* My experience, exhaustive as it was, left me in great difficulty and confusion. Of course I resigned myself, but not without some irritation, the effect of which was to leave me extremely susceptible with regard to proverbs, as if I were terrorized by them.[9] Through a strange conjunction, I was at the same time very skillful at detecting them. I could tell them coming a long way off. I guessed which phrases were getting ready to turn into proverbs. Even commonplaces provided me with a peculiar and irritating preoccupation.

The strangest is yet to tell. It is that this shame, or sort of fear, was not preventing me from using proverbs. Really, on the contrary, my progress along these lines was advancing, as if my hesitation and doubts, far from working against my expression, provided it with a favorable terrain. Frequently, and not without pride, I would happen to notice that I had just made rather skillful use of a proverb (and certainly without preparing it). Sometimes, knowing I would have to speak, I even prepared in advance several proverbs that I would use or not, depending on the circumstances.

Thus, rather pathetically, my experience of the proverb came to an end.[10] Around this time I was named director of courses in Malagasy at the École des langues orientales, and I gave up my idea of writing the thesis on proverbial effect I had proposed to the Sorbonne.[11] There were good reasons, if not for the first at least for the second of these two events. There is nothing in the world more humiliating than to be able to do perfectly something one is incapable of understanding.

III. Sacred Logic

On "high-flown words." Not one day passes in which one of our great men of politics does not allude, more or less directly, to the power of magic words or, as they are called, "high-flown words." A month ago[12] Hitler spoke of the power of slogans (like "futurism"), and Chamberlain of the power of words (like "equal rights"). André Maurois, speaking of politics, said the day before yesterday that we are separated only by words. And we know that Maurras and J. R. Bloch, one with the annoying power of the word "democracy" the other with the word "order" have an explanation for all our internal divisions. So we know that the question of sacred words or phrases is a constant one. There is no need to go to Madagascar to experience the proverb.

I doubt that this makes our experience any more satisfying. Our first impulse is to think that the great men are speaking foolishness. Novalis wrote that the word "freedom" overturned worlds. Yes. But we know why. It is because there were many brave people ready to be killed for freedom, who believed in it—people for whom *freedom* was the complete opposite of a word, the supreme reality. And so forth. It is fine for "cubism" to be only a word for Hitler, "order" a word for Jean Richard Bloch, "democracy" a word for Maurras. But for the democrat, the reactionary, or the cubist painter, they are the complete opposite of words; they are rather a knowledge and a secret conviction. And it is the painter, the reactionary, and the democrat that count. There is really a sort of drastic absurdity in speaking of the power of words, because the simplest experience shows us that where "words" are in evidence there is no power—but where there is power one doesn't even notice the words. I see no "power" that does not stem from ardor, conviction—from thought.

On "high-flown words," a sequel. Nevertheless, scarcely have we made this discovery before contradictory examples crop up all around. For there are words feared by everyone, words one avoids, which, therefore, exercise at least a negative power.

The word "devaluation" is to be avoided; you say instead "monetary alignment." For the word "war" you say "national defense." *La Revue des deux mondes* turns down titles with the word "death" in them. The last time the salary of the deputies was raised they did not say "an increase in the parliamentary compensation." They said "a coefficient taking into account the rise in the cost of living."

There are also words that are sought after: Certain lewd words bring good luck. Certain arrangements of words have a good effect. Advertisement is well aware of this, as is poetry. "Du beau . . . du bon . . . Dubonnet" is more effective than "Le Dubonnet est bel et beau." All of us, in our childhood have forged magical words that would throw us into the depths of devotion, into a sacred vertigo. We cared very little what they meant. Michel Leiris has given us two or three examples that seem to me quite striking.[13] One can love a woman because her name is Rose. One can side with "Freedom" or "Revolution" because these are words that sound good, without thinking very long about the nature of freedom or the chances of revolution.

But there is more. And the very demonstration we just used turns back against us. It was easy to explain the illusion of a Maurras or a Jean Richard Bloch by a common illusion: We imagine other people to be the way we would be in their place if we acted like them. Maurras and J. R. Bloch consider democracy and order to be mere words. Therefore (they think), republicans who agitate for democracy, reactionaries who follow the dictates of order, are stirred by mere words. The illusion is obvious.

But we must beware that this is no less common and natural than obvious. That's not hard: It is so common that it only has to appear to become true. True first of all for Maurras and Jean Richard Bloch, no doubt. But which confirmed reactionary, which confirmed democrat has *always* been a democrat or a reactionary? Who has never for one day questioned himself about the reasons for his faith? Who has not followed, or simply *understood*, one of the objections made to him? And so he too is led to consider "order" or "democracy" words. What is more, led to follow the dictates of a word, if he remains reactionary or a democrat.

And so, in this new realm of sacred language, as in the other, secret language throws us back again onto secret knowledge, and secret knowledge onto secret language. There is no way out of the circle.

On an attempt to set it straight. It seems there is no way out, unless through some vigorous effort to set it straight and get out.

Yes. But we might also wonder if we are not already out.

I said just now—and you certainly noticed—that my experience in Madagascar had been pathetic. Yes, but I was just beginning to discover that it was even more banal than pathetic. Naturally, at the moment I was able to think that I had come across a fine subject that might lead me to some important discovery. But I now registered that I had simply come across the subject that, if I had stayed at home, every newspaper and every conversation would have presented to me. And present to each of us, all the time. Because, in the end, if there is some serious question and we might have to act on it at any moment, it is good to know how it is possible for us to convince someone else, to make him believe what we believe and show him what we think we see. It is also good to know—since reflection is not much more than a conversation we hold with ourselves—how it is possible to convince ourselves, what means to use, what words. In short, I was posing for myself humanity's oldest and naivest question: How does one speak? how does one use language?

Now I have a sense that my failure itself—my failures—was giving me the beginnings of an answer.

It was that they were no less banal than the question. They were no less *ordinary* and were a sort of normal, official continuation of this sacred language, as if they were a constant effect of this language. I had certainly gone a great distance to look for a definition of sacred language, or rather, I had very conscientiously tested the banal (and moreover, contradictory) definitions of this sacred language, provided for me by common sense. This definition I finally had my hands on, thanks to my failure: Sacred language was *that* which necessarily brought about this failure. Considered as language, it was *that* which could evoke with the force of thought; considered as thought, *that* which could evoke with the force of language. In any case, it was such *that one could not think of it without completing it*: language with its equal thought, thought with its equal language.

What to do with thought. That this whole operation was not without its difficulties and obstacles is perfectly apparent. Now we simply have to admit that the difficulty or the obstacle is *also* part of sacred language. The rout of intelligence is also an event for intelligence.[14] And the terror—absolutely the excessive susceptibility regarding proverbs in which I was left by my Malagasy experience—this rout, this mystery, this effectiveness, above all this separation from every other phrase that I had to acknowledge in the proverb, were not, after all so different from the marks of distinction, effectiveness, and ambiguity with which we were trying to characterize the sacred. And as far as I was concerned, it was as if, rather than understanding it, I personally had *reinvented* this sacred.

But we are to find ourselves led, by other means, to an even more precise conclusion.

It suffices to apply the rules we set for ourselves at first. This rule, for example: After each observation of the language one should reconstitute the language as if it had not been an object of observation and thus deformed. Applying this is all the easier since we know from another source that the confusion into which the proverb throws us is also a *part* of that proverb in the sense that, far from preventing our use of it, it seemed that, it made its use easier. I never spoke a proverb better than following my disappointment. From which we can now conclude that every use of proverbs presupposes the same deception, which has become legitimate, normal—accepted.

That disappointment came from the fact that the proverb, through continual transmutation and metamorphosis, seemed to us like a thought where we took it to be a phrase, yet a phrase where we took it to be a thought. With the result that now we can define the use of a proverb. This use (and the clearer and more natural it is) presupposes a background level where language is not considered to be different from thought—or at least the difference between language and thought are no longer *likely to surprise us* and trouble us. Where the metamorphosis seems natural to us.

Clarity reversal. You might say about all this that it was hard to discover, slow and really quite banal. But, of course, the opposite is true. And, if it was particularly hard for us it is because we have been brought up badly. Our professor of geometry never told us that a triangle was also a square. Our sociology professor always asserted that the sacred was different from the profane. But every primitive man knows that a man, in certain cases, turns into a cow or a bat. Every child has learned that a pumpkin was also a carriage, and a lizard a footman. And it is not, undoubtedly, mere chance that tales are full of transformations and metamorphoses: Perhaps it is only a matter of imperceptibly preparing us to acknowledge more serious metamorphoses, ones that cannot even be spoken.

That cannot be spoken . . . because, in the end, I see no definition of thought that does not finally mean it is not language. It will be said that it cannot be seen (like a written sign), that it cannot be heard (like a spoken word), that it is never perfectly obvious (whereas words are obvious every which way). Yet neither do I see a definition of the word that does not state that it is not thought. What remains in place of this fearful formation—neither thought nor word, but utterly suited to be the densest word or the subtlest thought—presupposed by the clarity of a proverb? Nothing. Absolute void. Absolute chaos—which no one will escape for more than an instant. If there is one characteristic of the sacred that henceforth will be incapable of surprising us, it is that it is terrifying.

Terrifying, no doubt, but I return to the fact that it is habitual, and especially habitual in regard to language. Perhaps, to recognize this, it would have sufficed to remark that the words serving in every language as *keys* to the grammars and rhetorics are essentially ambiguous and designate thought as they do language. I do not mean to say that they are necessarily indifferent: They are able to be fantastically precise in meaning depending on whether it is a construction of pure language (without the least thought) or pure thought (without the least concern for language).

This is true of "logos," "oratio," and "discourse." Also of "literature." Also even of "proverb." Everything I have rather awkwardly concluded is contained in a name, but it was a question of managing to understand it and make it clear.

Concerning this understanding and this clarity, I have only one thing left to say: It bears only a slight resemblance to the clarity we were expecting. It is obtained not by extreme attention but by extreme absentmindedness. In short, one had to look *a little beyond* the proverb, abandoning it to its metamorphosis, its contradiction, and its obscurity. It is a matter of clarifying the particular object concerning us by the contrast of this obscurity.

Generally, it is acknowledged that an obscure or unknown fact has been explained when it has been reduced to familiar elements. But it seems that the clarity of a proverb—and doubtless of all sacred language—proceeds by an inverse operation, which might be called *clarity reversal*.

It is no longer a question of reducing the fact to some elements that are more clear but rather to set it off against a darker background. To give it the sort of light that, after surviving some great danger, shines from the simplest of acts: *eating*; the simplest of objects: *a cup*.

I don't like ending these remarks with a slightly absurd example. But the following is good enough for me to risk it all the same.

When a lady thinks her skin is too brown she has two ways to cure it: She can use makeup that makes her lighter. She can *reduce* it with makeup.

But she can also choose to have a black woman as her inseparable friend. The second procedure works just as well as the first. And it is evident that both our highest and our lowest reflection makes use of each of these in turn.

Joy in the Face of Death
Georges Bataille
Tuesday, June 6, 1939

[The month this lecture was held at the College of Sociology, the final issue of Acéphale *(it had been two years since the review last appeared, and this un-signed issue is entirely by Bataille's hand) published some pages entitled "La Pratique de la joie devant la mort" (The practice of joy in the face of death). The wording of the title was undoubtedly not the only common feature between the text as read and the published text. The article from* Acéphale *appears in the first volume of the* Oeuvres complètes. *Instead of the lecture itself (the text of which has not been found), I am publishing some posthumous pages by Bataille, doubt-lessly written in the same period and also entitled "Joy in the Face of Death." They were first published in the second volume of the* Oeuvres complètes *(pp. 242-47). It is not likely that they are what Bataille read on this June 6, 1939.*

The motif of joy in the face of death is not new for Bataille, whose inspiration had long owed a great deal to what certainly has to be called necrophilia. The heterology (or scatology) that he had been occupied with elaborating ever since his first publications placed the cadaver high among the various cast off objects that he made sacred. There are some old fragments (OC, vol. 2, pp. 72-76 and 127-33) of early, bookish information and firsthand autobiographical references assembled around these obsessions. It was from these notes that Le Bleu du ciel, *the novel Bataille finished in May 1935 and then decided not to publish, bor-rowed a scene of onanism induced by the presence of a nearby corpse.*

The tonic nature of this necrophilia must be stressed, however. There was a certain Nietzscheanism made of joy—above all, joy in the face of death—the tragic sentiment par excellence. "To see tragic natures sinking into destruction and to be able to laugh at it, *despite the deep comprehension, emotion, and sympathy one feels, that is divine." That was a slogan from Nietzsche Bataille liked to quote. One of these tragic figures for him was, no doubt, the young Chinese regicide subjected to the torture of the "hundred pieces." Bataille possessed several photos of this, given him by his psychoanalyst, Dr. Borel (in 1925, he says in* Les Larmes d'Éros). *They are unbearable pictures. In March 1942, Bataille used them to introduce the dramatic scenes around which "Torture," a section of* L'Expérience intérieure, *is organized. A significant parallel, this same section cites several meditation exercises for "the practice of joy in the face of death." The words "I teach the art of turning anguish into voluptuous pleasure"* (OC, *vol. 5, p. 47) refer to this torturing joy.*

One must also cite Hegel's phrase, to appear as an epigraph to Madame Edwarda: *"The life of the mind is not life that shies in the face of death." The life of the spirit is, in fact, life that laughs at death: laughs because of it and laughs with it. "Calaveras," a posthumous text in manuscript form, probably contemporary with this lecture, has another, crossed-out title: "Death laughs." Although there is sexual tragedy in Bataille, it is constantly closely doubled by a funereal comedy. In "The Sacred in Everyday Life," Leiris set out to find the "color" of his sacred. By the same token, one might wonder what was the color of Bataille's "laughter in the face of death." Sartre accused it of being yellow, which is doubtless even more right than he thought.*

But what death is it, in whose face this joy and this laughter are triggered? Whose death is it? The one who dies is never an enemy. Yet just the same no one is excluded. It is the death of God. But also Laure's death. It is also the collective and anonymous death whose shadow hung over the community with the threat of war. We should merely remember that Bataille, whose nostrils had long been after the scent of his own corpse, would always contrast the suave mari magno *of shore dwellers to the Dionysian joy of the one carried away by the storm. The death of the other touches him only because he can identify with him.*

In the spring of 1937, Bataille had participated in the establishment of a "Société de psychologie collective" that would meet during the same period as the College, between January and June 1938. For the subject to be studied during the first year the society decided on "attitudes in the face of death" (OC, *vol. 2, p. 444). Leiris, as well, took part in the venture (he spoke there March 28), as did Adrien Borel, who had been their psychoanalyst some ten years earlier. Among the attitudes in the face of death envisaged, none of the announced lectures mentions joy. I shall just bring two of these to your attention. On June 27, Dr. Lagache (a friend of the young philosopher-novelist whose novel had to change its title to be published,* Melancholia *becoming* La Nausée) *would evoke "the work of mourning" (his lecture was published that same year in the* Revue française de psychanalyse). *He viewed the problem of mourning and melancholy in a manner similar to that of Landsberg in his* Essai sur l'expérience de la mort:

"The death of someone else," wrote Lagache, "makes us 'become aware' of the 'interhuman reality' because this death is felt as a personal wound." The psychoanalytic portion of this essay essentially refers to Totem and Taboo, *and its ethnological portion to the "Contribution à une étude sur la représentation collective de la mort" by Robert Hertz. This is also a prominent reference in "La représentation artistique de la mort" by the art historian Georges Duthuit, announced but without a date on the Society's program. This piece would appear in 1939 in an issue of* Les Cahiers d'art *whose index also listed Bataille and Caillois. (Two weeks after Bataille spoke there on joy in the face of death, Duthuit delivered a lecture to the College entitled "The Myth of the English Monarchy"; see the following contribution).*

On January 18, 1938, Bataille himself opened the activities of the Société de psychologie collective. In his inaugural speech he, too, referred to Hertz's study, as well as to Freud, but especially to Hegel. He lingered over a remarkable case, however pathological, of joy in the face of death. It was borrowed from the work of an English psychologist, Valentine, and focused on a young woman who was seized with crazy laughter each time she heard a death announced. "To what extent is man likely to use depressions in a tonic sense?" Bataille wondered. Several days later he went back to the untimely laughter in the lecture given at the College on January 22: "The thing that provokes joy and exuberance," he commented, "is precisely what usually causes despondency." Following the model of the transformation of repulsion into attraction, the sacred of the left into the sacred of the right, reactions in the face of death are also able to exchange one sign for another, making death a stimulant, a stimulus, a source of positive energy and of reverse entropy. This sort of hydroelectric dam for psychic energy, where the fall in tension would have a dynamic effect, can be compared with Caillois's work at that time on psychasthenia and Carnot's principle.

The lecture on January 22 ("Attraction and Repulsion") clearly indicates that "social existence" itself is the transformer helping to accomplish this conversion, this metamorphosis of individual, negative, depressed attitudes into a collective ferment. Whence a comparatist sociology would conclude that each variety of social existence, in the face of death, induces its own specific reaction. This, in fact, was the focus of the "Declaration" circulated by the College after Munich. The signers refrained from intervening in the crisis on the political or diplomatic level. They addressed exclusively those whose anguish had revealed to them "that the only solution is the creation of a vital bond between men." The College, they announced, set out to reestablish "a form of collective existence" that would "allow one to behave onself when death threatens." This good behavior is not without its connections to the "virility" referred to by Bataille with a strange insistence in "The Sorcerer's Apprentice" a few months earlier, in July 1938. Moreover, in these two lectures during January 1938 (both the one at

the Société de psychologie collective and the one at the College), Bataille ac-
companied his story of the English girl's crazy laughter with another example of
a tonic reaction in the face of death: that of the young man who had had to leave
his father's burial because he had an erection. The "Declaration" deplored
"man's devirilization." The post-Munich debacle can be contrasted to the Oe-
dipal tumescence of the unidentified young man who, in the face of death,
showed in his own way an indisputably virile attitude.

Jean Bruno recalls that, starting in 1938, Bataille submitted himself to a real
"mystical training." "The practice of joy in the face of death" doubtless constitutes
the main rule of its etiquette. It is likely that the activist orthopraxy expressed in the
lectures of 1938 no longer corresponded, in its militancy, to Bataille's state of mind
at the time of this lecture. To go back to Caillois's contrast, he was in a more mys-
tical than shamanist state. In 1938, Bataille was trying to transform anguish into a
College, into a community, into a collective experience and not yet into a voluptuous
pleasure as joy in the face of death would do. The following month, Bataille, sus-
pending the activities of the College sine die, *would note that Caillois disapproved*
the role he assigned to mysticism (see "The College of Sociology," July 4, 1939):
This role was never more openly expressed than with joy in the face of death.]

The human spirit is dominated by a demand that makes bliss intolerable. Bliss
suddenly provokes a greater desire, one more demanding than the desire to be
happy: the desire to break up and destroy one's own bliss. In this action, which presupposes happiness and strength to begin with, man achieves in himself ''that which
makes him a man.'' The greatest and worst calm naturally serves as an avenue leading to ''joy in the face of death.'' Romantic images would give a wrong notion of
this action, which *necessarily* leaves one bare and sends one naked into the
desert. There, there is a great simplicity that causes objections to collapse on
their own when they claim that, since one does not die, it is fraudulent to speak
of ''joy in the face of death.'' It is not a question of dying at all but of being
transported ''to the level of death.'' Vertigo and laughter with no bitterness, a
sort of power that grows but is painfully swallowed up in itself to arrive at a sup-
pliant fierceness, that is something accomplished in great silence.

I

On the one hand, to consider death boldly leads to the ironic and angry sense of
a basic absurdity in human affairs: The solidarity of a man with his fellows often
seems laughable to someone who puts himself ''on the level of death.'' But on
the other hand, it is certain that solidarity and devotion to some cause are usually
necessary for those who use death to find their honest measure. Since joy in the
face of death is not the ordinary nostalgia resulting from fatigue, it is also unable
to serve as a pretext for men who would not want to risk their lives. It would be

easy to say "I belong to death. Why should I go get myself killed?" Anyone would be disquieted and would put some distance between himself and those who put on such an act. Joy in the face of death presupposes in the first place the sentiment of an inherent *greatness* as part of human life: It would be nonsense if not driven by an insurmountable desire for greatness. That is why those who feel it have no reason to search haphazardly for the cause (which *has* to be there) that will allow them effectively to use death as their measure. The *greatness* of individualities is required and guaranteed by the cause to which they are dedicated. What they must discredit and destroy—since it is true that the air they breathe, sunshine, and young women's smiles have to be part of their pride—is whatever requires and guarantees insignificance and pettiness. They are, truth to tell, condemned to rule other men and to maintain this uncompromising pride, if they are not willing to vanish. But it is not only their joy in knowing that they are perishable, that binds them to the physical destruction they confront, that puts them on the level of domination (from the beginning it is clear that a nonconfrontational humanity has no force to resist or conquer them); there is another element that contributes to providing them with a destiny that corresponds to the deepest requirements of social cohesion.

II

I said that the nuclei society gravitates around were "formed of small numbers of men bound to each other by deep emotional bonds." I tried later to define these "nuclei of social gravitation" as geometric loci where attitudes toward death were determined. Things as I have presented them, therefore, can have no coherence unless the "deep emotional bonds," around which discordant human reality is composed, are bound firmly into a necessary relationship with death. This is the paradox I have proposed: "Human hearts never beat as hard for anything else as they do for death." It seems that a sort of strange, intense communication is established between men each time the violence of death is near them. It is possible that they are bound by the simple sentiment of common danger. Even when only one of them is struck down by death, that does not, at that moment, threaten those present; the fragility brought to mind leads them to seek comfort by communicating among the survivors. But this coming together in the face of death has yet another sense that cannot be reduced to simple fear. For when fear is not present, the "realm of death," for all that, does not become a matter of indifference. It has an attraction that can affect a threatened man just as much as someone who is merely present. The grave, decisive change that results from death is such a blow to spirits that, far from their usual world, they are cast, transported and breathless, somewhere between heaven and earth, as if they suddenly perceived the dizzying, ceaseless motion possessing them. This motion then appears to be partly dreadful and hostile, but *external* to the one threatened by death or the one dying; it is all that is left, depriving the one who watches the dying as much as the one who dies. Thus it is that, when death is present, what remains of life only lives on outside, beyond and *beside itself.*

There is a suspended instant in which everything is carried away, in which everything vacillates: The deep, solid reality a person attributes to himself has disappeared, and all that remains there are presences that are much more loaded, completely mobile, violent, and inexorable. It is hard for the spirit, thus disconcerted, to see what is raging in the hell where his intoxication drags him and drowns him. His extreme emotion is translated by the dark diversity of phantoms, and nightmares he has with which to people it. All that survives are forces that themselves possess a violence comparable to that of the storm that has been unleashed. Then childish significance, attached normally to little things—idle pleasures ordering every day's stupidity—are carried away in the roar of a great wind. Existence, at bay, is incited to wholehearted greatness. The one isolated, driven from the "pettiness" of his person vanishes obscurely into the human community, but his disappearance would have no meaning if this community were not worthy of what took place. Whatever human destiny means by "unquenched" and "unquenchable," that incredible thirst for glory that robs one of sleep and gives no peace is the only possible thing energetic enough to respond to the need arising every time existence wavers when measuring itself against death.

III

If this shift outside, to beside oneself that is necessarily produced when death comes into play, is taken into account, it is easier to see why the army and religion alone are capable of satisfying the most consistent human aspirations. The former's profession is actually to confront death; the second has the sole knowledge of the language stamped by anguish and stormy majesty that is suitable for those on the threshold of the tomb. An attitude that is neither military nor religious becomes impossible to sustain in principle, from the moment death is present. It is impossible to be simultaneously in a position close to death and to communicate with those whose attitude is crudely profane. The shift outside, to beside oneself in the face of death, demands a sacred world such that, at the moment of one's being swallowed up, a vaster reality and forces able to confront terror appear. There is nothing like this in a café, a department store, or a bank: The silences, solemnities, and necessary violences belong, in essence, only to armies and churches.

IV

First I demonstrated that communities based on deep emotional bonds were essential to human existence; then that these deep emotional bonds belonged to those who deliberately approached death, determining the common attitudes in the face of our common fate. And consequently, linked to the ancient reality of the sacrifice, I have introduced a representation of joy in the face of death by means of which the intimate harmony of life with its violent destruction is affirmed. But not only does the formation of these deep emotional bonds require that an answer be given to the fundamental question of death, not only is it important that this answer not elude the problem; it seems that the very fact of coming into contact with the destruction of life entails an emotional community where those spirits gather who are also placed ''at death's level.'' Now I shall return to my premises, demonstrating that joy in the face of death would be an imposture if it were not bound to the commotion of a union. Those who look at death and rejoice are already no longer the individuals destined for the body's rotten decay, because simply entering into the arena with death already projected them outside themselves, into the heart of the glorious community of their fellows where every misery is scoffed at. Every instant dispelling, and annihilating the preceding one, the triumph of time seems to them bound up in their own people's conquering action. Not that they imagine they can thus escape their lot by substituting a community that is more durable than their persons. Quite the contrary, the community is necessary to them in order to become aware of the glory bound up in the instant that will see them torn from being. The feeling of cohesion with those who have chosen each other to share their great intoxication is, if need be, only the means of perceiving all of the glory and conquest signified by the loss, all of the renewed life, the rebounding, the ''alleluia'' signified by the dead person's fall. There is a connection there that does not easily allow of reduction to analytic formulas. One must have experienced, at least once, this excess of joy to know to what extent the fertile prodigality of the sacrifice is expressed in it, to what extent it can only be a movement of conquest, an overwhelming need to subject humanity to . . .

The Myth of the English Monarchy
Georges Duthuit

Tuesday, June 20, 1939

[Duthuit is an art historian (but not an academic). Among his published works, the earliest, Le Rose et le noir (de Walter Pater à Oscar Wilde), *1920 (The Pink and the black [from Walter Pater to Oscar Wilde]), gives evidence of an Anglophilia that will, perhaps, be echoed in the subject of this lecture presented before the College. More recently,* Mystique chinoise et peinture moderne *(1936)—simultaneously published in French and English—brings to mind somewhat the turn more and more clearly taken by Bataille's preoccupations. He is also the author of* Renoir *(1923),* Byzance et l'art du XIIe siècle *(1926), and* La sculpture copte *(1931). At the time of his connection with the College he was a regular contributor to* Cahiers d'art. *Very attentive to the tragic occurrences in Spain, in this luxurious review he expressed a position that refused to dissociate the battles of the artistic avant-garde and revolutionary struggles. In the fall of 1938 (just after Munich) he published in it, on pink paper, the manifesto "Pour l'art sans police": "After the panic caused by the Popular Front in its flirtatiousness, despite plenty of horrors, with progressive movements, after the immeasurable groveling of the September accord, we can expect as just recompense a harmonious alliance of pen, sword, and paintbrush." What he contrasted to this return to order is not foreign to the inspiration of the College: "It is, in fact, in the most oppressive darkness that Europe, or rather the human being, seeks himself. If the most talented brought this common confusion only magnificent solutions of anguish and distance, how can it be held against them?"*

Duthuit had been associated with the project of the "Société de psychologie collective'' in which Bataille had played an important role. The program circulated by this institution in the spring of 1938 announced that he was to read a paper, with Camille Schuwer, entitled ''La Représentation artistique de la mort.'' This text would appear (signed only by Duthuit) in 1939, in an issue of Cahiers d'art. *Bataille's ''Le Sacré'' (the pages written in November 1938, while Laure was dying) and an article by Caillois, ''Le Complexe de Polycrate, tyran de Samos,'' are also listed in this issue's index. Duthuit presented his study as an ''iconography of death.'' In it he shows that he is sensitive (pink and black leave him no choice) to the erotic resources of the macabre, but he denounces the progressive dedramatization of the representation of death: ''The corpse, which for ordinary men, is an object of fear, veneration, or anxious concern, which sometimes provokes attacks of delirium or orgiastic violence, has become in the studio a simple stage prop for a professional exercise.'' ''Why would death need a special representation in profoundly religious societies? It presents itself by itself without taking the detour of aesthetic fiction.'' The article ends with a denunciation of museums, those tombs of death, death buried under its own representation. (This is the same means of ''evading death'' that Caillois would describe somewhat later in ''La Représentation de la mort dans le cinéma américain,'' reprinted in* Instincts et société: *''What masks does the sacred adopt in a civilization whose originality consists precisely in eliminating it as much as possible?'' he asked, apropos the United States.)*

Duthuit would be in New York throughout the war. With Patrick Waldberg and Robert Lebel, he was to contribute to the issue of VVV *(''Vers un nouveau mythe? Prémonitions et défiances,'' [no. 4, February 1944]) that recalled and denounced what was brewing around Bataille between 1937 and 1939. This self-criticism by someone who had been close to the College was warmly greeted by Breton, who, moreover, was the one who provoked it. But suspicion was not yet in the air at the moment of Duthuit's address to the College.* Volontés *had just published the answers provoked by Monnerot's inquiry on spiritual directors: Duthuit's answer, as we have seen, was right in tune (for all of this, see Duthuit's response and the accompanying note).*

The English monarchy, which was the subject of his presentation, for the past three years had been sporadically at the top of the news. Thanks to the recent change of reigns, a certain nostalgia was mingled with the reflections inspired by a regime, surprisingly no longer considered merely anachronistic. George V died at the beginning of 1936. Nizan himself went to London to be present at the burial. It is not in the communist press but in the NRF *(March 1936) that his ''Funérailles anglaises,'' would appear—reporting that was aloof and sarcastic, emphasizing the outdated and ridiculous aspects of a pomp and ceremony taking place against a background of general indifference. It concludes with the inevitable touch of pink-and-black eroticism: ''On Shaftesbury Avenue, the stores where the Soho prostitutes buy their lingerie offered only black slips, pants, and stockings: Royal mourning was restoring to London the secrets of a lost eroticism.'' But this aloofness did not prevent Nizan's returning to London the next year to be present at the second act of this funeral, the coronation of the successor, George VI. His commentary would appear this time in* Ce soir *the communist paper, on May 9, 10, and 12, 1937.*

This spectacular ceremonial succession was to inspire commentators with wide-ranging reflections that are peculiarly like those that the theme of the death of the king (apart from regicide) would inspire among the driving forces of the College. Louis Gillet, for instance, a specialist in English literature, in the Revue des deux mondes *(''Au couronnement de George VI,'' June 1937) described the interregnum: ''This eclipse was regarded with the same anxiety as primitive beings felt seeing the omens darkening the sky and the threatening death agony of the sun.'' His article ended with praise for the British regime whose moderation and traditionalism were contrasted with the difficulties experienced by, or threatening, all the nations of the Continent. ''When one thinks of the sudden explosions, the unforeseen outbursts, the appearances of extraordinary characters that are the most striking phenomenon of our century, one comes to think that the English way of doing things, which for a long time was ours as well, is personally the most human, most prudent, most wise.'' There is the same envious tone in another conservative publication,* Revue de Paris *where Jean de Pange wrote (''Le Sacre du roi d'Angleterre,'' June 1937): ''Against the idea of a totalitarian State, which prevails throughout almost all of continental Europe, and which tends to nullify the moral value of the individual, they (= Anglo-Saxons) set the idea of trust, the act of faith that groups men of good will, freely united around the idea of autonomous work that is independent of the centralizing, leveling State.''*

It is true that these ceremonies were already two years past when Duthuit delivered his lecture at the College. However, the preceding year (in July 1938), the visit of the new British sovereigns had rekindled the flame of Anglophilia. It occasioned Wladimir Weidlé's reflections on the king of England, published in the NRF: *''The king reigns but does not govern. It might even be said that the less he governs the more he reigns, and that, having renounced the direct exercise of his power, he has gained immense latent power and prestige. He reigns over the imagination and heart of a great people, etc.'' In the same review Jean Guérin's ''Bulletin'' notes (to be added to our file on the myth of the power of words): ''Paris: On the occasion of the reception of the king of England, the word ''grandiose'' reappears in the French vocabulary (Paul Reynaud,* Paris-Soir, *etc.).''*

The Munich crisis followed, with no transition, the euphoria of these summer splendors. Remember that the second cycle of discussions at the College had begun, the preceding December 13, in a delayed reaction to the September crisis, with Bataille's reflections on the structure of democracies. It was within the same context that Paulhan, in March 1939, had defined democracy as the regime of the first comer, anyone at all, which "anyone at all," according to a somewhat formal logic, could only be a king, since both have a sovereignty that is unmotivated. A power that did not deny its arbitrariness would, for that very reason, reduce this arbitrariness to a minimum. In contrast to the dictatorial totalitarianism implied by the desire for a completely motivated power, monarchy—and particularly the British monarchy—thus can be defined in Leibnizian terms as the best of all possible democracies.

We cannot know what Bataille said that seemed to Paulhan to confirm his own views. But it is doubtful that Bataille ever had any profound affinity for the paradoxical elitism and affected Maurrassianism of the director of the NRF. *It is even more unlikely that in this lecture Duthuit (no matter how Anglophile he might have been) openly championed the British crown. The ambivalence of this period in regard to the idea of myth has been seen. Did Duthuit place himself among those who denounced its return to the modern world? His participation in the activities of the College would exclude the platitude of a rationalist mythophobe on his part. But, nonetheless, one can imagine that, speaking of the "Myth of the English Monarchy," he was more aligned with Paulhan's qualifications in speaking of the myth of the power of words, or with Étiemble's in analyzing the myth of Rimbaud than with Caillois's conviction in his conjuring up of "Paris, a Modern Myth." But to be sure, we would have to have read this lecture, and the text has not been found.]*

The College of Sociology
Georges Bataille
Tuesday, July 4, 1939

[What was to have been an assessment was a crisis. And Mars did not want it resolved: These collegians full of goodwill were prevented by war from being put to the test by a reality worthy of them. Three years earlier, in Acéphale, *Bataille wrote: "Civilization's apogee is a crisis." It must be said of this lecture that it constitutes, in the same manner, the apogee of the critical trajectory the College had opened for itself, the zenith at which it disintegrates. And more than a lecture, this moment must be called a communication in the precise sense of the word, which is here defined and illustrated simultaneously. If it is true that one never communicates except through wounds, that one is never united except by what separates, it would seem that the College had never, for one instant, been more communicative than on this day, when, turning its attention upon itself, it dissolved itself, carried away by the action of communal unity and discord that, as an apprentice sorcerer, it had vowed passionately to trigger. It was not an essential aim of the College to endure. It knew itself to be destined to death and even exalted its will to loss, obsessed as it was by its strange concern with making sociology be "harrowing." So it was in the order of things that this contrapuntal polyphony end with this orgasm, this little death, a perfect disharmony that history rapidly buried and confirmed, lost and multiplied.]*

This meeting was to be devoted to the College of Sociology itself. Since the College of Sociology, up to a certain point, is a singular venture, one difficult to reduce to usual forms of activity, there was good cause to specify its meaning and intentions, all the more because this singular nature has provoked misunder-

333

standings and confusion in the minds of those who watch us stir about. To tell the truth, circumstances are such, and relations are so strained between those who until now strove to carry things to a successful end, that I have more grounds for speaking of an organization in crisis than of its ordinary development. The presentation I am beginning now, will, therefore, be only the expression of a profound disagreement that has already opened a crack in the structure. It had been understood that there would be three of us speaking this evening, Caillois, Leiris, and myself, but I am alone. It is not without sadness that I acknowledge this. Caillois left for Argentina several days ago: his absence, obviously, is inevitable, but that does not make it less meaningful.[1] The few texts I have received from him since his departure are, in any case, of a sort that put an end to the harmony existing between us. I am not going to give an account of these today because it seems not impossible that an oral explanation—Caillois will return in September—will resolve the difference of opinion that they establish between us. I prefer, for the moment, to speak against the background of a disagreement rather than on terms accusing him, perhaps, through misinterpretation. Besides, it is possible that by raising the debate, shifting it to the point at which love and death are the only things at stake, all I am doing is ruling out any chance for a later appeasement. Though it seems that that is how things are, I maintain my conviction that at this moment I am acting in the opposite manner, but if I were aware that, doing so, I was destroying remaining possibilities, I would still do the same thing because there are other things more important than a College of Sociology. If I have come this evening, if I have come for the past two years, it is, in fact, less through concern with creating an influential organization than with the will to create a force on the basis of a consciousness of the wretchedness and greatness of this perishable existence that is our lot: CONFRONTATION WITH DESTINY is still, in my view, the essence of knowledge. It is because I perceived that the results advanced by the science of the sacred deprived human beings of the means they possess to evade what they are that it seemed to me appropriate to found an association with this science specifically as its object. There is no one more eager than I to find the virtues of association, more frightened than I of the deception upon which individual isolation is based; however, the *love of human destiny* is strong enough in me to relegate to a position of secondary importance any concern with what forms this can take to enter.

*It seems to me that the interest that, both internally and externally, gave rise to the College of Sociology, was due to its power to call everything into question. Each member had his own, perhaps different, intentions, and I did not intend, in speaking of the reasons I had, that anyone believe they were not specifically my own. Nevertheless, it is self-evident that only our remote intentions and our ability to define crucial problems all over again justified our existence. In truth, to the extent that the College of Sociology is not an open door to chaos in which each form stirs, arises, and perishes, an opening on the convulsion of festivals, forces, and human deaths, it represents only emptiness. That is why it hurts me to see Leiris, who abstains from speaking here today because he has had doubts about our activity's being well grounded—I am hurt to see Leiris reproach us for not better resembling those scholars who have inspired us. Leiris thinks we are not following the rules of Durkheim's sociological method and that the role we give to the sacred does not conform to Mauss's doctrine of the total phenomenon. To these thoughts he adds the fear of seeing our efforts end up by only creating the worst of literary cliques.[2] I have said that I would elevate the debate that results from the crisis I spoke of. I shall elevate it as high as I can. I think that Caillois's works, or mine, when published will arouse criticism but will compel respect. That is not at all the question. It is a matter, above all, of knowing if it is still possible to brandish fundamental questions, if we are in agreement to carry the possible questioning as regards life to the bitter end, to demand of ourselves *all* that our remaining powers are still capable of. Points of method and doctrine, inevitable obstacles, inevitable possibilities of failure, all of that is certainly important, but it is possible to have one's eyes also focused on what is beyond these inevitable difficulties.

That there is something beyond, I mean an earthly beyond, that belongs to contemporary beings is a truth that is hard to debate. It is no less debatable that the access to this beyond must present itself initially in the form of combat and danger. And no one doubts that *inner* dangers, the dangers within every movement are to be feared and are even more demoralizing.

The disagreement pointed out by Leiris is, moreover, far from excluding the possibility of later collaboration, once the aims and limits are well defined, especially once the forms of freedom necessary for the development of a venture that is still unsure of itself are made clear. The questions posed by the difference of opinion arising between Caillois and myself, no doubt, are more serious in the sense that they have to do more with the foundations than with the forms of an activity. But since, I am sure, they touch upon the very basis, I shall be allowed to speak about it through a detour, and distancing myself from the specific debate, I shall limit myself to speaking about the profound reality this debate calls into question. The very absence of Caillois, moreover, seems to me to make any other procedure impossible. It will suffice to point out in the beginning that the role I assign to mysticism, tragedy, madness, and death seems to Caillois hard to reconcile with our original principles.[3] I will add that Caillois is not the only one troubled by this feeling of incompatibility. Paulhan and Wahl also have communicated to me the same impression. Consequently, I have every reason to introduce an attempt at clarification today, as one of the expressions of a state of crisis. I shall try, therefore, to give a glimpse of how the development of the College of Sociology contained within itself the inevitability of the present crisis—only too happy to have had occasion to descend into the depths of my thought, not in the calm of solitary reflection, but in the disorder of contention.

Thus I am led to developing a general representation of things that will rank in the order of philosophical representations. And it is only when this representation has been completed that it will be possible for me to show how communifying unity is formed, namely, the power, and the sort of cerebral disturbance that goes back and forth between mysticism and madness. I should not, nevertheless, want anyone to worry about seeing me disappear into the discouraging maze of philosophical representation. Although I have to take on the central problem of metaphysics, I think I shall be able to remain clear: I am sure, in any case, that I speak of things directly touching upon every human being, provided he is averse to torpor.

One of the best established results, no doubt, of the efforts man has made to discover what he really is, is the absence of unity of person. Earlier beings represented themselves as an indivisible reality. There are some animals that can be cut in two, and after a certain amount of time the two sections form two complete animals that are distinct from each other. But, in the view of anyone sticking with the classical image of the human soul, there would be nothing more shocking than such an experience applied to man. Habits of thought are so well established that it remains difficult for any one of us to picture himself as split, one seeing the other, the one that loves or the one that flees. It is true that surgery working on humans or on slightly different animals is still far from any such brutal potential. It has only reached the stage of mixing things but leaving the essence of the creature intact. At the most we can glimpse in the distant future some really disturbing possibilities, such as the exchange of cerebral hemispheres in two of the great apes. I mention this less because I am interested in a possible experiment than because I wish to bring maximum disorder into habitual perspectives. I imagine that the idea of a composite being, the result of joining the brains of any two among us, is something that is disquieting to the point of vertigo. And yet this idea can become familiar. No longer is it anything more than banality to imagine a human being as whole that is not well closed, made up of distant parts that are badly attached, even unknown. It has been generally acknowledged that the individual is only an incomplete aggregate: An animal and a human being are simply regarded as restricted and stable compositions whereas a society is united only by very loose and easily revocable bonds. At the same time it is acknowledged that the individual or society is not an exception, that every element of nature is an aggregate of parts, at least until one comes to the simplest stage, the electron. Science lists atoms, despite their name, as collections of elementary particles, molecules as collections of atoms, and continuing step by step it arrives at the individual as a collection of cells and finally at society (where, it is true, it hesitates to acknowledge—but it is hard to see why—a simple case of a unity with multiple elements as its basis).

I don't want to insist on something that is only a scientific introduction to the essence of what I shall describe today. I am in a hurry, and this haste is perhaps understandable, to get to descriptions less external to the reality that we are. I am ready to speak directly of something each of us can experience, and I shall speak first of all about an aspect of our existence that is apparently the greatest possible departure from our union with the social group. I shall speak of the erotic activity that most of us maintain with one, or successively, with several of our kind. This detour has the advantage of bringing together realities that are not only the most obscure but also the most familiar. There is, in fact, nothing more vivid to our minds than the image of the union between two creatures of the opposite sex. But ordinary and convincing as it is, its sense is nonetheless concealed: All it is possible to say is that each being blindly obeys his or her instinct. Giving a name to this instinct, having it be the expression of a will to reproduce that belongs to nature, is not the way out of this darkness. In fact, there are other needs besides that of procreation that are satisfied in sexual union.

The introduction of a sociological point of view throws unexpected light on this natural obscurity.

If I take the reproduction of a simple, asexual cell, the birth of a new cell seems to result from an incapacity of the whole to maintain its integrity: a scission, a cut is produced. The effect of the growth of the minuscule creature is overflow, tearing, and a loss of substance. Two creatures communicate with each other in the first phase, through their hidden tears. No communication is more profound; Two creatures are lost in a convulsion that binds them together. But they communicate only by losing a portion of themselves. The communication binds them only through wounds where their unity, their integrity disperse in the heat of excitement.

Two beings of the opposite sex are lost in one another and together form a new being different from either. The precariousnes of this new being is obvious: It is never something whose parts are not distinct from it; there is no more than a tendency to lose consciousness in brief moments of darkness. But, while it is true that the individual's unity stands out far more distinctly, it is nonetheless precarious as well. Between the two instances there is, without a doubt, only a difference of degree.

Love expresses a need for sacrifice: Each unity must lose itself in some other that exceeds it. But the felicitous movements of flesh move in two directions. Giving in to the flesh, giving in to that point at which unity of the individual is torn within, is necessary if one wants to be lost finding oneself in the unity of love, but it does not follow that the moment of the tearing itself is meaningless for the existence that is torn. It is hard to know the part played by passion for another being in sexual union, the part played by erotic frenzy; the extent to which the being is in search of life and power, the extent to which he or she is driven to tear, to be lost at the same time as tearing and losing some other (and of course, the more beautiful the woman the more her tearing, her loss, or merely her being laid bare is desirable). Beyond the will to leave one's restricted being for a vaster one, there exists, very often mixed in with this first will to loss, a will to loss that finds that the only limit to its excessive actions is fear, and more, which uses this fear it provokes to make itself even more ardent, even more frenzied.

To this picture of the principal forms of being revealed by love must be added the union resulting from marriage. There exist many possibilities between the passionate impulse and that sort of oppressive conjugal existence where the heart is not at stake. In the extreme, self-interest and law are the bases for the joyless union of beings for whom physical love is only a concession to nature. If we now turn to the social groupings that correspond to the different, and contrasting, forms of sexual unions, the juridical and administrative society demonstrates a close connection with conjugal union based on interest; communities formed by deep emotional bonds recall the passionate union of lovers; and there is no lack of forms that have in common with erotic perversities that the loss of self in a vaster being occasions the loss of self in a chaotic universe and in death.

There is a paradoxical element here, I know: These connections will seem necessarily very arbitrary. However, I introduce them only with the intention of specifying their meaning. I propose to assume as a law that human beings are never united with each other except through tears or wounds, an idea that has a certain logical force in its favor. When elements arrange themselves to create the whole, this is easily produced when each of them loses, through a tear in its integrity, a portion of its particular being for the benefit of the communal being. Initiations, sacrifices, and festivals represent just such moments of loss and communication between individuals. Circumcisions and orgies are sufficient demonstration that there is more than one connection between sexual and ritual tearing. Add to this that the erotic realm itself has pointedly designated the act in which it is accomplished as a sacrifice, designating, as well, the denouement of this act as a "little death." However, one of the two domains extends beyond the other: The social tears coinciding with the sexes are the very ones that have a transformed and richer meaning, and the multiplicity of such forms stretches from war to the bloody cross of Christ. The execution of a king and the sexual act no longer have anything in common except that they unite through loss of substance. And it is in the creation or maintenance of a new unit of being that they are similar: It would be futile to claim that both are equally the effect of an obscure reproductive instinct whose action would account for all human forms.

I am now ready to say of the "sacred" that it is communication between beings[4] and, hence, formation of new beings. The notion developed by sociologists according to which, describing how it works, it is possible to compare it to electrical current and charges at least allows me to introduce an image that explains my proposition. The wounds or tears I speak of would intervene as if they opened just so many bursts of accumulated forces. But this burst of force outside oneself, produced for the profit of the social power, whether in religious sacrifice or in war, is, of course, not at all produced like those expenditures of money that must be made to acquire a desirable or necessary object. Although sacrifices and festivals are generally useful, they possess in themselves an attractive quality independent of the conscious or unconscious results they favor. Men gathering for sacrifice and for festivals satisfy the need they have to spend a vital overflow. The sacrificial tear opening the festival is a liberating tear. The individual who participates in the loss is vaguely aware that this loss engenders the community sustaining him. But a desirable woman is necessary for someone who wants to make love, and it is not always easy to know whether he makes love because he is attracted by this woman, or if he uses that woman out of a need to make love. By the same token, it is hard to know to what extent the community is only the propitious occasion for the festival and sacrifice or if the festival and sacrifice are proof of love given to the community.

In fact, it seems that this question, which might be thought merely picturesque, presents itself as our ultimate question, or, to take it further, the ultimate question of being. Being is, in fact, continually drawn in two directions; one leads to the creation of lasting organizations and conquering forces, the other leads, through the intermediary of expenditure of force and increasing excess, to destruction and death. We encounter this experience even in the most ordinary circumstances of life. In the background of any discussion about the appropriateness of a useful or tempting expense the principles of acquisition and loss are being weighed. But in everyday practice the extremes have disappeared to such an extent that this is all nearly unrecognizable. The interplay takes on meaning again when it is a question of sexual commerce. The union of lovers is confronted by this unending question: Supposing the unified being they form counts more for them than love, they are condemned to the slow stabilization of their relationship. The vacant horror of steady conjugality has already enclosed them. But if the need to love and be lost is stronger in them than the concern with being found, the only outlet is in tearing, in the perversities of turbulent passion, in drama, and if it is of a complete nature—in death. I would add that eroticism constitutes a sort of flight before the harshness of this dilemma. But I only mention it now in order to go on to a more general idea.

When a man and a woman are united by love, they form an association, a being that is completely closed back on itself, but when the initial equilibrium is compromised, it is possible that a nakedly erotic search can be added or substituted for the lovers' search whose original object was only themselves. Their need to lose exceeds their need to find each other. At this point the presence of a third person is not necessarily, as it was at the beginning of their love, the worst impediment. Beyond the common being met in their embrace, they seek infinite annihilation in a violent expenditure where the possession of a new object, a new woman or new man, is only the pretext for an even more annihilating expenditure. In the same fashion, those who are more religious than others cease being narrowly concerned with the community for which sacrifices are performed. They no longer live for the community, they live only for the sacrifice. It is in this manner that, little by little, they are possessed by the desire to spread their sacrificial frenzy through contagion. In the same way that eroticism slips easily into orgy, sacrifice that becomes an end in itself lays claim, beyond the narrowness of the community, to a universal value.

In the case of social existence, however, the initial impulses can spread only to the extent that the desire for sacrifice finds a god that will withstand it. Just as in its enclosed forms, that is to say, its simplest forms, the community provided some with the occasion for sacrifice, the equivalent of a community must be found in the form of a universal god, in order to spread the sacrificial orgy infinitely. Dionysus and the crucified god thus open a tragic procession of bacchants and martyrs. But the tear rent by the universal god's bursting outside the old, local community closes over in the long run. The Christian god, in his turn, is reduced to the state of a guarantor of social order. Yet he also becomes the wall against which the passion of love for love collides. And this, no doubt, is the point at which being's ultimate question takes shape. God's eternal vastness serves in the beginning as the object of loss for each being, who, in self-loss is found again in God. But what is lacking then is satisfaction for those who desire only to be lost without being found. When Teresa of Avila cried out that she was dying because she could not die, her passion opened an unstoppable breach into a universe where, perhaps, there is no longer any structure of form or being, where it seems that death rolls on from world to world. For the organized structure of beings is apparently senseless when it is a question of the totality of things: Totality cannot be analogous to the composite beings we know, beings driven by the same impulse.

So at this point I suppose my intention seems strange. However, I only wanted to describe the full extent of the problem whose dangers are apparent the moment man accepts to be questioned by the sociological sphinx. It seems to me that encountering this sphinx has remarkably increased the precision and brutality of metaphysical interrogation. What I want to say in essence is that a College of Sociology, in the form in which we conceived it, inevitably opened up this inexhaustible interrogation. It is possible that I sometimes give the impression of dwelling on a morose bias in considering something impossible. I could answer with a single sentence. I won't do that today. Today I shall content myself with introducing several practical proposals that are worthy of those means possessed by the College of Sociology.

Text of Caillois's letter[5]

Is it possible to find any reason for fighting and dying other than country or class, any reason for fighting that would not be based on material interests? Is it possible for the concern with human greatness that is shouldered by a few to constitute alone a sufficient reason for existence? But what, exactly, does one mean in speaking of greatness?

Since classes have been mentioned, could there be classes without a Church, without a sacred, without sacrifice?

Could there be a society without a spiritual power, radically separate from temporal power?

Appendixes

Records
(Bataille)

[These notes undoubtedly date from 1937. They are evidence that Bataille, at least, was concerned with having an independent review. It would have been jointly financed by the Société de psychologie collective designated here by the initials SPC (it was founded in April 1937) and by the College of Sociology, designated CS. To give some idea of the figures, I should mention that membership in the College amounted to 8 francs a month, 30 francs a year; a subscription to Acéphale *cost 10 francs and to the* NRF *85 francs.* L'Âge d'homme, *in 1939, was priced at 20 francs.]*

1. The question of bylaws. Election or not.
   Board constituted in principle by all those who give papers and elected by the members.
   Envisaging active and participating members. Fee for participants. Dues 10 francs.
2. Publication of a program of lectures.
   Each lecture having a title whenever possible.
   The question of place.
3. Trimestral public meetings.
4. Publication of a bulletin.
   100 monthly payments of dues at 10 francs = given a normal 50 percent loss would end up with 6,000 francs.

Advantageous to combine the available funds as much as possible with the

345

Société de psychologie collective, with the intent of publishing an existing review.

Given the possibility of assessable subscriptions, on the level of 200 x 25 or 5,000 francs a month, the 12,000 minimum francs that are necessary suppose

$$CS = 4,000$$
$$SPC = 3,000$$

5. Contents of the review.
   Articles.
   Impossibility of a bibliography.
   But a column of summary reviews.

Letter from Marcel Mauss to Élie Halévy

[On November 28, 1936, Élie Halévy gave a lecture at the Société française de philosophie whose subject was something he baptized "the age of tyrannies." Among the theses presented by the eminent liberal, Anglophile, Anglologist historian, the great admirer of Benthamite philosophical radicalism, we discover: "Socialism, in its primitive form, is neither liberal nor democratic; it is systematic and hierarchical." Also: "The age of tyrannies dates from August 1914, in other words, from the moment in which the warring nations adopted a regime that can be defined in the following manner: (a) From the economic point of view, an extremely widespread state takeover of all the means of production, distribution, and exchange;—and on the other hand, a governmental appeal to the heads of workers' organizations to help them in this state takeover—hence, syndicalism, and corporatism at the same time as state control; (b) from the intellectual point of view, a state takeover of thought, this state control, on its own, assuming two forms: one negative, through suppression of all expressions of an opinion that is judged unfavorable to the national interest, the other positive, by what we call the organization of enthusiasm." And finally: "It is from this war regime, much more than from Marxist doctrine, that all postwar socialism derives."

These theses were in no position to organize the enthusiasm of the intellectuals who came to hear them. When the acts of this meeting were being copied out for publication in the Bulletin de la Société française de philosophie, *Halévy was to prolong the debate by citing in an appendix some of the letters of reply his*

347

statements had earned him. The first letter is from Mauss. This one he will not have to answer because it is approving.

Halévy was dead when this Bulletin *appeared (no. 5, 1936). The material would be republished in 1938 in a posthumous volume taking its title,* L'Ère des tyrannies, *from it. It was subtitled* Études sur le socialisme et la guerre. *Mauss's letter appears in it on p. 230.]*

I agree completely with you on every point in your presentation. I should only like to add a very few things from my own experience.

Your conclusion that the two Italian and German tyrannies are based on bolshevism is entirely correct, but perhaps it was through lack of space that you left out two other traits I feel should be mentioned.

The fundamental doctrine from which all this is deduced is that of "minority agitation," as it was in the syndico-anarchist circles in Paris, and especially as it had been developed by Sorel at the time that I left the "socialist movement" rather than participate in his campaign. I saw with my own eyes the doctrine of minority, the doctrine of violence, and even corporatism propagated from Sorel to Lenin and to Mussolini. All three acknowledged this. I should add that Sorel's corporatism was intermediate between Pouget's and Durkheim's, and finally, for Sorel corresponded to a reactionary vision of our societies' past.

Austrian Christian-socialist corporatism, which became Hitler's, was originally of a different order; but in the end, emulating Mussolini, it became the same.

But this is my second point.

I place more importance than you on the fundamental fact of secrecy and conspiracy. I lived, for a long time, among active Russian Socialist Revolutionary party circles; I have followed the Social Democrats less well, but I knew the Bolsheviks of Parc Montsouris, and finally, I lived with them for a while in Russia. An activist minority was a reality over there; it was eternal conspiracy. This conspiracy lasted throughout the whole war, the whole Kerensky government, and won. But the formation of the communist party remained that of a secret sect, and its essential organism, the GPU, remained a secret organization's organization for combat. The communist party itself remained encamped in the middle of Russia, just as the Fascist party and the Nazi party are encamped, with no artillery or fleet, but with a complete police apparatus.

I can recognize easily here a phenomenon such as frequently occurred in Greece, which Aristotle described extremely well, but which is especially characteristic of archaic societies, and perhaps everywhere in the world. It is the "society of men," with its brotherhoods that are simultaneously public and secret; within such a society the youth society is the one that acts.

Even sociologically, it is, perhaps, a necessary form of action, but it is one that is backward, which is no reason for it not to be the fashion. It satisfies the need for secrecy, power, and action, the needs of youth and often of tradition. I should like to add that Aristotle's pages on the way in which tyranny is normally connected with war and with democracy itself are still perfectly applicable. One would think we were back in the time of the young people of Megara who swore in secret not to stop until they had destroyed the famous constitution.

This is just beginning it all over again, the same sequences.

[This letter needs to be read in the perspective of the essential "Appréciation sociologique du bolchevisme" published by Mauss in Revue de métaphysique et de morale January-March 1924. Until someone edits a collection of his militant articles, Mauss's politics can be read about in "Du socialisme au don," in Mauss, a special issue of L'Arc (no. 48, 1972).

It is likely that everything that seemed negative to Mauss in this technology of the conspiracy, made it, on the contrary, fascinating to his young disciple, Caillois. Moreover, for Caillois, Sorel was far from seeming devoid either of interest or, especially, of virtues. In a note that was approximately contemporary with Mauss's letter (NRF, April 1936), he demonstrates his admiration for this thinker who never was caught "being flagrantly witty." It concludes: "The voice of the public seems no longer to exaggerate when, hearing the names of Lenin, Mussolini and Hitler, it invariably recalls Sorel."

The French Communist party itself described its status and politics as "sectarian" during the thirties. Its numbers were still rather slim, its tactics tended toward conspiracy, and its public image was dependent on the romanticism of conspiracy (which Nizan planned to demystify in a novel bearing those words as its title). See H. Dubief, Le Déclin de la Troisième République (1929-1938) (Paris, 1976), particularly the chapter entitled "Les Communistes, entre le parti et la secte." This, no doubt, is what explains the appeal to the Communists concluding Caillois's "La Hiérarchie des êtres." The PCF (French Communist party) of the time was a more plausible guarantor of the sectarian fantasies that Caillois developed in that article than it would be today, though its participation in the Popular Front had already perceptibly damaged its plausibility.

"La Hiérarchie des êtres" (Les Volontaires no. 5, [April 1939]) concludes, in fact, by expressing the hope that the communist movement will delay no longer in realizing the compromise that its present collusion with democracy represented. "This would be the greatest guarantee of success for itself and for the notion of order. It would be sufficient for a determined minority, within the communist forces, to adopt and maintain its ideal." An erratum Pierre Missac added to the bottom of the page of an article, in which he accused Caillois of holding himself at the disposal of fascism refers, no doubt to this conclusion when it states: "Since these lines were written, Caillois has professed communism" ("Avec des cartes truquées," Cahiers du sud no. 216, [May 1939]).

This having been said, Meyer Schapiro's remarks several years later, upon reading texts contemporary with the College that Caillois was to gather in La Communion des forts *("French Reaction in Exile,"* The Kenyon Review, *Winter 1945, p. 33), were not lacking in intuition: "Despite all the scorn he feels for what he considers the dogmatism and irrationality of Marxism, Caillois would still be disposed to consider the Communists as acceptable agents for the social restoration he desires, on the sole condition that they continue to constitute themselves as a secret minority that keeps itself separate from the masses."*

Concerning the relationship between Caillois and the communists, it will be recalled that Inquisitions, *the review he (with, among others, Aragon) founded just before the preliminary discussions founding the College, was published by the Éditions sociales internationales, and that, in* Commune *(now Aragon's review, it too published by ÉSI), Sadoul's savage attack on "For a College of Sociology" (included here in Marginalia) is not without a favorable treatment of the author of "Winter Wind." He would benefit from this favorable treatment again, in the same columns, when Pierre Robin (formerly associated with* Inquisitions) *would conclude his review of* Le Mythe et l'homme *with a warning, rather than the condemnation pure and simple, that anyone other than Caillois would have merited.]*

Fragment
(Bataille)

[These are the few lines mentioned in note 10 of "Brotherhoods," in which Bataille picked up again the terminological quarrel pertaining to Bonapartism that he had eliminated from the lecture entitled "Secret Societies." No reliable indication of their purpose exists. It is no more than a likelihood that they are connected with the activities of the College. President Doumergue, described here as "the late," only earned this epithet in June 1937.]

Before going on to the presentations that are envisaged—which are to bear on the three questions of commune, community and federation—I am eager to recall quickly the object of this meeting.

We are all struck by the difficulties we meet each time we have to express ourselves on questions of social structure. A very few of the terms, such as State or nation, have a bit of precision to their meaning. Others, however, such as people, commune, order, democracy, and fascism, can be taken in a multitude of different senses.

Only the Marxists, in fact, have succeeded in agreeing on a certain number of definitions—agreeing, still, rather badly—but these definitions bear on a very limited aspect of things. As soon as it is a question of principal structures, the Marxists either shy away or introduce disastrous new definitions. I shall only cite Trotsky's introduction to the notion of Bonapartism, which alone is enough to show how little resistance habits of thinking about social matters offer to monstrous statements. Does not the Trotskyite Bonapartism cover, with the same word, not just the two Napoleons who ruled, but also Bismarck, Stalin, von

Papen, and the late President Doumergue?[1] Perhaps the worst is that Trotsky, recently defending these extravagant statements, came up with some arguments that had an air that was not only convincing but scientific.

I should like, as far as possible, to stick to precise statements, but I think that it is the greatest and most intimate parts of human nature that are currently tortured and anguished in the sinister vocabularies used by factions that have to have infinite falsifications at their disposal in order to exist. Never have such vacant verbal constructions been used to mislead passions or to exaggerate the anguish of those without the luck to be misled. I am not particularly hand in glove with what is called "the shining lights," "culture," or "rationalism," but I am persuaded that the aggressive, stealthy obstinacy, the quiet progress of science, is the surest means of destruction. We must work to destroy the pretentious phraseology used by both big and little [   ][2] that make our existence an absurdity today and something rotten tomorrow.

To the extent that we are concerned with human being's common existence, we need to use words that are as precise as surgical instruments. There will certainly be an occasion for us at some time or another to say why faculties do not provide us with these instruments. The fact remains that we shall have to forge them ourselves. This is, essentially, the object of this meeting. No doubt today we shall be approaching only the problematics of this work. But it is perhaps the problematics that is essential in these matters: It is the consciousness of a profound need that becomes clear, the consciousness also of the difficulty and the methods that are indispensable. A science that defines itself and comes into play, at the beginning, is as much a suffering and tough reserve as it is the certainty of winning.

Four Letters

I. Bataille to Leiris

July 3, 1939

Dear Michel,

I am sending you Caillois's text,[1] but it seems to me absolutely impossible to read it Tuesday.[2] This text is very *debatable*, in any case for me. It would be difficult indeed for the discussion not to take a polemical turn. And in Caillois's absence it would be impossible for me to express myself. So we have to wait for Caillois's return in order to polish it off. In addition to all this, Caillois speaks in the name of the College, even makes a commitment for the College; therefore, the text, in conformity with the bylaws enclosed with it, must be discussed *among us* before being read or published.

I don't think it is possible to read these bylaws as they stand. They seem very good to me, but there is a necessary clarification. And there is an advantage— Caillois, in any case, is keen on it—in not communicating them until they have been decided on.

There may be a number of excellent principles in Caillois's *Examen de conscience*. But there are useless exaggerations and a sort of emphasis on secrecy and silence. And finally flagrant contradictions (not to mention attacks against myself). In Caillois's mind, this is a text to go with the bylaws (at the very least one that could be connected to them). The bylaws, in fact, should still be published with a text of this sort. If Caillois is willing to be precise about what is obscure and seems contradictory, to suppress what takes the form of an internal polemics and substitute for this sort of harsh exercise in reprimand the kind of rigorous good sense that is the expression of any real thought process, the *Examen de conscience* might serve as the basis of such a text. (1) Make the general movement correspond to the logic of the development of an organization like ours (extreme reserve regarding propaganda, restraint, and withdrawal into oneself). (2) Make the expression of this reserve and this discretion have to be what is inscribed in the first instance, before any program of action (on condition that it lose its ostentatious nature).

Yours truly,
Georges Bataille

Without reading the bylaws, it is perhaps possible to speak of the project of achieving a structured organization in October, with bylaws defining the CS as an organization posing the question of spiritual power.

II. Leiris to Bataille[3]

Paris, July 3, 1939

Dear Georges,
   I am addressing this to you alone in Caillois's absence.[4]
   While I was working at writing the account of the College of Sociology's activity since its founding in March 1937—the account I was to read at tomorrow's session—I was led to reflect more closely than I had before upon what the activity of the College had been during these past two years. I was more and more assailed by doubts as to the rigor with which this venture has been conducted, and the result is that I cannot regard myself as qualified to take the position of speaking for our organization.
   If the idea of a congress that we were discussing with Caillois and several others takes shape next fall, I shall enlarge upon my objections during the meetings for discussion. Today I shall just mention the principal points with which I am in disagreement.
   1. In the first paragraph of the ''Note on the Foundation of a College of Sociology,'' which appeared in *Acéphale* and was reproduced in the *NRF* of July 1938,[5] it states that the College assigned itself the study of ''social structures'' as its main goal. Now, I think serious offenses against the rules of method established by Durkheim—whose spirit we continually evoke—have been committed many times at the College: working from badly defined ideas, comparisons made between data taken from societies of profoundly different natures, etc.
   2. In the second paragraph, the concern is with our forming a ''moral com-

munity'' that would represent something radically different from the usual scholarly associations. OK. But this ''moral community'' is still completely undefined, and I am extremely afraid that, if people coming from an intellectual group want to establish themselves as an Order or a Church, they will resort to forming what is merely a ''clique,'' as it is commonly called.

*As far as the foundation of an order is concerned, it seems premature in any event, as long as we have not managed to define a doctrine. An order is not founded to produce a religion; it is, on the contrary, in the heart of religions that orders are founded.

*3. The third paragraph of the same note speaks of the constitution of a ''sacred sociology.'' Although I am fully aware of the importance of the sacred in social phenomena, and of how vital it is for us, I think that emphasizing the role of this sort of thing to the extent that we have emphasized it—almost to the point of making the sacred the sole principle of explanation—is in contradiction with the acquisitions of modern sociology, and particularly, with the Maussian idea of ''total phenomenon.'' Far be it from me to want to make the College into a scholarly society where one would devote oneself to research in pure sociology. But, in the end, we have to choose, and if we take sociological science as it has been established by men like Durkheim, Mauss, and Robert Hertz as our reference, it is essential to stick to their methods. Otherwise, in order to clear up any ambiguity, we have to stop calling ourselves ''sociologists.''

*I am counting on the discussion meetings that will take place in the fall to clarify all of that and provide our movement with its decisive direction, and I want you (you and our friends as well) to know I am completely committed to the preparation of this congress, whose meeting I consider essential.

Michel Leiris
Member of the College of Sociology

III. Leiris to Bataille

Monday the third, 9 P.M.

Dear Georges,

I realize that I was wrong to wait until now to make an issue of my disagreement. It is my weakness not to be able to make up my mind—say yes or no—unless I have my back against the wall, and I realize full well that is inconvenient.

I am surprised, however, that you took this letter[6] as if it were directed at you personally: I do not take you and the College of Sociology to be identical, and, when I criticize the College of Sociology it is as a whole, as an organization of which I myself am a part.

It is my hope, in bringing you this letter, that we will discuss it and perhaps discover a way to get out of this, because I dislike putting you in a predicament by dropping out.

I was wrong, let me repeat, not to tell you bluntly, and soon enough, that I was not in a position to give such a paper. I thought that it was a case of my usual inhibitions and that I would, as so often happens, triumph over them at the last minute.

I refuse to believe that such a mistake, despite the momentary trouble it may cause you, is such that it can destroy our friendship.

Affectionately,
Michel

IV. Bataille to Caillois

Saint-Germain-en-Laye[7]
59 bis, rue de Mareil
July 20, 1939

Dear Caillois,

You have put me in a very difficult situation. Either your message would be read and I would have to say the extent to which I disagreed and what my criticisms were—without your being there to respond. Or I had to take the initiative of not presenting it to be read, contrary to the agreement. At the last moment, moreover, the situation was seriously aggravated: Leiris, refusing on the eve of the meeting to speak, presented me with a letter pointing out the extent of his disagreement with us.

I read Leiris's letter after having had an oral discussion with him: This discussion made it possible to say that we remained in essential agreement. Since then, moreover, everything has become very clear along these lines—and all the misunderstandings seem to have disappeared (to be exact, it was a question of methodology, and, no doubt, there will be good reasons to clear up a great many things on this subject).

About your message, I think that it will all remain unclear until we have had a similar oral discussion.

It was not read. I explained that you and I had profound problems between us, that I would not bring up the terms creating these problems but would simply speak about the heart of the question. You proposed as the basis for an "official doctrine" (1) "my theory of compound beings"; (2) "the opposition between the sacred and the profane in relation to the gift of self for the benefit of a vaster being." I developed this theory of beings in the direction of a problematic of the gift of self. I attempted to show that starting from this point inevitably introduced the need for drama. This took place under conditions making it seem impossible to resolve the question before seeing all its significance. (By the way, I did not exactly speak of drama, but of expenditure, loss, sacrificial madness, and, of course, I did not indulge in any criticism of your position: I simply defended myself after explaining that "the role I gave to mysticism, to drama, to madness and death" seemed to you "hard to reconcile with our original principles.") I added that you were not the only one "to be troubled by this feeling of incompatibility," which was shared, at least, by Paulhan and Wahl.

I think you would have a hard time disputing that the question I posed that day made sense. To tell the truth, I think if you cared about seeing what it is exactly that I want, you could easily see it: My insistence on taking Nietzsche as my reference, alone, indicates the direction I am taking. As much as anyone else, I am searching for a domination of whatever is monstrous, but on the condition that there be domination not of some foreign reality but of what precisely is acknowledged as oneself, and set free in festivals. (Obviously I am seeking to make possible certain states of mind that are like those of festival, and it is true that this is something that is important to me.) I cannot understand how, given this easily discerned position, you feel yourself obliged to seriously oppose me; in any case, I express myself well enough for *you* to grasp my intentions (but you grasp perhaps more readily, which seems to justify hostility against me).

That is in response to the portion of your "examination of conscience" concerning cheap cerebral agitation.

On your insistence on the necessity of being reserved, your message is so imprecise and gives so little the impression of being a practical method that it is very difficult for me to discuss it. I assume you regret having written *Winter Wind*. And, of course, I have no doubts as to the anxiety my "apocalyptic" tones arouse in you. It seems that your method of proceeding by allusion has many drawbacks. Stripped of that which, you would agree, is there just to amaze me and cannot be valued for its clarity—its method clarified, its assertions reduced to ones that are more precise (and perhaps less seductive)—it seems to me that this text should still be connected to the bylaws (usually bylaws have an introduction of this sort). I agree, in fact, about the very impulse you are expressing.

My greatest reservation has to do with how frantically you insist on describing yourself as "intellectual." You are perfectly aware that I am insistent upon totality, and at the time, you let pass everything I said about this in the *NRF*. Today it is the mysticism of my article that you speak of. By that you mean it irritates you. In any case you will acknowledge that it would be inconsistent on my part to see intentions within the College of Sociology that exclude the possibility of thinking the things expressed in this article. I am perfectly willing to acknowledge that I am an intellectual, but I do not want to add phrases that lead one to believe that an intellectual who willingly limits himself can still be called "honest'' and ''honorable.'' What Hegel called ''geistige Tierreich der Betrug'' (*geistige* must be translated as ''intellectual'') does not seem to me any less oppressive after your ''examination of conscience'' than before. There are weighty problems within the human spirit that no one can solve with a few words. Are you willing for the following (or something of the same sort) to be added to your statements? That the College of Sociology reserves the possibility of defining problems without quickly resolving them, for many difficult problems cannot be resolved by the decision that will be the result of the unforeseen course things may take (I don't insist expressly on this addition but rather on the principle itself).

This principle, moreover, seems to me to be critical in opposing the form you have given to the essential point of the bylaws. You want the College of Sociology in the long run to claim spiritual power. It seems to me that an organization that does not know the development to be caused by the ''course things may take'' cannot have any such claim. This organization can claim only to *pose* the question of spiritual power. It obviously has no answer beyond an assertion that a spiritual power is necessary. I even think that we begin to differ as soon as it is a question of the direction in which this power should be sought. Perhaps you believe that authority is possible for those who would possess knowledge and define its orthodoxy. I do not completely deny myself that hope. But I do not believe we can avoid here seriously overstepping the points you yourself have defined: namely, that society is a being no less true and no less rich than the person; that this being that requires the gift of self must be *Sacred* that is to say, possessing the powers, the virtues, the seductions that sacrifice demands and entails. Now the consequence of this is that spiritual power cannot refuse to define itself as a being similar to those it describes as no less true and no less rich than the person. Insofar as it is such a being, it must therefore possess the power of provoking sacrifice; it must therefore aspire to the sacred.

The principle you define as a closed ''council'' preceding open meetings seems to me the only answer to our need to discuss among ourselves, as soon as possible, all of these questions resulting from our exchange of letters. If you are as willing as I to discover *immediate* solutions that will allow us to continue, it will not even be difficult. The only trouble is that since the College, pending a completely new order, set itself an intellectual task, it is hard put to avoid confusing the immediate with the future. Moreover, it is up to you (I could not do it) to define what you call an immediate task and what must be the object of ''occultation.'' If, on top of it all, you proposed something viable, you would meet with no opposition, either from myself or from those who are really interested in our activity. Just now I received a letter that was entirely to your way of thinking in this respect. The College can make sense now only if it is able to close back on itself and provide itself with a solid constitution: The number is unimportant.

In June you saw me vacillating and hesitating, not seeing clearly what could be done after October. Today I think Leiris's statement alone gets us out of the impasse. Therefore, I take back what I myself proposed and what, perhaps exaggeratedly, made you uncomfortable. What I personally am proposing now may very well not meet with your hostility, and undoubtedly will demonstrate the possibilities for agreement that still exist between us. I should like to create a real course that systematically continues what I stated in the past in *Critique sociale*, this time examining things close up, organizing, clarifying, and, of course, elaborating. This would be for a few people who would commit themselves in advance to come more or less regularly.

For the review, I am expecting you to send your book reviews as soon as possible. It must absolutely come out October 1. So I have to send the final texts to the printer before August 25. Please—do your best so everything will be ready on time. If you can find the last issue of the *Revue internationale de sociologie*, it contains an article entitled *Montesquieu sociologue*.[8] I mention this because I have the impression that you would be happy to review this article (there will be other reviews of articles) to say what you think of Montesquieu.

The title *Religio* has to be rejected not only because it doesn't happen to be seductive but also because it is taken. The only names that did not seem impossible are NEMI, DIANUS, and URANUS. Most people to whom I spoke preferred the last one by far. For my part, I support it completely; the first two are too precious, too uncommon, I think.

The long delay of this long letter, begun July 6, is due to the little time I have had, combined with an *extreme* fatigue. Unfortunately, I have not had a chance to have the texts you sent me typed. On the whole I am very much in agreement with your conclusions about the sacred. It just seems to me possible to go beyond, and I hope we will attempt a discussion on this subject in the setting of the "council," but just a few of us. Your text and my paper given July 4, compared with some of Leiris's notes, would, I believe, provide the basis of a discussion that would get down to close examination.

I am hoping for a quick, brief answer from you, and especially the reviews.

Cordially,
Georges Bataille

Events

[This is a selection of news items Jean Guérin (Paulhan's pseudonym) put together with this title in the NRF Bulletin.]

October 1937:

Paris. The Academy revises its dictionary and replaces the example *This act of authority appalled* with a new example: *This act of authority was imperative*.

Paris. The death, of course unmentioned, of the best "expert" on socialism and also on English sociology: Élie Halévy.

Gijón. The heroic death of Abel Guidez, a young French academic, second in command to André Malraux in the España squadron, shot down by fascist planes.

July 1938:

Berlin. The *Arbeitsmann* mouthpiece of the Worker's Front, writes: "The external appearance of Czechs contradicts the ideal of Germanic beauty . . . There is a certain, undisputable, Asian tinge."

Leningrad. The Metropolitan Platanov converts to atheism and publicly explains "how religious miracles are made."

Dessau, May 29. "Ever since cannon merchants have been trying to get rich with people's blood . . . " Who wrote that? Goebbels.

Berlin. Creation of a "psychology laboratory" charged with studying foreign reactions to the visible results of the Berlin-Rome Axis.

Freiburg im Breisgau. The death, at the age of seventy-nine, of the metaphysician Edmund Husserl.

London, June 6. Freud, driven from Austria, arrives in London where he will live from now on.

Zurich. The Reich, claiming to be the successor of the Société d'éditions psychanalytiques de Vienne, asks for the copies of "its" books (to burn them) from Switzerland. It immediately gets what it wants.

Paris. Charles Maurras and André Maurois are elected members of the Académie française.

Canton. Approximately 10,000 civilians are killed by the Japanese, whom Claude Farrère proclaims "the most chivalrous race in the world."

Leningrad. Three schoolboys, convicted of theft, are given a suspended sentence of one year in prison. They will be put in jail for their first bad grade.

August 1938:

Paris. The Académie's latest choices have caused a sensation. Everyone thought Maurois was already in it and that Maurras never would be.

Tokyo. Twelve university professors, among them Takahashi Masao, are condemned for "doctrinal assistance to peasant workers' unions."

London. Lloyd George, a recent practitioner of divining, fears the excessive drought of the beginning of the year may have a drastic effect on international politics.

Reims. Celebrations in honor of the cathedral, restored with careful attention by Henri Deneux, who replaced the wooden framework with one of reinforced concrete.

Washington. "Women living in countries governed by warmongers should refuse to bear children," says Mrs. Roosevelt.

Prague, June 28-July 8. The annual Congress of Pen Clubs, in a gathering of a thousand delegates presided over by Romains, cheers Freud but refuses to come out against the *expression* of anti-Semitic theories.

Leipzig. The International Congress of Editors, with the French plentifully represented, sends a telegram "to the warm, enlightened friend of every cultural value": Dr. Goebbels.

Brussels. For the first time since Belgium has been free, the Belgian army maneuvers on the French border.

Vienna. The women of Vienna attack and claw the Nazis who were forcing women from Jewish high society to sweep the streets.

Rome. Mussolini declares that for the first time, in Spain, the forces of the last century's (that is, the French) revolution and this century's (fascist) revolution have met face to face. Among the fascist victories: Guadalajara.

New York. Following the legal institution of the marriage license (requiring a blood test) there are 21 marriages a day in 1938, as opposed to 498 in 1937.

Rome. Several university professors are charged with performing research on the Italian race, which is beginning to feel itself more and more Aryan and Nordic.

Paris. On the occasion of the reception of the king of England, the word "grandiose" reappears in the French vocabulary (Paul Reynaud, *Paris-Soir*, etc.)

Rome. Throughout all of Italy, a census is begun of Jews as well as of duplicate or "useless" works of art.

Tokyo. Japan decides against organizing the Olympic Games in 1940, not because, in ancient Greece, the games "suspended" wars, but for economic reasons.

October 1938:

Moscow. Arrest of a Russian Orthodox man who had a mass said in honor of Stalin.

London. Death, at the age of seventy-five, of the famous actor Walter Uridge, who played only a single role in his lifetime: that of Mugg in *The Belle of New York*.

Venice. F. T. Marinetti proposes that Italian poets put their imaginations at the disposal of the national cinema.

Budapest. Two thousand dwarfs, meeting at a congress, demand the concession of a territory in the Hungarian plains and protest the artificial production of dwarfs by unnatural mothers.

Tokyo. With the cellulose necessary for the manufacture of explosives becoming rare, women are forbidden to wear skirts with pleats and long-sleeved kimonos.

Leningrad. Death of Kuprin, a misfit in exile, a misfit in the USSR.

Rome September 2. Jews are excluded from the academies, universities and scientific associations.

Paris suburbs. Inauguration of Romain Rolland stadium, by himself.

Nuremberg. Extraordinary parades—derived from the mass, the military review, the plenary session, and the apotheosis of the music hall—with 800,000 Nazis assembled.

Some deaths: Max Factor, inventor of the sophisticated star; Frobenius, inventor of African civilization; J. Bédier, inventor of the Internationale des Fabliaux; Dr. Osty, inventor of metapsychics; Paul Arbelet, who discovered Stendhal's Louason; and Jean Longuet, Marx's grandson, who reconciled French and German traditions of socialism within himself.

Nuremberg, September 7. At the national socialist Congress: "We have here," says Rosenberg, "philosophers but no philosophy, sects but no religion."

Berlin. According to official statistics, in three months five thousand conversions to Islam would have been recorded.

Paris. Mr. A. de Châteaubriant returned from a private interview with Hitler with the assurance that the "the Führer will be the donor of peace to the world." Unfortunately, Hitler doesn't know French, nor Châteaubriant German.

Chitry. Death of Madame Jules Renard, who published half her husband's *Journal* and burned the other half.

London. The whole world is surprised and moved to see Neville Chamberlain, at the age of seventy, go up in an airplane for the first time in his life, to try to preserve the peace of the world.

November 1938:

Leningrad. From September 21 to 28, it is forbidden to pray for peace (according to the *Osservatore Romano*).

Munich. Through the Munich accords, peace is preserved. Peace in its dullest and most perishable sense.

Paris. Tailors spread the word: Because peace has provided us with joie de vivre, light-colored clothes will be worn this winter.

London-Paris. H. G. Wells and Léon Blum ask that the Nobel Peace Prize be given to President Bénès.

Berlin, October 7. Hitler is slightly wounded by a bouquet of flowers thrown at his automobile.

Paris. Jules Romains in the name of the *Pen Club* Aragon in the name of the Association des Écrivains et Artistes Révolutionnaires ask that the Nobel prize for literature be awarded to the Czechoslovakian writer Karel Čapek.

Paris. There is a question of erecting a monument to Czechoslovakia as martyr. It seems doubtful that the Czechs expected so many prizes and statues from us.

Leipzig. One of the new streets of Leipzig is named Sudetenland Street. Another, Saar Street. And another, Alsace Street.

Vienna. A Catholic demonstration takes place to cries of "Jesus is our Führer!" Cardinal Innitzer blesses the demonstrators.

Paris. After Stravinski and Chagall, Bruno Walter becomes French.

Vienna. Cardinal Innitzer sees his palace invaded and two of his priests defenestrated.

Rome. The measures taken against the Jews by the fascist Council are derived more from racial anti-Semitism than from State anti-Semitism.

Berlin. Any Israelite bearing an Aryan first name henceforth is to be called Israel or Sarah.

London. Trenches continue to be dug in the parks. Lovers are forbidden to take refuge there.

Paris. The human face is not the result of bursting buds, as was previously thought, according to Victor Veau, the eminent embryologist. It is a "rising tide."

Münster. The circulation of Catholic newspapers has not stopped increasing for two years. The *Westfaelische Landeszeitung* concludes from this that it is ridiculous to complain about persecution.

Chicago. Bénès accepts the position of professor at the university.

Amsterdam, October 17. Death of Karl Kautsky, friend and disciple of Marx, who was an adversary of Lenin.

London. "The lights go out, night falls," says Churchill in a speech broadcast to the Americans. "How long will I still be able to speak?"

December 1938:

London. People are fighting over the works of W. E. Hickson, author of a verse quoted by Chamberlain ("tenter encore, tenter toujours" [try, try again]). They are mediocre.

Berlin. According to Professor Hermann Bauch (*New Bases for Research on Race*), "It is not proven in the least that non-Nordics are unable to mate with monkeys."

Cairo. At the foot of the columns at Ahzar, René Guénon, completely Islamized and renouncing the world, studies the commentators of the Koran.

Berlin. Pogroms throughout Germany. Rosenberg, agreeing (he says) with Hitler, predicts the imminent disappearance of the Catholic and Protestant churches.

New York. The announcer O. Wells [Orson Welles], imitating President Roosevelt's voice, broadcasts H. G. Wells's *War of the Worlds*, provoking serious panic.

Stockholm. It was hoped that Czechoslovakia would win the Nobel prize for literature. It goes to China, in the person of the American, Pearl Buck.

Paris. Death of the philosopher Léon Chestov.

Munich. All art objects belonging to Jews are confiscated and placed in the national museums.

Paris. Claude Farrère, in a letter to *Le Figaro* accuses the Jesuit Reverend Fathers of taking their inspiration from Moscow.

April 1939:

Paris. Only two candidates apply for the post of executioner. One is the executioner from Alger. The other is Deibler's nephew.

June 1939:

Paris, May 4. *Paris-Soir* announces that during the celebrations organized to honor the 150th anniversary of the Revolution, "Mr. Albert Lebrun will be in exactly the same location as Louis XVI was."

September 1939:

Paris. Celebrations of the Revolution: The overall conclusion of the speeches delivered is that without the Revolution we would have no sciences or letters or freedom today.

Paris. Celebrations of the Revolution (sequel): Advertising capital punishments is suppressed by decree.

Berlin. After Van Gogh and Gauguin, Rembrandt, guilty of having taken Jewish history as his inspiration, is the next to be excluded from German museums.

Washington. Georgetown University Medical School offers 2,700 varieties of germs for sale at moderate prices.

Paris. Celebrations of the Revolution (sequel): The People's House of Representatives, replaced by full powers and statutory orders, is adjourned for two years.

Moscow. Death of Béla Kun, in prison.

Leningrad. Meyerhold, relapsed (into "formalism"), is reimprisoned.

December 1939:

(No longer will there be any question of "Events" here. Not that they are lacking. But some are too well known and, moreover, too serious; they can be discovered above, with comments. And the others are unverifiable.)

Marginalia

1938 René Bertelé, "À travers les revues: sciences de l'homme et sociologie sacrée," *(Human sciences and sacred sociology in the reviews)*. *Europe*, no. 190, (October 15, 1938), pp. 275-76.

It is not without interest to compare the preoccupations of the Centre d'Étude with those coming to light in the College of Sociology, whose foundations are laid by Roger Caillois and his friends in the July 1 issue of the *NRF*. Although their point of departure is similar, the tone and conclusions are certainly very different. The three essays grouped under the same title are themselves remarkably divergent: Georges Bataille's derives from an exasperated and confused Nietzscheanism that is, above all, anarchistic. Michel Leiris's interesting paper, in contrast, represents the maximum of objective rigor it is possible to bring to the description of the affective phenomena of early childhood. But it is particularly in Caillois's statements that the spirit of the group and the aim it proposes must be sought.

For half a century now, the human sciences have progressed with such rapidity that we are not yet sufficiently aware of the new possibilities they offer, and are further still from having the opportunity and audacity to apply them to the many problems posed by the interplay of instincts and "myths" that form or mobilize them in contemporary society. One particular result of this inadequacy is that an entire side of modern collective life, its most serious aspect, its deep strata, eludes the intellect. And this situation not only has the effect of sending man back to the futile capacities of his dreams, but also of changing the understanding of social phenomena as a whole and of vitiating at their very basis those maxims of action referred to and guaranteed by that understanding.

The precise object of this contemplated activity can be called Sacred Sociology, insofar as that implies the study of social existence in every manifestation where there is a clear, active presence of the sacred. The intention is, thus, to establish the points of coincidence between the fundamental obsessive tendencies of individual psychology and the principal structures governing social organization and in command of its revolutions.

There follows a rather correct analysis of the great types of individualists, "methodical iconoclasts," and their influence. What role, Caillois asks, can they play in present-day society? Moving from "riotousness" to a "broadly imperialist attitude," from being "banished" to being "elected," by grouping and instituting, in the very heart of society, and in order to conquer it, another "society" that is secret, active, triumphant, and aggressive: This is to be the reign of the "masters." Their attributes will be:

contempt, love of power, and courtesy, virtues that, while not necessarily cardinal, stem directly from the attitude described and are eminently characteristic of its originality. . . . It is healthy to desire power, whether over souls or bodies, whether prestige or tyranny.

These superior men, lords of the intellect, are to take their inspiration first and foremost from Baudelairean dandyism, "the privileged form of modern heroism." They are to be strong, prideful, and pitiless.

Thus, with Caillois, anarchic individualism becomes organized and active: It moves from revolt to revolution, which is its normal procedure. But at the same time it succumbs to the most "Luciferian" temptation: Instead of transforming the world, it conquers and enslaves it. This revolution will be made by a few for a few, and not by all for all. An aristocratic revolution, a revolution of self-interest, *a fascist revolution*—and you know how interesting that can be even for the intellect.

Finally, the problem of how to satisfy affective tendencies, the "sacred" as Caillois calls it, is put backward: Instead of reducing it to rational explanations, he demands that it be left all its obscure, mysterious, and virulent power—and you know what this taste for mysticism leads to. (This indulgence, which does not exclude a great display of scientific "rigor," is responsible for the equivocal and disappointing conclusions Caillois arrives at in his recent book *Le Mythe et l'homme.*)[*]

With Roger Caillois, no doubt great puerility goes along with an indisputable talent: The danger of the ideas he is putting forth, in too seductive a form, remains nonetheless real. Hitler, it is claimed, every morning, when he wakes up, reads a page from Nietzsche—a great misfortune for Nietzsche, who deserves better. It is to be feared that some possible dictator, lacking ideological justification, might someday arrive at the *College of Sociology* asking the support of its manifesto. It should be reasonably brought to Roger Caillois's attention that he is running this risk.

1938 Georges Sadoul, "Sociologie sacrée," *Commune. Revue littéraire pour la défense de la culture,* no. 60 (September-October 1938), pp. 1515-25 (the directors of the review are Romain Rolland, Aragon; it is published in the ÉSI, Éditions sociales internationales).

[Sadoul, the future author of the well-known Histoire du cinéma mondial, *was in charge of the "review of reviews" in* Commune. *Before that he had been a contributor to* Le Surréalisme au service de la révolution, *until the revolution passed up the services of surrealism. This episode no doubt gained him the acquaintance of Caillois and Monnerot. His allergy to Bataille dates from before the College of Sociology. In May 1934, in a review of* Le Chiendent, *he recalled the collaboration of Queneau and Bataille on "La Critique des fondements de la dialectique hégélienne," published by* La Critique sociale: *"Queneau, in collaboration with the distinguished psychanalo-scatologist, Georges Bataille, attempted in the renegade Suvarin's aperiodical review to reduce the dialectical process to the Oedipus complex." He is no sweeter to Leiris, in February 1935, in his review of* L'Afrique fantôme. *But this case did not seem totally hopeless to him: "The battles in the streets are even loud enough to wake a dreamer from his nap. We are certain that Leiris has made his choice between the two sides of the barricades." In July 1935, he mentioned Robert [sic] Caillois's* Procès intellectuel de l'art. *The first name was corrected a year later in his important review of the new journal* Inquisitions. *He introduced the readers of* Commune *to its two youngest editors, Roger Caillois and J.-M. Monnerot, "who, among the youth still frequenting the universities, are two particularly penetrating and inquiring minds."* Inquisitions, *he explains, is an instrument of research, but a research intending to be carried out "in the cadres of the Popular Front where all the members of the group have placed their sympathy."*

But Sadoul does not just make mincemeat of leftists. He also picks away at the publications of the far right in his column. This is how Blanchot's name turned up now and again under his pen. In August 1936, about the call to terrorism that

---

[*]One volume, *NRF.*

*Jeffrey Mehlman recently has given a certain publicity (*Legacies of Anti-Semitism in France *[1983]): "Those who would risk limiting the thought of* Combat *to the defense of Sundays and the hatred of non-Aryan accordion players will find a more general and even more explicit expression of this thought in Maurice Blanchot's article." After quoting this article, Sadoul concluded: "Of course, the saber rattling of these thoroughly literary combatants should not be taken too seriously, but let it not be forgotten that it was in a practically identical setting that the agents of the two hundred families would find the fanatical hand to assassinate Jaurès." In March 1937, another article from* Combat *would take its turn meeting his jabs. Blanchot and Bataille did not yet know each other. We can suppose that each read the other's name for the first time in Sadoul's writing. But it would be foolish to draw any conclusions at all from this.]*

Sacred Sociology

The Nouvelle Revue française for July opens with a series of article manifestos, signed by Georges Bataille ("The Sorcerer's Apprentice"), Michel Leiris ("The Sacred in Everyday Life"), and Roger Caillois ("Winter Wind"), gathered together with title and preface in common: "For a College of Sociology."

In this preface, signed with the initials of Roger Caillois, the aims of the College of Sociology and the reasons for its existence are defined.

> The preoccupation with rediscovering the primordial longings and
> conflicts of the individual condition transposed to the social
> dimension is at the origin of the "College of Sociology."

Studying society, starting not from social groups, nations, masses or classes, but from the individual, the "*individual condition*" seems, hence, to be the basis for the research of this "College of Sociology," whose program is defined thus.

> As soon as a particular importance is attributed to the study of social
> structures, one sees that the few results obtained in this realm by
> science not only are generally unknown but, moreover, directly
> contradict current ideas on these subjects. These results . . . remain
> timid and incomplete, on the one hand, because science has been too
> limited to the analysis of so-called primitive societies, while ignoring
> modern societies; and on the other hand, because the discoveries
> made have not modified the assumptions and attitudes of research as
> profoundly as might be expected.

The first aim of the College of Sociology seems, therefore, to be a critique of sociology, not of sociology in general and in every aspect, but sociology understood as totally represented by the sociological school of the French university system and illustrated by Durkheim and Lévy-Bruhl. Specifically, no attention is given to Marxist sociology, which, nonetheless, although it studied primitive societies, focused its efforts entirely on modern societies. But it does seem that, in the view of Bataille, Leiris, Caillois, and other professors of the College of Sociology, Marxist sociology has nothing to do with science and does not have to be treated with the same attention that must be accorded the labors of university sociology.

[A long quote followed that is not included here.]

If these phrases are stripped of the solemn, starched-shirt style that tries to claim a philosophical rigor and more often verges on chatter decked out in neologisms, if an attempt is made to set out the three points of this program, plain and simple, it seems to me possible to summarize them in ordinary language in this way.

The College of Sociology judges the labors of university sociology to be insufficient.

The College of Sociology wants to be not only a community of scholars but a *"virulent"* community.

The College of Sociology, above all, wants to apply itself to the study of the *"sacred,"* this notion found in institutions such as religion and the army, and it considers the sacred (as well as power and myth) to be a consequence of certain individual experiences.

Of the three articles that follow this manifesto, Roger Caillois's "Winter Wind" is, certainly, the one we should be advised to study most carefully because of the personality of its author. Georges Bataille's "Sorcerer's Apprentice" and Michel Leiris's "Sacred in Everyday Life" can be more or less disregarded.

Anyone who has followed in the past dozen years the writings of Bataille, published in a number of different avant-garde publications, has seen him perpetually, in rather obscure and pompous language, mix up and confuse scatology and eschatology, discourses on humanity's base functions and its mystical functions. In all of Bataille's work there is a will, or rather a vague impulse, to power that does not succeed in fooling one for long. In his philosophical writings, as well as in his novels published clandestinely, the author perpetually confuses—to repeat, in the wake of Marx and Engels, an expression of Feuerbach's—sperm and urine; one understands that the illusion of power is imperfect indeed. "The Sorcerer's Apprentice" does not bring new vigor to Bataille's earlier writings.

Leiris's article is no more than a sequence of childhood memories. He informs us that once he was much impressed by his father's revolver and top hat, his parents' bedroom, the bathrooms in their apartment, the fortifications and racetrack at Auteuil. Such memories can be useful for studying the psychology of a petit bourgeois born in the sixteenth arrondissement at the begining of the century, but their applications in sociology—even a sacred sociology—seem a bit limited to me.

If the third article deserves more attention it is, above all, because, whereas his sociological companions have wanted, for the past fifteen years, to embody the avant-garde and youth, and only end up in the rearguard of men of a certain age, Roger Caillois is, in age at least, a young man whose brilliance and intelligence have made university and literary circles consider him one of the hopes of his generation.

"Winter Wind" is the development of the three fundamental points of the College of Sociology and an attempt to apply them to the resolution of intellectual problems.

For Roger Caillois, the intellectual is, by definition, someone who cuts himself off from society and rejects it. This a priori definition does little more than bring out the old saw "nonconformism" which certainly has had time to become rusty since a certain Berl first introduced it long ago. On this subject, it is diverting to remark that the one tritely labeling certain intellectuals "Nonconformist," provided in his ensuing career the most magnificent example of bourgeois "conformism."

This is how Caillois takes his turn at expounding the nonconformism of intellectuals:

[The long quote that followed is deleted here.]

There are correct features to this analysis. But it makes the mistake of considering, among the intellectuals who rise up against society, only the romantic rebels, those who withdraw from the world to curse it and who remain alone in the privacy of their hopeless pessimism. But to want to reduce in this manner the refusal, or the "nonconformism" of intellectuals, even romanticism's intellectuals, is a conscious or unconscious mutilation of truth. Not only is an entire category of intellectuals eliminated from this picture, but certain episodes of their lives are deliberately obliterated.

Whereas Rimbaud cursed society and could mislead himself to glorify the convict, the one who was a communard glorified, in his greatest poems, the people and the Commune. Hugo, on his rock on Guernsey, sang of a convict and a prostitute in *Les Misérables* but also of the struggles of the people of Paris on the barricades; and, both in literary history and everyday language, Gavroche occupies more space than Cosette did in the time she was a prostitute. Baudelaire engaged himself in militant action and became a journalist in 1848. It would take forever to mention all the intellectuals who, in revolt against society, soon understood—for the rest of their lives or merely in a flash of thought that was all too brief—that the intellectual, in order to struggle against injustice, had to place himself alongside the people, the main victim of bourgeois injustice.

Roger Caillois just skips, pure and simple, this aspect of intellectual rebellion, this process that makes revolutionaries out of rebels. Apparently, for him the only intellectuals who are truly worthy of the name are "the great individualists" who claimed to oppose implacably their ego to any society, whatever it might be. And to quote a jumble of Nietzsche, Stirner, the cardinal de Retz, Rimbaud, Baudelaire, and Balzac all in one breath.

Let us continue to pursue Roger Caillois's reasoning, which, because it started with an incomplete postulate, because it never considered but one aspect of a problem, from this point on will be engaged in a course that is obviously false [etc.].

The metaphors employed in these phrases make Caillois's thought perfectly clear. This *island*, these *sharp, precipitous outlines*, these *moats* evoke the silhouette of an medieval castle where the masters of the world assembled, isolated by their drawbridges and their *armed neutrality* from the contemptible crowd of enslaved serfs, men "almost of another race."

Caillois obviously aspires, by banding together the intellectual ivory towers in this manner, to build a wall of fortifications, a fortified city, a feudal system whose center would be no longer the pope or emperor, but the sages of the College of Sociology. An ideal strangely similar to an active reality on the other side of the Rhine.

The objection will be made that all of this is not really serious, and that, despite the stylistic apparatus, the author's naivete is more striking than the rigor and absolute character of his theories. This is true, and I do not imagine that Caillois intends to use such a text to propose his candidacy for the government of the world, of France, or even of the Café des Deux-Magots.

These views are just as utopian (and just as worn out) as those of a Wells in *Modern Utopia* describing a new world governed exclusively by a caste of experts and other eminent brains, or again, describing the imaginary society of the moon ruled by a Grand Lunar, whose brain was so huge and whose thought was so intense that his skull was phosphorescent and so boiling with thought that slaves continually had to sprinkle the head of their great master with ice water.

But this utopianism expresses no less a formidable intellectual pride, a frightful scorn for the masses, a thirst for power strongly resembling the ambitiousness of a Rastignac (a member of the secret brotherhood of the Thirteen), which would be disturbing, if, by some remote chance, they expressed the spiritual preoccupations and immediate ambitions of a certain younger generation of academics. Such a position, cynically expressed with the redundancy and solemnity of a style that is sometimes skillful, is remarkably similar to the basic premises of the fascist adventurers, those Führers whose ambition, by means of secret and paramilitary organizations, have been able to establish the domination of a brotherhood over the masses of the people, to the benefit of a great capital whose existence seems not even to have been suspected by the professors of the College of Sociology.

This remarkable College of Sociology seems, moreover, to have postulated the negation of society, of economic structure and its classes, in order to leave standing a single distinction, that of the *Masters* intellectual and noble, and the immense multitude of the *Slaves* material and ignoble. For the esteemed professors of the College, sociology is the science of the negation of true sociology. And their conquering, aberrant, raving and paranoid imperialism is based on a complete misunderstanding of the most elementary social realities.

1938   Henri Mazel, "Revue de la quinzaine: Science sociale (Memento)," *Mercure de France*, no. 970 (November 15, 1938), p. 189.

Roger Caillois: *Le Mythe et l'homme*, Gallimard. The author successively studies myth's function, its role in the world, and its role in society. In order to redress modern reality, which, he informs us, gives those who study it almost every possible feeling of disgust, he demands a certain vigor of decision and a great harshness of execution. Indeed, indeed. But all of this, although the author founded a College of Sociology last year, is rather far removed from what is known as social science.—J. P. Reinach: *Du gouffre à l'espoir, essai social et politique*, Alcan. Here, we are once again on more solid ground . . .

1939   Robert Kanters, review of Roger Caillois, *Le Mythe et l'homme*, in *Cahiers du Sud*, 18, no. 214 (March 1939), p. 257.

Our civilization is dying (Nietzsche's observation) of its atomization: a double atomization of the individual who is isolated in relation to society and who is no longer capable, within himself, of anything except a disconnected existence (G. Bataille). Myth, acting simultaneously on the emotions and on the community, is the only possible remedy for this double, psychological and social, disconnection. It seems perfectly obvious to the members of the College of Sacred Sociology that every doctrine, henceforth, must be linked to the point at which individual and social determining factors meet, in order to have any hope for a subsequent grasp on men. The importance of these studies, in Caillois's view, resides in the fact that they are remote preparations, but still preparations, that will clear the way for a positive, future mythology. Here, unfortunately, his sociology of myths does not escape the perpetual problem of the passage from knowledge to action, from the indicative to the imperative. One cannot accept the purely verbal dialectic with which he endeavors (p. 10) to outline the process: the winter wind is to sweep all that away . . .

1939   Jean Paulhan, letter to Roger Caillois, dated October 7, 1939, published in the *NRF*, no. 197 (May 1969) (*Hommage à Jean Paulhan*), p. 1012.

Leiris is nowhere to be seen, sent off to southern Algeria. Bataille, according to the latest, was arranging rare books in the BN. He is sure to have gotten your letter. . .

I am awaiting impatiently the declaration of the College of Sociology. The moment I get it I will put my mind to the signatures. I assume Gide and Valéry, among others, would be ready and willing. But what, exactly, is this manifesto to say? I see rather well the points at which (Bataille, for all that, made rather a thing of it) nazism can be in agreement with the theses of the CS. When it would only be through the power accorded to those who feel worthy of it. I see less clearly what gives you the right to call it an "abscess to be emptied." Between the cause of the liberal democracies and that of communist fascism, Nietzsche, I fear, would have (sourly) chosen fascism, etc. But I await your declaration. . . .

1939   Pierre Prévost, "Le Collège de sociologie," *La Flèche*, May 26, 1939. [Bergery, leader of the Front Commun was director of the review, *La Flèche*. Further information concerning this is to be found in the introduction to Guastalla's lecture, "The Birth of Literature," on January 10, 1939, and in his reply to Monnerot's inquiry.]

France is currently in a paradoxical situation. Whereas it has often been the country originating movements that have transformed the social structures of humanity, it is now, on the contrary, isolated from the social upheavals that have been rocking Europe for the past twenty years. Corresponding to the radical actions of neighboring populations is the French population's inertia. Both when faced with threats and when faced with appeals the French population withdraws into itself, incapable of any significant initiative.

Though this state of affairs presents grave drawbacks, it also has serious advantages with respect to the unrest. Specifically, it allows those who in any other time or place would be heatedly involved in the battle to accomplish something to maintain the calm and cool lucidity required for the analysis of events and the formulation of an opinion.

It would, thus, be hard to imagine—in any formal sense, of course—an achievement analogous to the College of Sociology in Germany or Russia.

The College of Sociology was founded two years ago by a group of young men—spearheaded by Georges Bataille and Roger Caillois—who set themselves the goal of seeking out the fundamental structures of human societies.

Deliberately neglecting elements that are components of society's strictly political and economic forms—forms that, being constituted with the aim of assuring that it will endure, are essentially social—the College of Sociology more particularly latched onto the study of asocial forms, meaning those whose implicit goal is the destruction of society as a constituent body. These singular structures are typically represented by the military realm and the realm of tragedy, of the religious in the broad sense of the term. Each of these share one element, *conflict*; yet the expression of this conflict has completely opposite results with each. Military conflict wins over the whole social body from the outside, and it always risks overthrowing social forms by destroying people and things. Tragic conflict, on the contrary, is manifested in the heart of the individual and thus tends not to destroy social structures from the outside as do warlike manifestations, but from within, by seeking to free human beings from their constraint. But this attempt, far from weakening social cohesiveness, reinforces it by giving rise to communities that are the indispensable counterpart to the revolutionary effort at "personalization."

A series of sociological analyses has made it possible to judge rather clearly the massive movements that have turned the contemporary world upside down. *Marxism*, which is only interested in social forms and maintains that the necessary changes are not the responsibility of human initiative but the effect of historical processes, seems to be nonrevolutionary. In fact, the only thing that is revolutionary is political effort whose aim is the people's liberation from social tyranny (a conviction that we would translate for frontism with the phrase "economy in the service of man"). *National socialism*, which the College bent itself to studying at first, by dismissing the tragic and making the military of prime importance (similar, in this way, to Muslim society), has constructed a monstrous system. Everything making up this whole, social forms as well as religious forms, is in the service of the war apparatus whose ultimate outcome is the destruction of the social body.

Every human society, in order not to be reduced to a mere empty framework—uniquely composed of political and economic structures—must aggregate around a nucleus that is charged with providing life and meaning to the social group.

It is the fate of democracies to be reduced to a system laden with empty structures; such a weakness risks being fatal for them.

As for fascist systems, in an easy reaction against the impotence of democracies, their fundamental nature is military. But a social body that gives a preponderant position to war apparatus is headed for its own destruction, because war is, in its essence, the source of total ruin. It tends to destroy the social body waging it just as effectively as it destroys the one subjected to it.

Revolutionary efforts thus will focus above all on an enterprise for the restoration of tragic values.

There are many connections between the College of Sociology and frontism, connections that are located less on the doctrinal level than on that of a general *attitude*. Each of them, of course, pursues a different task: The former is bent on founding another table of values and on giving rise to the spiritual spark of a revolution, the latter wants to create new social forms, but plans and actions, far from opposing each other, are complementary.

1939   Jean Wahl, "La philosophie française en 1939," *Renaissance*, vols. 2 and 3 (New York, 1944-45), pp. 336-39. In a note added when it was published, Wahl mentioned that this assessment was written in 1939 for the *NRF*. The first philosopher mentioned is R. Ruyer, followed by Nogué, Souriau, Bachelard, Gurvitch, Jankélévitch, Raymond Aron, Dalbiez, Dr. Pihon, and Lacan.

It hardly seems necessary to discuss Sartre here. The readers of this review are familiar with *La Nausée*, *Le Mur*, and his opinions on Faulkner and Dos Passos. *La Nausée* alone would require a study. In any case, all its repercussions should be addressed. And the book fragment on *L'Imaginaire* that the *Revue de métaphysique* has given bodes well for the value of the work.

It is also not much use to expand at any great length about the College of Sociology, a somewhat ambiguous enterprise that is often fascinating. But is it possible to attempt to constitute the Sacred and simultaneously try to study it? Since the birth of this "College," that objection has come to mind, as it came to mind on being confronted with Durkheim's work, which suddenly is something the young people want to be linked with. A College of Psychology, rather, where one gets to know Bataille, Caillois, Leiris, patient-doctors, each of whom has given us wonderful things. The second, with *Le Mythe et l'homme*, has written a valuable philosophical work, as arid as he wishes, and fertile at the same time.

De Rougemont, with *L'Amour et l'Occident*, as with his earlier books, presents us with ideas that ask for discussion no doubt, but which are always keenly interesting. . . .

Klossowski, in his remarkable studies on the Marquis de Sade (also published in *Recherches philosophiques*), which conclude in *Esprit*, paradoxically, with a fine article full of Christian faith on the idea of the neighbor, demonstrates a thought that is surely still searching, even if it now believes it has the answer.

[At this point Wahl included a few remarks on Jean Grenier, Gabriel Marcel.]

Finally, we should also consider as already part of the philosophy developing on French soil, the works of Landsberg, who goes back to Saint Augustine via Scheler. And no doubt for him as for Berdiaeff and for Marcel in his last works, this French phenomenology and existentialism are somewhat thwarted in their development because of the ease of certain religious responses. But it also must be said that the religious appeal has been a powerful driving force in their thought and that Landsberg powerfully expresses important ideas.

[Wahl then mentions Lévinas, Rachel Bespaloff, Jeanne Hersch, Cavaillès, Lautmann, Chevalley. And in conclusion: "Since we are speaking of translation here, Hyppolite's beautiful translation of Hegel's Phenomenology *must be mentioned."]*

1940   Walter Benjamin, letter of January 17, 1940, to Gretel Adorno (written in French), in *Briefe*, edited by G. Scholem and Th. W. Adorno (Frankfurt am Main, 1966), vol. 2, p. 843. There is no mention of the College as such in Benjamin's correspondence, but here and there we find some mention of its members, and those lines are the ones I reproduce here. Affinities, such as in his letter of December 15, 1939, to Horkheimer, where he speaks of his "fierce enmity against the smug optimism of our leaders on the left." I recall also the note concluding the volumes of his correspondence. It points out that the folder containing "Passagenwerk" (the title of the project on which Benjamin was working at the end of his life) was hidden and preserved at the Bibliothèque nationale thanks to Bataille.

Apart from other projects, it will be fun to go back to analysis of new French publications. There is one, moreover, rather peculiar one that has just come out in Argentina. That is where Roger Caillois has just published a small volume that is a requisition [*sic*] against nazism, the argument of which repeats, without nuance or any modification at all, the same one occupying the daily papers of the entire world.[1] It was hardly necessary to go to the farthest reaches of the intelligible world or the earthly world to come back with that. It is true that Caillois publishes, on the other hand, in the *Nouvelle Revue française*, a theory of the festival, that I will discuss in my first account to Max. I shall also give my attention to a curious book by Michel Leiris, *Âge d'homme*, that received much notice before the war. . . .

. . . Our friend Klossowski, who is permanently unfit, has left Paris and has just found work in a municipal office in Bordeaux.

1940 Roger Caillois, "Seres del anochecer," *SUR* December 1940 (the quote is from the slightly revised French version of these pages: "Êtres de crépuscule," in *Le Rocher de Sisyphe* [Paris, 1946], pp. 159 ff.). About this text, Caillois in 1974 would say (*Approches de l'imaginaire*, p. 60) that, even more than "L'Esprit des sectes," it "constitutes the real lesson that [he] personally drew from the episode" of the College. In this "confession" he says, "I admit the private defeat that was mine then. That is the express reason that it concludes *Le Rocher de Sisyphe*, whose writing as well as thought put an end to juvenile and arrogant pipedreams for me."

We were just a few, scattered and awkward, lacking either energy or perseverance, but sensitive to the secret eddies of the universe, not at all anesthetized and not at all euphoric, very intelligent and always on the lookout, and not at all excited, not at all frantic, lost in the crowds that were blinded by frenzy and delirium, rancor and dread, or put to sleep by the torpor of gentle death throes. We were the last conscious beings in this world that pampered men too much, and we predicted that it would disappear, without sensing that we were not born to survive it, but rather destined, once its ruins were righted, to wretchedness, ridicule, and oblivion. . . . We were too delicate, too scholarly, too difficult, too incapable of being content with a game that did not fulfill us. And then we came too late, we were too small, our hearts were too weak. . . .

We will turn out to have been orators. . . . We did not belong to the dawn. We feel the cold and fly clumsily, we are quick to hide in holes in the walls; we lie in wait only for small prey. We are the sinister and cautious bat of twilight, the bird of experience and wisdom, who comes out after the rumblings of day, even fearing the shadows that day heralds. We should call ourselves twilight creatures. Men of ambiguities and false positions, we loudly proclaimed our taste for violence and would, perhaps, have been driven to despair to see our desires fulfilled. . . .

The house was burning and we were tidying the cupboard. We would have done better to fan the fire. We didn't dare. . . .

Not being guilty was our consolation for being weak in a time when weakness was the utmost guilt. Nor did we try to build any sort of ark to save what should be saved. . . .

We also lacked the generosity, the indifference to fate that, failing great joy, a familiarity with the worst downfalls provides and that the world to come will bring us. . . .

We were too weak, too much in love with very old and very frail things that we were holding onto more than we thought: beauty, truth, justice, every subtlety. We did not know how to sacrifice this. And when we understood that that was exactly what we had to consent to, we recoiled and found ourselves back again in our place, on the other side, in this old, spoiled world that has had its day and now must be liquidated.

Copyright © Éditions Gallimard, 1946

1941   Jean Paulhan, letter to Roger Caillois, dated Christmas Day, 1941, published in the *NRF*, no. 197 (May 1969) (*Hommage à Jean Paulhan*), p. 1015.

My dear friend, it is unpleasant to be at this juncture without any news of all of you except for the issue of *Cahiers du Sud* that is already out of date. Besides, except for you, this *Cahiers* is rather lamentable, taking prudence to unnecessary extremes.—Did you know that Guastalla committed suicide the same day as Prof. Boch of Paris?—The mysterious Petitjean, making all the obvious concessions (in his writings): apologizing for the boys he leads, and (he says) incites.—Georges Bataille, hardly forthcoming, entrenched in eroticism and mysticism. M. Leiris, violent, intense, raging.—But the College is long gone. What are you doing? . . .

1942   Julien Benda, *La Grande Épreuve des démocraties* (New York, 1942),
        pp. 190-91.

A False Rationalism

This is the name I give to the position attributed, not always incorrectly, to democracy, according to which every object of thought without exception must be
a matter of discussion, no one of them capable of representing authority as
dogma, no one capable of constituting the nourishment of something extremely
powerful, something possessed by any opposing system: blind belief. Recently,
certain members of a defeated democracy explained its defeat because it lacked,
they claim, a blind belief, whereas its enemy held a particularly strong one.

It seems obvious that the refusal to put any value above discussion is a death
wager for an organism that is subject to asserting its existence. The question is
whether, when it is observable in such a democracy, this refusal is there out of
corruption or if it is consubstantial with the system, and inscribed in its essence.
Certain pedants, hostile to democracy moreover, contend this, as well as that it is
the law of democracy to want a *total* rationalism, not to acknowledge any ground
in view of which criticism must suspend its preventive action, and to provide no
place for the "Sacred."[*] This assertion seems false to us. The law of democracy
is, like any system positing a will to live, to place certain objects above examination. These objects are precisely the right of examination itself, and, more
generally, the right to freedom, the primacy of justice and reason, national sovereignty, in short, the democratic principles themselves. For a democracy, these
must be like the principles of opposing systems, the object of a blind belief—
democratic belief—whose existence was proven by (to cite only two examples)
America in the war for its independence or France in 1792, giving proof also that
democracies intend for it to exist and that, like other blind beliefs, this one bears
fruit. Moreover, all of the democratic constitutions declare that there is one thing
they will not allow to be put in question, at least in their public debates; that is
precisely their democratic principle.

1943   Étiemble, review of Julien Benda, *La Grande Épreuve des démocraties*,
        published in *Les Lettres françaises*, no. 78 (February 1943), pp.
        100-101, the French language review published by *SUR* in Buenos Aires
        and directed by Caillois. Étiemble expresses his disagreement with
        Benda's judgment about the College in the passage taken from Benda's
        book published in New York in 1942.

Curiously, he accuses the College of Sociology of preaching a "complete ra-

---

[*] This was the thesis maintained in France by the "College of Sociology," whose principal representatives are Roger Caillois and Georges Bataille (see *NRF* 1938-39).

tionalism,'' which has no room for myths. Of course, every effort that does not rely at all on the force of the sacred to revive democracy is futile. But what is diverting is that, in the text Benda attacks (but does not quote), Bataille, Leiris, and Caillois precisely are asking that we return to ''a collective mode of existence that takes no geographical or social limitation into account and that allows one to behave oneself when death threatens'' (*Nouvelle Revue française*, November 1938). At the very most, if one's name is Benda and one takes Renouvier for inspiration, one might take the College of Sociology to task for the extreme indulgence it expresses for myths and the sacred. *Le Mythe et l'homme* is by Caillois; so is *L'Homme et le sacré*. And wasn't it Bataille who founded *Acéphale*? Yes, but in the meanwhile, between the ''Declaration of the College of Sociology'' and ''La Grande Crise des démocracies'' [*sic*], an article appeared in the *Nouvelle Revue française*, in August 1939, a ''Sociology of the Cleric,'' a rather brutal, but perhaps pertinent criticism of Eleuthère's position: ''The *cleric*, wanting to play the angel, plays the beast. . . . it is unbearable and anarchical, the very yeast of disorder and imposture.'' Benda may not have pardoned this article.

1943   Jean-Paul Sartre, ''Un Nouveau Mystique,'' *Cahiers du Sud*, no. 262 (December 1943) (printed in *Situations*, vol. 1 [Paris, 1947], p. 165).

It was not for nothing that Bataille was a member of that bizarre and famous College of Sociology that so astonished good old Durkheim (whom it expressly claimed as inspiration); every member of this College pursued extrascientific projects by means of a nascent science. Bataille learned there to treat man like a thing. These incomplete and volatile totalities, suddenly composed, then muddled, and just as suddenly decomposed and recomposed elsewhere, are more related to the ''unanimous lives'' of Romains, and above all to the ''collective consciousness'' of French sociologists, than they are to the Heideggerian *Mitsein*.

Is it just luck that these sociologists, Durkheim, Lévy-Bruhl, Bouglé, are the ones who, at the end of the last century, vainly attempted to lay the basis for a secular morality? Is it a coincidence that Bataille, the bitterest evidence of their bankruptcy, takes up their vision of the social again, surpasses it, and steals their notion of the ''sacred'' in order to adapt it to his personal ends. But the sociologist is incapable of being integrated with sociology: He remains the one who creates it. He can no more enter into it than Hegel into Hegelianism, Spinoza into Spinozism. In vain, Bataille attempts to integrate himself with the machinery he has erected: He remains outside, with Durkheim, with Hegel, with God the Father.

1943   Georges Bataille, *L'Expérience intérieure* (*Oeuvres complètes*, vol. 5 [Paris, 1973], p. 109).

I get angry when I think how much "active" time I spent—during the last peacetime years—in striving to have contact with my fellows. I had to pay this price. Ecstasy itself is empty when it is seen as a private exercise, mattering only to a single person.

Even when preaching to those who are convinced, there is some troubled element in the sermon. Profound communication requires silence. Last, the action implied by the sermon is limited to this: closing one's door in order to stop discourse (the external noise and mechanics). . . .

The war put an end to my "activity," and my life found itself even less separated from the object of its search.

Copyright © Éditions Gallimard, 1973

1945   Roger Caillois, "L'Esprit des sectes," Colegio de México, *Jornadas*, no. 41, (1945) (reprinted in *Instincts et société* [Paris, 1964], pp. 66-67, and in *Approches de l'imaginaire* [Paris, 1974], pp. 92-93).

It is time to read again *La Gerbe des forces* by Alphonse de Châteaubriant. [. . .] In a few forsaken fortresses in the heart of the Black Forest and in the Baltics, there is a great endeavor to prepare an elite of young, implacable, and pure leaders for the supreme role of dictators first of the nation then of the world destined for conquest by this nation. . . . But the undertaking fired more than one imagination.

It was particularly true among those of us who had founded the *College of Sociology*,[*] dedicated exclusively to the study of closed groups: male societies in primitive populations, initiatory communities, priestly brotherhoods, heretical or orgiastic cults, monastic or military orders, terrorist organizations, secret political associations of the Far East or of troubled periods in the European world. We were fascinated by the decision made throughout the course of history by men, who from time to time seem to want to provide consistent laws for an undisciplined society that was incapable of satisfying their desire for rigor. Sympathetically, we followed the steps taken by those who, withdrawing in disgust, left this society to live elsewhere under cruder institutions. But certain of us, extremely fervent, were not willing to resign ourselves to interpretation alone. They were impatient to act them out. Our research had convinced them that there was no obstacle that will and faith could not conquer, provided that the original alliance turned out to be truly indissoluble. In the rapture of the moment, nothing less than a sacrifice seems able to bind energies as profoundly as it was necessary to complete a task that was immense and, besides, had no definite object. Just as the ancient physicist required only one point to support the whole world, the sol-

---

[*]The aims of the institution were set out in three manifestos that were published simultaneously in the July 1, 1938, issue of the *Nouvelle Revue française* and signed respectively by Georges Bataille, Michel Leiris, and myself.

emn execution of one of their members seemed sufficient to the new conspirators to consecrate their cause and guarantee their faithfulness forever. By making their efforts invincible, it was to put the universe in their hands.

Who would believe it? It was easier to find a voluntary victim than a voluntary sacrificer. In the end it was all unresolved. At least I imagine it was, because I was one of the most reticent and perhaps things went further than I knew.[*]
Copyright © Éditions Gallimard, 1974

1945   André Rolland de Renéville, "La Poésie et le sacré" (a review of *La poésie moderne et le sacré* by Jean [*sic*] Monnerot), *La Nef*, no. 7 (June 1945), p. 110.

Monnerot is a friend of Roger Caillois. He took part in the group that, shortly before the war, published the first issue (which remained, unfortunately, without issue) of the review *Inquisition* [*sic*]. I mention these recollections because they portray rather well the mental landscape in which Monnerot evolved, and because they are capable of preparing us for a better understanding of his work. It is known that, in fact, through the impetus of Roger Caillois, the College of Sociology was founded in Paris for the objective and scientific study of all social behavior expressed in the form of the sacred. The description "sacred" applied not to a religious reality but to any manifestation that took as its pretext, or really was motivated by, a transcendent reality, and was accompanied by an outpouring toward a realm situated outside of influence. It is self-evident that poetry represents a form of activity that is, by choice, oriented toward the sacred. Monnerot's study, therefore, is very decisive in tackling the major problem that passages from Caillois and his friends maneuver around. And I assume that if by "poetry" Monnerot means "surrealism," it is because this movement seems to him to epitomize the essence of modern poetic research and, by its very nature, to go back far beyond the date at which surrealist activity, strictly speaking, made its appearance in literary life. If this seems surprising, one should remember that Caillois and his friends came, more or less, by way of surrealism and were deeply influenced by it.

1946   Jules Monnerot, "Sur Georges Bataille," *Confluences*, no. 9 (February 1946), p. 1016 (reprinted with the title "La Fièvre de Georges Bataille" in the collection of articles entitled *Inquisitions* [Paris, 1974], pp. 214 ff.).

---

[*]I allude here to the group Acéphale, which Bataille often talked about with me and which I always refused to participate in, though I contributed to the review of the same name, which was its organ. About this group, in which secrecy was required, there are interesting revelations in *VVV*, no. 4 (February 1944), pp. 41-49.

Between 1928 and 1939 one could find in Paris[†] four or five men, moreover utterly different—in favor of seeking, in the motives for action offered to them then by a historical existence, something that would represent all the elements of nostalgia and religion that they could not help deeply retaining. Submitting to something that remained permanently foreign—despite their possessing it—to that part of themselves they considered most authentic, seemed to them only a solution of lassitude. Prey to a silent interrogation, they saw those, whose anguish seemed to leave absolutely no other way out than effectiveness at any price, throwing themselves into militant action. It is hardly difficult to understand how the very idea of sociology is able to catch the attention of such men at such a moment. In the widest sense, sociology is the study by every means, even the riskiest, of the movements of attraction and repulsion that seem to govern human particles. The systematic determining factor of this particularity presented by human beings is the inability to remain isolated. Individuals are then considered only as *conductors* of currents that are themselves the object of research. The social phenomena that he boasted of "treating as things" were, in Durkheim's view, natural phenomena. Bataille meditated deeply on *Les Formes élémentaires de la vie religieuse*. Communication, he says, is more "real" than the elements that communicate.

1946   Georges Bataille, "Le Sens moral de la sociologie," *Critique*, no. 1 (June 1946) (review of J. Monnerot's book, *Les Faits sociaux ne sont pas des choses*).

The generation that reached maturity between the two wars tackled the problem of society under conditions that are worth remarking. From its elders, it received the heritage of a humanistic culture where every value was related to the individual. The implicit judgments linked to this culture reduced society to perhaps a necessary evil, but one whose very necessity was doubtful. A bit of juvenile importance and hotheadedness . . . . : This negation of instinct was expressed in a revolutionary will. Or at least, vague desire. For years on end I do not remember anyone who, in my presence, defended the rights of society against those of the individual. . . .

Until around 1930, the influence of Durkheim's sociological doctrine had scarcely gone beyond the sphere of the universities. It had had no repercussions in the groups stirred by an intellectual fever. Durkheim had been dead for a long time when some young writers, coming from surrealism—Caillois, Leiris, Monnerot—began to attend a course given by Marcel Mauss, whose outstanding

---

[†]These few lines allude to the exchange of ideas expressed by the foundation in 1938, by Georges Bataille and several others, of a College of Sociology that was not viable. See *Nouvelle Revue française*, July 1938, *in limine*.

teaching methods were strikingly faithful to those of the founder of the school. It is hard to say exactly what they were seeking there; it differed according to the person. We can only speak of a rather vague orientation, independent of whatever personal determining factors expressed it. Detachment from a society decomposed by individualism and the uneasiness resulting from limited possibilities in the individual sphere were all mixed in. At the most there was a serious attraction for realities that, taking the same value for each one, thus forming the social bond, are held to be sacred. These young writers, more or less clearly, felt that society had lost the secret of its cohesiveness and that that was exactly where the vague, uneasy, and sterile efforts of a poetic fever were aiming. Sometimes it happened that they no longer despaired and no longer considered the possibility of rediscovering this absurd. This search could be considered vital, and it alone seemed worthy of those efforts, which were undeserving of art's effeminate enchantment and tricks.

They were less interested in a new experiment that would have prolonged surrealism than in scientific research. They demonstrated a certain aversion toward a past linked to literary ferment, and what they most vehemently dismissed was any possibility of compromise, of a superficial science employed for the ends of a venture that was suspect. No doubt they wondered whether, in this manner, the sterility of pure knowledge would not be the successor to the impotence of art, but, for them the need for rigor and intellectual honesty was opposed to what was for others the stronger requirement, that thought engender action. This concern with a society that could create the rarest values, this movement of interest in sociological study, in fact did not result in action, and if today it is possible to discuss it, it is more in order to locate a sense of lack, and a nostalgia, both linked to the current state of social existence. In fact, it is doubtful that, on the limited level of scientific knowledge, any great results came of it. But the new realm of interest as thus defined demonstrates, without a doubt, important sorts of unrest. A work like *Les Faits sociaux ne sont pas des choses*—the most recent publication connected to these "sociological" tendencies[*] owes some of its importance to a rather remarkable coincidence: the categories that Monnerot bases his science of society upon correspond to the concerns I have just mentioned, and take into account their necessity.

1947   Roland-P. Caillois, "Roger Caillois ou l'inquisiteur sans Église," *Critique*, no. 8-9 (January-February 1947), p. 29.

---

[*]Jules Monnerot's first book, *La poésie moderne et le sacré* (Gallimard, 1945), gave evidence of this orientation already.

Seen altogether, Roger Caillois's works show several connections with this tendency. But today, Caillois disavows his initial position—at least in certain respects.

The sociological activity of Michel Leiris has remained more or less on purely scientific ground and is hardly apparent in his literary writing (except possibly in *L'Afrique fantôme*).

On the eve of the war he [Roger Caillois] founded, with Georges Bataille and Michel Leiris, the "College of Sociology." None of the founders of this Sacred College today approves of that foolhardy venture. How well we understand! It's hard to explain certain bonds. But it's not important. In Caillois's mind there was no doubt that the college should inherit the severe thought of Ignatius of Loyola, as long as that despotic saint had taken courses from Émile Durkheim—a Durkheim who was, moreover, an irrationalist or, as one put it curiously then, surrationalist—and, when necessary, had called for support on a secret brotherhood, one of Father Joseph's silent legions, in fact a moral synarchy. While Caillois may have retained nothing from surrealism, it is not so sure that he renounced *political* ambitions. I take the word in its finest sense, as describing temporal government.

1947 Pierre Klossowski, "Le Corps du néant," in *Sade, mon prochain* (Paris, 1947), p. 166.

The creation of a College of Sacred Sociology that would permit it to satisfy its proselytism represented the first attempt in the practical realm by Bataille's group to escape the dilemma with which events confronted it. [Klossowski then gives a quotation from the "Note on the Foundation of a College of Sociology."] Hostile to all social and political discrimination, the moral doctrine of any party at all representing in their view a mutilation of the totality of being, they did not lean toward political conspiracy. Considering that revolutionary destruction is usually followed by reconstitution of social structure and its head, everything in them aspired to the *formation of an "order developing and holding sway throughout the entire earth, as the only truly liberatory act and the only possible one"* (Caillois).[2]

Now, it seemed that this sacred community, universal though secret, must have been the result of a conspiracy that was already old, begun in the past by isolated individuals who conveyed the password among themselves, although apparently they had no relationship with each other; each existence formed something like a step in the conspiracy, and following his own destiny each one of them had elaborated the code of honor for this future community: Sade, Lautréamont, Hegel, Baudelaire, Rimbaud, Nietzsche were the names of some of these existences that Bataille considered to be *existences authentic in themselves to the extent that they all converged toward the formation of that order whose mission was to bring forth, from the heart of the profane world, from the world of functional servility, the sacred world of the totality of being.*
Copyright © Éditions du Seuil, 1947

1947 Claude Lévi-Strauss, "La Sociologie française," in G. Gurvitch, *La sociologie du XXe siècle* (Paris, 1947), p. 517.

It is not simply linguistics and geography but European archaeology and the

ancient history of the Far East that have been enriched by sociological influence. This influence even reached the "avant-garde." During the years immediately preceding the Second World War, the "College of Sociology," under the direction of Roger Caillois, became a meeting place for sociologies on the one hand and surrealist poets and painters on the other. The experiment succeeded.
Copyright © Presses universitaires de France, 1947

1949   Gaëtan Picon, *Panorama de la nouvelle littérature française* (Paris, "Le Point du jour," 1950; 2nd ed., 1959), p. 264.

In *Le Mythe et l'homme* (1938), Caillois anxiously turns his attention on contemporary civilization: He feels that we are "twilight beings," that we are living in rubble and ruins. And he examines the divided, split and incoherent, "critical" society that is ours, with nostalgia and hope for an "organic" and coherent society, where human communion could finally be reestablished. With his colleagues at the College of Sociology (Georges Bataille, Michel Leiris), at its inception he shared the desire for social coherence and human communication— the desire for the mythical and the sacred. He calls for "a new order" and exalts "the virtue of hope," the violent men, the heroes, the strong ones who are to create the future. However, *Le Rocher de Sisyphe* is also the defense of a threatened civilization. The circumstances persuade Caillois that not all should be rejected in this society, which elsewhere he describes in harsh terms: The new order he calls for has nothing in common with that of dictatorships and social regressions. It is simply a matter of rediscovering civilization's sense.
Copyright © Éditions Gallimard, 1950 and 1960

1950   Armand Cuvillier, *Manuel de Sociologie*, vol. 1 (Paris, 1950), chapter 2, sec. 18c (p. 40 of the 5th ed., 1967).

Once again, attempts at *working in teams* must be mentioned. One of the oddest of these was the College of Sociology; its manifesto, published in 1938, was signed by Roger CAILLOIS, Georges BATAILLE, and Michel LEIRIS. This was an attempt to remedy the individualism of research and to establish among the researchers "a moral community," bound moreover "to the virulent character of the realm studied." This realm was to be the mutual relations between man's "being" and society's "being." For that, it was necessary to study "the richest human phenomena," those related to myth and the notion of the *sacred*. The results of sociology thus were to correspond to "the most virile concerns, not to a specialized scientific preoccupation."
Copyright © Presses universitaires de France

1956   Georges Bataille, letter of January 1956, a draft of which is published in *Oeuvres complètes*, vol. 8, p. 615.

Durkheim's work, and even more, Mauss's, had a decisive influence on me,

but I always kept some distance on it. My thinking is nonetheless based on a subjective experience. When I and others founded the College of Sociology in 1937, I think it was my intention to rediscover a world that I wander from too easily, that of objectivity.
Copyright © Éditions Gallimard, 1976

1958   Georges Bataille, "Notice autobiographique," in *Oeuvres complètes*, vol. 7 (Paris, 1976), p. 461.

With Contre-Attaque disbanded, Bataille immediately decided to form, with those of his friends who had participated there (among them Georges Ambrosino, Pierre Klossowski, Patrick Waldberg), a "secret society" that would turn its back on politics and whose only goal would be *religious* (but anti-Christian, and essentially Nietzschean). This society was formed. Its intention was expressed in part in the review *Acéphale*, which published four issues from 1936 to 1939. The College of Sociology, founded in March 1936 [*sic*: for 1937], was somehow the external activity of this "secret society": This "college," whose realm was not sociology as a whole, but "sacred" sociology, made its presence felt through several series of lectures. Other than Bataille, its founders were Roger Caillois, and Michel Leiris. Lewitsky, Jean Paulhan, and Georges Duthuit were among the lecturers there.
Copyright © Editions Gallimard, 1976

1961   Jean-Louis Bédouin, *Vingt ans de surréalisme, 1939-1959* (Paris, 1961), p. 48.

The venture undertaken by surrealism has nothing in common with any sort of attempt at religious restoration. It does not aim at a mystical renaissance. Consequently, from the beginning the surrealists took as much distance as possible in relation to an enterprise such as the one Bataille attempted to found before the war—a sort of Dionysian cult, inspired, contradictorily, by Christian mysticism and the Nietzschean will to power. Among Breton's friends there were, to be accurate, some of the former audience of the "College of Sociology," who earlier and for various reasons had followed the experiment Bataille proposed and who, therefore, are even more than anyone else in a position to point out its dangers— not the least of which was the nonobservance of elementary rules of mental hygiene. This critical contribution, not negligible, comes from Robert Lebel, Patrick Waldberg, and Georges Duthuit, whose accounts Breton published in *VVV*, meaningfully entitled *Vers un Mythe nouveau? Prémonitions et défiances*.

1963   Roger Caillois, *L'Homme et le sacré* (Paris, 1963), Collection Idées, no. 24 ("Préface à la troisième édition").

. . . I imagined it was possible to transform ardent knowledge into an all-powerful lever within its own realm. Under these conditions, I scarcely distinguished the education I was to receive at the École pratique des Hautes Études from Marcel Mauss and Georges Dumézil, from that which, together with Georges Bataille and Michel Leiris, I ventured to propose in the modest room of the College of Sociology that we had just founded.

More than one page in this present volume is explained by this ambiguous origin, which puts the need of restoring an active sacred to society, a sacred that is indisputable, imperious, devouring, with a taste for cold, correct, together with scientific interpretation of what we (no doubt naively) then called the profound forces behind collective existence. I spoke of an active sacred: It was "activist" that we chose to say then, at least among us, to mean that we were thinking of something more than simple action. We were thinking of goodness knows what sort of vertiginous contagion, an epidemic ferment. Obviously, we did not give this epithet "activist" the very special sense it has gotten from current events.[3] We were referring to chemistry and to the sudden, irresistible explosive nature of certain reactions. It was wishing for miracles, and, in fact, these hollow ambitions went unheeded. I am persuaded that even without the war they would have misfired. I simply mention them to suggest that, more often than one imagines, enthusiasms of this sort have been able to inspire work that later seemed of an entirely different kind, less hot-blooded—in a word, the fruit of an effort at detachment.

Copyright © Éditions Gallimard, 1950

1967 Roger Caillois, "Divergences et complicités," *NRF*, April 1967 ("Hommage à André Breton"), p. 691. Reprinted in *Cases d'un échiquier* (Paris, 1970) under the title "Intervention surréaliste (Divergences et connivences)."

I distanced myself from surrealism to distance myself further from literature, learning only slowly and much later its reason for existence.

I then founded, with Georges Bataille—specifically to break bridges with literature—the College of Sociology. In a lifetime there are many things that repeat, all the more when one tries to avoid their repetition. With Georges Bataille I ran into the same difficulties I had encountered with André Breton, specifically a similar propensity for badly assessing what are words and what are things—or beings. This time, the conflict—which never broke out—bore on the possibility of conjugating and unleashing energies starting from the ritual execution of a consenting human victim. Bataille's attitude on this point was just as exasperated as Breton's definition of the simplest surrealist act: Go into the street with a revolver and shoot haphazardly at passersby.

Copyright © Éditions Gallimard, 1970

1969 Pierre Klossowski, "Entre Marx et Fourier," *Le Monde*, May 31, 1969, supplement to no. 7582 (special page devoted to Walter Benjamin).

I met Walter Benjamin during one of the meetings of Contre-Attaque—the name of the ephemeral fusion of groups headed by André Breton and Georges Bataille, in 1935. Later he assiduously attended the College of Sociology, an emanation intended to make "exoteric" the closed and secret group Acéphale (crystallized around Bataille, following his rupture with Breton). From this point on he was sometimes present at our secret meetings.

Disconcerted by the ambiguity of "acephalean" a-theology, Walter Benjamin disagreed with us, arguing that the conclusions he then was drawing from his analysis of German bourgeois intellectual evolution, namely, that the "increasing metaphysical and political buildup of what was incommunicable" (according to the antinomies of capitalist industrial society) was what prepared the favorable ground for nazism. For the time being he was trying to apply his analysis to our own situation. He wanted to keep us from slipping; despite an appearance of absolute incompatibility, we were taking the risk of playing into the hands of a "prefascist aestheticism." He clung to this interpretative scheme, thoroughly colored by Lukács's theories, in order to surmount his own confusion and sought to enclose us in this kind of dilemma.

There was no possible agreement about this point of his analysis, whose presuppositions did not coincide at all with the basic ideas and past history of the groups formed successively by Breton and Bataille, especially Acéphale. On the other hand, we questioned him even more insistently about what we sensed was his most authentic basis, namely, his personal version of a "phalansterian" revival. Sometimes he talked about it to us as if it were something "esoteric," simultaneously "erotic and artisanal," underlying his explicit Marxist conceptions. Having the means of production in common would permit substituting for the abolished social classes a redistribution of society into *affective classes*. A freed industrial production, instead of mastering affectivity, would expand its forms and organize its exchanges, in the sense that work would be in collusion with lust, and cease to be the other, punitive, side of the coin.

1979   Jules Monnerot, *Sociologie du communisme* (Paris, 1979), pp. 539ff. ("Le Collège de Sociologie ou le problème interrompu," appended by the author to the reedition published by Éditions Libres-Hallier of this work that originally appeared in 1963 at Gallimard).

What is this "College of Sociology" that you were evidently mixed up in when you were still a student? What were you doing there? Did you participate, yes or no? Since this "College" is directly, even, I would say, genetically related to *Sociologie du communisme*, I am taking the present occasion to satisfy— as far as I am able—my questioners' wishes. . . .

Between the two world wars of the twentieth century, some very young, and less young, men . . . spontaneously were able to come up with the idea, in order to put a necessary stop to the stagnation [that of a statelike monopoly control exercised by Durkheimians on sociology], of privatizing sociology in our country. At least that is what I began to think when I read in the review *La Critique sociale*, not at the date it appeared but much later, the text by Georges Bataille entitled "La Notion de dépense." I wanted to meet the author. It was easy. We were brought together by friends we had in common. And Bataille soon afterward published "La Structure psychologique du fascisme" in two installments (the last two issues of the review). Afterward, I introduced him to Roger Caillois whom I had met shortly before at André Breton's place on rue Fontaine.

Prompted by my taste for understanding certain dominant phenomena of the first half of the century (communism, fascism), I then conceived of a program of research composed mainly of *the approach to burning issues* that in France established sociology (in the sense the English speak of the established Church) either avoided or briefly touched on, bringing prejudices that dated from the nineteenth century. . . . Such a field of research was to be (though not exclusively) explored by a group I had internally baptized the "College of Sociology," created for this purpose. I confided in Bataille about this and it seemed to appeal to him. And to Caillois, the enthusiastic student of Georges Dumézil whom few of us knew at that time. The project I had just formulated thus "held together," but "in the absolute." When it came to realization, our conceptions, our ideas, and our behavior (Bataille's, Caillois's, and mine) rather quickly proved divergent. Bataille had frequently more or less stirred up "groupuscles," which were as quickly abandoned and were something of a literary coterie, a Trotskyite "fraction," a dissidence in the heart of dissidence. It was peculiar to the epoch and the milieu, and our friend had, it seems, the temperament of a heresiarch. Roger Caillois, born a great French writer, who had already at the age of eighteen the intellectual authority and grammatical infallibility that we have always known him to have since, was awaiting the publication at Gallimard of his first—brilliant—book *Le Mythe et l'homme*. Both of them envisaged starting forthwith into public activity, lectures, and statements. I thought it was first necessary, if not to perfect a method, which was far from having been done, at least to truly come to agreement. I expected no good to come of improvisation in such matters, and at my insistence, at Bataille's place on rue de Rennes, I asserted and developed a certain number of propositions on the subject. I remember how my argument went.

If, I said, the program of the "College of Sociology" is made up of the approach to "burning issues," we must expect to be burned ourselves by this inflammable material . . . excluded from scholarly bibliographies and societies, therefore from the organized and international system of established science. But we are up against a dilemma. What is its other horn? It is what you are very gradually in the process of choosing. I'll call it literary insignificance. . . .

My objections met with neither objection nor approval. They were declared to be extremely interesting. . . . Somewhat later, I noticed that Bataille, and doubtless Caillois, who were contributing to the *Nouvelle Revue française*, were turning in the direction of *literary eventuality*. I told Bataille straight off—curtly and with an impatience that I have no explanation or excuse for today—that I would not participate in the venture under these conditions. He did nothing to hold me back. I told him to consider it permanent and we left it there. A little later, I received a letter from Caillois with this sentence in it: "If you think people are making free with you, is the solution in abstaining? Come, and stand up for your point of view." But that was what I had already done. Consequently, I did not participate in the ways in which the "College of Sociology" made itself more or less known to the public—before an ultraspeedy disbanding that was easy to foresee.

Notes

Notes

Foreword: Collage

1. Georges Bataille, "L'Existentialisme," *Critique*, 41 (October 1950), p. 83.

2. Maurice Nadeau, *The History of Surrealism* (New York: Macmillan, 1968).

3. In "The Work of Art in the Age of Mechanical Reproduction," a text that first appeared in French (*Zeitschrift für Sozialforchung*, 1936) in a translation by Pierre Klossowski, who was to introduce Benjamin to the College. Also in "André Gide et ses nouveaux adversaires" (1936 also). See Walter Benjamin, *Illuminations* (New York: Schocken, 1969).

4. The example appears in Bataille's *Guilty*, trans. Bruce Boone (Los Angeles: Lapis Press, 1988). During the existence of the College, Bataille was living at Saint-Germain-en-Laye. His commuting train (to go to the Bibliothèque Nationale, or to meetings of the College) arrived at the Gare Saint-Lazare.

5. W. Benjamin, "Theses on the Philosophy of History," written at the beginning of 1940. See his *Illuminations*.

6. Philippe Lacoue-Labarthe and Jean-Luc Nancy, *The Literary Absolute: Theory of the Literature of the German Romanticism* (Albany, N.Y.: SUNY Press, in press).

7. Peter Bürger, *Theory of the Avant-Garde* (Minneapolis: University of Minnesota Press, 1984).

8. Sigmund Freud, "Group Psychology and the Analysis of the Ego," *Complete Works of Sigmund Freud*, vol. 18, pp. 65-143 (London: Hogarth Press, 1955).

9. Roger Caillois, *Man and the Sacred* (Glencoe, Ill.: Free Press, 1959), pp. 68-69; Marcel Granet, *Danses et légendes de la Chine ancienne* (Paris: PUF, 1959), vol. 1, p. 333; *La Pensée chinoise* (Paris: Albin Michel, 1934), p. 140; *Chinese Civilization* (New York: Knopf, 1930), p. 169.

10. Hans Mayer, *Ein Deutscher auf Widerruf, Erinnerungen* (Frankfurt: Suhrkamp, 1982), p. 241.

11. See the sections "Together," "Men without Women," and "A Winter's Tale," of my *The Politics of Prose: Essays on J.-P. Sartre*, trans. Jeffrey Mehlman (Minneapolis: University of Minnesota Press, 1987), pp. 175-88.

12. J.-L. Nancy, *La Communauté désoeuvrée* (Paris: C. Bourgois, 1986), p. 41. Bataille: "Be-

ing, it is true, is scarcely imaginable without sex—by general consent the absolute is accorded male attributes." "Qu'est-ce que le sexe?" *Critique*, 11 (April 1947), p. 372.

13. Maurice Blanchot, *La Communauté inavouable* (Paris: Éditions de Minuit, 1983), p. 17.

14. Pierre Klossowski, "Qui est mon prochain?" *Esprit*, 75 (December 1938) (cf. the introduction to "The Marquis de Sade and the Revolution").

15. Étiemble, "C'est le bouquet!" In *Hygiène des lettres* (Paris: Gallimard, 1952).

16. M. Foucault, *The History of Sexuality*, vol. 1 (New York: Pantheon, 1978), pp. 88-89.

17. Bataille, "Toward a Real Revolution," *October* [MIT Press], 36 (Spring 1986), pp. 32-41.

18. Rosalind Krauss, "No More Play," in *The Originality of the Avant-Garde and Other Modernist Myths* (Cambridge, Mass.: MIT Press, 1984).

19. Mayer, *Ein Deutscher auf Widerruf*, p. 241.

20. Cf. D. Hollier, "I've Done My Act: an Exercise in Gravity," *Representations*, 4 (Fall 1983), pp. 88-100 (for Sartre), and "Mimesis and Castration 1937," *October*, 31 (Winter 1984), pp. 3-15 (Caillois).

21. Jeffrey Mehlman, "Blanchot at *Combat*," in *Legacies of Anti-Semitism in France* (Minneapolis: University of Minnesota Press, 1983).

22. Blanchot, *La Communauté*, p. 37, and "L'Athenäeum," in *L'Entretien infini* (Paris: Gallimard, 1969), p. 517.

23. Raymond Aron, *Mémoires* (Paris: Julliard, 1983), p. 71.

24. Among those who answered Monnerot's inquiry one finds several specialists on the unconscious including Dr. R. Loewenstein (Lacan's psychoanalyst), who, as his analysand would reproach him, saw no wrong in intervention: "The function of the psychoanalyst, whether he is a doctor or an instructor, is to facilitate the adaptation of the unconscious and affective part of the human being with the new social and moral conditions of a society in the midst of evolution." Another response came from Dr. Jenny Roudinesco, the mother of Lacan's biographer. See Monnerot, "Il y a toujours eu des directeurs de conscience en Occident," *Volontés*, 14 (February 1939), pp. 202-204, 160-61.

25. "Le Mythe et l'art. Nature de leur opposition," *Congrès international d'esthétique et de science de l'art* (Paris: Alcan, 1937).

26. Michel Leiris, *La règle du Jeu, III. Fibrilles* (Paris: Gallimard, 1955), p. 153.

27. Denis de Rougemont, *Journal des deux mondes (1939-1946)*, in *Journal d'une époque (1926-1946)* (Paris: Gallimard, 1968), p. 507.

Note on the Foundation of a College of Sociology

1. Three points about this note that appeared at the bottom of the page: First, the signatories date the composition of this manifesto in March 1937, and therefore it is approximately contemporary with Caillois's reading of "Winter Wind"; second, it is not in October, but November 20, 1937, that the College will begin to be active; third, it is stated that this activity "*to start with . . . .* will consist in theoretical instruction." This discreet adverbial phrase is the only trace in this manifesto of the "practical" ambitions of the College and its intention to adopt and exploit what has just been defined as the "activist" character of collective representations. Bataille's opening lecture of November 20, 1937, will conclude with the provisory (and somewhat strategic) distinction between "knowledge" and "practice." In contrast, the conspiratorial ambition of these sociologists is made much more explicit in the 1938 version of this manifesto that appears in "For a College of Sociology," at the end of Caillois's "Introduction." We do not know if this final, explicit paragraph was cut from the first publication out of caution, or if it was added for the sake of clarity to the next.

2. First, Leiris does not figure among those who signed this "Note." Second, Georges Ambrosino, a physicist, will not speak at the College. Third, Klossowski will speak there, but like Ambrosino, his connection was more with *Acéphale*. Fourth, I do not know who Pierre Libra was. His reply to Monnerot's inquiry on the subject of "the directors of conscience" appears later. Fifth,

as for Monnerot (who signs himself sometimes Jules Monnerot, sometimes J.-M. Monnerot), along with Caillois he was on the editorial board of the short-lived *Inquisitions* before contributing to *Acéphale*. In 1974, more than thirty-five years later, he would adopt the title *Inquisitions* for his own use, giving it to a collection of articles the last of which is devoted to Bataille. Reading the College's reply to the inquiry concerning "directors of conscience" that he conducted in *Volontés* we will see that "the association [= the College] owes the name it bears" to Monnerot. He will not participate, however, in the activities of the College. His eclipse has to be linked with the "often stormy episodes" of what Caillois calls the "tortuous founding of the College of Sociology" (*Approches de l'imaginaire* [Paris, 1974], p. 58). In the first issue of *Critique* (June 1946), Bataille would publish a long article on Monnerot's book *Les Faits sociaux ne sont pas des choses*. In it Bataille mentions also the work of Leiris and Caillois but without naming the College. Monnerot's book *La Poésie moderne et le sacré* (Paris, 1945), completed in December 1940 (see his note 33), includes no mention of the activities of the College, despite the fact that their bibliography and their problematic are extraordinarily close.

P.S.: Monnerot added recollections about the College to the reedition of his *Sociologie du communisme*, which appeared in 1979. Some extracts from these will be found in the "Marginalia" collected in the Appendixes. It came out at the same time as the French edition of this volume, which thus was unable to take these into account.

For a College of Sociology: Introduction

1. Bataille, in *Acéphale*, played on the double meaning of this adjective—the activity of being critical, a state that is critical ("Chronique nietzschéenne," *OC*, vol. 1, p. 478). The ambition of the College could be said to be overdetermined, that is, the double resolve to critique democratic society and to put society's moving forces into a critical state.

2. These lines sound like Valéry (the Valéry of "La politique de l'esprit"; see *Variété III* [Paris, 1936], p. 196: "We have, in the space of a few decades, reforged, rebuilt, organized at the expense of the past, etc., etc."), taken up again by Bachelard's Nietzschean epistemology in *Le Nouvel esprit scientifique* (1934). This "Introduction," moreover, may be read as the "predication," in the Bachelardian sense, of a sociological experiment of which the College would be simultaneously the experimenter, the tool, and the guinea pig. The first (and only) issue (June 1936) of Caillois's review *Inquisitions* opened with Bachelard's text "Le Surrationalisme," in which one can read: "If one doesn't put one's reason at stake in an experiment, this experiment is not worth attempting." Bachelard would conclude his *Lautréamont* (1939) with wonderful pages on the theory of a forward and aggressive imagination underlying Caillois's *Le Mythe et l'homme*.

3. This is the text of "Note on the Foundation of a College of Sociology" that appeared in July 1937 in *Acéphale* and that opens the present collection.

4. In reality, the College was supposed to function on a relatively more selective (or elective) basis than this formula would have one understand. The program of meetings for the year 1937-38 stated: "Entry to the room will be reserved for members of the College, bearers of an invitation in their name, and (one time only) persons presented by a registered member." See the Appendixes: Records.

5. This last paragraph is not included in the text of the "Note on the Foundation of a College of Sociology" published a year earlier, in July 1937.

The invoking of the soul that concludes it is somewhat reminiscent of a remark by Maurice Halbwachs in his *Morphologie sociale*, which had just appeared (Paris, 1938). After having mentioned, in reference to the unanimist descriptions of Jules Romains, that there are social groups whose "body is apparent, but whose soul fluctuates," he insists that "at the opposite extreme, a society of saints, indeed of philosophers, is never a society of pure spirits: It has a body, even when it forgets it and tries to be detached from it" (p. 55).

The Sorcerer's Apprentice

1. (a) The paradox of sociology: Reaching the highest stage of the division of social work (sociologists as they constitute an independent and officially recognized professional body), sociology discovers at the same instant, however, what Mauss calls the total social phenomenon. It is, therefore, by its position incapable of drawing the lesson of its own discoveries for itself. Only an institution (a "College") will be able to do this, by grafting onto the total phenomenon an all-embracing, "totalizing" ambition (see Leiris's use of this term in Caillois's "Festival," note 22). (b). Contrary to Marxism and the theory of the ultimate economic determination of social phenomena, "French sociology" (Durkheim, Mauss, etc.) insists on the decisive nature, above all, of collective, religious representations where primitive societies are concerned.

2. Speaking of Sade, Klossowski will use the term "complete man" (*homme intégral*) (see "The Marquis de Sade and the Revolution"). There, too, the concept of totality and completeness will be linked to a proud and glorious incapacity to serve, a refusal to function: polymorphism vs. functionalism.

3. The *moral* devastations of science: In the "Note on the Foundation . . .," the College presented itself as "a moral community, different in part from that ordinarily uniting scholars." Caillois, in other texts, had already remarked on the demoralizing, simultaneously discouraging and corrupting, nature of modern science (see, among others, *Approches de l'imaginaire*, p. 27).

4. The following paragraph, which appears in the manuscript, was not kept in the published text: "The will to *re-action* is the only one that brings into play the great figures of destiny created by fatherland and flag. *Myths* without which there is no *totality* of existence, cannot be presented as the aim of action unless it is a question of a conflicting form. Even at that, myths of reaction are only old myths, with an impoverished content, that miss by a long shot the totality they claim. Reaction, no more than revolutionary action, is not compatible with a will to transform the world and to make it correspond to a profound exigency. Action always demands of the one who undertakes it that he renounce his dream."

5. The manuscript has here a sentence not preserved in the published version: "Even if vital exuberance obliterates the memory of the few inevitable interventions, only the part played by the impulsive element and by facts blindly *submitted to* contains the effective charm that binds the happy lover as much as the dying man or the murderer."

6. A quote from Luther used by Bataille the previous February 19 during the lecture entitled "Power" that he gave based on Caillois's notes (see Lectures: 1937-38). It is from the 1526 treatise *Can Men of War Also Achieve Beatitude?* Denis de Rougemont, in a note in *Esprit* (May 1937, "Retour de Nietzsche") discussing the issue of *Acéphale* devoted to Nietzsche and the Fascists, was scandalized by the Nazis' appropriation of the Germanic reformer: "They say also, doubtless for the rhyme, 'Luther precursor of Hitler.'" He goes on to say, "As if he were the ancestor not of Niemöller, Christian and Lutheran, but of Hitler, a pagan born a Catholic." See also the preface written at the same time by D. de Rougemont for Luther's *Traité du serf arbitre* (Paris, 1937).

7. Language much overused in 1938: The penetration of existentialism onto the left bank of the Rhine and its full-time installation on that of the Seine, are, if one may say so, translated into an intemperate use of the expression "human reality." It appears in Wahl's account of Leiris's lecture at the College (where there is a question of the future of the "science of human realities"). And Sartre, in *Esquisse d'une théorie des émotions* (1938), suggests that "as Heidegger believes, the ideas of world and of 'human reality' (*Dasein*) are inseparable." Corbin once again is responsible for this mistranslation (see Beaufret [1945]: "This word *Dasein* is rather generally translated by 'human reality.' Nothing is further from the exact, concrete sense of the word *Dasein* that seeks, on the contrary, to grasp the living nature of momentary presence bursting forth"; *Introduction aux philosophies de l'existence* [Paris, 1971], p. 16). Corbin, the "translator of Heidegger," was already responsible for the neologism *ipséité* that Sartre reproached Bataille for having borrowed from him

(*Situations I*, p.159); Cf. Bataille's recollections on this subject: "I am supposed to have borrowed the word *ipséité* from a translation by Corbin, but this translation (whose manuscript I never saw) came out after the text was published in the review (*Recherches philosophiques,* 1936 [the text in question was 'Le Labyrinthe ou la composition des êtres']) in which this word appears. Sartre is right to emphasize my interest in contemporary German philosophy. It was on my behalf that Henry Corbin proposed to my friend, Jean Paulhan, in 1929 the publication in the *NRF* of a translation of *Was ist Metaphysik?* (later I was told that Julien Benda protested. Anyway, the text was refused. The translation by Alexandre Koyré then appeared in *Bifur*" (*OC*, vol. 8, p. 666). Actually, the translation that came out in *Bifur* (no. 8, June 1931) is signed "M. Corbin-Petithenry"; the four introductory pages are by Koyré. It is noticeably different from the one Corbin did of the same text in *Qu'est-ce que la métaphysique?* (Paris, 1938). Thus *Dasein* is rendered not by "human reality" but, more simply, by "existence."

8. This sentence recalls something Bataille said in his letter to Kojève on December 6, 1937 (see Kojève, "Hegelian Concepts"): "As far as I am concerned, my own negativity only gave up on being used only when it no longer had any use; it is the negativity of a man with nothing left to do, not that of a man who prefers to talk."

9. On these distinctions, see the lecture on secret societies that Bataille gave the previous March 19, once again in place of Caillois.

The Sacred in Everyday Life

1. Cf. Baudelaire in *Fusées*: "I have found my definition of the Beautiful—of my Beautiful." Leiris refers to this definition in the *Miroir de la tauromachie* (note 8).

2. This "Smith and Wesson" will be mentioned in "Dimanche" (*La Règle du jeu*, vol. 1, [Paris, 1948], p. 196). In "Les Tablettes sportives" (*La Règle du jeu*, vol. 2, [Paris, 1955], p. 154), Leiris tells of how, during the war, he had to get rid of this revolver that he had inherited from his father.

3. "La Radieuse," whose trademark means "The Radiant One" is mentioned in *L'Âge d'homme* (p. 70 of the 1946 edition).

4. On this distinction between the two poles, the right and the left, of the sacred, see Bataille's later lecture "Attraction and Repulsion" (February 5, 1938). The distinction has its sociological origin in Robert Hertz's study "Prééminence de la main droite" (1909), reprinted in *Mélanges de sociologie religieuse et de folklore* (Paris, 1928). In 1933, Granet returned to the subject in "La Droite et la gauche en Chine" (reprinted in *Études sociologiques sur la Chine* [Paris, 1953]). This bipolarity is essential to the sacrificial aesthetic that Leiris develops in *Miroir de la tauromachie* (published in 1938 in the collection "Acéphale": "Always, everything will happen between these two poles acting as living forces: on the one hand, the right-hand element of immortal beauty, sovereign and plastic; on the other hand, the sinister left-hand element, located on the side of misfortune, accident, and sin." See also, in the same text, the importance (moral as much as aesthetic) of "left-handed passes" in bullfighting. Caillois, as well, fixes on the "polarity of the sacred" to which he devotes a chapter of *L'Homme et le sacré* (1939): "The right-hand and adroitness manifest divine purity and favor, the left-hand and clumsiness manifest pollution and sin." More recently he has reexamined it in *La Dissymétrie* (1973, reprinted in 1976 in *Cohérences aventureuses*).

5. This entire passage will be used again in "Dimanche" where Leiris compares the bathroom to "a secret society's den" [p. 215]. On the subject of the excretory function as the support propping up narrative, of the verbalization of anality, the German anthropologist K. Th. Preuss, cited by Bataille in his lecture "Attraction and Repulsion," had developed the idea of a magic proper to the different body orifices and, in particular, of an excretory magic. Durkheim, in *Les Formes élémentaires de la vie religieuse* (p. 328, 1912 edition), provides an excellent formulation of how this works: "The sacred character assumed by a thing is not implied in the intrinsic properties of that

thing: *It is in addition to these.*'' In *Psychologie collective et analyse du moi,* chapter 10, Freud contrasted the "excretory needs" that, "as can be seen nowadays among children and soldiers," allow of "a satisfaction in common" and the sexual act "during which the presence of a third person is superfluous at the very least."

6. *Miroir de la Tauromachie:* "All in all, everything is played out dangerously near a threshold as narrow as a razor's edge, a thin intervening zone or psychological *no-man's-land* that would constitute the epitome of the realm of the sacred." (p. 56 of the 1964 edition).

7. Conforming to a topography modeled on the principle "The good at the center, evil on the periphery," Caillois, in *L'Homme et le sacré,* makes the bush the specific locus of the impure forces that implement magic, insofar as it is opposed to religious orthodoxy: "Therefore it is in the bush, far from the village, that the sorcerer has his initiation." See also, in *Esquisse d'une théorie générale de la magie,* the places Mauss designates for the performance of magic ceremonies (in *Sociologie et Anthropologie* [Paris, 1960], p. 39).

8. Evocation of the races at Auteuil is one of the generating nuclei around which "Les Tablettes sportives" are organized.

9. On shamanism, see the lecture given by Lewitzky (Leiris's colleague at the Musée de l'Homme) March 7 and 21, 1939.

10. This "empty hall" reappears in "Il était une fois . . .," *Biffures,* p. 165).

11. These phonic associations—"Rebecca," "Mecca," "impeccable" are repeated in "Vois! Déjà l'Ange . . .," that concludes *Fourbis* (p.182).

12. ". . . Reusement!" is the first text of *La Règle du jeu. Biffures* opens with it.

13. Moïse, "Moisse," Seine-et-Oise, "osier": this sequence will be taken up again in "Alphabet" (*Biffures,* p. 55).

The Winter Wind

1. This formula from Origen is cited by Nietzsche, p. 341 in the edition of *The Will to Power* mentioned in note 3, this chapter ("The Christian with his formula *extra ecclesiam nulla salus* reveals his *cruelty* toward the enemies of his band of Christians"). This quotation and the one that follows are taken from the section edited by Würzbach under the title "L'Organisme social."

Klossowski will return to this after the war, in the chapter of *Sade, mon prochain* (Paris, 1947) evoking Bataille's ambitions during the College period, an enterprise intended, he says, for "souls who experience their life *extra ecclesiam* as a disembodiment and who go off in search of a body that they feel unable to acknowledge in the body of the Church" (p. 155).

2. See for this date, the first footnote in "Note on the Foundation of a College of Sociology": "This declaration was composed as early as March 1937."

3. "For the most part" is probably an allusion to Monnerot's desertion.

4. In the first and only issue of *Inquisitions* (June 1936), Caillois had given a brief review of the translation (by G. Bianquis) of the edition established by Würzbach of the work Nietzsche "took to be his essential work." He concludes with this homage to the editor: "His work, therefore, is destined to render the greatest service to all those who wish to study Nietzsche's ever-more-current thought." This review was followed by an equally short note on Thierry Maulnier's *Nietzsche,* from which the following comment is taken: "It is significant to see one of the youngest theoreticians of the extreme right begin with a work on Nietzsche and write, at the end of the preface: 'The taste for blood must be returned to philosophy. We must return to metaphysical systems their cruelty: their power of life and death.' This preoccupation is not foreign to us, far from it; and we count on taking lessons from Nietzsche also among others. The differences come from somewhere else." *Inquisitions,* as mentioned previously, was published by the official press of the French Communist party.

5. On the opposition of the *Luciferian* and the *Satanic* see "Paris, mythe moderne" (in *Le Mythe et l'homme,* p. 199) (commenting on "the intractable convict on whom the prison always shuts"):

"This is specifically the complex that I call the *Luciferian* spirit. It corresponds to the moment in which rebellion turns into a will for power and, losing none of its passionate and subversive character, attributes to intelligence, to the cynical and lucid vision of reality, a role of prime importance for the realization of its plans. It is the passage from *agitation* to *action*." See also "Naissance de Lucifer" in *Verve* (December 1937). And, in the interview with Lapouge, apropos Lewitzky's lecture on shamanism: "The question fascinated me . . . I felt I was very Luciferian then, I took Lucifer to represent effective rebellion."

It should be noted that Sartre (whose *La Nausée* had just come out in March 1938), in July 1938 began composing the novel that would appear seven years later under the title *Les Chemins de la Liberté*. In 1938 it was called *Lucifer* (see Contat and Rybalka, *Les Écrits de Sartre*, p. 27).

6. The concept of a society's density (not simply demographic but moral) had been introduced by Durkheim in *De la division du travail social* (1893); the progress made by lower societies as they became "higher" societies would be accompanied by a condensation. On the contrary, for Caillois this progress entailed a loosening that the College intended to remedy.

7. This neologism appeared in Caillois's review of Ph. de Felice's work, *Poisons sacrés, ivresses divines* in *Cahiers du Sud* [April 1937]: "Religion essentially appears as a force of reunification and communion, as a force not for social dispersion, but on the contrary, if I may risk a neologism, for *sursocialization* insofar as it is specifically the presence of the sacred that makes a community indissoluble." It appears again in "Les vertus dionysiaques" published by *Acéphale* in its July 1937 issue devoted to Dionysus: It is in Dionysism, Caillois writes, that what was marginal becomes the foundation of social life and it is, hence, the asocial that "gathers together collective energies, crystallizes them, rouses them—and demonstrates that it is a force of *sursocialization*."

At the beginning of the thirties, Bataille had lit into the prefix "sur" ("La Vieille taupe et le préfixe *sur* dans les mots *surhomme* et *surréalisme*," *OC*, vol. 2, p. 93). For his part he preferred to play around with *a*. But the epoch belonged more to overstatement than to the privative. Jarry's *surmale* (supermale) is already old, as is the Freudian *surmoi* (superego), when Dumézil risks a *surroi* (superking) (*Flamen-Brahman* [Paris, 1935], p. 40). In February 1938, Faulkner's *Sartoris* inspired Sartre to a *surprésent* (superpresent). As a matter of fact, Claude-Edmonde Magny soon would speak of the *sur-roman* (super-novel) apropos Sartre. It was in 1936 that Bachelard had introduced *surrationalisme* (superrationalism) in *Inquisitions*. Moreover, Bataille himself it is said, described *Acéphale* as a *surfasciste* (superfascist or beyond fascist) endeavor.

8. In the *NRF* of September 1939, Caillois would devote a note to the Cardinal de Retz (whose *Mémoires* had just appeared in the Pléiade edition) and several other leaders of the Fronde riots: "the sort of beings on whom passions, other than that for domination, have very little hold . . . beings that Corneille (it is not known whether he was their portrayer or the chief among them) defined in one stroke, writing that 'their nobility of temperament subjects everything to their glory'" (*Pompey*, p. 373). See also the school edition of *Le Cid* published by Caillois in 1939 (Classiques France).

9. In "La Hiérarchie des êtres" (*Les Volontaires*, no. 5 [April 1939], special issue entitled "Le fascisme contre l'esprit"), Caillois goes back to the distinction, which Bataille borrowed from Nietzsche, "between the *land of the fathers* (*patrie*, *Vaterland*, fatherland) and the *land of the children* (*Kinderland*)."

10. To be precise, this is "the temptation of St. Anthony" that both "La Mante religieuse" (pp. 72 and 87) and "Mimétisme et psychasthénie légendaire" (p. 141) cited in *Le Mythe et l'homme*. There is also a reference in "Les Démons de midi," a study of the forms of noontide *acedia*. (*Revue de l'histoire des religions*, December 1937, p. 162). Also a note on the importance of this theme for a "general phenomenology of the imagination" in *Cahiers du Sud*, September 1936, p. 676. In this note, Caillois refers to André Chastel's studies on *La tentation de Saint Antoine* (*Gazette des Beaux-arts*, April 1936; see also his "Légende de la reine de Saba," *Revue de l'histoire des religions*, *March-December 1939*). *Chastel himself was later to say that these works were indebted to Caillois's intuitions: "Acedia, 'spiritual' torment, twists its way through the innermost recesses of 'Mimétisme et

psychasthénie légendaire': I made it be the psychological key of the *Tentation de saint Antoine"* ("La Loyauté de l'intelligence," in *Roger Caillois, Cahiers pour un temps* [Paris, 1981], p. 30). On Chastel's relations with the College, see these recollections of the art historian himself: "We went to hear Dumézil or Granet rather than Alain who was all the rage then (we = Caillois and Chastel). It all went fast: The winter the College of Sociology was begun, based on new alliances, I was in the army, but I submitted a short text to *Inquisitions* whose title I did not find shocking" (ibid., p. 31). Chastel, as well, was himself to give a response to Monnerot's inquiry on spiritual advisers, the "directors of conscience," in the most orthodox and most militant terms (*Volontés*, no. 18 [June 1939], p. 31).

11. See "La Hiérarchie des êtres": "It will not seem senseless, speaking theoretically, to assume the principle of a *hierarchy of beings* that is universally valid, regardless of any sort of determining elements that are collective or external, such as race, nationality, religion, class, fortune, birth, etc. One is then led to imagine an *elective community* developing beyond the limitations that constitute those determining factors. This elective community would be an *order composed of men who are resolute and clear-headed, who are united by their affinities and by the common will to subjugate (unofficially at least) those of their fellows who have no talent for self-direction.* It would be an association of extreme density, imposing its own architecture on the various structures already in existence and working to decompose some of these while domesticating others. . . . Be that as it may, it is precisely this principle of equal rights, universal as democracy would have it or restricted as fascism would call for it to be, that is irrevocably rejected by the notion of *order* or of an elective community" (p. 323). To avoid any ambiguity, Caillois entrusts the realization of these ambitions to the Communist party, the only worthy successor to the Society of Jesus. Cf. on this subject, the remarks included with Mauss's letter to Élie Halévy (See Appendixes).

12. Balzac, in the preface to the *Histoire des Treize.* Baudelaire, in chapter 9 of "Le Peintre de la vie moderne." Caillois gives these references again in "Paris, mythe moderne" (*Le Mythe et l'homme,"* pp. 201-2). See also the notes that appeared in the *NRF:* for June 1936 on Ferran's book *L'Esthétique de Baudelaire* ("the problem precisely is in knowing if his [Baudelaire's] specific endeavour was not somehow to knock over (a violent term is necessary) aesthetics, tipping it in the direction of ethics. Never does he judge any work of art with the nuances of a man of taste, but rather with the *pious rages* of some inquisitor.") In March 1937, on the subject of Bouteron's Balzac in the Pléiade edition: "The *Comédie humaine* is intended to be *as imperative an illustration as possible* of a system of tastes rather than of ideas, which regards *passion* —that includes simultaneously *thought* and feeling—as both grounding and undermining social life to the greatest possible degree." Finally, in January 1938, the final volumes of this same edition of Balzac: "Vautrin reveals that he is as much the ruler as the rebel. He is less the survivor from among those irresolute romantic consumptives than the first figure and the portent of a race of conquerors who are both practical and voracious." D. H. Lawrence's name must also be included in this "set of the willful few"; see Caillois's "Brotherhoods," note 8.

In the eyes of Caillois, Corneille also was essentially "a student of the Jesuits" (see the edition of *Le Cid* mentioned in note 8 and "Résurrection de Corneille," *NRF,* October 1938). Last, I would recall *Inquisitions* (the review founded by Caillois in 1936) and the work announced (though it would never appear) on the flyleaf of *Le Mythe et l'homme —Le Saint-Office (textes militants).*

13. See "L'Agressivité comme valeur," *L'Ordre nouveau,* no. 41 (June 1937), p. 57, where Caillois writes: "Since various considerations, still least among which are economic data, tend, moreover, to divide people morally into *producers* and *consumers,* extraordinary emphasis must be placed on the infinite plasticity of the latter in respect to the refractory nature of the others." (On the review *L'Ordre nouveau,* see Bataille and Caillois's "Sacred Sociology," note 15.) These consumers are the satisfied victims of what Bataille in "The Sorcerer's Apprentice" calls "the absence of need." On this subject see Caillois, in "La Hiérarchie des êtres": "All the pleasures are theirs, pleasures of the flesh and the spirit as well, with the exception of the arid joys of independence and power

that they themselves, by means of the very things that make them happy and that dry up other thirsts at their source, render foreign, as though they were inconceivable.''

14. Caillois had published a review of *Service inutile* in *Inquisitions* (June 1936): ''It is possible to derive from it,'' we read there, ''a certain number of fundamental ethical principles that are suitable to include in the code of honor of a moral aristocracy: the importance accorded to contempt, to courtesy, and to restraint.'' In a note that appeared in February 1939 in *Volontés*, ''Le Mythe et l'imposture'' (a note full of allusions to themes debated by the College, and especially, to Guastalla's lecture, which took place several weeks before), Queneau also would praise *Service inutile* (the note is reprinted in *Le Voyage en Grèce* [Paris, 1973]). On the other hand, in the *NRF* of January 1939, Caillois published a very harsh article on *L'Équinoxe de septembre*, written by Montherlant on the heels of Munich. He does mention, however, that he still considers ''*Service inutile* to be the manual of a sound and important ethic.'' ''I regard,'' he goes on to say, ''his teaching as essential. Nearly all his maxims are golden rules.'' In fact, even very recently, in a posthumous tribute, Caillois wrote: ''There are many phrases if not pages of *Service inutile* that still ring in my memory'' (''Plaidoyer pour Tacite,'' *NRF*, February 1973). In ''L'Esprit des sectes'' (written during the war in Argentina and reprinted in *Instincts et société* [Paris, 1964]), Caillois would mention recollections that Montherlant published in 1941 in Drieu's *NRF* and in which he evokes ''a society that was somewhat codified and somewhat grim'' which he had founded, just after the other war, with several collegians among his friends. Leiris, in *Miroir de la tauromachie* (written in October 1937), cites Montherlant's *Les Bestiaires* in note 9. The table of contents of the (still Paulhanian) *NRF* of April 1940 included an article by Jean Wahl: ''Les 'Lépreuses' de Montherlant.''

15. See ''Jeux d'ombres sur l'Hellade'' (*Le Voyage en Grèce* and reprinted in *Le Mythe et l'homme*, p. 179): ''What vindicates Theseus is less that he conquered the Minotaur than that he had to fight it, and monsters predestine the ones to be demigods.''

16. Caillois proposed a collection to Gallimard that would concern ''tyrants and tyrannies'' (see the letter to Bataille quoted in ''Brotherhoods,'' the first projected titles: *Heliogabalus* and *Cheu Hoang-Ti* (to whom ''L'Ordre et l'empire,'' in *Le Mythe et l'homme*, was devoted). At the beginning of 1938, also at Gallimard, Élie Halévy's posthumous work *L'Ère des tyrannies* appeared; its title repeats that of an intervention that he made in November 1936 at the Société française de philosophie. It was following this intervention that Mauss sent him the letter that Caillois asked Bataille to allude to (included in the Appendixes). For all of this, see the lecture entitled ''Power'' given by Bataille, February 19, 1938.

Declaration of the College of Sociology on the International Crisis

1. On September 28, before departing for Munich, Daladier made a radio statement: ''Before my departure, I wish to address my thanks to the people of France for their extremely courageous and dignified attitude. I especially wish to thank those Frenchmen who were called to arms for their calm and their resolve, of which they have given new proof'' (the mobilization of certain categories of reservists had been ordered on September 24). In his speech at the Chamber of Deputies on October 4, Daladier repeated the same themes: ''It was the proven resolve of France that made success possible. We must render here to our beloved and great country the homage that is its due'' (Daladier, *Défense du pays* [Paris, 1939], p. 148).

2. Actually, the Germans in Sudetenland had only one desire, namely, to escape the Czechoslovakian dictatorship by returning to the ample bosom of the Third Reich. Chamberlain gave this report of his September 15 interview with Hitler to Commons: ''He says that if I could give him at once the assurance that the British government would accept the principle of self-determination, he would be entirely disposed to discuss the ways and means of applying it'' (quoted by Nizan, *Chronique de septembre* [Paris, 1939], p. 66).

3. Joseph Chamberlain (1836-1914) was the British colonial secretary from 1895 to 1903, and the leader during this period of the "imperialist" movement. On his support for Cecil Rhodes (owner-founder of Rhodesia) and his attitude during the Boer War (to which he sent General Kitchener, who, after a fragile victory, put down the tenacious Boer guerrillas with exemplary cruelty), one should read Élie Halévy's *Histoire du peuple anglais au XIXe siècle*, the volume entitled *Les Impérialistes au pouvoir (1895-1905)* [Paris, 1926]. Chamberlain, the self-made man, has many traits that prefigure those of twentieth century dictators. To oppose German and American competition, he made the British Empire into a commonwealth, whose independent members applied preferential tariffs to one another. This imperialist politics fit curiously into his dreams alongside the utopia of a united Teutonic race in which England, Germany, and the United States would be in agreement to counter the Franco-Russian schemes. This project was a product of an intention that could only have favorably impressed Hitler in respect to the author's son. On the subject of Chamberlain, there is also W. L. Strauss, *J. C. and the Theory of Imperialism* [Washington, 1942], and R. Koebner and H. Dan Schmidt, *Imperialism: The Story and Significance of a Political Word (1840-1960)* (Cambridge, 1964).

4. An allusion apparently to the letter he sent to Hitler on September 28, in which he says he is confident that Hitler can "get all the essentials without war and without delay"; see Nizan, *Chronique de septembre*, pp. 141, 164, 215. From the beginning of the crisis, Chamberlain made no secret of the fact: He was the advocate of peace—*at any price*.

5. The American public feared that its government would let it be dragged into a new "European" war because of the Czechoslovakian crisis. The approaching presidential elections made it particularly important, and Roosevelt gave reassurances in a speech delivered at Hyde Park on September 9. He ended with these words: "Including the United States in a British-French front against Hitler is a one hundred per cent false interpretation on the part of political columnists" (quoted by G. Bonnet, Foreign Affairs Minister of the Daladier government, in *Défense de la paix. De Washington au Quai d'Orsay* [Geneva, 1946], p. 211).

6. In June 1939, in issue 5 of *Acéphale* (written entirely by Bataille but not signed), two articles: "La Menace de guerre" and "La Joie devant la mort." This phrase is extracted from the first: "A man without strength to value his death as fortifying is something 'dead'" (*OC*, vol. 1, pp. 550 and 552).

Inquiry: On Spiritual Directors

1. [Normally, the French "directeur de conscience" is the equivalent of "spiritual adviser." This can be as banal as a "Dear Abby" or as time-honored as a "father confessor." But, as is the case both with other banalities and with religious terms in the context of the College, it is its revitalization that is at issue here. The contemporary concern with words rooted in the Latin *dirigere* (cf. Gramsci's *direzione*), as well as many of the stated intentions of the College (especially those of Caillois) led me to replace the weaker "adviser" with "director." (Occasionally, however, its more ordinary translation will appear in the text when it seems particularly appropriate.) The French "conscience" also poses problems because the morality implicit in "conscience" should be retained as well as the expandable knowing of "consciousness." "Spiritual" is the best I could do. All in all, "spiritual directors" is a real compromise, but for all these functions no common expression exists in English capable of revitalizing itself on its own terms as does "directeur de conscience."—Trans.]

2. Bataille's "La Notion de dépense" appeared in January 1933 in *La Critique sociale*. "La Structure psychologique du fascisme" was published a few months later, in the November 1933 and March 1934 issues of the same review. These two texts appear in volume 1 of the *Oeuvres complètes* and are translated in *Visions of Excess: Selected Writings, 1927-1939*, ed. Allan Stoekl (Minneapolis, 1985).

3. Klossowski's reply, along with those of Jacques Dehaut, Paul-Louis Landsberg, Marcel

Moré and Denis de Rougemont, together are introduced by these lines: "Some, who meet not only here, send to you in five different forms a common, but not collective, response." These five replies actually express a point of view that is personalist and Christian.

4. In these lines of Duthuit's one finds the proclamatory rhetoric borrowed from Balzac's *Histoire des Treize*, with which the participants in the College will habitually describe their venture; see particularly, in the Appendixes: Marginalia, the excerpts from Monnerot and Caillois quoted on pp. 383 and 381, respectively.

Duthuit delivered a lecture to the College of Sociology on June 20, 1939, entitled "The Myth of the English Monarchy," the text of which has not been found. He was to speak at the Société de Psychologie collective with Camille Schuwer on the theme "The Artistic Representation of Death." An article of his on the same subject would appear in the issue of *Cahiers d'art* (no. 1-4 [1939], p. 226) that he organized in connection with the College. Accompanying it were Bataille's "Le Sacré," and "Le Complexe de Polycrate, tyran de Samos" by Caillois.

See Robert Lebel, "Quand le feu fait des signes à Duthuit," *Critique*, no. 198 (November 1963), p. 973. "He was mixed up in the political and doctrinal battles of the moment. He appeared at the 'College of Sociology' where before the last war, a fruitful debate on the *sacred* was taking shape. Although his undertaking was related to that of Georges Bataille, who sought to reconstitute religious ecstasy without religion, their agreement was short-lived. The same misunderstanding later, in New York, when similar preoccupations temporarily brought him in contact with André Breton and the Surrealists."

5. Guastalla delivered a lecture to the College of Sociology on January 10, 1939; see Lectures: 1938-39. According to Georges Blin, it was through Monnerot that he became acquainted with the College.

6. Guastalla's book *Le Mythe et le livre* was published by Gallimard at the beginning of 1940.

7. Concerning *La Flèche*, the daily newspaper published by Bergery and his "front Commun," see Guastalla's lecture, "The Birth of Literature," January 10, 1939.

8. Pierre Libra's name is among those signing the July 1937 "Note" of *Acéphale*; see "Note on the Foundation of a College of Sociology." I have not encountered it elsewhere except in this inquiry. I am reproducing here only about a third of his rather long reply. The unqualified Maurrassian racist point of view that it develops shamelessly will be apparent. Perhaps the disappearance of this signatory from the College's scene may have something to do with one of the rites Bataille insisted on bestowing upon it. Caillois recalls these in his interview with Lapouge: "Bataille always was determined to reinforce the College with a sect endowed with a very precise ritualism. For him the Sacred would only reappear thanks to the celebration of rites. Some of his rites were rather impractical, for example, the idea of celebrating the death of Louis XVI, January 21 on the Place de la Concorde. Other rites were less complicated, like our sticking to the obligation to refuse to shake hands with anti-Semites."

Maurras's joke about the Republic as the "headless woman" is well known, and not to be confused with Acephalus who is the headless man. I was informed by Monnerot that Pierre Libra died in combat in April 1940.

9. This judgment does not reflect the sentiment of the College on this best-seller whose success almost made Caillois regret the invention of the printing press (in a note in the *NRF* of March 1936). In view of the truisms it diffuses, "popular wisdom suddenly looks like enigmatic suggestions and unfathomable paradoxes." Caillois continues: "The author writes: 'Those who are proletarians today owe their situation to hereditary defects of mind and body' (*sancta simplicitas*), and proposes that appropriate measures come to accentuate this situation so that social inequalities are more clearly concomitant with biological inequalities. Society would then be directed by a hereditary aristocracy formed from the descendants of Crusaders, heroes of the Revolution, great criminals and financial and industrial magnates. A few pages later, apparently unaware of the abrupt mutation, he contemplates suppressing the proletariat, on the contrary, by making all young men perform obligatory ser-

vice in the factories." There is no doubt we are looking at an unpardonable contradiction. The first solution, however, heredity aside, is not far removed from the dreams the College was to develop two years later.

10. See comments on Paulhan and his relations with the College in the Introduction to "For a College of Sociology," and his lecture "Sacred Language," delivered May 16, 1939.

Sacred Sociology

1. First, modified by the vocabulary and ambitions of the College, we find here the stance with which French sociology confronts the Marxist trend. For Marxists society is defined by a conflict (class struggle). For French sociology, society is defined by what it calls cohesions. See Mauss, apropos Durkheim: He "strongly objected to any war of the classes or of nations" (*Oeuvres*, ed. Karady [Paris, 1969], vol. 3, p. 507). A society, Mauss said elsewhere, is defined "by its will to be one" (ibid., p. 315). Second, this unitarianism is not, however, expressed in the objective language of French sociology, much more in that of Simmel, Weber, and Tonnies whom Raymond Aron had just introduced to France (*La Sociologie allemande contemporaine* [Paris, 1935]). Caillois praises this book highly in a brief review of Sorokin's *Les Théories sociologiques contemporaines* (*NRF*, April 1939, p. 707). Aron for his part would publish a review of Caillois's book *Le Mythe et l'homme* in Horkheimer's Parisian review *Zeitschrift für Sozialforschung*.

2. Durkheim's *De la division du travail social* (sec. 1 and 7) and Mauss's *Essai sur le don* disproved the theory identifying the social with the contract: The contract presupposes an already established social body and could not be its origin.

3. Remember that Georges Ambrosino (signer of the note in *Acéphale* was a physicist. He attended the discussions of the College throughout. Bataille, after the war, while editor of *Critique* asked him to write several articles on physical questions. The preface of *La Part maudite* (1949) ends with Bataille's thanks to Ambrosino for all that the book owes to him (*OC*, vol. 7, p. 23).

4. Durkheim, in *Les Règles de la méthode sociologique* (Paris, 1895, p.127); "Society is not a simple sum of individuals, but the system formed by their association represents a specific reality that has its own characteristics." This type of formula (X is more than or different from the sum of its parts), vitalist in origin, was very much in vogue in gestaltian circles. Bataille gives a definition of this "more" that is interesting in its precision: the whole is the *movement* that takes over the parts.

5. Émile Belot, "Le Rôle capital de l'astrophysique dans la cosmogonie," *Scientia*, 304 (1937), pp. 74-82.

6. On the definitions of "being" that this "compound ontology" inspires in Bataille, see first, "The Sorcerer's Apprentice": "Not the being that rational philosophy represents by giving it the attribute of immutability, but the being that a first name and a patronymic express, and then the double being who is lost in endless embraces—in a word a city being who 'tortures, beheads, and makes war.' And second, "Le Labyrinthe" (1936): "'Being' grows in the tumultuous excitement of a life that knows no limits: It languishes, and slips away if the one who is simultaneously 'being' and knowledge mutilates himself by reducing himself to knowledge" (*OC*, vol. 1, p. 434).

7. "Equally granting perception to the inorganic world; an absolutely precise perception—there "truth" reigns!—Uncertainty and illusion begin with the organic world." Bataille quotes this phrase of Nietzsche's in the second issue of *Acéphale* ("Propositions sur le fascisme"), in January 1937, See *OC*, vol. 1, p. 470.

8. Bataille's analyses in "La Notion de dépense" (1933) and Caillois's in the texts of *Le Mythe et l'homme* brought phenomena of consciousness and phenomena of nature together into the same homogeneous and continuous series: Consciousness *qua* consciousness would obey the same laws as inorganic matter.

9. We should note what it is in the College's inspiration that is more or less expressly dependent on Jules Romains's unanimism. Caillois, in his "Préambule pour L'Esprit des sectes" (see Appen-

dixes: Marginalia), will refer to *Recherche d'une Église*, the seventh volume of the novelistic series of *Les Hommes de bonne volonté*, which had appeared in 1934. He acknowledged from it the expression of a "taste for darkness and for power" shared by the College. André Cuisenier's *Jules Romains et l'unanimisme* was published in 1935. "Psychic reality," said Jules Romains, "is not an archipelago of solitude" ("Petite introduction à l'unanimisme" [1925] in *Problèmes européens* [Paris, 1933], p. 232). "If, a certain number of men brought together by the most arbitrary chance, in addition form a lasting union, where some action germinates, they tend to become something other than a certain number of men" (p. 235). And, in *Puissances de Paris*: "We will teach groups to become gods."

10. The concept of "person" (not to be confused with "individual") had recently taken on a particular intensity with the manifestos of the personalist movement just published by Mounier (see especially *Anarchie et personnalisme* [1937]). The movement had regrouped around *Esprit*, edited by Mounier. Klossowski was a contributor. Other contributors connected to the College were Paul-L. Landsberg, Denis de Rougemont, Marcel Moré. In the May 1937 issue of this review, there is a note from de Rougemont apropos *Acéphale* that confirms what Bataille says here: " 'Acéphale' is the sign of radical antistatism, that is to say, of the only antifascism worthy of the name. This society, which has no single head, is more or less what, in less romantic terms, we call a federation. On this crucial point, it seems much easier to make Nietzsche and his disciples agree with personalism than with any other political doctrine" (p. 314). In the same issue, a note from Landsberg on the same subject expresses the same opinion: "The contributors to the Acephalus [*sic*] are here writing as personalists in defending the personal essence of a thought that one cannot separate from the life of a man or from the totality of his experience" (p. 296). *Esprit* was a Catholic review. See J.-L. Loubet del Bayle, *Les Non-conformistes des années 30* (Paris, 1969).

11. On the subject of secret societies, refer to the lecture Bataille delivered the following March 19.

12. On this concept borrowed from Rabaud, see Caillois's lecture "Animal Societies."

13. The College refuses to belong to de facto communities. The elective communities that it opposes to them, communities of persons brought together by elective affinities, could be defined as communities of value. What value? Precisely that of the community as such: a community of those for whom the community is a value and not a fact. One's country is only a fact: It would be stupid to deny it, it is morally inadmissible to limit oneself to it.

Here the College departs from the opinions of its masters in the school of French sociology, in order to approximate the terminology and inspiration from across the Rhine that Raymond Aron had just brought to France.

14. In the margins of the manuscript, Bataille added these notes: "(1) De facto communities: clan, phratry, tribe, nation, civilization, humanity. (2) Elective communities, based on Lowie: a) army, b) simple organizations, administrations, production teams." Robert Lowie, the anthropologist from Berkeley, had just had two of his works translated into French by Éva Métraux, the first wife of Bataille's "oldest friend" (Métraux herself was connected with the Ethnographic Museum at the Trocadéro): his *Manuel d'anthropologie culturelle* and his *Traité de sociologie primitive* (Paris, 1935). Chapters 10 and 11 of the latter are entitled respectively: "Associations" and "Theory of Associations." In the *Cahiers du Sud* in 1937 (shortly after this lecture), Caillois published a review of these two books: "The part concerning government," he wrote, "remains too perfunctory, but the two chapters on the half-secret, half-official associations that have such an important place in the life of those who are not civilized are a remarkable clarification, in fact, of one of the questions figuring among those whose investigation has been put on the agenda by events."

15. These sentences refer to the groups (like Contre-Attaque, both literary and political, toward which Bataille rather strongly inclined in the thirties. The last of these, the so-called secret society of Acéphale, was contemporary with the College.

16. Bataille's note at the bottom of the page: "For *elective community* as opposed to traditional community see Ordre Nouveau—Cuvillier pp. 32-36."

The first part of the footnote doubtless refers to an article by Caillois in the June 1937 number of *L'Ordre nouveau*. The issue's theme was "Revolutions and revolution," the title of the article, "Aggressivity as a Value." The note seems to refer to what one reads there: "Each time one comes upon a community of men whose union is not the result of an enslaving or clever past or fate, but the concerted result of a mutual choice, dictated by a convergent will and an image of the goal to be pursued, this community (whether the Society of Jesus or the Ku Klux Klan), though absurdly restricted in size to begin with, has always, however, known a success that is oddly disproportionate to its beginnings." On the movement "L'Ordre nouveau," one can consult J. Touchard, "L'esprit des années 1930," in *Tendances politiques de la vie française depuis 1789* (Paris, 1960), and J.-L. Loubet del Bayle, *Les Non-conformistes des années 30*. Its founders were Arnaud Dandieu (librarian at the Bibliothèque Nationale, who died in 1933 at the age of thirty-six) and Robert Aron (who was working at Gallimard). Several of its members, like Denis de Rougemont, were also involved in *Esprit*. None of the members of the College took part in it, despite the affinities evidenced by Caillois's contribution to the review of the same name, *L'Ordre nouveau*. Besides, "The New Order" was to lose much of its audience as the Popular Front rose to power. After 1937 the review had troubles with publication. It disappeared in 1938.

The second part of the note refers to Armand Cuvillier's *Introduction à la sociologie* (Paris, 1936), in which pages 32-36 are devoted to *Organicism* and summarize the theses of Herbert Spencer, Albert Schäffle, G. de Greef, Espinas, and René Worms. Of Schäffle we are told that for him "society is an 'intentional organism,' an *organization* rather than an organism."

17. Bataille's descriptions hesitate, as we shall see, between a pyramidal and a labyrinthine depiction of social structure. Feudalism is pivotal in this fluctuation: depending on its submission to the central (monarchistic) power or, on the contrary, its rebelliousness. On this point, refer to Klossowski's lecture, "The Marquis de Sade and the Revolution."

18. See Caillois's "Paris, mythe moderne" and Walter Benjamin's "Paris, Hauptstadt des XIXe Jahrhundert."

Hegelian Concepts

1. Kojève contrasts the conflict and impotence of Novalis when faced with Napoleonic power to the harmony that made the couple, Napoleon-Hegel, prevail. Caillois also targeted Novalis for attack in the special number of the *Cahiers du Sud* (1937) devoted to German romanticism, but he took his departure from Fichte's theory of knowledge, not from the exigencies of action, attending to the intellectual process of the romantic lie and not to a political critique. Bataille will dissociate himself, by his statements in "The Sorcerer's Apprentice" about the "man of fiction," from the depiction of the "beautiful soul," the *belle âme*, that Kojève gives here: that truth is not satisfying is not sufficent cause for one to be satisfied with dreams or lies.

2. It is not because it is afraid to act but because action fails it that negativity finds it has no use. Its situation is different from that of the "beautiful soul": Disinvolvement with historical and political action is not the result of an initial choice.

3. The version of this letter published in *Le Coupable* has at this point: "It is introduced into a system that nullifies it and only affirmation is 'recognized.' The algebra of recognition prohibits negativity, in effect, from making itself recognized as such, as Bataille is to remind us on the following February 5. Paradoxically, he will even go so far as to illustrate this law using Hegel himself as an example, saying that his work, "insofar as it recognizes negativity, has itself not been recognized."

4. What follows was not printed in *Le Coupable*. This censorship, like the addition mentioned in the preceding note, is indicative of the direction in which Bataille took his "self-criticism" after the failure of the College of Sociology. At the time he writes this letter, he thinks that negativity must be able to make itself be recognized, that even without a historical use, it must, at least as a last resort, apply itself to making itself recognized. When he publishes it, he thinks that recognition focuses only

on how negativity *betrays* itself, positively. In 1937 he sides with Hegel whom he wants to have recognized as the father of the negative. In 1944 he dissociates himself from Hegel because he is far too recognizable.

5. The owl is the bird of Minerva. Hegel said that it took flight only at nightfall: just like the philosopher who has the distinction of always arriving too late, when everything is over and done.

6. The *Tierreich*; Kojève translates this as "bestiary," and Hyppolite translates it as "the mind's animal kingdom."

Animal Societies

1. See "Corps célestes" (published in *Verve*, Spring 1938): "The absence of radiance, or 'cold,' abandons the Earth's surface to an 'overall movement' that appears to be a universally *devouring* movement, whose predominant form is life. At its peak anthropocentrism is the culmination of this tendency: The weakening of the terrestrial globe's material energy has made possible the constitution of human existences that are just so many ignorances about the movement of the universe." (*OC*, vol. 1, p. 518).

2. See "Le Labyrinthe" (published in *Recherches philosophiques*, 5 [1936] and reprinted in *L'Expérience intérieure* with the title "Le Labyrinthe [ou la composition des êtres]"): "Being is never found except as a unity composed of particles whose relative autonomy is maintained" (*OC* vol. 1, p. 437). This text gives later (p. 440) two illustrations of "compound ontology": the city and laughter. Bataille is to pick up again on these in his lectures; see especially pp. 84 and 111.

3. The reference is to Étienne Rabaud, *Phénomène social et sociétés animales* (Paris, Alcan), 1937. Chapter 3 describes and defines what the author means by "interattraction" (pp. 100-103). This is an extract: "Its essential characteristic is to operate between individuals independently of their sex, to operate in a very prolonged, often permanent manner. It does not, therefore, result in any way from a momentary physiological condition, renewing itself at various intervals in some animal or other, whether solitary or social, but rather from a fundamental physiological condition, of a constitutional nature one might say." Concerning Rabaud, see "Attraction and Repulsion I." Rabaud's (antisociological) thesis in the work just quoted consists in maintaining that the insertion of an individual into a group does not change in any way either the nature or the behavior of that individual: "Interattraction is reduced strictly to itself. . . . Life in common involves no consequences for its constituents. . . . The effect of interattraction is limited to the secondary bonding of individuals with each other" (pp. 107-8).

4. This no doubt refers to Rabaud's observation: "One day I watch a cow alone in a pasture that is surrounded by a hedge and separated from the road. On the other side of this road, in the neighboring pasture that is also hedged, four cows are grazing. The behavior of the isolated animal is both very curious and characteristic: She trots back and forth along the hedge; every now and then she stops, stubbornly looking at the four cows across the way who are peacefully browsing. . . . Finally, she knocks the gate down and would go into the next field if no one intervened. The attraction exerted by her fellow creatures is so obvious that the peasants notice it and tell someone. She is quickly limited to just herself; in groups, or isolated, the cow's way of life doesn't change" (p. 110).

5. Opposition to Durkheimian sociology appears in numerous passages of Rabaud's book, see in particular, pp. 6-10 and 274ff.

The Sacred in Everyday Life

1. The philosopher Paul-Louis (or Ludwig) Landsberg had been the pupil of Max Scheler. Born (Bonn, 1901) of a Jewish family but baptized by a Protestant minister, it was said to be only the Church's condemnation of suicide that kept him from converting to Catholicism (see his *Essai sur l'expérience de la mort* [Paris, 1936], which appeared in a French translation by the author in col-

laboration with Pierre Klossowski). He must first have left Germany in 1933 for Barcelona (where Bataille, who was there completing *Le Bleu du ciel*, met him in 1935; see "Les Présages," *OC*, vol. 2, pp. 266-70). Driven out of Spain by the civil war, he next took refuge in Paris where he would actively participate in the personalist movement (writing in *Esprit* and in *Les Nouveaux Cahiers*). In 1937, he gave a course at the Sorbonne on the philosophy of existence. In his response to Monnerot's inquiry (included with those of Jacques Dehaut, Klossowski, Marcel Moré, Denis de Rougemont), he would oppose "spiritual directors" and "crowd leaders" (*Volontés*, no. 18 [June 1939], p. 43). Interned in 1940, Landsberg refused to emigrate to the United States where Maritain wanted to have him invited. Arrested by the Gestapo in March 1943, he died at Oranienburg (a concentration camp) in 1944. His *Einführung in die philosophische Anthropologie* (Frankfurt am Main, 1934) was republished in 1960. He was also author of works devoted to medieval philosophy, to Plato's Academy, to Pascal, and to the Augustinian theory of grace.

Attraction and Repulsion I

1. November 20, "Sacred Sociology."

2. Also November 20 (but Caillois's presentation was not written down).

3. December 4, "Hegelian Concepts." (I have not turned up any text in which Kojève mentions the problem of "the foundations of sociological science.")

4. The lecture of December 19 on "Animal Societies."

5. An allusion, apparently, to Leiris's lecture "The Sacred in Everyday Life" (January 8, 1938).

6. These are the reflections that I have included here in place of the missing lecture by Caillois ("Animal Societies").

7. Bataille showed his disagreement with Rabaud in his lecture at the Society of Collective Psychology: "Primitive disgust is perhaps the only violently *active* force that can account for the characteristic clear-cut exteriority specific to social things. I have the impression that if only immediate sympathy (what Rabaud calls interattraction) constituted society, it would not quite appear as we see it" (*OC*, vol. 2, p. 285).

8. For Bataille (for organicism) society is an individual. For Rabaud it is made up of individuals. These two propositions are mutually exclusive. See the quotation from Rabaud, included by Cuvillier in *Introduction à la sociologie*: "A society is made of individuals, and the individual only exists free of any material tie; as soon as a material link, a physiological dependency, is produced, the individual disappears" (p. 37).

9. Rabaud is a biologist. Most of the examples in his book are taken, in fact, from the insect world: bees, wasps, ants . . .

Two of the studies Caillois collected in *Le Mythe et l'homme* focus also on insects: the one describing the praying mantis, and the one treating mimetic phenomena. Although the latter twice cites Rabaud (pp. 112 and 122), it is not hard to see the difference between these two authors. For Caillois, a sociologist at that point, the insect world does not serve to prime a theory of interattraction but as the magnetic inductor of a series of fascinated repulsions. He outlines a theory of what one might call the taboo of the insect.

10. Freud "Psychologie collective et analyse du moi," in *Essais de psychanalyse*: "The social sentiment thus is based on the transformation of an originally hostile sentiment into a positive attachment."

11. "Attraction and Repulsion II: Social Structure," delivered on February 5, 1938.

12. In the manuscript margin, Bataille noted: "nucleus of silence."

13. It was doubtless following this remark that Caillois came to recall the ambiguity of a line from Virgil: "incipe, parve puer, risu cognoscere matrem" (*risu*: his or her smile?). Bataille mentions this intervention in a note in *Le Coupable* (*OC*, vol. 5, p. 389).

14. C. W. Valentine, "La psychologie génétique du rire," trans. by S. Dalinier, *Journal de psychologie normale et pathologique*, 33 (November-December 1936). This article had been cited by Bataille in his lecture at the Society of Collective Psychology: "Valentine . . . thus cites a young girl who is generally very humane and very good, who, every time she heard a dead person mentioned, could not keep from laughing. There is, likewise, an example of a man who could not see a burial without having an erection, so much so that he had to leave his father's burial" (*OC*, vol. 2, p. 287). This last example, whose origin is undetermined, would reappear quite later in *La Littérature et le Mal* ("Sade"): "A young man could not see a burial without feeling physically aroused; for this reason he had to leave his father's funeral procession" (*OC*, vol. 9, p. 254).

15. This definition is given by Rabaud on page 101 of his work *Phénomène social et sociétés animales* (1937). See "Animal Societies," note 3, this volume. To this positivity as the basis of society, Bataille would oppose the Hegelian negativity, which he rewrote into "unemployed negativity" in his next lecture.

16. On the problem of recognizing one's kind, see Caillois who in "Winter Wind" bases his hierarchical ethic on this recognition: "In that manner an ideal line of demarcation hardens, along which each of us distributes those who are his *fellow creatures* and the others." Remember, in regard to this, that it is in 1936 (in Marienbad) that Lacan proposed for the first time his theory of the "mirror stage" in which he links the recognition of a fellow creature and the elaboration of the ego (identification of the ego and identification with the other). In the version that he gives of this in 1949, he mentions Caillois's work and his ideas "newly at odds with the sociological background where they were formed" (*Écrits*, 1966, p. 96).

17. Edith S. Bowen, "The Role of the Sense Organs in Aggregations of *Ameiurus melas*," *Ecological Monographs*, I, (January 1931): The cutting of the olfactory nerves has no effect upon the positive reactions to other fishes in either blinded or normal individuals. . . . Vision is an important factor in the integration of these aggregations. Neither blinded fishes nor normal fishes in the dark ever aggregate, and normal fishes follow a small moving object in a way which, if continued, would result in aggregation formation" (p. 33). In 1934, Queneau published a novel, *Gueule de pierre* (later recast in *Saint-Glinglin*), the first part of which, entitled "Fish," began with a mention of schools of fish: "Papa! Mama! Life in a school of fish is really too dreadful" (p. 10).

18. Pierre Janet, "Les troubles de la personnalité sociale," *Annales médico-psychologiques*, 95, part 3 (1937), pp. 421-68. Note that Janet was "quite willing to accept the presidency" of the Society of Collective Psychology. In the lecture he would give in the context of this society (even more short-lived than the College), Bataille would also mention this article by Janet: "Professor Janet emphasized that the individual subject is not easily distinguished from the fellow creature that he relates to, from the *socius*" (*OC*, vol. 2, p. 287). A little later, at the time he was drafting *L'Expérience intérieure*, Bataille would closely read Janet's book *De l'angoisse à l'extase* (*OC*, vol. 5, pp. 429 and 430). It was also Janet's definition of psychasthenia that Caillois borrowed to use in "Mimétisme et psychasthénie légendaire" (*Le Mythe et l'homme*, p. 130).

In the article cited here, Janet disputes Rabaud's theses (but grants that the sexual act is not a "social act") and refers with the highest praise (p. 447) to Lacan's thesis *De la psychose paranoïaque dans ses rapports avec la personnalité* (published in 1932).

19. "The Sorcerer's Apprentice," the section entitled "The True World of Lovers."

Attraction and Repulsion II

1. Was this in a discussion following an earlier presentation? Or perhaps in the "Chronique nietzschéenne" in *Acéphale* (July 1937) where Bataille gives a sort of account of *Numance*, Cervantes's play that Barrault had just staged. It has phrases such as "existence, that is to say tragedy" or "life requires united men and men are only united by a chief or by a tragedy" (*OC*, vol. 1, pp. 482 and 489). See also "La Mère-Tragédie" (1937) and in "L'Obélisque" (1938), the section entitled "Les 'Temps tragiques' de la Grèce" (*OC*, vol. 1, p. 493 and 507). Bataille will come back

to the question of tragedy in "Power" (February 19, 1938). Leiris also, in the *Miroir de latauromachie*, refers the Spanish bullfight to the organization of "ancient tragedy."

2. Phenomenology here should be understood in a sense that is as much Hegelian as Husserlian. See Bataille's references at the beginning of "La Structure psychologique du fascisme" (1933): This discussion, he says, "will not fail to shock those persons unfamiliar either with French sociology or with modern German philosophy (phenomenology) or with psychoanalysis" (*OC*, vol. 1, p. 339).

3. Bataille inserted a page here on which he notes the following reflections: "Difference between science and this doctrine. Working hypotheses (general interpretations) are not simply instruments of research as in science: They are that also. But, independent of anyone, the instrument of research in a particular case can be, simultaneously, an instrument of life. All sciences with medicine as their result are in the same situation." The opposition: (Hegelian) phenomenology /psychoanalysis (or, if one prefers, "human sciences") that is to be developed now had already been mentioned in the lecture at the Society of Collective Psychology. It was resolved there, specifically on the issue of attitudes when confronted with the dead, to Hegel's advantage: "Hegel's explanation," said Bataille, "has at least one advantage over Freud's" (*OC*, vol. 2, p. 286).

4. This is doubtless an allusion to the following anecdote, reported by Rosenkranz and quoted by Wahl (*Le Malheur de la conscience dans la philosophie de Hegel* [1929], 2nd ed. [Paris, 1951], p. 72): "This negativity that Hegel speaks of is finally death. A disciple of Hegel's, Rosenkranz tells us, during one lesson in which the master demonstrated systems destroying each other, succeeding each other, said of him: 'See, this man is death itself, that is how everything must perish.'" Bataille was struck by this anecdote, living his own contacts with Kojève on the same model, as these notes pertaining to *Sur Nietzsche* demonstrate: "From '33 (I think) to '39 I attended the course that Alexandre Kojève devoted to the analysis of *La Phénoménologie de l'esprit* (an inspired analysis, measuring up to the book: How many times were Queneau and I staggered as we left the small room—staggered, stunned). In that same period, by reading a great deal, I kept up with scientific trends. But Kojève's course broke me, crushed me, killed me ten times over" (*OC*, vol. 6, p. 416). We see that Bataille, too, crucified himself at Kojève's hours.

5. On the difficulties encountered by the recognition of the negative, see Bataille's letter to Kojève included at the end of "Hegelian Concepts."

6. It is difficult, in regard to these pages where the description of the village church is expanded to the point of evoking royal coronations, not to mention *Notre-Dame de Rheims*, this first short piece of a Bataille who was then considering attending seminary, published in 1918, and which I reprinted as the center of *La Prise de la Concorde* [Paris, 1974]. That its shadow reappears, in the very midst of the College of Sociology, is all the more significant in that it is cast by the light of the war threat. Remember that Caillois was born in Reims (no *h*) in 1913, or one year before Bataille left this city ahead of advancing German troops.

Remember also that in May 1937 the coronation of George VI took place. From an account of the event published in the *Revue des deux mondes* (June 1937) by Louis Gillet comes this description of the throne: "Neutral and secular, in its immemorial form and its attitude of impersonal expectation, this piece of furniture, pensive and enigmatic, seemingly fateful, is frightening. An intimidating solitude surrounds it. One feels that the man who soon will come to take his seat there is doomed to share in this immense solitude, which cuts him off from the world while exposing him to all eyes."

Finally, Gabriel Le Bras, who taught religious sociology at the École pratique des Hautes Études (in 1939 his seminar dealt with Christian brotherhoods), had promised Marc Bloch a volume entitled *L'Église et le village* (cf. F. Le Bras, *Études de sociologie religieuse*, vol. 2 [Paris, 1956], p. 493).

7. See, for example, the pages in *L'Afrique fantôme* where Leiris describes the sacrifice to Abba Moras Worquié (pp. 374ff.). The narrative is introduced by these restrospective remarks: "Never had I felt the degree to which I am religious; but with a religion where it is necessary that I be made to see the god . . ." (September 14, 1932). Another remark, on August 25, is certainly the remark of a "sorcerer's apprentice": "Resentment against ethnography, which causes one to take this very inhuman position of observer, in circumstances in which one should abandon oneself" (p. 350).

8. Bataille and Leiris were both psychoanalyzed by Dr. Adrien Borel (who participated in the Society of Collective Psychology mentioned earlier), Bataille in 1927, Leiris in 1929.

9. Bataille wrote initially: "or even high and low."

10. A reference to the "double funerals" described by Robert Hertz in his "Contribution à une étude sur la représentation collective de la mort" (1907), reproduced in the collection published by Mauss as *Mélanges de sociologie religieuse et de folklore* (Paris, 1928). Bataille had already cited this study in his lecture at the Society of Collective Psychology: "Facts relative to 'attitudes in the face of death' as regards primitive peoples have been developed in a sufficiently meaningful way by Robert Hertz in his *Étude sur la représentation de la mort*. These facts convey the most complex form of behavior in relation to the dead, taboo and violation of taboo, the attitude in relation to putrefaction and the attitude in relation to the skeleton, the necessity of a second funeral—subsequent to the bones' bleaching . . ." (*OC*, vol. 2, p. 282). This study will also be used by Caillois in his May 2, 1939, lecture. It is cited by Georges Duthuit in an article in *Cahiers d'art* (1939, nos. 1-4), "Représentations de la mort," which was accompanied by illustrations, some of which had figured ten years earlier in *Documents* and many of which will be reprinted in *Les Larmes d'Éros*. Duthuit had participated in the College's activities but left no recognizable trace of it—except, perhaps, this article. His response to Monnerot's inquiry on the spiritual directors is published here (see "Inquiry").

11. Konrad Theodor Preuss. It seems Bataille is referring to the article "Der Ursprung der Religion und Kunst" (*Globus*, 86 [1904], and 87 [1905]) that is mentioned in the bibliography of Caillois's *L'Homme et le sacré*. Caillois acknowledges how much this book, in fact, was influenced by the climate of the College, written in intimate proximity to Bataille. In volume 9 of *L'Année sociologique*, p. 239, Mauss praised this study in which Preuss connects the action of magic to different body openings (*Körperöffnungen*): the magic of defecation, of cohabitation (sexual emissions), and, for the mouth, the voice and breath. In 1937 Preuss had published, under Mauss's direction, a *Lehrbuch der Völkerkunde*, which has recently been reissued. It was his last work.

12. Freud, *Totem and Taboo*: "Society is based on a crime committed in common."

13. The last page of the manuscript is lost. The text of the lecture stops in the middle of this unfinished sentence. As we shall see, Caillois's participation in the activities of the College will become rarer for reasons of health. This is also the moment in which Caillois publishes, at Gallimard, his first important collection, *Le Mythe et l'homme* (in print March 28, 1938).

Power

1. See Caillois, *L'Homme et le sacré* (I quote from the 1950 edition), p. 64: "The configuration of modern cities on a certain level still makes the partly mythical, partly objective value of this disposition perceptible—at the center the church or cathedral (the seat of the divine), city hall, official buildings, the courthouse (the symbols and temples of power and of the authorities) . . ."

2. *L'Homme et le sacré* (referred to from now on as *HS*), p. 116: The king "has at his disposal every means of coercion that could force resisters into submission. But one must not overlook the fact that his intermediaries explain less than they demonstrate the effectiveness of power."

3. "Attraction and Repulsion I," delivered January 22, 1938.

4. Vimy, in the Pas-de-Calais, in September 1915 and then in April and September 1917, was the scene of violent fighting during World War I.

5. Albert Lebrun (1871-1950), elected President of the Republic in 1932 (after the assassination of Paul Doumer) and reelected in 1939. After the defeat of 1940, Pétain would call on him at the Élysée and tell him: "President, the painful moment has come." Lebrun then dropped the curtain on the Third Republic with which he was born. He recounted all of this in *Témoignage* (Paris, 1945).

6. The name of this fabric, Vichy, did not yet evoke a special political regime.

7. *HS*, p. 113: "a principle of individuation is asserted."

8. *HS*, p. 116: "Power appears as the realization of a will. . . . It comes as an invisible, addi-

tional, and irresistible virtue that is manifested in the chief as the source and principle of his authority.''

9. *HS*, p. 118: ''His person harbors a holy force that creates prosperity and maintains the order of the world.''

10. This priest is the king of the woods, ''the *rex nemorensis* who died so often before encountering Frazer and immortality'' as Dumézil puts it with erudite wit (*Mitra-Varuna* [1940] [1948], p. 100). Frazer organized his *Golden Bough* around this figure. The name of the priest-king-criminal was Dianus, soon to be taken by Bataille as a pseudonym (''L'Amitié,'' in *Mesures*, 1940).

11. The sixth part of the *Golden Bough* was entitled *The Scapegoat*. Caillois would make use of it in his May 2, 1939, lecture, ''Festival'' (see note 35).

12. Georges Dumézil, *Ouranos-Varuna. Étude de mythologie comparée indo-européenne* (Paris, 1934). In the *Cahiers du Sud* of June 1935, Caillois had published a brief commentary on this little book.

13. A power initially religious or magic and then an armed force: This is the period in which Dumézil is beginning his research on the sovereign function and its double aspect. The research will continue through 1938-39 and result in the publication in 1940 of *Mitra-Varuna. Essai sur deux représentations indo-européennes de la souveraineté*. In the preface to this work, Dumézil thanks Caillois whose questions obliged him to go into detail at several points in his investigation. For the army, see the next lecture (March 5).

14. On this point, see Mauss's letter to Élie Halévy that Bataille will quote in his lecture on secret societies (March 19, 1938) and that is reproduced in the Appendixes.

15. On this opposition between ''power'' and ''tragedy,'' refer to ''Attraction and Repulsion II,'' note 1.

16. In the margin Bataille noted ''repression.''

17. This phrase of Luther's will be cited again by Bataille in ''The Sorcerer's Apprentice.''

18. See, however, concerning the break with Christianity, a more cautious statement in ''Nietzsche et les fascistes'' in *Acéphale*, no. 2, (January 1937): ''The whole scene of the place made in Hitler's Germany for a free, anti-Christian enthusiasm, while pretending to be Nietzschean, thus comes to a shameful end'' (*OC*, vol. 1, p. 459).

19. See in Sade's *La Philosophie dans le boudoir*, Dolmancé's declaration, ''More effort, Frenchmen, if you want to be republicans. . . .'' And there is the following statement: ''An already old and corrupt nation that bravely shakes off the yoke of its government to adopt a republican one will only maintain itself through many crimes.'' This phrase is twice quoted by Bataille in *Acéphale* (*OC*, vol. 1, pp. 442 and 489). The lecture that Klossowski is to make at the College the following year, February 7, 1939, is also constructed around it.

The Structure and Function of the Army

1. This first fragment is entitled ''The mystical army'' (*OC*, vol. 2, pp. 232-37).

2. A first version of this sentence was ''a small strong animal with a large weak animal: the small and the large possessing each other. . .'' Opposition of the force produced by concentration and the weakening connected with extension. The sexual opposition of masculine and feminine is connected to this: Man tends in toward himself, woman extends herself. He is tight, she relaxes. Cf. the use of the word ''virile'' in ''The Sorcerer's Apprentice.''

3. The word is illegible in the manuscript.

4. This section comes from the fragment entitled ''Sacrifice'' (*OC*, vol. 2, p. 238).

5. What follows constitutes the fragment entitled ''Social Structure'' (*OC*, vol. 2, pp. 248-49).

Brotherhoods, Orders, Secret Societies, Churches

1. The letter is dated February 3, 1938:

Dear Bataille:

Here are the promised notes on secret societies. No doubt you will find them too brief and schematic. But I think, all things considered, that they are rich and easy to expand on. I am more and more struck by the importance of this point of view and the facility it provides for classifying every sort of thing. The structure owes almost everything to Dumézil: I have only abstracted and generalized (I have not even put things together). It is important to mention this and to refer to the works of D. (the *Centaures* and *Brahman-Flamen* especially) and to his course this year. I have been unable to give precise examples to fill in the outline because Dumézil is not eager for the detail of his research to become public domain. Send these two pages back to me as quickly as you can, please. I'd like to work a bit on them.

Take them to the session on Saturday. If I am in Paris, I'll make an appearance and comment on them myself (but there's one chance in a thousand).

I'd really like to have some news of the College: Will you send me, in as much detail as possible, an account of how it went last time and how it goes on Saturday?

Yours,

R. C.

P.S. How far have you gotten on your article for the *NRF?* I've proposed a collection "Tyrants and Tyrannies" at Gallimard—studies on the extreme forms of power. What do you think of the idea?

[Caillois refers here to Dumézil's *Le Problème des Centaures* (Paris, 1929) and *Flamen-Brahman* (Paris, 1935). The first of these works treats, especially, youth societies, which Dumézil's course at the Hautes Études would study again in 1937-38, in particular the Roman ones (Lupercalia). The article for the *NRF* mentioned in the postscript is "The Sorcerer's Apprentice." As for the collection "Tyrans et tyrannies," which never existed, it was to open with a book on Emperor Cheu Hoang-Ti and another on Heliogabalus.]

2. Further indented are the commentaries Bataille mixed in with Caillois's notes.

3. In Bataille's sense, the College must not be a conspiratorial society; its secret is not clandestine in the sense of political underground. See note 11, this chapter, and accompanying text.

4. Bataille had already copied this quotation in a file meant for *Acéphale* (*OC*, vol. 1, p. 645). It comes from volume 4 of Andler's book, *Nietzsche, sa vie et sa pensée* (p. 309).

5. All of these points are studied by Dumézil in his book about centaurs. Caillois will return to them in "Festival". It is the *winter wind*, remember, that rekindles the activity of the secret societies.

6. This dichotomy is at play less in society than in the function of sovereign power: alongside the gravity of the old (Mitra), the rapidity—in the etymological as well as the usual sense—of the young (Varuna). Dumézil will give this opposition its definite form in *Mitra-Varuna* (1940).

7. This letter was addressed by Mauss to the historian Élie Halévy after a lecture made by the latter at the Société française de philosophie on "The Age of Tyrannies." Halévy died shortly after reading this paper, which was to be reprinted (with Mauss's letter) in the posthumous collection edited by Raymond Aron that bears its title. The letter from Mauss is reproduced here in the Appendixes.

8. The meeting, March 1937, during which a first version of "The Winter Wind" was presented. Along with Balzac and Baudelaire, D. H. Lawrence (who is present in Caillois's "Paris, mythe moderne") must be referred to as well; Caillois will mention him again in a note in the *NRF* (May 1940) on *Ends and Means* of Aldous Huxley: "On the question of obedience, Huxley balks. He shies at Loyola's 'superior militarism.' . . . On this point, his confused friend, D. H. L. showed more lucidity when he *dreamed* of a sort of brotherhood of implacable aristocrats, governing the world with their mercenary ancestors' ancient cunning."

9. See the section entitled "Secretive."

10. Here Bataille had originally introduced a comparison of "secret societies" with that other Procrustean bed, "Bonapartism": Both terms proved to have an almost boundless conceptual hospi-

tality. "Is this not the place," he wrote, "to recall Trotsky defining Bonapartism and assigning to it in addition to Napoleon I, Napoleon III, Bismarck, von Papen, Stalin, and to top it all off President Doumergue." Bataille will return to these ideas in a note that is published here in the Appendixes: Fragment.

11. In the letter to Élie Halévy that Bataille just read. But it is a concept to which Mauss regularly had recourse; see, for example, the notes that make up his *Manuel d'ethnographie* (Paris, 1947) in the chapter entitled "Secondary Forms of Social Organization. Societies of Men. Secret Societies. Castes. Classes": "The question of the legality or illegality of the secret society will be asked. The way in which we too generally interpret the secret society as hostile to the State is an error. We always imagine secret societies from our society's point of view. There are, in fact, conspiratorial societies that, however, play a role in line with the law." In the same passage, Mauss indicates the "international character of secret societies" (p. 123).

As for Bataille, who already has had recourse to this distinction in the first lecture, he will again make use of it in "The Sorcerer's Apprentice."

12. Bataille is the one who forges this concept of an "existential" secret society. The influence of German philosophy actually is beginning to assume this tone, although we have not yet arrived at out-and-out existentialism.

Sacred Sociology of the Contemporary World

1. Hence, the College was going to create its own publication (meanwhile, it was welcome at the *NRF*). In the appendix I have given several notes on the subject by Bataille (Records). See also his letter to Caillois (Four Letters). I have done my best to recreate in the notes this bibliography that the College was unable to publish.

2. The manuscript stops in the middle of this sentence.

Tragedy

1. This is a good place to recall that Klossowski, alongside his work on sadism, had translated *Le Sens de la souffrance* by Max Scheler and participated in the translation into French of Landsberg's book *Essai sur l'expérience de la mort*.

2. See Bataille's "La Mère-Tragédie."

The Structure of Democracies

1. On the subject of Benda's remarks in this discussion, see the passage of *La Grande Épreuve des démocraties* (1942) quoted in the Marginalia as well as Étiemble's review of this book. Caillois's "Sociologie du clerc," which appeared in the August 1939 *NRF* (reprinted, minus his notes, in *Approches de l'imaginaire*), constitutes another important item in the file. Composed "on the occasion of a debate at the *Union for Truth* on the subject of a paper by Benda," Caillois writes, "this study can, in certain respects seem an attempt to refute the theories maintained by Julien Benda." The cleric, *clerc*, Caillois demonstrates, is not the defender of eternal values; he is someone promoting an order.

2. "Hitler is the president of an elective democracy," Paulhan reminds us, in "Retour sur 1914," *NRF*, October 1939 (*Oeuvres*, vol. 5, p. 283).

3. In *La Revue universelle* no. 15 (November 1, 1938), Thierry Maulnier entitles his review of the reflections on the crisis of Munich, put together that same month by the *NRF*, "The Intellectuals Arrive Too Late." In it he does not mention the College of Sociology, which, however published there its "Declaration on the International Crisis." However, it is possible that that is what he is thinking of when he mentions the "dangerous mixture of moral aesthetics and politics" that, according to him, was demonstrated by a number of the positions expressed there. After a few remarks on the disappointed warmongering of someone like Schlumberger, Arland, or Montherlant, he makes a

particularly violent attack on Benda: How can someone who, for twenty years, has argued for clerics staying out of secular struggles, complain about this setback? In *Inquisitions* (June 1936), Caillois hailed with a very sympathetic note, the *Nietszche* of the extreme right that Maulnier had just published (see "The Winter Wind," note 3).

The Birth of Literature

1. This probably refers to the June 6 lecture, "Joy in the Face of Death." G. Blin recalls a "demoralizing" meeting held in the rue Gay-Lussac, that was interrupted by extreme rightist and by communist groups. It ended in a scramble with the bookseller afraid for his books, Caillois stuttering like hell, and Bataille, voiceless, unable to make himself heard.

2. This was an interesting misprint: *s'écroule* "Everything falls apart." It should read *tout s'écoule* "Everything passes."

The Marquis de Sade and the Revolution

1. There is a fine three-page "Chamfort" signed by Klossowski in the review *Les Nouvelles Lettres*, no. 1 (June 1938): "Chamfort's heart was taken from behind by this revolution in which he had placed his hope of making mankind a partner in celebrating his sensitivity." On the subject of his suicide: "Charged with choosing fraternity or death, he preferred to inflict an exemplary punishment on himself, but, in the light of this punishment the clouds of fraternity were torn asunder, revealing the inevitable pair, Cain and Abel." On the subject of luck: "Chamfort's venture is that of a man who claims all have a right to the luck whose very nature requires that one be alone to enjoy it." On the subject of Sade: "The ethical imperative of natural man keeps Chamfort from giving in to the protean temptations of the Marquis de Sade's complete man" (p. 63). The second issue of *Les Nouvelles Lettres* (August 1938) would publish Klossowski's translation of Kierkegaard's *Antigone* which he had read at the College at the session on the preceding May 19.

2. On the subject of this *homme intégral* (complete man), see "The Sorcerer's Apprentice," note 2: Here the theme of polymorphy is more important than that of totalization.

3. A reference here to "Qui est mon prochain?" (Who is my fellow man?), an article that appeared in *Esprit* (December 1938, pp. 402-23) to inaugurate a short-lived series of columns entitled "The Strength of Hatreds," introduced as follows: "The break that became explicit in the French soul is one of the surest signs of the totalitarian upsurge. We must pay attention to how it acts deep inside our heart of hearts; for it is there that it turns healthy struggle into hatred that breaks with what is human. This column will be devoted to seeking out the roots of hatred instead of capitulating to a vague moralism of reconciliation. Today the following will serve as a sort of metaphysical introduction." Two pages of this article (412-13) are reproduced in the appendix of *Sade, mon prochain*.

4. A problem for the sacred in everyday life.

5. The first edition of *Sade, mon prochain* (1947) here referred to the following note: "The Nazi experience demonstrated, on the contrary, how an entire nation *can accept* such systematization when an idea that is hypostatized as the sole idea of race furnishes the fundamental *pretext*. What existed sporadically in 1793 was rationally exploited from 1933 to 1945." This note does not appear in the 1967 reedition.

6. *Français, encore un effort si vous voulez être républicains*, in *La philosophie dans le boudoir*. The emphasis is Klossowski's.

7. On feudalism, see note 17 of "Sacred Sociology" and the accompanying text.

8. This is the first appearance of the motif of the vicious circle. Klossowski later will make particularly intensive use of it in works devoted to Nietzsche; see *Nietzsche et le cercle vicieux* (Paris, 1969) and "Circulus vitiosus," in *Nietzsche aujourd'hui?* vol. 1 (Paris, 1973). There he connects the Nietzschean vicious circle to fantasies of conspiracy and a secret society ("Nietzsche's conspiracy is

only conceivable insofar as it would be conducted by some secret, elusive community whose action can hold sway under any regime"). Its logic is not very different from that employed here on the subject of Sade: the sovereign structures to which this conspiracy would lead are in effect caught in the same vicious circle as Sade's republican aristocrat: "they would have to merge their domination with their own disintegration" (*Nietzsche aujourd'hui?* p. 93). In many respects the College of Sociology could also claim to be a rather vicious "circle."

9. In his speech before the Convention on November 13, 1792: "The king must be judged as an enemy," "it is impossible to rule innocently." About all of this, see *Le Procès de Louis XVI* as presented by A. Soboul, Collection Archives (Julliard 1966).

10. "Maximilien Robespierre's opinion on the conviction of Louis XVI," speech delivered at the Convention December 3, 1792 (I have corrected the quotation following the text given in volume 9 of Robespierre's *Oeuvres* [PUF, 1958] where Robespierre's "conclusion" is formulated as follows: "But Louis must die because the country must live").

11. Caillois also makes reference to de Maistre in "Sociology of the Executioner." Klossowski gave his lecture five days after the death of the executioner Anatole Deibler, which was to be the pretext for Caillois's lecture.

12. On the subject of the incompatibility of any cult of the *mère patrie*, "mother-fatherland" with a Sadian attitude, see Klossowski's exposition demonstrating that the mother is the target par excellence of his characters' aggressions and the aggressions of their discourse, particularly "Éléments d'une étude psychanalytique sur le marquis de Sade," *Revue française de psychanalyse*, vol. 6 (1933), which includes "Le Père et la mère dans l'oeuvre de Sade," published in the appendix of *Sade, mon prochain*.

In "Qui est mon prochain?" (cited earlier) we find: "For the Eternal Father before whom they were still guilty, the Revolutionaries substituted the Mother Country (*Mère Patrie*) who was to ensure them the innocence of natural man" (p. 413).

13. Also in the speech of December 3, 1792.

14. In the program of the "Cahiers de 'Contre-Attaque'" (November 1935, reprinted in volume 1 of Bataille's *Oeuvres complètes*, pp. 384-92) there is an announcement of a small work devoted to Fourier by Klossowski. This is the text: "The moral discipline of an outdated rule is based on economic misery, which rejects, as the most formidable danger, the free play of passions. Fourier envisaged an economy of abundance resulting, on the contrary, in the free play of passions. At the moment that abundance is within reach of men and eludes them only because of their moral destitution, is it not time to finish off the cripples and castrati who today impose this destitution, in order to open the way for man freed from social constraint, a candidate for all the pleasures that are his due—the way shown by Fourier a century ago?" In "Le Corps du néant," a text devoted to Bataille and the groups he masterminded before the war, Klossowski will connect the College of Sociology to a genealogy that includes the Fourierist phalanstery: "Youth of France, Saint-Simonians, Fourierists, Proudhonian Anarchists and Communards" (*Sade, mon prochain*, 1947, p. 158; this text is not in the 1967 reedition).

More recently: "Sade et Fourier," Klossowski's contribution, appeared in the issue of the review *Topique* devoted to Fourier (October 1970).

15. Here the 1967 edition gives a long note where Klossowski "rectifies" these positions that were nearly thirty years old. Since it has a bearing on the final two paragraphs, I have put it at the end of the lecture. 1939: Evil secretes boredom in the long run; that is why Sade's permanent immorality is only a utopia. 1967: What lies in wait for immorality is not boredom, it is the institution in which its rebellious intensity risks getting stuck. 1939: A law of all or nothing set crime against law. 1967: An assertion of partiality and exception opens the possibility of a perverse use of the institution.

The Sociology of the Executioner

1. For the theory of imagination implied in these remarks, see *Le Mythe et l'homme* (especially

"La Mante religieuse") and more recently, *La Pieuvre. Essai sur la logique de l'imaginaire* (Paris, 1973).

2. This short news item provided by Jean Guérin in the *NRF*: "*Paris*, May 4. *Paris-Soir* announces that during the festivities organized in honor of the 150th anniversary of the Revolution, 'Mr. Albert Lebrun will be in exactly the same location as Louis XVI was.'"

3. Hans Mayer was to deliver a lecture at the College on the following April 18: "The Rituals of Political Associations in Romantic Germany."

4. On the subject of this volume of the *Golden Bough*, see Caillois's "Festival," note 35.

5. In *Les Soirées de Saint-Petersbourg* (1821), first interview.

6. Caillois quoted this phrase in the article on Léon Blum reproduced in the introduction to Bataille's lecture on "Power." Klossowski also referred to it in his lecture on Sade.

7. This winter zenith stirs the College's imagination far more intensely than the 14th of July and the taking of the Bastille. We know that, ever since "Contre-Attaque," Bataille had been dreaming of celebrating the 21st of January with some bizarre event on the Place de la Concorde.

Shamanism

1. I have taken the following definition of shamanism from the chapter Lewitzky wrote for *L'Histoire générale des religions* (*HGR*): "In the hierarchy of powers men, of course, occupy a rather modest position. Some, however, have a soul that is superior to others, one capable of rivaling the spirits, even to surpass certain of them. These individuals, men or women, naturally high in the ranks of the spirits, possess the power of entering into contact with them, and can, with their help, penetrate effectively into the other worlds. They have a special name. The Tungus-Manchus call them *shaman* or *sama*, the Altaic Turks *kam* or *gam*, the Kazak-Kirghizes *baksa*, the Yakuts *oyun* (masculine) and *udagan* (feminine), the Samoyeds *tadibey*, the Buryats *bo* (masculine) and *odegon* (feminine), the Ostyak *tytebe*, the Eskimo *angakkoq, angalthkok,* etc. In ethnographic literature the term shaman, chamane, or chaman is generally used."

2. In *HGR* Lewitzky notes: "It is certainly the drum that is the most characteristic attribute of shamanism . . . a shaman's drum is made out of a skin stretched over a wooden frame that is circular or oval . . . On the instrument for beating there is always the figure of a genie, who is to carry the shaman's voice. . . . But the drum is not solely a musical instrument; it is also an instrument for levitation. In a number of myths it appears as the shaman's flying carpet, in fact, and the beliefs of certain shamanist peoples frequently attribute to it the ability to fly."

3. Radlov, *Aus Siberien* (Leipzig, 1884).

4. Hangalov, *Novye materialy o shamanstve u Buryat* (Irkutsk: Zapiski Vost.-Sibir. Otd. IRGO, 1890).

5. Bogoras, *The Chukchee* (Leiden-New York, 1904-09).

6. Lewitzky notes in *HGR*: "Every shaman is chosen by a spirit who comes—usually in a dream—to offer to be his ally and thus his connection to the invisible world. This alliance is of a rather particular nature. Most frequently it has the appearance of a true tender affection that the spirit feels toward the one he has chosen. . . . There are certain shamanic initiation rituals that have the character of real marriage ceremonies.

7. Chachkov, *Shamanstvo v Sibiri*, kniga II (Saint-Petersburg: Zapiski Imp. Russk. Gruz. Obshch., 1847).

8. See, however, what Lewitzky writes in *HGR*: "Several mythologies represent the first shamans with titanic traits, as defenders of human interests against the omnipotence of the gods." On the subject of titanism and the echoes this theme could evoke at the College of Sociology, see Caillois's note in the *NRF* of November 1937 apropos V. Cerný's work, *Essai sur le titanisme dans la poésie romantique occidentale entre 1815 and 1830* (Prague, no date). This review ends on an almost prophetic note: "Soon we will have to greet either fearfully or enthusiastically the birth of a new

titanism that is remarkably more voracious, more active, more realistic, locating problems on the level required. It would not be to their disadvantage if the ones designated to take over learned something about the example of their elders. Of course, they are not people who are likely to neglect their education'' (p. 848).

9. See *HGR*: It is shamans ''who return to heaven the arrows that the gods send to earth, guaranteeing somehow the relations between gods and men.'' The gods, therefore, are somehow dependent on the shamans. A connection can be made between this Asian reply to Loyola's question ''How does one speak to God?'' and the last lines of a note by Caillois on a work on Chaldean archaeology (*Cahiers du Sud*, 206 [June 1938]). There he draws a connection between the arrows shot at heaven and the construction of the Tower of Babel: ''How did these monuments raised by the piety of the faithful become the work of pride and revolt against the divinity?'' asks Caillois. ''It must be observed that in certain versions the story of the Tower of Babel is connected to the character of Nimrod, 'the great hunter in the eyes of the Eternal' and a typical hero of the *conquest of heaven*. And soon we come upon the myth of the arrow shot at the canopy of heaven and falling back bloody. This time we have to look in China in order to reconstitute the rites that occasioned these prestigious ambitions of earthly sovereigns.'' This connection between Chinese and Mesopotamian phenomena was outlined in *La Civilisation chinoise* by Granet (p. 239). See also Caillois's lecture on festival.

10. Sternberg, *Pervobytnaya religya v svete etnografii* (Leningrad, 1936).

11. Concerning the ''bridge,'' we can read Marcel Mauss's suggestions as Caillois reported them in ''Le Grand Pontonnier'' (*Cases d'un échiquier* [Paris, 1970]). Mauss suggests a derivation of the word ''religion'' based on the activity of bridge builders: ''The proof of this,'' he goes on, ''is that in Rome the religious leader, the highest priest, is called the 'bridge-builder': *pontifex*. But today, when someone speaks of the pope as the Sovereign Pontiff, does he know he is calling him the Great Pontonnier?'' This conversation took place in 1937. In 1939, in ''Le Complexe de Polycrate, tyran de Samos'' (*Cahiers d'art*, nos. 1-4), Caillois gives this activity, which he calls for the occasion ''pontifiante'' an aggressivity that is specifically titanic, evoking the activity of the shaman. Thus he speaks of ''Xerxes' *hubris* in throwing a bridge across the Hellespont and crossing something not meant to be crossed.'' He concludes: ''The religious dangers connected to the construction of bridges are well known.'' Taken at his word, transgression can, in fact, be reduced to a mere bridge crossed.

12. Tengheri: a great god, one of whom reigns in each heaven.

13. Shirokogorov, *Opyt postroeniya obshchey teorii shamanizma sredi Tungusov* (Vladivostok, 1919).

14. Castren, *Reiseerinnerungen aus den Jahren 1838-1844* (Saint Petersburg, 1853).

15. Radlov, *Aus Siberien*.

16. Krasheninnikov, *Opisanie zemli Kamchatki* (Saint Petersburg, 1755).

The Rituals of Political Associations in Germany

1. The concept of ''residue'' and its complement, ''derivation,'' provide the material for chapters 6 to 11 in Pareto's *Traité de sociologie générale* (1916; French translation, 1919). Shortly before this lecture, its definition had appeared in two articles in *Zeitschrift für Sozialforschung*. In the first, Raymond Aron, after having recalled that the Italian economist and sociologist (who died in 1923) ''was acknowledged by the Fascists as one of their masters,'' proposed the following formulation: ''Residues are what is relatively constant in human behaviors, and derivations represent the most superficial and most changeable aspect of these behaviors. To make an analogy with philological analysis, residues are the sentimental roots of actions, and derivations are comparable to the numerous words extracted from the same root'' (''La Sociologie de Pareto,'' *Zeitschrift* . . ., 6 [1937], Part 3, p. 494). The second definition is Halbwachs's: ''residues, that is to say, what is found when all justifications and rationalizations are set aside,'' and ''that which resists society's rational action'' (''La Psychologie collective du raisonnement,'' *Zeitschrift* . . ., 7 [1938], part 3, p. 361).

Pareto is to figure in Caillois's response to the inquiry *Pour une bibliothèque* published by Queneau in 1956. His *Sociologie générale* rubs shoulders there with Huizinga's *Homo Ludens* Weber's *Wirtschaft und Gesselschaft* and Spengler's *Le Déclin de l'Occident*.

2. The exact title of these articles, which appeared in *L'Action française* of February 23, March 3, and March 14, was "Goethe à n'en pas finir."

3. "In my opinion, I maintain that because of its morality, the modern German collectivity is one of the plagues of the world and if all I had to do to exterminate it completely was to push a button, I would do it instantly, free of any tears for the few righteous people who would fall in the process. Let me add that I have a hard time believing in these righteous people and see too seldom a German of the Reich, whether named Nietzsche or Wagner, who, deep within does not have scorn for civilizations founded on reason, the certainty that hegemony is his race's due and a belief in the moral primacy of force." These lines by Julien Benda are found in *Un Régulier dans le siècle* (Paris, 1938), and reprinted in the complete volume of his autobiographical writings, *La Jeunesse d'un clerc*, followed by *Un Régulier dans le siècle* and *Exercices d'un enterré vif*, with a foreword by Étiemble (Paris, 1968), p. 228. This quote has also been cited (with no more sympathy) by Walter Benjamin in a review of Benda's autobiography that he provided to the *Zeitschrift* (7 [1938]) and that he signed, for the occasion, "J. E. Mabinn." In this review, moreover, he also attacks Caillois's "Aridité," an article that had just been published by *Mesures*, no. 2 (1938) and that, in 1942, would figure in the Mexican edition of *La Communion des forts*.

4. Valéry, *Variété IV* (Paris, 1938). In it we find, side by side with "Discours en l'honneur de Goethe," the famous "Discours de l'histoire," which also dates from 1932. That is where the expression "History is the science of things that don't repeat themselves" appears. In *Regards sur le monde actuel* (1931), the challenge mentioned by Hans Mayer was already there to be read, particularly in the pages entitled "De l'histoire." ("History justifies anything you want it to. It teaches absolutely nothing because it contains everything and gives examples of everything.")

5. Raymond Aron, *Introduction à la philosophie de l'histoire. Essai sur les limites de l'objectivité historique* (Paris, 1938), p. 285. It was also in 1938 that Aron published his *Essai sur la théorie de l'histoire dans l'Allemagne contemporaine*. He participated in the discussion following Halévy's lecture "The Era of Tyrannies" at the Société française de philosophie in November 1936. Furthermore, he contributed regularly to the *Zeitschrift*, where his review of Caillois's *Mythe et l'homme* (7 [1938], p. 414) contested the "parallel made between insect behavior and human myths." In the same issue of the Frankfurt School's journal Adorno spoke of the chapter of *Mythe et l'homme* devoted to the praying mantis (just issued separately by Adrienne Monnier) in the most positive terms: "Die Kritik der Isolierung der Sphären von Gesellschaft und Natur . . . hat ihre progressive Seite" and even "eine echt materialistischen Aspekt" (p. 410).

6. On nazism's neopaganism and other pseudo-Nietzschean farces, see Bataille, "Nietzsche et les fascistes," *Acéphale*, no. 2 (January 1937) (*OC*, vol. 1, pp. 458ff.).

7. Jakob Wilhelm Hauer (1881-1962), author of works such as *Eine indoarische Metaphysik des Kampfes und der Tat* (1934), *Glaube und Blut* (1938), *Germany's New Religion* (1937), *Ein arischer Christus?* (1939).

8. Ernst von Salomon, *Die Geachteten* (Gutersloh, 1930; translated into French as *Les Réprouvés* by Andhrée Vaillant and Jean Kuckenburg, 1931). *La Ville*, by the same author, was translated by Norbert Guterman in 1933. In a column of July 1938 entitled "Une Seule Défaite manque aux marxistes," Drieu La Rochelle wrote, apropos *Les Réprouvés*: "For a long time we have only had the remarkable book, not well enough known, by Ernest von Salomon, *Les Réprouvés*, which recounted the venture of the first irregulars doing battle in Germany against despair, annihilation, giving up. To this now must be added Benoist-Méchin's fine work, *Histoire de l'armée allemande*" (*Chronique politique* [Paris, 1943], p. 152).

9. Ernst Röhm, *Die Geschichte eines Hochverräter* (Munich, 1928). An organizer of Silesian irregulars, then of the SS, he wrote this in Bolivia, where he reorganized the local army after a first

clash with Hitler following the failure of the Munich putsch. The next clash, as we know, had to end for this homosexual condottiere in the blood of the night of the long knives.

10. *OS* (Ober-Schlesien) appeared in 1929. Arnolt Bronnen is the author of a number of plays (*Die Exzesse* [1923]; *Die Geburt der Jugend* [1922]) and novels.

11. Emil Julius Gumbel, editor of numerous documents (*Verschwörer, Beiträge zur Geschichte und Soziologie der deutschen nationalistischen Geheimbünde seit 1918* [Vienna, 1924]; *"Lasst Köpfe rollen"; faschistische Mörde 1924-1931*; in the *Aufträge des deutschen Liga für Menschenrechte* as presented by E. J. Gumbel [Berlin, 1931]). Les Cahiers Bleus published *Les Crimes politiques en Allemagne, 1919-1920* (Paris, 1931).

12. On the translation of the Hegelian *aufheben*, see Hyppolite's note on page 19 of the first volume of his translation of *La Phénoménologie de l'esprit* that came out in 1939: "This cancellation is, furthermore, a preservation, as Hegel requires that we allow that the term 'preserve' implies a negation, because for him every preservation is a *salvation.*"

13. Arthur Moeller van den Bruck (1876-1925), *Das dritte Reich* (Berlin, 1923); French translation by J. L. Lénault, with an introduction by Thierry Maulnier (Paris: Rieder, 1933).

14. M. van den Bruck, *Sozialismus und Aussenpolitik* (Breslau: Schwarz, 1933).

15. *Die Revolution der Nihilismus; Kulisse und Wirklichkeit im dritten Reich* (Zurich-New York, 1938); French translation by Paul Raboux and Marcel Stora (Paris, 1939). Drieu La Rochelle would refer to this work by the former mayor of Danzig in the article he published in *Je suis partout*, January 12, 1940, concerning Dumézil's *Mythes et dieux des Germains* (the article was entitled "Eternal Germany"): "Thus the present subversion led by Hitler that is described for us with alarming precision by Hermann Rauschning in his *Révolution du nihilisme* would be part of our neighbors' constant temperament" (*Chronique politique*, p. 215).

16. "History is a cemetary of aristocracy," Pareto, *Traité*, vol. 2, sec. 2053, p. 1034.

17. *Après* is the title of the French translation (Paris, 1931) of *Der Weg Zurück* (Berlin, 1931); *Trois Camarades* (Paris, 1938) that of *Drei Kamaraden* (Amsterdam, 1938).

18. Hans Blüher (1888-1919) wrote, among other things, two volumes entitled *Die Rolle der Erotik in der männlichen Gesellschaft; eine Theorie der menschlichen Staatsbildung nach Wesen und Wert* (Jena, 1919); its second volume is devoted to *Familie und Männerbund*. When Dumézil discusses Germanic secret societies, he refers to Stig Wikander: *Der arische Männerbund* (Lund-Uppsala, 1938). Mauss's study on the Eskimo also contains a number of reflections on societies of men.

Festival

1. See *Les Formes élémentaires de la vie religieuse* (Paris, 1912), in which Durkheim describes "the two phases alternating in the life of Australian societies: dispersion and concentration." "In the first, economic activity is preponderant, and it is in general of little or no intensity. . . . The state of dispersion in which society then finds itself has the effect of making life uniform, flat, and dull. But let there be a *corrobbori* [= festival] and everything changes. . . . The mere fact of agglomeration acts as an exceptionally potent stimulant" (p. 308).

2. M. Mauss, "Essai sur les variations saisonnières des sociétés Eskimos. Étude de morphologie sociale" (in collaboration with H. Beuchat), *L'Année sociologique 1904-1905* (Paris, 1906), pp. 39-131. This study has been reprinted in recent editions of Mauss's book entitled *Sociologie et anthropologie* (Paris, 1968). The following propositions are taken from it: "There is no religion in summer. . . . Life seems to be secularized. . . . On the contrary, the winter settlement lives, so to speak, in a continual state of religious exaltation. . . . In short, it is possible to imagine the whole of winter life to be a sort of long festival" (pp. 96-100). Later, speaking of the Indians of the American Northwest: "In winter the clan disappears and gives way to groups of an entirely different kind, secret societies, or more precisely, religious brotherhoods in which all the nobles and

free people are organized in a hierarchy'' (p. 126). Remember that Caillois had opened the activities of the College in March 1937 by reading a manifesto entitled ''The Winter Wind'' that aspired to no other end than to *cast a chill* because cold goes hand in hand with density, agglomeration, festival, and hierarchy.

3. The quote is from Boas (''The Social Organization and Secret Societies of the Kwakiutl Indians,'' *Report of the U.S. National Museum for 1895* [Washington, D.C., 1897]) and is cited in the conclusion of Mauss's study (p. 126).

4. Durkheim, *Les Formes*, p. 309.

5. This saying of Confucius appears in Granet's *La Civilisation chinoise. La vie publique et la vie privée* (Paris, 1929), p. 181. Caillois, in a review of Alexis Carrel's book, *L'Homme, cet inconnu*, published in the March 1936 *NRF* was already remarking, ''We still are expecting this *general theory of the instincts*, initiated here and there by Moll and Weissmann, which already proves capable of accounting for some very disconcerting things that don't seem to make sense psychologically. They do so, moreover, by evoking only such simple principles as, for example, contraction and dilation, tumescence and detumescence, paroxysm and relaxation.'' ''La Mante religieuse,'' reprinted in *Le Mythe et l'homme*, would illustrate this theory of an orgiastic chaos: ''Sexual detumescence is a phenomenon of remarkable violence, freeing in one convulsion a considerable amount of energy that has been gradually accumulated and brought to the breaking point'' (p. 93). But then he would be referring not to Confucius, nor to Moll, but rather to the Freud of *Beyond the Pleasure Principle*.

6. The contents of this paragraph, and much of those that follow, are taken from Lucien Lévy-Bruhl's book *La Mythologie primitive. Le monde mythique des Australiens et des Papous* (Paris, 1935), particularly the first chapter, ''Le Monde mythique.'' There the concept of *Urzeit*, borrowed from K. Th. Preuss, is mentioned. There also are quotes from Fortune and Elkin, ethnographers responsible for the descriptions of the customs of both the natives of the island of Dobu and the primitive Australian peoples. In the August 1938 *NRF* Caillois had published a review of Lévy-Bruhl's last book, *L'Expérience mystique et les symboles chez les primitifs*. These remarks are taken from it: ''One often has the impression, reading Lévy-Bruhl, that he considers only the religious aspect of the life of primitive peoples and that he contrasts it, not to the religious life of civilized peoples, but to the critical and scientific forms of their intellectual activity. Hence, he is comparing a sensitivity to an intelligence, not to another sensitivity.'' Thus, instead of the diachronic succession of a primitive mentality replaced by a logical mentality, one must substitute a synchronic opposition of different realms, one sacred, the other profane, alternating but mutually supportive.

The first part of L.-B.'s work was that of a historian of philosophy. Only the study on Auguste Comte foreshadows the orientation it was to take subsequently: sociological, or more precisely psychological, since Lévy-Bruhl from then on would devote himself to a survey of ''primitive thought.'' *La Morale et la science des moeurs* is pivotal, developing the impossibility of changing an indicative into an imperative. The result was a pessimism (''a society can only be given the morality it already has'') in marked contrast to the activism of the College. Leiris mentions in ''Dimanche'' (*Biffures*, p. 213) the influence L.-B.'s books had in his own choice of an ethnographic career. Lévy-Bruhl died in March 1939, a few months before the *Revue philosophique*, which he directed, published the special issue he had prepared to celebrate the 150th anniversary of the French Revolution.

7. The bibliography of *L'Homme et le sacré* (*HS*) refers to A. P. Elkin, ''The Secret Life of the Australian Aborigines,'' *Oceania*, 3 (1932).

8. This Netsilik Eskimo myth was recorded by Knud Rasmussen. Lévy-Bruhl cites it in *La Mythologie primitive* (*MP*), p. 210.

9. A Caribou Eskimo myth, recorded by Rasmussen and cited by Lévy-Bruhl in *MP*.

10. G. Dumézil, ''Temps et mythe,'' *Recherches philosophiques*, 5 (1935-36).

11. Elkin, ''The Secret Life'' cited by Lévy-Bruhl, *MP*, p. 17.

12. C. Daryll Forde, *Ethnography of the Yuma Indians* (Berkeley, 1931), p. 214. (Caillois cites this work in the bibliography of *L'Homme et le sacré*.)

On the subject of these rock paintings, see A. P. Elkin, "Rock-Paintings of North-West Australia," *Oceania*, 1 (1930). Lévy-Bruhl cites this study in *MP*, p. 134ff.

13. This ceremony is described by Durkheim (following Spencer and Gillen) in *Formes*, p. 532.

14. P. Wirz, *Die Marind-anim von holländisch-Süd-Neu-Guinea* (cited by Lévy-Bruhl, *MP*, p. 121).

15. C. Strehlow, *Die Aranda—und Loritja—Stämme in Zentral-Australien* (cited by Lévy-Bruhl, *MP*, p. 123.)

16. See Marcel Granet, *La Civilisation chinoise* (Paris, 1929), particularly "Rivalités de confréries" (pp. 229-41). Granet meant to study this great winter "drinking bout" in a book that remained only a project: *Le Roi boit*. For more on shooting arrows at heaven, see Lewitzky's lecture on shamanism, especially note 9.

17. See Granet, *La Pensée chinoise* (Paris, 1934), pp. 106-9.

18. See Dumézil, *Le Problème des centaures. Étude de mythologie comparée indo-européenne* (Paris, 1929).

19. Robert Hertz, "La Représentation collective de la mort," in *Mélanges de sociologie religieuse et de folklore* (Paris, 1928).

20. See the death of Cheu Hoang-Ti in "L'Ordre et l'empire" (*Le Mythe et l'homme*, p. 154).

21. This description is borrowed from Durkheim (*Formes*, p. 311), who borrowed it from Spencer and Gillen.

22. Maurice Leenhardt, *Gens de la Grande Terre*, volume 1 of *L'Espèce humaine* (Paris, 1937). Chapter 8 is entitled "Le Pilou. Moment culminant de la société." The following remarks are taken from a review of this book by Leiris (*NRF*, November 1938, the same issue in which appeared *Le Miroir de la tauromachie* and the articles pertaining to Munich; see the editor's introduction to "Declaration of the College of Sociology on the International Crisis"). "In the picture he gives us of Kanakan life and thought, as well as in those pages in which he describes how this thought has been changed by contact with European civilization, the author seems never to depart from this principle, which should be every ethnographer's golden rule: There is no real understanding except through identification." Further on: "Leenhardt keeps a vision of things that is *totalizing* (in the occultist sense of 'all is in all'), rather than disconnected, linear like the one that is due to our own activities, which are themselves broken up and mechanized to a far greater extent than in so-called primitive societies."

23. The bibliography of *HS* refers to Lord Raglan, *Le Tabou de l'inceste* (French trans., Paris, 1935). The book first appeared in New York with the title *Jocasta's Crime* (1932). Caillois reviewed it for *Les Cahiers du Sud* in November 1935. He observes that the author, rather than being interested in incest itself, is more interested "in the creation myths and rituals that are, in fact, continually connected to the etiology of incest. Lord Raglan, whose daring idea continues to be felicitous, reconstitutes the ideal scenario for the rituals of the recreation of the world." This review, despite its modest pretensions, ended with a call to arms: "We must make these questions perfectly clear: not to reduce them, but rather to perceive, and if need be, to exalt them. In order for an action to be something other than agitation, it must know how to hit only where it hurts."

24. Mauss, "Variations saisonnières," p. 100. The author comments on solstice festivals: "Sexual communism is a form of communion, and perhaps the most intimate one there is. When it rules, a sort of fusion of individual personalities into each other is produced. Here we are far from the state of individuation and isolation in which, dispersed during the summer, the little family groups exist."

25. Mauss, "Variations saisonnières," p. 114.

26. Lévy-Bruhl, *MP*, pp. 137, 139.

27. Granet, *La Civilisation chinoise*, p. 182.

28. These facts come from Frazer's *The Scapegoat* (London, 1913).

29. Dumézil, *Le Problème des centaures*, pp. 169, 187.

30. L. R. Farnell, *The Cults of the Greek States* (Oxford, 1921).

31. See Frazer, *The Scapegoat*, 35.

32. Granet, *La Civilisation chinoise*, p. 201.

33. Mauss, "Variations saisonnières," p. 121 (The chief does not remain chief, or rather the rich man does not remain rich and influential, except under the condition that he periodically distributes his wealth. . . . He alternately enjoys his fortune and pays for it; and expiation is the condition for the enjoyment."

34. See Durkheim, *Formes*, p. 312.

35. The information in this paragraph is borrowed from Frazer's *The Scapegoat*. The French translation of his *Le Bouc Émissaire* appeared in 1925 and is cited by Caillois in his bibliography. He reviewed it in the November 1936 *Cahiers du Sud*. On this occasion he recalled the British anthropologist's interpretation of "the passion of Christ as the false king of the Jews with a reed for his scepter, thorns for a crown, and mocking robes of crimson, his entrance into Jerusalem on an ass with palms overhead." "The sacrificed God is no longer the magical sovereign who lives, dies, and is born again with the vegetation, but a false king, the king of Saturnalia, the king of Carnival." Chapter 8 of *The Scapegoat* (chapter 58, 3, in *The Golden Bough*) is devoted to the Saturnalia. It ends with a long note that develops the carnivalesque interpretation of the Crucifixion that Caillois refers to here and that he will bring up again in 1961, in his narrative *Ponce Pilate* (especially p. 78). Dianus, the priest at Nemi, is a central character in *The Golden Bough*. *The Scapegoat* gives, as it were, the comic version of this.

36. Leenhardt, *Gens de la Grande Terre*, p. 170 (Leenhardt's text reads: "Exalt the ancestors").

37. There are three different versions of what follows: first, that of *HS* (1939), which I give first; second, the *NRF* version (1940), longer and forming a separate paragraph ("Festival and Vacation"); third, the 1950 edition of *HS* which adds thoughts about the war.

38. This is where the variation of these final lines given in the *NRF* begins.

39. Mauss ended his "Variations saisonnières" with similar (even if less derogatory) remarks on the vacation. In our Western societies, he says, "from about the beginning of July, as a consequence of the summer dispersal, city life enters a period of continual languor, the *vacation*, which comes to an end at the end of autumn" (p. 127).

40. Here, in place of the following, *HS* gives the lines about war that appear later in this text.

Sacred Language

1. Who is this somewhat Rimbaldian Botzarro to whom Paulhan, a master of invention, had already attributed (1921) the epigraph to *Jacob Cow le Pirat ou Si les mots sont des signes?* (Jacob Cow the pirate, or Whether words are signs). The first epigraph of *Les Fleurs de Tarbes* is also borrowed (if that is the right word) from him: "This kind native, as I was about to repeat the words I had been taught, exclaimed 'Stop! Each person can only use them once.'" The source would be *Voyages de Botzarro*, XV.

2. This is Madagascar, where Paulhan lived from January 1908 until December 1910.

3. This passage repeats, sometimes word for word, the beginning of "L'Expérience du proverbe," which appeared in *Commerce*, 1925 (and is reprinted in the second volume of Paulhan's *Oeuvres* [Paris, 1966]). Most of the Malagasy examples that are quoted further on already figured in this article, but were rendered generally in a different French.

4. The original text would read more like: "the wily care, the solemn discretion, the *morituri sumus* of this good people, when they pronounced the musty sentences bequeathed them by the centuries and that they will transmit to their children?" Léon Bloy, *Exégèse des lieux communs* (1st ser., 1902; 2nd ser., 1913), vol. 8 of his *Oeuvres*, ed. Jacques Petit (Paris, 1968), p. 19.

5. "The true Bourgeois, that is to say in a modern sense and as generally as possible, the man who makes no use of the faculty of thought and who lives or seems to live without having been

tempted, for a single day, by the need to understand anything at all, the authentic and indisputable Bourgeois is necessarily limited in his language to a very small number of formulas," Bloy, *Exégèse*, p. 19.

6. "L'Expérience du proverbe" of 1925 did not mention secret societies. Paulhan adapted his vocabulary to the College's thematic (but he would still, in March 1946, publish in *Les Temps modernes*: "Rhetoric was a secret society"; rebaptized in *Oeuvres*, vol. 3, "Rhetoric had its password").

7. Charles Bally, *Précis de stylistique* (Geneva, 1905), intended his book for foreigners studying French (p. 14). He notes: "One is a better etymologist for a foreign language than for one's own language" (p. 22). Moreover, he denounces the confusion between "the etymological connection and the semantic connection" (p. 23). Paulhan is to return to this question in *La Preuve par l'étymologie* (1953). He discusses Bally's theses in *Clef de la poésie* (1944).

8. Paulhan's first work, *Les Hain-Tenys merinas, poésies populaires malgaches*, collected and translated by J. P. (Paris, 1913), was devoted to these. "As to their name 'hain-teny,'" we read in the version of this book that is reprinted in the second volume of the *Oeuvres* (p. 70), "it can mean equally, 'knowledge of the language,' or 'knowledge of the words'; also: 'learned words'; if you push it a bit: 'wise words.'" "The hain-tenys are popular poems current among the Merinas who inhabit the central portion of Madagascar. They are enigmatic poems, difficult from more than one point of view and similar to those that literary history calls obscure poems—medieval fatrasies or the poems of troubadours."

9. *Les Fleurs de Tarbes* in 1941 was to have the subtitle "Terror in Letters."

10. This is the title of the first article published by Paulhan on the subject ("L'Expérience du proverbe," *Commerce*, 1925).

11. Paulhan would only teach for a year following his return from Madagascar (1910-11). About his thesis one can read what pertains to it and is said about it in the second of the *Cahiers Jean Paulhan* (*Jean Paulhan et Madagascar*) (Paris, 1982). The subject had been accepted by Lévy-Bruhl in 1910 or 1912. Paulhan soon lost interest in it. But in 1922 and, it appears, in 1936 (see Wahl's letter on p. 264) he would think of it again.

12. One month? Jean Guérin (alias Jean Paulhan) had noted in August 1937, in the *Bulletin* where he summarized the news for the readers of the *NRF* (no. 287, p. 365): "*Munich*: Hitler, inaugurating the Hall of German Art, announces that he 'will rid German existence of these hollow words: cubism, Dadaism, futurism, impressionism.'"

In what follows Paulhan returns to the argument and some of the formulations of his "Letter to the *Nouveaux Cahiers* on the power of words (*Les Nouveaux Cahiers*, April-May 1938; reprinted by J.-Cl. Zylberstein in his edition of the *Fleurs de Tarbes* for the collection "Idées" in 1973). Paulhan had already spoken out on this subject on December 20, 1937, before the "Groupe des *Nouveaux Cahiers*." Founded in March 1937, the review *Les Nouveaux Cahiers* had published de Rougemont, Moré, S. Weil, Landsberg. The quotes from Maurras and J.-R. Bloch (the latter a communist, the former a monarchist) are taken, respectively, from the *Dictionnaire* (entry for *Mot* [word]) and from *Destin du siècle*. For more on this debate, which was to occupy an essential position in *Les Fleurs de Tarbes*, see Paulhan's correspondence with Parain published in the *NRF*, October, November, and December 1983.

13. "The Sacred in Everyday Life," read before the College on January 8, 1938, ended with the beginnings of a list of "sacred language" by Leiris. But Paulhan could equally be thinking of *Glossaire: j'y serre mes gloses*, whose formulas were collected in a volume this very year (1939) at Galerie Simon. Ten years earlier, the author introduced them with: "A monstrous aberration makes men believe that language was born to facilitate their mutual relations" (M. Leiris, *Brisées* [1966], p. 11). The sacred "in" everyday life, it should be noted, is a similar motif to the one Paulhan latches onto here: the sacred in the profane.

14. Intelligence taking into account its own blind spot and its blackouts is a knotty enigma that is

related to Bachelardian superrationalism. This is especially true of Caillois's version ("combine into a system whatever until now an incomplete reason eliminated systematically," "Procès intellectuel de l'art" [1934], in *Approches de l'imaginaire*). By the same token, sacred disorder is not opposed to the order of the world; the order of things implies the violence of Varuna. This systematic blacking out refers also to the absorption of the observer by his object, the epistemological "engagement" that Bataille, in "The Sorcerer's Apprentice," had assigned as the College's goal. (Jean Wahl had just published a collection of poems whose title, significantly, was *Connaître sans connaître* [Knowing without knowing]).

The College of Sociology

1. For more about this voyage from which Caillois was not about to return, see the editor's introduction to "Festival."

2. See his letter to Bataille, written on the eve of this lecture and included here in the Appendixes.

3. In June 1939, Bataille published anonymously issue no. 5 of *Acéphale* (the review had not appeared since it announced the foundation of the College). In the index: "La Folie de Nietzsche" (in which madness is described as an integral part because it disintegrates "human integrality") and "La Pratique de la joie devant la mort" (mystic dramatizations: "There is good reason to use the word 'mystic,'" Bataille himself would comment about these exercises). Whereas Loyola's example led Caillois to dream up *Inquisitions* and found the College of Sociology, through the intermediary of "spiritual exercises," he would lead Bataille onto paths of "inner experience." On the subject of Caillois's condemnation of the mysticism toward which Bataille was turning, remember that in *Le Mythe et l'homme*, he contrasted the aggressive, Luciferian virility of the shaman to the effusion and confusion of mystics.

4. This formulation, itself, is the ashes of a communication. It is the echo of a dramatic coincidence that Bataille had just been struck by. In "Le Sacré," which he wrote while Laure was dying (and which *Les Cahiers d'art* was to publish in 1939), we read that the sacred is "only a privileged moment of communal union, a moment of convulsive communication of something ordinarily stifled." In the margins of the manuscript he had noted : "identity with love" (*OC*, vol. 1, p. 562 and note). After the death of his companion, in the papers left by her, he was to discover—concerning this subject about which, however, they had never spoken—an identical formulation: "Poetic work," she noted, "is sacred in that it is the creation of a local event, 'communication' felt as *nakedness.*—It is a violation of oneself, stripping oneself bare, communication to others one's reasons to exist" (quoted by Bataille, *OC*, vol. 5, p. 508). At the time this last lecture was held, Bataille was finishing up with Leiris the volume entitled *Le Sacré* in which they gathered certain posthumous notes by Laure. They come back to the link between communication and the sacred: "Communication, here, must be understood in the sense of a fusion, a loss of oneself, whose integrity is accomplished only through death and of which erotic fusion is an image. Such a conception is different from that held by the French school of sociology, which only considers men's communication with each other. This conception tends to identify what is apprehended in mystic experience and what is set in action by the rituals and myths of the community."

5. This letter by Caillois has not been found. Bataille's response to him two weeks later (July 20, 1939) is found in the Appendixes.

Fragment (Bataille)

1. Trotsky, "Où va la France," *La Vérité*, November 9 ,1934 (see the collection entitled *Le Mouvement communiste en France* [Paris, 1971]), edited by Broué: p. 450 for Doumergue, p. 452 for von Papen). Doumergue had succeeded Daladier after the riots of February 1934.

After several presidencies (of the Council in 1914, of the Senate in 1923), Gaston Doumergue (also called Gastounet) was elected president of the Republic in 1924. Paul Doumer succeeded him in 1931 and was assassinated a year later. Lebrun (Albert) was then elected for a first seven-year term (he would begin a second in 1939): It is he who, after the riots organized by the far right on the Place de la Concorde had, in February 1934, resulted in the fall of the government of a unified left led by Daladier, would appeal to Doumergue to form a new government. The latter would be president of the Council from February until November 1934. It is obviously to this last episode of his political career that Trotsky is referring in this article, which appeared several days after the fall of his government.

2. A blank space occurs at this point in the manuscript.

Four Letters

1. This text, "Examination of Conscience," has not been found. Caillois would use this title again, putting it in the plural (and in Spanish) in a note appearing in April 1941 in *SUR*. (The note focuses on three French works published in New York: A. Maurois, *Tragédie en France*; J. Romains, *Sept mystères du destin de l'Europe*; and J. Maritain, *À travers le désastre*). It will be noted that "Seres del anochecer," an extract from "Êtres de crépuscule," would also appear in the Buenos Aires review in December, 1940 (see the Marginalia). This text contains no explicit "attack" on Bataille. But Caillois will describe it, in *Approches de l'imaginaire* as having marked for him a definitive abandonment of the "juvenile and arrogant pipedreams" crystallized by the College.

2. Tuesday, July 4, that is the day after this letter was written: It was to be the final session of the College (see Bataille's lecture for that day).

3. Bataille would summarize the objections formulated by Leiris in this letter in the lecture he was to give the next day.

4. Caillois was, in fact, in Buenos Aires where at the invitation of Victoria Ocampo, he was giving a series of lectures on "the great mythological themes." Since war had not broken out, everyone thought he would return at the end of the summer.

5. This "Note" is included at the beginning of this volume.

6. This refers to the preceding letter, dated the same day. Leiris, consequently, would not be present at the final lecture of the College, which Bataille would deliver alone the next day.

7. This is the address given in the last issue of *Acéphale* (June 1939) as that of Patrick Waldberg. Bataille lived in Saint-Germain with Laure, who died there in November 1938 (about this house, see the posthumous fragments, dated September 1939, published in connection with *Le Coupable* in *OC*, vol. 5, pp. 492ff.). Whereas the College of Sociology could be considered a Parisian institution, Saint-Germain and its wooded surroundings would constitute the setting for the activities of the "secret" society Acéphale (the instructions for "meeting" in the forest at Marly are found in *OC*, vol. 1, p. 277).

8. A. Robinet de Cléry, "Montesquieu sociologue," *Revue internationale sociologie*, May-June 1939.

Marginalia

1. "Naturaleza del Hitlerismo," published by Caillois in *SUR*, no. 61, (October 1939), pp. 93-107, in a collection entitled "Testimonio Francès," which also included texts by Jean Cazaux and Armand Petitjean.

2. Caillois, "Natureleza del Hitlerismo."

3. During the Algerian war this designated terrorist groups of the extreme right who, like the Organisation de l'Armée Secrète were opposed to Gaullist politics in Algeria.

Bibliography

Bibliography

I. Publications by Founders, Directors, and Speakers of the College

Ambrosino, Georges, G. Bataille, R. Caillois, P. Klossowski, P. Libra, and J. Monnerot. "Note sur la fondation d'un Collège de Sociologie." *Acéphale* 3-4 (July 1937): 26.

Bataille, Georges. *Le Bleu du ciel.* Paris: J.-J. Pauvert, 1957 (written in 1935).

_____. *Le Coupable.* Paris: Gallimard, 1944.

_____. *L'Expérience intérieure.* Paris: Gallimard, 1942.

_____. *La Littérature et le mal.* Paris: Gallimard, 1957.

_____ [under pseud. Pierre Angélique]. *Madame Edwarda.* Paris: Éditions du Solitaire, 1941; [under real name] J.-J. Pauvert, 1956.

_____. *Oeuvres complètes* (9 vols. to date). Paris: Gallimard, 1970-.

_____, ed. *L'Ordre de chevalerie* (medieval poem, 13th C.). Paris: Picard, 1922.

_____. *Sur Nietzsche.* Paris: Gallimard, 1945.

_____ [Dianus, pseud.]. "L'Amitié." *Mesures* 2 (Apr. 1940): 129-50. Rpt. in *Le Coupable.*

_____. "L'Apprenti sorcier." ("Pour un Collège de Sociologie") *NRF* 298 (July 1938): 8-25.

_____. "Calaveras." In *Oeuvres complètes, II.* (Probably written in 1936.)

_____. "Chronique nietzschéenne." *Acéphale* 3-4 (July 1937): 15-23.

_____. "La Conjuration sacrée." *Acéphale* 1 (June 1936): 2-4.

_____. "Corps célestes." *Verve* 1 (Spring 1938): 97-100.

_____, and R. Queneau. "La Critique des fondements de la dialectique hégélienne." *La Critique sociale* 5 (Mar. 1932): 209-14.

_____, R. Caillois, and M. Leiris. "Déclaration du Collège de Sociologie sur la crise internationale." ("Pour un Collège de Sociologie"). *Esprit* 74 (Nov. 1938): 301-3; *NRF* 302 (Nov. 1938): 874-76; *Volontés* 11 (Nov. 1938): 60-62.

_____. "L'Existentialisme." *Critique* 41 (Oct. 1950): 83-86.

_____. "La Folie de Nietzsche." *Acéphale* 5 (June 1939): 1-8.

_____. "La Guerre et la philosophie du sacré." *Critique* 45 (Feb. 1951): 133-43. (Review of R. Caillois, *L'Homme et le sacré.*)

_____. "Le Labyrinthe." *Recherches philosophiques* 5 (1935-36): 364-72.

_____. "La Menace de guerre." *Acéphale* 5 (June 1939): 9.

_____. "La Mère-Tragédie." *Le Voyage en Grèce* 7 (Summer 1937): 20-21.

_____. "Nietzsche et les fascistes." *Acéphale* 2 (Jan. 1937): 3-13.

_____. "La Notion de dépense." *La Critique sociale* 7 (Jan. 1933): 7-15.

_____. "Notre-Dame de Rheims" (1918). Rpt. in Denis Hollier, *La Prise de la Concorde*. Paris: Gallimard, 1974.

_____. "L'Obélisque." *Mesures* 2 (Apr. 1938): 35-50.

_____. "La Pratique de la joie devant la mort." *Acéphale* 5 (June 1939): 11-23.

_____. "Propositions sur le fascisme." *Acéphale* 2 (Jan. 1937): 17-21.

_____. "Qu'est-ce que le sexe?" *Critique* 11 (April 1947): 387-89.

_____. "Le Sacré." *Cahiers d'art* 1-4 (1939): 47-50.

_____. "Sade." *La Littérature*. (First published as "Le Secret de Sade." *Critique* 15-16 (Aug.-Sept. 1947): 147-60; 17 (Oct. 1947): 304-12). (Review of P. Klossowski, *Sade, mon prochain*.)

_____. "Le Sens moral de la sociologie." *Critique* 1 (June 1946): 39-47. (Review of J. Monnerot, *Les Faits sociaux ne sont pas des choses*.)

_____. "La Structure psychologique du fascisme." *La Critique sociale* 10 (Nov. 1933): 159-65; 11 (Mar. 1934): 205-11.

Caillois, Roger. *Approches de l'imaginaire*. Paris: Gallimard, 1974.

_____. *Bellone ou la pente de la guerre*. Paris: Nizet, 1963.

_____, ed. *Le Cid*, by P. Corneille. Paris: Hachette, Classiques France, 1939.

_____. *Circonstancielles (1940-1945)*. Paris: Gallimard, 1946.

_____. *La Communion des forts*. Mexico City: Ediciones Quetzal, 1943; Marseille: Sagittaire, 1944.

_____. *L'Homme et le sacré*. Paris: E. Leroux, 1939; Gallimard, 1950.

_____. *Instincts et société*. Paris: Gonthier, Bibliothèque Médiations, 1964.

_____. *Le Mythe et l'homme*. Paris: Gallimard, 1938; [in Spanish] Buenos Aires: Éditions SUR, 1939.

_____. *Procès intellectuel de l'art*. Marseille: Éditions des Cahiers du Sud, 1935. Rpt. in *Approches de l'imaginaire*.

_____. *Puissances du roman*. Marseille: Sagittaire, 1942; Buenos Aires: Éditions du Trident, 1945. Rpt. in *Approches de l'imaginaire*. [in Spanish] *Sociología de la novela*. Buenos Aires: Éditions SUR, 1942.

_____. *Le Rocher de Sisyphe*. Paris: Gallimard, 1946.

_____. *Le Roman policier*. Buenos Aires: Éditions des Lettres françaises, 1941. Rpt. in *Puissances du roman*.

_____. "L'Agressivité comme valeur." *L'Ordre nouveau* 41 (June 1937): 56-58.

_____. "L'Alternative." *Cahiers du Sud* 194 (May-June 1937): 111-21. Rpt. in *Approches du l'imaginaire*.

_____. "Ambiguïté du sacré." *Mesures* 2 (Apr. 1939): 35-64. Rpt. in *L'Homme et le sacré*.

_____. "L'Aridité." *Mesures* 2 (Apr. 1938): 7-12. Rpt. in *La Communion des forts*.

_____. "Le Complexe de Polycrate, tyran de Samos." *Cahiers d'art* 1-4 (1939): 51-55.

_____. "Les Démons de midi." *Revue de l'histoire des religions* 115 (Mar.-June 1937): 142-73; 116 (July-Aug. 1937): 54-83; 116 (Sept.-Dec. 1937): 143-86.

_____. "Divergences et complicités." *NRF* 172 (Apr. 1967): 686-98. Rpt. in *Cases d'un échiquier*. Paris: Gallimard, 1970.

_____. "Ensayo sobre el Espíritu de las Sectas." (Coll. *Jornadas*, 41). Mexico City: El Colegio de México (1945): entire issue. Rpt. in *Instincts et société*. (Includes "Préambule pour L'Esprit des sectes.")

_____. "Exámenes de conciencia." *SUR* 79 (Apr. 1941): 102-7.

_____. "La Hiérarchie des êtres." *Les Volontaires* 5 (Apr. 1939): 317-26. Rpt. in *La Communion des forts.*

_____. Introduction, "Pour un Collège de Sociologie." *NRF* 298 (July 1938): 5-7. Rpt. in *Approches de l'imaginaire.*

_____. "Jeux d'ombres sur l'Hellade." *Le Voyage en Grèce.* Rpt. in *Le Mythe et l'homme.*

_____. "La Mante religieuse." *Minotaure* 5 (1934): 23-26; *Mesures* 2 (Apr. 1937): 89-119. Rpt. in *Le Mythe et l'homme.*

_____. "Mimétisme et psychasthénie légendaire." *Minotaure* 7 (1935): 4-10. Rpt. in *Le Mythe et l'homme.*

_____. "Naturaleza del Hitlerismo." *SUR* 61 (Oct. 1939): 93-107.

_____. "Paris, mythe moderne." *NRF* 284 (May 1937): 682-99. Rpt. in *Le Mythe et l'homme.*

_____. "Pour une orthodoxie militante." *Inquisitions* 1 (June 1936): 6-14. Rpt. in *Le Mythe et l'homme.*

_____. "Résurrection de Corneille." *NRF* 301 (Oct. 1938): 659-65.

_____. "Seres del anochecer." *SUR* 75 (Dec. 1940): 95-99. Rpt. as "Êtres de crépuscule," in *Labyrinthe* [Geneva] 15 (Dec. 15, 1945): 1-2 and in *Le Rocher de Sisyphe.*

_____. "Sociología del verdugo." *SUR* 56 (May 1939): 17-38. Rpt. as "Sociologie du bourreau" in *La Communion des forts* and in *Instincts et société.*

_____. "Sociologie du clerc." *NRF* 311 (Aug. 1939): 291-301. Rpt. in *La Communion des forts.*

_____. "Théorie de la fête." *NRF* 315 (Dec. 1939): 863-82; 316 (Jan. 1940): 49-59. Rpt. in *L'Homme et le sacré.* Rpt. as "Teoría de la fiesta." *SUR* 64 (Jan. 1940): 57-83.

_____. "Le Vent d'hiver" ("Pour un Collège de Sociologie"). *NRF* 298 (July 1938): 39-54.

_____. "Les Vertus dionysiaques." *Acéphale* 3-4 (July 1937): 24-25.

_____. Reviews of:

Le Bouc émissaire, by J. G. Frazer. *Cahiers du Sud* 188 (Nov. 1936): 848-50.

La Comédie humaine, by Balzac (Ed. Bouteron). *NRF* 282 (Mar. 1937): 452-55.

L'Équinoxe de septembre, by H. de Montherlant. *NRF* 304 (Jan. 1939): 150-54.

Essai sur le titanisme dans la poésie romantique occidentale entre 1815 et 1830, by V. Cerny. *NRF* 290 (Nov. 1937): 847-49.

L'Esthétique de Baudelaire, by A. Ferran. *NRF* 273 (Nov. 1936): 900-904.

L'Exercice du pouvoir, by Léon Blum. *NRF* 289 (Oct. 1937): 673-76.

L'Expérience mystique et les symboles chez les primitifs, by L. Lévy-Bruhl. *NRF* 299 (Aug. 1938): 321-24.

La Fin et les moyens, by Aldous Huxley. *NRF* 320 (May 1940): 702-04.

La Guerre dans les sociétés primitives, by M. Davie. *NRF* 275 (Aug. 1936): 384-86.

L'Homme, cet inconnu, by A. Carrel. *NRF* 270 (Mar. 1936): 438-39.

Manuel d'anthropologie culturelle and *Traité de sociologie primitive*, by Robert H. Lowie. *Cahiers du Sud* 200 (Dec. 1937): 743-46.

Mémoires du Cardinal de Retz. *NRF* 312 (Sept. 1939): 489-91.

Nietzsche, by Thierry Maulnier. *Inquisitions* 1 (June 1936): 55.

Ouranos-Varuna, by G. Dumézil. *Cahiers du Sud* 173 (June 1935): 499-501.

Poisons sacrés, ivresses divines, by Ph. de Felice. *Cahiers du Sud* 193 (Apr. 1937): 304-06.

Propos de Georges Sorel, ed. J. Variot. *NRF* 271 (Apr. 1936): 600-2.

Service inutile, by H. de Montherlant. *Inquisitions* 1 (June 1936): 56.

Le Tabou de l'inceste, by Lord Raglan. *Cahiers du Sud* 177 (Nov. 1935): 777-79.

Les Tentations de Saint-Antoine, by Claude Roger-Marx. *Cahiers du Sud* 186 (Aug.-Sept. 1936): 676-77.

Les Théories sociologiques contemporaines, by P. Sorokin. *NRF* 307 (Apr. 1939): 705-7.

Ur en Chaldée, by Leonard Wooley. *Cahiers du Sud* 206 (June 1938): 471-72.

La Volonté de puissance, by F. Nietzsche (Trans. G. Bianquis). *Inquisitions* 1 (June 1936): 55.

Duthuit, Georges. *Byzance et l'art du XIIe siècle*. Paris: Stock, 1926.

_____. *Le Musée inimaginable*. Paris: José Corti, 1956.

_____. *Mystique chinoise et peinture moderne*. Paris: Chroniques du jour, 1936.

_____. *Le Rose et le noir (de Walter Pater à Oscar Wilde)*. Paris: Renaissance du livre, 1920.

_____. "Byzantines and Decadents." *XXème siècle* 5-6 (1938): 11-12.

_____. "Grandeur du cérémonial." *XXème siècle* 1-3 (1938): 3-8.

_____. "Pour l'art sans police." *Cahiers d'art* 3-10 (Autumn 1938): 69-72.

_____. "Représentations de la mort." *Cahiers d'art* 1-4 (1939): 25-39.

_____. "Vers un nouveau mythe? Prémonitions et défiances." *VVV* 4 (Feb. 1944): 41-49.

Guastalla, René M. *Le Mythe et le livre, Essai sur l'origine de la littérature*. Paris: Gallimard, 1940.

_____, and P. Sammartino. *Survey of French Literature*. New York and London: Longmans, Green, 1937.

_____. Reviews of:

Le Drapeau noir, by J. Romains. *La Flèche*, Dec. 18, 1937.

La Fin de l'après-guerre, by Robert Aron. *La Flèche*, Dec. 30, 1938.

La Fin et les moyens, by A. Huxley. *La Flèche*, Mar. 24, 1939.

Harmonies de la Grèce, by J.-G. Tricot. *La Flèche*, July 28, 1939.

Journal d'une révolution (1937-1938), by Jean Guéhenno. *La Flèche*, May 26, 1939.

Mythes et dieux des Germains, by G. Dumézil. *La Flèche*, June 16, 1939.

Vie de Jaurès, by P. d'Esanges. *La Flèche*, Dec. 2, 1938.

_____, and G. Blin, trans. *Traité de la Monarchie divine*, by Philo. *Mesures* 4 (Oct. 1939): 155-76.

Klossowski, Pierre, trans. *Le Marquis de Sade*, by Otto Flacke. Paris: B. Grasset, 1933.

_____. *Nietzsche et le cercle vicieux*. Paris: Mercure de France, 1969.

_____, and P.-J. Jouve, trans. *Poèmes de la folie*, by Friedrich Hölderlin. Paris: J. O. Fourcade, 1930.

_____. *Sade, mon prochain*. Paris: Éditions du Seuil, Collection Pierres vives, 1947; [modified 1967].

_____, trans. *Le Sens de la souffrance*, by Max Scheler. Paris: F. Aubier, 1936.

_____, trans. "L'Angoisse mythique chez Goethe" (from "Goethe's *Elective Affinities*," by W. Benjamin). *Cahiers du Sud* 194 (May-June 1937): 342-48.

_____, trans. "Antigone," by S. Kierkegaard, *Les Nouvelles Lettres* 2 (Aug. 1, 1938): 21-57.

_____. "Chamfort." *Les Nouvelles Lettres* 1 (June 1, 1938): 60-63.

_____. "Circulus vitiosus." In *Nietzsche aujourd'hui?* Paris: UGE, 1973.

_____. "Le corps du néant." In *Sade, mon prochain*, 1st ed. (1947).

_____. "Don Juan selon Kierkegaard." *Acéphale* 3-4 (July 1937): 27-32. Rpt. in *Sade, mon prochain*, 1st ed.(1947).

_____. "Éléments d'une étude psychanalytique sur le marquis de Sade." *Revue française de psychanalyse* 6 (1933): 458-74. (Includes "Le Père et la mère dans l'oeuvre de Sade.") Rpt. in *Sade, mon prochain*.

_____. "Entre Marx et Fourier." *Le Monde*, May 31, 1969 (supplement to issue 7582).

_____. "Lettre sur Walter Benjamin." *Mercure de France* 1067 (July 1952): 456-57.

_____. "Le Mal et la négation d'autrui dans la philosophie de D. A. F. de Sade." *Recherches philosophiques* 4 (1934-35): 268-93. Rpt. in *Sade, mon prochain*.

_____, trans. "L'Oeuvre d'art à l'époque de sa reproduction mécanisée," by Walter Benjamin. *Zeitschrift für Sozialforschung* 5 (1936): 40-63.

_____. "Qui est mon prochain?" *Esprit* 75 (Dec. 1938): 402-23. Partially rpt. in *Sade, mon prochain*.

_____. "Sade et Fourier." *Topique* 4-5 (Oct. 1970): 79-98.

_____. "Temps et agressivité. Contribution à l'étude du temps subjectif." *Recherches philosophiques* 5 (1935-36): 100-111. Rpt. in *Sade, mon prochain*.

_____, trans. "Le Verdict," by Franz Kafka. *Bifur* 5 (Apr. 1930): 5-17.

Kojève, Alexandre [A. Kojevnikov], trans. *L'Idée socialiste*, by Henri de Man. Paris: B. Grasset, 1935.

_____. *Introduction à la lecture de Hegel*. Ed. R. Queneau. Paris: Gallimard, 1947.

_____, trans. "Autonomie et dépendance de la Conscience de soi," by Hegel (with commentaries). *Mesures* 1 (Jan. 1939): 109-39.

_____. Review of *La Pensée chinoise*, by Granet. *Recherches philosophiques* 4 (1934-35): 446.

Landsberg, Paul-Louis [Ludwig]. *Essai sur l'expérience de la mort*. Paris: Desclée de Brouwer, 1936.

_____. "Introduction à une critique du mythe." *Esprit* 64 (Jan. 1938): 512-29.

_____. Report on *Acéphale*. *Esprit* 56 (May 1937): 296.

Leiris, Michel. *L'Afrique fantôme*. Paris: Gallimard, 1934.

_____. *L'Âge d'homme*. Paris: Gallimard, 1939.

_____. *Brisées*. Paris: Mercure de France, 1966.

_____. *Contacts de civilisations en Martinique et en Guadeloupe*. Paris: UNESCO/Gallimard, 1955.

_____. *Glossaire: j'y serre mes gloses*. Paris: Éditions de la Galerie Simon, 1939. Rpt. in *Mots sans mémoire*.

_____. *La Langue secrète des Dogons de Sanga*. Paris: Institut d'ethnologie (Travaux et mémoires, 50), 1948.

_____. *Mots sans mémoire*. Paris: Gallimard, 1969.

_____. *Nuits sans nuit et quelques jours sans jour*. Paris: Fontaine, 1945; Gallimard, 1961.

_____. *La Règle du jeu. I: Biffures*. Paris: Gallimard, 1948. *II: Fourbis*. Paris: Gallimard, 1955.

_____. "La Cabeza de Holofernes." *SUR* 42 (Mar. 1938): 41-52. Rpt. in *L'Âge d'homme*.

_____. "Lucrèce et Judith." *Mesures* 3 (July 1936): 71-95. Rpt. in *L'Âge d'homme*.

_____. "Miroir de la tauromachie." *NRF* 302 (Nov. 1938): 799-809. Rpt. as a book: Paris: G.L.M., Collection Acéphale, 1938.

_____. "Du Musée d'Ethnographie au musée de l'Homme." *NRF* 299 (Aug. 1938): 344-45.

_____. Review of *Gens de la Grande Terre*, by M. Leenhardt. *NRF* 302 (Nov. 1938): 853-54.

_____. "Un Rite médico-magique éthiopien: le jet du danquârâ." *Aethiopica* 3, 2 (Apr. 1935): 61-74.

_____. "Le sacré dans la vie quotidienne." ("Pour un Collège de Sociologie"). *NRF* 298 (July 1938): 26-38.

Lewitzky, Anatole. "Autour du Pôle Nord." *L'Espèce humaine*. Ed. Paul Rivet. *L'Encyclopédie française*. VII. Paris: 1936.

_____. "Mythes et rites du chamanisme." *Diogène* 17 (Jan. 1957): 33-44. (Also available in English.)

_____. "Quelques aspects de la vie religieuse des peuples de l'Asie centrale et septentrionale." *Histoire des religions*. Ed. M. Gorce and R. Mortier. Paris: A. Quillet, 1944-51.

Mayer, Hans. *Ein Deutscher auf Widerruf. Erinnerungen*. Frankfurt am Main: Suhrkamp, 1982-84.

_____. *Georg Büchner und seine Zeit*. Wiesbaden: Limes, 1946.

Monnerot, Jules-Marcel. *Les Faits sociaux ne sont pas des choses*. Paris: Gallimard, 1946.

_____. *Inquisitions*. Paris: José Corti, 1974.

_____. *La Poésie moderne et le sacré*. Paris: Gallimard, 1945.

_____. *Sociologie du communisme*. Paris: Éditions Libres-Hallier, 1979.

_____. "Le Collège de Sociologie ou le problème interrompu." In *Sociologie du communisme*.

_____. "Déclaration de la Délégation des Antillais français." *Commune* 23 (July 1935): 1250.

_____. "Dionysos philosophe." *Acéphale* 3-4 (July 1937; special "Dionysos" issue): 9-14.

_____. "Il y a toujours eu des directeurs de conscience en Occident." *Volontés* 14 (Feb. 1939): 3-6.

_____. Résultats de l'enquête sur les directeurs de conscience. *Volontés* 18 (June 1939): 5-236.

_____. "Sur Georges Bataille." *Confluences* 8 (Oct. 1945): 874-82; 9 (Feb. 1946): 1009-18. Rpt. as "La Fièvre de Georges Bataille," in *Inquisitions*.

Paulhan, Jean. *Les Fleurs de Tarbes, ou: La terreur dans les lettres.* Paris: Gallimard, 1941; 1973. First published in *NRF* 273 (June 1936): 856-69; 274 (July 1936): 177-91; 275 (Aug. 1936): 338-54; 276 (Sept. 1936): 495-505; 277 (Oct. 1936): 676-98.

_____. *Les Hain-Tenys merinas, poésies populaires malgaches.* Paris: Geuthner, 1913; Gallimard, 1938.

_____. *Oeuvres.* 5 vols. Paris: Cercle du Livre précieux, 1970.

_____ [Jean Guérin, pseud.]. "Bulletin." *NRF* 287 (Aug. 1937): 365.

_____ [Jean Guérin, pseud.]. "Bulletin." *NRF* 298 (July 1938): 173-76.

_____ [Jean Guérin, pseud.]. "Bulletin." *NRF* 317 (Feb. 1940): 287. (Second review of *Mythes et dieux des Germains*).

_____. Review of *Mythes et dieux des Germains*, by G. Dumézil. *NRF* 312 (Sept. 1939): 527.

_____, and B. Parain. "Correspondance." *NRF* 369 (Oct. 1983): 172-91; 370 (Nov. 1983): 176-92; 371 (Dec. 1983): 142-48.

_____. "La Démocratie fait appel au premier venu." *NRF* 306 (Mar. 1939): 478-83.

_____. Lettre à Roger Caillois (Oct. 7, 1939). *NRF* 197 (May 1969; special Paulhan issue): 1012-13.

_____. Lettre à Roger Caillois (Christmas Day, 1941). *NRF* 197 (May 1969): 1015-16.

_____. Lettre aux *Nouveaux cahiers* sur le pouvoir des mots. *Les Nouveaux cahiers* 22-25 (Apr.-May 1938). Rpt. in *Les Fleurs de Tarbes* (1973).

_____. "Retour sur 1914." *NRF* 313 (Oct. 1939): 529-32.

_____. "La Rhétorique était une société secrète." *Les Temps modernes* 6 (Mar. 1946): 961-84. Rpt. as "La Rhétorique avait son mot de passe," in *Oeuvres, III.*

_____. "Une semaine au secret." In *Écrivains en prison.* Paris: P. Seghers, 1945.

Rougemont, Denis de. *L'Amour et l'Occident.* Paris: Plon, 1939.

_____. *Journal d'une époque (1926-1946): Le Paysan du Danube (1926-1929); Journal d'un intellectuel en chômage (1933-1935); Journal d'Allemagne (1935-1936); Journal des deux mondes (1939-1946).* Paris: Gallimard, 1968.

_____. "Retour de Nietzsche." (Review of *Acéphale*). *Esprit* 56 (May 1937): 313-15.

Wahl, Jean. *Connaître sans connaître.* Paris: G.L.M., 1938.

_____. *Études kierkegaardiennes.* Paris: F. Aubier, 1938.

_____. *Le Malheur de la conscience dans la philosophie de Hegel.* Paris: Rieder, 1929.

_____. "Au Collège de Sociologie." *NRF* 293 (Feb. 1938): 345-46.

_____. "La Philosophie française en 1939." *Renaissance* [New York] 2 and 3 (1944-45): 336-39.

_____. Review of *Les Lépreuses*, by H. de Montherlant. *NRF* 319 (Apr. 1940): 459-74.

II. Related Works

Aron, Raymond. *La Sociologie allemande contemporaine.* Paris: F. Alcan, 1935.

_____. Review of *Le Mythe et l'homme*, by R. Caillois. *Zeitschrift für Sozialforschung* 7 (1938): 413-18.

Aron, Robert. *La Fin de l'après-guerre.* Paris: Gallimard, 1938.

Bachelard, Gaston. *Lautréamont.* Paris: José Corti, 1939.

_____. "Le Surrationalisme." *Inquisitions* 1 (June 1936): 1-6.

Benda, Julien. *La Grande Épreuve des démocraties.* New York: Éditions de la Maison française, 1942.

_____. *La Jeunesse d'un clerc (1936); Un Régulier dans le siècle (1938); Exercice d'un enterré vif*, (1946), foreword by Étiemble. Paris: Gallimard, 1968.

_____. Review of *Socialisme fasciste*, by Drieu la Rochelle. *NRF* 257 (Feb. 1935): 295-96.

Benjamin, Walter. *Briefe*. Ed. G. Scholem and Th. W. Adorno. Frankfurt am Main: Suhrkamp, 1966.

_____. "Paris, Hauptstadt des XIXe Jahrhundert." In *Schriften*. Frankfurt am Main: Suhrkamp, 1955.

_____. [J. E. Mabinn, pseud.]. Review of "L'Aridité," by R. Caillois. *Zeitschrift für Sozialforschung* 3 (1938): 463-66.

_____. "Über einige Motive bei Baudelaire." *Zeitschrift für Sozialforschung* 8 (1939): 50-91.

_____. Lettre à Gretel Adorno (Jan. 17, 1940). In *Briefe*.

Caillois, Roland-P. "Roger Caillois ou l'inquisiteur sans Église." *Critique* 8-9 (Jan.-Feb. 1947): 28-43.

Chastel, André. "La Loyauté de l'intelligence." In *Roger Caillois, Cahiers pour un temps*. Paris: Centre G. Pompidou, Éditions Pandora, 1981.

_____. Réponse à l'enquête de Monnerot. *Volontés* 18 (June 1939): 31-33.

Drieu la Rochelle, Pierre. *Chronique politique (1934-1942)*. Paris: Gallimard, 1943.

Dubief, Henri. *Le Déclin de la Troisième République (1929-1938)*, vol. 13 of *Nouvelle Histoire de la France contemporaine*. Paris: Éditions du Seuil, 1972-76.

Dumézil, Georges. *Mitra-Varuna. Essai sur deux représentations indo-européennes de la souveraineté*. Paris: Leroux, 1940.

_____. *Mythes et dieux des Germains*. Paris: Leroux, 1939.

_____. *Ouranos-Varuna. Étude de mythologie comparée indo-européenne*. Paris: Adrien-Maisonneuve, 1934; 1948.

_____. Réponse à Carlo Ginsburg. *Annales* 5 (Sept.-Oct. 1985): 985-88.

Durkheim, Émile. *Les Formes élémentaires de la vie religieuse*. Paris: F. Alcan, 1912.

Étiemble [René]. *Le Mythe de Rimbaud (I: Genèse du mythe; II: Structure du mythe)*. Paris: Gallimard, 1952.

_____. "Deux Masques de Roger Caillois." *NRF* 320 (Sept. 1979): 137-42.

_____. "Le mythe de Rimbaud." *Revue de littérature comparée* 19 (Jan.-Mar. 1939): 172-77.

_____. Reviews of:

La Communion des forts, by Caillois. *L'Arche* 6 (Oct.-Nov. 1944): 146-57.

La Grande Épreuve des démocraties, by J. Benda. *Les Lettres françaises* [Buenos Aires] 78 (Feb. 1943): 100-101.

"Réparation à Nietzsche." (*Acéphale*, special issue "Nietzsche et les fascistes"). *NRF* 283 (Apr. 1937): 634-35.

Fardoulis-Lagrange, Michel. *G.B. ou un ami présomptueux*. Paris: Soleil noir, 1969.

_____. "Un Art divin: l'oubli." *Tel quel* 93 (Autumn 1982): 76-90.

Groethuysen, Bernard. Review of *Le Mythe et le livre*, by R. Guastalla. *NRF* 320 (May 1940): 698-700.

Hollier, Denis. *La Prise de la Concorde*. Paris: Gallimard, 1974.

Jamin, Jean. "quand le sacré devint gauche." *L'Ire des Vents* 3-4 (1981): 98-118.

Janet, Pierre. "Les Troubles de la personnalité sociale." *Annales médico-psychologiques* 95 (1937): 421-68 (part III).

Koyré, Alexandre. "La sociologie française contemporaine." *Zeitschrift für Sozialforschung* 5 (1936): 260-64.

Lapouge, Gilles. "Entretien avec R. Caillois." (Special issue "Présence de Georges Bataille".) *La Quinzaine littéraire* 97 (June 16-30, 1970): 6-8.

Laure [Colette Peignot]. *Écrits, fragments, lettres*. Ed. Jérôme Peignot. Paris, UGE, 10/18, 1978.

Lebel, Robert. "Quand le feu fait des signes à Duthuit." *Critique* 198 (Nov. 1963): 970-76.

Lévi-Strauss, Claude. "La sociologie française." In *Twentieth-Century Sociology*. Ed. Georges Gurvitch, New York: Philosophical Library, 1945.

Mabille, Pierre. *Égrégores ou la vie des civilisations*. Paris: J. Flory, 1938.

Mauss, Marcel. "Appréciation sociologique du bolchevisme." *Revue de métaphysique et de morale* 31, (Jan.-Mar. 1924): 103-32.

———, and H. Beuchat. "Essai sur les variations saisonnières des sociétés Eskimos. Étude de morphologie sociale." *L'Année sociologique 1904-1905* 9 (1906): 39-131. Rpt. in *Sociologie et anthropologie*. Paris: PUF, 1968.

———. Lettre à Élie Halévy. *Bulletin de la Société française de philosophie* 5 (Oct.-Dec. 1936): 234-35.

Picon, Gaëtan. *Panorama de la nouvelle littérature française*. Paris: Le Point du jour, 1950.

Queneau, Raymond. *Le Dimanche de la vie*. Paris: Gallimard, 1952.

———. *Le voyage en Grèce*. Paris: Gallimard, NRF, 1973.

———. "Le Mythe et l'imposture." *Volontés* 14 (Feb. 1939): 14-17. Rpt. in *Le Voyage en Grèce*.

———. "Naissance et avenir de la littérature." (Review of *Le Mythe et le livre*, by R. Guastalla. *Volontés* 22 [May 1940]: issue never published). Rpt. in *Le Voyage en Grèce*.

———. "Premières confrontations avec Hegel." *Critique* 195-96 (Aug.-Sept. 1963): 694-700.

Sadoul, Georges. "*Inquisitions*. Pierre-Jean Jouve et les chants de la liberté." *Commune* 35 (July 1936): 1390-98.

———. Reviews of:

L'Afrique fantôme, by M. Leiris. *Commune* 18 (Feb. 1935): 630-31.

Le Chiendent, by R. Queneau. *Commune* 9 (May 1934): 1018-19.

Procès intellectuel de l'art ("Notice sur l'impureté de l'art"), by R. Caillois. *Commune* 23 (July 1935): 1333.

———. "Sociologie sacrée." *Commune* 60 (Sept.-Oct. 1938): 1515-25.

Sartre, Jean-Paul. "Un Nouveau Mystique." *Cahiers du Sud* 260 (Oct. 1943): 783-90; 261 (Nov. 1943): 866-86; 262 (Dec. 1943): 988-94. Rpt. in *Situations I*. Paris: Gallimard, 1947.

———. Review of *L'Amour et l'Occident*, by D. de Rougemont. *Europe* 198 (June 1939): 242-48. Rpt. in *Situations I*.

Schapiro, Mayer. "French reaction in Exile." *Kenyon Review* 7 (Winter 1945): 29-42.

III. Related Material Available in English

Aron, Raymond. *Introduction to the Philosophy of History*. Boston: Beacon Press, 1960.

Bataille, Georges. *Blue of Noon*. New York: Urizen Books, 1978.

———. *Guilty*. Trans. Bruce Boone. Los Angeles: Lapis Press, 1988.

———. *The Naked Beast at Heaven's Gate* [*Madame Edwarda*]. Paris: Olympia Press, 1956.

———. *Visions of Excess: Selected Writings, 1927-1939*. Ed. Allan Stoekl. Minneapolis: University of Minnesota Press, 1985.

———. "Autobiographical Note." *October* [MIT Press] 36 (Spring 1986): 107-10.

———. "The College of Sociology." In *Visions of Excess*.

———. "Le Coupable." *Semiotext(e)* 4 (1979): 136-44.

Benjamin, Walter. *Illuminations*. New York: Schocken Books, 1969.

Benoist-Méchin, Jacques. *History of the German Army since the Armistice*. Zurich: Scientia, 1939.

Blumenson, Martin. *The Vildé Affair: Beginnings of the French Resistance*. Boston: Houghton Mifflin, 1977.

Caillois, Roger. *Man and the Sacred*. Glencoe, Ill.: Free Press, 1959.

———. "The *Collège de Sociologie*: Paradox of an Active Sociology." *Sub-Stance* 11-12 (1975): 61-64.

———. "Mimicry and Legendary Psychasthenia." *October* [MIT Press] 31 (Winter 1984): 17-32.

Daladier, Édouard. *In Defense of France*. New York: Doubleday, Doran, 1939.

Dumézil, Georges. *Gods of the Ancient Northmen*. Berkeley: University of California Press, 1973.

Durkheim, Émile. *The Elementary Forms of the Religious Life*. London: Allen & Unwin, 1915; Glencoe, Ill.: Free Press, 1954.

Flacke, Otto. *The Marquis de Sade*. London: Davies, 1931.

Frazer, Sir James G. *The Golden Bough*. London: Macmillan, 1955.

_____. "The Dying God." *Golden Bough*, vol. IV, part 3.

_____. "The Scapegoat." *Golden Bough*, vol. IX, part 4.

Freud, Sigmund. *Beyond the Pleasure Principle*. New York: Liveright, 1970.

_____. *Totem and Taboo*. New York: Knopf, 1946.

_____. "Group Psychology and the Analysis of the Ego." *Complete Psychological Works of Sigmund Freud*, vol. 18. London: Hogarth Press, 1955.

Granet, Marcel. *Chinese Civilization*. London: Kegan Paul, Trench, Trubner, 1930; New York: Meridian Books, 1959.

Halévy, Élie. *The Era of Tyrannies: Essays on Socialism and War*. New York: New York University Press, 1966.

Hertz, Robert. *Death and The Right Hand*. Aberdeen: University Press, 1960.

Kojève, Alexandre. *Introduction to the Reading of Hegel*. New York: Basic Books, 1969.

Landsberg, Paul. *The Experience of Death*. London: Rockliff, 1953.

Leiris, Michel. *Manhood: A Journey from Childhood into the Fierce Order of Virility*. New York: Grossman, 1963.

Mauss, Marcel. *A General Theory of Magic*. London & Boston: Routledge & Kegan Paul, 1972.

_____. *The Gift: Forms and Functions of Exchange in Archaic Societies*. New York: Norton, 1967.

Michels, Robert. *Political Parties: A Sociological Study of the Oligarchical Tendencies of Modern Democracy*. New York: Hearst's International Library, 1915.

Pareto, Vilfredo. *The Mind and Society*. New York: Harcourt, Brace, 1935.

Queneau, Raymond. *The Sunday of Life*. London: Calder, 1976.

Rauschning, Hermann. *The Revolution of Nihilism*. New York: Alliance; Longmans, Green, 1939.

Romains, Jules. *The Lonely*. [Recherche d'une Église]. New York: Knopf, 1935.

Rougemont, Denis de. *Love in the Western World*. New York: Torch Books, 1972.

Compiled by Renée Morel

Index

Index

Prepared by Andreas Michel

443

of myth, 160; social function of, 22-23;
space-time of, 289
Le Mythe et l'homme (Caillois), 8, 50, 68,
159, 164, 201, 215, 250, 280, 350, 376,
380, 386, 390, 397n2, 400n5, 401n10,
402n12, 403nn15, 16, 406n8, 410n9,
411n18, 413n13, 418n1, 423n5, 427n3;
critiqued by Aron, 421n5; reviews of, 373
Mythical times, as Chaos and Golden Age,
286-87
Mythological invention, and fictional
invention, 23
Mythology, zoomorphic elements in, 258-60

Nadeau, Maurice, ix
Nancy, Jean-Luc, xvii; and desubjectified
enunciation, xxi
Napoléon, 89, 270, 271, 272, 275, 276; and
Christianity, 87; and Kant, Fichte, 87; and
Stalin, 86, 87
National socialism, 268; and history of
unification of Germany, 265; as monstrous
system, 375; and patrimony of signs, 264-
66; vs. universalism of the Catholic
church, 274
Nationalism: and globalized Germanity, 268;
and masculine order, 272, 275-77; vs.
national socialism, 267; and racism, 62-64;
and universalism, 52-67 *passim*
Nature: and distinctions between people, 37-
39; power as force of, 41; and the
uninitiated, 40
Necessity: vs. existence, 155; and fate, 179;
and world of tragedy, 148
Necrophilia, and Bataille, 322
Negativity: Bataille vs. Hegel, 117; as
destructive action (Hegel), 116-17; laughter
and sexuality and, 117; and nullification,
91; as sin, 91
Neopaganism, 265, 274
Neurosis, as diversion of subject's fervor, 54
Niemöller, Pastor, 59
Nietzsche, Friedrich, 34, 35, 39, 48, 63, 73,
151, 153, 195, 202, 203, 217, 275, 322,
323, 356, 366, 368, 372, 385, 387, 398n6,
401n9, 407n10, 414n18, 421n6; and
atomization of individual, 373, 374; the
defascizing of, 164; Derrida on, xxii;

Klossowski on, 417n8; and knowledge, 79;
and tragedy, 122
Nizan, Paul, 44, 48, 145, 163, 349, 403n2,
404n4; "Funérailles anglaises," 330-331
Nogué, 376
Nord-Sud, 304
Les Nouveaux Cahiers, 410n1
Nouvelle Revue française, 7, 8, 43, 44, 51,
99, 158, 159, 163, 189, 304, 305, 369,
416n1
Les Nouvelles Lettres, 167, 193
Novalis, xiv, 317, 408n1; and anti-Catholic
Catholicism, 274; condemned by Caillois,
219; peak of romantic imagination, 89
Novel: vs. cathedral (Caillois), xi-xii; as
countermyth, 202; and democracy
(Bataille), xvi
Novelist, vs. city, 202
Nuremberg Congress, 281

Obscenity, 91
Ocampo, Victoria, 99, 163
Octavius, 133
Odon, Yvonne, 249
Order (association), masculine, 272
Order, 215-17, 416n1; and doctrine, 355; and
elective community, 217; and festival, 281-
303; and homogeneity, 217
Organism, simple vs. linear, 76, 79-81
Orthopraxy, 68
Osty, Dr., 362
Other, as raw material, 39
Others, and fellow creatures, 37
"Overall movement": as animating human
societies, 126-36 *passim*; and conscious
will, 158; and nucleus, 128; pluralism as,
191; and power, 128

Pange, Jean de, 331
Papen, Franz von, 351
Parain, Brice, 85, 426n12
Pareto, Vilfredo, 49; and history, 267; on
residue in *Traité de sociologie générale*,
264
Paris Commune, 371
Parody, and festival, 299
Pascal, Blaise, 410n1
Passion, and dialectic, 181
Pasternak, Boris, 48

Theory and History of Literature

Denis Hollier is a professor of French at Yale University and previously taught at the University of California, Berkeley. His books include *Panorama des Sciences Humaines*, *La prise de la Concorde: Essais sur Georges Bataille* and *The Politics of Prose: Essay on Sartre* (in translation from Minnesota, 1987). Hollier's articles appear in *Raritan*, *Representations*, *Enclitic* and *October*.

Betsy Wing has a B.A. in art history from Bryn Mawr College; she also attended Columbia University and Miami University, Ohio, and is currently a candidate for the M.F.A. at Louisiana State University. Her translations include Hélène Cixous and Catherine Clément's *Newly Born Woman* (Minnesota 1986) and Catherine Clément's *Opera, or the Undoing of Women* (forthcoming from Minnesota). Wing's translations and fiction have also appeared in *Representations*, *boundary 2*, and *Southern Review*.